Lecture Notes in Computer Sc

Commenced Publication in 1973
Founding and Former Series Editors:
Gerhard Goos, Juris Hartmanis, and Jan van Leeuwen

László Kovács Norbert Fuhr
Carlo Meghini (Eds.)

Research and Advanced Technology for Digital Libraries

11th European Conference, ECDL 2007
Budapest, Hungary, September 16-21, 2007
Proceedings

Springer

Volume Editors

László Kovács
Hungarian Academy of Sciences
Computer and Automation Research Institute
Department of Distributed Systems
H-1111 Budapest, XI. Lágymányosi u. 11., Hungary
E-mail: laszlo.kovacs@sztaki.hu

Norbert Fuhr
University of Duisburg-Essen
Information Systems Department of Computational and Cognitive Sciences
47048 Duisburg, Germany
E-mail: norbert.fuhr@uni-due.de

Carlo Meghini
Consiglio Nazionale delle Ricerche
Istituto di Scienza e Tecnologie della Informazione
56124 Pisa, Italy
E-mail: meghini@isti.cnr.it

Library of Congress Control Number: 2007934833

CR Subject Classification (1998): H.3.7, H.2, H.3, H.4.3, H.5, J.7, J.1, I.7

LNCS Sublibrary: SL 3 – Information Systems and Application, incl. Internet/Web and HCI

ISSN	0302-9743
ISBN-10	3-540-74850-4 Springer Berlin Heidelberg New York
ISBN-13	978-3-540-74850-2 Springer Berlin Heidelberg New York

Springer is a part of Springer Science+Business Media

springer.com

Printed in Germany

Typesetting: Camera-ready by author, data conversion by Scientific Publishing Services, Chennai, India
Printed on acid-free paper SPIN: 12121076 06/3180 5 4 3 2 1 0

Preface

We are proud to present the proceedings of the 11th European Conference on Research and Advanced Technology for Digital Libraries (ECDL 2007) which, following Pisa (1997), Heraklion (1998), Paris (1999), Lisbon (2000), Darmstadt (2001), Rome (2002), Trondheim (2003), Bath (2004), Vienna (2005) and Alicante (2006), took place on September 16-21, 2007 in Budapest, Hungary. Over the last 11 years, ECDL has created a strong interdisciplinary community of researchers and practitioners in the field of digital libraries, and has formed a substantial body of scholarly publications contained in the conference proceedings.

ECDL 2007 featured separate calls for paper and poster submissions, resulting in 119 full papers and 34 posters being submitted to the conference. All papers were subject to an in-depth peer-review process; three reviews per submission were produced by a Program Committee of 69 members from 27 countries. In total 36 of 119 full paper submissions were accepted at the Program Committee meeting for presentation at the conference and publication in the proceedings with Springer, resulting in an acceptance rate of 30%. Also, 24 poster/demo submissions and another 15 papers from the full paper submissions were accepted for poster presentation and publication in the proceedings volume.

ECDL 2007 was devoted to discussions about hot issues and applications and primarily provided a forum to reinforce the collaboration of researchers and practicioners.The main conference consisted of 12 technical sessions and a poster /demo session on the following topics: Ontologies, Digital Libraries and the Web, Models, Multimedia and Multilingual Digital Libraries, Grid and Peer-to-Peer, Preservation, User Interfaces, Document Linking, Information Retrieval, Personal Information Management, New DL Applications and User Studies.

The conference featured two panels, which addressed timely and important topics, namely, experiences of DL projects in synergy with the European Commission's initiatives in the panel "On the Move Towards the European Digital Library: BRICKS, TEL, MICHAEL and DELOS converging experiences" chaired by Massimo Bertoncini and the special challenges of Digital Library research and development in the host region of the conference in the panel "Digital Libraries in Central and Eastern Europe: Infrastructure Challenges for the New Europe" chaired by Christine Borgman.

The keynote talk by Seamus Ross (Humanities Computing and Information Management, University of Glasgow) addressed the questions of digital preservation, while the keynote talk by Arne Solvberg (Dept. of Computer and Information Science, Norwegian University of Science and Technology) focused on the challenges of WiFi-Trondheim – an experiment in providing Broadband Everywhere for All.

The preceding tutorials provided further in-depth looks at areas of current interest, including "Thesauri and Ontologies in DLs by Dagobert Soegrel, Introduction to DLs" by Ed Fox, "Approaches for Large Scale Digital Library Infrastructures" by Thomas Risse, and "Building DLs On-Demand by Sharing Content, Services and Computing Resources" by Donatella Castelli.

The workshops, held in conjunction with ECDL2007, covered wide areas of interest: CLEF 2007 – Cross-Language Evaluation Forum, Workshop on "Foundations of Digital Libraries"; LADL 2007 – Cross-Media and Personalized Learning Applications on Top of Digital Libraries, Curriculum Development in Digital Libraries: An Exercise in Developing Lesson Plans , Towards a European Repository Ecology: Conceptualizing Interactions Between Networks of Repositories and Services, NKOS -Networked Knowledge Organization Systems and Services, and Libraries in the Digital Age: What If...?

We would like to take the opportunity to thank everybody who made this conference possible, all the conference participants and presenters, who provided an exciting full-week program of high technical quality. We greatly appreciate the contribution of the Program Committee members, who did an outstanding reviewing job under tight time constraints; and we are grateful to all Chairs and members of the Organization Committee, who worked hard to make the best out of the Conference.

Finally, we would also like to thank the conference sponsors and cooperating agencies: the Computer and Automation Research Institute of the Hungarian Academy of Sciences (MTA SZTAKI), the DELOS Network of Excellence on Digital Libraries, and the Hungarian Tourism Office.

September 2007

László Kovács
Norbert Fuhr
Carlo Meghini

Organization

Organization Committee

General Chair

László Kovács	Department of Distributed Systems, Computer and Automation Research Institute, Hungarian Academy of Sciences, Hungary

Program Co-chairs

Norbert Fuhr	Information Systems Faculty of Engineering Sciences, University of Duisburg-Essen, Germany
Carlo Meghini	Consiglio Nazionale delle Ricerche Istituto di Scienza e Tecnologie dell'Informazione, Italy

Workshops Chairs

Maristella Agosti	University of Padua, Italy
Birte Christensen-Dalsgaard	State and University Library, Denmark

Poster and Demo Chairs

Ulrike Steffens	OFFIS, Germany
José Borbinha	DEI/IST/UTL and INESC-ID, Portugal

Tutorials Chair

Rudi Schmiede	Darmstadt University of Technology, Germany

Publicity and Exhibit Chairs

Yuzuru Tanaka for Asia	Meme Media Laboratory, Hokkaido University, Japan
Jane Hunter for Australia	School of ITEE, Australia
Hussein Suleman for Africa	University of Cape Town, South Africa

Panel Chairs

Seamus Ross	University of Glasgow, UK
Edward Fox	Virginia Tech / Dept. of Computer Science, USA

Doctoral Consortium Chairs

Tiziana Catarci	University of Rome 1, Italy
Nicolas Spyratos	Université de Paris-Sud, France

Local Arrangements Chair

Gusztáv Hencsey	Computer and Automation Research Institute, Hungarian Academy of Sciences, Hungary

Program Committee

Hanne Albrechtsen	Institute of Knowledge Sharing, Denmark
Margherita Antona	FORTH, Greece
Tom Baker	State and University Library, Germany
Nicholas Belkin	Rutgers University, USA
Maria Bieliková	Slovak University of Technology in Bratislava, Slovakia
George Buchanan	University of Wales, Swansea
Gerhard Budin	University of Vienna, Austria
Tiziana Catarci	University of Rome 1, Italy
José H. Canós Cerda	Universidad Politecnica de Valencia, Spain
Hsinchun Chen	University of Arizona, Tucson, USA
Anita S.Coleman	University of Arizona, USA
Gregory Crane	Tufts University, USA
Sally Jo Cunningham	University of Waikato, New Zealand
Mário J. Gaspar da Silva	Universidade de Lisboa, Portugal
Pablo de la Fuente	University of Valladolid, Spain
Susanne Dobratz	Humboldt University, Germany
Boris V.Dobrov	Moscow State University, Russia
Jacques Ducloy	CNRS-INIST, France
Lim Ee-Peng	Nanyang Technological University, Singapore
Floriana Esposito	University of Bari, Italy
Schubert Foo	Nanyang Technological University, Singapore
Edward Fox	Virginia Tech, USA
Richard Furuta	Texas A & M University, USA
Stefan Gradmann	University of Hamburg, Computing Center, Germany
Allan Hanbury	Vienna University of Technology, Austria
Donna Harman	NIST, USA
Djoerd Hiemstra	Twente University, The Netherlands
Jen-Shin Hong	Department of Computer Science, National ChiNan University, Taiwan
Leonid Kalinichenko	Russian Academy of Sciences, Russia
Sarantos Kapidakis	Ionian University, Greece
Claus-Peter Klas	University of Duisburg, Germany
Traugott Koch	Max Planck Digital Library, Germany
Harald Krottmaier	Graz University of Technology, Austria
Carl Lagoze	Cornell University, USA
Mounia Lalmas	Queen Mary University of London, UK
Ronald Larsen	University of Pittsburgh, USA

Table of Contents

Multimedia and Multilingual DLs

Grid and Peer-to-Peer

Preservation

User Interfaces

User Studies

Panels

Posters and Demos

The Semantic GrowBag Algorithm: Automatically Deriving Categorization Systems

Jörg Diederich and Wolf-Tilo Balke

L3S Research Center and Leibniz Universität Hannover, Hanover, Germany
{diederich,balke}@l3s.de

Abstract. Using keyword search to find relevant objects in digital libraries often results in way too large result sets. Based on the metadata associated with such objects, the faceted search paradigm allows users to structure and filter the result set, for example, using a publication type facet to show only books or videos. These facets usually focus on clear-cut characteristics of digital items, however it is very difficult to also organize the actual semantic content information into such a facet. The *Semantic GrowBag* approach, presented in this paper, uses the keywords provided by many authors of digital objects to automatically create light-weight topic categorization systems as a basis for a meaningful and dynamically adaptable *topic facet*. Using such emergent semantics enables an alternative way to filter large result sets according to the objects' content without the need to manually classify all objects with respect to a pre-specified vocabulary. We present the details of our algorithm using the DBLP collection of computer science documents and show some experimental evidence about the quality of the achieved results.

Keywords: faceted search, category generation, higher-order co-occurrence.

1 Introduction

Due to today's sophisticated ranking techniques, the simple keyword search paradigm has been remarkably successful in finding relevant resources in huge data collections, such as digital libraries or even the world wide web. One remaining problem, however, is that users are often unsure which actual keywords to choose so that finding a particular resource often involves several search queries, which then have to be manually refined step-by-step according to the result set of the previous keyword search.

The *faceted search* [1,2,3,4] paradigm makes this process of refining queries explicit and presents the results along with several orthogonal facets, which characterize the result set (e.g., a 'publication type' facet might reveal that there are only two videos among possibly 10,000 relevant results) and thus allow the user to restrict the result set in an easy and intuitive way by exploiting metadata.

This paper is focused on facets based on the actual content of the objects, which allow to restrict the result set to a specific topic. To limit the size of such a *topic facet*, a hierarchical system is typically used to structure the facet, for example, using the Dewey Decimal Classification System, the ACM curriculum or any other cataloguing system (cf. Fig. 1). Such a topic facet can be used in several different ways:

L. Kovács, N. Fuhr, and C. Meghini (Eds.): ECDL 2007, LNCS 4675, pp. 1–13, 2007.

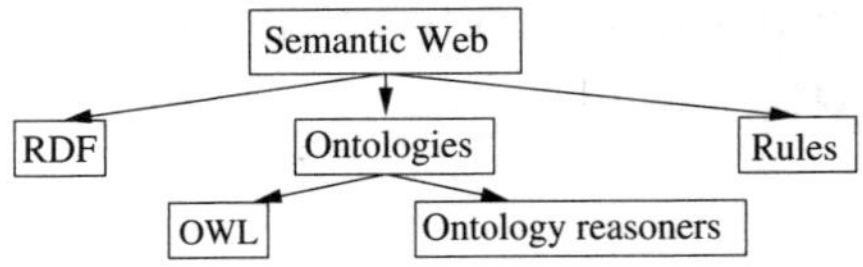

Fig. 1. Example categorization system for topics

- To filter results according to a whole subtree (e.g., if a user selects 'ontologies' in a facet based on the categories in Fig. 1, all objects about 'OWL' and 'Ontology reasoners' can be automatically included in the result set, too).
- To find communities (e.g., for a query 'XML', the facet might show a large number of objects in 'RDF' and in 'OWL', but not in 'Rules').
- To characterize authors or groups of authors (e.g., showing that the objects authored by a particular person are mainly about the topics 'OWL' and 'Rules').
- To characterize the object collection as a whole (e.g., if a query 'rules' only provides results related to 'Semantic Web', but not about 'business rules').

The main problem, however, is creating and maintaining the underlying topic categorization system, which is often done manually and especially difficult for very dynamic domains such as computer science research.

We have already presented first demonstrations of the basic applicability of our approach [5,6] for topic categorization, but not yet disclosed and evaluated our algorithm's specifics. This paper details our *Semantic GrowBag approach* to automatically organize topics in light-weight hierarchical categorization systems (so-called *GrowBag graphs*), starting from the author keywords available in large digital object collections such as DBLP for the computer science domain, or Medline for the medical domain. In Sect. 2 we briefly investigate related work for faceted searches and taxonomy generation. Section 3 presents our Semantic GrowBag algorithm and its basic characteristics. Using the DBLP data set we explain our algorithm in detail in Sect. 4 along practical use cases and evaluate the derived GrowBag graphs. In this way, we give a good intuition about the algorithm's practical impact and show that the (rather limited) tagging with keywords in today's collections is already useful to derive good and intuitive topic facets. The paper closes with a short summary and outlook.

2 Related Work

The basic idea of faceted search was built on the scatter/gather clustering approaches [7] for document browsing. The hierarchical organization of result documents according to certain faceted categories has been shown to enable intuitive user interfaces superior to the presentation of ranked lists [8]. But for the actual creation of good faceted categories some degree of manual interaction is still needed and all categories of interest must always be known in advance, thus, important emerging trends in the data may not be shown in faceted interfaces [1,2,3]. We will see in the practical use cases that the Semantic GrowBag algorithm overcomes some of these problems by automatically deriving faceted categories on the fly and can even reflect trends in the taggings by selecting only parts of the underlying document base.

Another related technology are so-called topic maps [9] that were defined as an XML-based data format (standardized in 1999 as ISO/IEC 13250) to formulate simple structures for knowledge representation. The topic maps defined 'associations' between topics and 'occurrences' that linked topics to documents, e.g., on the WWW. In contrast to our approach, topic maps therefore base on the idea of reflecting more or less static thesauri and indexes like e.g., the topic hierarchy of the Open Directory Project (ODP).

For the (to some degree) automatic creation of ontologies there are several approaches mostly relying on (supervised) learning techniques based on natural language processing, e.g., using language models or syntactic contexts [10,11]. These approaches identify synonyms, sub-/superclass hierarchies, etc. from full texts by relying on the sentence structure, where phrases like 'such as...' imply a certain hierarchy between terms. Moreover, the belief in the correctness of derived classes and/or hierarchies can be supported by comparison to general ontologies like WordNet or counting co-occurrences, e.g., in documents retrieved by Google. In contrast to our approach these techniques aim to understand the whole information space concerned with a topic and not the most discriminating facets as given by a collection.

Sanderson and Croft [12] have proposed a basic approach to automatically create categorization systems by exploiting keyword co-occurrences. Keyword Y is defined as subsuming keyword X if at least 80% of the objects tagged with X are also tagged with Y, and Y occurs more frequently than X. Although manually determined subsumption relations usually have a much stronger semantics, already this simple subsumption definition has shown a nice performance for navigational purposes [12] when using keywords extracted from full text. However, for manually specified keywords, authors tend to use only 'leaf' categories they have in mind, so two subsuming keywords hardly co-occur in more than 80% of the cases.

3 The Semantic GrowBag Algorithm

The basic idea of the Semantic GrowBag algorithm is to automatically create categorization systems from a corpus of digital objects (like documents, images, etc.) annotated with keywords. This is done by exploiting *higher-order co-occurrence*, known from computational linguistics [13]. As shown in Fig. 2, keywords X and Z are associated with one object (C), which is a *first order co-occurrence* or simply *co-occurrence*. Keywords Y and Z are not associated with the same object, but there may still be a subsuming keyword (X) which is associated with objects (B and C) that are tagged by both keywords Y and Z, respectively. Such *second order co-occurrences* (or generally higher-order co-occurrences) occur more often than first-order occurrences alone

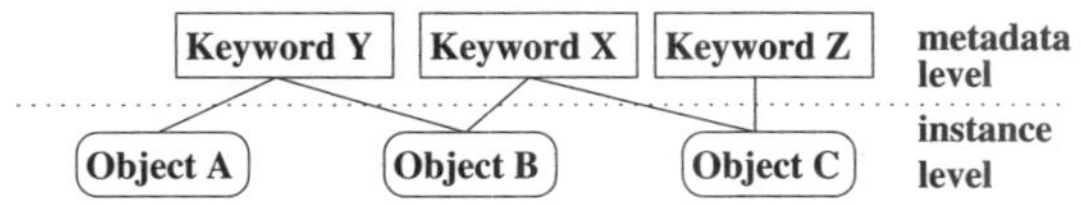

Fig. 2. Example {first|second}-order co-occurrence

and, hence, reduce the sparsity of the co-occurrence dataset. They have also been found to be more robust than first-order co-occurrences, for example, improving word sense disambiguation algorithms [13].

Including higher-order co-occurrences has two main effects: (1) Finding additional ('hidden') relations between keywords which cannot be found using first-order co-occurrences only. (2) Changing the 'strength' (i.e., the number) of existing first-order co-occurrences to include higher-order co-occurrences.

The Semantic GrowBag algorithm uses a biased PageRank algorithm [14] for the computation of the higher-order co-occurrences, as the properties of PageRank are well understood, it can be computed very efficiently and converges to a stable solution for appropriate input data (e.g., in the SimRank approach [15], PageRank has been used in a similar way to compute transitive similarities). Our algorithm comprises the following three steps, which are explained in more detail in the upcoming sections.

I. Compute a new co-occurrence metric including higher-order co-occurrence.
II. Find relations between keywords, based on the new co-occurrence metric.
III. Construct for each keyword i a single GrowBag graph to present a limited view on the 'neighborhood' of keyword i instead of having one manually crafted graph as for legacy classifications/thesauri which covers the whole object collection.

3.1 Part I: Higher-Order Co-occurrences

In a nutshell, computing the co-occurrence metric including higher-order co-occurrences comprises the following three basic steps:

1. Create an (nxn) matrix M based on weighted (first-order) co-occurrence relations for the n keywords.
2. For each keyword i, determine the most often co-occurring keywords (the *direct neighbors*).
3. For each keyword i, compute the Biased PageRank scores using matrix M and biasing on the direct neighbors of keyword i.

The resulting n PageRank score vectors are complementary to the n lists of most often co-occurring keywords, but additionally include higher-order co-occurrences due to the flow of the scores in the PageRank graph. Specifically, the ranking imposed by the scores in the PageRank score vector of keyword i now determines the *hidden related keywords* to keyword i and is, hence, an enhancement of the legacy 'related keywords' notion.[1] The following sections provide more details.

Co-occurrence Matrix M. The elements $m(j, i)$ of matrix M are defined as follows:

$$m(j, i) = \frac{cooc(i, j) * ICF(i)}{\sum_j cooc(i, j) * ICF(i)} \tag{1}$$

[1] Latent semantic analysis [16,17] is very related here, which basically performs a singular value decomposition on the co-occurrence matrix to find 'latent' topics, i.e., abstract topics given by linear combinations of keywords. However, it cannot find subsumption hierarchies.

with $cooc(i, j)$ being the (first order) co-occurrences of keywords i and j, i.e., the number of objects that are tagged with both keywords[2]. The inverse co-occurrence frequency (ICF) much resembles the inverse document frequency as known from information retrieval [18] and is defined as follows:

$$ICF(i) = \log(\frac{\text{Overall \# of keywords}}{\text{total \# of keywords co-occurring with keyword } i}) \quad (2)$$

Multiplying the ICF of i to $cooc(i, j)$ in eq. (1) has the effect that $m(j, i)$ is decreased for those keywords i that co-occur with many other keywords. These have, thus, a less discriminating power.

The above defined matrix M has the following properties: It is symmetric in terms of links, i.e., if $m(j, i) \neq 0$ then $m(i, j) \neq 0$. Hence, the PageRank graph defined by M does not contain dangling nodes or rank sinks. Though symmetric in terms of links, it is **not** symmetric in terms of weights: The normalization in the denominator of eq. (1) ensures that $m(j, i) \neq m(i, j)$ since the sum of all co-occurrences is typically not the same for all pairs of keywords. Therefore, the PageRank graph defined by M is a **directed** graph so that the PageRank scores do not converge to the number of co-occurring keywords for each keyword. Hence, matrix M is stochastic, irreducible, and primitive because of normalization and because we apply the Random Jump vector as defined by Page and Brin [14] (with the usual 15% random jump probability). Therefore, the PageRank computation converges to the principal Eigenvector [19].

Direct Neighbors: Top-X. To find the direct neighbors for a given keyword t_i, we first sort the vector with all co-occurring keywords for t_i. We then define the direct neighbors as the *top-X elements* of the sorted vector which accumulate the first P% of the sum of all vector values (i.e., the integral of the co-occurrence graph). P is the essential parameter of our algorithm that controls to which degree higher-order co-occurrence should be included. A typical value found useful in practice is $P \in [10 : 30]\%$.

Biasing on Top-X. For computing the biased PageRank scores, we initialize the start vector and the random jump vector with 1 to provide each node in the PageRank graph with some default score. This step is the most costly part of our approach in terms of time complexity, but as the overall set of author keywords will remain stable (they are never changed and changes are relatively small for large object collections), our algorithm can be computed off-line and re-run periodically to update the results according to the added author keywords.

3.2 Part II: Finding Hidden Relations

To find relations between two keywords i and j, the PageRank score vectors for the keywords i and j are used as follows:

---

[2] Using Dice or Jaccard similarity instead of co-occurrences has been found inferior as they give a rather high weight for rarely occurring terms, which does not support the notion of 'emergent' semantics.

1. Sort the power-law distributed PageRank score vectors and cut the tail to filter out all keywords with too low scores.
2. Compare the scores of keywords i and j in those two sorted and filtered score vectors. If both i and j exist in both vectors and either i or j has a higher score in *both* vectors, the one with the higher score is a candidate for subsuming the one with the lower ranks.
3. Post-filter candidates based on their rank in both score vectors and determine the confidence of the final subsumption relation.

The resulting list contains triples (keyword i, keyword j, confidence), denoting that keyword i subsumes keyword j with the given confidence.

As the PageRank scores are power-law distributed for power-law distributed graphs (and co-occurrences are typically also power-law distributed), the tail of the PageRank score vector comprises many keywords which are only very weakly related to the keyword, on whose neighborhood we biased the PageRank computation. Hence, we can safely apply *tail cutting* in step 1 and keep only those elements in the sorted PageRank score vector, which accumulate 80% of the overall score in the score vector (following the well-known 80-20 rule).

In the third step, we apply the following rules to filter too weak relations and determine the confidence of the remaining subsumption relations:

1. If neither keyword i is among the *top-*X_j elements of the PageRank score vector of keyword j nor keyword j is among the *top-*X_i elements of the vector of keyword i, then both are assumed to be too weakly related and are deleted from the list of subsumption candidates.
2. If the subsumed keyword is among the *top-*X elements of the score vector of the subsuming keyword, then we set the confidence in the subsumption relation to 'low' (*weak relation*).
3. If both keywords are among the *top-*X elements of both score vectors, then we set the confidence in the subsumption relation to 'high' (*strong relation*).

3.3 Part III: Creating GrowBag Graphs

In the third and final part, the Semantic GrowBag algorithm finally uses the hidden related keywords of i as 'seed nodes' and 'grows' the set of nodes to create a specific GrowBag graph for keyword i using the following steps:

1. Add those keywords as nodes that subsume the latent related keywords of i directly.
2. Add recursively all keywords as nodes that are subsumed by already collected keywords.
3. Add all relations as edges where both involved keywords have already been collected. Use different edge visualizations to account for the 'strength' of the relation (dashed lines for weak relations and two-headed arrows for strong relations).

The intention is to visualize only the most important *related neighbors* and the keywords subsumed by them to limit the size of the graph.

4 Use Case and Experimental Evaluation with Practical Data

This section explains the Semantic GrowBag algorithm in detail along one use case for the start keyword 'RDF' and additionally shows how the GrowBag graph for 'RDF' changes over time. We used a subset of the computer science publications listed in DBLP and extracted the author keywords from the web, post-processed them using acronym replacement and Porter stemming [20] and removed those, which are mentioned less than five times, resulting in $13,200$ keywords. The relation DocumentID $\rightarrow$ keywords comprises about $500,000$ entries for $93,000$ publications.[3]

4.1 Creating a GrowBag Graph for 'RDF'

This use case shows how to find the GrowBag graph for the keyword 'RDF' for the period 2001–2005. The description follows the three main parts of the algorithm to (1) create a co-occurrence matrix including higher order co-occurrences, (2) find relations between keywords, and (3) create a GrowBag graph for the keyword 'RDF'. In out GrowBag demonstrator,[4] all graphs are periodically updated (so the version in the Web might differ from the graphs presented here).

Part I: Top-X and Biased PageRank. After creating the co-occurrence matrix M, the algorithm first extracts the corresponding 'RDF' row of M, comprising the weighted co-occurrences of 'RDF' (using the ICF as weight) with all other keywords. This matrix row is sorted according to the matrix values (cf. left part of Table 1; the plain co-occurrence values are shown for comparison.

In this example, the direct neighbors of 'RDF' are 'RDF' itself (the start keyword is included by definition), 'Semantic Web' and 'Metadata' as they accumulate $P = 20\%$ of the total sum of matrix values of all keywords in that list.[5]

Table 1. Direct neighbors (left) / the PageRank score vector (right) for 'RDF' ($top\text{-}X = 3$)

Rank	Keyword	$m(j,i)$	$cooc(i,j)$
1	RDF	259.8	55
2	Semantic Web	112.1	31
3	Metadata	55.3	15
4	XML	41.4	15
5	Annotation	26.3	6
6	Ontology	26.1	8
7	DAML	23.1	4
8	RDF Schema	20.6	3
9	DAML+OIL	18.0	3
10	OWL	16.0	3
...	...	...	

Rank	Keyword	Score
1	Semantic Web	828.1
2	Metadata	755.0
3	RDF	746.4
4	Ontology	127.1
5	XML	120.2
6	Web Service	74.6
7	Information Retrieval	50.2
8	Data Mining	49.3
9	Clustering	49.3
10	Annotation	49.0
...	...	...

[3] Titles, authors, citations etc. are planned to be included in future versions.

[4] `http://dblp.l3s.de/GrowBag`

[5] This heuristics to find P was confirmed by manual inspection of a large set of resulting graphs but is subject of further research.

Afterwards, the algorithm uses PageRank (biasing to 100% on the three direct keywords of 'RDF') to find a new ranking. The resulting *PageRank score vector* includes higher-order co-occurrences, which are not reflected in the sorted co-occurrence vector. Practically speaking, the main objective of the first part is to see whether the start keyword 'RDF' itself remains the 'top keyword' in the score vector after running the Biased PageRank or if other keywords are more relevant and 'overtake' (in the sorted co-occurrence vector, the start keyword stays always on top). As shown in the right part of Table 1, indeed 'Semantic Web' and 'Metadata' achieve a higher score than 'RDF' and are candidates for subsuming 'RDF'.

Part II: Deriving Relations. The basic idea of the second part to identify 'subsumption' relations between 'RDF' and its direct neighbors is to do a pairwise comparison of the scores of two vectors: the PageRank score vector of 'RDF' and of its direct neighbors (cf. Table 2).

Table 2. PageRank score vectors for 'Semantic Web' (left; $X = 8$) & 'Metadata' (right; $X = 16$)

Rank	Keyword	Score
1	Semantic Web	407.7
2	Ontology	373.0
3	XML	358.4
4	Web Service	330.6
5	RDF	311.4
6	Metadata	303.5
7	Description Logics	288.5
8	OWL	284.3
9	Data Mining	47.8
10	Security	45.6
...	...	...

Rank	Keyword	Score
1	Metadata	262.6
2	XML	125.1
3	Semantic Web	207.1
4	Digital Libraries	199.5
5	Ontology	197.5
6	Interoperability	172.3
7	Annotation	171.8
8	RDF	167.1
9	web	151.1
10	OAI	149.7
...	...	...

For the direct neighbor 'Semantic Web', the score of 'RDF' is lower than the score of 'Semantic Web' in both the PageRank list of 'Semantic Web' (cf. Table 2 (left)) and the PageRank list of 'RDF' (cf. Table 1 (right)). Hence, 'RDF' is defined to be subsumed by 'Semantic Web' (RDF achieves a sufficiently high score in both lists not to be affected by tail cutting). Since 'RDF' is among the top-$X = 8$ elements of the PageRank score vector of 'Semantic Web', the confidence in this relation is defined as 'strong'. Analogously, 'RDF' is found to be subsumed by 'Metadata'.

Part II is repeated to find subsumption relations between all pairs of keywords.

Part III: Combining the Relations into a Graph. For the final graph, the set of keywords N related to 'RDF' and the corresponding edges between the keywords in N have to be found. An excerpt of the resulting graph when starting from 'RDF' is depicted in Fig. 3:

To determine N, the Semantic GrowBag algorithm includes all direct neighbors of 'RDF' in N as initial 'seed', i.e., the start keyword 'RDF' itself (depicted as box with a black background), and the keywords 'Semantic Web', and 'Metadata' (grey boxes).

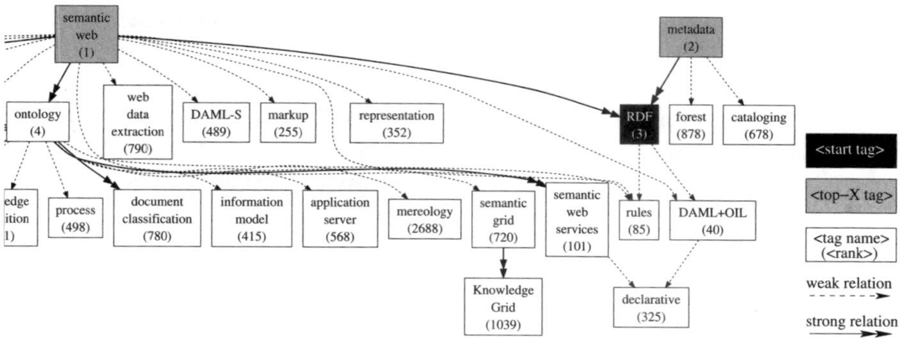

Fig. 3. Excerpt of the GrowBag graph for 'RDF' in the period 2001–2005

This set is grown by recursively collecting all subsumed keywords in N (transparent boxes). Finally, the immediate 'parents' of the direct neighbors are added to the final set N to put these direct neighbors into their immediate context (which does not add keywords to the graph in this example). To connect the nodes, all known subsumption relations involving keywords from N are added.

Two additional pieces of information are also shown in the graph: First, the Semantic GrowBag algorithm additionally provides a 'confidence' for an edge that depends on the underlying data. Second, all keywords in the graph are also associated with their rank in the PageRank score vector of the start keyword 'RDF', which gives evidence on how closely related the keyword is to 'RDF'. As an example, 'ontology' (rank 4; sibling of 'RDF') has a closer relation to 'RDF' than 'web data extraction' (rank 790; also a sibling of 'RDF').

4.2 Graph Development over Time

Whereas facets are usually considered to be static, the Semantic GrowBag algorithm can also show the development of the categorization over time for our input data. The previous figure depicted the GrowBag graph using all documents in the main period of

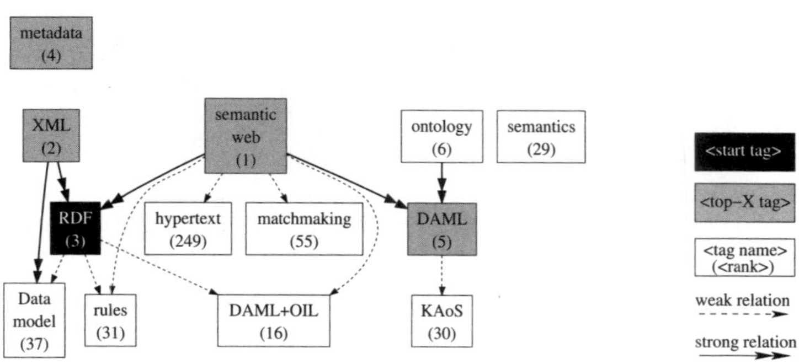

Fig. 4. GrowBag graph for 'RDF' (2002-2003)

'RDF' (2001-2005). In contrast, figures 4 and 5 show the relations restricted to 2002–2003 and 2003–2004 respectively[6].

In 2002/03, for example, 'Semantic Web' subsumes 'DAML' whereas in 2003/04, 'Semantic Web' subsumes 'OWL'. Very interesting is the relation between 'Semantic Web' and 'Alloy' in 2003/04: Alloy is a modelling language from the Formal Methods community, that has been used to validate Semantic Web ontologies for consistency.

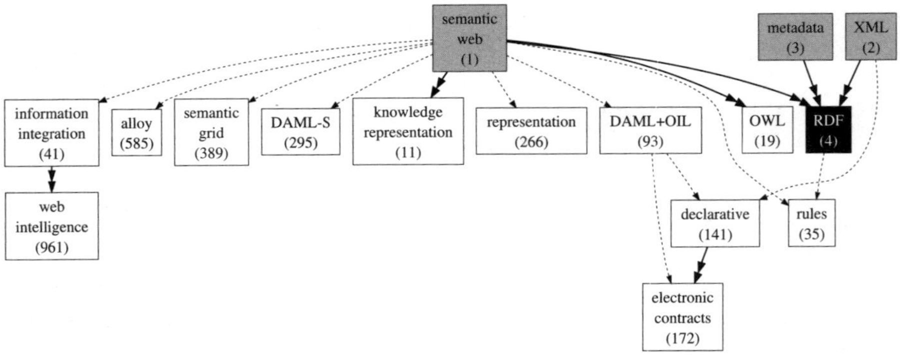

Fig. 5. GrowBag graph for 'RDF' (2003-2004)

4.3 Comparison with the Baseline Approach

In general, the quality of categorization systems is a very subjective issue and can hardly be evaluated automatically. One objective of the Semantic GrowBag approach is finding additional relations between keywords based on higher-order co-occurrences. Hence, we compared the number of relations found by our approach with the relations found using the baseline approach [12] (cf. Sect. 2, to which we also applied the 'tail cutting' to eliminate too shallow relations). Table 3 shows the number of found relations in all GrowBag graphs and for the baseline approach for three different periods.

Table 3. Identified relations and overlap for 1996-2000, 2001–2005, and 2004–2005

Approach	2001–2005		1996-2000		2004-2005	
	Relations	Overlap	Relations	Overlap	Relations	Overlap
GrowBag	2150 (929)	n.a.	2494 (988)	n.a.	853 (413)	n.a.
Baseline 51%	2297	96 (63)	2101	414 (168)	1427	63 (35)
Baseline 55%	2297	80 (50)	2101	394 (152)	1427	59 (31)
Baseline 60%	1793	60 (41)	1859	334 (120)	1245	41 (18)
Baseline 70%	727	29 (18)	605	130 (49)	458	19 (8)
Baseline 80%	324	8 (7)	352	58 (20)	232	3 (2)
Baseline 100%	260	5	270	40	215	1

[6] We coupled the data from two years, since the data was too sparse in single years. We omitted the children of XML for space reasons.

For the originally proposed 80% threshold in the baseline approach, only about $230 - 350$ relations are found ($15 - 30\%$ compared to GrowBag), of which $8 - 58$ overlap with the relations identified by our approach. Hence, our approach finds additional relations using higher-order co-occurrences compared to the original baseline approach, which assumes that subsuming keywords and the keywords they subsume are used together pretty often (e.g., $> 80\%$) to annotate one resource. This is true for automatically extracted keywords from full text, but in general happens less often for manually assigned keywords.

Furthermore, most of those relations being found by both approaches are actually 'strong' relations as found by the Semantic GrowBag scheme (shown in parentheses in Table 3). This indicates that the distinction between 'strong' and 'weak' relation is reasonable, though there is a high variance between the different periods. As an alternative way to increase the identified number of relations in the baseline approach, the threshold could be decreased to $51 - 60\%$ (cf. Table 3). However, the overlap in the identified relations between GrowBag and the baseline approach remains still very small.

We also examined the depth of the hierarchies created by GrowBag and the baseline approach with 60% and found that less than 10% of the nodes have a depth larger than one (i.e., have 'grand-children' nodes) with an average depth of 1.1 as opposed to 22% and an average depth of 1.3 in the GrowBag approach. Hence, the introduction of higher-order co-occurrences helps in creating deeper hierarchies as expected.

While this section does not allow to judge the quality of the relations found by our approach, it shows that the same results cannot be achieved with a (simpler) system based on first-order co-occurrences only.

4.4 The Top-X Threshold

Finding an appropriate *top-X* is important for high quality graphs. In this context, the threshold $P = 20\%$ for the accumulated sum of the PageRank scores was determined empirically for our specific data set. We varied this threshold between 10% and 30%, but already in the 15% case very many keywords have two or less keywords as direct neighbors, so that too few PageRank lists can be computed. In the 25% case, the maximum size of the *top-X* list becomes too high (up to 49 compared to 34 in the 20% case). This threshold P will be subject of further research and always has to be adapted to the underlying corpus. This is because it influences the quality of the identified relations and depends on characteristics of the particular object collection such as the average number of keywords per object, the average number of co-occurring keywords, etc.

5 Summary and Future Work

In this paper we presented the Semantic GrowBag approach for the automatic creation of hierarchical categorization systems for usage in topic facets. Exploiting existing author keyword annotations, we have strong evidence that the automatically derived facets generally are indeed semantically meaningful. Even at this preliminary stage of applying the algorithm to real world collections (which are often not yet thoroughly annotated) the existing annotations allow to get sufficiently good facets for result presentation. Moreover, we have shown that also the evolution of topics over time can be derived and may provide an added value for collection browsing. This benefit for result presentation has already been demonstrated in the FacetedDBLP prototype [6] that also can be accessed online[7]. It provides a faceted view on the DBLP data using GrowBag graphs to create topic facets (with respect to a chosen time interval).

As future work, we want to further improve the quality of the topic facets, e.g., using a more sophisticated detection of the direct neighbors (i.e., the top-X). Furthermore, we envision a change detection scheme to automatically detect keywords in quickly changing environments. We have also started to look at different input data sets, such as the Medline Database, or data sets stemming from collaborative tagging, which in general require a much stronger pre-processing stage to clean the corpus of keywords/tags.

Acknowledgments

This work was partially funded by the European NoE Knowledge Web and the Emmy-Noether Program of the German Research Foundation DFG. The authors gratefully acknowledge the many fruitful discussions with our colleagues.

References

1. Hearst, M.A.: Clustering versus faceted categories for information exploration. Commun. ACM 49(4), 59–61 (2006)
2. Rodden, K., Basalaj, W., Sinclair, D., Wood, K.: Does organisation by similarity assist image browsing? In: Proc. of SIGCHI conference, pp. 190–197 (2001)
3. Ross, K., Janevski, A.: Querying faceted databases. In: Bussler, C.J., Tannen, V., Fundulaki, I. (eds.) SWDB 2004. LNCS, vol. 3372, pp. 199–218. Springer, Heidelberg (2005)
4. Weber, A., Reuther, P., Walter, B., Ley, M., Klink, S.: Multi-layered browsing and visualization for digital libraries. In: Gonzalo, J., Thanos, C., Verdejo, M.F., Carrasco, R.C. (eds.) ECDL 2006. LNCS, vol. 4172, Springer, Heidelberg (2006)
5. Diederich, J., Thaden, U., Balke, W.T.: The semantic growbag demonstrator for automatically organizing topic facets. In: Proc. of the SIGIR Workshop on Faceted Search (2006)
6. Diederich, J., Thaden, U., Balke, W.T.: Demonstrating the Semantic GrowBag: Automatically Creating Topic Facets for FacetedDBLP. In: Proc. of the JCDL (2007)
7. Cutting, D.R., Karger, D.R., Pedersen, J.O., Tukey, J.W.: Scatter/gather: a cluster-based approach to browsing large document collections. In: Proc. of SIGIR conference, pp. 318–329 (1992)
8. Pratt, W., Hearst, M.A., Fagan, L.M.: A knowledge-based approach to organizing retrieved documents. In: Proc. of the AAAI conference, Menlo Park, CA, USA, pp. 80–85 (1999)
9. Park, J., Hunting, S.: XML Topic Maps: Creating and Using Topic Maps for the Web. Addison-Wesley, Reading (2002)
10. Hearst, M.A.: Automatic acquisition of hyponyms from large text corpora. In: Proc. of the Conference on Computational Linguistics, pp. 539–545 (1992)
11. Cimiano, P., Völker, J.: Text2onto - a framework for ontology learning and data-driven change discovery. In: Montoyo, A., Muñoz, R., Métais, E. (eds.) NLDB 2005. LNCS, vol. 3513, pp. 227–238. Springer, Heidelberg (2005)
12. Sanderson, M., Croft, B.: Deriving concept hierarchies from text. In: Proc. of the SIGIR conference, pp. 206–213 (1999)

[7] `http://dblp.l3s.de`

13. Schütze, H.: Automatic word sense discrimination. Comput. Linguist. 24(1), 97–123 (1998)
14. Page, L., Brin, S., Motwani, R., Winograd, T.: The pagerank citation ranking: Bringing order to the web. Technical report, Stanford University (1998)
15. Jeh, G., Widom, J.: SimRank: A Measure of Structural-Context Similarity. In: Proc. of the SIGKDD conference (2002)
16. Deerwester, S.C., Dumais, S.T., Landauer, T.K., Furnas, G.W., Harshman, R.A.: Indexing by latent semantic analysis. JASIS 41(6), 391–407 (1990)
17. Hofmann, T.: Probabilistic latent semantic indexing. In: Proc. of SIGIR conference, pp. 50–57 (1999)
18. Baeza-Yates, R.A., Ribeiro-Neto, B.A.: Modern Information Retrieval. ACM Press /Addison-Wesley (1999)
19. Langville, A., Meyer, C.: Deeper inside pagerank. Internet Mathmatics 2(1), 335–380 (2004)
20. Porter, M.: An algorithm for suffix stripping. Program 14(3), 130–137 (1980)

Ontology-Based Question Answering for Digital Libraries

Stephan Bloehdorn[1], Philipp Cimiano[1], Alistair Duke[2], Peter Haase[1], Jörg Heizmann[3], Ian Thurlow[2], and Johanna Völker[1]

[1] Institute AIFB, University of Karlsruhe, D-76128 Karlsruhe, Germany
{bloehdorn,cimiano,haase,heizmann,voelker}@aifb.uni-karlsruhe.de
[2] British Telecom, Adastral Park, Ipswich IP5 3RE, UK
{alistair.duke,ian.thurlow}@bt.com
[3] ontoprise GmbH, Amalienbadstr. 36, D-76227 Karlsruhe, Germany
heizmann@ontoprise.de

Abstract. In this paper we present an approach to question answering over heterogeneous knowledge sources that makes use of different ontology management components within the scenario of a digital library application. We present a principled framework for integrating structured metadata and unstructured resource content in a seamless manner which can then be flexibly queried using structured queries expressed in natural language. The novelty of the approach lies in the combination of different semantic technologies providing a clear benefit for the application scenario considered. The resulting system is implemented as part of the digital library of British Telecommunications (BT). The original contribution of our paper lies in the architecture we present allowing for the non-straightforward integration of the different components we consider.

1 Introduction

In the last decade, *Digital Libraries* [1] have emerged as a standard means for accessing published resources maintained electronically by libraries. Many digital libraries have evolved from traditional libraries and concentrated on making their information sources available to a wider audience. Today, many companies maintain their own digital libraries, and research and development for digital libraries now includes processing, dissemination, storage, search and analysis of all types of digital information. In contrast to physical libraries, digital libraries enable concurrent access at any time without physical boundaries. As such, digital libraries can be regarded as indispensable tools for today's knowledge workers. Digital libraries have always been an appealing playground for innovative computer science solutions. To name just a few examples, cross-referencing functionalities, document digitalization and optic character recognition (OCR), improved information retrieval techniques and recommender functionalities have changed the way we interact with digital libraries far beyond their basic functionalities. So far, functionalities of digital libraries are typically implemented in a specific context and are tuned to meeting the requirements of a specific audience. Currently missing are *generic methods* for the smooth integration of content stemming

L. Kovács, N. Fuhr, and C. Meghini (Eds.): ECDL 2007, LNCS 4675, pp. 14–25, 2007.

from different sources and for a flexible framework for implementing new functionalities. Further, fine-grained access to resources (resource retrieval) and facts (fact retrieval) in the form of structured queries combining fine-granular metadata and fulltext content is typically not provided. In this paper we show that with the help of semantic technologies we can bridge this gap. In particular, ontologies offer a generic solution to the problem of integrating various sources. The documents in the knowledge sources are annotated and classified according to the ontology. Hereby, an ontology is essentially a logical theory conceptualizing relevant aspects of an underlying domain, in our case the domain of publications. Our ontology model consists of concepts organized hierarchically in terms of subsumption as well as of (binary) relations together with appropriate domain/range restrictions. The ontological metadata can then be exploited for advanced knowledge access, including navigation, browsing, and semantic search. Advanced semantics-based mining technology can extract fine-grained metadata from articles contained in the digital library. Finally, current reasoning techniques allow to answer structured queries to access full-text content as well as fine-grained metadata from articles from different sources in a uniform way.

In this paper, we present a principled framework for integrating digital library knowledge sources as well as facts extracted from the content under consideration by means of an ontology-based digital library system that can be used for several adaptions of the standard digital library scenario. As an example, we then present a system that allows the posing of structured natural language queries against the digital library with a well-defined semantics provided by the underlying ontology. The resulting system has been implemented as part of a case study with the Digital Library of British Telecommunications plc (BT) within the EU IST integrated project Semantic Knowledge Technologies (SEKT)). It combines a variety of tools for natural language question interpretation, information extraction, query answering and reasoning which are glued together by ontology-based knowledge representation formalisms and a corresponding ontology and metadata management system.

This paper is organized as follows: In section 2 we introduce a scenario which will serve as a running example throughout this paper. From this scenario, we derive a number of requirements for an ontology-based digital library system. In section 3, we present the architecture and the components of our system. In section 4 we refer back to the earlier requirements and describe how they are addressed and handled in our implementation. Section 5 discusses related work while Section 6 summarizes the main contribution of the paper.

2 The Scenario

In this section, we present a short scenario which will be used as a running example throughout this paper:

Scenario (BT Digital Library). *Bob works as technology analyst for British Telecom. His daily work includes research on new technological trends, market developments as well as the analysis of competitors. Bob's company maintains a digital library that gives access to a repository of internal surveys and analysis documents. The company also has a license with an academic research database which is accessed via a separate* *interface. Depending on his work context, Bob uses the topic hierarchies, the full-text search functionalities or metadata search facilities provided by the two libraries to get access to the relevant data. However, Bob is often annoyed by the differing topic hierarchies and metadata schemes used by the two libraries as well as by a cumbersome syntax for metadata queries. Questions which Bob might be interested in could include:*

1. *What articles were published by William Arms in "Communications of the ACM"?*
2. *Who wrote the book "Digital Libraries"?*
3. *What article deals with Grid Computing?*
4. *What are the topics of "The future of web services"?*
5. *Which conference papers were classified as "emerging technology trends 2007"?*
6. *Which articles are about "Intellectual Capital"?*

The user Bob in this scenario can be seen as a typical example of a knowledge worker who is using digital libraries for everyday research tasks. The scenario also points to a number of deficiencies of many of the current interfaces to digital libraries. From the initial scenario and the above questions, we derive the following requirements:

Support for Structured Queries Against Metadata and Documents: With current interfaces to Digital Libraries, users either pose keyword-based queries on document full-texts or abstracts or they use metadata search facilities to perform document retrieval. However, question 1 requires as answers articles which fulfill the condition of having been published by William Arms in a certain journal, i.e. Communications of the ACM, and thus a structured query against the metadata of the articles. Question 2 requires the author of a certain publication, i.e. the book with title "Digital Libraries". This shows that in general we are interested in receiving as answers facts from the knowledge base rather than only relevant documents. We thus require the capability to pose structured queries to the underlying digital library which can be evaluated against the articles' metadata as contained in the knowledge base. For metadata queries, current interfaces either offer preselected attribute fields (which are interpreted as conjunctive queries over a attribute-specific fulltext search) or they require some kind of formal query language.

Integration of Heterogeneous Knowledge Sources: In general, answering questions as the above might however require uniform access to different sources or repositories. However, a common limitation is that different providers of digital libraries use different taxonomies and different metadata schemes to describe the stored content, which requires a user to switch between different representations depending on the back-end system searched. A particular challenge is the integration of structured knowledge sources (e.g. document metadata) and unstructured sources (e.g. document fulltexts). We would like to access heterogenous knowledge sources via a single, unified interface that integrates different metadata schemes as well as different topic hierarchies.

Automatic content extraction and classification: Questions 3 and 4 might require fine-grained access to the topics of articles. Hereby, with topics we mean items of some classification scheme to which documents are related. Though in many cases articles are classified, we can not expect that all relevant categories are actually explicitly stated.

Thus, some support for automatically capturing the content of new documents added to the library seems necessary. The content of the Digital Library is not static, but changes over time: New documents come in, but also documents may be removed from the document base. We here require means to automatically extract relevant knowledge and to classify the new content.

Natural Language Interface: Finally, in order to provide intuitive access and not to impose the burden on the user of learning a formal query language, we would like to allow the user to use an intuitive query language, ideally arbitrary natural language queries. In our running scenario, Bob should thus be able to ask the questions directly in the way they are stated in the scenario above.

All of the above requirements can, of course, be tackled by ad-hoc modifications of the interfaces. The approach we take is, however, generic and can be flexibly extended. We have implemented an approach that enables the user to perform structured natural language queries against the information contained in the Digital Library. The semantics of the information and the user queries is defined by an underlying ontology. As a result, users are able to ask queries such as "What article deals with Grid Computing?", i.e. a query that allows for relating different knowledge sources and that does not only allow to return documents, but structured answers to the query.

3 Architecture and Components

In this section we discuss the overall architecture of the proposed digital library system. The architecture – as shown in Figure 1 – consists of the following main components:

- The *Knowledge Portal* is the user interface to the digital library. The user interacts with the portal by asking queries in natural language. The underlying transformation and query answering processes are completely transparent to the user. Figure
- The *Query Translation* component translates the natural language queries into structured logical queries against the ontology. This translation relies on a deep parsing of the questions using a lexicon that describes the possible lexical realizations of the elements in the ontology. The resulting logical queries are expressed in SPARQL [2], a query language standardized by the W3C for the Semantic Web.
- The *Query Answering* component manages the integrated ontologies and performs the answering of SPARQL queries against the knowledge sources. Extensions can be integrated that enable additional search functionalities at query time, e.g. for online-*text classification* of content. The query results are tuples of variable bindings that satisfy the query.
- The *Knowledge Base* of the digital library consists of a number of heterogeneous knowledge sources, partially structured in the form of metadata and topic hierarchies, but largely unstructured in the form of fulltext documents. All these data sources are integrated using an *ontology*. The *Ontology Learning* component is used to automatically extract structured ontologies from the unstructured text documents in the library. This allows the integration of the text documents with the other data sources such that they can be queried in a uniform way.

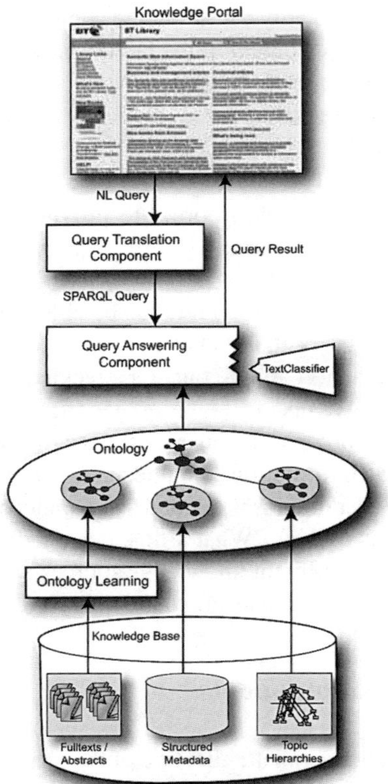

Fig. 1. Conceptual Architecture of the Application

In the following, we will discuss the individual components in more detail. While the architecture is generic in principle, we illustrate it using the components used for the implementation of the BT Digital Library.

3.1 Knowledge Base and Ontology

As shown in the bottom of Figure 1, the knowledge base of the digital library comprises a number of different knowledge sources. In the BT Digital Library, it consists of databases with bibliographic metadata, topic hierarchies, such as INSPEC[1], but also unstructured sources such as full text documents with different formats. All these heterogeneous knowledge sources are integrated using a common ontology, which is based on a designed general ontology, which we call PROTON (PROTo ONtology)[2]. Within PROTON, we adapt a layered approach: The classes in this ontology are a mixture of very general classes, e.g. `Person`, `Role`, `Topic`, `TimeInterval`, and classes which are more specific to the world of business, e.g. `Company`, `PublicCompany`,

[1] `http://www.iee.org/publish/inspec/about/`

[2] `http://proton.semanticweb.org`

MediaCompany. Finally, the ontology contains domain specific aspects, including classes relating to the specifics of the library, e.g. to the particular information sources available. Within PROTON there is a class Topic such that each individual topic is an instance of this class. However, frequently a topic will be a subtopic of another topic, e.g. in the sense that a document 'about' the former should also be regarded as being about the latter. The hierarchy of topics is modeled using a special relation subTopic. This relationship is defined to be transitive, in the sense that if A is a subtopic of B and B is a subtopic of C, then A is also a subtopic of C.

The structured information sources are integrated using a mapping of the underlying structures to the ontology. As a simple example, a database table describing persons would be mapped to the class Person in the ontology along with its properties, such as name affiliation, etc. The mapping formalism [3] also supports more complex mappings that establish correspondences between conjunctive queries over the sources and the ontology. For the unstructured sources – such as fulltext documents – the mapping is not as direct. Instead, we obtain structured ontologies from the unstructured sources with the help of the ontology learning tool Text2Onto [4], as explained in the following.

3.2 Ontology Learning

Ontology Learning aims at learning and extending ontologies on the basis of textual data. In our system, ontology learning is used to dynamically extract new topics, concepts and relations in the underlying document collection. For this purpose, we exploit Text2Onto, a framework for ontology learning and data-driven ontology evolution [4]. It relies on a combination of natural language processing and machine learning techniques for extracting ontologies from unstructured textual resources. In particular, it implements algorithms for learning the following ontological primitives: **concepts** and **instances** as well as **subconcept**, **subtopic**, **instance-of** and arbitrary **binary relations** between concepts. The algorithms implemented in Text2Onto build on a variety of techniques from information retrieval (e.g. statistical measures such as tf.idf for term extraction), natural language processing (e.g. lexico-syntactic patterns for extracting subconcept and instance-of relations) as well as machine learning (e.g. clustering for learning concepts hierarchies, association rules for extracting binary relations), etc.

To illustrate the ontology learning process consider the following excerpt from a digital library document about collaborative development environments: *To support remote authoring of Web pages and file contents, as well as remote source code access, GForge uses several network protocols, including SSH, SFTP, CVS pserver, and FTP.* Given a lexico-syntactic pattern matching a sequence of noun phrases such as $NP_{concept}$, *including* $NP^1_{\text{instance}} \ldots NP^n_{\text{instance}}$ Text2Onto would conclude from this sentence that SSH, SFTP, CVS pserver and FTP are instances of network protocol. If the user later asks for documents about network protocols, the learned concept instantiation will enable a reasoner to infer that a document dealing with SSH might be relevant for the user – even if the term *network protocol* is not explicitly mentioned in the text.

We apply the algorithms to extract the above mentioned primitives from each of the relevant information spaces in the digital library, and merge the resulting ontologies. Most importantly, Text2Onto keeps a document pointer to the document where a certain ontological primitive was extracted from. This allows fine-grained queries to be posed to the document collections by asking for the topics, concepts, instances, as well as different types of taxonomic and non-taxonomic relations occurring in a document. By the integration of Text2Onto we could for example answer questions like: *What network protocols are talked about in the article "The Future of Web Services"?* or *What articles are about "Intellectual Capital"?*.

3.3 Query Answering

The integrated ontology is managed by the KAON2 ontology management system[3], which acts as the query answering component. As mentioned before, the queries are logical conjunctive queries against the ontology. Query answering amounts to a reasoning process over the knowledge sources according to the semantics of the underlying ontology language OWL. To represent the conjunctive queries, we here rely on SPARQL as the query language, an ontology query language standardized by the W3C [2]. The query answering is not a mere retrieval of explicitly stated facts (as in a conventional database), but involves a deduction of answers over the knowledge base [5]. As an example, consider the following SPARQL query which asks for articles that are associated with the topic "Intellectual Capital"?:

```
SELECT  ?x WHERE {
   ?x rdf:type <http://proton.semanticweb.org/2005/04/protonu#Article> .
   ?x <http://proton.semanticweb.org/2005/04/protont#hasSubject> ?y  .
   ?y rdfs:label ?z .
   match(?z,"Intellectual Capital")
```

For the answering of queries, we follow a virtual integration approach that does not require a full integration of all knowledge sources: The actual data still resides in the individual knowledge sources, and the mapping between the ontology and the knowledge sources is only used at runtime to retrieve the facts that are actually relevant for answering a query. In a query, predicates can be used that require access to different knowledge sources. The evaluation of these predicates is automatically *pushed down* to the respective knowledge sources, e.g. as a relational query in the case of a relational database, or to a fulltext index in the case of the fulltext match predicate `match` over the topic hierarchy contained in the above query. In Section 3.5, we discuss the evaluation of a special predicate for the classification of text documents. At last the result set is processed and sent back to be displayed by the BT knowledge portal.

3.4 Query Translation from Natural Language

ORAKEL [6] is a natural language interface which translates natural language queries to structured queries formulated with respect to a given ontology. This translation relies essentially on a compositional semantic interpretation of the question guided by two lexica: a domain-specific and a domain-independent lexicon. As the name suggests, the domain-independent lexicon is a priori encoded into the system and captures the domain-independent meaning of prepositions, determiners, question pronouns etc., which typically remain constant across domains. The domain-specific lexicon needs to

[3] `http://kaon2.semanticweb.org`

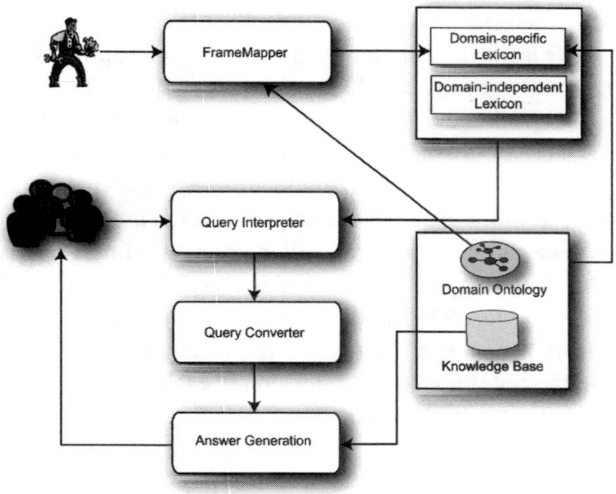

Fig. 2. Overview of the ORAKEL system

be created by a *lexicon engineer* who is assumed to create the lexicon in various cycles. In fact, ORAKEL builds on an iterative lexicon development cycle in which the lexicon is constantly updated by the lexicon engineer on the basis of the questions the system failed to answer so far. The end users then are able to directly interact with the BT digital library portal by accessing the library data via natural language questions, which are translated into SPARQL queries by the ORAKEL system. The underlying mechanism however is hidden from the users - the only thing users need to do is to input the query just as their normal questions and then get the result from the portal. The obvious advantage of using such a natural language interface is that users do not have to learn nor struggle with a formal query language, while they can still benefit from the possibility to pose structured queries.

Further, ORAKEL was also modified to process quoted text by matching it against a text index of the metadata in the database using a special purpose predicate *match*. The question *"What articles are about "Intellectual Capital"?"* is translated into the SPARQL query presented above.

Figure 2 gives an overview of the ORAKEL system, which has been designed in a flexible manner allowing the system's target query language to be easily replaced. As the architecture described here relies on the KAON2 system as inference engine and knowledge repository, ORAKEL was adapted to generate SPARQL queries. Further, a lexicon was generated for the Proton ontology, which specifies the possible lexical representations of the ontology elements in the user queries.

3.5 Text Classification

Often query answering requires the evaluation of predicates whose extensions need to be determined using special purpose algorithms at query time. This is for example the case if the text documents need to be classified against parameters that are provided at query time by the user. Automated text classification [7] is a standard tool for adaptive categorization of textual data. In essence, given a collection of positive and negative examples, machine learning techniques are used to discover patterns in the text that will help in the categorization of unseen documents in the future. For topics for which no explicit library classification exists, e.g. personalized interests or emerging topics, one can train and use such a classification module. Of course, the classification accuracy for text mining tasks will depend on many factors such as representation, training algorithm, number of training documents and parameter setting. We have used a simple approach that has been shown to perform well in practice, namely the bag-of-words representation together with Support Vector Machine (SVM) classification. While training is performed offline, the resulting models can be simply integrated into the system by means of the Built-In mechanism. As a result, the special-purpose predicate "classified-as" is contained in the ontology but its extension is evaluated at query time against the document fulltext and the stored model(s)[4].

4 Scenario Revisited

The architecture described in the previous section has been implemented and deployed at BT. In contrast to the previously existing system, the resulting question answering prototype does not only allow for asking questions about existing metadata in the BT library, but also about topics found by Text2Onto as well as to invoke the automatic text classification system at runtime. The net result is that a variety of queries about authors, topics, about documents etc. could be answered successfully against the BT ontology and database. The questions introduced in section 2 are examples of supported natural language queries.

We will revisit two of these questions. Consider the question *What articles were published by "William Arms" in "Communications of the ACM"?*. The corresponding SPARQL query would look as follows:

```
SELECT ?x WHERE {
 ?x rdf:type <http://proton.semanticweb.org/2005/04/protonu#Article> .
 ?x <http://proton.semanticweb.org/2005/04/protont#documentAuthor> ?y .
 ?x <http://proton.semanticweb.org/2005/04/protonu#publishedWithin> ?z .
 ?y rdfs:label ?ys .
 match(?ys,''William Arms'')
 ?z rdfs:label ?zs .
 match(?ys,''Communications of the ACM'') }
```

As another example, consider the question *"Which conference papers are classified as "emerging technology trends 2007?"*. By means of ORAKEL and a small set of rules, the question would result in the following SPARQL query, which would use the SVM classification on document abstracts of documents of type article and the (previously trained) SVM model "emerging technology trends 2007":

```
SELECT ?x WHERE {
 ?x rdf:type <http://proton.semanticweb.org/2005/04/protonu#Article>.
 ?x <http://proton.semanticweb.org/2005/04/protont#documentAbstract> ?y.
 EVALUATE ?margin:=tgclassify(?y,'emerging technology trends 2007').
 FILTER ?margin>0 }
```

[4] The underlying module for text classification and corresponding training is part of the TextGarden library. See `http://www.textmining.net/` for further information.

Table 1. Results for the different iterations

Iteration	Recall (avg.)	Precision (avg.)
1	42%	52%
2	49%	71%
3	61%	73%

Furthermore, an evaluation of the system was carried out with BT and other users. A primary goal was to evaluate the performance of the natural language question answering over several iterations of the ontology lexicon. The lexicon was constructed in three iterations: one initial iteration of 6 hours and 2 follow-up iterations of each 30 minutes in which the questions not answered by the system were examined. The end users received written instructions describing the conceptual range of the knowledge base, asking them to ask at least 10 questions to the system. In each of three iterations, 4 end users asked questions to the system and a graduate student updated the lexicon on the basis of the failed questions after the first and second round for about 30 min., respectively. The end users were also asked to indicate whether the answer was correct or not, which allowed for the evaluation of the system's performance in terms of precision and recall. The results of the evaluation are presented in Table 1, which clearly shows that the second iteration performed much better than the first one, both in terms of precision and recall. In the third iteration, there was a further gain in recall with respect to the second iteration. Concluding, we can on the one hand indeed say that the precision of the system is fairly high. On the other hand, the lower recall is definitely compensated by a fallback strategy. In case the semantic understanding and answering of the query fails, our system resorts to standard information retrieval techniques to provide a number of relevant documents to the user's query. This move thus makes the implemented system very robust. Overall, the application of our prototype showed that we could indeed improve the access to BT's digital library by (i) integrating of data and sources using an inference engine (ii) precise question answering, (iii) exploitation of new topics detected by Text2Onto, as well as (iv) on-the-fly text classification functionality.

5 Related Work

While traditional digital library systems such as e.g. DSpace [5] or e Prints[6] have mostly focused on providing a generic infrastructure for storing digital content and metadata, the relation to Semantic Web technologies has been mostly restricted to metadata import/export functionalities. The actual combination of semantic technologies and Digital Libraries has only received increased attention in recent years. In the following, we discuss some related projects that apply Semantic Web technologies for digital libraries.

An initiative that is in many aspects similar to our work, is the JeromeDL project[7] [8], which employs Semantic Web technologies mainly for user management and

[5] `http://dspace.org/`

[6] `http://www.eprints.org/`

[7] `http://www.jeromedl.org/`

personalized search within a digital library. In JeromeDL, full text content, bibliographic entries etc. are described with respect to the Jerome ontology. JeromeDL is distinguished by the extensive conceptualization and advanced search and personalization algorithms. However, in contrast to our approach, JeromeDL lacks any kind of knowledge extraction or natural language query functionalities. The SIMILE Project[8] ([9]), aims at enhancing interoperability among digital assets, vocabularies, metadata and services. SIMILE tackles the challenge that collections can be distributed but should be queried in a uniform way. Semantic Web technologies, in particular the Resource Description Framework (RDF) [10] are used to tackle the challenge that collections can be highly distributed but need to be queried in a uniform way. While SMILE shares the interoperability-related aspects with our work, it does not go beyond this. Recently, some initiatives have emerged with the aim of moving from a content-centered organization of digital libraries towards more service-oriented architectures. The main idea of projects such as FEDORA project[9] ([11]) is to support the whole digital content value chain from data creation, sharing, search and dynamic provision of appropriate services.

6 Conclusions

We have presented an approach that combines a number of semantic technologies, including ontology management, ontology learning and reasoning, keyword-type search and text classification in order to allow the flexible and versatile answering of natural language questions on top of a digital library. The users are able to perform structured natural language queries against a variety of knowledge sources in an integrated manner with a well-defined semantics provided by the underlying ontology. The novelty of our system lies in the combination of different tools for natural language question interpretation, ontology learning, query answering as well as reasoning. Our experience showed that with reasonable effort it is possible to apply semantic technologies to enhance a semantic library so that: (i) natural language questions can be answered precisely relying on standard (logical) querying techniques, (ii) topics can be automatically spotted over time and integrated into the system, and (iii) text documents can be classified on-the-fly given a user query. Though the integration of semantic technologies which have been developed recently at our institute (ORAKEL, Text2Onto, Text classification modules, KAON2) was far from straightforward mainly due to technical and infrastructure problems, the case study proved that semantic technologies are indeed mature enough to be integrated with reasonable effort and deliver a clear added value. In this sense we can only encourage other people to venture out and experiment with semantic technologies in order to foster the exchange of experiences between the Semantic Web and Digital Library communities.

Acknowledgements. This work was partially supported by the European Commission under contracts IST-2003-506826 SEKT, IST-2006-027595 NeOn, and IST-FP6-026978 X-Media.

[8] `http://simile.mit.edu/`

[9] `http://www.fedora.info/`

References

1. Arms, W.Y.: Digital Libraries. MIT Press, Cambridge (2001)
2. Prud'hommeaux, E., Seaborne, A.: SPARQL query language for RDF. W3C Working Draft (2007), available at http://www.w3.org/TR/rdf-sparql-query/
3. Haase, P., Motik, B.: A mapping system for the integration of OWL-DL ontologies. In: Hahn, A., Abels, S., Haak, L. (eds.) Proceedings of the first international ACM workshop on Interoperability of Heterogeneous Information Systems (IHIS'05), CIKM Conference, Bremen, Germany, November 4, 2005, pp. 9–16. ACM Press, New York (2005)
4. Cimiano, P., Völker, J.: Text2Onto - a framework for ontology learning and data-driven change discovery. In: Montoyo, A., Muńoz, R., Métais, E. (eds.) NLDB 2005. LNCS, vol. 3513, pp. 227–238. Springer, Heidelberg (2005)
5. Motik, B., Sattler, U., Studer, R.: Query answering for OWL-DL with rules. In: McIlraith, S.A., Plexousakis, D., van Harmelen, F. (eds.) ISWC 2004. LNCS, vol. 3298, pp. 549–563. Springer, Heidelberg (2004)
6. Cimiano, P., Haase, P., Heizmann, J.: Porting natural language interfaces between domains – a case study with the ORAKEL system. In: Proceedings of the International Conference on Intelligent User Interfaces (IUI), pp. 180–189 (2007)
7. Sebastiani, F.: Machine learning in automated text categorization. ACM Computing Surveys 34, 1–47 (2002)
8. Kruk, S.R., Decker, S., Zieborak, L.: Jeromedl - adding semantic web technologies to digital libraries. In: Andersen, K.V., Debenham, J., Wagner, R. (eds.) DEXA 2005. LNCS, vol. 3588, pp. 716–725. Springer, Heidelberg (2005)
9. Mazzocchi, S., Garland, S., Lee, R.: Simile: Practical metadata for the semantic web. XML.com (2006)
10. Manola, F., Miller, E.: Resource description framework (RDF) model and syntax specification (2004), http://www.w3.org/TR/rdf-primer/
11. Payette, S., Staples, T.: The mellon fedora project: Digital library architecture meets xml and web services. In: Calzarossa, M.C., Tucci, S. (eds.) Performance 2002. LNCS, vol. 2459, pp. 406–421. Springer, Heidelberg (2002)

Formalizing the Get-Specific Document Classification Algorithm

Fausto Giunchiglia, Ilya Zaihrayeu, and Uladzimir Kharkevich

Department of Information and Communication Technology
University of Trento, Italy
{fausto,ilya,kharkevi}@dit.unitn.it

Abstract. The paper represents a first attempt to formalize the get-specific document classification algorithm and to fully automate it through reasoning in a propositional concept language without requiring user involvement or a training dataset. We follow a knowledge-centric approach and convert a natural language hierarchical classification into a formal classification, where the labels are defined in the concept language. This allows us to encode the get-specific algorithm as a problem in the concept language. The reported experimental results provide evidence of practical applicability of the proposed approach.

1 Introduction

Classification hierarchies have always been a natural and effective way for humans to organize their knowledge about the world. These hierarchies are rooted trees where each node defines a topic category. Child nodes' categories define aspects or facets of the parent node's category, thus creating a multifaceted description of the objects which can be classified in these categories. Classification hierarchies are used pervasively: in conventional libraries (e.g., the Dewey Decimal Classification system (DDC) [8]), in web directories (e.g., DMoz [2]), in e-commerce standardized catalogues (e.g., UNSPSC [3]), and so on.

Standard classification methodologies amount to manually organizing objects into classification categories following a predefined system of rules. The rules may differ widely in different approaches, but there is one classification pattern which is commonly followed. The pattern is called the *get-specific principle*, and it requires that an object is classified in a category (or in a set of categories), which most specifically describes the object. Following this principle is not easy and is constrained by a number of limitations, discussed below:

- the meaning of a given category is implicitly codified in a natural language label, which may be ambiguous and may therefore be interpreted differently by different classifiers;
- a link, connecting two nodes, may also be ambiguous in the sense that it may specify the meaning of the child node, of the parent node, or of both;
- as a consequence of the previous two items, the classification task also becomes ambiguous in the sense that different classifiers may classify the same objects differently, based on their subjective opinion.

L. Kovács, N. Fuhr, and C. Meghini (Eds.): ECDL 2007, LNCS 4675, pp. 26–37, 2007.

In the present paper we propose an approach to converting classifications into *formal classifications*, whose labels are encoded in a propositional concept language. Apart from this, we present a classification model and show how the get-specific algorithm can be described in this model. We then show how the model and the algorithm can be encoded in the concept language, which allows us to fully automate document population in formal classifications through propositional reasoning. Note that by doing this, we eliminate the three ambiguities discussed above. In order to evaluate our approach, we have re-classified documents from several branches of the DMoz directory without any human involvement or an a priori created training dataset. The results show the viability of the proposed approach, which makes it a realistic alternative to the standard classification approaches used in Information Science.

The remainder of the paper is organized as follows. In Section 2 we introduce the classification model, we show how the get-specific algorithm can be described in this model, and we identify the main problems peculiar to the algorithm. In Section 3 we show how classifications can be translated into formal classifications, how the get-specific algorithm can be encoded in the concept language, and how its peculiar problems can be dealt with in the concept language. In Section 4 we present and discuss evaluation results of our approach. In Section 5 we discuss the related work and, in particular, we compare our approach to that used in Information Science. Section 6 summarizes the results and concludes the paper.

2 The Get-Specific Classification Algorithm

Classifications are hierarchical structures used for positioning objects in such a way, that a person, who navigates the classifications, will be facilitated in finding objects related to a given topic. To attain such organization of objects, in standard classification approaches, objects are manually classified by human classifiers which follow a predefined system of rules. The actual system of rules may differ widely in different classification approaches, but there are some generic principles which are commonly followed. These principles make the ground of the *get-specific* algorithm, described in the rest of this section.

2.1 Classifications and a Classification Model

To avoid ambiguity of interpretation, in Definition 1 we formally define the notion of classification; and in Figure 1 we give an example of a classification, extracted from the DMoz web directory and adjusted for sake of presentation.

Definition 1. *A classification is a rooted tree $C = \langle N, E, L \rangle$ where N is a set of nodes, E is a set of edges on N, and L is a set of labels expressed in a natural language, such that for any node $n_i \in N$, there is one and only one label $l_i \in L$.*

We see the process of classification as a decision making procedure in which the classification tree is divided into a set of minimal decision making blocks. Each block consists of a node (called the root node of the block) and its child

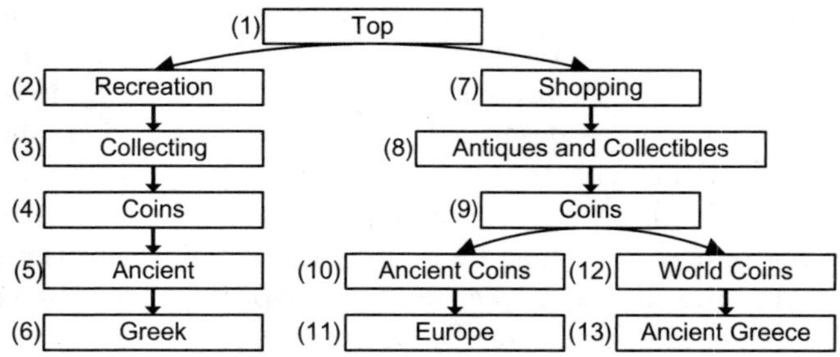

Fig. 1. A part of the DMoz web directory

nodes (see Figure 2). While classifying an object, the classifier considers these blocks in a top-down fashion, starting from the block at the classification root node and then continuing to blocks rooted at those child nodes, which were selected for *further consideration*. These nodes are selected following decisions which are made at each block along two dimensions: *vertical* and *horizontal*. In the vertical dimension, the classifier decides which of the child nodes are selected as candidates for further consideration. In the horizontal dimension, the classifier decides which of the candidates are *actually* selected for further consideration. If none of the child nodes are appropriate or if there are no child nodes, then the root node of the block becomes a *classification alternative* for the given object. The process reiterates and continues recursively until no more nodes are left for further consideration. At this point, all the classification alternatives are computed. The classifier then decides which of them are most appropriate for the classification of the object and makes *the final classification choice*.

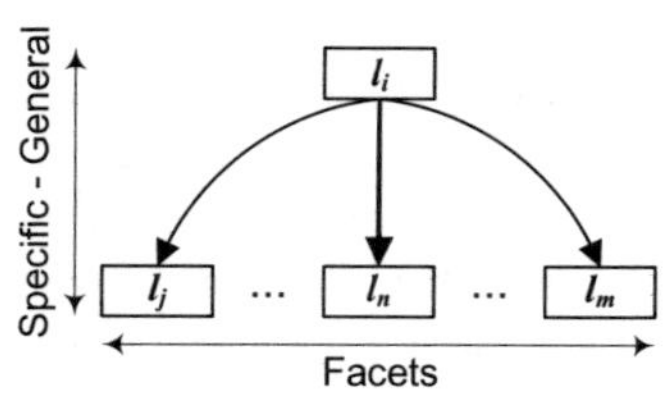

Fig. 2. The decision making block

2.2 Modelling the Get-Specific Classification Algorithm

In this subsection we discuss the general principles lying behind the get-specific algorithm and we show how these principles can be implemented within the model introduced in the previous subsection. Particularly, we discuss how vertical and horizontal choices, as well as the final classification choice are made.

- **Vertical choice.** Classification hierarchies are organized such that upper level categories represent more general concepts, whereas lower level categories represent more specific concepts. When the classifier searches for an appropriate category for the classification of an object, she looks for the ones which most specifically describe the object and, therefore, when making a vertical choice, she selects a child node as a candidate if it describes the object more specifically than the parent does. For example, if a document about ancient Greek coins is classified in the classification from Figure 1, then node n_6 is more appropriate for the classification than node n_5. When this principle is applied recursively, it leads to the selection of the category which lies as deep in the classification hierarchy as possible. The principle described above is commonly called the *get-specific principle.* Let us consider, for instance, how Yahoo! describes it:

> *"When you suggest your site, get as specific as possible. Dig deep into the directory, looking for the appropriate sub-category."* [4]

- **Horizontal choice.** Child nodes may describe different aspects or *facets* of the parent node and, therefore, more than one child node may be selected in the vertical choice if a multifaceted document is being classified. As a consequence of this, the classifier needs to decide which of the several sibling nodes are appropriate for further consideration. When one sibling node represents a more specific concept than another, then the former is usually preferred over the latter. For example, node n_{10} is more appropriate for the classification of ancient Greek coins than node n_{12}. As a rule of thumb, the horizontal choice is made in favor of as few nodes as possible and, preferably, in favor of one node only. We call the principle described above, the *get-minimal principle.* Consider, for instance, how DMoz describes it.

> *"Most sites will fit perfectly into one category. ODP categories are specialized enough so that in most cases you should not list a site more than once."* [1]

- **Tradeoff between vertical and horizontal choices.** The two principles described above cannot always be fulfilled at the same time. Namely, if the vertical choice results in too many candidates, then it becomes hard to fulfill the principle of minimality in the horizontal choice. In order to address this problem, a tradeoff needs to be introduced between the two requirements, which usually means trading specificity in favor of minimality. The following is an example of a tradeoff rule used in DMoz:

> *"If a site offers many different things, it should be listed in a more general category as opposed to listing it in many specialized subcategories."* [1]

- **The final classification choice.** When all classification alternatives are determined, the classifier confronts all of them in order to make her final classification choice. Note that now the choice is made not at the level of a minimal decision making block, but at the level of the whole classification. However, the classifier uses the same selection criteria as those used in the horizontal choice. For example, nodes n_6 and n_{13} are more appropriate for the classification of documents about ancient Greek coins than node n_{11}.

2.3 Problems of the Get-Specific Classification Algorithm

As discussed in [10], there are several problems which are common to document classification algorithms. The problems are caused by the potentially large size of classifications, by ambiguity in natural language labels and in document descriptions, by different interpretations of the meaning of parent-child links, and so on. All these problems lead to nonuniform, duplicate, and error-prone classification. In addition to the problems discussed in [10], the get-specific algorithm has two peculiar problems, related to the two decision dimensions. We discuss these problems below on the example of a document titled *"Gold Staters in the Numismatic Marketplace"*, being classified in the classification from Figure 1.

- **Vertical choice: the "I don't know" problem.** The classifier may make a mistake because she does not (fully) understand the meaning of a child node or the relation of the document to that node, whereas the node is a valid candidate. For example, the classifier may not know that "Gold Stater" is a coin of ancient Greece and, therefore, will erroneously classify the document into node n_5, whereas a more appropriate node is n_6.
- **Horizontal choice: the "Polarity change" problem.** The classifier may make a mistake when one of the sibling candidate nodes is more appropriate for further consideration than another, but a descendent of the latter is more appropriate for the classification than a descendant of the former node. For instance, the label of node n_{10} more specifically describes the document than the label of node n_{12}. Therefore, the classifier will choose node n_{10} only as a candidate and will finally classify the document in node n_{11}, whereas a more appropriate node for the classification is node n_{13}, a descendent of n_{12}.

3 Formalizing the Get-Specific Classification Algorithm

In this section we formalize the get-specific classification algorithm by encoding it as a problem expressed in propositional Description Logic language [5], referred to as L^C. First, we discuss how natural language node labels and document descriptions are converted into formulas in L^C. Second, we discuss how we reduce the problems of vertical, horizontal, and final classification choices to fully automated propositional reasoning. Finally, we show how the problems discussed in Section 2.3 can be dealt with in a formal way.

3.1 From Natural Language to Formal Language

Classification labels are expressed in a natural language, which is ambiguous and, therefore, is very hard to reason about. In order to address this problem, we encode classification labels into formulas in L^C following the approach proposed in [10]. This allows us to convert the classification into a new structure, which we call *Formal Classification* (FC):

Definition 2. *A Formal Classification is a rooted tree $FC = \langle N, E, L^F \rangle$ where N is a set of nodes, E is a set of edges on N, and L^F is a set of labels expressed in L^C, such that for any node $n_i \in N$, there is one and only one label $l_i^F \in L^F$.*

Note that even if L^C is propositional in nature, it has a set-theoretic semantics. As proposed in [10], the interpretation of a concept is the set of documents, which are *about* this concept. For instance, the interpretation of concept `Capital` (defined as "a seat of government") is the set of documents about capitals, and *not* the set of capitals which exist in the world.

Below we briefly describe how we convert natural language labels into formulas in L^C. Interested readers are referred to [10] for a complete account. Figure 3 shows the result of conversion of the classification from Figure 1 into a FC.

1. **Build atomic concepts.** Senses of nouns and adjectives become atomic concepts, whose interpretation is the set of documents about the entities or individual objects, denoted by the nouns, or which possess the qualities, denoted by the adjectives. We enumerate word senses using WordNet [17], and we refer to them as follows: `pos-lemma#i`, where `pos` is the part of speech, `lemma` is the word lemma, and `i` is the sense number in WordNet.
2. **Disambiguate word senses.** Irrelevant word senses are identified and corresponding to them atomic concepts are discarded. As proposed in [15], if there exists a relation (e.g., synonymy, hypernymy, or holonymy) in WordNet between any two senses of two words in a label (or in different labels on a path to the root), then corresponding to them concepts are retained and other concepts are discarded. If no relation is found, then we check if a relation exists between two WordNet senses by comparing their glosses [13].
3. **Build complex concepts.** Complex concepts are built as follows: first, words' formulas are built as the logical disjunction ($\sqcup$) of atomic concepts corresponding to their senses (remaining after step 2). Second, syntactic relations between words are translated into logical connectives of L^C. For example, a set of adjectives followed by a noun group is translated into the logical conjunction ($\sqcap$) of the formulas corresponding to the adjectives and to the nouns; prepositions like "of" and "in" are translated into the conjunction; coordinating conjunctions "and" and "or" are translated into the logical disjunction ($\sqcup$); words and phrases denoting exclusions, such as "except" and "but not", are translated into the logical negation ($\neg$).

Before a document can be automatically classified, it has to be assigned an expression in L^C, which we call the document concept, written C^d. The assignment of a concept to a document is done in two steps: first, a set of n keyphrases is retrieved from the document using text mining techniques (see, for example, [22]); the keyphrases are converted to formulas in L^C, and the document concept is then computed as the conjunction of the formulas.

3.2 The Algorithm

In the following we describe how we make vertical and horizontal choices, compute the tradeoff, and make the final classification choice in FCs.

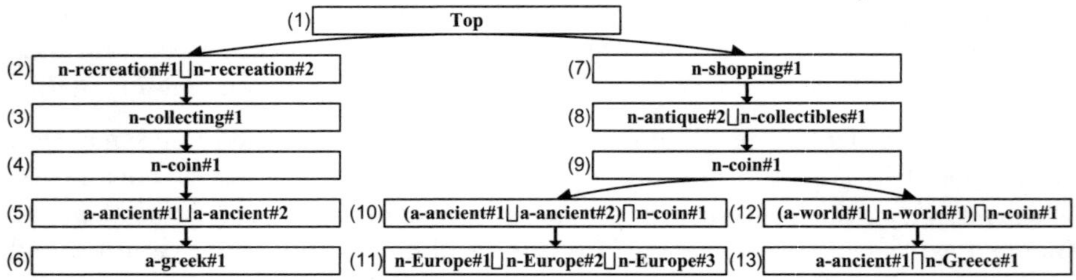

Fig. 3. Formal Classification

- **Vertical choice.** A child node n_i is a candidate, given that a document with concept C^d is being classified, if the label of the node, l_i^F, subsumes C^d, i.e., if the following holds: $C^d \sqsubseteq l_i^F$. In formulas, if N_c is the set of child nodes in the block, then we compute the vertical choice $V(C^d)$ as:

$$V(C^d) = \{n_i \in N_c | C^d \sqsubseteq l_i^F\} \tag{1}$$

If the vertical choice results in no candidates, then root node n_r of the current block is added to the set of classification alternatives $A(C^d)$:

$$\textbf{if } |V(C^d)| = 0 \textbf{ then } A(C^d) \leftarrow A(C^d) \cup \{n_r\} \tag{2}$$

In Figure 4a we show an example of a situation when two child nodes n_2 and n_4 are selected for further consideration, and in Figure 4b we show an example of a situation when no child node can be selected.

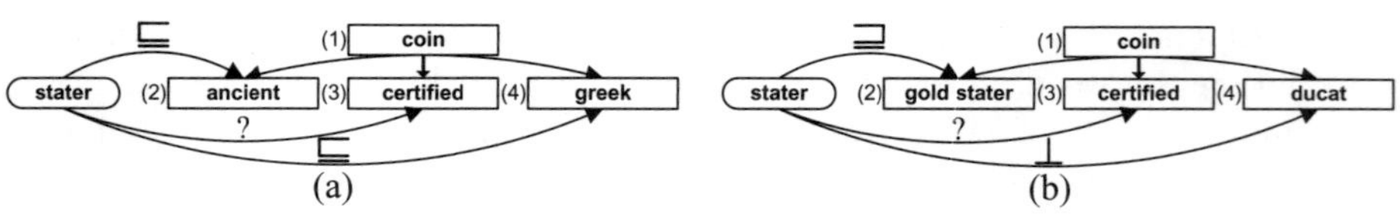

Fig. 4. Vertical choice ("?" means no relation is found)

- **Horizontal choice.** Given the set of candidates $V(C^d)$, we exclude those nodes from the set, whose label is more general than the label of another node in the set. In formulas, we compute the horizontal choice $H(C^d)$ as:

$$H(C^d) = \{n_i \in V(C^d) | \nexists n_j \in V(C^d),\ s.t.\ j \neq i, l_j^F \sqsubseteq l_i^F, and\ l_j^F \not\sqsupseteq l_i^F\} \tag{3}$$

We introduce the last condition (i.e., $l_j^F \not\sqsupseteq l_i^F$) to avoid mutual exclusion of nodes, whose labels in the FC are equivalent concepts. For instance, two syntactically different labels "seacoast" and "seashore" are translated into two equivalent concepts. When such situation arises, all the nodes, whose labels are equivalent, are retained in $H(C^d)$.

- **The tradeoff.** Whenever the size of $H(C^d)$ exceeds some threshold k, the nodes of $H(C^d)$ are discarded as candidates and root node n_r of the block is added to the set of classification alternatives $A(C^d)$. In formulas:

$$\textbf{if}|H(C^d)| > k \textbf{ then } H(C^d) \leftarrow \emptyset \textbf{ and } A(C^d) \leftarrow A(C^d) \cup \{n_r\} \quad (4)$$

- **The final classification choice.** When no more nodes are left for further consideration, set $A(C^d)$ includes all the classification alternatives. We compare them to make the final classification choice, but, differently from vertical and horizontal choices, we compare the *meanings* of nodes given their path to the root, and not their labels. We encode the meaning of node n_i into a concept in L^C, called *concept of node* [11], written C_i, and computed as:

$$C_i = \begin{cases} l_i^F & \text{if } n_i \text{ is the root of the } FC \\ l_i^F \sqcap C_j & \text{if } n_i \text{ is not the root, where } n_j \text{ is the parent of } n_i \end{cases} \quad (5)$$

  Similar to how the horizontal choice is made, we exclude those nodes from $A(C^d)$, whose concept is more general than the concept of another node in the set. In formulas, we compute the final classification choice $C(A)$ as:

$$C(A) = \{n_i \in A(C^d) | \nexists n_j \in A(C^d),\ s.t.\ j \neq i,\ C_j \sqsubseteq C_i,\ and\ C_j \not\sqsupseteq C_i\} \quad (6)$$

  The last condition (i.e., $C_j \not\sqsupseteq C_i$) is introduced to avoid mutual exclusion of nodes with the same meaning in the classification hierarchy. For instance, two paths *top/computers/games/soccer* and *top/sport/soccer/computer_games* lead to two semantically equivalent concepts. When such situation arises, all the nodes with the same meaning are retained in $C(A)$.

Computing Equations 1, 3, and 6 requires verifying whether the subsumption relation holds between two formulas in L^C. As shown in [10], a problem expressed in L^C can be rewritten as an equivalent problem expressed in propositional logic. Namely, if we need to check whether a certain relation *rel* (which can be $\sqsubseteq$, $\sqsupseteq$, $\equiv$, or $\perp$) holds between two concepts A and B, given some knowledge base $\mathcal{KB}$ (which represents our a priori knowledge), we construct a propositional formula according to the pattern shown in Equation 7 and check it for validity:

$$\mathcal{KB} \rightarrow rel(A, B) \quad (7)$$

3.3 Dealing with Problems

Encoding a classification algorithm into a problem in L^C allows it to avoid many problems, which are common to classification algorithms [10]. Particularly, since the problem is encoded in a formal language, there is no ambiguity in interpretation of classification labels, of edges, and document contents. Apart from this, since computation is performed by a machine, the problem of classification size becomes largely irrelevant. Finally, since the formal algorithm is deterministic, the classification is always performed in a uniform way.

In Section 2.3 we discussed two problems, peculiar to the get-specific algorithm. Below we discuss what they mean in L^C and how they can be dealt with.

- **Vertical choice: The "I don't know" problem.** This problem arises when the specificity relation in Equation 1 cannot be computed while a human observes that it exists. The problem is caused by lack of background knowledge and it can be dealt with by adding missing axioms to the underlying knowledge base [12]. For instance, if we add a missing axiom which states that concept `Stater` (defined as "any of the various silver or gold coins of ancient Greece") is more specific than concept `Greek` (defined as "of or relating to or characteristic of Greece ..."), then the algorithm will correctly classify document *"Gold Staters in the Numismatic Marketplace"* into node n_6 in the classification shown in Figure 1.
- **Horizontal choice: The "Polarity change" problem.** The problem arises when the label of node n_i is more specific than the label of its sibling node n_j (i.e., $l_i^F \sqsubseteq l_j^F$), but the concept of a n_i's descendant node n_k is more general than the concept of a n_j's descendant node n_m (i.e., $C_k \sqsupseteq C_m$). In the simplest case, this problem can be dealt with by not performing the horizontal choice. In this case, both n_k and n_m will be in the classification alternative set for some document, and n_k will then be discarded when the final classification choice is made.

4 Evaluation

In order to evaluate our approach, we selected four subtrees from the DMoz web directory, converted them to FCs, extracted concepts from the populated documents, and automatically (re)classified the documents into the FCs. We extracted document concepts by computing the conjunction of the formulas corresponding to the first 10 most frequent words appearing in the documents (excluding stop words). We used WordNet 2.0 [17] for finding word senses and their relations, and we used S-Match [11] for computing Equation 7. Parameter k for tradeoff computation was set to 2.

In the evaluation we employ standard information retrieval measures such as micro- and macro-averaged precision, recall, and F1 [19]. In Table 1 we report dataset statistics and evaluation results for each of the four datasets. We performed a detailed analysis of the "Languages" dataset results (see Figure 5). In Figure 5a we show how precision and recall are distributed among nodes. Figure 5b shows how far (in terms of the number of edges) an automatically classified document is from the node where it was actually classified in DMoz.

From Figure 5a we observe that about 40% of nodes in the "Languages" dataset have precision and recall equal to 0[1]. After manual inspection of the results, we concluded that this problem is caused by lack of background knowledge. For instance, 8 documents about Slovenian language were misclassified because there was no WordNet synset "Slovenian" defined as "the Slavic language spoken in Slovenia" and a hypernym relation of it with synset "Slavic language". Figure 5b shows that about 20% of documents are classified in one edge distance from the node where they were originally populated, whereas 89% of them were

[1] Precision for nodes with no documents was counted as 0.

Table 1. Dataset statistics and evaluation results

Dataset	Nodes	Docs	Max. subtree depth	Mi-Pr	Mi-Re	Mi-F1	Ma-Pr	Ma-Re	Ma-F1
Photography[a]	27	871	4	0.2218	0.1871	0.2029	0.2046	0.1165	0.1485
Beverages[b]	38	1456	5	0.4037	0.4938	0.4442	0.3848	0.3551	0.3693
Mammals[c]	88	574	5	0.3145	0.3014	0.3078	0.3854	0.2677	0.3159
Languages[d]	157	1217	6	0.4117	0.4503	0.4301	0.4366	0.4187	0.4275

[a] http://dmoz.org/Shopping/Photography/

[b] http://dmoz.org/Shopping/Food/Beverages/

[c] http://dmoz.org/Health/Animal/Mammals/

[d] http://dmoz.org/Science/Social_Sciences/Linguistics/Languages/Natural/Indo-European/

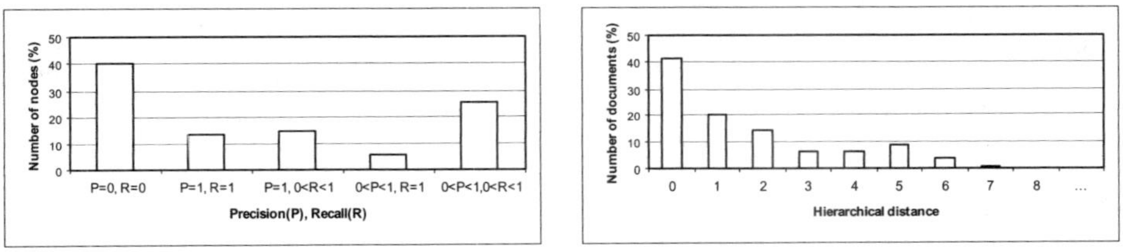

(a) (b)

Fig. 5. Analysis of the “Languages” dataset results

classified one node higher on the path to the root. Note that this still allows it to find a document of interest by browsing the classification hierarchy.

5 Related Work

The idea of that the get-specific classification algorithm can be encoded in a formal language and the first formal specification of the algorithm were reported in [10]. The current paper extends [10] in several respects. First, it proposes a classification model and shows how the algorithm can be implemented in this model. Second, it discusses how the model can be described and implemented in L^C. Third, it identifies the main problems peculiar to the get-specific algorithm and shows how they can be dealt with in L^C. Finally, for the first time, the current paper presents experimental results, which demonstrate that document classification can be fully automated using a knowledge-centric approach.

The idea of that natural language labels in classifications can be translated in a formal language was first introduced in [7], and, in [15], the authors provided a detailed account of the translation process using Description Logic as the target formal language. The current paper uses the translation rules described in [10], which originates from [15], but which uses the less computationally expensive propositional subset of Description Logics. In [10], the authors define a set-theoretic semantics for the translation rules and show that a propositional concept language is enough to capture the semantics of a large amount of labels.

In Information Science, hierarchical document classification usually refers to supervised or unsupervised text categorization [19]. Differently from the supervised case (e.g., see [14,9,21]), in our approach we do not need to have a pre-classified set of documents. In fact, classification choices depend on the *meaning* of classification labels and not on the documents already classified in nodes. Differently from the unsupervised approach (e.g., [16,23]), we do not need to annotate classification nodes with a relatively large (w.r.t. the label size) set of keywords to classify documents. Apart from this, in formal classification labels, the terms are connected through logical connectives, which increases the expressiveness of the category description. However, unsupervised classification is the approach closet to ours from the text categorization domain. The results, reached by the two approaches, are comparable. For instance, in [23], the authors report to reach max 42.70% in micro-F1 measure on different web directory datasets.

Noteworthy, some text categorization approaches rely on an underlying knowledge base (e.g., WordNet [17]) in order to find relations among words to optimize the construction of the feature space (e.g., see [6,18]). However, these approaches still require a training dataset to operate, i.e., they are supervised in nature.

6 Conclusions and Future Work

The current paper makes a contribution at the turn of several disciplines. First, it takes the notion of classification from Library Science and shows how it can be converted in a form of ontology – the fundamental notion on the Semantic Web. Interestingly, the two notions are often used interchangeably in the two communities [20]. Second, we provide a classification model and show how the get-specific algorithm, commonly used in hierarchical document classification systems, can be described in this model. Third, it shows how document classification can be fully automated using a knowledge-centric approach, an approach which is conceptually different from the one used in Information Science. Finally, evaluation results reported in this paper demonstrate the proof of concept of our approach, which makes it a viable alternative to the conventional way of automated document classification.

Our future work includes: (a) development of more accurate document concept extraction algorithms; (b) evaluation of our approach in specific domains using domain ontology as the underlying knowledge base; (c) development of knowledge base enrichment algorithms which take into account the classification semantics (which, for example, will define concept `Stater` as more specific than concept `Greek`); and (d) automatic document re-classification when the structure of the classification hierarchy changes.

References

1. DMoz guidelines: See, `http://dmoz.org/guidelines/site-specific.html`
2. DMoz: See, `http://dmoz.org/`
3. UNSPSC: See, `http://www.unspsc.org/`

4. Yahoo! guidelines: See, `http://docs.yahoo.com/info/suggest/appropriate.html`
5. Baader, F., Calvanese, D., McGuinness, D., Nardi, D., Patel-Schneider, P.: The Description Logic Handbook: Theory, Implementation and Applications. Cambridge University Press, Cambridge (2003)
6. Bloehdorn, S., Hotho, A.: Text classification by boosting weak learners based on terms and concepts. In: ICDM 2004, pp. 331–334. IEEE Computer Society Press, Los Alamitos (2004)
7. Bouquet, P., Serafini, L., Zanobini, S.: Semantic coordination: a new approach and an application. In: Proc. of the 2nd International Semantic Web Conference (ISWO'03). Sanibel Islands, Florida, USA (October 2003)
8. Chan, L.M., Mitchell, J.S.: Dewey Decimal Classification: A Practical Guide. Forest P., U.S (December 1996)
9. Dumais, S.T., Chen, H.: Hierarchical classification of web content. In: Proc. of SIGIR-00, 23rd ACM International Conference on Research and Development in Information Retrieval, pp. 256–263. ACM Press, Athens, GR (2000)
10. Giunchiglia, F., Marchese, M., Zaihrayeu, I.: Encoding classifications into lightweight ontologies. JoDS VIII (Winter 2006)
11. Giunchiglia, F., Shvaiko, P., Yatskevich, M.: Semantic schema matching. In: Proc. of CoopIS, pp. 347–365 (2005)
12. Giunchiglia, F., Shvaiko, P., Yatskevich, M.: Discovering missing background knowledge in ontology matching. In: Proc. of ECAI (2006)
13. Giunchiglia, F., Yatskevich, M.: Element level semantic matching. In: McIlraith, S.A., Plexousakis, D., van Harmelen, F. (eds.) ISWC 2004. LNCS, vol. 3298, Springer, Heidelberg (2004)
14. Koller, D., Sahami, M.: Hierarchically classifying documents using very few words. In: Proc. of ICML-97, 14th International Conference on Machine Learning, pp. 170–178. Morgan Kaufmann Publishers, Nashville (1997)
15. Magnini, B., Serafini, L., Speranza, M.: Making explicit the semantics hidden in schema models. In: Fensel, D., Sycara, K.P., Mylopoulos, J. (eds.) ISWC 2003. LNCS, vol. 2870, Springer, Heidelberg (2003)
16. McCallum, A., Nigam, K.: Text classification by bootstrapping with keywords, em and shrinkage. In: Proc. of ACL99 - Workshop for Unsupervised Learning in Natural Language Processing (1999)
17. Miller, G.: WordNet: An electronic Lexical Database. MIT Press, Cambridge (1998)
18. Peng, X., Choi, B.: Document classifications based on word semantic hierarchies. In: Proc. of International Conference on Artificial Intelligence and Applications, pp. 362–367 (2005)
19. Sebastiani, F.: Machine learning in automated text categorization. ACM Computing Surveys 34(1), 1–47 (2002)
20. Soergel, D.: The rise of ontologies or the reinvention of classification. Journal of the American Society for Information Science 50(12), 1119–1120 (1999)
21. Sun, A., Lim, E.P.: Hierarchical text classification and evaluation. In: Proc. of ICDM, pp. 521–528 (2001)
22. Turney, P.D.: Learning algorithms for keyphrase extraction. Information Retrieval 2(4), 303–336 (2000)
23. Veeramachaneni, S., Sona, D., Avesani, P.: Hierarchical dirichlet model for document classification. In: Proc. of ICML (2005)

Trustworthiness Analysis of Web Search Results

Satoshi Nakamura, Shinji Konishi, Adam Jatowt, Hiroaki Ohshima, Hiroyuki Kondo, Taro Tezuka, Satoshi Oyama, and Katsumi Tanaka

Department of Social Informatics, Graduate School of Informatics, Kyoto University
Yoshida-Honmachi, Sakyo, Kyoto 606-8501, Japan
{nakamura, konishi, adam, ohshima, kondo, tezuka, oyama, tanaka}@dl.kuis.kyoto-u.ac.jp

Abstract. Increased usage of Web search engines in our daily lives means that the trustworthiness of searched results has become crucial. User studies on the usage of search engines and analysis of the factors used to determine trust that users have in search results are described in this paper. Based on the analysis, we developed a system to help users determine the trustworthiness of Web search results by computing and showing each returned page's topic majority, topic coverage, locality of supporting pages (i.e., pages linked to each search result) and other information. The measures proposed in the paper can be applied to the search of Web-based libraries or can be useful in the usage of digital library search systems.

Keywords: Web search, trustworthiness, page locality, user study.

1 Introduction

Web search engines have become indispensable tools for acquiring information over the Internet. Web search engines accept user queries consisting of a few keywords, retrieve relevant pages available from the Web, and rank the found results by using their own ranking systems. One of the most important problems with such a search process is that the search engine does not indicate the extent to which returned page is trustworthy for the user's request except for computing the rank of the page. That is, conventional search engines do not provide information concerning whether:

1. The significance of the content of each returned page is a majority or minority in the Web.
2. The extent to which each returned page contains typical query topics contained on the Web.
3. The extent to which each returned page is supported uniformly throughout the world.

If this information is displayed to users by search engines, users will be able to determine which page is trustworthy, and which page they should choose from the search results listed.

L. Kovács, N. Fuhr, and C. Meghini (Eds.): ECDL 2007, LNCS 4675, pp. 38–49, 2007.

Fogg *et al.* analyzed factors with which the user determines the trustworthiness of Web pages [1,2]. This work was performed by analyzing a questionnaire based on the Prominence-Interpretation theory [3] and means that the level of the user's trust depends on *prominence*, the strength of appeal of the page, and the user's *interpretation* of the page. Based on these results, they proposed guidelines to determine the credibility of the information about authors that is displayed on Web sites [4]. Zaihrayeu *et al.* attempted to calculate the trustworthiness of search results [5]. They computed the degree of trustworthiness by classifying search results based on IWTrust evaluation, which can be used to learn feature vectors created by linguistic analysis of browsed pages among search results. Yanbe *et al.* recently developed a new page reranking system using social bookmark information [6]. This system allows users to rerank Web search results based on a returned page's bookmark information. Yamamoto *et al.* also developed a system [7] that helps to determine the trustworthiness of sentences by searching and aggregating related Web pages.

We surveyed the search engine usage of users to understand the context in which users search, and which factors cause the user to trust the search results and to understand the requirements of the search system. In this paper, we describe these user studies and analyze the factors determining the trust that users have in search results. Based on this analytic work, we developed a system to help users determine the trustworthiness of Web search results independently from a conventional search engine's ranking mechanism. We computed and displayed measures including *topic majority*, *topic coverage*, *locality of supporting pages*, and others for each page. The topic majority measures the significance of the content of a returned page. The topic coverage measures how many topics concerned with a search query the returned page contains. The locality of supporting pages for a returned page denotes the localness of distribution of the supporting pages. These measures are useful for users to determine the trustworthiness of searched results.

We also describe our prototype system, in which those measures are displayed together with the standard search results. Additionally, we describe a two-dimensional display interface for the measures.

2 Survey

In this section, we describe the results of the user studies performed in order to gather information regarding the use of search engines. We especially focused on analyzing factors used to determine the trustworthiness of the search results by users. The objectives of this survey were to:

1. investigate the frequency of Web searches by users
2. determine the circumstances in which users search the Web
3. understand the motivation of users for searching in the Web, i.e. why users do search in general
4. analyze how many results do users check, i.e. what is the lowest ranked item that users view before they decide to modify the query and search again

5. estimate the number of times users access search results before they decide to modify query terms
6. investigate whether users are aware of the underlying mechanisms by which search engines determine ranks of pages
7. analyze how much users trust the ranking method used by search engines
8. examine the features of a page used by users to determine the trustworthiness of its contents
9. determine whether users had experienced obtaining information from search engines that was incorrect, obsolete, or untrue
10. analyze what additional information should be provided by search engines, such as URLs and page snippets, to improve search efficiency
11. understand what kind of search engines users would like to use in the future.

We created an online questionnaire consisting of 26 questions that were answered by 1000 Internet users between 25th and 26th December 2006. Users were divided into four categories depending on their age: 20-29, 30-39, 40-49 and 50-59 years old. Each group consisted of 250 respondents; half males and half females. Respondents could choose several answers for some questions. The findings we obtained are discussed below based on the analysis of the survey results:

1. The analysis revealed that 68.7% of users usually use search engines less than 10 times a day. 27.5% of users search more than 11 but less than 30 times a day, and the rest search the Web more than 30 times per day.
2. Users decide to use search engines when they want to research particular information or browse the Web (Figure 1). It is also common for users to search without any particular reason. Two other common situations in which searches were performed are when watching TV and reading e-mails.
3. Users search the Web mostly because they require basic (46%) or detailed (36.8%) information about particular things (Figure 2). Another motivation for searching the Web is to do some comparison (7.4% of respondents selected it as a first reason). Few users chose other reasons for searching the Web. These results suggest that the depth and the coverage of topics in pages relevant to a query can improve the search experience.
4. More than 50% of users analyze only the top five search results. By this we mean that users read titles and snippets or pages that are provided by search engines. Only about 20% of users actually go further than the top five search results. These results indicate the need for creating more efficient search techniques.
5. On average, users visit between one to three pages before they decide to modify the search query or finish search in the Web (78.37% users). Relatively few users analyze more than 11 search results. An interesting result is that more than 20% of respondents do not actually access the pages but only read the returned snippets.
6. Users often believe that the more frequently visited a page is, the higher rank it has in search results. Another common belief is that the relevance of a page to the search query is a major factor when determining its rank in search results. A third belief is that the freshness level considerably influences search

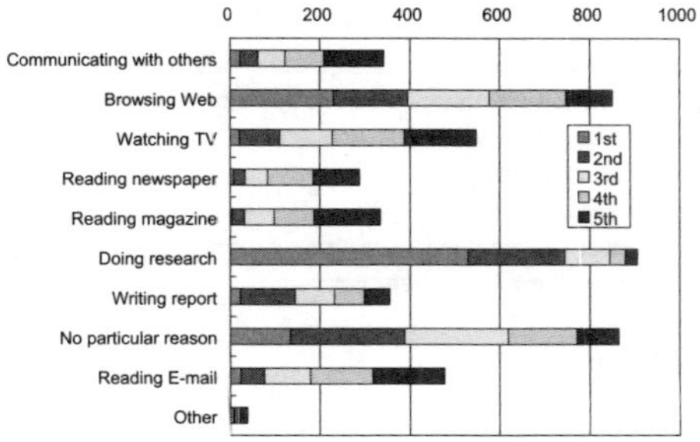

Fig. 1. Situations when users search Web

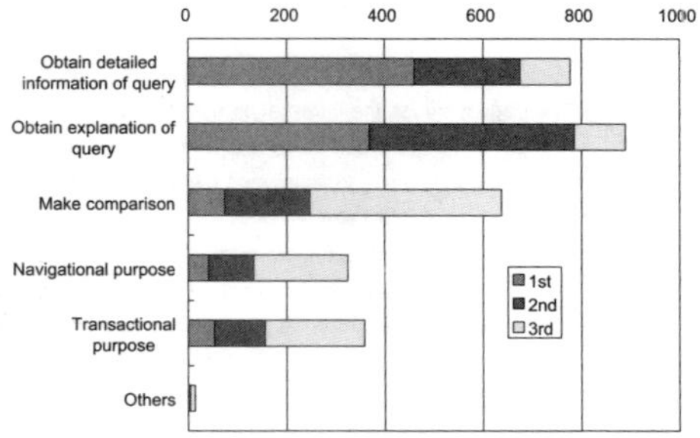

Fig. 2. Reasons for searching Web

Fig. 3. User beliefs about ranking methods used by search engines

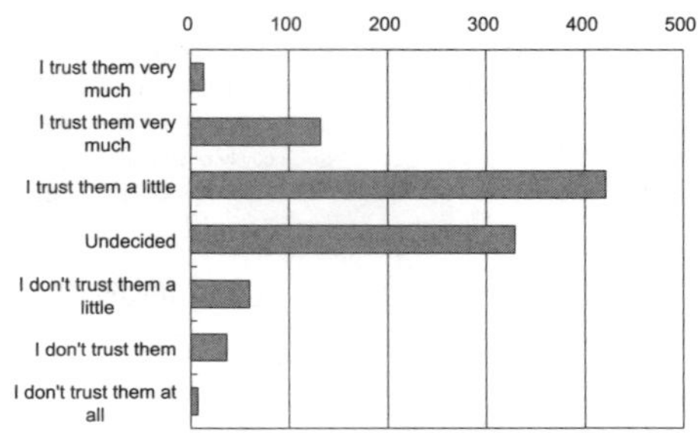

Fig. 4. User trust levels of search results

ranking. An interesting observation is that 17.1% of users actually think that the ranking depends on the amount of money paid by Web authors to search engine companies. Figure 3 shows the popularity of common beliefs among users about the ranking mechanisms used by current search engines.

7. Analysis revealed that 56.7% of respondents generally trust ranking methods used by search engines, and only 10.4% of users do not trust them (Figure 4). This observation indicates the necessity of providing trustworthy search mechanisms as Internet users often assume the correctness of information provided by search engines.
8. Users take into account information about the author or the owner of the page when deciding whether to trust the information. The second trust-invoking characteristic of pages is their relevance to the search query. Respondents tend not to trust pages if they contain spelling errors, grammatical mistakes, or biased information. Users also consider the page creation date as an important factor to determine the trust level of pages. Additionally, users do not trust information that is unique among different sources. The results of this analysis are shown in Figure 5.
9. Some users (12.3%) experienced obtaining information which, after subsequent inspection, turned out to be erroneous, obsolete, or untrue, 3.5% of

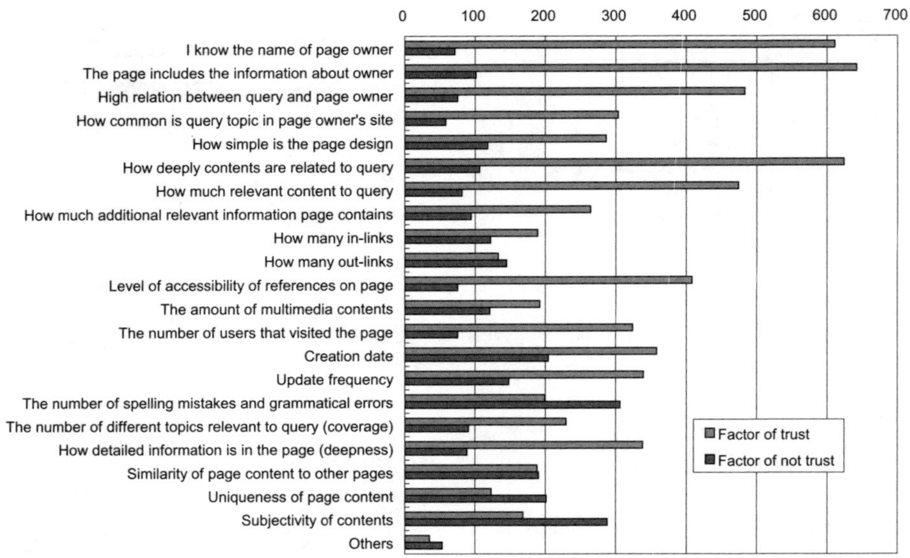

Fig. 5. Characteristics of pages that users trust

users accessed adult content, pages containing viruses, or phishing sites, and 5.2% of users detected untrue, obsolete or subjective information when using search engines.

10. Our study indicated that users would like search engines to provide the following types of information: publication date, related words, information about the page author or owner, scoring reflecting trustworthiness of pages, page type, thumbnail image of pages, and third party evaluations.
11. The main search engine characteristics that users wish to use in future are the capability to provide additional information about the results (48.08%) and domain-focused searching (45.7%) (Figure 6). Other common features are: automatic analysis of trust levels of pages, context-aware search and indication of the current popularity levels measured by the number of users visiting pages at query time. Respondents also wished search engines provided summaries of search results or performed result clustering.

3 Prototype System for Determining Trustworthiness of Web Search Results

Based on the survey results described in the preceding section, we designed a prototype system that helps a user to determine the trustworthiness of information on the Web. The purpose of our system is not to determine the trustworthiness of content by itself but to provide the user with supplementary information to help determine the trustworthiness. We did not largely change the user interface

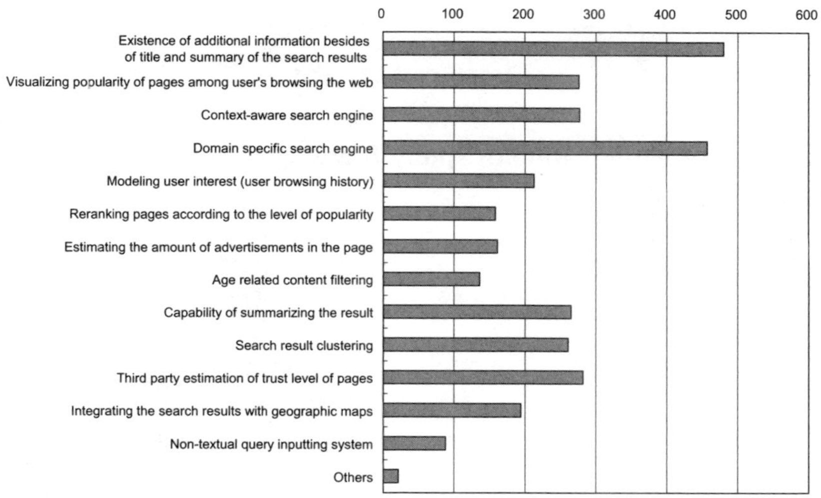

Fig. 6. Search engine characteristics that users would like to use in future

of a current search engine that is familiar to the user but added supplementary information as *add-ins* beside the ranked results returned by the search engine. This enables the system to raise the user's awareness of the trustworthiness of the search results without unnecessarily disturbing the user.

3.1 Information Presented in Prototype System

There are many kinds of information available to assist users to determine the trustworthiness of search results. The major information presented with standard search results are as follows:

Topic majority. Nearly half the respondents (43.4%) paid attention to how many similar pages to the search result exist when determining the trustworthiness of the search results. Topic majority is the number of similar pages to the search result that exist in the Web or in the set of pages related to the query. We calculated this by analyzing the number of pages related to the query and the number of pages similar to or containing the same topics.

Topic coverage. More than half the respondents (63.2%) tended to trust search results that contain many topics about the search query when searching something they have little or no knowledge about. Topic coverage is how many topics about the query the search result contains. We calculate this number by analyzing the number of topics about the query that the search result contains.

Locality of link sources. Spatial information can also play an important role in estimating the trustworthiness of Web contents. For example, if a certain page is only linked by pages in a limited area, the user can consider that the page has only a limited local support. On the other hand, if the page

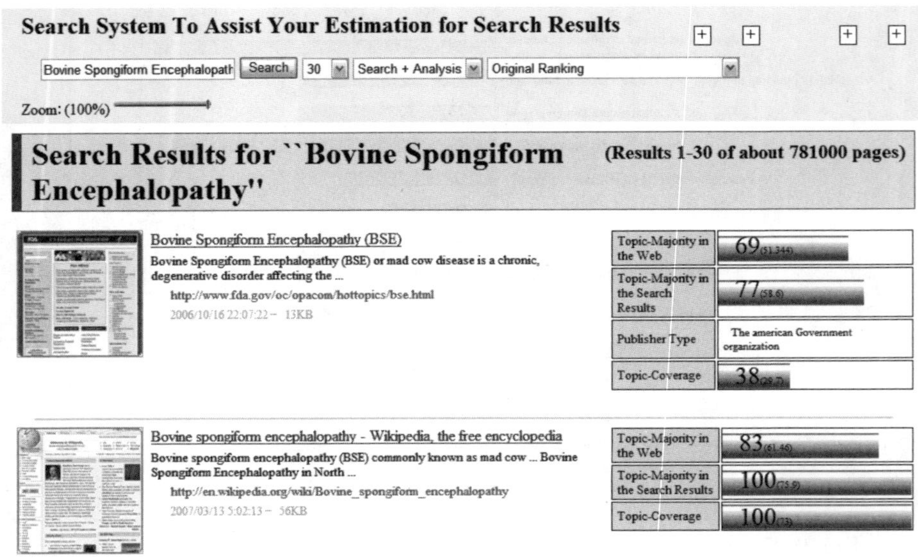

Fig. 7. User interface of prototype system

is linked from pages distributed over a large area (e.g. many countries), the user may think that the page has higher reliability. To support such judgements, our system visualizes the geographic distribution of link sources and illustrates how uniformly they are distributed. In related work, Ma and Tanaka described "localness degrees" as a ranking measure of Web pages [8]. Zhang et al. proposed LocalRank, based on a graph structure of semantic and geographic relationships [9]. Such works are different from ours in that they analyze the content itself, whereas we focus on link sources.

Other information. Other types of information exist that are often requested by users and are provided by our prototype system. One is topic details because nearly three quarters of the respondents (72.6%) tended to trust pages describing specific topics about the query. Also, our system provides publisher information (because 85.1% of the respondents paid attention to the publisher's details), the social bookmark number for each returned page (because 38.3% of the respondents paid attention to how many users browsed the search result), and the last-modified date (since 61.4% of the respondents paid attention to when the page was last modified or created.)

3.2 Calculating Topic Majority and Topic Coverage of Pages Using Query Topic Terms

To calculate topic majority and topic coverage, we need to find *representative topics* for user-specified query words.

Wikipedia and Web search results returned by a search engine are used to identify topic terms for a query. First, the system sends the user-specified query terms to Wikipedia to retrieve entries that match the query term. If such an entry is found, the system chooses terms as topic terms whose frequencies in the entry page are larger than a given threshold. If no entries match the query, the system sends the query term to a Web search engine and retrieves top ranked pages. The system then chooses terms whose frequencies in the result pages are higher than the given threshold as topic terms. The system optionally applies statistical tests proposed by Oyama and Tanaka [10] to improve the accuracy of identifying topic terms.

Let q be the user-specified query terms and t be a potential topic term extracted from a Wikipedia page. We compare the values of the following two formulas:

$$p(t \mid q) = \frac{\mathrm{DF}(q \wedge t)}{\mathrm{DF}(q)}$$

$$p(t \mid \mathrm{intitle}(q)) = \frac{\mathrm{DF}(\mathrm{intitle}(q) \wedge t)}{\mathrm{DF}(\mathrm{intitle}(q))},$$

where DF is the number of results returned by the search engine for a query in the argument, and intitle(x) is the number of pages containing term x in their title. If $p(t \mid \mathrm{intitle}(q))$ is larger than $p(t \mid q)$, we determine that t is a topic term of q.

Let $T = \{t_1, \ldots, t_n\}$ be the set of identified topic terms for q. The system calculates topic majority and topic coverage as follows:

Topic majority(in the Web). This is the number of Web pages that have similar topics to the topic of the page being evaluated. Let P be the set of terms appearing in the page. We calculate Topic majority (in the Web) as

$$\mathrm{TopicMajority(in\ the\ Web)} = \mathrm{DF}(q \wedge s_1 \wedge \ldots \wedge s_m)$$

where $s_i \in T \cap P$ and i is up to three.

The higher this indicator, the more the page includes topics considered significant to the search query. This indicator depends on the search query.

Topic majority(in the search results). This is the number of search results similar to the search results that are to be evaluated. Let p_k be the page to be evaluated, $\boldsymbol{v}(p_k)$ be the feature vector of page p_k, $R(p)$ be the set of the search results for q, $\|\boldsymbol{v}\|$ be the norm for the vector $\boldsymbol{v}$, and θ be a threshold for the similarity between two vectors. We calculated Topic majority (in the search results) as follows.

$$\mathrm{TopicMajority(in\ the\ search\ results)} = \left| \left\{ p_i \mid p_i \in R(q), \frac{\boldsymbol{v}(p_k) \cdot \boldsymbol{v}(p_i)}{\|\boldsymbol{v}(p_k)\| \|\boldsymbol{v}(p_i)\|} > \theta \right\} \right|$$

The topic majority (in the search results) indicator can be used to determine whether the search terms are significant in the search results. This indicator depends on the search query and the number and size of the search results.

Topic coverage. Topic coverage is the rate of topic terms appearing in the page to be evaluated and is calculated as follows:

$$\text{TopicCoverage} = \frac{|T \cap P|}{|T|}.$$

In the formula, no weight is assigned to topic terms to reflect topics, which are minor in the Web. Considering this indicator and other information, i.e. topic details, users can determine the bias of a page's contents.

3.3 Calculating Locality of Supporting Pages Using Link Structure

As described in the previous section, spatial factors can help the user determine trustworthiness of Web content. We define Locality of Supporting Pages (L) of a Web page as follows.

$$L(p) = \frac{n}{\sum_{i=1}^{n} ln(d(p, p_i) + 1)} \tag{1}$$

In the formula, p and p_i are the coordinates of the target Web page and pages that link to it, respectively. $d(p, p_i)$ indicates the distance between p and p_i. n is the number of pages that link to the target page.

The system obtains the URLs of pages that link to the target page using the "link" operator of a regular search engine. The system then converts these URLs to IP addresses using DNS. Finally, it obtains geographical coordinates corresponding to these IP addresses using GeoLite City by MaxMind [11]. At this moment, our system can only support judgments on the trustworthiness of the Web page. It can not help the user in judging the trustworthiness of pieces of information on it. Providing finer granularity is a part of our future work.

Figure 8 illustrates that the locality of supporting pages is only weakly correlated with the number of links toward the target Web pages. It shows that the locality of supporting pages can provide a ranking different from conventional search engines, since they are basically based on the amount of links coming in. Figure 9 illustrates the system's visual interface. In this example, it shows the spatial distribution of pages that link to the government of South Africa[1]. The locality of supporting pages was $L = 2.427$. This is close to that of Google[2] ($L = 2.939$) and the government of Australia[3] ($L = 2.792$) whereas far from that of a locally targeted page, such as Alachua County Today[4], a local news site in Florida ($L = 42.240$).

3.4 User Interface

We show a screenshot of the prototype system's user interface in Figure 7. This interface has an input field for a search query, the number of results the user

[1] http://www.gov.za
[2] http://www.google.com
[3] http://www.australia.gov.au
[4] http://www.alachuatoday.com

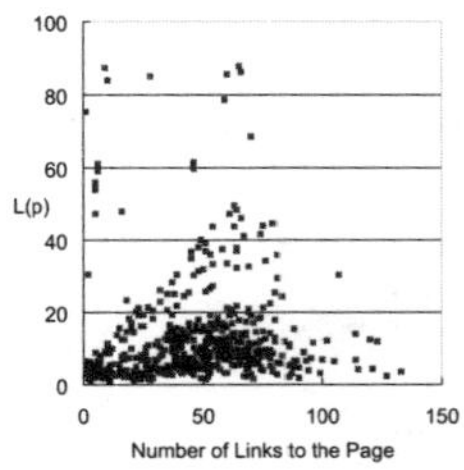

Fig. 8. Locality and Amount of Supporting Pages

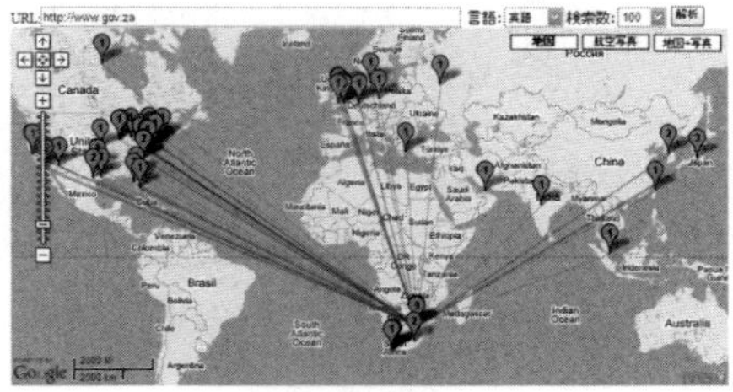

Fig. 9. Visual Presentation of Locality Support

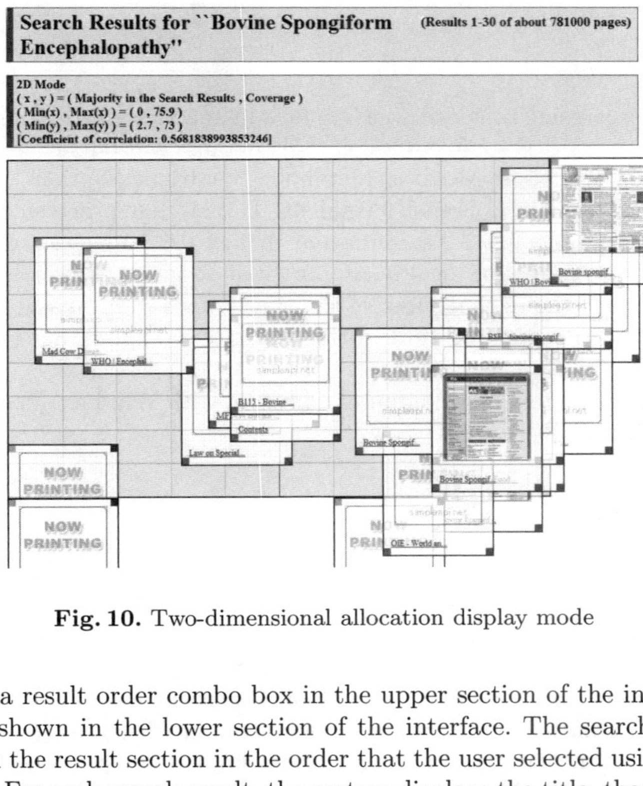

Fig. 10. Two-dimensional allocation display mode

wants, and a result order combo box in the upper section of the interface. The results are shown in the lower section of the interface. The search results are displayed in the result section in the order that the user selected using the order combo box. For each search result, the system displays the title, the snippet, the URL, the thumbnail, the date when the page was last updated, and the page size on the left. Additional information the system has analyzed for the search result is displayed on the right. Moreover, a bar is displayed for each item to indicate the relative value, (the max value is changed to 100 and the min value is changed to zero). We also implemented a toggle display function for each additional piece of information.

We implemented a two-dimensional allocation display mode as shown in Figure 10 (the horizontal axis is the topic majority (in search results) and the

Table 1. Time Analysis for Locality Support

Steps	Avg. time (sec)
Mapping of URLs	0.416
Link analysis	7.619
Retrieval of link sources (for 50 links)	1.088
Locating of link sources (for 50 links)	3.899
Graph consruction	0.090
Calculation of locality support	0.000
Rendering	0.004
Storing of cache	0.015
Total time	8.150

vertical axis is the topic coverage). This mode will enable users to better understand the relationship among search results.

3.5 Evaluation

To evaluate processing time, we used snippets in analysis and obtained site information, topic majority, topic coverage, topic details, and publisher information. We submitted 5 queries: Measles, Metabolic Syndrome, National Referendum Bill, Tokyo Midtown, and French President. The average processing time of top 10 pages for each query is 7.2 seconds and that of top 50 pages is 28 seconds.

The calculation time for locality support was obtained as average values of 9 pages. The result shows that most of the time comes from link analysis, which is dependent on the response time of the Web search engine that returns URLs of link sources (Table 1).

We tested our system on a computer equipped with Windows Vista, processor 1.83GHz, RAM 2GB.

4 Conclusion

We developed a way to help search engine users to determine the trustworthiness of Web search results by computing and showing several different types of information concerned with the search results. We first surveyed users to understand the way they search the Web, how they determine the trustworthiness of search results, and user expectations of search engines. The supporting information that our system provides must be computed in real-time when users execute queries on search engines. Because of limited computation time, we restricted the supporting information to that which could be computed efficiently by accessing search engines. The future problems are how to extract valuable supporting information in a more efficient manner from Web search engines and the Internet.

Acknowledgments

This research was supported by MEXT Grant-in-Aid for Scientific Research in Priority Areas entitled: "Content Fusion and Seamless Search for Information

Explosion" (Project Leader: Katsumi Tanaka, A01-00-02, Grant#: 18049041) and "Design and Development of Advanced IT Research Platform for Information" (Project Leader: Jun Adachi, Y00-01, Grant#: 18049073), by MEXT Grant-in-Aid for "Development of Fundamental Software Technologies for Digital Archives", Software Technologies for Search and Integration across Heterogeneous-Media Archives (Project Leader: Katsumi Tanaka), and by MEXT Grant-in-Aid for Young Scientists (B) (Grant#: 18700086, 18700111, 18700129).

References

1. Fogg, B.J., Marshall, J., Laraki, O., Osipovich, A., Varma, C., Fang, N., Paul, J., Rangnekar, A., Shon, J., Swani, P., Treinen, M.: Web credibility research: A method for online experiments and some early study results. In: CHI 2001, pp. 295–296 (2001)
2. Fogg, B.J., Kameda, T., Boyd, J., Marshall, J., Sethi, R., Sockol, M.: Stanford-Makovsky web credibility study 2002: Investigating what makes web sites credible today. Report from the Stanford Persuasive Technology Lab, Stanford University (2002)
3. Fogg, B.J.: Prominence-interpretation theory: Explaining how people assess credibility online. In: CHI2003, pp. 722–723 (2003)
4. Stanford Guidelines for Web Credibility: `http://www.webcredibility.org/guidelines/index.html`
5. Zaihrayeu, I., da Silva, P.P., McGuinness, D.L.: IWTrust: Improving user trust in answers from the web. In: Herrmann, P., Issarny, V., Shiu, S.C.K. (eds.) iTrust 2005. LNCS, vol. 3477, pp. 384–392. Springer, Heidelberg (2005)
6. Yanbe, Y., Jatowt, A., Nakamura, S., Tanaka, K.: Can social bookmarking enhance search in the web? In: JCDL 2007 (to appear, 2007)
7. Yamamoto, Y., Tezuka, T., Jatowt, A., Tanaka, K.: Honto? search: Estimating trustworthiness of web information by search results aggregation and temporal analysis. In: APWeb/WAIM 2007 (to appear, 2007)
8. Ma, Q., Tanaka, K.: Retrieving regional information from web by contents localness and user location. In: Myaeng, S.-H., Zhou, M., Wong, K.-F., Zhang, H.-J. (eds.) AIRS 2004. LNCS, vol. 3411, pp. 301–312. Springer, Heidelberg (2005)
9. Zhang, J., Ishikawa, Y., Kurokawa, S., Kitagawa, H.: LocalRank: Ranking web pages considering geographical locality by integrating web and databases. In: Andersen, K.V., Debenham, J., Wagner, R. (eds.) DEXA 2005. LNCS, vol. 3588, pp. 145–155. Springer, Heidelberg (2005)
10. Oyama, S., Tanaka, K.: Query modification by discovering topics from web page structures. In: Yu, J.X., Lin, X., Lu, H., Zhang, Y. (eds.) APWeb 2004. LNCS, vol. 3007, pp. 553–564. Springer, Heidelberg (2004)
11. MaxMind: `http://www.maxmind.com/`

Improved Publication Scores for Online Digital Libraries Via Research Pyramids

Sulieman Bani-Ahmad and Gultekin Ozsoyoglu

Department of Electrical Engineering and Computer Science
Case Western Reserve University
Cleveland, Ohio 44106
{sulieman, tekin}@case.edu

Abstract. Ranking publications of *Online Digital Libraries* (ODLs) is useful for (i) providing comparative assessment of publications and (ii) listing relevant ODL search results first in search outputs, enabling users to aggregate pertinent results quickly and easily. Studies show that effective citation-based scoring functions, namely, PageRank, HITS and Citation Count, are highly skewed, and have accuracy problems, possibly due to topic diffusion. In this paper, based on the notion of research pyramids, we propose an a priori technique to assign more effective publication scores. Using the ACM SIGMOD Anthology ODL as a testbed, we show that our approach provides more accurate and less skewed publication scores.

1 Introduction

Searching on-line Digital Libraries (ODLs) efficiently and effectively is becoming more and more important as the size and use of ODLs expand at a very high rate. As examples, (i) in Computer Science, ACM Digital Library [1] has close to 1 million full-text publications collected over 50 years, to search and download; (ii) in Electrical Engineering and Computer Science, IEEE Xplorer [2], another ODL, provides users with on-line access to more than 1,700 selected conferences proceedings; and, (iii) ScienceDirect [3], the world's leading scientific, technical and medical information resource celebrated its billionth article download in November'06 since launched in 1999.

Providing accurate publication scores for search results and ranking publications returned as search results accurately can help users in reducing the time spent in searching ODLs. And, better publication rankings are also useful for comparative assessments of publication venues and scientists as well. At the present time, ODLs lack effective and accurate publication rankings [4]. For instance, ACM Digital Library returns rankings of publication search results that are unexplained and not useful to users [1]. Moreover, search outputs of ODLs tend to suffer from the "topic diffusion" problem, where commonly, keyword-based searches produce a large number of publications over a large number of topics, thereby producing scores that are nonspecific to topics.

L. Kovács, N. Fuhr, and C. Meghini (Eds.): ECDL 2007, LNCS 4675, pp. 50–62, 2007.

Using social networks or bibliometrics, a number of publication score functions has been defined [8, 9, 23]. In an earlier work [23], we compared and evaluated several publication score functions, including *PageRank* [8] and *Authorities scores* [9], both adopted from the www search domain, and *citation-count scores* from the bibliometrics domain [5]. We observed the *separability* problem with all of these functions which is that none of these scoring functions assigns scores that distribute well over a given scale, e.g., [0, 1]. Instead, distributions of existing publication score functions are highly skewed, and decay very fast [6], resulting in a much less useful comparative publication assessment capability for users. This lack of separability is caused by the "rich gets richer" phenomena [6, 17], i.e., a very small number of publications with relatively high numbers of in-citations have even higher chances of receiving new citations. Yet, these scoring functions are still not very accurate, probably caused by topic diffusion in search outputs [18].

The research evolution model proposed in [12] suggests that citation relationships between research publications produce multiple, small *pyramid-like* structures, where each pyramid represents publications related to a highly specific research topic. A *research pyramid* is defined [12] as a set of publications that represent a highly specific research topic, and usually has a *pyramid-like* structure in terms of its citation graph [12]. Publications within an individual research pyramid are (i) *motivated by* earlier publications in the topic area (e.g., this paper is motivated in part by citations [4], and [12]), or (ii) *use techniques* proposed in publications from other research pyramids (e.g., this paper in part uses some of the techniques presented in citations [8] and [9]). Other "reasons" for citations may also be observed [12].

In this paper, our goals are to (a) provide a solution to the ODL search output ranking problem due to the topic diffusion problem, by grouping search outputs at the most-specific (detailed) topic level and without identifying the topics themselves, (b) eliminate the low separability problem of score functions, and (c) improve the accuracy of three score functions, namely, PageRank, Authorities and Citation Count score functions. Our approach uses the research pyramid (RP-) model to improve the separability and accuracy of publication scores, and is based on normalizing publication scores within a limited scope, namely, *within individual research pyramids*. These improvements come from the fact that publications are now compared to their peers within their peer groups, namely, their own research pyramid publications that are on the same topic.

This paper proposes and empirically evaluates two approaches to identify research pyramids. The first, called *LB-IdentifyRP*, uses Link-Based Research Pyramid identification, which captures research pyramids by identifying pyramid-like structures *from the citation graph of the publication set*. The second approach, called *PB-IdentifyRP*, uses Proximity-Based Research Pyramid identification, utilizes a graph-based proximity measure, namely SimRank [13], to compute similarities between publications, and then restructures the k-most-similar publications into a research pyramid.

This paper's contributions are:

- Validate the research pyramid model of research evolution.
- Propose and evaluate two algorithms to identify research pyramids.
- Improve publication scores in terms of accuracy and separability via publications' research pyramids.

As a testbed, we have utilized *AnthP*, a publication set of 14,891 publications from the ACM SIGMOD Anthology. Our experimental results show that

- The complete publication citation graph (of *AnthP*) is highly clustered.
- Each cluster of the complete publication set has a pyramid-like structure in terms of the citation graph of the cluster.
- Each cluster represents a highly specific research topic.

Note that the above three findings validate the research pyramid model proposed in [12].

- Topic similarities decay over both the citation age and citation paths.

We used the two topic similarity decay curves to guide the RP construction.

- Within RP citation graphs, the average number of in-citations per paper varies, pointing to the importance of comparative publication scores within RPs.
- Publication scores within RPs are accurate, due to our approach where each publication is compared only to its peer (research pyramid paper) group.

The rest of the paper is organized as follows. Section 2 presents publication score functions, and introduces the notion of normalizing publication scores within their research pyramids. Section 3 lists the properties of the research pyramid model. In section 4, we present two algorithms to identify research pyramids, namely, *LB-IdentifyRP,* and *PB-IdentifyRP.* Section 5 empirically validates the research pyramid model of research evolution, and evaluates the effectiveness of employing research pyramids for score separability and accuracy.

2 Publication Scores

Existing citation-based publication score functions are all based on the notion of prestige in social networks [7] and bibliometry [5]. In this paper, as publication score functions we use:

* *PageRank* [8] algorithm: PageRank score P_{PgRank} of a publication P is recursively computed as the normalized sum of PageRank scores of documents citing P.
* *Authority score* of the HITS (Hyperlink Induced Topic Search) algorithm [9]: Each document P gets two scores, namely *hub* and *authority* scores. Hub score of P is computed

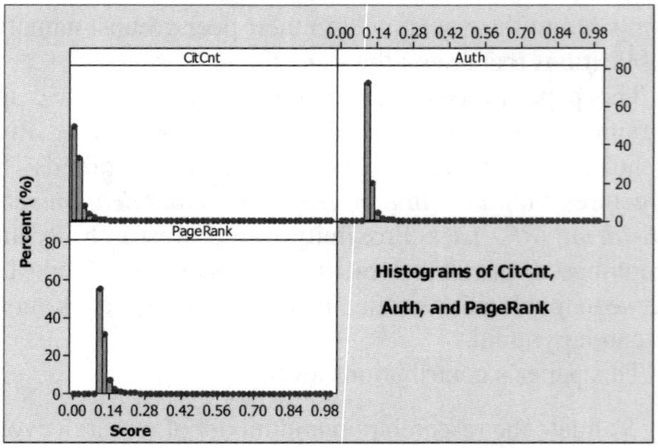

Fig. 1. Score distribution of the three publication score functions

by summing up authority scores of the publications that P cites, and the Authority score of P, denoted by P_{Auth}, is computed by summing the hub scores of publication citing P.

* Normalized *citation count score*: For a particular paper P that receives C_P citations, the normalized citation count P_{CitCnt} is the ratio of C_P to the number C_{Pmax} of in-citations of the most cited paper in the publication set.

Figure 1 shows that the three score functions, namely, P_{PgRank}, P_{Auth}, and, P_{CitCnt} are highly skewed, and do not separate scores well. In [21], the author observed the skewness and inseparability of these functions independently in computer science and life sciences publications (70,000 documents in each) as well. And, it is shown [6, 17] that distributions of citation-based score functions are also highly skewed and decay very fast. We think that the cause is topic diffusion since scores are computed with respect to the full publication set. By using the research-pyramid model proposed in [12], we normalize scores of publications within their own research pyramids, which allows for a fair comparative assessment of publications as publications are compared to their peers in their own research pyramids.

3 Properties of Research Pyramid Model

We have observed three properties of research publications in three separate data sets, namely, ACM Anthology (AnthP; 15,000 publications) [10], and computer sciences and life sciences publication sets (each with 70,000 publications) [21]. In the next section, we utilize these properties in the identification of research pyramids.

Property 1 (*Maximum Citation Age*). In online digital libraries (ODLs), most publications receive most of their in-citations within a fixed number of years after their publication dates. We refer to this value as the *Maximum Citation Age,* and denote it by C_{AgeMax}.

We have observed [16, 21] that, in *AnthP* and Computer Sciences and Life Sciences ODLs, most publications receive 90% of their in-citations in 10 years, i.e., $C_{AgeMax}=10$. Figure 2 presents the citation age distributions in AnthP. Below in Property 4, we give a tighter bound for citation age within which topical similarity within an RP is maintained between citing and cited publications.

In rare cases, publications may cite works older than C_{AgeMax}. It is found [19] that a great proportion of these citations are for historical reasons, which we interpret as: old cited works (a) have coarse similarity to citing papers, and (b) do not belong in the RP of the citing publication.

Property 2 (*Topic Specificity Over Time*). Scientific research publications quickly become very topic-specific over time, usually referable via a highly specific topic.

As illustrated in Figure 3, an old research pyramid that covers a certain research topic leads to instantiations of new research topics, and thus to creations of new RPs, that *use* techniques proposed in the publications of parent RP(s). Again, such old citations carry topical similarity between the citing and cited publication at a coarse granularity level. Possible citation exchanges between different RPs also occur and are of type "uses", i.e., the citing paper *uses* techniques proposed by the cited paper.

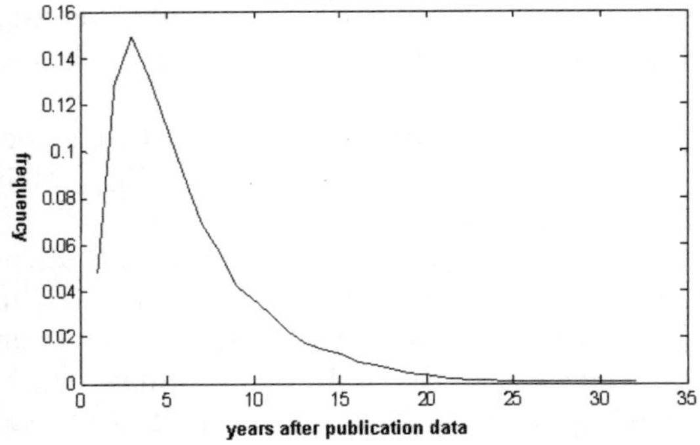

Fig. 2. Citation age distribution curve of AnthP

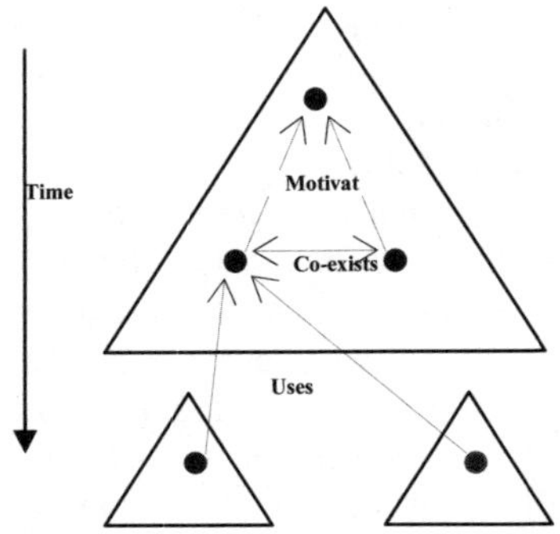

Fig. 3. The RP-Based Model

Example. Codd's paper "*E. F. Codd, "A Relational Model of Data for Large Shared Data Banks", Commun. ACM 13(6): 377-387(1970)*" is about the topic *relational model,* and cited around 580 times. A new and more specific topic of 2000's (i.e., citation to Codd's work is 30+ years old), say, *rank-aware join algorithms*, is coarsely related to the more general topic *relational model* in that, a publication P in the RP of *rank-aware join algorithms* and citing Codd's paper "uses" the techniques proposed in the RP of the *relational model.*

Property 3 (*Topic Similarity Decay Over Citation Path)***.** After *very small* citation path distances, topical similarity between papers decays significantly.

From Figure 5, in AnthP, after a citation path of length 3, the topical similarity, as measured by SimRank, significantly decays. We refer to this value by $L_{Max\text{-}TopicDecay}$. This observation led us to build RPs of height at most 3 in the experimental results section.

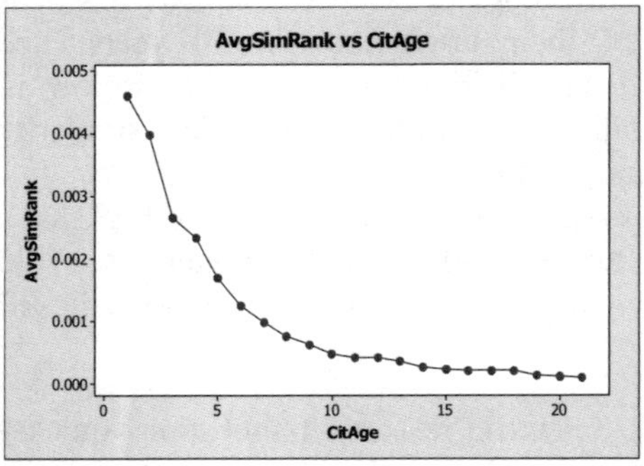

Fig. 4. SimRank score change with citation age

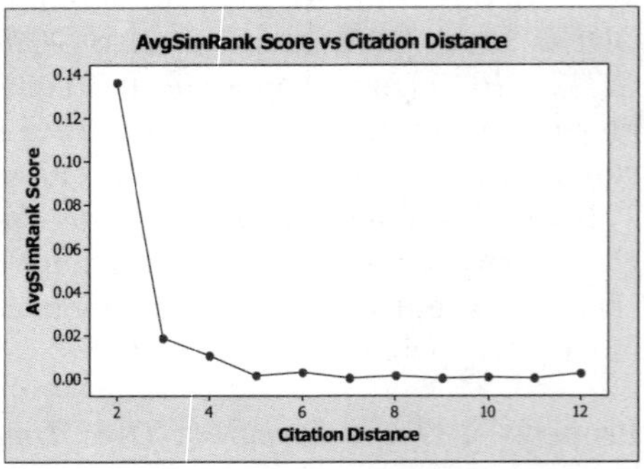

Fig. 5. SimRank score change with citation distance

Property 4 (*Topic Similarity Decay over citation age*)**.** After a certain citation age, topical similarity between the citing and the cited papers significantly decays.

From Figure 4, in the AnthP set, after a citation age of about 5 years, the topic similarity between the citing and cited papers decays significantly. We refer to this value by $C_{AgeMax\text{-}TopicDecay}$. This observation led us to build RPs in the experimental results section such that the maximum citation age *within an RP* is 5 years.

Next we present the two characteristics that identify a *research pyramid RP*.

RP-Property 1 (*High Topic Specificity*). An RP, usually organizable into a pyramid, is a set of publications that represent a *highly specific research topic*.

We maintain high topic specificity of RPs by applying properties 3 and 4, and keeping the height of research pyramids low (property 3). Note that we make no attempts to identify the topic associated with an RP, as our approach does not need the topics explicitly. But, in interactive environments, providing topics to users is useful [22].

RP-Property 2 (*Research Pyramid Construction*). RPs are arranged into *pyramid* structures either directly by using citation graphs (i.e., the link-based approach) [12] or indirectly using the publication times and close proximity of papers (i.e., the proximity-based approach).

4 Research Pyramid Identification Procedures

Based on the properties of publications and characteristics of RPs, next we propose two *offline* research pyramid identification procedures, namely, the link-based (LB) and the proximity-based (PB) RP identification procedures.

Both procedures start by choosing a candidate root node for an RP, called the *cornerstone paper*. The paper that is located at the root of a research pyramid receives more citations than others as other publications within the research pyramid are "motivated" by it, and directly or indirectly cite it. Thus, our approach is to *identify papers with high in-citations as cornerstone papers* (i.e., the roots) of RPs to be constructed.

The *link-based* procedure locates research pyramids by identifying pyramid-like structures in the citation graph of the publication set. In summary, within an individual RP, publications are topically related [12], and motivated by each other (see figure 3) [12], and we use the four properties of section 3 to identify citations within RPs—as summarized next.

In *AnthP,* the average number of citations to a paper ("in-citations"), denoted by C_I, is 2.066. Note that, in our experiments, we consider *only* the *AnthP* citations that are completely within AnthP; any citation from a paper within AnthP to a paper that is not in AnthP is removed. Using Property 3 and RP-Property 1, we limit RP heights to 3. Thus, the expected number of papers within a research pyramid RP_P with paper P as the root and with height 3 is $|RP_P| = 1 + C_I + C_I^2 + C_I^3 \approx 15$. Of course, the actual identified RP sizes (the number of papers in RP_P) vary. Some RPs may deal with active research topics, and, in such cases, the number of in-citations of publications are noticeably higher than C_I, leading to noticeably higher RP sizes as well.

Figure 6-(a) presents the link-based *LB-IdentifyRP()* procedure. The proximity-based *PB-IdentifyRP()* is similar, except that the function call to *LB-FormRP()* is replaced by the function call *PB-FormRP()*. The procedure *LB-IdentifyRP()* (a) selects a cornerstone paper P from the existing publication set (originally, say, AnthP) as an RP root, by simply picking the current most-cited publication (only citations that are

$C_{AgeMax\text{-}TopicDecay}$ old according to property 4 above), (b) calls *LB-FormRP()* to locate the RP set RP_P of P, and (c) eliminates RP_P from the current publication set *CurrAnthP*, and repeats (a)-(c) again, until no more publications are left in *CurrAnthP*.

Note that our approach in this paper is to create distinct and nonoverlapping research pyramids. An alternative approach, not reported here due to space limitations, is to allow *overlapping research pyramids* as follows: Do not to eliminate *any* papers from the original publication set (i.e., remove step (c) above); instead, simply *color each* selected publication, and continue until all publications are colored, meaning that, when the algorithm ends, each paper belongs to at least one RP set, and possibly more.

The two main functions of the link-based *LB-IdentifyRP()* procedure are *ChooseRoot()* and *LB-FormRP(). ChooseRoot()* (See Figure 6.b) chooses publications that are cornerstone papers, or roots of research pyramids. The function *LB-FormRP()* (Figure 6.c) forms the RP_P of a root publication *P* by adding direct citers of *P* (i.e., *level-1 citers*) into RP_P, and indirect citers of *P* at a level up to the L_{Max}; in experiments, we choose L_{Max} as 3, by following the property 3. The function *Citers*(*P*, *l*, $C_{AgeMax\text{-}Topic\text{-}Decay}$) returns the set of publications that cite P at a level *l* (which is at most L_{Max}) where the citation age of the citing paper with respect to P is less than the maximum citation age $C_{AgeMax\text{-}Topic\text{-}Decay}$, (Properties 1 and 4). In more detail,

1. Paper-id pid_P of root *P* along with its level *0* is inserted into RP_P and the queue *Q*, which holds paper-ids for future expansions and their distances to the root paper *P*.
2. Two-tuple $<P_i, \ell>$ in *Q* is dequeued, and expanded by locating direct or indirect citers of P_i so long as their levels with respect to *P* is at most $L_{Max\text{-}TopicDecay}$ (i.e., 3) and their citation age with respect to *P* (the root) is less than the maximum citation age $C_{AgeMax\text{-}TopicDecay}$ (i.e., 5). All expanded publications and their level info with respect to *P* are inserted into the queue *Q*.
3. The above two steps are repeated until *Q* is empty; then RP_P is returned.

```
proc LB-IdentifyRP(AnthP, RP-Sets)
{RP-Sets := Ø;
 CurrAnthP := AnthP;
 while (CurrentAnthP = Ø)
  {Root:=ChooseRoot(CurrAnthP);
   RP_Root:=LB-FormRP(Root,L_Max-TopicDecay);
   RP-Sets:=RP-Sets U RP_Root;
   CurrAnthP:=CurrAnthP - RP_Root;
  } }
```
(a) Procedure LB-IdentifyRP

```
funct ChooseRoot(CurrAnthP)
 return TopCited_TopicDecay(CurrAnthP);
```
(b) Function ChooseRoot

```
funct LB-FormRP(P, L_Max)
{Set RP_P:={P};    Queue Q;
 Q.Enqueue({P},0);
 while(Q is not empty)
 {<P_i, ℓ>:=Q.Dequeue;
   if(ℓ<L_Max)then
   {CiterSet=Citers(P_i, ℓ,
                     C_AgeMax-TopicDecay);
     Q.Enqueue(CiterSet,(ℓ+1));
      RP_P = RP_P +CiterSet;
      } } }
  Return RP_P}
```
(c) Function LB-FormRP()

```
Funct PB-FormRP(P, L_Max)
{Set RP_P={P}; Queue Q;
 Q.Enqueue(P,0);
 while(Q is not empty)
 {<P_i, ℓ>:=Q.Dequeue;
 if(ℓ<L_Max) then
 {CiterSet(P_i):=Citers(P_i, ℓ,
                     C_AgeMax-TopicDecay)

  TopSimSet:=TopSim(P_i,|CiterSet(P_i)|,
                 C_AgeMax-TopicDecay);
  Q.Enqueue(TopSimSet, ℓ+1);
  RP_P= RP_P+TopSimSet;
  } }
  Return RP_P}
```
(d) Function PB-FormRP()

Fig. 6. Functions of *LB-* and *PB-IdentifyRP* algorithms

The function *PB-FormRP()* (figure 6.d) of the proximity-based approach utilizes a graph-based proximity measure, namely *SimRank* [13], to compute similarities between publications. It captures RP_P of the root publication by locating publications that are most similar to *P* and yet (a) are linked to *P* with a citation path length of at most $L_{Max\text{-}TopicDecay}$, and (b) have a citation time distance less than $C_{AgeMax\text{-}TopicDecay}$. *SimRank* iteratively computes similarity scores between nodes in a graph G following the rule that "two nodes are similar if they are linked with similar nodes". In other words, the *SimRank* similarity between two nodes *a* and *b*, *S(a, b),* is iteratively computed using the formula (until the similarity scores converge):

$$S(a,b) = \left[C / |I(a)||I(b)|\right] * \sum_{i=1}^{|I(a)|} \sum_{j=1}^{|I(b)|} S(I_i(a), I_j(b))$$

where $I(a)$ and $I(b)$ are sources of in-links of a and b, respectively. C is the decay factor between 0 and 1. We choose C=0.8 [13]. If $|I(a)| or |I(b)|=0$ then *S(a, b)*=0 by definition, in the case where a=b, *S(a, b)*=1. The space complexity of the naive SimRank algorithm is $O(N^2)$ where N is the graph size (the citation graph in publication domain). We prune as in [13] by considering node pairs that are near each other in the range of radius *r*. We choose *r*=6, which is twice the value of the expected research pyramid height as also explained in Section 5.

PB- FormRP() receives as input the root *P,* the maximum level L_{Max} from root, and utilizes the maximum citation age $C_{AgeMax\text{-}TopicDecay}$ (as 5) and returns the RP set RP_P of publication *P* following the same main steps of *LB- FormRP()* with one main difference: the way the two-tuple $<P_i, \ell>$ dequeued from *Q* is expanded, as follows:

- Top $|Citers(P_i, \ell, C_{AgeMax\text{-}TopicDecay})|$ similar papers, based on *SimRank*, to P_i are identified. The number of citers of P_i is used to capture the density of the RP being identified, and thus to expand RP at P_i accordingly.
- The identified similar papers are added to RP_P and also enqueued to *Q* for further expansion, this time with the level increased by 1. Similar to *LB- FormRP()* a maximum level of $L_{Max\text{-}TopicDecay}$ (which is 3) is employed.

Advantage of PB-FormRP() over *LB-FormRP()* is that it successfully captures co-existing members of RP as well as those that are not reachable through any citation path from RP's root (as illustrated in Figure 3 above). We give an example.

Example. Figure 7 shows two RPs; RP_1 and RP_2. RP_1 contains two co-existing roots *A* and *B*. Such a case occurs when two researchers work on the same problem simultaneously. At some point of our RP identification process, *A* will probably be recognized as a root of a new RP, say RP_3, as it has more in-citations than *B*. And, since B is not reachable through any path from

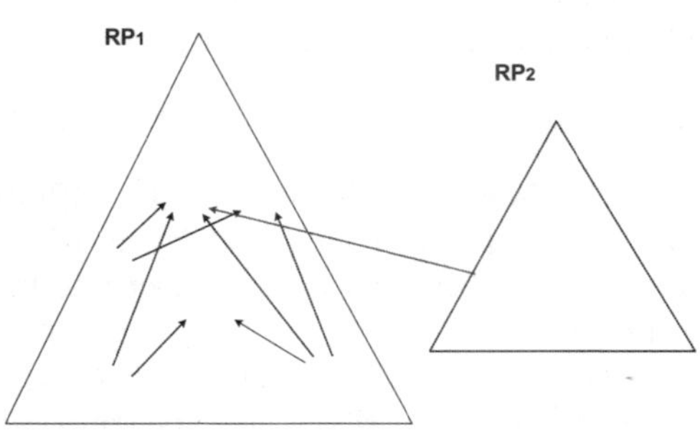

Fig. 7. Examples where *PB-FormRP()* is more successful than *LB-FormRP()*

A, *LB-FormRP()* will fail to identify *B* as a member of RP_3. *PB-FormRP()* will succeed to place both A and B into RP_3 in this case as *B* is very similar to *A*. A similar problem will be observed with paper *C* that is not reachable through any path from the root. Furthermore, *LB-FormRP()* may incorrectly identify *F*, that probably "uses" a technique proposed in *A*, as a member of RP_3 when *F* is really a member of RP_2 which co-exists with RP_3. *PB-FormRP()* successfully repels *F* from RP_3 as *F* is not similar to *A* or any of RP_3's members, based on *SimRank*.

We observe here that *PB-FormRP()* may capture *pyramid-like* structures, but not exactly pyramid structures. SimRank computes similarity between two papers P_1 and P_2 by averaging the similarity of the citers of both. However, note that similar papers to a member of an RP will be the other members of the same RP since members of an RP are usually cited by each other (as they are motivated by each other).

5 Empirical Evaluations of Score Functions

AnthP, utilized as the ODL testbed here, is a publication set of 14,891 publications from the ACM SIGMOD Anthology. After eliminating citations to papers outside *AnthP*, the average in-citations per AnthP paper is 2.066.

The three citation-based publication score functions (*PageRank*, *Authorities*, and *Citation count*) have separability (high skew) and accuracy problems. We have observed that 99% of AnthP publications have scores below 0.1. This is because in-citations conform to the *Power Law* distribution, which describes the scale invariance found in many natural phenomena including publication citation graphs. As for low accuracy (probably due to "topic diffusion" problem [18]), different research topics differ in their citation graph densities. Thus, a paper P's chances of receiving new citations depends on how dense the citation graph of the research topic of P is.

Observation: *AnthP* RPs (that represent specific research topics) have an almost normal distribution in the average in-citations received by members of an RP (figure 8).

For separability, first we verify the RP model on the *AnthP* set. We have experimentally observed that only 3.32% of SimRank scores are higher than 0.1, indicating that *AnthP* is highly clustered.

Observation: Average size of *AnthP* RP is 15 (as expected from section 4).

Figure 9 shows the distribution of the observed RP sizes within AnthP. Note that the PB approach identified larger RP sizes as it can identify co-existing RP roots and members that are not reachable through any citation path from the roots (section 4).

Figures 10 and 11 illustrate that $P_{PgRank\text{-}LB}$, $P_{PgRank\text{-}PB}$, $P_{CitCnt\text{-}LB}$ and $P_{CitCnt\text{-}PB}$ publication scores distribute much better over the interval [0, 1].

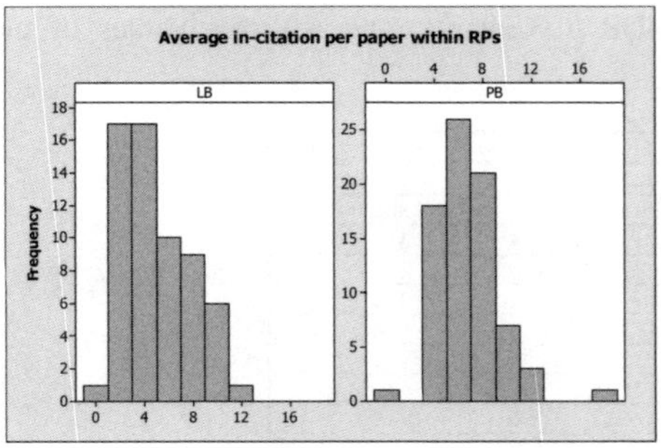

Fig. 8. Variance of citation-graph densities in different topics

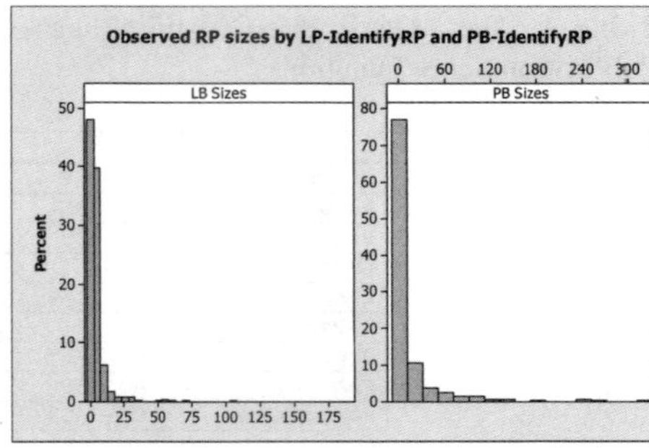

Fig. 9. Observed RP sizes by LP-IdentifyRP and PB-IdentifyRP

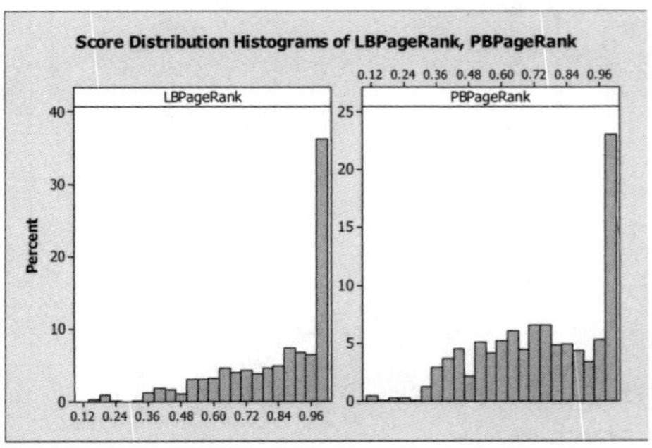

Fig. 10. Score distributions of PageRank normalized within RPs

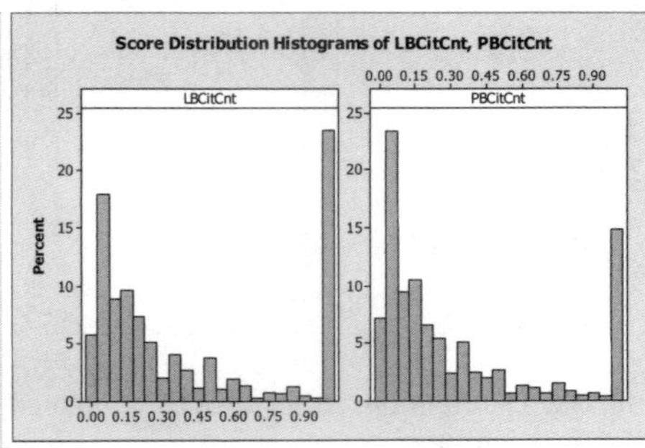

Fig. 11. Score distributions of CitCnt normalized within RPs

Observation: For RP-based scores, the observed skew values (table 1) range between (-0.05) and (1.88) in the RP-based scores (zero skew indicates that the distribution is symmetric).

In comparison, the original scores showed highly skewed values that range between 8.12 and 13.04, which means that they are sharply left-skewed.

Observation: For RP-based scores, kurtosis values (that measure how sharply peaked a distribution is) range between (-0.26) to (2.65) (near zero Kurtosis values indicate normally peaked data).

In comparison, in the case of globally normalized scores, Kurtosis values range between (113.28) and (291.10). The enhancement of score distribution comes from the fact that publications are being compared to their peer groups, i.e., publications that belong to the same scope, and thus have the same chances of receiving new citations.

The above observations on *PageRank* (P_{PgRank}, $P_{PgRank\text{-}LB}$, $P_{PgRank\text{-}PB}$) also apply to *Authorities* scores (P_{Auth}, $P_{Auth\text{-}LB}$, $P_{Auth\text{-}PB}$). Here we report only PageRank-related results as we have observed that P_{Auth} and P_{PgRank} scores are highly correlated with a correlation coefficient of 0.98, and the correlation between P_{PgRank} and P_{CitCnt} is 0.74. [23]

Table 1. The Means, InterQuartile Ranges (IQR), Skewness, and Kurtosis values of the Publication Score Functions

	Mean	IQR	Skewness	Kurtosis
CitCnt	0.02527	0.01845	8.12	113.28
Auth	0.11352	0.01134	13.04	291.10
PageRank	0.12091	0.01733	8.84	134.65
LBCitCnt	0.55698	0.88462	-0.05	-1.81
LBAuth	0.81266	0.37723	-1.02	-0.26
LBPageRank	0.77649	0.46181	-0.80	-0.84
PBCitCnt	0.20802	0.21910	1.88	2.65
PBAuth	0.62386	0.32036	-0.07	-0.58
PBPageRank	0.55653	0.31615	0.30	-0.60

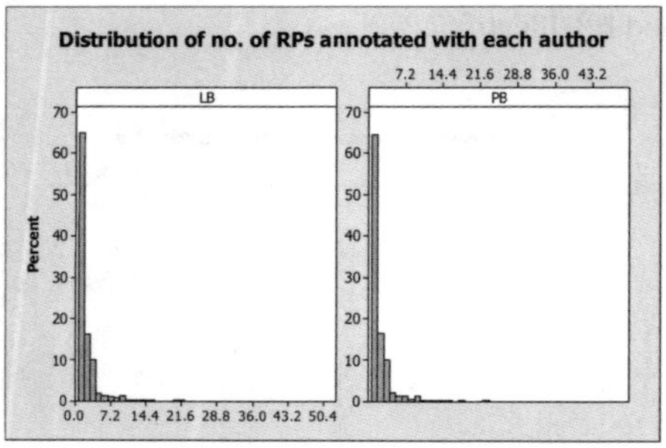

Fig. 12. Distribution of no. of RPs annotated with each author

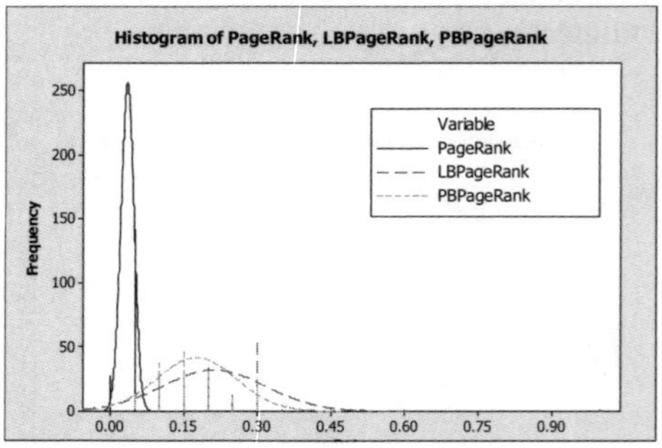

Fig. 13. Quality values distribution of the search results

Observation: Each author in *AnthP* is identified with (i.e., author papers in) 2.19 and 2.16 LB and PB research pyramids (figure 12).

This indicates that publications within an RP are highly related, and, thus, the identified RPs are accurate.

We used expert knowledge in the data management field to manually evaluate the accuracy of searching via RPs. For this purpose, we built a prototype keyword-based search system that

- Sends search keywords to Microsoft's Fulltext Search engine (MsFTS), that indexes the titles of AnthP publications. In turn, MsFTS generates a list of relevant publications (*result set*) along with *rank values* (which measures text-based relevancy between the publications and the search keywords).
- For each publication *p* in the result set, aggregates *p's* rank value returned by MsFTS with its scores, measured in two ways, namely globally-normalized PageRank and LBPageRank. We refer to this final score as the *quality* of paper *p* or **Q**(p). The quality scores are then used to sort the search output list so that high quality results appear at the top. The idea behind this aggregation is to push down publications that have high PageRank/LBPageRank scores and yet also have low rank values Rank(*p*), i.e., low relevancy to the search keywords. **Q**(*p*) is computed according to the following formula

$$\mathbf{Q}(p) = \text{Rank}(p) * [\text{LB}]\text{PageRank}(p)$$

Sample 1

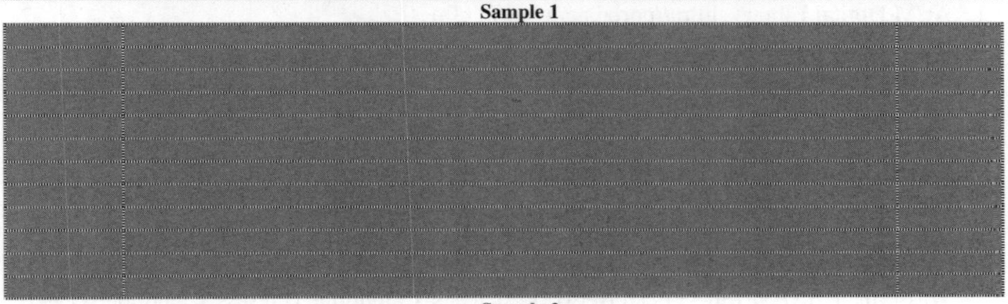

Sample 2

Fig. 14. Sample results of the "complexity of join" query. Quality is computed using RP-based (sample 1) and the globally-normalized PageRank (sample 2) along with the average relevancy scores as assigned by experts.

We performed multiple searches and manually evaluated the accuracy of our system's outputs. We observed that LBPageRank-based quality scores resulted in 16% - 25% more accurate search outputs than the PageRank-based quality scores. Accuracy was measured for the top-k publications in the result sets, where k is 10. In figures 13 and 14, we report our observations on one search experiment for the keywords "complexity of join".

Observation: Quality scores of search results distribute better when computed based on RP-based publication score functions (figure 13).

Each publication in the Figure 14 is evaluated by several domain experts who assigned a score between 0 and 10 (0: non-relevant and 10: completely relevant).

Observation: The average expert relevancy scores assigned to publications of Samples 1 and 2 are 7.07 and 5.77 (figure 14).

The above observation indicates that searching via RP-based publication scores is more accurate than globally normalized publication scores.

6 Conclusions

In this paper, we used the Research-Pyramid model proposed in [12] to solve the separability and accuracy problems of publication score functions. We showed that (i) normalizing publication scores within their research pyramids provides more accurate and less skewed scores, moreover (ii) ranking search results by these scores promises to give higher accuracy compared to ranking by globally normalized publication scores due to reduction of topic diffusion effect.

As the next work in this on-going research, we are working on the problem of automatically annotating research pyramids with keywords representing fine-grained research topics. Also, by using the identified research pyramids, we are working on visualization, namely, building a hierarchical structure that places research pyramids into a hierarchical structure.

References

1. ACM Digital Library, http://portal.acm.org/dl.cfm
2. IEEE XPlore, http://ieeexplore.ieee.org
3. ScienceDirect, www.sciencedirect.info
4. Nattakarn, et al.: Evaluating utility of different ranking functions in context-based environment. In: DBRank Workshop, Istanbul, Turkey (April 2007), http://vorlon.case.edu/7Enxr27/Publications/DBRank07.pdf
5. Chakrabarti, S.: Mining the Web. Morgan-Kauffman, Seattle (2003)
6. Redner, S.: Citation statistics from more than a century of physical review. physics 0407137 (2004)
7. Wasserman, S., Faust, K.: Social Network Analysis. Cambridge U. Press, Cambridge (1994)
8. Brin, S., Page, L.: The anatomy of a large-scale hypertextual web search engine. Computer Networks and ISDN Systems (1998)
9. Kleinberg, J.: Authoritative sources in hyperlinked environments. In: The 9th ACM-SIAM Symposium on Discrete Mathematics (SODA) Conference (1998)
10. Al-Hamdani, A.: Querying web resources with metadata in a database. PhD thesis, EECS Dept., CWRU (2003)
11. CiteSeer Scientific Digital Literature Library, http://citeseer.ist.psu.edu
12. Aya, S., Lagoze, C., Joachims, T.: Citation Classification and its Applications. In: International Conference on Knowledge Management (2005)
13. Jeh, G., Widom, J.: SimRank: A measure of structural-context similarity. In: ACM SIGKDD International Conference on Knowledge Discovery and Data Mining (2002)
14. PubMed, http://www.ncbi.nlm.nih.gov/entrez/query.fcgi
15. Google Scholar, http://scholar.google.com/scholar
16. Bani-Ahmad, S., Cakmak, A., Ozsoyoglu, G., Al-Hamdani, A.: Evaluating Publication Similarity Measures. IEEE Data Eng. Bull. 28(4), 21–28 (2005)
17. Li, X., Chen, G.: A local-world evolving network model. Physica A 328, 274–286 (2003)
18. Haveliwala, T.H.: Topic-sensitive PageRank. In: WWW Conference, Hawaii (2002)
19. Ahmed, T., Johnson, B., Oppenheim, C., Peck, C.: Highly cited old papers and the reasons why they continue to be cited. Part II., The 1953 Watson and Crick article on the structure of DNA, Scientometrics 61, 147–156 (2004)
20. Case, D.O., Higgins, D.M.: How can we investigate citation behavior? A study of reasons for citing literature in communication. Jour. Of American Society of Information Science 51(7), 635–645 (2000)
21. Pan, F.: Comparative Evaluation of Publication Characteristics in Computer Science and Life Sciences. MS Thesis, EECS, Case Western Reserve University (2006)
22. Nattakarn, R., Ozsoyoglu, G.: Finding Related Papers in Literature Digital Libraries (submitted for publication), http://vorlon.case.edu/~nxr27/CRelatedPapers/ContextRelatedPapers.pdf
23. Bani-Ahmad, S., et al.: Evaluating Score and Publication Similarity Functions in Digital Libraries. In: International Conference of Asian Digital Libraries (2005)
24. Kohlschutter, C., Chirita, P., Nejdl, W.: Using Link Analysis to identify aspects in faceted web search. In: SIGIR workshop on Faceted Search (2006)

Key Element-Context Model: An Approach to Efficient Web Metadata Maintenance

Ba-Quy Vuong, Ee-Peng Lim, Aixin Sun, Chew-Hung Chang, Kalyani Chatterjea, Dion Hoe-Lian Goh, Yin-Leng Theng, and Jun Zhang

Nanyang Technological University, Singapore
{vuon0001,aseplim}@ntu.edu.sg

Abstract. In this paper, we study the problem of maintaining metadata for open Web content. In digital libraries such as DLESE, NSDL and G-Portal, metadata records are created for some good quality Web content objects so as to make them more accessible. These Web objects are dynamic making it necessary to update their metadata records. As Web metadata maintenance involves manual efforts, we propose to reduce the efforts by introducing the **Key element-Context** (**KeC**) model to monitor only those changes made on Web page content regions that concern metadata attributes while ignoring other changes. We also develop evaluation metrics to measure the number of alerts and the amount of efforts in updating Web metadata records. KeC model has been experimented on metadata records defined for Wikipedia articles, and its performance with different settings is reported. The model is implemented in G-Portal as a metadata maintenance module.

1 Introduction

In a digital library (DL), creating and maintaining metadata records for Web pages with high quality content serve three important purposes. Firstly, the Web content is largely uncensored and it requires some domain knowledge and experience to distinguish the good content objects from the poor ones. Digital librarians therefore play a critical role in selecting the good quality contents and creating metadata records. Secondly, the existence of metadata records allows one to organize and present the Web content objects according to some classification or grouping (e.g., task-based grouping) schemes adopted by a digital library. In this case, the metadata records serve as proxies of Web content objects. Accessing these Web content objects will be of no different from accessing other non-Web content objects. Finally, metadata records contain attributes that are searchable. Again, this allows Web content objects to be queried like other digital library objects.

There are already several metadata creation efforts for Web pages in digital library projects [1,2,6]. The National Science Digital Library[1] (NSDL) funded by the National Science Foundation has been indexing and creating metadata

[1] `http://www.nsdl.org`

L. Kovács, N. Fuhr, and C. Meghini (Eds.): ECDL 2007, LNCS 4675, pp. 63–74, 2007.

for quality Web resources in science, technology, engineering, and mathematics domain for research and education. The Digital Library for Earth System Education[2] (DLESE) project maintains a collection of metadata records about Web pages and other resources relevant to earth science education. In our digital library system known as G-Portal, we also create and maintain metadata for selected Web content objects related to geography education, and provide a wide range of services to help learners organize and collaborate in the learning process [2].

Once created, metadata records of Web content objects often require updates due to the changes made on the referenced Web pages. This is known as the **Web metadata maintenance problem**. Web metadata maintenance is a challenging problem due to several reasons:

- *Autonomous changes to Web content.* Web pages, residing on different sites, can be changed anytime by their owners. Such changes often happen without alerting those DL systems maintaining metadata about the affected pages.
- *Manual efforts to update metadata records.* Whenever changes are detected on Web pages, the respective metadata owners have to update the affected metadata records and the updates require manual inpection and judgement.

Web metadata maintenance consists of three major subtasks, namely (a) *scheduled monitoring*, (b) *change detection*, and (c) *metadata record update*. Scheduled monitoring is to periodically fetch the latest versions of the Web content objects so as to detect changes. Here, we assume that the Web content objects do not publish changes to DL systems as soon as changes occur. A pull-based monitoring is therefore required. Change detection refers to comparing different versions of a Web content object to determine if there are changes made. Once changes are detected, metadata records have to be updated for those changed Web content objects in subtask (c).

We observe that metadata record(s) may be derived from only some content region(s) in a Web page. Therefore, not all changes to a Web page result in changes to its metatdata. To reduce false alarms in subtask (b) and to minimize manual efforts in subtask (c), we propose a **Key element-Context (KeC)** model that allows metadata owners to select Web page content regions for monitoring. The main idea is to narrow the scope of Web page change detection using the concepts of **key element** and **context**.

Given a metadata attribute, there is a *content region* in the Web page which is used to derive the value of the attribute directly. We call this content region *key element* and introduce a concept known as *context* to help locating a key element. For a given metadata attribute, different choices of context(s), options to locate context(s), and options to locate the key element, may lead to different amount of alerts and maintenance efforts. We therefore develop evaluation metrics to measure the two types of overheads. The KeC model was tested on a set of metadata records created for Wikipedia pages. The empirical results showed that the maintenance overheads could be reduced by making the appropriate

[2] `http://www.dlese.org`

choices of context and key elements, and the options to locate them. Compared with the naive approach to monitor Web page changes, our proposed model has shown significant improvements. This KeC model has been implemented as a part of G-Portal as a Web metadata maintenance module. Details of this module is not covered in this paper due to space constraint.

The rest of the paper is organized as follows. Section 2 describes the related research. We present the KeC model in Section 3 and define the evaluation metrics in Section 4. After reporting our experiments in Section 5, we conclude the paper in Section 6.

2 Related Work

Monitoring dynamic Web pages for metadata maintenance is a new and challenging problem. Sharaf and Labrinidis proposed a model of freshness-aware scheduling of continuous queries [5]. Continuous queries are those registered by user and are executed whenever a new update occurs in the Web page in order to maintain an up-to-date result in a real-time fashion [7]. Pandey proposed a Continuous Adaptive Monitoring (CAM) method consisting of a few phases in which Web pages are monitored based on the resources allocated [4]. The main purpose of this approach is to optimize a schedule for monitoring each Web page. Both work did not provide any mechanism for monitoring specific Web content regions for metadata maintenance. They assumed Web changes are "pushed" from Web sites to applications. Nevertheless, in real life, it is more common to detect changes to Web pages using a "pull" (polling) approach.

One of the general-purpose approaches close to detecting relevant Web page changes for metadata maintenance is WebCQ [3]. This approach allows a user to specify Web objects for monitoring and tracks information at Web page level. However, it does not support structured Web objects and is not designed for Web content regions where metadata attributes are derived from.

3 KeC Model

3.1 Key Element and Context

Our proposed KeC model requires metadata owner to define for each metadata attribute a **key element**. A key element is some content region in the Web page referenced by the metadata record, and the content region is directly used to *derive* the value of the attribute. A key element can be in various forms including text, table, image, etc.. Consider the following metadata record created for the Wikipedia's Singapore page shown in Figure 1. It consists of three metadata attributes all related to economy.

Metadata Attribute	Value
`Total GDP:`	`$123.4 billion`
`Per capita:`	`$28,368`
`Manufacturing Contribution:`	`$34.55 billion`

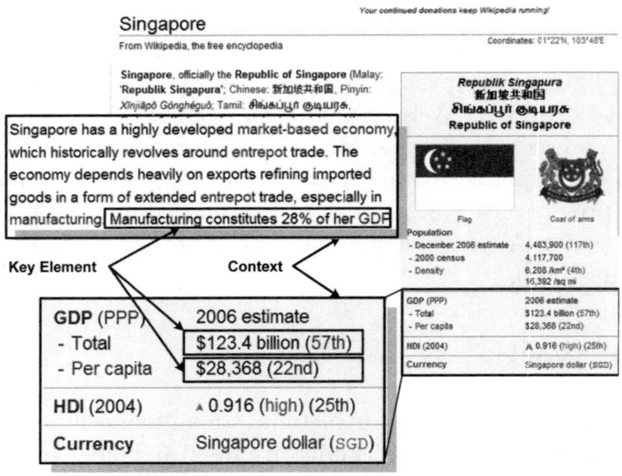

Fig. 1. Wikipedia Article on Singapore

As illustrated in the figure, the key elements of `Total GDP` and `Per capita` attributes are two cells in an information box on the right of the page where the values of the two attributes are found. The `Manufacturing Contribution` attribute, on the other hand, has a key element that is a sentence in the page and the value is derived manually from the information provided as $0.28 \times \$123.4$ billion $= \$34.55$ billion. The fact that some metadata attribute values are not directly extractable from the Web page is not uncommon and should be considered in the design of Web metadata maintenance module.

A change to a key element most likely implies an update to be made on the corresponding metadata attribute. The kind of metadata attribute value update to be made, however, very much depend on the way the attribute value is "derived" from key element.

With key elements defined for metadata attributes, a Web metadata maintenance module can focus on only those changes to the Web page that affect the key elements. Alerts caused by other unimportant changes to the Web page are known as **false alarms**. A good Web metadata maintenance module should therefore aim to reduce false alarms by monitoring changes to key elements only.

A key element in a Web page can be identified either by its *content* or *location*.

- *By content*: This uses the latest key element's content to identify the key element content region. For example, for key elements that are text regions, text content can be used for identification. For key elements that include media objects such as image, audio, and video files, we can check for their file names, timestamps, and/or hash values. This works well for the key elements whose contents are unique. By using the content to identify a key element, we are indirectly detecting the changes to it. The main drawback however is that one would have to scan through the corresponding Web page to locate the key element(s).

– *By location*: This uses some location information to identify a key element. The location can range from byte offset from the beginning of the Web page (the most rigid form), to some combination of HTML tag path and byte offset. The advantage of using location is that it does not require scanning the Web page for key element content. It however cannot accommodate minor changes to the key element location that does not really affect the metadata attribute value, especially when the location of key element is rigidly defined.

To overcome the inherent limitations of using key element alone to track a Web page content region, we introduce **context** as a larger content region enclosing a key element. In other words, we define for each key element a context that cover the former's content region. Within a context, exactly one occurrence of the key element of a metadata attribute is expected. The content of context may not have any relationship with the metadata attribute. Its main role is to demarcate a content region where an occurrence of the key element is to be found. This is important to a key element to be identified by content in case key element's content is not unique in the Web page. In addition, we only need to scan for the key element within the context covering a smaller region compared with the entire Web page.

Context is also important to a key element that is to be identified by location because it gives more flexibility to the specification of key element's location. Instead of a key element's location defined with respect to the entire Web page, it can be defined with respect to the context. Hence, changes outside the context will not be taken as location changes to the key element within the context. For example, in Figure 1, the `Total GDP` attribute has key element defined by a cell in the information box. The context of this key element could be the information box. It does not really matter where the `Total GDP` cell is located as long as it is found within the information box (or the context) or is said to *float* within the context. The identification of context and the accompanying options for the key element and context identification is discussed in the next section.

3.2 Identification Options

Given a context, one can specify any of the two *identification options* for finding the *key element* within it, namely:

– **Fixed key element:** The key element is assigned a fixed location within its context. This is specified when it is necessary for the key element to stay at the same place in the context, even when the context itself may move around in the Web page (i.e., the context has floating location).
– **Floating key element:** The key element is free to move within the context and is to be identified by content (e.g., the `Total GDP` example).

The fixed location of key element within the context can either be a byte offset, or a combination of HTML tag path from the beginning of the context and byte offset.

Fig. 2. Wikipedia Article on FIFA Standings Table

Each *context* itself, similar to key element, is also assigned an identification option of either *fixed* or *floating location.*

– **Fixed context:** A context is designated a fixed location if it has to stay at the same place in the Web page identified by a byte offset, or an offset from the beginning of a HTML element located by a tag path.
– **Floating context:** A floating context is used when its location in the Web page is not important. In this case, we can use the *content of context* for identification; or a *pair of signature patterns* to mark the begin and end of the context.

To sum up the above, the KeC model provides the following four combinations of identification options for a given pair of key element and context: *fixed context and fixed key element*, *fixed context and floating key element*, *floating context and fixed key element* and *floating context and floating key element.*

These options have different ways of generating alerts with respect to a change in the Web page. For example for the *fixed context and fixed key element* option, the metadata owner is alerted whenever the location of context is not found in the Web page, or the key element's location within the context is not found, or the key element's content has changed. The details of other options are discussed in Section 4.

3.3 Nested Context

So far in the KeC model, a key element is identified using one context. In the other words, it adopts a *single context.* This is appropriate for cases where the Web page or the monitored information are not structurally complex, e.g., the information box containing `Total GDP` in Figure 1. For more complicated cases where the key element cannot be easily identified by using just one enclosing context, we define *nested context* to be a context that can enclose another context and this enclosed context may in turn contain one or more smaller contexts. The largest context contains all other contexts while the smallest one only contains the key element. Each nested context can also be identified either by fixed or floating location within the enclosing context.

For example, Figure 2 shows the standings table of national football teams. Assume that a metadata attribute concerns the position of Brazil team, not their points. An appropriate combination of identification options is to use a context nested in another context and the key element as shown. Context 2 is identified by floating location, Context 1 is identified by fixed location and the key element is also identified by floating location. As long as both contexts are found and the key element's content does not change, no alert will be fired. On the other hand, changes to the location of Context 1 suggest changes in position of Brazil team. Changes in the key element's content may also be the result of removal of the team from the standings table. In both cases, the metadata owner should be alerted to make appropriate revision to his/her metadata. When this example is handled by a single context by assigning the standings table as the context with fixed location option and the particular row containing Brazil team as the key element with floating location option, much higher number of alerts are generated compared with the nested context approach due to frequent changes in the team's point.

4 Evaluation Metrics

To evaluate the performance of our proposed KeC model, we propose a set of evaluation metrics which assumes that there is a set of metadata attributes to be monitored. Each attribute has one key element and all attributes share the same context. Although these metrics only apply to the single context model, they can be easily extended to evaluate performance of the nested context.

The set of evaluation metrics can be further divided into **total number of alerts** and **true user effort**. The total number of alerts refers to the number of messages that a metadata owner receives to examine metadata attributes for possible revisions. Some of these alerts may eventually result in changes of metadata attributes but others may not. The true user effort measures the amount of efforts that a metadata owner spends to revise metadata attributes. To keep it simple, we only consider the effort of searching and checking the key elements' content of the affected attributes. This effort is measured by the amount of Web page content (in bytes) that the owner needs to examine. All notations used in our proposed evaluation metrics are given in Table 1.

Let $\mathcal{K}$ be the set of key elements sharing the same context. In the simplest case where KeC model is not used, any single change to the Web page will trigger a user alert on all attributes. In terms of effort, the user will need to scan the entire Web page to see if the change would cause some update to metadata attribute values. The number of alert and true user effort for this option are defined in Equations 1 and 2 respectively.

$$A_1 = N_W \tag{1}$$

$$E_1 = \sum_{v=2}^{N_W} L_{Wv} \tag{2}$$

If the KeC model is used, each metadata attribute can have one of following four available options: *fixed context and fixed key element, fixed context and floating key element, floating context and fixed key element, floating context and*

Table 1. Notations in Evaluation Metrics

N_W	# of times a Web page W is changed
N_{Cl}	# of times a context's location is not found
N_{Cs}	# of times context is not found
N_{Kli}	# of times ith key element's location within context is not found
N_{Kci}	# of times ith key element's location is found but not its context
N'_{Kci}	# of times ith key element's content is not found within context
L_{Wv}	Length of the Web page at version v
L'_{Wv}	Equals L_{Wv} if context's location is not found and 0 otherwise
L''_{Wv}	Equals L_{Wv} if context is not found and 0 otherwise
L_{Cv}	Length of the context at version v if context is found but key element's location within context is not found, and 0 otherwise
L'_{Cv}	Length of the context at version v if the context is found but key elements content is not found within context, 0 otherwise
L_{Kvi}	Length of the key element i at version v if its location is found but its content is not found within context, 0 otherwise

floating key element. To make it simple, we assume that all attributes use the same option.

Fixed context and fixed key element: The metadata owner is alerted whenever the location of context is not found in the Web page, or the a key element's location within the context is not found, or the a key element's content is changed. In these cases, user effort is determined by:

- Location of context is not found: The user effort involves the length of Web page since the new context's location has to be determined.
- Location of a key element is not found: Since context can be found, its region can be highlighted for user to scan for the key element. Thus, the user effort involves the length of context region.
- A key element's content is changed: Since the key element's location is unchanged, the user effort involves finding the new key element's content within the key element's region to help the metadata owner identify changes.

The number of alerts and true user effort are defined in Equations 3 and 4 respectively.

$$A_2 = N_{Cl} + \sum_{key\ element\ i \in \mathcal{K}} (N_{Kli} + N_{Kci}) \tag{3}$$

$$E_2 = \sum_{v=2}^{N_W} (L'_{Wv} + L_{Cv} + \sum_{key\ element\ i \in \mathcal{K}} L_{Kvi}) \tag{4}$$

Fixed context and floating key element: Metadata owner is alerted when the context's location is not found or a key element's content within the context is not found. If the context's location is not found, the metadata owner needs to search the entire Web page for the key element. If context's location is found but not the key element's content, the context's region can be highlighted to guide the search for key element. Thus, the total number of alerts and true user effort are defined in Equations 5 and 6 respectively.

$$A_3 = N_{Cl} + \sum_{key\ element\ i \in \mathcal{K}} N'_{Kci} \tag{5}$$

$$E_3 = \sum_{v=2}^{N_W} (L'_{Wv} + L'_{Cv}) \tag{6}$$

Floating context and fixed key element: If a context is not found or a key element's location within context is not found, an alert will be sent to the metadata owner. When the context is found but not all key element's locations, the context region can be highlighted to guide the key element search. Thus, the total number of alerts and user effort are defined by Equations 7 and 8 respectively.

$$A_4 = N_{Cs} + \sum_{key\ element\ i \in \mathcal{K}} (N_{Kli} + N_{Kci}) \tag{7}$$

$$E_4 = \sum_{v=2}^{N_W} (L''_{Wv} + L_{Cv} + \sum_{key\ element\ i \in \mathcal{K}} L_{Kvi}) \tag{8}$$

Floating context and floating key element: An alert is sent to the metadata owner whenever the context's content or a key element's content is not found. Context region, if found, can be highlighted to guide the search for the key element. Thus, the total number of alerts and user effort are defined by Equation 9 and Equation 10 respectively.

$$A_5 = N_{Cs} + \sum_{key\ element\ i \in \mathcal{K}} (N'_{Kci}) \tag{9}$$

$$E_5 = \sum_{v=2}^{N_W} (L''_{Wv} + L'_{Cv}) \tag{10}$$

5 Experiment

To evaluate the effectiveness of our proposed models, we conducted experiments on some Wikipedia articles. The objective is to see how well the proposed models perform in terms of reducing the amount of alerts and true user effort. We also investigated situations in which each identification option performed best.

5.1 Data Sets

We use two data sets. The first comprises 174 Wikipedia articles of randomly selected countries obtained from a publicly available listing of countries. We simulated the Web page evolution process by retrieving the edit history of each article and extracting versions from this edit history. The country articles' edit histories are retrieved in the period from July 1, 2006 to December 31, 2006. The second set consists of only one article about FIFA World Ranking[3]. The edit history used is from July 1, 2004 to December 31, 2006.

5.2 Experiment Setup

We applied the proposed models and evaluation metrics to measure the performance in three cases: monitoring changes for metadata derived from the information box tables of country articles, monitoring changes for metadata derived from sentences in the Economy paragraph of the country articles, and monitoring changes for metadata derived from the FIFA standings table.

Experiment 1: Information box table of country articles. In this experiment, we built metadata record for each country. Each metadata record consists of 15 attributes whose values are derived from the information box table. The attributes were selected so that the 1st versions of most articles contain them. For those articles that cover less than 15 attributes, we just used a subset of these attributes that appear in the article's first version. Our statistics showed that there were no articles contain less than 12 attributes in their first version. The identification options shown in Table 2 were used, in which *Content Region 1* is "Information box" and *Content Region 2* is "a cell in the information box".

Experiment 2: Sentences in Economy paragraph of country articles. In this experiment, we built one metadata record for each country. Each metadata record contains one attribute which was derived from the third sentence in the first version of the Economy paragraph. The identification options are shown in Table 2 where *Content Region 1* is "Economy Paragraph" and *Content Region 2* is "the third sentence in the first version of the Economy paragraph".

Experiment 3: FIFA standings table. In this experiment, we built one metadata record with eight attributes corresponding to the position of 8 football teams in the standings table. The identification options are shown in Table 2 where *Content Region 1* is "Standings table", and *Content Region 2* is "a cell in the standings table"

For the cases of floating context in all the 3 experiments, we used the context's signature patterns to locate content region 1.

5.3 Experimental Results

Table 3 shows the averaged total alerts and true user efforts for different identification options of the three experiments.

Experiment 1: Information box table of country articles. As shown in Table 3, Options 5 and 7 gave the least number of alerts (60). Both options assigned the information box as context and each info box cell as a key element.

[3] `http://en.wikipedia.org/wiki/Fifa_world_rankings`

Table 2. Identification options for experiments

Option	Context	Context location	Key element	Key element location
Opt 2:	Full Web pages	Fixed location	Content region 1	Fixed location
Opt 3:	Full Web pages	Fixed location	Content region 1	Floating location
Opt 4:	Content region 1	Fixed location	Content region 2	Fixed location
Opt 5:	Content region 1	Fixed location	Content region 2	Floating location
Opt 6:	Content region 1	Floating location	Content region 2	Fixed location
Opt 7:	Content region 1	Floating location	Content region 2	Floating location
Opt 1:	No monitoring models are deployed.			

Table 3. Experimental Results

Experiments	Metrics	*Opt 1*	*Opt 2*	*Opt 3*	*Opt 4*	*Opt 5*	*Opt 6*	*Opt 7*
Exp 1	Total Alerts	823	103	103	165	60	165	60
(823 versions)	True User Effort (MB)	38.07	4.48	4.57	0.65	0.68	0.659	0.68
Exp 2	Total Alerts	823	37.4	37.6	41.9	41	31	30
(823 versions)	True User Effort (MB)	38.07	1.78	1.70	1.78	1.80	0.81	0.82
Exp 3	Total Alerts	1113	241	241	588	116	588	116
(1113 versions)	True User Effort (MB)	23.47	0.35	0.41	0.22	0.06	0.22	0.06

Option 5 considered fixed context and Option 7 considered floating context. Their numbers of alerts were much smaller than that caused by not using the proposed metadata monitoring model.

In terms of user effort, it turns out that Option 4 was the best instead of Options 5 and 7. It is because fixed context, fixed key element always help to visually guide the metadata owner to the new context or key element more easily, thus reducing the efforts in metadata attribute updating.

Experiment 2: Sentences in the Economy paragraph of country articles. It is shown that Option 7 (floating paragraph, floating sentence) returned the best result in terms of total number of alerts. Option 7 also had better result than Options 2,3,4 and 5 and slightly better than option 6.

In terms of true user effort, Option 6 (floating paragraph, fixed sentence) was the best. This option reduced the effort very significantly compared with no monitoring. This option also halved the amount of user efforts for Options 2,3,4 and 5. It also had a slightly better result than Option 7.

Experiment 3: FIFA standings table. As shown in Table 3, Options 5 and 7 returned the best results in terms of number of alerts. They help to reduce the number of alerts very much. We also notice that the options of assigning Web page as context and standings table as key element (Options 2 and 3) generated smaller number of alerts than the options of assigning standings table as context and cells as key element with fixed key element (Options 4 and 6). This is because in Options 2 and 3, any important change alerts once to the metadata owner while in Options 4 and 6, the same change may be alerted more than once if there are more than one metadata attribute monitored. However, in terms of true user effort, Options 4 and 6 had better results as alerts in these options already contain information to reduce maintenance effort.

In terms of user effort, the best options in this experiment were also 5 and 7. The use of these options helps to reduce effort of Option 1 by 372.8 times.

6 Conclusions

As Web increasingly becomes the preferred source of information, it is necessary to create and maintain metadata for useful Web content. This paper introduces the KeC model to reduce the maintenance effort by tracking only the relevant content regions in Web pages. With various identification options provided, a metadata owner can select the most appropriate key element and context specifications and identification options for the monitored data. This paper also introduces some evaluation metrics to measure the performance of proposed models by the number of alerts generated and the user's maintenance effort. We conducted some experiments on three different Web metadata monitoring scenarios. The results showed that our proposed KeC model significantly reduced the number of alerts as well as the amount of user effort. The proposed KeC model has been implemented in the Web metadata monitoring subsystem of G-Portal, a digital library system for geography education.

References

1. Lagoze, C., Krafft, D., Cornwell, T., Dushay, N., Eckstrom, D., Saylor, J.: Metadata aggregation and automated digital libraries: a retrospective on the NSDL experience. In: Proceedings of ACM/IEEE-CS Joint Conference on Digital Libraries, Chapel Hill, NC., pp. 230–239 (2006)
2. Lim, E.-P., Goh, D.H.-L., Liu, Z., Ng, W.-K., Khoo, C.S.-G., Higgins, S.E.: G-portal: A map-based digital library for distributed geospatial and georeferenced resources. In: Proceedings of ACM/IEEE Joint Conference on Digital Libraries, Portland, Oregon, pp. 351–358 (2002)
3. Liu, L., Pu, C., Tang, W.: WebCQ-detecting and delivering information changes on the web. In: Proceedings of ACM CIKM, McLean, Virginia, pp. 512–519 (2000)
4. Pandey, S., Ramamritham, K., Chakrabarti, S.: Monitoring the dynamic web to respond to continuous queries. In: Proceedings of World Wide Web Conference, Budapest, Hungary, pp. 659–668 (2003)
5. Sharaf, M.A., Labrinidis, A., Chrysanthis, P.K., Pruhs, K.: Freshness-aware scheduling of continuous queries in the dynamic web. In: Proceedings of ACM Workshop on the Web and Databases, Baltimore, Maryland, pp. 73–78 (2005)
6. Sumner, T., Dawe, M.: Looking at digital library usability from a reuse perspective. In: Proceedings of ACM/IEEE Joint Conference on Digital Libraries, Roanoke, VA, pp. 416–425 (2001)
7. Terry, D., Goldberg, D., Nichols, D., Oki, B.: Continuous queries over append-only databases. In: Proceedings of ACM SIGMOD, San Diego, California, pp. 321–330 (1992)

A Cooperative-Relational Approach to Digital Libraries

A. Malizia[1], P. Bottoni[2], S. Levialdi[2], and F. Astorga-Paliza[1]

[1] Computer Science Department, Universidad Carlos III de Madrid.
Avda. de la Universidad, 30. 28911 Leganés, Madrid, Spain
{amalizia,jastorga}@inf.uc3m.es
[2] Computer Science Dept., Universitá "Sapienza" of Rome,
Via Salaria 113, 00198 Rome, Italy
{bottoni,levialdi}@di.uniroma1.it

Abstract. This paper presents a novel approach to model-driven development of Digital Library (DL) systems. The overall idea is to allow Digital Library systems designers (e.g. information architects, librarians, domain experts) to easily design such systems by using a visual language. We designed a Domain Specific Visual Language for such a purpose and developed a framework supporting it; this framework helps designers by automatically generating code for the defined Digital Library system, so that they do not have to get involved into technical issues concerning its deployment. In our approach, both Human-Computer Interaction and Computer Supported Collaborative Work techniques are exploited when generating interfaces and services for the specific Digital Library domain.

1 Introduction

Digital Libraries are complex information systems involving many different areas: Library and Information Science (LIS), Information Retrieval (IR) and Human-Computer Interaction (HCI), to name a few. Google books, the ACM Portal, or Springer on line are examples of Digital Libraries that we use on a dayly basis. But from the designer point of view, there is a need for case tools or modeling support for describing not only the contents but also the interactions and the collaboration work that can happen within such complex systems. For example, scenario or activity-based approaches can be mutuated from HCI in order to model the society of users cooperating within a Digital Library. For example, a scenario can happen in which users have to concurrently access the same document to contribute to its tagging, or to provide advanced services through shared content. Indeed, services like: cross-references, focus groups on special subjects, deployment of collective tagging can be of great interest to Digital Libraries users. Moreover, there are mainly two categories of designers involved in such systems: Librarians and Information Scientists, plus Software engineers (experts in various fields from Information Retrieval to Database Management Systems). These categories of users are generally in contrast when deploying Digital Libraries. Librarians are the domain experts able to deal with faceted categories

L. Kovács, N. Fuhr, and C. Meghini (Eds.): ECDL 2007, LNCS 4675, pp. 75–86, 2007.

of documents, taxonomies and document classification, while engineers usually concentrate on services and code development. With our framework, we aim to propose an approach that is suitable for both, allowing librarians to categorize and model the documents as well as their collections, and software engineers to focus on service development and requirements. The paper is organized as follows: Section 2 presents an overview of the definitions of Digital Library systems and previous work relevant to the presented approach. Section 3 is about modelling Digital Libraries environments considering a model-driven approach for collaborative work scenarios. Section 4 explains the elements of the meta-model at the core of our work. Section 5 illustrates a working example of a Digital Library automatically generated by our framework, and describes more general applications, while Section 6 draws the conclusion and discusses future works.

2 Background and Related Work

There are many definitions of DLs; for example the Delphi study by Kochtanek *et. al.* [1] of digital libraries coalesced a broad definition: organized collection of resources, mechanisms for browsing and searching, distributed networked environments, and sets of services objectified to meet users' needs. The President's Information Technology Advisory Committee (PITAC) Panel on Digital Libraries treats digital libraries as the networked collections of digital text, documents, images, sounds, scientific data, and software, that make up the core of today's Internet and tomorrow's universally accessible digital repositories of all human knowledge. Underlying all these definitions there is a consensus that digital libraries are fundamentally complex. Such complexity is due to the inherently interdisciplinary nature of this kind of systems. Digital libraries integrate findings from disciplines such as hypertext, information retrieval, multimedia services, database management, and human-computer interaction [2]. Designers of digital libraries are most often library technical staff, with little to no formal training in software engineering, or computer scientists with little background in the research findings of information retrieval or hypertext. Thus, digital library systems are usually built from scratch using specialized architectures that do not benefit from digital library and software design experiences. Wasted effort and poor inter-operability can therefore ensue, raising the costs of digital libraries and risking the fluidity of information assets in the future. Formal models and theories are crucial to specify and clearly, understand the characteristics, structure, and behavior of complex information systems. It is not surprising that most of the disciplines related to digital libraries have underlying formal models that have properly steered them: databases, information retrieval [3,4], and hypertext and multimedia [5]. Furthermore, formal models for information systems can be used for the design of a real system, providing a precise specification of requirements against which the implementation can be compared for correctness. Currently, there is a huge bibliography on digital libraries, while there are only a few papers dealing with DL within CSCW environments. The Digital Libraries Group at Universidad de las Americas-Puebla (UDLA - Mexico) [6] introduced the concept of personal and group spaces which are relevant in a CSCW domain in the DL system context. Users can share information stored in their personal spaces or share their agents for allowing other users to perform the same search on the document collections in the DL. In [7], the authors describe a formal foundation theory, on digital libraries, called 5Ses based on the following concepts: streams, data structures, spaces (for the resource space), scenarios, societies. This approach is an evidence of a good modeling endeavour but it doesn't specify formally how to derive a system implementation from the model. In the CRADLE framework we chose the E/R formalism, mainly for two reasons: it is powerful and general enough for describing digital libraries' models (at least it is frequently used for modeling DBMS applications which are foundations for digital libraries) [8], and is supported by many tools as a meta-modeling language. Although most approaches to entity-relationship modeling do not deal deeply with dynamic aspects, because the entity-relationship approach is used for modeling static structure it ought not to be separated from the behavior alone. Temporal entity-relationship extensions [9] add dynamic aspects to the entity-relationship approach, but most of them are not directed to object-oriented approaches. Recently, the advent of object-oriented based technology calls for and demands information systems design approaches and tools resulting in object-oriented systems. These considerations drove the research towards modeling approaches like the Unified Modeling Language (UML) [10]. Since UML metamodel is specified by a combination of UML class diagrams (abstract syntax), OCL (well-formedness rules) and English (detailed semantics), it lacks the rigor of a language precisely defined using formal language techniques. The imprecision of the UML specification has undesirable consequences for users, since engineers might use implementation decisions that are inconsistent with the specification and other implementations.

3 Modeling Collaborative Scenarios in Digital Libraries

Our approach generates code from tools built after modeling a digital library (according to the rules defined by the proposed meta-model); we use an automatic transformation and mapping from model to code so as to generate software tools for a given digital library model. We call our methodology **Cooperative-Relational Approach to Digital Library Environments** (CRADLE model). In CRADLE, the specification of a digital library encompasses four complementary dimensions: 1. multimedia information supported by the DL (Collection Model); 2. how that information is structured and organized (Structural Model); 3. the behavior of the DL (Service Model); and the different societies of actors; 4. groups of services that act together to carry out the DL behavior (Societal Model). Initially, a DL designer is responsible for formalizing a conceptual description of the digital library using the meta-model concepts. This phase is normally preceded by an analysis of the DL requirements and characteristics (Figure 1a). Model specifications in CRADLE are then fed into a DL generator (written in Python for ATOM3 [12]), to produce the tailored DL, suitable for specific platforms and requirements (Figure 1b). We chose ATOM3 for its meta-meta-model specification which describes the basic elements that can be used to design a meta-model modelling formalism. If newer concepts and structures need to be introduced, they can be modelled at a meta-meta-level. The advantage of the AToM3 approach is the flexibility that can be achieved. In fact, by adopting the model of a modelling formalism, and automatically generating a prototype of the modelling environment, design choices can be rapidly evaluated. These are built upon a collection of stock parts and configurable components that provide the infrastructure for the new DL (Figure 1c). This infrastructure includes the classes of objects and relationships that make up the DL, and processing tools to create/load the actual library collection from raw documents, as well as services for searching, browsing, and collection maintenance. Finally, the `LibGen` module (Figure 1d) generates tailored DL services code stubs by composing and specializing components from the component pool. CRADLE is in its alpha version but we have already used it to build pilot systems and prototypes.

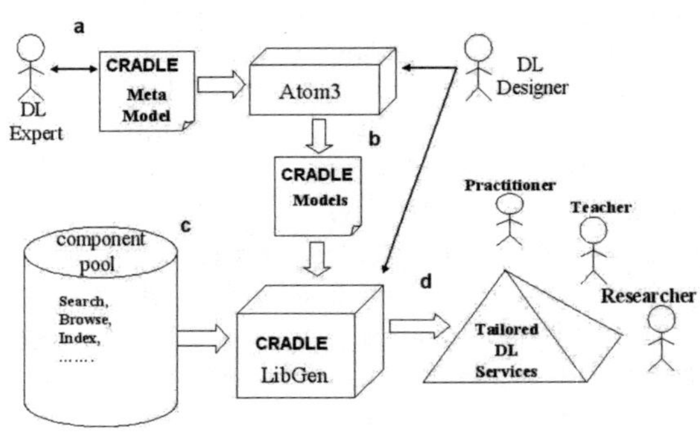

Fig. 1. The CRADLE scheme

Most of the CRADLE model primitives are defined as XML based elements, which can enclose other sublanguages that help define DL concepts. The XML User Interface Language (XUL) is used to represent appearance and visual interfaces [13], while the XDocLet [14] (also XML based) standard is used for deploying service templates.

4 The Cradle Meta-model

In the CRADLE formalism, the specification of a DL, includes: multimedia documents supported by the DL - Collection Model; how that information is structured and organized - Structural Model; the behavior of the DL - Service Model; and the different societies of actors and groups of services that act together to carry out the DL behavior - Societal Model. In our approach a society is an instance of the CRADLE model defined according to a specific collaboration framework in the digital library domain. A society is the highest-level component of a digital library, which exists to serve the information needs of its set of actors and to describe the context it is used in. Digital libraries are used for collecting, preserving, and sharing information artefacts between society members. In fact, cognitive models for information retrieval [15,16], for example, focus on users information-seeking behavior (i.e., formation, nature, and properties of a users' information need) and on the ways in which information retrieval systems are used in operational environments. After carefully reviewing literature on digital libraries topics, we selected basic entities among the facets from the categorizations presented in [7]. In fact, in the digital library context, we can model actors as the users of digital libraries. Actors interact with the DL through services (interfaces) that are (or can be) affected by the actors preferences and messages (raised events). Another class selected from the proposed study are Activities. Activities within cooperation digital libraries consist of: collecting, creating, disseminating, evaluating, organizing, personalizing, preserving, requesting, and selecting. All these activities can be described and implemented using scenarios and appear in the DL setting as a result of actors using services (thus societies). Digital libraries can contain repositories of documents (Components), information, data, metadata, relationships, logs, annotations, and user profiles, all of which are interpreted as distinct types of digital objects, according to their specific structure, metadata, and relation. The Socio-economic class represents what surrounds the DL. This facet is mainly related to the societal aspects of the DL and their interactions abstracting aspects surrounding the DL such as: policies, economic issues, standards, and organizational attributes. Finally, the Environment class defines the context a DL is embedded in. The environment involves a set of spaces (e.g., the physical space, or a concept space defined by the words of a natural language) that defines the use and the context of a DL.

In a previous paper [17] we presented an early model called SADDLE, which had limitations with respect to the complexity of the Digital Libraries which could be developed with it, due to the incomplete specification of some elements. In the new meta-model presented here, we introduced for instance the notion of Document detached from (but related to) to the Collection and introduced a mechanism for managing the responses to events, as described in the following paragraph. In the CRADLE model, a Society is a group space made of several personal spaces, and, agents are modeled as services interacting with actors and collections (resources). The idea of personal and group spaces and agents is interesting and stimulating; nevertheless a concurrent and cooperative task model should be included in digital libraries both for managing services (synchronous/asynchronous) interactions and for specifying operative scenarios as we describe in the following paragraph. This means that the CRADLE approach aims at filling the gap to support models for the design of user interface and interaction among collaboration in digital libraries systems. The meta-model in Figure 2 includes the basic entities:

- The Actor entity has three attributes: Role, Status and Events.
    - Role: a description of the role (i.e. librarian, server,)

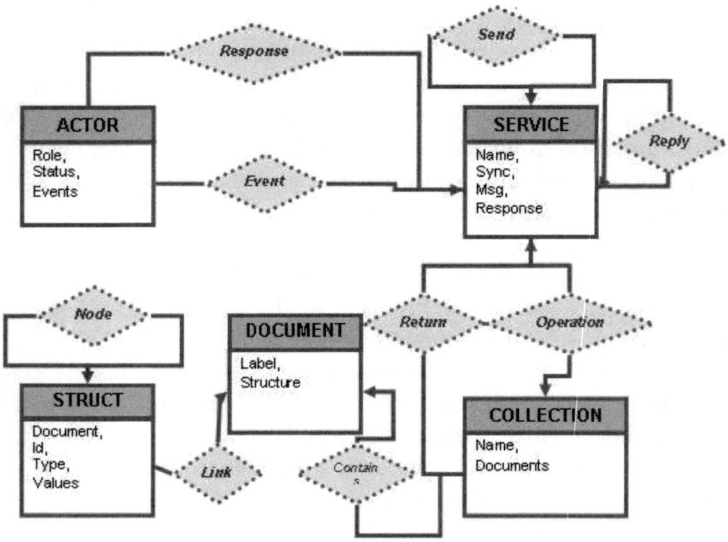

Fig. 2. The CRADLE meta-model with the E/R formalism

  - Status: None (N.A.), Active (present in the model and actively generating events), Inactive (present in the model but not generating events), Sleeping (present in the model and awaiting for a response to a raised event)
  - Events: describes a list of events that can be raised by the Actor, or received as response message from a Service (which is treated as an event by an Actor). Examples of events (for a library environment) can be: borrow, reserve, return, etc.
- The Service entity has four attributes: Name, Sync, Events, Responses.
  - The Name attribute is a string representing a textual description of the service.
  - The Sync attribute states whether the service employs a synchronous or asynchronous communication, and has two possible values: wait (synchronous) or nowait (asynchronous).
  - The Messages attribute is a list of messages that can trigger actions among services (tasks); for example valid or not valid in case of a parsing service.
  - The Responses attribute contains a list of response messages that can reply to raised events; they are used as communication mechanism among actors and services.
- The attributes of Collection are: Name and Documents; Name is a string which specifies the logical name of the Collection, while Documents is a list of couples made of Document name and Document Label (a pointer to the Document entity).

- In the Document entity two different attributes are present: Label and Structure.
  - The Label defines a textual string which can be referenced by a Collection entity. We can view it as a document identifier, specifying a class or a type of documents.
  - The Structure defines its semantics and area of application. For example, any textual representation can be seen as a set of characters, so that text documents, such as scientific articles and books, can be considered as a structured set of elements.
- Structures are represented as graphs and the Struct entity (a vertex) contains four attributes: Document, Id, Type, Values.
  - The Document attribute is a pointer to the Document entity the structure refers to.
  - The Id is a unique identifier for structures elements.
  - The Type attribute takes three possible values: Metadata, Layout, and Item. Metadata indicates that the structural element is a content descriptor, for instance title, author, etc. Layout indicates that the structural element is mapped on a layout, such as: left frame, columns, header, etc. Item indicates a generic structure element that can be used for extending the model while keeping it general.
  - The Values attribute is a list of single or multiple values the structure element can take; it describes the element content, like for instance title, author, etc.

The Relationships between the entities shown in Figure 2 are quite self-explanatory. Actors interact with Services by an event-driven communication model. Services are connected to each other by synchronous or asynchronous messages (send and reply). Services can perform operations (like: get, add and del) on Collections and these operations return Collections of Documents as results. Documents are contained in Collections and Struct elements are connected to each other as nodes of a graph representing metadata structures associated to documents. In the next section we present a basic example of how to use our framework to generate a simple Digital Library.

5 Generating Digital Library Environments

As a first step in designing the DL environment in the CRADLE framework, designers model the *Society* involved in the specific scenario. We define a running example, called *Library*, modeling a simple digital library environment to show the overall process, starting from the basic entities of the model. The *Actors* (represented by circles) involved in this *Library* are: *Students* and *Librarians*. The digital library *Collection* (represented by multiple rectangles) consists of *Digital Paper Documents* structured with *Publication, Author* and *Title* metadata information (*Struct entities*). There are two basic services available in this example, the *Front Desk* and the *Search* services. The *Front Desk* is responsible for managing communication between *Students* and *Librarians*, while the

Search service executes queries on the digital library. In Figure 3, the CRADLE environment is shown together with the defined entities. The rectangles render the *Services* appearance, while the single rectangle connected to a *Collection* represents a *Document* entity; the circles linked to the *Document* entity are the *Struct* (metadata) entities. The represented scenario is about a *Student* trying to borrow a *Paper* from the *Library*; she interacts with the *Front Desk* service requesting a paper and obtaining a response message about its availability within the digital library. The *Front Desk* service is asynchronous (see Section 4) and forwards the borrow request (Borrow_Request) to the *Librarian* actor. The *Librarian* sends a Doc_Request message to the *Search* service (Do_Search). The *Search* service is synchronous (see Section 4). It queries the document collection looking for the requested document and waits for the *get* result (a collection of documents) to send the response back. The service returns an *Is_Available* boolean message which is then propagated as a response to the *Librarian* and eventually to the *Student* (see Figure 3).

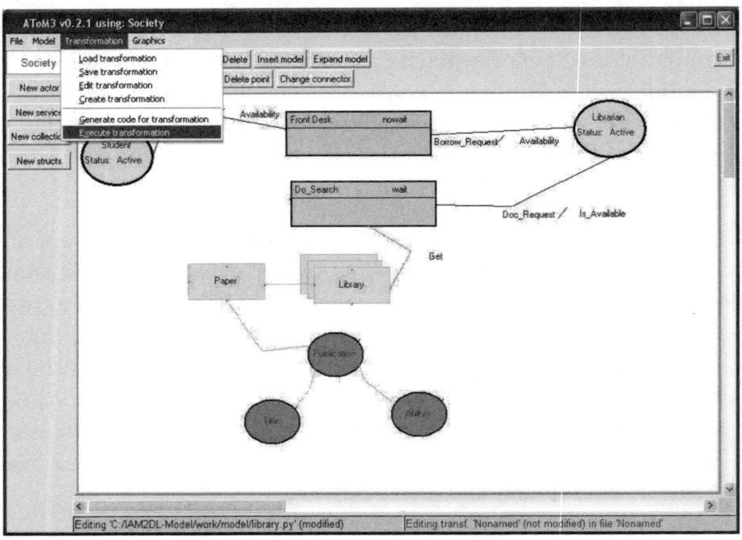

Fig. 3. Starting the code generation process by transformation execution

When the library designer has built the model, if the *execute transformation* menu item is selected, the framework runs the transformation process, executing the code generation actions associated with the entities and services represented in the model. The user interface generation occurs according to the XUL and XDocLet templates and the entities defined in the model. In this example the generated UI is presented in Figure 4.

The generated UI is based on the template code, enriched with information from the modeled entities. On the right side of Figure 4(A) the document area is presented according to the XUL template. Documents are managed in this

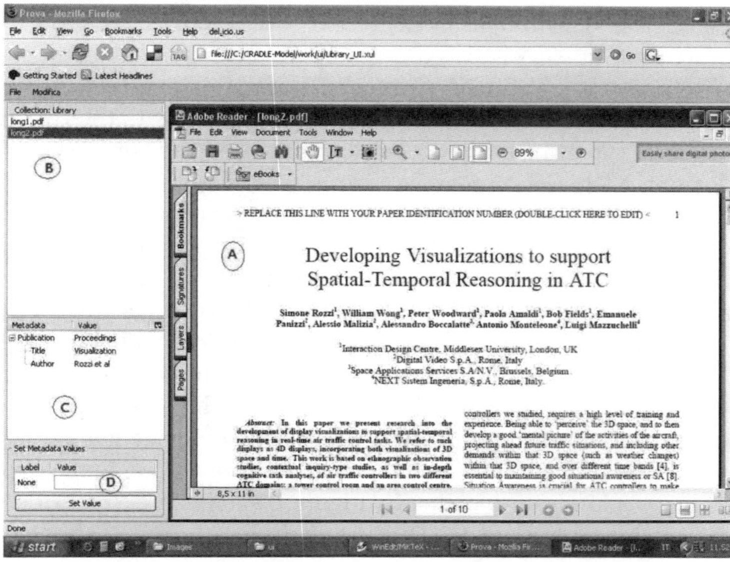

Fig. 4. The UI generated by CRADLE transforming the Library model in XUL code

area according to their MIME type; in this example, since the documents are *PDF* files, they are loaded with the appropriated *Acrobat Reader* plug-in. On the left column of the UI are three basic boxes. The *Collection* box, Figure 4(B), presents the list of documents contained in the *Collection* specified by the *Documents* attribute of the *Library Collection* entity, and allows users to interact with documents. After selecting a document by clicking on the list, it is presented in the document area (Figure 4(A)) where it can be managed. In the *MetaData* box, Figure 4(C), the tree structure of the metadata is depicted according to the metadata categorization modeled by the designer. The XUL template contains all the basic layout and action features for managing a tree structure. The generated box contains the parent and child nodes according to the attributes specified in the corresponding *Struct* elements included in the model. The user can click on the root for compacting or exploding all the tree nodes, and by selecting one, the UI activates the *MetaData operations* box, Figure 4(D). After the selected metadata item is presented in the "set MetaData Values" box, the user can edit its values and by clicking on the "set value" button save this information. Not only does the "set value" operation save the metadata information, but it also displays it in the intermediate box (tree-like structure) for changing the UI visualization according to the new values. The code generation process for the designed services is based on the XDoclet templates. The CRADLE framework generates the code for the messages and events as designed in the *Library* model. In particular, for the *Front Desk* service, a *message listener* template is used to generate the Java code. The *Actors* classes are also generated by using the services templates since they have attributes, events and messages just like the services. The *Do_Search* service code is based on the producer and consumer templates since it is synchronous by definition in the modeled scenario. The overall code generation process is based on template code snippets generated from AToM environment; the ATomM graph transformation engine works following the generative rules specified by our meta-model. To generate the tree structure for the metadata, the Transformation action is invoked and some Python code is executed loading XUL section templates from external files; exploring the metadata tree in the visual model with a breadth-first search and attaches the XUL code for displaying the *Struct* node in the appropiate position within the graph structure in the visual interface according to the metadata String specified in the model. Summarizing, in the CRADLE approach the code generation process is based on templates provided for basic interfaces, services and actors behaviors.

We have explored a variety of personal and group interfaces and environments to place the digital collections wealth at the user's disposal. For instance, we considered the case of an international scientific conference management with all the roles played by the chairs and committees in reviewing and accepting (or rejecting) different kinds of documents. Figure 5 shows en extract of a detailed conference model view in the CRADLE framework.

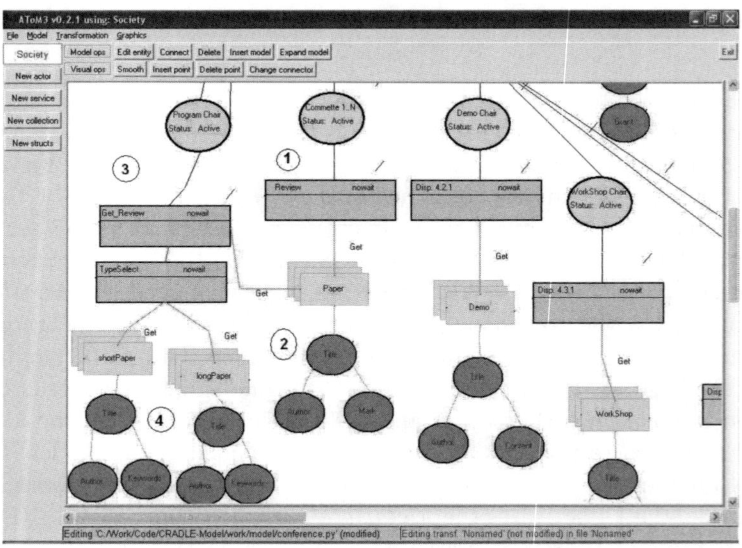

Fig. 5. Extract from the CRADLE visual model for the reviewing process in an academic conference environment

As shown in Figure 5, the Committee actor (this is an example of a generic Committee that can change depending on the task purpose), by using the Review service, uploads the reviewed papers (Figure 5(1)) in the Paper Collection, populating the corresponding metadata (Figure 5(2)): Title, Author, Mark (representing the review synthesis, e.g. fair, poor, good, etc.). Among the Program Committee actor duties is the management of the submitted reviews (get other

Committees' reviews) and making the final decision for acceptance and form of publication (short or full papers). The Program Committee actor gets the submitted reviews using the Get Review service and select the type of publication, e.g. short or full by invoking the TypeSelect service (Figure 5(3)). Finally, documents are uploaded into the different collections with their basic metadata (Figure 5(4)): Title, Author, Keywords. Some components are ready to be incorporated into regular user activities (searching, browsing, tagging), others are at different stages of development, from preliminary prototypes to usability testing.

6 Conclusion and Future Work

Summarising, Digital Libraries (DLs) are extremely complex information systems that integrate findings from disciplines such as hypertext, information retrieval, multimedia services, database management, and human-computer interaction. Designers of DLs are often multidisciplinary teams, which include library technical staff and computer scientists. Wasted effort and poor inter-operability can therefore ensue (raising the costs of DLs and hindering the fluidity of information assets). Examining the related bibliography we noted that there is a lack of tools or computer-aided systems for designing and developing Cooperative DL systems. Moreover, there is a need for modeling interactions among DL systems and users (as proposed in the HCI field) such as: scenario or activity-based approaches.

The CRADLE framework aims to fill this gap by providing a meta-model based approach for generating visual interaction oriented tools for DLs. We experimented with it within a group of graduate students from the School of Library and Information Science (Scuola Speciale per Archivisti e Bibliotecari - SSAB), at University La Sapienza of Rome, Italy. They are trained as librarians and information architects and thus their help was crucial in developing our approach. Moreover, we involved some graduate students from the Computer Science Dept. at University La Sapienza of Rome, Italy, who worked as the service engineers. The early results (with documents in Italian) were very encouraging but further investigation is needed. In fact, recently, AToM3 has been provided with the possibility to describe multi-view DSVLs, such as the UML or VisMODLE formalism to which this work directly contributed [18]. The XML User Interface Language (XUL) is used to represent appearance and visual interfaces. It is a language derived from XML that describes user interfaces. XUL is not a public standard yet, but it uses many existing standards and technologies which make it easily readable for people with a background in web programming and design. The main benefit of XUL is that it provides a simple definition of common user interface elements (widgets). This drastically reduces the software development effort required for visual interfaces, which has represented the basic motivation for interpreting it in the CRADLE framework. These are notations made of a set of different diagram types, each one describing a different aspect or viewpoint of the system, and are suitable for the future enhancements of our framework.

References

1. Kochtanek, T.R., Hein, K.K.: Delphi study of digital libraries. Inf. Process. Manage 35(3), 245–254 (1999)
2. Fox, E.A., Marchionini, G.: Toward a worldwide digital library. Commun. ACM 41(4), 29–32 (1998)
3. Turtle, H.R., Croft, W.B.: Evaluation of an inference network-based retrieval model. ACM Trans. Inf. Syst. 9(3), 187–222 (1991)
4. Baeza-Yates, R.A., Ribeiro-Neto, B.A.: Modern information retrieval, ACM Press/Addison-Wesley (1999)
5. Lucarella, D., Zanzi, A.: A visual retrieval environment for hypermedia information systems. ACM Trans. Inf. Syst. 14(1), 3–29 (1996)
6. Reyes-Farfan, N., Sanchez, J.A.: Personal spaces in the context of OA. In: ACM/IEEE 2003 Joint Conference on Digital Libraries (JCDL 2003) Proceedings, Houston, Texas, USA, May 27-31, 2003, pp. 182–183. IEEE Computer Society, Los Alamitos (2003)
7. Gonçalves, M.A., Fox, E.A., Watson, L.T., Kipp, N.A.: Streams, structures, spaces, scenarios, societies (5s): A formal model for digital libraries. ACM Trans. Inf. Syst. 22(2) (April 2004)
8. Gogolla, M., Herzig, R., Conrad, S., Denker, G., Vlachantonis, N.: Integrating the ER approach in an OO environment, ER, pp. 376–389 (1993)
9. Bettini, C.: Review - temporal entity-relationship models - a survey, ACM SIGMOD Digital Review 2 (2000)
10. Berkem, B.: Aligning it with the changes using the goal-driven development for UML and MDA. Journal of Object Technology 4(5), 49–65 (2005)
11. Reeves, J.W.: What is software design? (1992), available at `bleading-edge.com`
12. de Lara, J., Vangheluwe, H.: AToM3: A Tool for. In: Kutsche, R.-D., Weber, H. (eds.) ETAPS 2002 and FASE 2002. LNCS, vol. 2306, pp. 174–188. Springer, Heidelberg (2002)
13. `www.mozilla.org/projects/xul/`
14. `xdoclet.sourceforge.net`
15. Oddy, R.N., Robertson, S.E., van Rijsbergen, C.J., Williams, P.W. (eds.): Information retrieval research. In: proc. joint acm/bcs symposium in information storage and retrieval, cambridge, june 1980, Butterworths (1981)
16. Ellis, D.: The dilemma of measurement in information retrieval research. JASIS 47(1), 23–36 (1996)
17. Levialdi, S., Malizia, A.: Modeling Collaborative Interactions in a network of Digital Libraries. In: Proceedings of the I International Conference on Multidisciplinary Information Sciences and Technologies (INSCIT 2006), Merida (Spain), vol. I, pp. 181–185 (October 2006)
18. Malizia, A., Guerra, E., de Lara, J.: Model-driven development of digital libraries: Generating the user interface. In: Proceedings of the ACM/IEEE 9th International Conference on Model Driven Engineering Languages and Systems (MDDAUI 2006 workshop), vol 214, CEUR (2006) ISSN 1613-0073

Mind the (Intelligibility) Gap

Yannis Tzitzikas[1,2] and Giorgos Flouris[3]

[1] Computer Science Department, University of Crete, Greece
[2] Institute of Computer Science, FORTH, Greece
[3] Istituto della Scienza e delle Tecnologie della Informazione, CNR, Italy
tzitzik@ics.forth.gr, flouris@isti.cnr.it

Abstract. Intelligibility, evolution and emulation are some of the key notions for digital information preservation. In this paper we define formally these notions on the basis of modules and inter-module dependencies. Subsequently, we discuss how we can handle the evolution of modules and dependencies. This work can be exploited for building advanced preservation information systems and registries.

1 Introduction

Modern society and economy is increasingly dependent on a deluge of only digitally available information. The preservation of digital information within an unstable and rapidly evolving computing environment is a challenging problem of prominent importance. [8] proposed tackling this problem on the basis of the notion of *dependency*. In this paper we adopt the same abstract notion of *module* and *dependency* but in a more expressive framework. We formalize the concept of *intelligibility* of digital objects and we extend the model with *emulators*. As preservation is an endless process, we also focus on the evolution of dependencies and describe change operations and notification services. This work can be exploited for building advanced preservation information systems and registries.

2 Dependencies and Dependency Graphs

2.1 Definitions and Notations

An archive's digital collection consists of a set of *objects*, containing all the data objects in the archive, as well as of a set of *modules* (or components) needed for understanding/executing/managing such objects. In this paper, we adopt a very general interpretation of the term module. It can be a software or hardware module; it could also be a knowledge model expressed either formally or informally, explicitly or tacitly; it could even be a digital object describing how another module functions (*e.g.*, a manual). For instance, it could be an English-To-Greek dictionary that is useful for a Greek-speaking person to understand a piece of text written in English, or an ontology that is useful for understanding the contents of a metadata file. Thus, the distinction between digital objects

L. Kovács, N. Fuhr, and C. Meghini (Eds.): ECDL 2007, LNCS 4675, pp. 87–99, 2007.

and modules is often vague, so, we will keep our terminology simple by using the term module to refer to both modules and objects.

There is no standard method for defining what a module is, as we may have modules of various levels of abstraction. An element modeled as one module could in fact correspond to a large number of interconnected finer modules, depending on the level of detail that we are interested at and/or is useful for the application at hand. Similarly, a software module replicated in several places can be viewed as a single module, or as a compound module consisting of a number of replicas, either of which needs to be intelligible. Finally, complex modules, *e.g.*, a web page, may consist of images, text etc, and could be viewed as a single module, or as many, all of which should be intelligible.

Modules (or objects) may require the availability of one or more other modules in order to function (or be understood). We can model this using a *dependency relation*, denoted by $>$, where $t > t'$ means that t depends on t', *e.g.*, it may mean that t cannot function without the existence of t'. In principle, t' also depends on some other module an so on, and such dependencies may continue indefinitely, as probably nothing in this world is self-existent. Nevertheless, depending on the application, we may consider some modules to be understandable by all users of a digital archive; such modules will be called *primitive*.

Modules, in general, do not depend on one module but many. Consider for example a file `README.TXT` written in English; the intelligibility of the file depends on the availability of a suitable text editor (*e.g.*, Notepad), plus a good understanding of the English language by the reader. This can be modeled using two dependencies of the form $t_{README} > t_{NOTEPAD}$, $t_{README} > t_{ENG}$. This pair of dependencies has conjunctive semantics, in the sense that t_{README} requires both $t_{NOTEPAD}$ and t_{ENG} in order to be understood.

In other cases, dependencies could have disjunctive semantics; for example, the above file can be read using, *e.g.*, Wordpad, even if Notepad is not available. To capture this kind of semantics, we will generalize our notations, by defining the concept of the *generalized module*, which is just a set of modules (*e.g.*, $\{t_1, t_2\}$). A generalized module is interpreted disjunctively, in the sense that $\{t_1, t_2\}$ means "either t_1, or t_2". Standard modules can be captured using singleton sets, *e.g.*, $\{t\}$.

Generalizing our notations, we will henceforth use $>$ to denote the dependency relation between generalized modules. This way, the dependency $\{t_{README}\} > \{t_{NOTEPAD}, t_{WORDPAD}\}$ means that the intelligibility of the module t_{README} depends on the availability of at least one of $t_{NOTEPAD}$, $t_{WORDPAD}$.

Thus, there are two basic dependency types. The first is conjunctive dependencies, which are useful when there are some modules (*e.g.*, $t_1, t_2, \ldots$) which are all necessary for the intelligibility of a module t; this type is modeled using a number of different dependencies, *i.e.*, $\{t\} > \{t_1\}$, $\{t\} > \{t_2\}$, ... The second is disjunctive ones, used when t requires the existence of at least one of $t_1, t_2, \ldots$ for its intelligibility; this type is captured using generalized modules, *i.e.*, $\{t\} > \{t_1, t_2, \ldots\}$.

The above basic types allow us to model many different types of dependencies, including quite complex ones. For example, if we want to model that "the readability of t_{README} depends on the existence of t_{ENG}, and either $t_{NOTEPAD}$ or $t_{WORDPAD}$", we can capture it using the pair of dependencies $\{t_{README}\} > \{t_{ENG}\}$ and $\{t_{README}\} > \{t_{NOTEPAD}, t_{WORDPAD}\}$. A more difficult case is if we want to model that "the readability of t_{README} depends on either knowledge of English (t_{ENG}), or knowledge of Greek (t_{GR}) and an English-to-Greek dictionary (t_{ENG2GR})"; this would require the extra step of transforming this description into the equivalent one: "t_{README} depends on either t_{ENG} or t_{GR} and either t_{ENG} or t_{ENG2GR}", which can be captured using the pair: $\{t_{README}\} > \{t_{ENG}, t_{GR}\}$ and $\{t_{README}\} > \{t_{ENG}, t_{ENG2GR}\}$[1].

We now have all the necessary ingredients for the formal definition of our model. We denote by $\mathcal{T}$ the set of all *modules* (which include digital objects as well); a *generalized module*, also called a *node*, is any set S of modules ($S \subseteq \mathcal{T}$), interpreted disjunctively. Thus, the set of all generalized modules is just the powerset of $\mathcal{T}$, denoted by $2^{\mathcal{T}}$. A *dependency relation* is a binary relation $> \subseteq 2^{\mathcal{T}} \times 2^{\mathcal{T}}$; the notation $S_1 > S_2$ implies that at least one module of S_1 depends on at least one module of S_2. These notions can be more intuitively represented in a graph $\Gamma = (2^{\mathcal{T}}, >)$, which we will call the *dependency graph*. Sometimes, it will be useful to refer to *families of nodes*, which are conjunctively interpreted sets of generalized modules, denoted by $\mathbf{S}$; notice that $\mathbf{S} \subseteq 2^{\mathcal{T}}$, *i.e.*, each element of $\mathbf{S}$ is a generalized module S (*i.e.*, a set of modules, interpreted disjunctively).

As explained before, certain notions, like module, primitive module, dependency etc are just application-dependent conventions. In the following, we assume that a dependency graph contains (models) all the modules and their dependency-related information that is important for the application at hand. Moreover, we make no assumptions as to the properties of $>$ (*e.g.*, acyclic, transitive etc), as such assumptions may be invalid for certain applications.

2.2 Types of Dependencies

Consider a relationship $S_1 > S_2$. We can distinguish the following general cases, depending on the size of S_1:

- $|S_1| = 1$, $|S_2| \geq 1$ (*e.g.*, $S_1 = \{t_1\}, S_2 = \{t_{21}, t_{22}, \ldots, t_{2m}\}$). Here, $S_1 > S_2$ means that t_1 depends on one of $t_{21}, t_{22}, \ldots, t_{2m}$. Such dependencies will be called *basic*.
- $|S_1| > 1$, $|S_2| \geq 1$ (*e.g.*, $S_1 = \{t_{11}, t_{12}, \ldots, t_{1n}\}$, $S_2 = \{t_{21}, t_{22}, \ldots, t_{2m}\}$). Here, $S_1 > S_2$ means that one of $t_{11}, t_{12}, \ldots, t_{1n}$ depends on one of $t_{21}, t_{22}, \ldots, t_{2m}$. Such dependencies will be called *complex*.

The above distinction is motivated by our belief that complex dependencies are artificial and probably not useful in practice. For example, the (complex) dependency $\{t_1, t_2\} > \{t_3, t_4\}$ implies that either t_1 or t_2 depend on either t_3 or t_4. Most often, this will be just because, for example, t_1 (alone) depends on t_3, and t_2 (alone) depends on t_4. It is hard to find an example where a complex dependency is not just a consequence of a number of basic ones. Another type

[1] This idea is based on the algorithm transforming logical formulas in CNF.

of dependencies is *trivial* dependencies. A dependency $S_1 > S_2$ is called trivial iff $S_1 \subset S_2$. Trivial dependencies can be either basic or complex and they are always true. For example, $\{t_1, t_2\}$ always depends on $\{t_1, t_2, t_3\}$ because, if neither of t_1, t_2, t_3 is understandable, then, obviously, none of t_1, t_2 is understandable either. Trivial dependencies could be considered as the counterpart of tautologies in a logical theory. Finally, dependencies where either $S_1 = \emptyset$ or $S_2 = \emptyset$ are not intuitively useful, as they have no real-world counterpart.

The above observations imply that the only interesting dependencies are those that are both basic and non-trivial; such dependencies will be called *editable.* In the rest of this paper, the symbol $>$ will always refer to editable relations, and a dependency graph will be assumed to contain only editable arcs.

3 Intelligibility

3.1 Profiles

Now, let us consider a preservation system, say s, which supports a finite number of users, say $u_1, \ldots, u_n$, by archiving the digital objects that may be of interest to them, as well as the modules that are useful for their intelligibility. The related information (dependencies), that is useful for the system to determine the useful modules is modeled in a dependency graph $\Gamma = (2^{\mathcal{T}}, >)$. This graph Γ is assumed to capture the (known and interesting) state of affairs regarding the dependencies between the various models and objects available in the "world", and may contain information on modules that are not available to the system and/or any of its users.

The system s, as well as any of the users $u_1, \ldots, u_n$, are assumed to have access to some of the modules in $\mathcal{T}$; the sets of modules that they have access to are called (system or user) *profiles* and denoted by T_s and T_{u_i} respectively. Notice that only atomic modules are included in a profile, as it makes no intuitive sense to say that someone has access to either module t_1 or module t_2.

3.2 Modules' Intelligibility, Self-Intelligibility, Intelligibility Gaps

It is often useful to be able to determine whether a user u, with a profile T_u, can understand a module $t \in \mathcal{T}$. Using our definitions, in order for t to be understood, the modules that it depends upon should be available. To capture this notion, we define the family of nodes that are *directly required for intelligibility*, denoted by $req(t)$, as follows: $req(t) = \{S \subseteq \mathcal{T} \mid \{t\} > S\}$. Given the disjunctive nature of nodes, in order for t to be understood by u, he must have access to at least one module from each node $S \in req(t)$; that is: $S \cap T_u \neq \emptyset$ for all $S \in req(t)$.

But this is not enough, because the modules required for understanding t, should themselves be intelligible (not just accessible) by u. Normally, we can assume that this is true; if a user can access some module t', he has probably taken actions already so as to make t' intelligible, by importing all the necessary modules, thus making his profile *self-intelligible*: T_u is self-intelligible, iff for all $t \in T_u$ and for all $S \in req(t)$ it holds that $S \cap T_u \neq \emptyset$.

Using the notion of self-intelligibility, our original question on the intelligibility of a module t can be answered as follows: if the user's profile is self-intelligible, all we need to check is whether $S \cap T_u \neq \emptyset$ for all $S \in req(t)$. It can be easily shown that this will be true iff the set $T_u \cup \{t\}$ is self-intelligible. In the general case, we can say that a module t is intelligible by a user u iff there is some profile $T_u{}' \subseteq T_u$ such that $T_u{}' \cup \{t\}$ is self-intelligible.

A module t not being understandable by u, means that there are certain "missing" modules, which, if added to T_u, will make t intelligible; such modules are denoted by $Missing(t, u)$ and form an *intelligibility gap*. Similarly, we can define $Missing(t, s)$ for the system.

3.3 Algorithmic Aspects

Let's now see how the above quantities can be determined algorithmically. Firstly, the algorithm for determining self-intelligibility is trivial and follows from the definition. Moreover, if T_u is self-intelligible, then, determining whether t is intelligible by u is equivalent to determining whether $T_u \cup \{t\}$ is self-intelligible.

Unfortunately, this technique cannot be applied for a non-self-intelligible profile T_u, because we would have to check the self-intelligibility of $T_u{}' \cup \{t\}$ for all $T_u{}' \subseteq T_u$; this is not an efficient calculation. To address this problem we reduce it to the problem of query answering in monadic and negation-free Datalog. For reasons of space below we just sketch this reduction. If S is a node, we denote by $S^{\vee}$ the disjunction of all modules in S, *i.e.*, $S^{\vee} = \vee_{t \in S} t$. If $t \in \mathcal{T}$, then for each S such that $t > S$ we can define $S^{\vee}$ and then take the conjunction of these disjunctions, *i.e.*, for each t we define the logical formula $E^{CNF}(t) = \wedge_{t>S} S^{\vee}$. Let $E^{DNF}(t)$ be the equivalent logical formula in DNF. For each conjunction, say $t_1 \wedge t_2$ in $E^{DNF}(t)$ we derive the Datalog rule $t(X) : -t_1(X), t_2(X)$. Let $R(t)$ denote the resulting set of rules and $R(\Gamma)$ the union of the rules for each module in Γ. Now for each $t \in T_u$ that is *primitive*, we derive the fact $t(Const)$ where $Const$ is a constant, and let $R(T_u)$ denote these facts. We use the same constant $Const$ for each $t \in T_u$. It can be easily proved that if the answer of the query $q = t$ in the knowledge base $R(\Gamma) \cup R(T_u)$ is not empty, specifically if it equals $\{Const\}$, then t is intelligible by u. Otherwise, it is not intelligible, so it belongs to the gap. Figure 1, illustrates the reduction with an example. Notice that the profile $T_u = \{t_1, t_2, t_4\}$ is not self-intelligible because t_1 is not intelligible since $t_1 > \{t_5, t_6\}$ and $\{t_5, t_6\} \cap T_u = \emptyset$. In this example t is not intelligible by u, however t_8 is intelligible by u. Indeed the answer of the query $q = t$ is empty, while the answer of the query $q = t_8$ is not empty[2].

As Γ is expected to change less frequently than the profiles, we can keep the rules $R(\Gamma)$ stored (to avoid recomputing them); on the other hand, recomputing $R(T_u)$ is faster, so frequent changes in the profiles should not cause major delays.

Computing $Missing(t, u)$ is more difficult, as, due to the disjunctive nature of dependencies, there may more than one possible solution. Thus, different criteria

[2] Notice that if T_u were self-intelligible, then t would be intelligible simply because for each $S \in req(t)$, we have $S \cap T_u \neq \emptyset$.

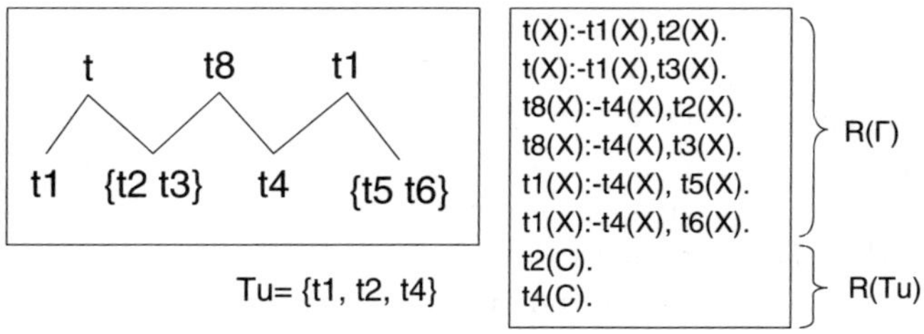

Fig. 1. Deciding intelligibility using Datalog

of minimality (*e.g.*, cardinality) could be adopted to select a single solution. This problem is quite relevant with abduction [2] and is a subject for future research.

4 Emulators

When a module, say t, requires (depends on) a particular module, say t_1, which is not available, we may consider using some kind of emulator, say t_2, which would make t dependent on another, available module, say t_3. In this case, we say that t_1 (the *emulated module*) was *emulated* by t_2 (the *emulator*) and t_3 (the *emulation target*); the emulator and the emulation target will be collectively referred to as the *emulation scheme* and the whole process will be called *emulation*. Emulation is a common practice for achieving interoperability in information systems and can take several different forms (conversion, transformation, translation etc).

In our `README.TXT` example (Section 2), the module t_{README}, which normally requires knowledge of the English language (t_{ENG}), can alternatively be read using t_{GR} (knowledge of the Greek language), provided that we use some translator tool, or a dictionary t_{ENG2GR}, that would translate it in Greek. In this example, t_{ENG} is the emulated module, t_{ENG2GR} is the emulator and t_{GR} is the emulation target.

As described in Section 2, the net effect of this emulation process is that dependencies involving t_{README} are captured by the pair: $\{t_{README}\} > \{t_{ENG}, t_{GR}\}$ and $\{t_{README}\} > \{t_{ENG}, t_{ENG2GR}\}$. Notice that the emulation process causes t_{README} to be no longer dependent on the emulated module (t_{ENG}) alone; also t_{README} does not depend on the emulation scheme (*i.e.*, the emulator t_{ENG2GR} or the emulation target t_{GR}) alone.

In the general case, emulation can take more complex forms: a module t may depend on a number of nodes, some of which may be replaceable by an emulation scheme, which may also consist of a number of nodes. Thus, in its most general form, the "emulated module" and the "emulation scheme" can be families of nodes, say $\mathbf{S}_1, \mathbf{S}_2$ respectively, but the general idea is the same.

Formally, $\mathbf{S}_2 = \{S_{21}, \ldots, S_{2m}\}$ will be called an *emulation scheme* for $\mathbf{S}_1 = \{S_{11}, \ldots, S_{1n}\}$ with respect to t iff:

- For all $i = 1, \ldots, n$, it is *not* the case that $\{t\} > S_{1i}$.
- For all $i = 1, \ldots, m$, it is *not* the case that $\{t\} > S_{2i}$.
- For all $i = 1, \ldots, n$, $j = 1, \ldots, m$, it holds that $\{t\} > S_{1i} \cup S_{2j}$.

In the README.TXT example, we have: $t = t_{README}$, $\mathbf{S}_1 = \{\{t_{ENG}\}\}$, $\mathbf{S}_2 = \{\{t_{ENG2GR}\}, \{t_{GR}\}\}$. Emulation schemes are quite useful in preservation because every user or system that has access to either $\mathbf{S}_1$ or $\mathbf{S}_2$ will be able to understand the content of t; thus, whenever some member of the family $\mathbf{S}_1$ is close to becoming obsolete, it makes sense to consider using (or developing) an emulation scheme for it (with respect to all the interesting modules in our system), so as to retain their intelligibility when $\mathbf{S}_1$ becomes obsolete. Notice that this idea can also be used to model migration, where the role of the emulator in that context is played by the software (module) that applies the migration.

5 Handling Changes

Modules and dependencies may change over time and such changes should be supported. For this reason we describe a number of operations to handle change; such operations can be exploited for defining a protocol between a preservation information system and its users (information providers and consumers).

Following the general trend in fields dealing with changes, we define two general classes of operations: *atomic* and *complex* [6]. Atomic operations are simple, fine-grained operations, whereas complex are more coarse-grained operations, being decomposable into a set of atomic ones. Complex operations usually represent some intuitive and frequently performed type of change, while atomic ones represent some trivial change. Atomic operations are used as "building blocks", in terms of which more complex operators are built, thus facilitating the definition of the semantics of a complex change. Moreover, atomic operations allow the engineer to override the default behavior of some complex change whenever necessary. Notice that, in principle, any sequence of atomic operations can be considered a complex one, so there is no limit on the number of complex operations that can be defined.

A change operation may cause all sorts of problems upon the related structures. To avoid this, two conditions must be verified following a change:

1. All related structures should be *valid*. Valid means that all dependencies ($>$) in Γ are editable and refer to nodes from $2^{\mathcal{T}}$; moreover, all profiles should contain known modules only, *i.e.*, modules in $\mathcal{T}$ (so: $T_s \subseteq \mathcal{T}$, $T_u \subseteq \mathcal{T}$).
2. The system's and users' profiles should be self-intelligible.

There are several options regarding the correct reaction if one of the above conditions fail; our policy is the following: if the first condition fails (invalidity), the change should be either blocked, notifying the engineer of the issue, or some side-effects should be spawned to render the validity condition true (the exact reaction depends on the type of invalidity); if the second condition fails (self-intelligibility), a notification should be issued to the engineer and/or the respective profile owner in order to correct the situation. Non-self-intelligibility is not handled automatically because (a) it is not a very severe problem and (b) there is no single way to restore it, so whatever automatic method we may devise is potentially problematic for certain applications.

5.1 Atomic Changes

Atomic changes should handle changes in modules and dependencies. For modules, we should consider addition and deletion in each of $\mathcal{T}, T_s, T_u$; only the addition and deletion of atomic modules is considered, as it makes no sense to add (or delete) a generalized module (*e.g.*, $\{t_1, t_2\}$). Regarding dependencies, for reasons explained in Section 2, only editable dependencies will be amenable to change, so we consider the addition and deletion of editable dependencies from the graph Γ. This gives a total of 8 atomic operations to consider. All other operations, including replacement, will be handled by complex operations (see subsection 5.2). Table 1 shows the change operations (atomic and complex) considered in this paper and where each one is applied.

Table 1. Change Operations

Operation	Applicable on		
	$\mathcal{T}$	T_s	T_u
$Add\_Mod(t)$	•	•	•
$Del\_Mod(t)$	•	•	•
$Add\_Dep(t, S)$	•		
$Del\_Dep(t, S)$	•		
$Replace\_Mod(t_1, t_2)$		•	•
$UpgradeBackComp\_Mod(t_1, t_2)$	•		
$AddEmulScheme(t, \mathbf{S}_1, \mathbf{S}_2)$	•		

Adding modules to the model ($\mathbf{Add\_Mod_T(t)}$). This operation is applicable when a new module is created, or when we learn the existence of a module that was previously unknown; in such cases, a new module (t) is added in $\mathcal{T}$. This operation cannot cause invalidity or self-intelligibility problems (so it has no side-effects). It is rarely executed alone; usually, the new module will be associated with a number of dependency arcs with other (generalized) modules, but this kind of information should be added separately, using other operations.

Adding modules to a profile ($\mathbf{Add\_Mod_s(t)}$ and $\mathbf{Add\_Mod_u(t)}$). These operations are used in order to add a new module (t) in T_s or T_u. They may cause invalidity if t is not already part of the model ($t \notin \mathcal{T}$). Should this be the case, the operation is blocked and the engineer is notified in order to take proper action. The alternative option to deal with this problem would be to automatically add t to $\mathcal{T}$; this may in fact seem more attractive. However, we chose otherwise because the addition of a new module in $\mathcal{T}$ should be authorized by the engineer and anyway accompanied with a number of dependency additions describing the dependencies associated with t (otherwise we end up with an incomplete model). By notifying the engineer on the issue, we invite him to authorize the addition by introducing the module and the relevant dependencies himself before allowing the addition of the new module to the profile. These operations may also cause non-self-intelligibility, in which case the operation should be executed normally, but a notification should be issued to the engineer and/or respective profile owner to correct the situation somehow.

Deleting modules from the model ($\mathbf{Del\_Mod_T(t)}$). This operation is applicable when we spot a modeling error, *i.e.*, when a non-existing module is modeled in Γ; it is not applicable to obsolete modules, as such modules should not be removed from Γ, but from the respective profiles.

This operation may cause invalidity, because there may be dependency arcs involving the deleted module, or involving a generalized module that includes it; moreover, the module may belong to some profile. Thus, the following actions (side-effects) should be taken along with the module deletion, in this order:

1. For each editable dependency of the form $\{t'\} > S$, where $t \in S$, $S \neq \{t\}$ and $t' \neq t$, add a new dependency $\{t'\} > S - \{t\}$ (see operation *Add_Dep* below). Formally, the executed operation is $Add\_Dep(t', S - \{t\})$.
2. Delete all editable dependencies of the form $\{t'\} > S$ where $t \in S \cup \{t'\}$ (see operation *Del_Dep* below). Formally, the executed operation is $Del\_Dep(t', S)$.
3. Delete module t from the system's and users' profiles (see operations Del_Mod_s and Del_Mod_u respectively below). Formally, the operations executed are $Del\_Mod_s(t)$ and $Del\_Mod_u(t)$ for all users u, respectively.
4. Upon execution of side-effects (steps 1-3), module t can be deleted from $\mathcal{T}$.

Notice that the removal of t from the profiles (step 3) should be accompanied with a notification to the respective profile owner that module t was non-existent and is removed from the model. Normally, this should not be an issue, as no user could have claimed to have access to a non-existent module, unless he did so by mistake. Also, note that the fact that other operations (side-effects) are executed along with $Del\_Mod_T(t)$ does not classify $Del\_Mod_T(t)$ as a complex operation, as there is no other atomic operation that can handle step 4 above. An operation having side-effects is different from an operation being decomposable into an equivalent sequence of other operations.

Deleting modules from a profile ($\mathbf{Del\_Mod_s(t)}$ and $\mathbf{Del\_Mod_u(t)}$). These operations are used in order to delete a non-existent or obsolete module (t) from a profile (T_s or T_u); they may cause non-self-intelligibility, in which case a notification should be issued after the execution of the operation, as usual.

Adding dependencies to the model ($\mathbf{Add\_Dep(t, S)}$). This operation is used to add a new editable dependency ($\{t\} > S$) to the model. This operation is useful when a new dependency is created (*e.g.*, as part of the addition of a new module), or when we learn about a previously unknown dependency.

Before executing this operation, it should be verified that the dependency to be added ($\{t\} > S$) is editable and that $\{t\} \cup S \subseteq \mathcal{T}$, *i.e.*, only already known modules are used. Should this be the case, the addition of the dependency can proceed normally, and no invalidities can occur; in a different case, we should reject the operation, as it would cause an invalidity. Moreover, the addition of the new dependency could render the system's and/or some users' profiles non-self-intelligible; as usual, this problem is handled by issuing a notification.

Deleting dependencies from the model (Del_Dep(t, S)). This operation is applicable when we realize that an existing editable dependency is not really true; it is also useful (as a side-effect) when a module is deleted from $\mathcal{T}$. As usual, only editable dependencies can be deleted. This operation cannot cause invalidity or self-intelligibility problems (so it has no side-effects).

5.2 Complex Changes

In this subsection we define a number of complex operations that we consider useful; as already mentioned, such a list cannot possibly be complete. All operations will be defined in terms of the atomic operations of the previous subsection; notice that the order of execution may be important. The various atomic operations should be performed in a transactional manner, *i.e.*, if one operation in the list fails, the whole complex operation fails and should be rolled back.

Replacing a module in a profile (Replace_Mod$_\mathbf{s}$($\mathbf{t_1}, \mathbf{t_2}$) and Replace_Mod$_\mathbf{u}$($\mathbf{t_1}, \mathbf{t_2}$)). These two operations are used in order to replace a module t_1 with t_2 in T_s or T_u and are especially useful when a particular module is becoming obsolete and is being replaced (*e.g.*, by a newer version). A replacement consists of a deletion of t_1, followed by the addition of t_2 in the profile; the model $\mathcal{T}$ is not affected. Any more sophisticated functionality should be captured using other operations. If t_2 is in the respective profile, or if t_1 is not, then the operation is rejected; otherwise the following actions should be taken to implement these operations:

1. Perform the operation $Add\_Mod_s(t_2)$ (or $Add\_Mod_u(t_2)$).
2. Perform the operation $Del\_Mod_s(t_1)$ (or $Del\_Mod_s(t_1)$).

Upgrading a module with a backwards compatible version in the model (UpgradeBackComp_Mod($\mathbf{t_1}, \mathbf{t_2}$)). Often, modules (*e.g.*, software applications) are being upgraded; such upgrades (new versions) are handled as new modules in our model. However, in many cases, the newer and the older version of the module share some properties, such as dependency relations. To save the engineer from the burden of defining such dependency relations whenever a new, backwards compatible version of a module is inserted, we offer the operation $UpgradeBackComp\_Mod(t_1, t_2)$.

This operation adds a new module (t_2) in $\mathcal{T}$ and automatically creates a number of dependencies involving t_2, based on the information on the dependencies involving t_1. In particular, any module depending on t_1 should now depend on t_1 *or* t_2; in addition, t_2 should depend on all (generalized) modules that t_1 depends on. This behavior is justified by the fact that a backwards compatible version normally depends on the same generalized modules as the older version, and can be used as an alternative (to t_1) way of understanding a module; any possible deviation from this default behavior should be captured using additional operations that would restore the desired behavior, overriding the default one.

This operation presupposes that t_1 is already in $\mathcal{T}$ ($t_1 \in \mathcal{T}$), while t_2 is not ($t_2 \notin \mathcal{T}$); if either condition is false, the operation is rejected. Following this operation, the old and the new version (t_1, t_2) will coexist in the graph. The following actions should be taken to implement it:

1. Perform the operation $Add\_Mod_T(t_2)$.
2. For each editable dependency $\{t_1\} > S$ do: $Add\_Dep(t_2, S)$.
3. For each editable dependency $\{t\} > S$, for which $t_1 \in S$, do: $Add\_Dep(t, S \cup \{t_2\})$.
4. For each editable dependency $\{t\} > S$, for which $t_1 \in S$ and $t_2 \notin S$, do: $Del\_Dep(t, S)$.

Following the successful execution of this operation, the users (and the system) should be notified on the existence of a new, backwards compatible version of t_1; this might motivate many users (or the system) to upgrade.

Adding an emulation scheme to the model (AddEmulScheme($\mathbf{t}, \mathbf{S_1}, \mathbf{S_2}$)). This operation is used to denote that $\mathbf{S}_2$ is an emulation scheme for $\mathbf{S}_1$ with respect to t. The structures $\mathbf{S}_1, \mathbf{S}_2$ are, as usual, families of nodes. This operation automatically determines the relevant dependency changes and executes them, saving us from the burden of updating all the dependencies manually.

Let $\mathbf{S}_1 = \{S_{11}, \ldots, S_{1n}\}, \mathbf{S}_2 = \{S_{21}, \ldots, S_{2m}\}$; it is assumed, as usual, that all related modules (*i.e.*, t and those in $\mathbf{S}_1, \mathbf{S}_2$) are already in the graph (*i.e.*, that $\{t\} \cup S_{11} \cup \ldots \cup S_{1n} \cup S_{21} \cup \ldots \cup S_{2m} \subseteq \mathcal{T}$) and that t depends on the modules of $\mathbf{S}_1$, *i.e.*, $\{t\} > S_{1i}$ is in the graph for all $i = 1, \ldots, n$. If any of these conditions is not true, the operation is rejected. After the execution of the operation, $\mathbf{S}_2$ should be an emulation scheme for $\mathbf{S}_1$ with respect to t. The following actions should be taken to implement this operation:

1. For all $i = 1, \ldots, n$, $j = 1, \ldots, m$ do: $Add\_Dep(t, S_{1i} \cup S_{2j})$.
2. For all $i = 1, \ldots, n$ do: $Del\_Dep(t, S_{1i})$.
3. For all $i = 1, \ldots, m$ do: $Del\_Dep(t, S_{2i})$.

Other operations. Apart from the above complex operations, one could consider a number of other operations, such as operations on renaming modules, replacing dependency relations, or cleaning up the system (referring to the removal of modules that are no longer necessary for the intelligibility of any module in the system's profile). Such operations can be defined in a similar way and are omitted due to lack of space.

6 Concluding Remarks

Recently, there has been a number of theoretical attempts (like [1], [3]), standards (like OAIS[3]) and ongoing international projects (like CASPAR[4] and PLANETS[5])

[3] OAIS reference model (ISO:14721:2003).
[4] http://www.casparpreserves.eu/

dealing with digital preservation, indicating a growing interest on the problem and resulting to the study of several of its aspects, such as the definition of metadata and services for preservation, cost-related strategies for data preservation planning etc.

In this paper, we formalized the notions of profile, intelligibility, emulation and evolution based on the notion of dependency and described the services that should be supported by a modern information preservation system. Dependency management has been a subject of research in several (old and newly emerged) areas, from software engineering [4], [9], [10], [11] to ontology engineering [5], [7]; to the best of our knowledge, this is the first paper that uses these notions for digital preservation, so it is quite different from other theoretical attempts on the problem ([1], [3]). Issues for further research include measuring computational complexity and extending the model with complex dependencies, composite modules and dependencies of different granularity.

Acknowledgements

This work was partially supported by the EU project CASPAR (FP6-2005-IST-033572) which aims at building a pioneering framework to support the end-to-end preservation lifecycle for scientific, artistic and cultural information.

References

1. Cheney, J., Lagoze, C., Botticelli, P.: Towards a Theory of Information Preservation. In: Constantopoulos, P., Sølvberg, I.T. (eds.) ECDL 2001. LNCS, vol. 2163, pp. 340–351. Springer, Heidelberg (2001)
2. Eiter, T., Gottlob, G.: The complexity of logic-based abduction. Journal of the ACM 42(1), 3–42 (1995)
3. Flouris, G., Meghini, C.: Steps towards a theory of information preservation. In: Proceedings of the International Workshop on Database Preservation (2007)
4. Franch, X., Maiden, N.A.M.: Modeling Component Dependencies to Inform their Selection. In: 2nd Intern. Conf. on COTS-Based Software Systems (2003)
5. Jarrar, M., Meersman, R.: Formal Ontology Engineering in the DOGMA Approach. In: Meersman, R., Tari, Z., at.al. (eds.) CoopIS 2002, DOA 2002, and ODBASE 2002. LNCS, vol. 2519, pp. 1238–1254. Springer, Heidelberg (2002)
6. Stuckenshmidt, H., Klein, M.: Integrity and change in modular ontologies. In: Proceedings of the 18th International Joint Conference on Artificial Intelligence (IJCAI-03) (2003)
7. Sunagawa, E., Kozaki, K., Kitamura, Y., Mizoguchi, R.: An Environment for Distributed Ontology Development Based on Dependency Management. In: Fensel, D., Sycara, K.P., Mylopoulos, J. (eds.) ISWC 2003. LNCS, vol. 2870, pp. 453–468. Springer, Heidelberg (2003)
8. Tzitzikas, Y.: Dependency Management for the Preservation of Digital Information. In: Procs. of the 18th Intern. Conf. on Database and Expert Systems Applications, DEXA'2007, Regensburg, Germany, September 2007, Springer, Heidelberg (2007)

9. Vieira, M., Dias, M., Richardson, D.J.: Describing Dependencies in Component Access Points. In: Procs. of the 23rd Intern. Conf. on Software Engineering, ICSE'01, Toronto, Canada, pp. 115–118 (2001)
10. Vieira, M., Richardson, D.: Analyzing dependencies in large component-based systems. ASE 00, 241 (2002)
11. Walter, M., Trinitis, C., Karl, W.: OpenSESAME: an intuitive dependability modeling environmentsupporting inter-component dependencies. In: Procs. of 2001 Pacific Rim International Symposium on Dependable Computing, pp. 76–83 (2001)

Using XML Logical Structure to Retrieve (Multimedia) Objects

Zhigang Kong and Mounia Lalmas

Queen Mary, University of London
{cskzg,mounia}@dcs.qmul.ac.uk

Abstract. This paper investigates the use of the logical structure in XML documents for the retrieval of XML multimedia objects. We study different logical levels and their combinations. Our investigation is carried on a purpose-built test collection based on the INEX test collection. Our findings are the followings. First, all logical levels allow discriminating between elements contained in different documents, whereas the lower logical levels allow discriminating between elements within a same document. Second, combining the logical levels improve retrieval performance.

1 Introduction

In XML document collections, a multimedia[1] object is referenced as an external entity in the attribute of an XML multimedia element that is specifically designed for multimedia content. Some textual content can appear within the element, describing (or 'annotating') the multimedia object itself. The elements that surround the multimedia element in the document's logical structure can have textual content that provides additional descriptions of the object. Therefore, the textual content within a multimedia element and the elements in the document's logical structure can be used to calculate a representation of the multimedia object that is capable of supplying direct retrieval of this multimedia data by a textual (or 'natural language') query. We believe that exploiting the logical structure can play an essential role in providing effective retrieval of XML multimedia objects.

The main motivation behind this paper is to investigate the use of the document's logical structure for representing and retrieving XML multimedia objects. This work performed extensive experiments to understand how the approach of combining logically disjointed document parts works, and to demonstrate why we need this logical structure for the combination rather than using directly the whole document.

The paper is organised as follows. In Section 2, we present related work. In Section 3, we describe our approach. In Section 4, we describe the test collection built to evaluate our approach. In Section 5, we present our experiments and results. Finally we conclude in Section 6.

[1] The work described in this paper was carried out with image objects; nonetheless, the approach can be applied to any other media.

L. Kovács, N. Fuhr, and C. Meghini (Eds.): ECDL 2007, LNCS 4675, pp. 100–111, 2007.

2 Related Work and Background

The work related to ours is mainly in the area of text-based retrieval of multimedia objects, and in particular images. Document parts have been used in a number of web image retrieval approaches. [3] investigates the retrieval of images on the web by dividing the textual parts of web pages into image caption, neighbouring image captions, the rest of text in the page, and text in the pages pointing to that page. These parts are often combined and different weights (in addition to the standard term frequency and inverse document frequency) are assigned to the terms extracted from different parts. Other approaches combine the textual- and content-based retrieval. In [10], the combination is done after a relevance feedback step. Again weights are used to emphasise the contribution of the various text parts. In [1], a face recognition system and semantic-based retrieval approach are used to analyse the surrounding text of facial images to locate person names and determine their degree of association with each image. Thus using surrounding "bits" to index images has already been investigating, which is also what our work is doing, but through the exploitation of the XML logical structure.

The work reported in [6] is concerned with collections of images with associated descriptions in the form of captions or metadata that were often manually generated during for example a cataloguing phase. Even though these descriptions can be semi-structured (i.e. formatted in XML or MPEG-7), they remain descriptions of the images. This is different from our work, where the multimedia objects are themselves embedded within the logically structured XML content.

XML-related work was carried out as part of the INEX 2005 multimedia track [14]. For instance, [5] used the linear combination of evidence to merge the retrieval scores from content-based image retrieval and text-based XML retrieval. Other similar approaches include [13,12]. However, these were developed for the Lonely Planet collection, which, as described in Section 4, is not appropriate for our investigation.

Approaches in XML text retrieval have exploited the surrounding "bits" (e.g. related elements) for retrieving XML text elements. For instance, [11] applied the language models both at element level and at article (document) level. Then they mixed evidence from the two language models to retrieve elements. [9] developed a hierarchical language model, taking advantage of the logical structure of XML documents. The score used for ranking an XML element was estimated by mixing evidence of the element with its parent element. Using surrounding "bits" to represent and retrieve XML elements has shown to be beneficial, and this is what is being done in our work, but with respect to XML multimedia elements.

3 Indexing and Retrieving XML Multimedia Objects

The general idea of our approach is to use the surrounding text to represent the content of multimedia (or in fact any) XML elements. The XML logical structure, for example *article-> section->subsection->paragraph*, can be interpreted to describe a *topic->subtopic->sub-subtopic->one aspect*. It is reasonable to assume that paragraphs in the same subsection are used to describe the subsection's topic, and paragraphs in different subsections but in the same section are used to describe the section's topic. This would indicate that the text content closer to the multimedia object in the document's logical hierarchy would provide a better description of the multimedia object and thus could produce more accurate representation of the object.

We divided XML documents into different granularities based on their logical structure. We call these granularities *regions*. For a given multimedia object referenced in a multimedia element, the multimedia element is named the multimedia object's own region, a sibling element to the multimedia element is named its sibling region, the parent of the multimedia element is named its 1st ancestor region, etc.

Figure 1 shows an example. The two <p> elements are the sibling region of the <fig> element, the multimedia (in our case image) element, which is the own region. The other regions are depicted in the figure. The regions are disjoint from their lower level regions so that the regions have no overlapping content with their lower level regions. For example, the lightly dashed line area is the 1st ancestor (4rd highest) region and the thick dashed line area is the 2nd ancestor (3th highest) region.

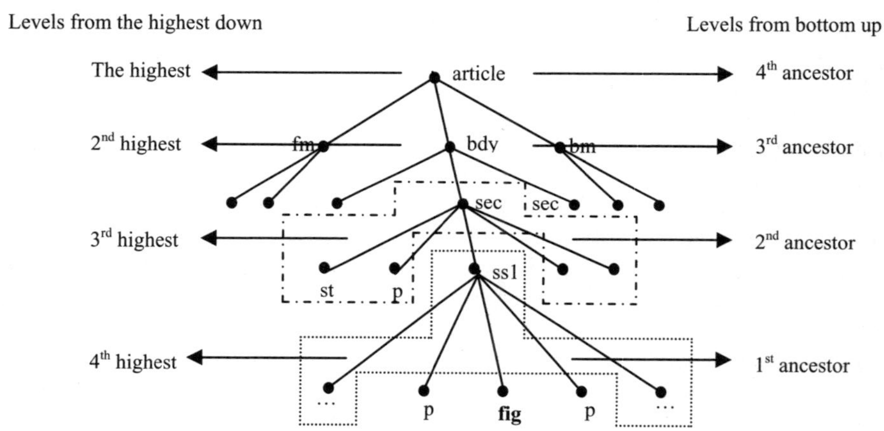

Fig. 1. The logical regions

A region can be treated as an atomic retrieval unit, like a document, and then any standard IR model can be applied to a region just as it might be applied to a document. At this stage of our work, we focus on investigating the impact of the XML logical structure on retrieving XML multimedia objects. Therefore, we use simple indexing and retrieval methods, where it is straightforward to perform experiments that will inform us on the suitability of our approach. For this purpose indexing is based on the basic tf-idf weighting and retrieval is based on the vector space model. The ranking score of a multimedia element is computed as follows:

$$rsv_o = \sum_{r \in o} \alpha_r rsv_r \tag{1}$$

where α_r is a weight assigned to a logical region *r*, where $\sum_{r \in o} \alpha_r = 1$. Finally, rsv_r is the retrieval status value of the region *r* computed by the vector space model.

This approach was previously presented in [7] and an evaluation on a small test collection [8] showed the approach to be promising. In particular, it was showed that using elements higher in a document's logical structure works well in selecting the documents containing relevant multimedia objects, whereas elements lower in the structure are necessary to select the relevant images within a document. However, as the evaluation was performed on a very small data set (7864 images and 37 MB text), it is necessary to perform a large-scale evaluation to properly validate the proposed approach.

4 Building the Test Collection

INEX started a multimedia track in 2005 [14]. However, the test collection is not appropriate for the evaluation of our approach due to the following reasons. First, the images in this test collection have been organized together in the same parent element (the <images> element). Therefore, the logical context of the images within the same XML document is almost the same so that it cannot be used to investigate the impact of the logical structure on discriminating between the multimedia objects within a document. Second, there is no diversity in the depths of the multimedia objects as all images are located in the same logical level. Third, it has a relatively flat hierarchy (the depth of image elements is 3). Finally, the test collection is still small in size (2633 images contained in 14.5 MB text). As such, this test collection is not suitable for a large-scale evaluation of our approach. We therefore built a large test collection, where XML text elements are used to simulate multimedia elements[2].

4.1 Methodology

In [2], a text only document collection is used to test the validity of a cluster-based multimedia retrieval approach. Two sets of experiments were carried out. The first set compared the cluster-based representations with representations based on randomly generated citations. The second set showed that the cluster-based representations provided approximately 70% of the retrieval effectiveness of directly indexing the original content.

Our methodology is inspired by [2]: using an XML text collection to validate XML multimedia retrieval approach. The retrieval of a multimedia object will be viewed as retrieval of a multimedia element. The proposed methodology selects a number of text elements from XML documents to simulate multimedia elements, and we refer to them as simulated multimedia elements. Based on this, we apply our proposed approach to represent and retrieve these elements.

In an XML document, a multimedia element is an element that has an attribute value referencing an external entity (a multimedia object). Therefore, there is no difference between the retrieval of a text element and the retrieval of a multimedia element, especially when the retrieval is based on the representations of surrounding texts, i.e. the regions.

---

[2] The INEX 2006 multimedia track provides a large and more suitable multimedia collection. We are currently continuing our work with this collection.

4.2 The Document Collection, Topics and Relevant Elements

We use the INEX 2004 text collection, which consists of 12,107 articles, totalling 494MB in size, where the average depth of an element is 6.9 [4]. The INEX collection can be considered an adequately sized data set due to the large number of documents and the fact that the elements are distributed in an appropriate tree structure, having deep logical relationships. The benefit of using the INEX collection is that we can we use its topics and its relevant assessments.

Our approach is to make use of the regions to represent the content of multimedia elements and then apply content-oriented retrieval as defined in INEX based on this representation. For this reasons, we use the CO (content-only) topics in INEX, which are free-text queries. Our test collection thus contains a subset of the INEX 2004 CO topics.

For this subset of topics (the precise numbers and how the set was selected are described below), we need to identify the relevant simulated XML multimedia elements. We aim to study how the use of regions impacts on the retrieval of the most relevant multimedia elements. Thus, only the highly relevant elements will be considered as relevant in our test collection. Relevance in INEX 2004 is defined according to two dimensions, Exhaustivity (E) and Specificity (S), each of which is measured on a 4-point scale: not (0), marginally (1), fairly (2), and highly (3). We define the highly relevant elements as those at least highly exhaustive or highly specific. In addition, if only highly exhaustive, then the element should be at least fairly specific, and vice versa. In summary, only elements that have been assessed as (3,3), (3,2) and (2,3) are considered for building the relevant simulated XML multimedia elements, where (x,y) stands for (exhaustive value, specificity value).

We exclude any overlapping elements in our test collection as the real multimedia objects would not be overlapping with each other (in INEX, two overlapping elements, e.g. an element and its parent element, may both be assessed as (3,3) for a given topic). To make sure each topic has an appropriate number of simulated relevant elements, we do not select the topics that have less than 10 relevant elements. As a result, our test collection has 25 topics, following from [15] who show that to obtain any significant results when comparing approaches, at least 25 topics should be used. These selected 25 topics have in total 5773 selected relevant simulated multimedia elements, on average 231 relevant elements per topic. The maximum depth is 9 and minimum depth is 2, with an average of 5.21.

4.3 Select a Collection of Simulated Multimedia Elements

The selection of the non-relevant simulated multimedia elements in the test collection is done by a random process, performed by traversing the XML document, where overlapping elements are excluded. To avoid that the selected elements are contained within a small number of documents, whilst other documents have no selected elements, the process will select at least 10 elements from each document. The depth distribution of selected elements in this process is kept similar to the depth distribution of the relevant simulated elements. Those selected elements are viewed as irrelevant elements as they are randomly selected. In total, the built test collection contains 143,034 (including the relevant ones) simulated multimedia elements, on average 12 elements per document. For simplicity, we will use “multimedia element” instead of “simulated multimedia element” in the remaining of this paper.

5 Experiments, Results and Analysis

Extensive experiments were carried out using the built test collections to test the use of the regions. The title field of 25 selected INEX topics are used as query terms. In section 5.1 we present the results obtained using regions from the lowest level up. Section 5.2 presents the results using regions from the document root level down. Subsequently, in section 5.3, we compared the results using any types of region with the element’s self content (own region). In section 5.4, we compare the results using combinations of regions with those using the whole document. At last, we present the results obtained using a weighted combination of regions in section 5.5.

In all our experiments, the retrieval status values are calculated according to formula 1. When the representations are composed of single regions, α_r =1 (Sections 5.1 to 5.3). In addition, stop-words were removed and stemming was applied. We report the precision values for the 11 standard recall values. In addition, we present the Mean Average Precision (MAP) and sometimes the precisions at element cut-off (5, 10, 15 and 20).

5.1 Using Lowest Level Region to Up Level Regions

These experiments were performed to investigate the use of region levels for retrieving multimedia elements. The results from using the sibling region to the highest level region (8th ancestor in this collection) are shown in figure 2. The MAP values obtained using regions from sibling level to 8th ancestor level are: 0.1166, 0.1383, 0.1900, 0.1828, 0.0807, 0.0196, 0.0047, 0.0067, and 0.0019.

We can see that effectiveness decreases from the 2nd ancestor level to the highest level. This is what we expected, the region closer to a given multimedia element in the document’s logical hierarchy produces a more accurate representation of the element. However, the MAP obtained with the 2nd (or 3rd) ancestor regions is better than that with the 1st ancestor (or sibling) regions. We expected that the 1st level regions, which are closer to the multimedia elements in the document hierarchy, should lead to better performance than when using 2nd ancestor regions. There is, however, a clear explanation why this is not the case. As the regions are disjoint from each other, and due to the nested logical structure, the 2nd ancestor regions have more terms than the 1st ancestor regions (as shown in figure 1). The greater number of terms increases the number of matches between a query and the region having more terms, which is why 2nd ancestor regions led to better performance.

Therefore, the impact of the regions on retrieval performance could be a balance of two aspects. A lower level region offers more accurate representation than a higher level region and a higher level region supplies more terms than a lower level region. The difference between 1st and 2nd ancestor regions clearly demonstrates this to be the case. As presented in table 1 of section 5.3, using 1st ancestor regions produces better

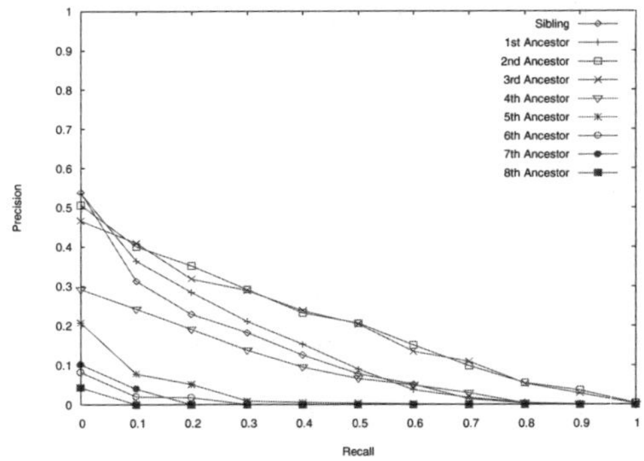

Fig. 2. Regions from sibling upwards

performance at top 20 cut-off values than using 2nd ancestor regions. The higher performance at top cut-off level obtained using 1st ancestor regions is due to them providing more accurate representations and the higher performance of MAP using 2nd ancestor regions is due to them having more terms.

We observed that the highest levels, the 7th and 8th ancestor level, almost retrieved nothing. We found that only 0.09% of the relevant multimedia elements have 8th ancestor region and 1.44% of those have 7th and higher level ancestors. This means that those not having these level regions will certainly not be retrieved.

5.2 Using Regions from Document Root Level Down

This section presents a second set of experiments to investigate the use of regions to represent multimedia objects, starting from regions at the document root level and going down the logical structure. In the built test collection, most of the multimedia elements are located in the <bdy> element. Thus, the highest region level is the document root element, /article, the 2nd highest level region is the element /article/bdy, and the 3rd highest level region is the element /article/bdy/sec/. We stop at this level because the lower level regions of some elements may not exist. If they do not exist, it makes sense that the elements will not be retrieved. The results are given in figure 3. The MAP values of regions from the highest level to the 3rd highest level are: 0.1294, 0.1858, and 0.1868.

Looking at the results of the 2nd and 3rd highest level regions, it is clear that the 3rd highest level region leads to higher precision for low recall values and the 2nd highest level region leads to higher precision for high recall values. The lower level (3rd highest) region offers more accurate representation than the higher level (2nd highest) region, so the former led to better precision for lower recall values. The latter contains more terms and thus led to better precision than the former for higher recall values. This is also what we observed in section 5.1. Due to the balancing effect of the above two, there is only a small difference between their MAP values.

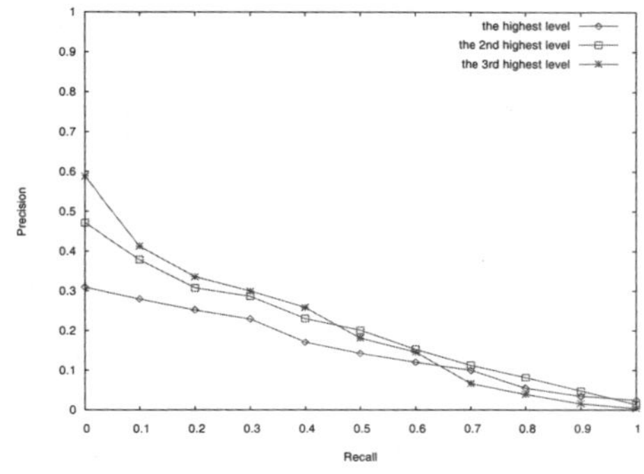

Fig. 3. Regions from root level down

The results show that the highest level region is still useful for retrieving multimedia elements, although it performs worse than its lower levels. This indicates that the regions at all logical levels seem useful.

5.3 Effectiveness of Self Content

The aim of this section is to compare the use of regions and the element itself (the own region). As the multimedia elements are actually simulated by text elements, the own region here simply refers to the text element itself. Table 1 compares the results from using the own region up to the 3rd ancestor level.

Table 1. MAP values and precisions at element cut-off from own regionup to 3rd level region

	MAP	precision @ 5	precision @ 10	precision @15	precision @ 20
Own	0.1587	0.3680	0.3920	0.3520	0.3340
Sibling	0.1166	0.3760	0.3320	0.3013	0.2900
1st	0.1383	0.4240	0.3920	0.3707	0.3400
2nd	0.1900	0.3120	0.3600	0.3360	0.3260
3rd	0.1828	0.2400	0.2320	0.2427	0.2560

The results show that the self content obtained poorer MAP than the 2nd and 3rd ancestor levels (table 1), although its precisions at 5, 10, 15 and 20 are higher than those of the 2nd and 3rd ancestor levels. The results illustrate that other parts of documents (here the regions) are necessary to lead to better representation, thus more effective retrieval, of the text element. This is not a new result in itself, and has been observed in INEX, where it is now common to include collection and article statistics in representing and/or retrieving elements [4].

5.4 Using Regions Instead of Document

This section provides two sets of experiments, each of which contains three experiments. The first set represents multimedia objects in three ways: 1. Using the whole surrounding document text (excluding the self content) to represent the multimedia element. 2. Using the whole document text (including the self content) to represent the multimedia element. 3. Combining surrounding logical regions from sibling up to the highest level. The second set is as follows: 1. Combining own region with the whole surrounding document text. 2. Combining own region with the whole document text (including the self content). 3. Combining regions from own region up to the highest level. All the combinations above are based on the average combination (formula 1).

The results of the first set of experiments are presented in figure 4. The MAP values of the first set are 0.1922, 0.1900, and 0.3114. There is almost no difference between representation using the whole document and that using the surrounding text. However, combining regions led to higher performance than either of these methods. It obtained 62.02% higher MAP than that of using surrounding text and 63.89% higher MAP than that of using whole document. The combination of the text in the regions is the same as the text of the whole surrounding text. The terms in the whole surrounding text that match query terms are exactly the same as those in the hierarchical regions (from sibling to the highest level). So why did combining the term matching of regions obtained distinctly better performance?

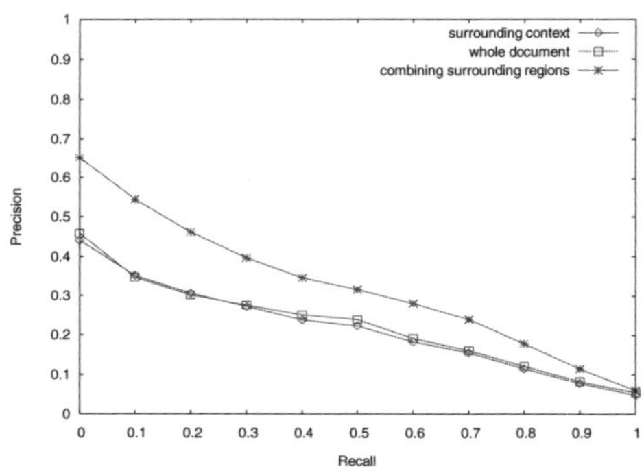

Fig. 4. Combination vs. whole document (1)

In the combination formula, each region is treated as an atomic unit to which the standard cosine function is applied. As the regions are logically nested within each other, a higher region has more terms. Thus a term occurring in a lower region can obtain a higher weight than one occurring in a higher region due to the smaller value of the normalization factor. When we use the text as a whole unit to apply the vector space model, a term located at different positions in the whole text obtains the same term weight. Therefore, the terms in the combination of regions that match the query terms are the same as those in the whole text that match the query terms. The matched terms' frequencies in the combination of regions are also the same as those in the whole text. However, the terms' weights in the combination are different from those in the whole text. A term matching the query located in the lower level region is weighted higher and thus provides more impact on the retrieval than the same term located in its higher level region.

The results further demonstrate the conclusions of previous sections: a lower level region offers more accurate representation and thus leads to better performance; the higher level region contains more terms and the "more" terms involved in higher level make the region more effective. The combination of regions benefits from both of the these points, as it assigns higher weight to the terms matching the query in the lower level region and provides the whole terms of the text from sibling to the highest level regions. This is the reason why combining regions performs better.

Furthermore, when using the whole text or whole document to represent the multimedia elements in the XML documents, the representations can only be used to discriminate the multimedia elements located in different XML documents. However, combining the logically structured regions offers different weights in the representations of multimedia elements within the same XML documents. This can further discriminate between elements within the same documents in addition to multimedia elements located in different XML documents. This is another reason why combining regions led to better performance than using whole surrounding text and using whole document.

The aim of the second set of experiments is to further demonstrate the advantage of using the logical structure. We combine the self content (own region) with the whole surrounding text or whole document to further discriminate between elements within the same documents and thus to improve performance. Then, the results will be compared with the combination of logically structured regions (including the own region).

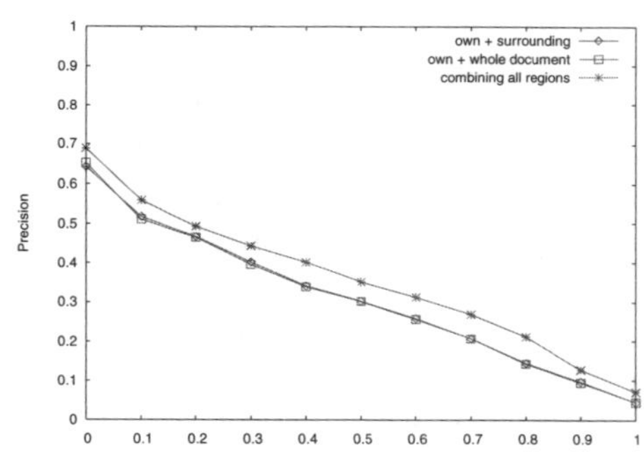

Fig. 5. Combination vs. whole document (2)

The results of the second set experiments are presented in figure 5. The MAP values of the second set are 0.2918, 0.2911, and 0.3488. Compared with figure 4, the results show that the MAP of combining the own region with the whole surrounding text increase by 51.82% from using the whole surrounding text and that of combining the own region with whole document leads to an increase of 53.21% over using the whole document. Combining the self content improves the effectiveness due to the further discrimination between elements within the same documents.

However, combining logically structured regions (including the own region) obtained obviously better result than the combination of own region and whole document. The MAP of the former is an increase of 19.53% over the latter. Even combining logically structured regions without the own region (figure 4) gained better MAP than the latter. This demonstrates that combining logically structured regions not only discriminate between elements contained in different documents as well as discriminate between elements within the same documents but also improve the accuracy of the overall representation. This is because combining logically structured regions emphasizes the lower level regions, which can offer more accurate representation than the higher level ones. Therefore, combining logically structured document regions proves essential in XML multimedia retrieval.

5.5 The Weighted Combination

We applied a number of weighted combinations. All led to little effectiveness improvement. The best one, which emphasizes the own, 2nd highest and 3rd highest regions, leads to an increase of 0.49% compared to the average combination. This is due to the following reason: In the average combination, the terms in a lower level region have already been highly weighted compared to those in a higher level region, as discussed in section 5.4. Therefore, further weighting the lower level regions can only lead to very limited improvement.

6 Conclusions and Future Work

This paper investigated the use of the logical structure in XML documents to retrieve XML multimedia objects. We studied the use of region levels and their combination for retrieving multimedia elements. We showed that all levels allow discriminating between multimedia elements contained in different XML documents, whereas the lower level regions allow discriminating between elements within a document. In addition, we found that the lower level regions provide more precise representation than the higher level regions, leading to improved precision, whereas higher level regions contain more terms than lower level regions, leading to improved recall. We compared the combination of the logically structured regions with using the whole document as representation. We showed that the former was better for representing and retrieving multimedia elements. Therefore, we can conclude that using the XML logical structure is important in XML multimedia retrieval.

A strong challenge to the validity of the experiments described in this paper comes from using text elements to simulate multimedia elements. However, as a multimedia element is just an element, there is no difference between the retrieval of a multimedia element and the retrieval of a text element, when using their regions to represent them. Further work needs to be carried out into the use of these methods, or more sophisticated ones, within a large XML multimedia document collection. We are currently working with the collection of INEX 2006 multimedia track [16].

Acknowledgements

This work was carried in the context of INEX, an activity of the DELOS Network of Excellence.

References

1. Aslandogan, Y.A., Yu, C.T.: Diogenes: A Web search agent for content based indexing of personal images. In: Proceedings of the eighth ACM international conference on Multimedia, pp. 481–482 (2000)
2. Dunlop, M.D., van Rijsbergen, C.J.: Hypermedia and free text retrieval. Information Processing & Management 29(3), 287–298 (1993)
3. Harmandas, V., Sanderson, M., Dunlop, M.D.: Image retrieval by hypertext links. In: Proceedings of SIGIR-97, Philadelphia, US, pp. 296–303 (1997)
4. Fuhr, N., Lalmas, M., Malik, S., Kazai, G. (eds.): INEX 2005. LNCS, vol. 3977. Springer, Heidelberg (2006)
5. Iskandar, D.N.F.A., Pehcevski, J., Thom, J.A., Tahaghoghi, S.M.M.: Combining Image and Structured Text Retrieval. In: Fuhr, N., Lalmas, M., Malik, S., Kazai, G. (eds.) INEX 2005. LNCS, vol. 3977, pp. 525–539. Springer, Heidelberg (2006)
6. Jones, G., Groves, D., Khasin, A., Lam-Adesina, A., Mellebeek, W.A.: Dublin City University at CLEF 2004: Experimentswith the ImageCLEF St Andrew's Collection. In: Peters, C., Clough, P.D., Gonzalo, J., Jones, G.J.F., Kluck, M., Magnini, B. (eds.) CLEF 2004. LNCS, vol. 3491, Springer, Heidelberg (2005)
7. Kong, Z., Lalmas, M.: Integrating XLink and XPath to Retrieve Structured Multimedia Documents in Digital Libraries. In: Proceedings of RIAO (2004)
8. Kong, Z., Lalmas, M.: XML Multimedia Retrieval. In: Consens, M.P., Navarro, G. (eds.) SPIRE 2005. LNCS, vol. 3772, pp. 218–223. Springer, Heidelberg (2005)
9. Ogilvie, P., Callan, J.: Hierarchical language models for XML component retrieval. In: Fuhr, N., Lalmas, M., Malik, S., Szlávik, Z. (eds.) INEX 2004. LNCS, vol. 3493, Springer, Heidelberg (2005)
10. Sclaroff, S., La Cascia, M., Sethi, S., Taycher, L.: Unifying Textual and Visual Cues for Content-based Image Retrieval on the World Wide Web. Computer Vision and Image Understanding 75(1-2), 86–98 (1999)
11. Sigurbjornsson, B., Kamps, J., de Rijke, M.: An Element-based Approach to XML Retrieval. In: Proceedings of INEX 2003 Workshop (2003)
12. Tjondronegoro, D., Zhang, J., Gu, J., Nguyen, A., Geva, S.: Integrating Text Retrieval and Image Retrieval in XML Document Searching. In: Fuhr, N., Lalmas, M., Malik, S., Kazai, G. (eds.) INEX 2005. LNCS, vol. 3977, pp. 511–524. Springer, Heidelberg (2006)
13. van Zwol, R.: Multimedia strategies for B -SDR, based on Prinicipal Component Analysis. In: Fuhr, N., Lalmas, M., Malik, S., Kazai, G. (eds.) INEX 2005. LNCS, vol. 3977, pp. 540–553. Springer, Heidelberg (2006)
14. van Zwol, R., Kazai, G., Lalmas, M.: INEX 2005 multimedia track. In: Fuhr, N., Lalmas, M., Malik, S., Kazai, G. (eds.) INEX 2005. LNCS, vol. 3977, Springer, Heidelberg (2006)
15. Voorhees, E.M., Buckley, C.: The effect of topic set size on retrieval experiment error. In: Proceedings of the 25th ACM SIGIR, pp. 316–323 (2002)
16. Westerveld, T., van Zwol, R.: Multimedia Retrieval at INEX 2006. 2007 SIGIR forum (2007), http://www.acm.org/sigs/sigir/forum/2007J-TOC.html

Lyrics-Based Audio Retrieval and Multimodal Navigation in Music Collections

Meinard Müller, Frank Kurth, David Damm, Christian Fremerey, and Michael Clausen*

Department of Computer Science III, University of Bonn,
Römerstraße 164, 53117 Bonn, Germany
{meinard,frank,damm,fremerey,clausen}@iai.uni-bonn.de
http://www-mmdb.iai.uni-bonn.de

Abstract. Modern digital music libraries contain textual, visual, and audio data describing music on various semantic levels. Exploiting the availability of different semantically interrelated representations for a piece of music, this paper presents a query-by-lyrics retrieval system that facilitates multimodal navigation in CD audio collections. In particular, we introduce an automated method to time align given lyrics to an audio recording of the underlying song using a combination of synchronization algorithms. Furthermore, we describe a lyrics search engine and show how the lyrics-audio alignments can be used to directly navigate from the list of query results to the corresponding matching positions within the audio recordings. Finally, we present a user interface for lyrics-based queries and playback of the query results that extends the functionality of our SyncPlayer framework for content-based music and audio navigation.

1 Introduction

Recent activities in integrating music and audio documents into the holdings of existing digital libraries have emphasized the importance of appropriate tools for automatically organizing and accessing large music collections. As opposed to existing collections of homogeneous document types like text databases, musical information is represented in various different data formats such as text, score, or audio, which fundamentally differ in their structure and content. Hence there is a particular challenge to develop suitable techniques for searching and navigating through existing heterogeneous collections of digital music document.

As an example, consider a user who only recalls a few words of a song's lyrics like, for example, parts of the hook line or of the chorus. Using these words as a query, a music search engine based on classical text-based retrieval may be used for searching a database of *text documents* containing the lyrics of a collection of songs. In this case, the retrieval results displayed to a user would consist of text passages corresponding to occurrences of the query terms within

* This work was supported in part by Deutsche Forschungsgemeinschaft (DFG) under grant 554975 (1) Oldenburg BIB48 OLof 01-02.

L. Kovács, N. Fuhr, and C. Meghini (Eds.): ECDL 2007, LNCS 4675, pp. 112–123, 2007.

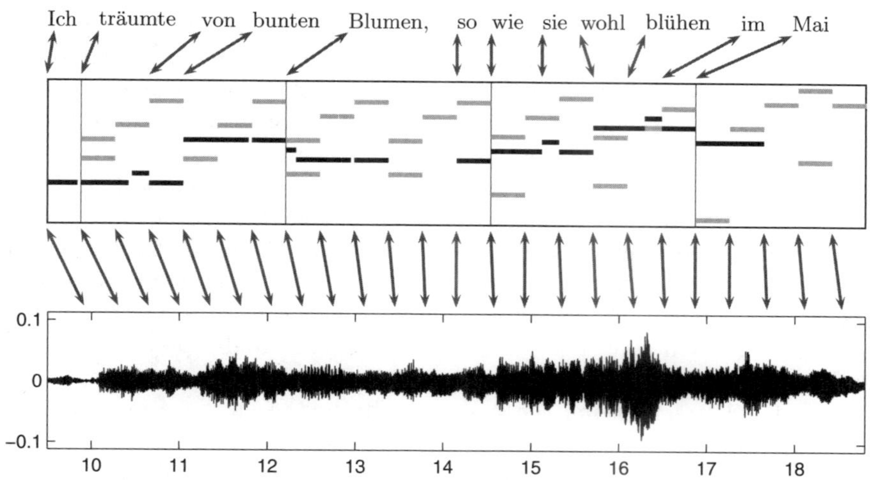

Fig. 1. Lyrics, MIDI version, and the waveform of an audio recording by Allen of measures 5 to 8 of Schubert's piano song D 911, No. 11 from the Lied cycle "Winterreise". The MIDI version is shown in piano-roll, where the black bars encode the vocal and the gray bars the piano track. The generated time alignments are indicated by the two-headed arrows.

the lyrics. However, in the music domain, the retrieval results are most naturally presented by acoustically playing back parts of an actual *audio recording* that contain the query terms, while a *musical score* may be the most appropriate form for visually displaying the query results. Such applications for *multimodal* music retrieval and navigation rely on the availability of suitable annotations and time alignments for connecting or *linking* the different types of available information related to a particular piece of music. In the latter example, an alignment of the lyrics to time positions in a corresponding audio recording would constitute such linking information.

Making lyrics-based audio retrieval feasible for larger scale music collections, this paper presents techniques for automatic lyrics-audio synchronization, for text-based lyrics search, as well as for multimodal music access and data presentation. As our first contribution, in Sect. 2 we describe a method to automatically generate audio *annotations* by temporally aligning the lyrics of a piece of music to audio recordings of the same piece. To solve this task, we exploit the availability of music documents in different data formats that describe a given piece of music at various semantic levels. In particular, we assume the availability of a MIDI representation (a kind of mid-level representation in between audio and score as will be described in Sect. 2), which serves as a "connector" in the lyrics-audio synchronization process: first we align the lyrics to the MIDI representation and then align the MIDI to an actual audio recording. This idea is illustrated by Fig. 1, which shows the lyrics, a MIDI version, and the waveform of an audio recording for measures 5 to 8 of Schubert's piano song D 911, No. 11 from the Lied cycle "Winterreise". This piece, in the following simply referred to as Schubert example, will serve as running example throughout this paper. Fig. 1 also shows two time alignments (a lyrics-MIDI and a MIDI-audio alignment), which are indicated by the bidirectional arrows. The availability of such alignments allows for accessing the audio recording exactly at the positions where a particular lyrics' term is sung by the vocalist.

In Sect. 3, we present effective as well as efficient methods for *searching* music collections based on textual queries by using a combination of indexing techniques from text retrieval and prior knowledge on the particularities of music lyrics. For evaluating this query-by-lyrics scenario, we integrated the proposed retrieval algorithms in the existing SyncPlayer framework, as will be discussed in Sect. 4. The SyncPlayer is basically an enhanced audio player providing a plug-in interface for multidmodal presentation, browsing, and retrieval of music data, see [1]. For *presenting* the query results to the user, we implemented a SyncPlayer plug-in for synchronously displaying the lyrics along with the audio playback. Based on the lyrics-audio alignments, the user may directly navigate from the list of lyrics-based query results to the corresponding matching positions within the audio recordings. Finally, in Sect. 5, we give an example to illustrate the interplay of various multimodal navigation and visualization tools and give prospects on future work. References to related work are given in the respective sections.

2 Alignment of Lyrics and Music Audio

In this section, we present a procedure for automatically annotating audio recordings of a given song by its corresponding lyrics. To this end, we will exploit the existence of various music representations in different data formats conveying different types of information on a piece of music. Before describing the actual lyrics-audio alignment procedure, we briefly discuss the involved data types and give references to related work on music alignment.

We start with the symbolic *score format*, which contains explicit information on the notes such as musical onset time, pitch, duration, and further hints concerning dynamics and agogics. In contrast, the purely physical *audio format* encodes the waveform of an audio signal as used for CD recordings. In generally, it is very difficult or even infeasible to extract musical note parameters from a given waveform, in particular for complex polyphonic music. The *MIDI format* may be thought of as a hybrid of the last two data formats which explicitly represents content-based information such as note onsets and pitches but can also encode agogic and dynamic subtleties of some specific interpretation. Finally, the *lyrics* represent the textual information of a song or opera. For an example, we refer to our Schubert example shown in Fig. 1.

A key idea for automatically organizing and annotating large music collections is to exploit the availability of different music representations at various semantic levels. To this end, one needs *alignment* or *synchronization* algorithms that automatically link and interrelate the differently formatted information sets related to a single piece of music [2]. Here, *synchronization* is taken to mean a

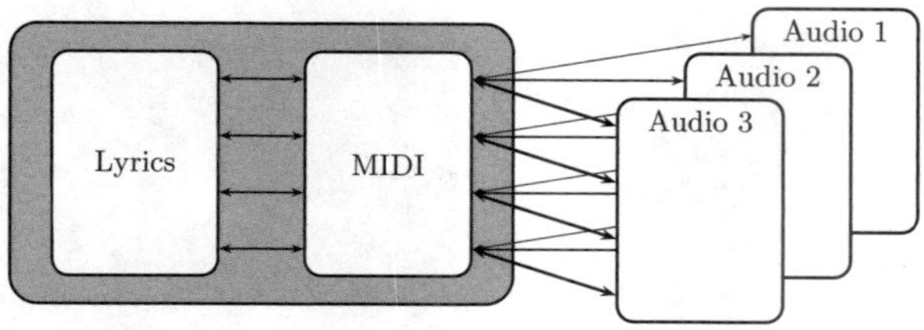

Fig. 2. Lyrics-audio alignment via MIDI-audio synchronization

procedure which, for a given position in one representation of a piece of music, determines the corresponding position within another representation, see Fig. 1. In the last few years, extensive research has been conducted on automatic music synchronization and great advances have been achieved in aligning score, MIDI, and audio representations of a given piece, see [2,3,4,5,6,7,8] and the references therein. In contrast, the automatic alignment of lyrics to a corresponding audio recording of the underlying song, also referred to as *lyrics-audio synchronization*, is a very hard problem. In particular, the automatic recognition of vocals within a song seems infeasible without any additional assumptions. To alleviate the problem, Wang et al. [9] present an approach to automatic lyrics-audio alignment, which strongly relies on musical a priori knowledge of the song's and the lyrics' structure. Furthermore, the authors aim at a relatively coarse per-line alignment roughly estimating the start and end times for each lyrics line within the audio.

In the following, we describe a simple but effective procedure for automatic lyrics-audio synchronization, which works for large classes of music and generates precise alignments on the word or even syllable level. In our approach, we assume the existence of a MIDI file, which represents the symbolic score information and contains the lyrics along with MIDI time stamps. Then, the lyrics can be located within a given audio recording by aligning the MIDI note parameters to the audio data. In other words, we solve the original problem by computing a lyrics-MIDI alignment and then by applying a MIDI-audio synchronization, which can be done very efficiently as described below. To legitimate this procedure, we note that attaching lyrics to MIDI data has to be done only *once* independent of a particular interpretation or instrumentation. At the end of this section, we describe how this can be done using a semi-automatic procedure. Such an enriched MIDI can then be used for lyrics-audio alignment for *all* available audio recordings of the respective piece, see Fig. 2. This situation applies to a wide range of pieces from Western classical music, where one often has a few dozens of different CD recordings of an opera or a song.

In the first step of our algorithm for MIDI-audio synchronization, we transform the MIDI as well as the audio data into a common mid-level representation, which allows for comparing and relating music data in various realizations and formats. In particular, we use chroma-based features, where the *chroma*

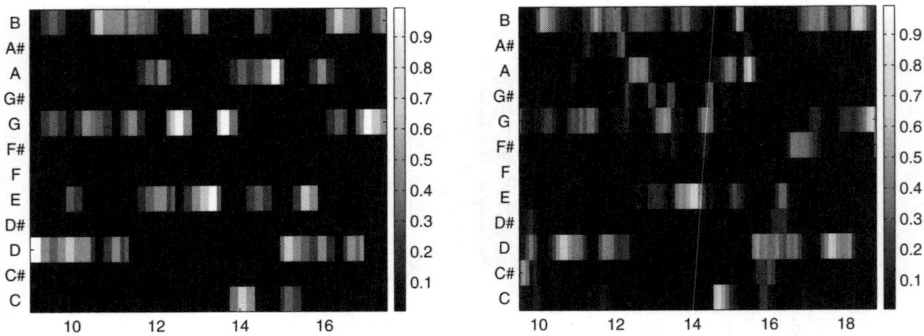

Fig. 3. Normalized chroma representations for the Schubert example (Fig. 1) derived from a MIDI representation (left) and an audio recording by Allen (right)

correspond to the twelve traditional pitch classes of the equal-tempered scale. These features account for the well-known phenomenon that human perception of pitch is periodic in the sense that two pitches are perceived as similar in "color" if they differ by an octave [10]. Assuming the equal-tempered scale, the chroma correspond to the set $\{C, C^\sharp, D, \ldots, B\}$ that consists of the twelve pitch spelling attributes as used in Western music notation. Note that in the equal-tempered scale, different pitch spellings such $C^\sharp$ and $D^\flat$ refer to the same chroma. Now, using the explicit MIDI pitch and timing information, one can directly transform a MIDI data stream into a sequence of normalized 12-dimensional chroma vectors, where each vector covers a specific time interval. Such a chroma representation is also referred to as *chromagram*. To compute a MIDI chromagram, as suggested in [4], each pitch is associated to a corresponding chroma unit vector. Then, for a fixed time interval, one adds up the chroma unit vectors of all active MIDI pitches and normalizes the resulting sum vector. In our implementation, we work with a resolution of 10 features per second, where each feature vector corresponds to a 200 ms time interval. Similarly, the audio data stream is transformed into a chromagram representation. This can be done by suitably binning spectral coefficients [10] or by employing a suitable pitch filter bank [11]. Fig. 3 shows a MIDI chromagram as well as an audio chromagram for our Schubert example. Note that a normalized 12-dimensional chroma vector expresses the relative distribution of the signal's local energy content within the 12 chroma bands. A chromagram shows a high degree of robustness to variations in dynamics, timbre, as well as articulation and strongly correlates to the harmonic progression of the underlying pieces.

In the second step, the MIDI and audio data streams can be directly compared on the chroma representation level. Denoting the feature sequence of the MIDI file by $V := (v_1, v_2, \ldots, v_N)$ and of the audio file by $W := (w_1, w_2, \ldots, w_M)$, one builds an $N \times M$ cross-similarity matrix by calculating a similarity value for each pair of features (v_n, w_m), $1 \leq n \leq N$, $1 \leq m \leq M$. An alignment path of maximum similarity is determined from this matrix via dynamic programming. Note that the time and memory complexity of this problem is proportional in the product $N \times M$, which becomes problematic for long pieces. To overcome this issue, the calculation is iteratively performed on multiple scales of temporal resolution going from coarse to fine. The alignment results of the coarser scale are used to constrain the calculation on the finer scales. For details we refer to [6]. The resulting optimal path encodes the MIDI-audio alignment as indicated by the bidirectional arrows in Fig. 1.

Extensive tests on a large corpus of Western music as described in [6] have shown that our synchronization algorithm yields accurate MIDI-audio alignments at a 100 ms resolution level (only in few cases there are some deviations of up to a second), which is sufficient for our lyrics-based audio retrieval and navigation application. As was mentioned above, we need enriched MIDI files that contain the lyrics along with MIDI time stamps. Since such MIDI files are rarely available, we semi-automatically annotated the lyrics for several popular songs as well as the 24 songs of Franz Schubert's Lied cycle Winterreise (op. 89, D. 911). To this end, we collected freely available lyrics (often already containing suitable syllable divisions) as well as corresponding MIDI files from the WWW. We then manually processed the lyrics by attaching the number of musical notes corresponding to the respective word or syllable. As it turns out, this process is not too laborious since in most cases each given word or syllable corresponds to exactly one note. Actually, this information was sufficient to automatically derive the desired MIDI time stamps for the lyrics simply by sequentially reading off the MIDI note onsets from the vocal track. In Sect. 4, we describe how the synchronization results are integrated into our SyncPlayer system.

3 Lyrics-Based Music Retrieval

We now describe our index-based method for lyrics-based retrieval. In the following, we assume that the lyrics for our collection of N audio recordings are stored in N text files $\mathcal{L} := (L_1, \ldots, L_N)$ where a file L_i consists of a sequence $(t_{i1}, \ldots, t_{in_i})$ of terms. Our indexing technique uses inverted files which are well known from classical text retrieval [12]. In lyrics-based music retrieval, users are likely to query catchy phrases as they frequently occur in the chorus or hook line of a song. Therefore, our basic indexing strategy presented next is designed to efficiently retrieve exact sequences of query terms. Later on, this basic strategy is extended to allow fault tolerant retrieval.

In a preprocessing step, for each term t an inverted file $H_{\mathcal{L}}(t)$ is constructed from our text files. $H_{\mathcal{L}}(t)$ contains all pairs (i, p) such that t occurs as p-th lyrics term within text file L_i, i.e., $t_{ip} = t$. Using inverted files, query processing may then be performed simply by using intersections of inverted files: assume a query is given as a sequence of words $q := (t_0, \ldots, t_k)$. Then, the set of *matches*

$$H_{\mathcal{L}}(q) := \bigcap_{j=0}^{k} H_{\mathcal{L}}(t_j) - j \tag{1}$$

can be easily shown to contain all pairs (i, p) such that the exact sequence of terms q occurs at position p within the i-th document. To make this basic matching procedure robust towards errors such as misspelled or wrong words, we introduce several methods for incorporating fault tolerance. To account for typing errors, we preprocess each query term t_j and determine the set T_j of all terms in our dictionary of inverted files (i.e., the set of all terms with an existing inverted file) having a small edit distance to t_j. Then, instead of only considering the exact spelling t_j by using $H_{\mathcal{L}}(t_j)$ in (1), we consider the union $\cup_{t \in T_j} H_{\mathcal{L}}(t)$ of occurrences of all terms which are close to t_j with respect to their edit distance. To account for term-level errors such as inserted or omitted words, we first preprocess all word positions occurring in (1) by a suitable quantization. This amounts to replacing each of the inverted files $H_{\mathcal{L}}(t)$ by a new set $\lfloor H_{\mathcal{L}}(t)/Q \rfloor \cdot Q$, where each entry (i,p) of $H_{\mathcal{L}}(t)$ is replaced by a quantized version $(i, \lfloor p/Q \rfloor \cdot Q)$ for a suitably chosen integer Q ($Q = 5$ was used in our tests). Furthermore, we replace $H_{\mathcal{L}}(t_j) - j$ of (1) by $H_{\mathcal{L}}(t_j) - \lfloor j/Q \rfloor \cdot Q$ prior to calculating the intersection. The latter yields a list $(m_1, \ldots, m_\ell)$ of matches which is subsequently ranked.

For each match m_i we obtain a ranking value r_i by combining classical ranking criteria (r_i^1, r_i^2 and r_i^3 in what follows) with criteria accounting for the peculiarities of the lyrics-based scenario (r_i^4 in what follows). As for the classical criteria, each match m_i is assigned a ranking value r_i^1 that essentially measures the deviation of the query terms occurring in m_i from their correct ordering as specified by q. To account for term-level mismatches, a ranking value r_i^2 counts the total number of query terms occurring in m_i. Note that r_i^2 may be obtained efficiently by using a dynamic programming technique [13] while simultaneously calculating the set of matches (1). A further ranking value r_i^3 accounts for the total edit distance of the query terms to the terms matched in m_i. Exploiting the lyrics-audio alignment corresponding to m_i, we obtain a ranking value r_i^4 by suitably weighting the temporal distance (within the audio recording) of the first and the last query term occurring in m_i. Finally, an overall ranking value for each match is obtained as $r_i := \sum_{j=1}^{4} w_j r_i^j$, where $w_1, \ldots, w_4$ denote some suitably chosen real-valued weighting factors. In future work, it will be interesting to include even more music-specific knowledge into the ranking procedure. As an example, one might exploit available information about the structure of the audio recording to give lyrics terms more weight if they occur in structurally salient passages such as in the chorus sections.

The proposed methods for indexing and retrieval can be realized by properly adapting well-known text retrieval techniques. To verify the efficiency of the proposed methods, we created an index for a test corpus of approximately 110.000 lyrics documents of mainly popular music crawled from the web. As described in [13], retrieval using the proposed inverted-file based approach can be performed very efficiently in both of the cases of exact and fault tolerant retrieval including the proposed ranking.

To conclude this section, we note that in the above we have tacitly assumed that the aligment information for linking the lyrics to the audio recordings is stored in some suitable secondary data structure that can be accessed efficiently. In our implementation, we use an additional file format to store this information which turns out to perform sufficiently well.

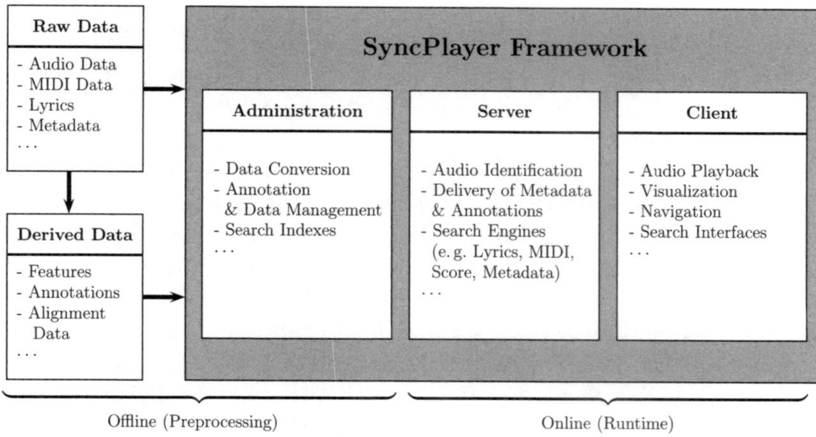

Fig. 4. Overview of the SyncPlayer framework

4 A Prototypical System for Lyrics-Based Audio Retrieval

In this section, we present a prototypical implementation of a system for lyrics-based audio retrieval. Our system has been realized based on the existing SyncPlayer framework, which basically consists of an advanced audio player offering a plug-in interface for integrating content-based MIR applications. In Sect. 4.1, we first briefly summarize the SyncPlayer framework and its components. Subsequently, Sect. 4.2 demonstrates how the methods for annotation and retrieval presented in Sect. 2 and Sect. 3 are integrated into this framework.

4.1 The SyncPlayer Framework

The SyncPlayer is a client-server based software framework that integrates various MIR-techniques such as music synchronization, content-based retrieval, and multimodal presentation of content-based audiovisual data [1]. The framework basically consists of three software components as depicted in Fig. 4: a server component, a client component, and a toolset for data administration.

The user operates the *client component*, which in its basic mode acts like a standard software audio player for `*.mp3` and `*.wav` files. Additional interfaces, e.g., for performing content-based queries as well as various visualization tools, are provided through plug-ins (see Fig. 5). A remote computer system runs the *server component*, which supplies the client with annotation data such as synchronization information and controls several query engines for different types of content-based audio retrieval. Several server-side *administration tools* are used for maintaining the databases and indexes underlying the SyncPlayer system.

The SyncPlayer framework offers two basic modes for accessing audio documents and corresponding content-based information. First, a user operating the client system may choose locally available audio recordings for playback. The client then extracts features from the audio recordings which are sent to the remote SyncPlayer server. The server subsequently attempts to *identify* the audio recording based on the submitted features. Upon success, the server searches its database for available annotations (such as lyrics or notes) which are then sent back to the client. The client system offers the user several visualization types for the available annotations. Two examples are a karaoke-like display for lyrics information and a piano-roll style display for note (MIDI-) information. Fig. 5 shows the SyncPlayer client (top left) along with the MultiVis plug-in for displaying lyrics synchronously to audio playback (bottom left).

The second method for accessing audio documents using the SyncPlayer is by means of appropriate query engines. In this scenario, the user operates a query plug-in offered by the client. Queries are submitted to the SyncPlayer server which, depending on the query type, schedules the queries to an appropriate query engine. A ranked list of retrieval results is returned to the client and displayed to the user. The user may then select particular query results for playback which are subsequently streamed from the server along with available annotation data. Note that the latter type of streaming is generally only allowed for authorized users. For more detailed information on the SyncPlayer framework, we refer to [1,14]. A demo version of the SyncPlayer is available for download at the SyncPlayer Homepage [15].

4.2 The Lyrics Search Plug-In

The methods for aligning lyrics to audio recordings presented in Sect. 2 as well as the procedures for creating the lyrics-based search index (see Sect. 3) have been integrated into the SyncPlayer administration tools. A query engine for lyrics-based search according to Sect. 3 has been implemented and connected to the SyncPlayer server.

On the client side, a query interface for textual queries has been developed. The interface is shown in the right part of Fig. 5. Query results returned by the server are displayed in the same window according to the formerly described ranking criterion. Fig. 5 shows a query and corresponding query results for a lyrics fragment taken from the song *Yellow Submarine* by the Beatles. The first two matches are displayed in the lower part of the interface. Note that due to our matching strategy, a match not only consists of a particular document ID but also of the precise position (in seconds) of the query terms within the corresponding audio recording. Upon selecting one of the matches in the result list, the audio recording is transfered to the SyncPlayer client (provided the audio recording is available for download) and playback starts directly at the matching position.

At the moment, lyrics search in the online version of the SyncPlayer framework works on our test corpus of about 100 audio recordings including the 24 piano songs as discussed above. A larger scale evaluation of the Lyrics Seeker including relevance-based measures for retrieval performance will be conducted within the Probado library project which is summarized in the next section.

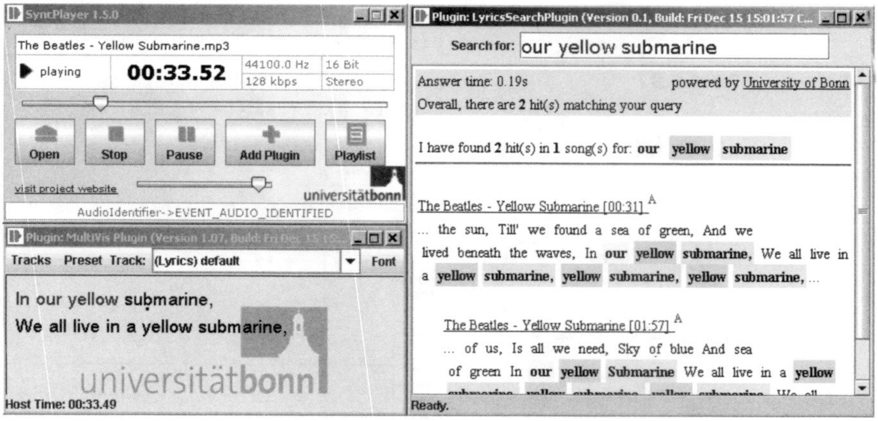

Fig. 5. SyncPlayer client (top left), MultiVis plug-in for displaying lyrics synchronously to audio playback (bottom left) and Lyrics Search plug-in for textual queries (right)

5 Conclusions and Future Work

In this paper, we have introduced a combination of methods facilitating lyrics-based audio retrieval in digital music collections. Based on automatically generated lyrics-audio alignments, the user is enabled to directly access audio material from the result list obtained by our query engine for text-based lyrics retrieval. As illustrated by Fig. 6, these functionalities can be combined with further browsing and visualization tools to allow for multimodal inter- and intra-document navigation in inhomogeneous and complex music libraries. Here, the SyncPlayer plug-in concept allows any number of plug-ins to be opened at the same time. For example, the lyrics search plug-in affords lyrics-based audio retrieval, while the lyrics visualization plug-in displays the text as in typical karaoke applications. At the same time the audio structure plug-in facilitates intra-document browsing on the basis of the repetitive structure of the respective audio recording, where the audio structure has been extracted in a fully automated process, see, e. g., [11]. Similar to our lyrics-based audio retrieval scenario, the availability of MIDI-audio alignments can be used to facilitate score-based audio access as well as synchronous score visualization as indicated by the piano-roll representation in Fig. 6. Further plug-ins may be used for displaying the waveform, a spectogram, a chromagram, or other derived audio representations.

There are many meaningful ways to add functionalities for content-based, multimodal music retrieval and navigation. For example, a functionality for synchronously displaying high quality scanned scores is currently being developed. This also requires an automated procedure to time align the pixels of scanned sheet music to corresponding time positions within an audio recording.

In future work, we will investigate novel ways for automatic lyrics to audio alignment based on scanned score material. Furthermore, we plan to integrate several other query engines into the SyncPlayer framework facilitating,

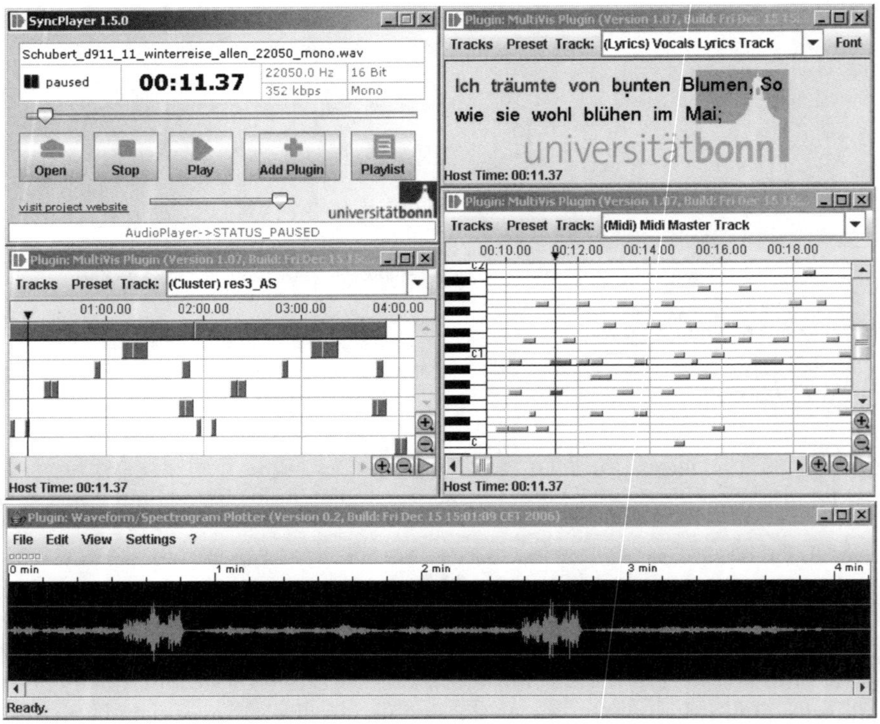

Fig. 6. SyncPlayer client with several of the available plug-ins for browsing and visualization illustrated for the Schubert example from Fig. 1. The figure shows the main audio player (upper left) as well as plug-ins for visualizing lyrics (upper right), audio structure (middle left), piano-roll (middle right), and the waveform signal (bottom).

e.g., audio matching [16] and score-based retrieval [13]. The methods and software components presented in this paper will be used within the German digital library initiative *Probado* [17] that aims at integrating (non-textual) multimedia documents into the workflow of existing digital libraries. In the Probado project, we are currently setting up a repository of digitized music documents consisting of audio recordings and scanned sheet music. In this context, the proposed methods will be used for the tasks of automatic annotation of music documents (lyrics-audio alignment, Sect. 2), content-based audio retrieval (lyrics search, Sect. 3), and content-based navigation in audio recordings (SyncPlayer and plug-ins, Sect. 4).

In conclusion, we hope that our advanced audio player opens new and unprecedented ways of music listening and experience, provides novel browsing and retrieval strategies, and constitutes a valuable tool for music education and music research. For the future, large-scale evaluations and systematic user studies have to be conducted to identify user needs and to convert the SyncPlayer into a system which is suitable for permanent application in existing digital libraries.

References

1. Kurth, F., Müller, M., Damm, D., Fremerey, C., Ribbrock, A., Clausen, M.: SyncPlayer — An Advanced System for Multimodal Music Access. In: ISMIR, London, GB (2005)
2. Arifi, V., Clausen, M., Kurth, F., Müller, M.: Automatic Synchronization of Musical Data: A Mathematical Approach. Computing in Musicology 13 (2004)
3. Dannenberg, R., Raphael, C.: Music score alignment and computer accompaniment. Special Issue, Commun. ACM 49(8), 39–43 (2006)
4. Hu, N., Dannenberg, R., Tzanetakis, G.: Polyphonic audio matching and alignment for music retrieval. In: Proc. IEEE WASPAA, New Paltz, NY (October 2003)
5. Müller, M., Kurth, F., Röder, T.: Towards an efficient algorithm for automatic score-to-audio synchronization. In: Proc. ISMIR, Barcelona, Spain (2004)
6. Müller, M., Mattes, H., Kurth, F.: An efficient multiscale approach to audio synchronization. In: Proc. ISMIR, Victoria, Canada, pp. 192–197 (2006)
7. Soulez, F., Rodet, X., Schwarz, D.: Improving polyphonic and poly-instrumental music to score alignment. In: Proc. ISMIR, Baltimore, USA (2003)
8. Turetsky, R.J., Ellis, D.P.: Force-Aligning MIDI Syntheses for Polyphonic Music Transcription Generation. In: Proc. ISMIR, Baltimore, USA (2003)
9. Wang, Y., Kan, M.Y., Nwe, T.L., Shenoy, A., Yin, J.: Lyrically: automatic synchronization of acoustic musical signals and textual lyrics. In: MULTIMEDIA '04: Proceedings of the 12th annual ACM international conference on Multimedia, pp. 212–219. ACM Press, New York (2004)
10. Bartsch, M.A., Wakefield, G.H.: Audio thumbnailing of popular music using chroma-based representations. IEEE Trans. on Multimedia 7(1), 96–104 (2005)
11. Müller, M., Kurth, F.: Towards structural analysis of audio recordings in the presence of musical variations. EURASIP Journal on Advances in Signal Processing, Article ID 89686 2007, 18 (2007)
12. Witten, I.H., Moffat, A., Bell, T.C.: Managing Gigabytes, 2nd edn. Van Nostrand Reinhold (1999)
13. Clausen, M., Kurth, F.: A Unified Approach to Content-Based and Fault Tolerant Music Recognition. IEEE Transactions on Multimedia 6(5) (2004)
14. Fremerey, C.: SyncPlayer – a Framework for Content-Based Music Navigation. Diploma Thesis, Dept. of Computer Science, University of Bonn (2006)
15. Multimedia Signal Processing Group Prof. Dr. Michael Clausen: SyncPlayer Homepage. Website (January 2007), `http://www-mmdb.iai.uni-bonn.de/projects/syncplayer/index.php`
16. Müller, M., Kurth, F., Clausen, M.: Audio matching via chroma-based statistical features. In: Proc. ISMIR, London, GB (2005)
17. Steenweg, T., Steffens, U.: Probado – non-textual digital libraries put into practice. In: ERCIM News Special Theme: European Digital Library, pp. 47–48 (July 2006)

Automatic Identification of Music Works Through Audio Matching

Riccardo Miotto and Nicola Orio

Department of Information Engineering, University of Padua, Italy
{miottori,orio}@dei.unipd.it

Abstract. The availability of large music repositories poses challenging research problems, which are also related to the identification of different performances of music scores. This paper presents a methodology for music identification based on hidden Markov models. In particular, a statistical model of the possible performances of a given score is built from the recording of a single performance. To this end, the audio recording undergoes a segmentation process, followed by the extraction of the most relevant features of each segment. The model is built associating a state for each segment and by modeling its emissions according to the computed features. The approach has been tested with a collection of orchestral music, showing good results in the identification and tagging of acoustic performances.

1 Introduction

Automatic identification of music works is gaining increasing interest because it can provide new tools for music accessing and distribution. Manual identification of music works is a difficult task that, ideally, should be carried out by trained users who remember by heart hundreds, or even thousands, of hours of music. Non expert users, instead, are usually able to recognize only well known works, and they may require the aid of an automatic tool for labeling the recordings of performances of unknown works. Automatic tools are particularly useful with instrumental music, when lyrics are not available for recognizing a particular work. Metadata about music works are needed also during the creation of a music digital library. For instance, theaters, concert halls, radio and television companies have usually hundreds of hours of almost unlabeled analog recordings, which witness the activities over the years of the institution and that need to be digitized and catalogued for preservation and dissemination. Moreover, music is extensively used as the background of commercials, television shows, and news stories. The automatic identification of music works employed as audio background may be useful for users, that can access for new interesting material.

A common approach to music identification is to extract, directly from a recording in digital format, its *audio fingerprint*, which is a unique set of features that allows for the identification of digital copies even in presence of noise, distortion, and compression. It can be seen as a content-based signature that summarizes an audio recording. Applications of audio fingerprinting include

L. Kovács, N. Fuhr, and C. Meghini (Eds.): ECDL 2007, LNCS 4675, pp. 124–135, 2007.

Web-based services that, given a sample of recording, provide the users with metadata about authors, performers, recording labels, of given unknown digital recordings. A comprehensive tutorial about audio fingerprinting techniques and applications can be found in [1]. Audio fingerprinting systems are designed to identify a particular performance of a given music work. This assumption is valid for many applications. For instance, users are interested to particular recordings of a given music work, e.g. the one of a renown group rather than of a garage band. Moreover, digital rights management systems have to deal also with the rights of the performers. For these reasons, the audio fingerprint is computed from recordings, and usually it is not able to generalize the features and to identify different performances of the same music work. On the other hand, the identification of a music work may be carried out also without linking the process to a particular performance. Music identification of broadcasted live performances may not benefit from the fingerprints of other performances, because most of the acoustic parameters may be different. In the case of classical music, the same works may have hundreds of different recordings, and it is not feasible to collect all of them in order to create a different fingerprint for each recording. To this end, a methodology that allows the user to recognize the different instances of a given music work, without requiring the prior acquisition of all the available recordings, could be a viable alternative to audio fingerprinting.

An alternative approach to music identification is *audio watermarking*. In this case, research on psychoacoustics is exploited in order to embed in a digital recording an arbitrary message, the watermark, without altering the human perception of the sound [2]. The message can provide metadata about the recording (such as title, author, performers), the copyright owner, and the user that purchases the digital item. The latter information can be useful to track the responsible of an illegal distribution of digital material. Similarly to fingerprints, audio watermarks should be robust to distortions, additional noise, A/D and D/A conversions, and compressions. On the other hand, watermarking techniques require that the message is embedded in the recording before its distribution and it is almost impossible to watermark the millions of digital recordings already available on the Internet. Moreover, watermarks can be made unreadable using audio processing techniques.

This paper reports a novel methodology for automatic identification of music works from the recording of a performance, yet independently from the particular performance. Unknown music works are identified through a collection of indexed audio recordings, ideally stored in a music digital library. The approach can be considered a generalization of audio fingerprinting, because the relevant features used for identification are not linked to a particular performance of a music work. Clearly the approach allows the user to identify the metadata related to a musical work and not to the particular performance used for the identification. The limitation of not identifying the performers can be balanced by the fact that only a single instance of a given work needs to be stored in the database. Moreover, as already mentioned, audio fingerprinting techniques are not able to identify live performances. The methodology reported in this paper extends previous work on music identification based on audio to score matching [3], where performances were modeled starting from the corresponding music scores. Also in this case, identification is based on hidden Markov models (HMMs). The application scenario is the automatic labeling of performances of tonal Western music through a match with pre-labeled recordings that are already part of an incremental music collection. Audio to audio matching has been proposed in [4,5] for classical music audio to audio matching and audio to audio alignment respectively, and in [6] for pop music.

2 Automatic Identification of Music Performances

The automatic identification of music performances is based on a *audio to audio* matching process, which goal is to retrieve all the audio recordings from a database or a digital library that, in some sense, represent the same musical content as the audio query. This is typically the case when the same piece of music is available in several interpretations and arrangements.

The basic idea of the proposed approach is that, even if two different performances of the same music work may dramatically differ in terms of acoustic features, it is nevertheless possible to generalize the music content of a recording in order to model the acoustic features of other, alternative, performances of the same music work. A recording can thus be used to statistically model other recordings, providing that they are all performed from the same score. It has to be noted that the proposed methodology is particularly suitable for tonal Western music, and other music genres where performers strictly adhere to a give music score. This may not be the case of jazz music, where musicians may change the melodic and rhythmic structure of a given song. To cope with this genre, other dimensions may be more suitable, for instance the harmonic structure. Applications to rock and pop music are under current development, generalizing the concept of music score with a representation similar to the lead-sheet model proposed in [7].

With the aim of creating a statistical model of the score directly from the analysis of a performance, the proposed methodology is based on a number of different steps, as depicted in Figure 1. In a first step, *segmentation* extracts audio subsequences that have a coherent acoustic content. Audio segments are likely to be correlated to stable parts in a music score, where there is no change in the number of different voices in a polyphony. Coherent segments of audio are analyzed through a second step, called *parameter extraction*, which aims at computing a set of acoustic parameters that are general enough to match different performances of the same music work. In a final step, *modeling*, a HMM is automatically built from segmentation and parametrization to model music production as a stochastic process. At matching time, an unknown recording of a performance is preprocessed in order to extract the features modeled by the HMMs. All the models are ranked according to the probability of having generated the acoustic features of the unknown performance.

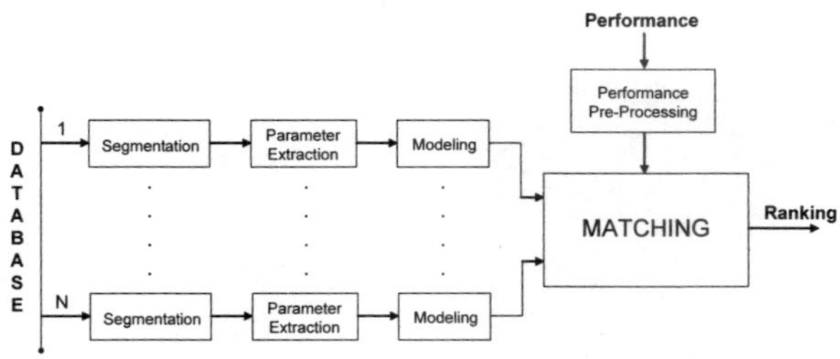

Fig. 1. Audio to audio matching process

2.1 Segmentation

The audio recording of a performance is a continuous flow of acoustic features, which depends on the characteristics of the music notes – pitch, amplitude, and timbre – that vary with time according to the music score and to the choices of the musicians. In order to be structured, the audio information has to undergo a *segmentation* process. According to [8], the word segmentation in the musical world can have two different meanings: one is related to musicology and is normally used in symbolic music processing, whereas the other one follows the signal processing point of view and it is used when dealing with acoustic signals. In the latter case, the aim of segmentation is to divide a musical signal into subsequences that are bounded by the presence of music events. An event, in this context, occurs whenever the current pattern of a musical piece is modified. Such modifications can be due to one or more notes being played, possibly by different instruments, to active notes being stopped, or to a change in pitch of one or more active notes. This approach to segmentation is motivated by the central role that pitch plays in music language. In fact the segmentation of the acoustic flow can be considered the process of highlighting audio excerpts with a stable pitch.

The representation of a complete performance can then be carried out through the concatenation of its segments. In the proposed approach, segmentation is carried out by computing the spectrogram of the signal, and then taking the correlation of different frames represented in the frequency domain. Frames were computed using windows of 2048 samples – approximately 46 msecs – with an hopsize of 1024 samples. High correlation is expected between frames where the same notes are playing, while a drop in correlation between two subsequent frames is related to a change in the active notes. Thus correlation has been used as a similarity measure between audio frames. Similarity between different parts of an audio recording can be represented as in the left part of Figure 2, that is with a symmetric matrix where high similarity values are represented by bright pixels, top-left and bottom-right pixel show the self-similarity for the first and last frame and bright square regions along the diagonal represent the potential similar regions.

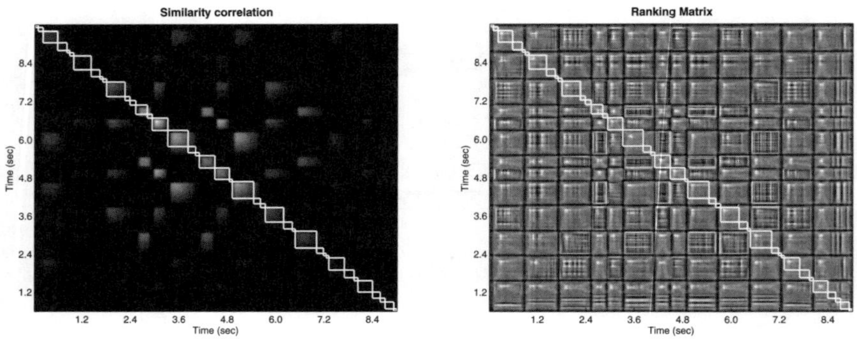

(a) (b)

Fig. 2. Similarity (a) and rank (b) matrices with highlighted segments

Segmentation has been carried out according to the methodology proposed in [9], which has been developed in the context of text segmentation. In particular, hierarchical clustering on the similarity matrix is exploited to segment a sequence of features – being either textual elements or acoustic parameters – in coherent passages. According to [9], segmentation effectiveness can be improved if clustering is performed on a ranking matrix, which is computed by replacing each value in the similarity matrix with its rank in a local region, where the local region size can vary according to the context. The rank parameter is defined as the number of neighbors with a lower similarity value and it is expressed as a ratio between the number of elements with a lower value and the number of elements examined to circumvent normalization problems along the matrix bounds. Figure 2 shows the two different matrixes depicting the segments along the main diagonal.

The clustering step computes the location of boundaries using Reynar's maximization algorithm [10], a method to find the segmentation that maximizes the inside density of the segments. A preliminary analysis of the segmentation step allowed us to set a threshold for the optimal termination of the hierarchical clustering. It is interesting to note that it is possible to tune the termination of hierarchical clustering, in order to obtain different levels of cluster granularity, for instance at note level or according to different sources or audio classes. In our experiments, audio samples have been normalized to obtain similar levels of segmentation granularity between the performances.

Figure 3 depicts the segments computed with the proposed techniques, superimposed to the energy trend of an audio recording, the same that have been used to represent matrixes of Figure 2. It is important to note that these figures depicts the results of segmentation applied to a quite simple audio excerpt – monophonic plain audio – and they are shown in order to have a clearer visual representation than polyphonic audio segmentation, which is the scope of our approach. In this case, it can be seen that the spectral based segmentation is highly correlated with the energy envelope.

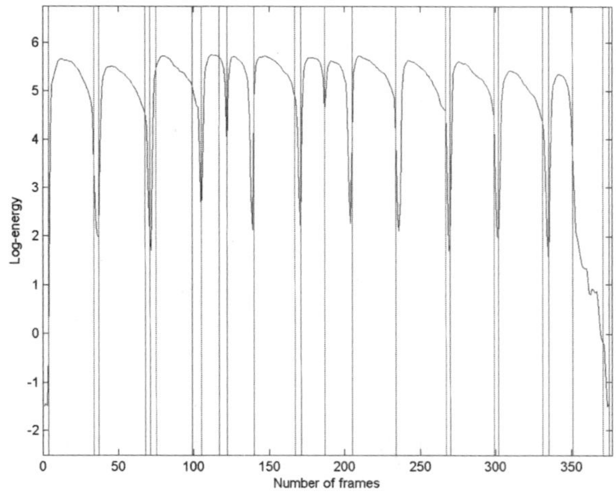

Fig. 3. Example of segmentation of a recording represented by its energy envelope

2.2 Parameter Extraction

In order to obtain a general representation of an acoustic performance, each segment needs to be described by a compact set of features that are automatically extracted. In line with the approach to segmentation, also parameter extraction is based on the idea that pitch information is the most relevant for a music identification task. Because pitch is related to the presence of peaks in the frequency representation of an audio frame, the parameter extraction step is based on the computation of local maxima in the Fourier transform of each segment, averaged over all the frames in the segment.

In general, the spectra of different real performances of the same music work may vary because of differences in performing styles, timbre, room acoustics, recording equipment, and audio post processing. Yet, for all the performances the positions of local maxima are likely to be related to the position along the frequency axis of fundamental frequency and the first harmonics of the notes that are played in each frame. Thus a reasonable assumption is that alternative performances will have at least similar local maxima in the frequency representations, that is the dominant pitches will be in close positions.

When comparing the local maxima of the frequency representation, it has to be considered that Fourier analysis is biased by the windowing of a signal, which depends on the type and of the length of the window. These effects are expected both on the reference performances and on the performance to be recognized. Moreover, small variances on the peaks positions are likely to appear between different performances of the same music work, because of imprecise tuning and different reference frequency. For these reasons, instead of selecting only the peaks in the Fourier transform, each audio segment has been described by a set of bin intervals, centered around the local maxima and with the size of

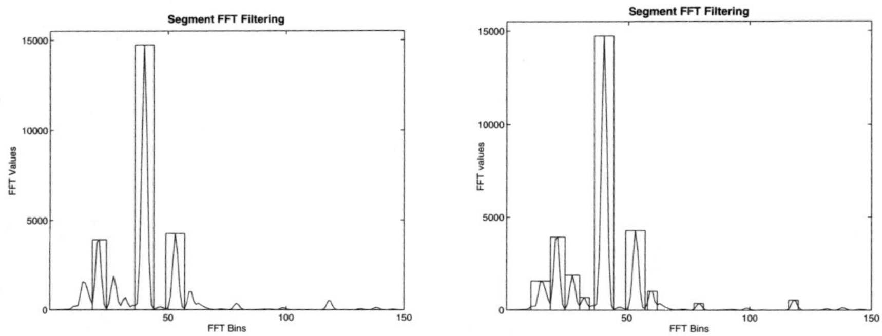

(a) (b)

Fig. 4. Parameters extraction considering 70% (a) and 95% (b) of the overall energy

a quarter tone. The number of intervals is computed automatically, by requiring that the sum of the energy components within the overall intervals is above a given threshold. Figure 4 depicts two possible sets of relevant intervals, depending on the percentage of the overall energy required: 70% for case (a) and 95% for case (b). It can be noted that a small threshold may exclude some of the peaks, which are thus not used as content descriptors.

2.3 Modeling

Each music work is modeled by a hidden Markov model, which parameters are computed from an indexed performance. HMMs are stochastic finite-state automata, where transitions between states are ruled by probability functions. At each transition, the new state emits a random vector with a given probability density function. A HMM λ is completely defined by:

- a set of N states $Q = \{q_1, \ldots, q_N\}$, in which the initial and final states are identified;
- a probability distribution for state transitions, that is the probability to go from state q_i to state q_j;
- a probability distribution for observations, that is the probability to observe the features r when in state q_j.

Music works can be modeled with a HMM providing that: states are labeled with events in the audio recording, transitions model the temporal evolution of the audio recording, and observations are related to the audio features previously extracted that help distinguishing different events. The model is hidden because only the audio features can be observed and it is Markovian because transitions and observations are assumed to depend only on the actual state.

The number of states in the model is proportional to the number of segments in the performance. In particular, experiments have been carried out using n

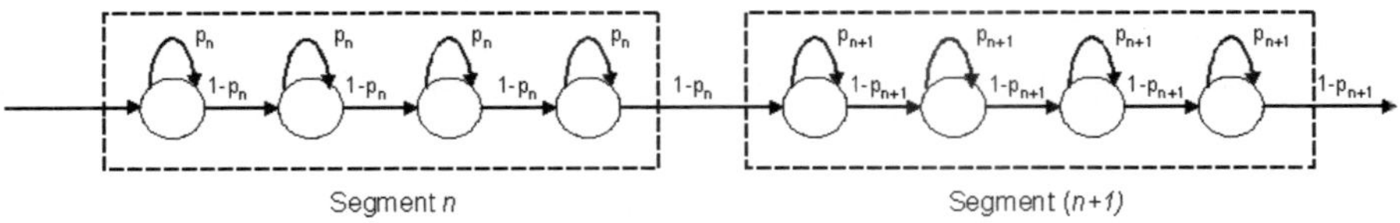

Fig. 5. Graphical representation of HMM corresponding to two general segments

states for each segment. Figure 5 shows the HMM topology corresponding to two segments of four states each. It is proposed that states can either perform a self-transition, which models segments duration, or forward-transitions, which model the change from a segment to the following one. All the states in a given segment have the same probability p of performing a self-transition. Given this limitation, the probability of having a given segment duration is a negative binomial:

$$P(d) = \binom{d-1}{n-1} p^{d-n}(1-p)^n$$

The values n and p can be computed on the basis of the expected duration of the segments and transition probabilities, information that can be extracted from the actual duration of each segment. Durations need to be statistically modeled because different performances of the same music work may remarkably differ in timing. Each state in the HMM is labeled to a given segment and, accordingly with the parameter extraction step, emits the probability that a relevant fraction of the overall energy is carried by the frequency intervals computed at the previous step.

The modeling approach is similar to the one presented in [3], and, in fact, one of the goals of this work was to create a common framework where an unknown performance could be recognized from either its score or an alternative performance.

2.4 Identification

Recognition, or identification, is probably the application of HMMs that is most often described in the literature. The identification problem may be stated as follows:

- given an unknown audio recording, described by a sequence of audio features $R = \{r(1), \cdots, r(T)\}$,
- given a set of competing models λ_i,
- find the model that more likely generates R.

The definition does not impose a particular evolution of models λ_i, that is the path across the N states that corresponds to the generation of R. This allows us to define a number of criteria for solving the identification problem, depending on different constraints applied to the evolutions of the states of λ_i. Three different approaches are proposed, whose names are derived from the notation proposed in a classical tutorial on HMMs [11].

Approach α. The most common approach to HMM-based identification, is to compute the probability that λ_i generates R regardless of the state sequence. This can be expressed by equation

$$\lambda_\alpha = argmax_i P(R|\lambda_i)$$

where the conditional probability is computed over all the possible state sequences of a model. The probability can be computed efficiently using the *forward probabilities*, also known as alpha probabilities. Even if approach α is the common practise for speech and gesture recognition, it may be argued that also paths that have no relationship with the actual performance give a positive contribution to the final probability. For instance, a possible path, which contributes to the overall computation of the forward probabilities, may consist in the first state of the HMM that continuously performs self-transitions. These considerations motivate the testing of two additional approaches.

Approaches δ and γ. Apart from recognition, another typical HMM problem is finding the most probable path across the states, given a model and a sequence of observations. A widely used algorithm is Viterbi decoding, which computes a path that is *globally* optimal according to equation

$$q^\delta = argmax_q P(q|R, \lambda_i)$$

Alternatively, a *locally* optimal path [12] can be computed, according to equation

$$\overline{q}(t) = argmax_q P(q(t)|R, \lambda_i)$$
$$q^\gamma = \{\overline{q}(1), \overline{q}(2), \ldots, \overline{q}(T)\}$$

Both global and local optimal paths can be used to carry out an identification task, for finding the model that more likely generates R while state evolution is constrained. This approach leads to equations

$$\lambda_\delta = argmax_i P(R|q^\delta, \lambda_i)$$
$$\lambda_\gamma = argmax_i P(R|q^\gamma, \lambda_i)$$

that show how the probability of R is conditioned both by the model λ_i and by the state sequence of the global or optimal paths.

2.5 Computational Complexity

All the presented approaches allow the computation of the probabilities using a dynamic programming approach. In particular, it is known in the literature that each of the approaches requires $\mathbf{O}(DTN^2)$ time, where D is the number of competing models, T is the duration of the audio sequence in analysis frames, and N is the average number of states of the competing HMMs. Considering that, as described in Section 2.3, each state may perform a maximum of two transitions, it can be shown that complexity becomes $\mathbf{O}(DTN)$. In order to increase efficiency, the length of the unknown sequence should be small, that is the method should give good results also with short audio excerpts.

An important parameter for computational complexity is the number of states N. A first approach to reduce N is to compute a coarse segmentations, which corresponds to a smaller number of group of states. On the other hand, a coarse segmentation may give poor results in terms of emission probabilities, because a single segment could represent parts of the performance with a low internal coherence. Another approach to reduce the computational complexity is to use a small number of states n for each segment, and model the durations with higher values of the self-transition probabilities p. As previously mentioned, in our experiments we found that setting $n = 4$ for each segment gave a good compromise.

3 Experimental Evaluation

The methodology has been evaluated with real acoustic data from original recordings taken from the personal collection of the authors. Tonal Western music repertoire has been used as a test-bed because it is a common practice that musicians interpret a music work without altering pitch information, which is the main feature used for identification.

The audio performances used to create the models were 100 incipits of orchestral works of well known composers of Baroque, Classical, and Romantic periods. All the incipits used for the modeling had a fixed length of 15 seconds. The audio files were all polyphonic recordings, with a sampling rate of 44.1 kHz, and they have been divided in frames of 2048 samples, applying a hamming window, with an overlap of 1024 samples. With these parameters, a new observation is computed every 23.2 milliseconds. The recordings to be recognized were 50 different performances of the same music works used to build the models. Also in this case they were an incipit of the music works, with a length of 10 seconds. The shorter lengths guaranteed that the performances to be recognized were shorter than the ones used to build the models, even in the case the two performances had a different tempo. The actual requirement is that the performance to be recognized is at least as long as the performance used for the recognition.

The 50 audio excerpts have been considered as unknown sequences to be identified, using the alternative approaches presented in Section 2.4. Table 1 reports the identification rates for the three approaches in terms of mean Average Precision, which is a well known measure in information retrieval and, for an identification task, it is equal to the mean of the reciprocal of the rank of the musical work to be identified.

With this experimental setup the average identification rate was quite different among the approaches, with α outperforming the two approaches that take into account also the global an local optimal paths. A more detailed analysis of the results highlighted that, in some cases, local differences between the reference and the unknown performances gave unreliable results in the alignment, affecting the overall identification rates.

Table 1. Identification rates for the different approaches, in terms of Average Precision

Approach	Mean Average Precision (%)
α	78.7
γ	39.3
δ	51.1

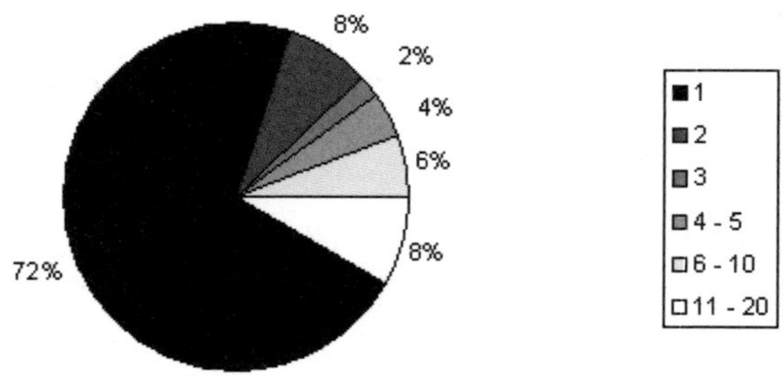

Fig. 6. Rank distributions of correct matches in the α identification test

For the particular case of α, more detailed results are reported in Figure 6 that shows the percentages at which the correct audio recording was ranked as the most similar one, and when it was ranked within the first two, three, five, ten and twenty positions. As it can be seen, 43 out of 50 queries (86%) returned correct match among top 3 models, and 36 among them (72%) were correctly identified. Moreover, only 4 queries (8%) returned the correct match after the first 10 positions. These encouraging results allow us to consider the methodology suitable for the development of a supervised system for music identification. A typical scenario could be the one of an user that, after running the identification routines, is provided with a list of potential matches, together with a link to the reference performances that he can listen to, in order to finally identify the unknown recording.

4 Conclusions

A methodology for automatic music identification based on HMMs has been proposed. Three approaches to compute the conditional probability of observing a performance given the model of an indexed audio recording have been tested on a collection of digital acoustic performances. Experimental results showed that, at least for tonal Western music, it is possible to achieve a good identification rate. In particular, the typical approach to recognition based on the used of forward probabilities, which has been defined as the α approach, achieved an identification rate of 72%. Alternative approaches, which take into account the alignment between the reference and the unknown performances, did not have comparable performances.

These results suggest that the approach can be successfully exploited for a retrieval task, where the user queries the system through an acoustic recording of a music work. The automatic identification of unknown recordings can be exploited as a tool for supervised manual labeling: the user is presented with a ranked list of candidate music works, from which he can choose. In this way, the task can be carried out also by non expert users, because they will be able to directly compare the recordings of the unknown and of the reference performances. Once that the unknown recording has been correctly recognized, it can be indexed and joint to the musical digital library, allowing us to increment the information stored inside it.

A prototype system has been developed, which allows a user, after recording or downloading an excerpt of a performance of classical music, to obtain after few seconds the relevant metadata of the music work.

References

1. Cano, P., Batlle, E., Kalker, T., Haitsma, J.: A review of audio fingerprinting. Journal of VLSI Signal Processing 41, 271–284 (2005)
2. Boney, L., Hamdy, A.T.K.: Digital watermarks for audio signals. IEEE Proceedings Multimedia, 473–480 (1996)
3. Orio, N.: Automatic recognition of audio recordings. In: Proceedings of the Italian Research Conference on Digital Library Management Systems, pp. 15–20 (2006)
4. Müller, M., Kurth, F., Clausen, M.: Audio matching via chroma-based statistical features. In: Proceedings of the International Conference of Music Information Retrieval, pp. 288–295 (2005)
5. Dixon, S., Widmer, G.: MATCH: a music alignment tool chest. In: Proceedings of the International Conference of Music Information Retrieval, pp. 492–497 (2005)
6. Hu, N., Dannenberg, R., Tzanetakis, G.: Polyphonic audio matching and alignment for music retrieval. In: Proceedings of the IEEE Workshop on Applications of Signal Processing to Audio and Acoustics, pp. 185–188. IEEE Computer Society Press, Los Alamitos (2003)
7. Seifert, F.: Semantic music recognition – audio identification beyond fingerprinting. In: Proceedings of the International Conference of Web Delivering of Music, pp. 118–125 (2004)
8. Aucouturier, J.: Segmentation of Music Signals and Applications to the Analysis of Musical Structure. Master Thesis, King's College, University of London, UK. (2001)
9. Choi, F.Y.: Advances in domain independent linear text segmentation. In: Proceedings of the Conference on North American chapter of the Association for Computational Linguistics, pp. 26–33 (2000)
10. Reynar, J.: Topic Segmentation: Algorithms and Applications. PhD Thesis, Computer and Information Science, University of Pennsylvania (1998)
11. Rabiner, L., Juang, B.: Fundamentals of Speech Recognition. Prentice-Hall, Englewood Cliffs, NJ (1993)
12. Raphael, C.: Automatic segmentation of acoustic musical signals using hidden markov models. IEEE Transactions on Pattern Analysis and Machine Intelligence 21(4), 360–370 (1999)

Roadmap for MultiLingual Information Access in the European Library

Maristella Agosti[1], Martin Braschler[2], Nicola Ferro[1], Carol Peters[3], and Sjoerd Siebinga[4]

[1] University of Padua, Italy
{maristella.agosti, nicola.ferro}@unipd.it
[2] Zurich University of Applied Sciences Winterthur, Switzerland
martin.braschler@zhwin.ch
[3] ISTI-CNR, Area di Ricerca – 56124 Pisa, Italy
carol.peters@isti.cnr.it
[4] The European Library, The Netherlands
Sjoerd.Siebinga@KB.nl

Abstract. The paper studies the problem of implementing MultiLingual Information Access (MLIA) functionality in The European Library (TEL). The issues that must be considered are described in detail and the results of a preliminary feasibility study are presented. The paper concludes by discussing the difficulties inherent in attempting to provide a realistic full-scale MLIA solution and proposes a roadmap aimed at determining whether this is in fact possible.

1 Introduction

This paper reports on a collaboration [1,4,5] conducted between DELOS[1], the European Network of Excellence on Digital Libraries funded by the EU Sixth Framework Programme, and The European Library (TEL)[2], a service fully funded by the participant national libraries members of the Conference of European National Librarians (CENL)[3], which aims at providing a co-operative framework for integrated access to the major collections of the European national libraries.

The ultimate goal of MultiLingual Information Access (MLIA) in TEL is to enable users of TEL to access and search the library in their own (or preferred) language, retrieve documents in other languages and have the results presented in an interpretable fashion (e.g. possibly with a summary of the contents in their chosen language). The problem is complex and many factors are involved. These include: the number of languages involved, the current heterogeneous setup of TEL, the lexical tools and resources needed.

[1] http://www.delos.info/
[2] http://www.theeuropeanlibrary.org/
[3] http://www.cenl.org/

L. Kovács, N. Fuhr, and C. Meghini (Eds.): ECDL 2007, LNCS 4675, pp. 136–147, 2007.

- *Number of Languages.* The number of different languages represented in TEL constitutes a major hurdle for MLIA, as ideally it should be possible to launch a query in any one of the national languages of the TEL collections and retrieve relevant material in any one of the collections. Possible approaches to the problem might be the use of multilingual ontologies, metadata and subject authority data, statistical translation resources, or some kind of interlingua.
- *Heterogeneous set-up.* A serious problem is represented by the heterogeneous set up of TEL, as there are severe limitations on how the existing infrastructure is able to process a cross-language query result.
- *Resources Needed.* Any cross-language strategy implies the acquisition and development of appropriate lexical tools and linguistic resources such as stemmers, morphologies, bilingual dictionaries, etc. As more languages are involved, not only does the number of resources increase, but the type of resources needed becomes more complex and more difficult to acquire.

The implementation of MLIA in TEL is thus an ambitious task and must be considered a medium/long-term goal, to be achieved through a series of intermediate steps. In this paper, we will try to determine the scope of implementation, attempt to identify the main obstacles, and devise a road-map which could help us to determine whether the full implementation of free-text MLIA in TEL is in fact practicable.

This document is organised as follows: section 2 describes the current TEL architecture; in section 3 we discuss the underlying motivations for our study and the main goals; Section 4 presents solutions studied so far; finally Section 5 proposes further experimentation and outlines a Roadmap for future investigations.

2 TEL Architecture Overview

Figure 1 shows the architecture of the TEL system. The TEL project aims at providing a "low barrier of entry" for the national libraries that should be able to join TEL with only minimal changes to their systems [7]. This ease of integration is achieved by extensively using the Search/Retrieve via URL (SRU)[4] protocol in order to search and retrieve documents from national libraries. In this way, the user client can be a simple browser, which exploits SRU as a means for uniformly accessing national libraries.

With this objective in mind, TEL is constituted by three components:

- a Web server: provides users with the TEL portal;
- a central index: harvests catalogue records from national libraries which support the Open Archives Initiative Protocol for Metadata Harvesting (OAI-PMH)[5] and provides integrated access to them via SRU;

[4] `http://www.loc.gov/standards/sru/`

[5] `http://www.openarchives.org/OAI/openarchivesprotocol.html`

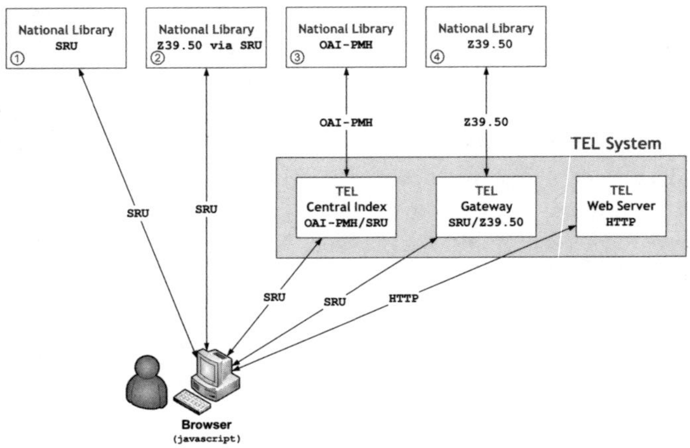

Fig. 1. Architecture of the TEL system

- a gateway between SRU and Z39.50: allows national libraries which support only Z39.50[6] to be accessible via SRU.

This light architecture allows TEL to support and integrate as follows:

1. a national library which natively uses SRU can be directly searched by the client;
2. a national library can have a local gateway between Z39.50 and SRU, so that the client can access it as if it were a native SRU library;
3. a national library which supports only Z39.50 can rely on the central SRU/Z39.50 gateway offered by the TEL system in order to be searched by clients;
4. a national library able to share metadata records by using OAI-PMH can be searched via the TEL central index, which harvests those records and makes them accessible to the client via SRU.

Figure 2 illustrates an example of interaction with the TEL system using the sequence diagram notation of Unified Modeling Language (UML)[7]. The example considers the case in which a user wants to query, simultaneously, a national library which exported its records to the TEL central index, a Z39.50 national library, and a native SRU national library.

- the user asks the browser to connect to the Uniform Resource Locator (URL) of the TEL portal;
- the browser connects to the TEL Web server, which downloads all the TEL portal on the client. From now on, there is no more interaction with the TEL Web server, but all the computation and interaction with the user is managed by the browser using Javascript.

---

[6] http://www.loc.gov/z3950/agency/

[7] http://www.omg.org/technology/documents/formal/uml.htm

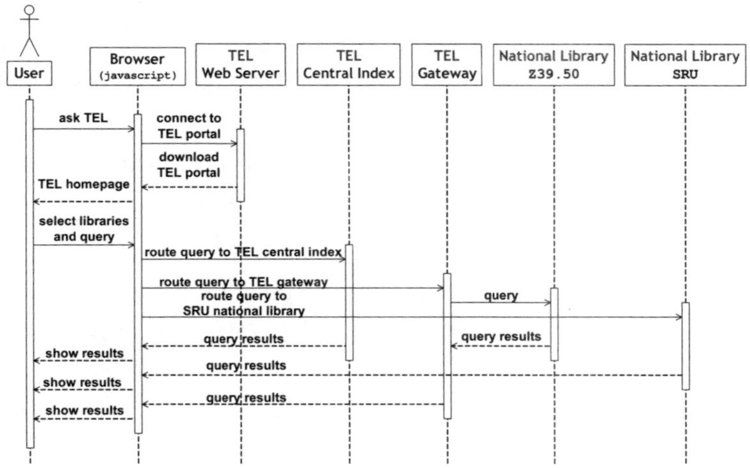

Fig. 2. Sequence diagram of the functioning TEL system

If the user decides to send a query to the national libraries mentioned above:

- the browser, using SRU, routes the user's query to, respectively: the TEL central index for the national library which exported its record via OAI-PMH, the TEL gateway for the Z39.50 national library, and directly to the native SRU national library, and waits for the results to come back;
- the browser receives the query results back from each system and displays them to the user.

3 Motivations and Goals

True multilingual access is more than just being able to search in more than one language. It means that the intended result is retrieved in each target collection regardless of language, character-encoding, metadata-schema, or normalisation rules. TEL is a heterogeneous federated search service for national libraries in Europe. This heterogeneous set-up poses a wide variety of problems for the implementation of MLIA functionality.

MLIA in TEL can be roughly divided into three areas: 1. Multilingual user interface; 2. Multilingual mapping/linking of controlled vocabulary; 3. Multilingual search on free-text.

1. The TEL Portal interface and help texts are currently available in the 20 languages of the full partners.[8] Localization is the responsibility of the individual libraries and translation files are updated with each new release.

[8] Languages of full-partners (20): Croatian, Czech, Danish, Dutch, English, Estonian, Finnish, French, German, Greek, Hungarian, Italian, Latvian, Lithuanian, Maltese, Polish, Portuguese, Serbian, Slovakian, Slovenian. Languages to be added in the near future (8): Bulgarian, Icelandic, Irish, Norwegian, Romanian, Russian (?), Spanish, Swedish.

2. Under the EDLProject[9] a study is currently underway to determine how existing controlled vocabulary initiatives can be integrated into the TEL service. This study builds on previous work done under the TEL-ME-MOR project[10]. The initiatives being examined include:

- Subject Headings: Multilingual ACcess to Subjects (MACS), Multilingual Subject Access to Catalogues (MSAC), CRISSCROSS, etc.
- Authority Files: Linking and Exploring Authority Files (LEAF), Virtual International Authority File (VIAF).
- Classification Schemata: feasibility of linking various translations of classification schemata like Universal Decimal Classification (UDC), Dewey Decimal Classification (DDC), and so on.

3. Studies in the MLIA domain have mostly focused on the remaining area: multilingual search on free-text. The main reason is that it is very difficult to use controlled vocabularies for MLIA unless a multilingual version is available covering all the languages in the collection and all documents have been classified using this. We thus decided to make free-text MLIA the main focus of this paper.

3.1 Issues to Be Considered

The implementation of free-text MLIA in TEL is an ambitious aim and success is not guaranteed. Although great advances have been made in recent years in the field of multilingual information access[11], it remains difficult to implement this functionality outside a controlled setting with unified full-text data-resources. In TEL, MLIA must be applied to hybrid resources that contain only snippets of free-text (often only keywords or ungrammatical sentences) in rigidly structured bibliographic files.

We list here the main questions that must be asked when considering free-text MLIA-implementation in TEL.

1. How can we implement MLIA with the TEL "low barrier of entry" approach.
2. How can we implement a multilingual component for multiple federated targets that is scalable both with respect to content and languages?
3. Is it actually possible to have a one to many and many to one cross-language access to 20-31 languages and still get good results?
4. Are the necessary language processing tools and resources available for all target languages?
5. Is it possible to use pivot-languages to reduce the amount of linguistic resources needed?
6. How should we deal with languages that have small collections and a relatively small number of native speakers?

[9] http://www.edlproject.eu

[10] http://www.telmemor.net/

[11] See, for example, the results published by the Cross Language Evaluation Forum: http://www.clef-campaign.org

7. Which metadata fields are relevant for free-text multilingual search: 1) title; 2) description; 3) keywords; 4) type; 5) abstract?
8. How do we solve the problem of limited context? The content of these fields is generally very short and often ungrammatical.
9. Can response times be sufficiently fast in an operational web environment?

3.2 TEL User and System Requirements

User interaction and empowerment have always been key principles of The European Library. The same should apply with respect to MLIA. MLIA functionality must be integrated in the portal in a non-obtrusive and intuitive manner. From a system design perspective the following key requirements for MLIA can be identified: 1. similar functionality on local and federated targets; 2. reduction of query complexity; 3. scalability; 4. speed and reliability; 5. full Unicode compliance; and finally 6. focus on open-source software and linguistic resources. These requirements are examined in more detail in the rest of this section.

1. TEL aims to provide a unified integrated access to the resources of European National Libraries. It is therefore important that any MLIA solutions proposed provide the user the same functionality regardless of the type of targets being queried, i.e. the local TEL central index or federated targets. Another important constraint is that due to the TEL 'low barrier of entry' principle, the implementation of MLIA must be on the portal-side, i.e. no data manipulation on the partner side.

2. The question of how to query tens - sometimes hundreds - of collections/targets with a large number of translated query terms, has no easy answer. Bag-of-words or concatenated OR queries are often very complex and could lead to serious retrieval degradation. In order to reduce query complexity and improve response time, the option of creating target-specific queries could be explored.

3. Any MLIA solution should be flexible and scalable, in order to deal with the explosive growth of The European Library both in the number of targets and languages. Currently, TEL offers content from 23 National Libraries in 242 collections. In 2007, the numbers are expected to rise to 32 National Libraries and over 350 collections. Other relevant future expansions will be the addition of much more full-text in addition to the bibliographic records and integration with non-library Cultural Heritage institutions, like museums and archives.

4. An important aspect of scalability is reliable and consistent retrieval performance. During the prototyping phase, performance benchmarking should be done against very large amounts of data to ensure reliability. Because TEL is a fully operational service, response time is an important consideration. From an operational viewpoint, what would be an acceptable upper threshold for MLIA transactions in TEL (5-10 seconds)? This is not a easy question when search engines, like Google, give subsecond results. If multilingual retrieval is too slow, maybe returning a monolingual result first and presenting multilingual results later via pop-up or URL-link, would be a good intermediate solution.

5. All aspects of the MLIA implementation should be fully Unicode compliant, in order to properly handle the profusion of special diacritics and character encodings found in Europe[12]. Even though most targets support Unicode, the problem of composed vs. decomposed Unicode characters still gives incomplete results. For example, ¨a and a" are usually displayed in the same way to the user but, when processed, give back different results. Special attention should also be paid, to how target-side normalisation affects retrieval. For example, some of the database search interfaces of our targets replace ž with a * wildcard. This leads to large numbers of unwanted results.

6. It is necessary to focus on open-source software and linguistic resources to support the community and reduce cost of the working system. The European Library is funded by the national libraries themselves and therefore does not have the capital to buy expensive licensing for translation software and linguistic resources.

4 Implementing MLIA Functionality: A Feasibility Study

The architecture and functioning of the TEL system as described in the previous sections pose some problems when planning to introduce MLIA.

TEL has no control on queries sent to the national libraries, since the client browser directly manages the interaction with national library systems via SRU. As a consequence, introducing MLIA functionality into the TEL system would have no effect on the national library systems. Thus, in order to achieve full MLIA functionality, not only the TEL system but also all the national library systems would have to be modified. This is an unviable option as it would require a very big effort and disregards the "low barrier of entry" guideline adopted when designing the TEL system.

A two-step solution is suggested and two complementary approaches are proposed: *isolated query translation* and *pseudo-translation* [1,4,5]. The first provides a basic cross-language search functionality for the entire TEL system; the second operates on the TEL central index.

Figure 3 shows the architecture of the TEL system with the two new components: the first performs the "isolated query translation", while the second is responsible for the "pseudo-translation".

Note that the "isolated query translation" component can be directly accessed by the client browser by using the SRU protocol and thus the interaction with this new component is explicit. On the other hand, the "pseudo-translation" component is not directly accessed by the client browser but represents an extension of the TEL central index, which would be enhanced with MLIA functionalities. These two approaches are outlined below. They have both been well tested: the former via a set of mock-up implementations; the latter via a comparative evaluation setup. A full description of these studies is given in the literature cited above.

[12] Under the TEL-ME-MOR project, an extensive survey was done on Unicode support and several recommendations were made to TEL partners.

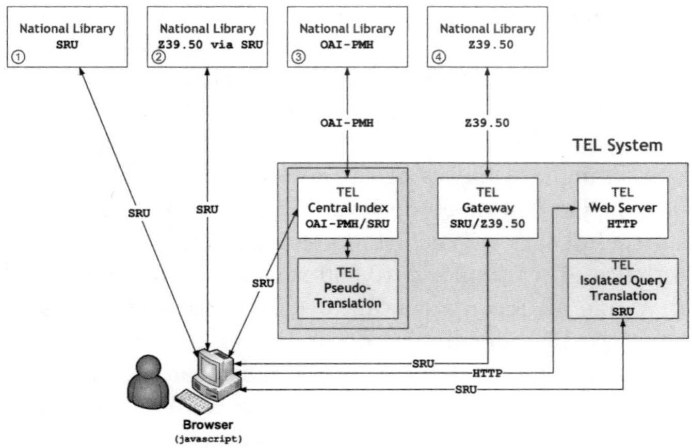

Fig. 3. Architecture of the TEL system with new MLIA functionalities

4.1 Isolated Query Translation

"Isolated query translation" can be considered as a sort of pre-processing step where the translation problem is treated as completely separate from the retrieval.

Before actually submitting the query, the user asks the browser to translate it. The browser sends the query via SRU to the "isolated query translation" component which translates it and can also apply query expansion techniques to reduce the problem of missing translations [3]. At this point, the user can interactively select the translation which best matches his needs or can change some query term to refine the translation. In this latter case, the translation process may be iterated. Once the desired translation of the query is obtained, the retrieval process is executed using both the translated query and the original one.

"Isolated query translation" requires some user interaction, because the users may need to choose among multiple translations of the same term in order to disambiguate them or may need to modify the original query if the translated query does not match their needs.

The main advantage of this solution is its ease of implementation and its compliance with the "low barrier of entry" approach of TEL. No changes to the national library systems are required and this new functionality can be transparently added to them, even if it is actually performed in the TEL system.

The main drawback is that, as the translation is separated from the retrieval process, relevant documents may be missing in the result set and thus the performance may be low. Moreover, huge linguistic resources, such as dictionaries, are needed since the vocabulary used in queries is expected to be very large; translation components are needed for each pair of source/destination language the system is going to support.

4.2 Pseudo-translation

The aim of the "pseudo-translation" approach was to tackle two problems that can arise when applying MLIA strategies developed for information retrieval on collections of lengthy full-text documents to library records.

In fact, a preliminary analysis of the records accessible in TEL originating from the Bibilothèque Nationale de France and the British Library confirmed that there is little full text in the TEL documents that can be used for retrieval. The characteristics of a sample of 10,000 random French and English records were studied. While all records contain a (short, basically one-sentence) title, only approximately 13% of all records in the French data sample contained additional data suited for retrieval. In the English sample, approximately 88% of records contain subject keywords that may prove to be suitable for retrieval. Other fields interesting for retrieval are only contained in a small number of records (11% contain an alternative title, 6% a listing of the table of contents, and 1% an abstract).

Having only a small number of content-bearing words to work with means that translation failures (out-of-vocabulary words) can be expected to have serious consequences. If several key words go untranslated, a record can easily "disappear", i.e. it becomes impossible to retrieve it.

This problem was addressed by applying methods originally developed for query expansion to the records, adding additional terms that may be used for subsequent retrieval. Using this strategy, the key concepts expressed in the limited text fields of the record were strengthened, and the probability that these concepts "survive" translation was increased.

The feasibility study simulated an environment in which as large a sample as possible of the bibliographic records - namely 151,700 - was enriched by expansion terms. Each record was run as a query against all other records of the sample, selecting those terms from expansion with highest weight that did not originally appear in the record. To simulate this process for analysis, any retrieval system that allows query expansion can potentially be used.

The resulting additional terms formed no sentences. This was deemed to be unproblematic for the following translation stage, as the nature of the existing text in the records does not also lend itself specifically to machine translation (short, often ungrammatical text). For this reason, any translation resource that covers an extensive vocabulary should be suitable . The same expansion idea can be applied to the query in an analogous way.

This second component of the feasibility study was evaluated carefully and the results were very encouraging. We tested the method by performing cross-language retrieval with German queries on the pseudo-translated English records.

When applying overlap analysis, 55% of queries analyzed showed evidence of good retrieval results, and 83% of queries showed evidence that they did not suffer significantly from the cross-language setup when compared to the monolingual baseline (note that for some of these queries there simply will be no relevant records in the collection!). The latter number is encouraging, being in line with what has been reported as state-of-the-art for Cross Language

Information Retrieval (CLIR) in the Cross-Language Evaluation Forum (CLEF) campaign on lengthy documents. A full description of the evaluation is given in [4]. Please note, however, that the numbers have to be treated with care, owing to the limitations described above. This approach should actually benefit in terms of effectiveness when scaling up to larger collections, which would occur when implementing the approach in the actual TEL system.

Combining Both Approaches. It is important to note that these two approaches can be implemented in conjunction in order to improve the MLIA functionality offered to TEL users. The implementation is facilitated as they share common components at the architectural level. For example, the translation engine or the translation resources, whether machine translation, machine readable dictionaries, or a combination of methods, can be shared by both approaches in order to reduce the development effort.

5 Towards Full MLIA

Although the results of the feasibility study were encouraging, they are a long way from solving the problem of implementing true MLIA functionality in TEL. Both solutions were proposed only in an language-to-language context (i.e. with queries in one language against target collections in a second language). This is very far from the one to many problem represented by TEL and mentioned in Section 3.

To a large extent, the isolated query translation approach may be the only feasible solution for cross-language querying on all the TEL collections with the existing TEL architecture, and it has the advantage that it offers the possibility for user interaction, giving the user the chance to check and modify the translation proposals offered. However, this approach also has significant limitations. In particular, it is impossible to perform additional query or preliminary results refinement on the basis of the contents of the target collections as these are held by national libraries and are not available for further processing in the TEL system. Furthermore, once we begin to talk about one-to-many querying with both collections and queries in more than 20 languages, problems clearly arise. The number of translation resources needed to cover all the possible language pairs would be enormous and, for many pairs of languages, probably non-existent. It seems clear that this solution is not viable to meet TEL's ambitious goal of enabling its users to search all target collections in their own language.

The pseudo-translation method appears to have more potential than the isolated query strategy but can only be applied to collections present in the TEL central index and lacks any kind of user interaction. In this method, the key concepts expressed in the limited text field of the bibliographic records are strengthened via an expansion process; the expanded record is then translated into the language of the query (German in the example cited) and monolingual retrieval is performed. These procedures (both document expansion and pseudo-translation) can be performed off-line with regular refreshings as the collections in the central index expand. However, again, once we begin to talk about queries and collections in a large number of languages, the problems are all too evident. The need to pseudo-translate each collection of expanded records into more than 20 languages would mean that the TEL archives and indexes would become enormous and, as already stated, the number of translation resources needed would be very large.

In our opinion, the only possibility for true multilingual retrieval when we are faced with such a large number of languages is to use an interlingua or pivot language of some sort. The obvious candidates are English or French, as these are the languages for which bilingual dictionaries and machine translation resources are most easily available. Although the adoption of an interlingua involves multiple translation steps and thus considerably increases translation errors, it becomes a feasible option when faced with a potentially large number of query and target languages. A number of studies have attempted to evaluate the performance loss that can be expected with a pivot language and strategies to reduce this have been proposed [2,6]. Therefore, our proposal for a future feasibility study is to experiment again with both approaches in a truly multilingual context, introducing an interlingua and employing machine translation and/or bilingual dictionary sources which translate between English and the other languages involved in the experiments, ideally the same languages as those listed in point 5 of the roadmap below.

With the pseudo-translation approach on the central index, the idea would be to pseudo-translate a large set of the expanded documents from their source language (whatever it is) to English. A set of queries in a number of languages will then also be translated into English. The results will be evaluated and compared with the results that would have been obtained from a monolingual search.

In order to test the isolated translation approach using an interlingua, two alternatives can be explored. The first option would be to convince national libraries to also provide an English translation of their main metadata fields, e.g. title, keywords, and abstract. In this way, it would be possible to test this method, translating queries formulated in a number of languages into English and then sending them to the local collections selected. The second option, perhaps preferable as it does not require action from the national libraries, would be to perform multiple translations: instead of doing a language-to-language translation, we should perform a query language-to-interlingua and an interlingua-to-target language translation. Again, in both cases, evaluation would be done by comparing the results obtained against a monolingual search of the same collections.

Roadmap. Here below we propose a Roadmap. The main purpose of the Roadmap is to investigate whether full-scale MLIA in TEL is actually possible. In order to determine this, we propose the following steps:

1. Set up a survey to determine the availability of linguistic resources for the 20 languages of TEL-full-partners, paying special attention to languages with relatively small number of native speakers (e.g. Estonian and Slovenian).
2. Simultaneously, identify an exhaustive list of TEL user requirements, with sets of sample queries and possible use-cases. The sample queries should also contain queries which should give problems with partner-side normalisation and Unicode character-encoding;

3. Perform a feasibility study on how the inter-lingua approach can be used to meet the TEL user requirements.
4. TEL must design a component-based prototype which allows for easy scalability with new language components and integrates well in a federated architecture.
5. Test and benchmark the prototype's retrieval performance with a realistic number of representative languages from TEL-partners, e.g. Germanic (English, German), Romance (French, Portuguese), Slavic (Polish, Czech), Greek, Baltic (Latvian) and Finno-Ugric (Finnish).
6. Determine if retrieval performance (speed and accuracy) of the prototype is reliable and scalable enough to take into production.

Acknowledgements

The work reported in this paper has been partially supported by the DELOS Network of Excellence on Digital Libraries, as part of the Information Society Technologies (IST) Program of the European Commission (Contract G038-507618).

References

1. Agosti, M., Braschler, M., Ferro, N.: A Study on how to Enhance TEL with Multilingual Information Access. DELOS Research Activities 2006. ISTI-CNR at Gruppo ALI, Pisa, Italy, pp. 115–116 (August 2006)
2. Ballestreros, L.A.: Cross-Language Retrieval via Transitive Translation. In: Advances in Information Retrieval: Recent Research from the CIIR, pp. 203–234. Kluwer Academic Publishers, Dordrecht (2000)
3. Ballesteros, L., Croft, W.B.: Phrasal Translation and Query Expansion Techniques for Cross-language Information Retrieval. In: Proc. 20th Annual International ACM SIGIR Conference on Research and Development in Information Retrieval (SIGIR 1997), pp. 84–91. ACM Press, New York (1997)
4. Braschler, M., Ferro, N.: Adding MultiLingual Information Access to The European Library TEL. In: DELOS Conference 2007 Working Notes. ISTI-CNR, Gruppo ALI, Pisa, Italy, pp. 39–49 (February 2007)
5. Braschler, M., Ferro, N., Verleyen, J.: Implementing MLIA in an existing DL system. In: Proc. International Workshop on New Directions in Multilingual Information Access (MLIA 2006) [last visited 2006, October 2], pp. 73–76 (2006), `http://ucdata.berkeley.edu/sigir2006-mlia.htm`
6. Lehtokangas, R., Airio, E.: Translation via a Pivot Language Challenges Direct translation in CLIR. In: Proc. SIGIR 2002, pp. 73–76. ACM Press, New York (2002)
7. van Veen, T., Oldroyd, B.: Search and Retrieval in The European Library. A New Approach. D-Lib Magazine 10(2) (February 2004)

MinervaDL: An Architecture for Information Retrieval and Filtering in Distributed Digital Libraries*

Christian Zimmer, Christos Tryfonopoulos, and Gerhard Weikum

Department for Databases and Information Systems
Max-Planck-Institute for Informatics, 66123 Saarbrücken, Germany
{czimmer, trifon, weikum}@mpi-inf.mpg.de

Abstract. We present MinervaDL, a digital library architecture that supports approximate information retrieval and filtering functionality under a single unifying framework. The architecture of MinervaDL is based on the peer-to-peer search engine Minerva, and is able to handle huge amounts of data provided by digital libraries in a distributed and self-organizing way. The two-tier architecture and the use of the distributed hash table as the routing substrate provides an infrastructure for creating large networks of digital libraries with minimal administration costs. We discuss the main components of this architecture, present the protocols that regulate node interactions, and experimentally evaluate our approach.

1 Introduction

In this paper we present MinervaDL, a digital library (DL) architecture that supports *approximate* information retrieval and filtering functionality in a single unifying framework. Our architecture is hierarchical like the ones in [24,12,21,26] and utilizes a Distributed Hash Table (DHT) to achieve scalability, fault-tolerance, and robustness in its routing layer. The MinervaDL architecture allows handling huge amounts of data provided by DLs in a distributed and self-organizing way, and provides an infrastructure for creating large networks of digital libraries with minimal administration costs.

There are two kinds of basic functionality that we expect our architecture to offer: *information retrieval* (also known as *one-time querying*) and *information filtering* (also known as *publish/subscribe* or *continuous querying* or *selective dissemination of information*). In an information retrieval (IR) scenario a user poses an one-time query and the system returns all resources matching the query (e.g., all currently available documents relevant to the query). In an information filtering (IF) scenario, a user submits a continuous query (or *subscription* or *profile*) and will later be notified from the system about certain events of interest that take place (i.e., about newly published documents relevant to the continuous query).

Our DL architecture is built upon the Minerva P2P search engine [3,2] and contains three main components: *super-peers*, *providers* and *consumers*. Providers are implemented by information sources (e.g., digital libraries) that want to expose their content to the rest of the MinervaDL network, while consumers are utilized by users to query for

* This work has been partly supported by the DELOS Network of Excellence and the EU Integrated Project AEOLUS.

L. Kovács, N. Fuhr, and C. Meghini (Eds.): ECDL 2007, LNCS 4675, pp. 148–160, 2007.

and subscribe to new content. Super-peers utilize the Chord DHT [19] to create a conceptually global, but physically distributed directory that manages aggregated statistical information about each provider's local knowledge in compact form. This distributed directory allows information consumers to collect statistics about information sources and rank them according to the probability to answer a specific information need. This reduces network costs and enhances scalability since only the most relevant information sources are queried. In MinervaDL, both publications and (one-time and continuous) queries are interpreted using the vector space model (VSM), but other appropriate data models and languages could also be used (e.g., LSI or language models).

As an example of an application scenario for MinervaDL let us consider John, a professor in computer science, that is interested in constraint programming and wants to follow the work of prominent researchers in the area. He regularly uses the digital library of his department and a handful of other digital libraries to search for new papers in the area. Even though searching for interesting papers this week turned up nothing, a search next week may turn up new information. Clearly, John would benefit from accessing a system that is able to not only provide a search functionality that integrates a big number of sources (e.g., organizational digital libraries or even libraries from big publishing houses), but also capture his long term information need (e.g., in the spirit of [24,16,28]). This system would be a valuable tool, beyond anything supported in current digital library systems, that would allow John to save time and effort. In our example scenario, the university John works in is comprised of three geographically distributed campuses (Literature, Sciences and Biology) and each campus has it own local digital library. In the context of MinervaDL, each campus would maintain its own super-peer, which provides an access point for the provider representing the campus' digital library, and the clients deployed by users such as John. Other super-peers may also be deployed by larger institutions, like research centers or content providers (e.g., CiteSeer, ACM, Springer, Elsevier), to provide access points for their users (students, faculty or employees) and make the contents of their digital libraries available in a timely way. MinervaDL, proposed in this paper, offers an infrastructure, based on concepts of P2P systems, for organizing the super-peers in scalable, efficient and self-organizing architecture. This architecture allows seamless integration of information sources, enhances fault-tolerance, and requires minimum administration costs.

Contrary to approaches like LibraRing [24] that focus on *exact* retrieval and filtering functionality (e.g., by disseminating documents or continuous queries in the network), in MinervaDL publications are processed locally and query or subscribe to only selected information sources that are most likely to satisfy the user's information demand. In this way, efficiency and scalability are enhanced by trading faster response times for some loss in recall, achieving *approximate* retrieval and filtering functionality. MinervaDL is the first approach to provide a comprehensive architecture and the related protocols to support approximate retrieval and filtering functionality in a digital library context. In the following sections, we position our paper with respect to related work, and discuss the MinervaDL architecture and an related application scenario. Subsequently, we present the protocols that utilize node interactions and experimentally show the efficiency of our approach both in terms of retrieval effectiveness and message efficiency. Finally, in the last section we give directions for future work.

2 Related Work

In this section, we survey related work in the context of information retrieval and filtering in P2P networks. Initially we focus on retrieval approaches in super-peer networks and structured overlay networks as these are the two areas conceptually closer to our approach. Subsequently we discuss work in the area of P2P IF and position our work with respect to the approaches presented here.

IR in super-peer networks. In [12] the authors study the problem of content-based retrieval in distributed digital libraries focusing on resource selection and document retrieval. They propose to use a two-level hierarchical P2P network where digital libraries are clients that cluster around super-peers that form an unstructured P2P network in the second level of the hierarchy. In a more recent work, [13] uses also an unstructured P2P architecture to organize the super-peers and uses the concept of neighborhood to devise a method for super-peer selection and ranking. In a similar fashion, [11] proposes an architecture for IR-based clustering of peers in semi-collaborating overlay networks.

ODISSEA [21] was one of the first attempts to utilize a DHT in a super-peer environment, by focusing on architectural issues of building a P2P search engine. There, a two-tier architecture is again adopted, and the lower tier nodes of the system are implemented on top of Pastry DHT. Later, OverCite [20] was proposed as a distributed alternative for the scientific literature digital library CiteSeer. This functionality was made possible by utilizing a DHT infrastructure to harness distributed resources (storage, computational power, etc.).

IR in structured networks. With the advent of DHTs as a remedy for the node location problem that existed in unstructured networks, a significant number of approaches tried to support VSM on top of structured overlays. Meteorograph [9] was one of the early papers to deal with the problem of similarity search over structured P2P overlays. pSearch [23] was the first P2P system that used LSI to reduce the feature vectors of the documents. In pSearch the authors propose the usage of a multi-dimensional CAN to efficiently distribute document indices in the P2P network. In [18] a similar approach is proposed, and Chord DHT is used to index the documents and route the queries to appropriate peers. While most of related papers utilize a DHT to route the queries to appropriate peers, Minerva [3] follows a different approach. In Minerva the structured overlay offers a conceptually global, but physically distributed directory, that maintains IR-style *statistics* and *quality of service information*. This information is exploited by querying peers, and most relevant ones according to resource selection algorithms [2] are contacted. The research presented in this paper extends the Minerva approach with information filtering functionality and adapts the protocols to a DL environment.

IF in P2P networks. New approaches that use a DHT as the routing infrastructure to build filtering functionality have lately been developed. Scribe [17] is a topic-based publish/subscribe system based on Pastry. Hermes [16] is similar to Scribe because it uses the same underlying DHT (Pastry) but it allows more expressive subscriptions by supporting the notion of an event type with attributes. pFilter [22] uses a hierarchical extension of CAN DHT to filter unstructured documents and relies on multi-cast trees to notify subscribers. VSM and LSI can be used to match documents to user queries. Finally, supporting prefix and suffix queries in string attributes is the focus of the

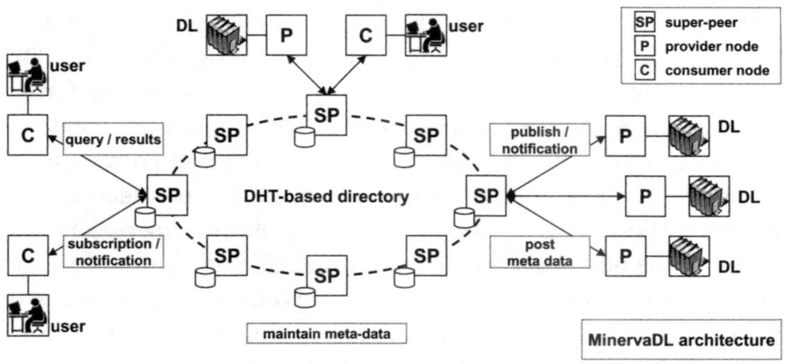

Fig. 1. A high level view of the MinervaDL architecture

DHT-Strings system [1], which utilizes a DHT-agnostic architecture to develop algorithms for efficient multi-dimensional event processing.

None of the works discussed above provides a comprehensive architecture and the related protocols to support both IR and IF in DLs using DHTs. P2P-DIET [10] and LibraRing where the first approaches that tried to support both functionalities in a single unifying framework. P2P-DIET utilizes an expressive query language based on IR concepts and is implemented as an *unstructured P2P network* with routing techniques based on shortest paths and minimum weight spanning trees. An extension of P2P-DIET [7] considers a similar problem for distributing RDF meta-data in an Edutella [15] fashion. LibraRing [24] was the first approach to provide protocols for the support of both IR and IF functionality in DLs using DHTs. In LibraRing, super-peers are organized in a Chord DHT and both (continuous) queries and documents are indexed by hashing words contained in them. This hashing scheme depends heavily on the data model and query language adopted, and the protocols have to be modified when the data model changes [24]. The DHT is used to make sure that queries meet the matching documents (in the IR scenario) or that published documents meet the indexed continuous queries (in the IF scenario). In this way the retrieval effectiveness of a centralized system is achieved, while a number of routing optimizations (such as value proxying, content based-multicasting, etc.) are used to enhance scalability.

Contrary to the LibraRing approach, in MinervaDL the Chord DHT is used to disseminate and store *statistics* about the document providers rather than the documents themselves. Avoiding per-document indexing granularity allows us to improve scalability by trading recall for lower message traffic. This approximate retrieval and filtering approach relaxes the assumption of potentially delivering notifications from every producer that holds in all the works mentioned above and amplifies scalability. Additionally, it allows us to easily support different data models and query languages, without modifications to the protocols, since matching is performed locally in each node.

3 MinervaDL Architecture

Figure 1 shows a high level view of the MinervaDL architecture, composed of three types of nodes: *super-peers*, *consumer nodes*, and *provider nodes*.

Super-peers run the DHT protocol and form a distributed directory that maintains statistics about providers' local knowledge in compact form. The Chord DHT is used to partition the term space such that each directory node is responsible for the statistics of a randomized subset of terms. Directory nodes are super-peers, nodes with more capabilities than consumer or provider nodes (e.g., more cpu power and bandwidth) that are responsible for serving information consumers and providers and act as their access point to the MinervaDL network. When the number of super-peers is small, each node can easily locate others in a single hop by maintaining a full routing table. When the super-peer network grows in size, the DHT provides a scalable means of locating other nodes. Super-peers can be deployed by large institutions like universities, research centers or content providers (e.g., CiteSeer, ACM, Springer, Elsevier) to provide access points for their users (students, faculty or employees) or digital libraries.

Consumer nodes are utilized by users to connect to the MinervaDL network, using a single super-peer as their *access point*. Utilizing a consumer node allows users to pose one-time queries, receive relevant resources, subscribe to resource publications with continuous queries and receive notifications about published resources (e.g., documents) that match their interests. Consumer nodes are responsible for selecting the best information sources to query (resp. monitor) with respect to a given one-time query (resp. continuous query). If consumer nodes are not online to receive notifications about documents matching their submitted continuous queries, these notifications are stored by their access point and are delivered upon reconnection.

Provider nodes are implemented by information sources that want to expose their content to the MinervaDL network. Provider nodes use a directory node as their access point and utilize it to distribute statistics about their local resources to the network. Providers answer one-time queries and store continuous queries submitted by consumers to match them against new documents they publish. More than one provider nodes may be used to expose the contents of large digital libraries, and also an integration layer can be used to unify different types of DLs.

4 The MinervaDL Protocols

In this section, we explain in detail the way consumers, providers and super-peers join and leave the network, publish new documents, submit one-time or continuous queries and receive answers and notifications for their submitted queries. We use functions $key()$, $ip(n)$ and $id(n)$ to denote the key, the IP address and the identifier of node n respectively. $key(n)$ is created the first time a consumer or provider joins the MinervaDL network, and is used to support dynamic IP addressing and $id(n)$ is produced by the Chord hash function and is used to identify a super-peer within the Chord ring.

4.1 Provider and Consumer Join

The *first time* a provider P wants to connect to the MinervaDL network, it has to follow the join protocol. P hast to find the IP address of a super-peer S using out-of-band means (e.g., via a secure web site that contains IP addresses for the super-peers that are currently online). P sends to S a NEWPROV($key(P), ip(P)$) message and S adds P in its *provider table* (PT), which is a hash table used for identifying the providers that use S as their *access point*. Here, $key(P)$ is used to index providers in PT, while each PT slot stores contact information about the provider, its status (connected/disconnected) and its stored notifications (see Section 4.7). Subsequently, S sends to P an acknowledgement message AckNewProv($id(S), ip(S)$). Once P has joined, it can use the connect/disconnect protocol described next to connect to and disconnect from the network. Consumers use a similar protocol to join the MinervaDL network.

4.2 Provider and Consumer Connect/Disconnect

When a provider P wants to connect to the network, it sends to its access point S a ConnectProv($key(P), ip(P), id(S)$) message. If $key(P)$ exists in PT of S, P is marked as connected. If $key(P)$ does not exist in PT, this means that S was not the access point of P the last time that P connected (Section 4.8 discusses this case). When a provider P wants to disconnect, it sends to its access point S a DisconnectProv($key(P), ip(P), id(S)$) message and S marks P as disconnected in its PT.

Consumers connect/disconnect from the network in a similar way, but S has also to make sure that a disconnecting consumer C will not miss notifications about resources of interest while not online. Thus, notifications for C are stored in the *consumer table* CT of S and wait to be delivered upon reconnection of C (see Section 4.7).

4.3 Maintaining the Directory

In MinervaDL, the super-peers utilize a Chord-like DHT [19] to build-up a distributed directory, while each provider P uses its access point to distribute per-term statistics about its local index to the directory using Post messages. At certain intervals (e.g., every k publications or time units) the provider has to update its statistics in the directory. We now describe the updating process done by a provider.

Let $T = t_1, t_2, \ldots, t_n$ denote the set of all terms included in the documents a provider P has published after the last directory update. For each term $t \in T$, the provider computes statistics: (i) the maximum term frequency of occurrence within P's document collection (tf_t^{max}); (ii) the number of documents in its document collection containing t (df_t); (iii) the size of P's document collection (cs). Using its IP address, P forwards the Post($key(P), ip(P), tf_t^{max}, df_t, cs, t$) message to the super-peer S that is P's access point to the directory. Next, S uses the Chord `lookup()` function to forward a modified Post message (including in addition S's IP address $ip(S)$ and identifier $id(S)$) to the super-peer node responsible for identifier $H(t)$ (i.e., this node is responsible for maintaining statistics for term t). This node S_t stores the received Post message in its local statistics table ST to be able to provide the term statistics to nodes requesting them.

4.4 Submitting an One-Time Query

In this section we show how to answer one-time vector space queries. Let us assume that a consumer C wants to submit a query q containing terms $t_1, t_2, \ldots, t_n$. The following steps take place. In step one, C sends to its access point S a SUBMITQ($key(C), ip(C)$, q) message. In the second step, for each term $t \in q$, S computes $H(t)$ to obtain the identifier of the super-peer responsible for storing statistics about term t. Then, it sends GETSTATS($key(C), ip(C), t$) message by using the Chord `lookup()` function.

In step three each super-peer S_t that receives a GETSTATS message, searches its local statistics table ST for term t to retrieve a list L of provider nodes storing documents containing the term t. Each element in list L is a tuple ($key(P), ip(P), tf_t^{max}, df_t, cs, t$) containing contact information about providers and statistics about terms contained in documents that these providers publish. Subsequentlyt, S_t creates a RETSTATS($id(S_t)$, $ip(S_t), L$) message and sends it to consumer C using $ip(C)$ included in the GETSTATS message. In this way, the consumer receives provider statistics for all query terms.

In step four, C uses the scoring function $sel(P, q)$ described in Section 5.1 to rank the providers with respect to q and identify the $top - k$ providers that hold documents satisfying q. Subsequently, C creates a GETRESULTS($ip(C), key(C), q$) message and forwards it, using the contact information associated with the statistics, to all provider nodes selected previously. Once a provider node P receives a GETRESULTS message containing a query q, it matches q against its local document collection to retrieve the documents matching q. The local results are ranked according to their relevance to the query to create a result list R. Subsequently, P creates a RETRESULTS($ip(P), R, q$) message and sends it to C. In this way, C collects the local result lists of all selected providers and uses them to compute a final result list that is then presented to the user. To merge the retrieved result lists, standard IR scoring functions (e.g., CORI [4] or GlOSS [8]) are used.

4.5 Subscribing with a Continuous Query

This section describes how to extend the protocols of Section 4.4 to provide information filtering functionality. To submit a continuous query $cq = \{t_1, t_2, \ldots, t_n\}$, the one-time query submission protocol needs to be *modified*. The first three steps are identical while step four is modified as follows.

C uses the scoring function $pred(P, cq)$ described in Section 5.2 to rank the providers with respect to cq and identify the $top-k$ providers that may publish documents matching *cq in the future*. These are the nodes that will store *cq* and C will receive notifications from these nodes only. This query indexing scheme makes provider selection a critical component of the filtering functionality. Notice that, in a filtering setting, resource selection techniques like $sel(P, cq)$ described in Section 5.1 and used for one-time querying, are not appropriate since we are not interested in the current document collection of the providers but rather in their future publishing behavior.

Once providers that will store *cq* have been determined, C creates an INDEXQUERY ($key(C), ip(C), id(S), ip(S), cq$) message and sends it to these providers using the IP addresses associated with the GETSTATS messages C received in the previous step. When a provider P receives an INDEXQUERY message, it stores *cq* in its local continuous query data structures to match it against future publications. P utilizes these data structures at publication time to find quickly all continuous queries that match a publication. This can be done using e.g., algorithms BestFitTrie [25] or SQI [27].

4.6 Publishing a New Document

Contrary to approaches such as [24] that distribute the documents or the index lists among the nodes to achieve exact retrieval and filtering functionality, publications in MinervaDL are kept locally at each provider. This lack of publication forwarding mechanism is a design decision that offers increased scalability in MinervaDL by trading recall. Thus, only monitored provider nodes (i.e., indexing a continuous query cq) can notify a consumer C, although other providers may also publish relevant documents. As already stated, this makes the scoring function $pred()$ a critical component.

Thus, when a provider node P wants to publish a new document d to the MinervaDL network, the document is only matched against P's local continuous query database to determine which continuous queries match d, and thus which consumers should be notified. Additionally, at certain intervals P creates POST messages with updated statistics and sends them to its access point S.

4.7 Notification Delivery

Assume a provider P that has to deliver a notification for a continuous query cq to consumer C. It creates a NOTIFICATION($ip(P), key(P), d, cq$) message, where d is the document matching cq, and sends it to C. If C is not online at that time, then P sends the message to S, where S is the access point of C, using $ip(S)$ associated with cq. S then is responsible for storing the message and delivering it to C upon reconnection. If S is also off-line then the message is sent to S', which is the access point of P, and S' utilizes the DHT to locate the $successor(id(S))$ (as defined in Chord [19]), by calling function `lookup()`. Answers to one-time queries are handled in a similar way.

4.8 Super-Peer Join/Leave

To join MinervaDL network, a super-peer S must find the IP address of another super-peer S' using out-of-band means. S creates a NEWSPEER($id(S), ip(S)$) message and sends it to S' which performs a lookup operation by calling `lookup(id(S))` to find $S_{succ} = successor(id(S))$, similarly to the Chord joining procedure. S' sends a ACK-NEWSPEER($id(S_{succ}), ip(S_{succ})$) message to S and S updates its successor to S_{succ}. S also contacts S_{succ} asking its predecessor and the data that should now be stored at S. S_{succ} updates its predecessor to S, and answers back with the contact information of its previous predecessor, S_{pred}, and all continuous queries and publications that were indexed under key k, with $id(S) \leq k < id(S_{pred})$. S makes S_{pred} its predecessor and populates its index structures with the new data that arrived. After that S populates its finger table entries by repeatedly performing lookup operations on the desired keys.

When a super-peer S wants to leave LibraRing network, it constructs a DISCONNECTSPEER($id(S), ip(S), id(S_{pred}), ip(S_{pred}), data$) message, where $data$ are all the continuous queries, published resources and stored notifications of off-line nodes that S was responsible for. Subsequently, S sends the message to its successor S_{succ} and notifies S_{pred} that its successor is now S_{succ}. Clients that used S as their access point connect to the network through another super-peer S'. Stored notifications can be retrieved through $successor(id(S))$.

5 Scoring Functions

Selecting the appropriate provider nodes to forward an one-time or a continuous query, requires a ranking function that will be used to determine the most appropriate sources for a given information demand. Although, both IR and IF protocols utilize the same meta-data stored in the distributed directory, the node ranking strategies differ significantly and have to consider varying objectives: in the case of IR, the scoring algorithm has to identify authorities with respect to a given query, i.e., nodes that have already made available a lot of relevant document *in the past*. These nodes should receive high scores, and thus be ranked high in the respective node ranking that will result. For this purpose, standard resource selection algorithms known from the IR literature can be utilized. Section 5.1 discusses our scoring function for one-time querying.

In contrast, in the IF case the scoring function has to determine the most appropriate provider nodes that given a continuous query cq, will publish documents matching cq *in the future*. In this setting, relying on existing resource selection algorithms similar to the ones utilized for one-time querying leads to low recall, as these algorithms are able to capture past publishing behavior, and cannot adapt to the dynamics of the filtering case. To better illustrate this consider the following example.

Assume two providers, where the first is specialized in soccer (i.e., in the past has published a lot of documents about soccer), although now it is rarely publishing new documents. The second provider is not specialized in soccer but currently it is publishing many documents about soccer. Now, a consumer subscribes for documents with the continuous query *soccer Euro 2008*. A ranking function based on resource selection algorithms would always choose the first provider. To get a higher ranking score, and thus get selected for indexing the query, the second provider has to specialize in soccer, a long procedure that is inapplicable in a filtering setting, which is by definition dynamic. The above example illustrates that our ranking formula should be able to predict the publishing behavior of providers by observing both their past and current behavior and projecting it to the future. To achieve this, we rely on statistical analysis tools to model a provider's publishing behavior. In Section 5.2 we discuss a novel technique that is based on time-series analysis of IR statistics.

5.1 Resource Selection

A number of resource selection methods (e.g., tf/idf based, CORI [5], GlOSS [8] and others) are available to identify authorities with respect to a query q. We use a tf/idf based approach to compute a score for provider P using the formula shown below:

$$sel(P,q) = \sum_{t \in q} \beta \cdot \log\left(df_{P,t}\right) + (1-\beta) \cdot \log\left(tf_{P,t}^{max}\right)$$

The parameter β can be chosen between 0 and 1 and is used to stress the importance of df or tf^{max} (experiments have shown that $\beta = 0.5$ is an appropriate value in most cases [2]). Using the scoring function presented above we can identify providers that store high-quality documents for query q and thus achieve high recall by querying only a few providers. To further improve recall we have developed overlap-aware node selection strategies [2] and techniques that exploit term correlations [14].

5.2 Publishing Behavior Prediction

Our prediction mechanism collects IR statistics from the distributed directory and treats them as time-series data to perform statistical analysis over them. Statistical analysis assumes that the data points taken over time have some sort of internal structure (e.g., trend etc.), and uses this observation to analyze older values and predict future ones [6]. There exist various approaches that differ in their assumptions about the internal structure of the time-series (e.g., whether it exhibits a trend or seasonality). *Moving average techniques* are a well-known group of time-series prediction techniques that assign equal weights to past observations (e.g., averaging is the simplest form of moving average techniques), and thus cannot cope with trends or seasonality. In our setting, it is reasonable to put more emphasis on a node's recent behavior and thus assign higher weights to recent observations. *Double exponential smoothing* assigns exponentially decreasing weights to past observations and assumes that the time-series data present some trend to predict future values. Since many queries are expected to be short-lived so that no seasonality will be observed in the IR statistics time-series, we do not consider seasonality in our predictions (and thus we do not use *triple exponential smoothing*).

The scoring function $pred(P, cq)$ returns for a score representing the probability that provider P will publish in the future documents relevant to the continuous query cq. In MinervaDL, we use double exponential smoothing to predict the following two statistical values. Initially, for all terms t in cq, we predict the value for $df_{P,t}$ (denoted as $df^*_{P,t}$), and use the difference (denoted as $\delta(df^*_{P,t})$) between $df^*_{P,t}$ and the last received value from the directory to calculate the score for P. $\delta(df^*_{P,t})$ reflects the number of relevant documents concerning t that P will publish in the next period. Secondly, we predict $\delta(cs^*)$ as the difference in the collection size of P reflecting the provider node's overall expected future publishing activity. In this way we model two aspects of the node's behavior; its ability to publish relevant documents in the future and its overall expected publishing activity. The consumer node that submits cq obtains the IR statistics that are needed as an input to our prediction mechanism by utilizing the distributed directory. The following formula is used to compute the prediction score for a provider P with respect to a continuous query cq:

$$pred(P, cq) = \sum_{t \in cq} \log\left(\delta(df^*_{P,t}) + \log\left(\delta(cs^*_P) + 1\right) + 1\right)$$

In the above formula, publication of relevant documents is accented compared to publishing rate. If a node publishes no documents at all, or, to be exact, the prediction of $\hat{cs}^*$, and thus the prediction of $\hat{df}^*$, is 0 then the $pred(P, q)$ value is also 0. The addition of 1 in the log formulas is used to yield positive predictions and to avoid $\log(0)$.

6 Experiments

In our experimental evaluation we assume a total number of 1000 providers and the same number of consumers, which are connected to a MinervaDL network using 400 super-peers as access points. At bootstrapping, each provider stores 300 documents and is mainly specialized in one out of ten categories (e.g., *Music*, *Sports*, *Arts* etc.) such

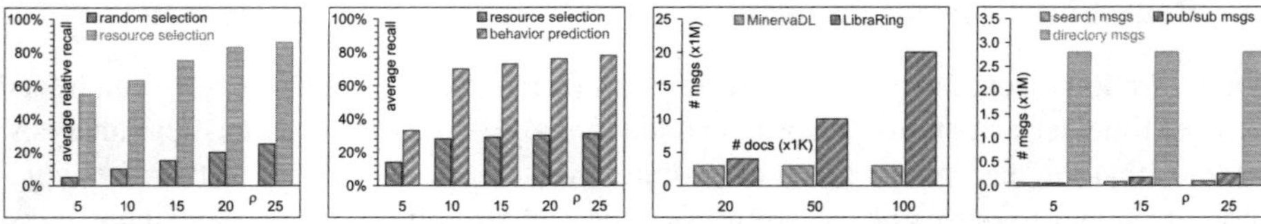

(a) IR scenario (b) IF scenario (c) approx. vs exact IF (d) message costs

Fig. 2. Retrieval effectiveness and message costs for MinervaDL

that we have 100 specialized information sources per category. We construct 30 queries[1] containing two, three or four terms that are strong representatives of a certain document category and are used both as one-time and continuous queries. Figure 2 shows the retrieval effectiveness of MinervaDL in terms of recall and its efficiency compared to exact matching approaches.

IR scenario. In figure 2(a), the experimental results of the information retrieval functionality of MinervaDL are presented. We assume that a consumer requests the 30 one-time queries and we are interested in the relative recall to a centralized search engine hosting a joint collection: the ratio of top-25 documents included in the merged P2P result. Thus, we apply the selection strategy as described before and increase the percentage ρ of providers in the system that are requested to answer the query. Figure 2(a) shows that the retrieval performance of MinervaDL manages to retrieve more than 90% of the top rated documents by asking only a fraction of the providers, whereas the baseline approach of random node selection reaches a much lower recall (around 20%).

IF scenario. To evaluate the IF functionality of MinervaDL, we assume that providers publish 30 documents within a specific time period (called publishing round) and we investigate the results after ten publishing rounds. We consider a scenario that models periods of inactivity in the publishing behavior and assume that consumers subscribe with 30 continuous queries and reposition them in each publishing round. In the experiments, we vary the percentage of monitored providers ρ and rank them using the two scoring functions approaches described in Section 5. As a retrieval measurement, we use recall as the ratio of total number of notifications received by the consumers to the total number of published documents matching a subscription. As illustrated in Figure 2(b), the use of behavior prediction improves recall over resource selection as it manages to model more accurately the publishing behavior of providers. In this way, our proposed scoring function manages to achieve a recall of around 80% by monitoring only 20% of the providers in the network. Notice that for resource selection, this number is only 35% which makes it an inapplicable solution to a filtering environment.

Message Costs Analysis. Figures 2(c) and 2(d) show different aspects of our message costs analysis. Here, we assume that in each round, the subscriptions are repositioned and the one-time queries are requested again (e.g., by another consumer). In this setting, we have three types of messages: directory, retrieval, and filtering messages. Figure 2(c)

[1] Example queries are *museum modern art*, or *space model*.

compares MinervaDL with an implementation of the exact matching protocols of LibraRing [24]. We consider the overall message costs as a function of the total number of documents published in the system for both approaches. As shown, message costs of MinervaDL are independent of the number of publications, whereas LibraRing, and all exact matching approaches, is *sensitive* to this parameter since documents have to be disseminated to the network. This imposes a high network cost especially for high publication rates expected by nodes exposing the contents of DLs.

Finally, in Figure 2(c) we can observe that directory messages dominate both retrieval and filtering messages. This is expected since matching and filtering mechanisms are by design local to accommodate high publication rates. This means that building both IR and IF functionality on top of the routing infrastructure imposes no extra cost on the architecture, compared to one that supports only one type of functionality. Since other types of information can also be stored in the directory in the same fashion (e.g., QoS statistics or load balancing information) building extra functionality will increase the added value of the directory maintenance, and come at almost no extra cost.

7 Outlook

We are currently implementing MinervaDL and plan to deploy it over a wide-area testbed such as PlanetLab. We are also focusing on the IF case and investigate the automatic adaptation of prediction parameters and the usage of different prediction techniques.

References

1. Aekaterinidis, I., Triantafillou, P.: Internet Scale String Attribute Publish/Subscribe Data networks. In: CIKM (2005)
2. Bender, M., Michel, S., Triantafillou, P., Weikum, G., Zimmer, C.: Improving Collection Selection with Overlap-Awareness. In: SIGIR (2005)
3. Bender, M., Michel, S., Triantafillou, P., Weikum, G., Zimmer, C.: Minerva: Collaborative P2P Search (Demo). In: VLDB (2005)
4. Callan, J.: Distributed Information Retrieval. Kluwer Academic Publishers, Dordrecht (2000)
5. Callan, J.P., Lu, Z., Croft, W.B.: Searching Distributed Collections with Inference Networks. In: SIGIR (1995)
6. Chatfield, C.: The Analysis of Time Series - An Introduction. CRC Press, Boca Raton (2004)
7. Chirita, P.-A., Idreos, S., Koubarakis, M., Nejdl, W.: Publish/Subscribe for RDF-based P2P Networks. In: ESWC (2004)
8. Gravano, L., Garcia-Molina, H., Tomasic, A.: GlOSS: Text-Source Discovery over the Internet. In: ACM TODS (1999)
9. Hsiao, H.-C., King, C.-T.: Similarity Discovery in Structured P2P Overlays. In: ICPP (2003)
10. Idreos, S., Koubarakis, M., Tryfonopoulos, C.: P2P-Diet: An Extensible P2P Service that unifies ad-hoc and Continuous Querying in Super-Peer Networks. In: SIGMOD (2004)
11. Klampanos, I., Jose, J.: An Architecture for Peer-to-Peer Information Retrieval. In: SIGIR (2003)
12. Lu, J., Callan, J.: Content-based Retrieval in Hybrid Peer-to-Peer Networks. In: CIKM (2003)
13. Lu, J., Callan, J.: Federated Search of Text-based Digital Libraries in Hierarchical Peer-to-Peer Networks. In: Losada, D.E., Fernández-Luna, J.M. (eds.) ECIR 2005. LNCS, vol. 3408, Springer, Heidelberg (2005)

14. Michel, S., Zimmer, C., et al.: Discovering and Exploiting Keyword and Attribute-value Co-occurrences to Improve P2P Routing Indices. In: CIKM (2006)
15. Nejdl, W., Wolf, B., Qu, C., Decker, S., Sintek, M., Naeve, A., Nilsson, M., Palmér, M., Risch, T.: Edutella: A P2P Networking Infrastructure based on RDF. In: WWW (2002)
16. Pietzuch, P., Bacon, J.: Hermes: A Distributed event-based Middleware Architecture. In: DEBS (2002)
17. Rowstron, A., Kermarrec, A.-M., Castro, M., Druschel, P.: Scribe: The Design of a Large-scale Event Notification Infrastructure. In: COST264 (2001)
18. Sahin, O., Emekci, F., Agrawal, D., Abbadi, A.: Content-based Similarity Search over Peer-to-Peer Systems. In: Ng, W.S., Ooi, B.-C., Ouksel, A.M., Sartori, C. (eds.) DBISP2P 2004. LNCS, vol. 3367, Springer, Heidelberg (2005)
19. Stoica, I., et al.: Chord: a Scalable Peer-to-Peer Lookup Protocol for Internet Applications. In: ACM TON (2003)
20. Stribling, J., Councill, I., Li, J., Kaashoek, M., Karger, D., Morris, R., Shenker, S.: Overcite: A Cooperative Digital Research Library. In: Castro, M., van Renesse, R. (eds.) IPTPS 2005. LNCS, vol. 3640, Springer, Heidelberg (2005)
21. Suel, T., et al.: Odissea: A Peer-to-Peer Architecture for Scalable Web Search and Information Retrieval. In: WebDB (2003)
22. Tang, C., Xu, Z.: pfilter: Global Information Filtering and Dissemination Using Structured Overlays. In: FTDCS (2003)
23. Tang, C., Xu, Z., Dwarkadas, S.: Peer-to-Peer Information Retrieval Using self-organizing Semantic Overlay Networks. In: SIGCOMM (2003)
24. Tryfonopoulos, C., Idreos, S., Koubarakis, M.: Libraring: An Architecture for Distributed Digital Libraries based on DHTs. In: Rauber, A., Christodoulakis, S., Tjoa, A.M. (eds.) ECDL 2005. LNCS, vol. 3652, Springer, Heidelberg (2005)
25. Tryfonopoulos, C., Koubarakis, M., Drougas, Y.: Filtering Algorithms for Information Retrieval Models with Named Attributes and Proximity Operators. In: SIGIR (2004)
26. Tryfonopoulos, C., Zimmer, C., Koubarakis, M., Weikum, G.: Architectural Alternatives for Information Filtering in Structured Overlay Networks. IEEE Internet Computing (2007)
27. Yan, T.W., Garcia-Molina, H.: The SIFT Information Dissemination System. In: ACM TODS (1999)
28. Yang, B., Jeh, G.: Retroactive Answering of Search Queries. In: WWW (2006)

A Grid-Based Infrastructure for Distributed Retrieval

Fabio Simeoni[1], Leonardo Candela[2], George Kakaletris[3], Mads Sibeko[4], Pasquale Pagano[2], Giorgos Papanikos[3], Paul Polydoras[3], Yannis Ioannidis[3], Dagfinn Aarvaag[4], and Fabio Crestani[1]

[1] Department of Computer and Information Sciences, University of Strathclyde, Glasgow, UK
{fabio.simeoni, f.crestani}@cis.strath.ac.uk
[2] Istituto di Scienza e Tecnologie dell'Informazione "Alessandro Faedo" – CNR, Pisa - Italy
{candela, pagano}@isti.cnr.it
[3] Department of Informatics and Telecommunications, University of Athens – Athens, Greece
{g.kakaletris, g.papanikos, p.polydoras, yannis}@di.uoa.gr
[4] Fast Search & Transfer ASA, Oslo, Norway
{mads.sibeko, dagfinn.aarvaag}@fast.no

Abstract. In large-scale distributed retrieval, challenges of latency, heterogeneity, and dynamicity emphasise the importance of infrastructural support in reducing the development costs of state-of-the-art solutions. We present a service-based infrastructure for distributed retrieval which blends middleware facilities and a design framework to 'lift' the resource sharing approach and the computational services of a European Grid platform into the domain of e-Science applications. In this paper, we give an overview of the DILIGENT *Search Framework* and illustrate its exploitation in the field of Earth Science.

1 Introduction

The problem of retrieving information which is widely disseminated and autonomously managed has a wide range of possible solutions. Variability is in terms of:

- *models*: from those in which queries and data are structured or semi-structured (data retrieval), to those in which they are mostly or entirely unstructured (document or content-based retrieval) [1];
- *approaches*: from those in which queries are distributed along with the data (distributed retrieval) [2,3], to those in which the data is centralised around the queries (content crawling and metadata harvesting) [4];
- *architectures*: from those in which queries emanate from clients and data is held at servers (client-server architectures), to those in which both may originate from any of a number of peers (peer-to-peer architectures) [5].

Across the spectrum, the core challenges remain those associated with the latencies of the underlying network and the heterogeneity of data, tools, means, and purposes which may be observed across communicating nodes. It is increasingly recognised that the scale of these challenges requires infrastructural support to reduce the development costs normally associated with state-of-the-art solutions [6]. It is equally recognised

L. Kovács, N. Fuhr, and C. Meghini (Eds.): ECDL 2007, LNCS 4675, pp. 161–173, 2007.

that, in most areas, infrastructural support remains piecemeal and revolves around open-source implementations of standard protocols and formats.

Issues of large scale distribution and heterogeneity are particularly acute in e-Science communities, where infrastructures are called upon to enable secure, cost-effective, and on-demand *resource sharing* [7]. This is the Grid vision [8], and current-generation infrastructures increasingly realise it under a service-based paradigm and for low-level computational resources, such as networks, storage, and processing cycles [9,10]. Building on these platforms, next-generation infrastructures set out to extend the vision into application domains, where the scope for resource sharing broadens to include, among others, retrieval services [11]. The impact is potentially non-trivial, for co-ordinated sharing of application resources may invalidate cost analyses of retrieval solutions which assume more conventional deployment scenarios: solutions with high adoption costs may be *outsourced* to the Grid infrastructure.

The DILIGENT project[1] is one of the first attempts to systematically lift into the Digital Library (DL) domain the facilities of a European Grid platform[2] (see also [12,13]). The expected outcome is a rich infrastructure of internetworked machines, *middleware services*, *domain services*, and *application services* in which resource sharing is an implication of *virtual digital libraries*, i.e. DLs that are: (*i*) assembled *declaratively* from community-provided datasets and application services; and (*ii*) deployed and re-deployed *on-demand* across machines by middleware services, according to availability, performance, and functional constraints. This is genuinely ambitious, for it reflects a model of application-level sharing which encompasses not only data resources but also domain and application services: like computing cycles, storage, and data before, application logic becomes a commodity within an infrastructure which abstracts over its physical location at any given time. The dynamic deployment of services is the key challenge of DILIGENT and its primary contribution to the Grid vision for application domains.

The DILIGENT infrastructure retains the service-orientation of the underlying platform and organises its services across three layers: the *Collective Layer* (CL), where middleware services define, deploy, secure, and otherwise support the operation of DLs; the *Digital Library Layer* (DLL), where domain services manage the data and orchestrate processes against it; and the *Application Specific Layer* (ASL), where application services mediate between users and the services of the CL and DLL layers. Within the DLL layer, in particular, the infrastructure offers novel opportunities for supporting application development: not only may its domain services be *invoked* to offer sophisticated functionality, they may also be designed so as to be *specialised and extended* into application services which are tailored to the bespoke needs of adopting communities. In this case, a service-oriented infrastructure becomes a *service-oriented framework*.

In this paper, we focus on a core part of the DILIGENT DLL layer in which infrastructural support is largely in terms of a framework for application services. In particular, we abstract away from DLL services dedicated to content, metadata, annotation, and workflow management, and concentrate instead on the DILIGENT *Search Framework*, i.e. the set of DILIGENT services for the distributed retrieval of both data and

[1] `http://www.diligentproject.org/`

[2] Enabling Grids for E-sciencE, `http://public.eu-egee.org/`

documents. We discuss the framework in Section 2 and we report on its exploitation within the domain of Earth Science, a challenging e-Science, in Section 3. Finally, we conclude in Section 4, where we outline directions for further work.

2 The DILIGENT Search Framework

Within a service-oriented framework, the notion of 'service' acquires structure and granularity to accommodate functional composition and abstraction, respectively (cf. Figure 1). Precisely, our service model distinguishes between: (*i*) *service classes*, i.e. flat groupings of services within the same functional area (e.g. the *Index* class), (*ii*) *services*, i.e. abstract instances of service classes (e.g. the *LookupService* in the Index class), and (*iii*) *web services*, i.e. entry-points to concrete implementations of abstract services *LookupFactoryService*). (e.g. the Service implementations are dynamically deployable, and doing so on one or more *Host Nodes* of the DILIGENT infrastructure (DHNs) yields *running instances* of the service (RIs).

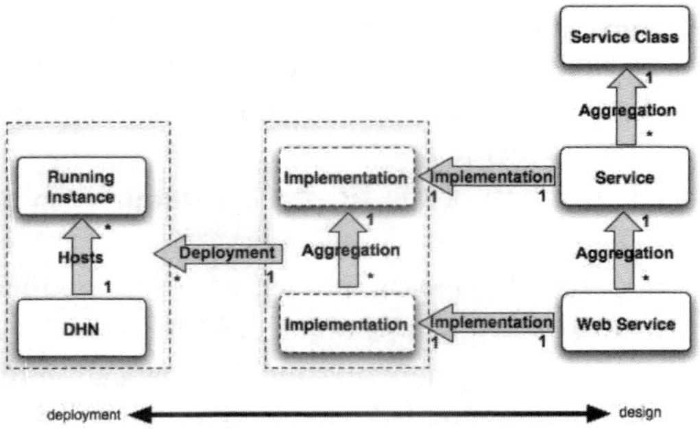

Fig. 1. Service Model

Against this model, the support offered by the framework is twofold. Firstly, it provides a set of *core services* which coordinate the functionality of application and domain services towards a wide range of distributed search processes; depending on the semantics of the orchestrated services, processes may fall at arbitrary points within the content-based vs. data-based spectrum and operate upon different forms of content and metadata (full-text or multimedia search, similarity search, structured and semi-structured search, etc.). Discussed in Section 2.1, the core services provide foundations to support the heterogeneity and dynamicity of data and processing requirements which can be observed within e-Science scenarios. Secondly, the Search framework offers design blueprints, partial implementations, and libraries for the development of application and domain services compliant with second-generation Web Service standards [14,15]. Two distinguished classes of such services, namely the index management services and the service for content description, selection and result fusion, are outlined in Sections 2.2 and 2.3, respectively.

2.1 The Core Services

The DILIGENT *Search Service* is a *Service Class* that groups all fundamental functional elements (i.e. Services) related to Information Retrieval (IR), but not directly bound to a more specific thematic area, such as Indexing, Distributed Information Retrieval (DIR), etc. The overall search management as well as several gluing elements fall within its scope. In contrast, we refer to the *Search Engine* as the full fledged set of elements that serve IR in DILIGENT. Finally, we refer to *Search Framework* when implying not only software but also protocols, rules and even guidelines for implementing and extending DILIGENT IR.

Search Overview. DILIGENT Search Engine, modular even in its internal structure, captures its requirements through a complex, yet straightforward, set of concepts and mechanisms, which are depicted in Figure 2.

The main idea behind the presented architecture is that the actual work of retrieving and processing the information and data contained in DILIGENT or other sources, is not an integral part of the Search Service, but can rather be off-loaded to entities that focus on different (D)IR and data processing aspects. Yet, the Search Service comes bundled with a set of such entities to enable the out-of-the-box use of the system.

The search task is captured by a set of steps which manage:

- Interaction with the ultimate consumer of the service (e.g. the User Interface) through a query language and various alternative interaction staging facilities;
- Consolidation of information regarding the status and availability of resources in need / reach;
- Preparation of the IR process through advanced facilities that potentially impose changes over the initial query;
- Operation planning, producing a near-optimal workflow of low-level search operations, in terms of resource utilisation;
- Execution of the workflow, i.e. invocation of the low-level search operations, (potentially off-loaded to external engines) and progress monitoring;

In this operation, the *Search Orchestrator*, which falls is the class of *Services* in the service model, is the entry point of the Search Engine, and acts as the manager of the IR procedure. Under its co-ordination, collaborating, yet independent, sets of service classes, such as the DIR, the Index and the Metadata Management ones, form the backbone of DILIGENT Search Engine.

The major hooks for extending functionality that renders the overall engine capable of capturing the requirements for custom processing, raised by its addressed communities, have been sketched in the above. These entail both the IR preparation steps, masked under the *Query Preprocessor* concept, as well as the run time processing performed by single components of the *Search Operators* set. Within the adopted architecture,

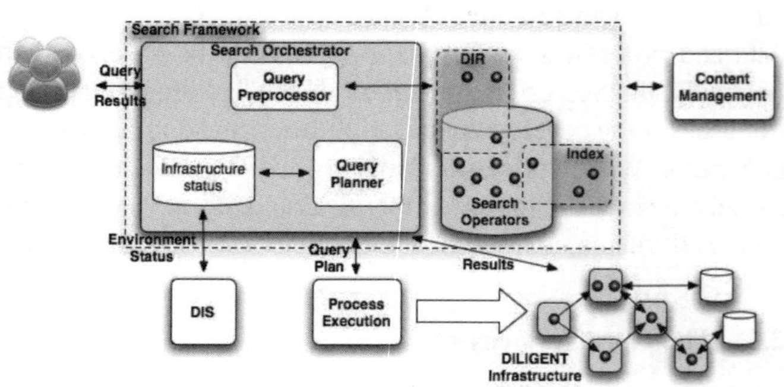

Fig. 2. The DILIGENT Search Framework

the quality and performance of the IR operations are, to a large degree, subject to the performance of particular elements plugged-in at these predefined placeholders.

In the following paragraphs we deepen on selected aspects of the DILIGENT Search Engine and its operation.

Serving a Request. The first step, even prior to searching, is the construction of a user query, i.e. an XML based, tree-like, abstract representation of the IR processing tasks involved in a search operation, that the engine must perform on behalf of the user. This query, formulated in a strict structure, is passed to the *Search Orchestrator* and has its validity thoroughly verified.

This procedure, i.e. validation, is an informed decision based on the availability of infrastructure resources. This information is gathered by the DIS, the DILIGENT CL service playing the role of global registry commonly used in both SOA architectures and Grid infrastructures to monitor and discover resources. The DIS has a two-fold role in the context of Search. The first is the discovery of the hosting environment the engine resides and the resources it can allocate to a task, e.g. Web Services, RIs, DHNs. This environment does not only drive the construction of query execution plans, but in conjunction with the dynamic deployment feature and the modular nature of service oriented approaches, it can imply the need to create new resources to utilise in future evaluations. The second key role of the DIS is to actually enable the modular architecture the Search framework provides. Available service instances define their semantics within the search context by publishing them to the DIS in a common way. These semantics are used by the *Query Planner* to produce execution plans.

The *Search Orchestrator* is constantly aware of the environment, through repetitive interactions with the DIS. Given a user query, the service supervises the individual steps that produce the query results. These steps include validation, preprocessing, such as injecting personalised information and pre-selection over the available sources, and linguistic processing. The enriched query and the environment information are passed to the *Query Planner*, in order for it to construct the execution plan.

The individual steps of this plan are performed by elements which are labelled as *Search Operators*. These operators are actually services that enable both information retrieval and data processing. Processing can refer to standard operations, e.g. sort, join, merge, but also to more complex ones, such as mathematical and logical expression evaluation, aggregation and even branching evaluation, all within the same workflow. Following the service-oriented approach, search operators build up a pool of dynamically selectable services, allowing unconstrained extensibility of the Search Service through the addition of new, custom, processing blocks. These very concepts equip the Search Engine with the capability to exploit elements such as DataFusion, Indices and Metadata handling services, as Search Operators themselves, even if they are distinct components. Search Operators follow the aforementioned Service Model, thus it is possible to have the domain-specific Services embedding multiple operation steps in a single Operator Service, leaving room for trade-off evaluation of distributed computational power versus highly optimised local transactions.

Planning and Optimising Execution. In order to produce the execution plan, the *Query Planner* matches abstract queries to concrete service instance invocations. This is accomplished using templates that specify the query sub-trees a service can satisfy.

The outcome of the procedure is a graph of service invocations, adopting the orchestration model of the Business Process Execution Language (BPEL). According to this, there is a global view of the participant service instances, under the central control of the execution engine (the DILIGENT Process Execution Service). This paradigm accommodates, among others, better performance, sophisticated control and fine grained error handling. The final plan is subsequently passed to the available execution engine which executes and monitors it so that the desired results are produced and passed back to the user.

Due to the dynamic nature of the underlying infrastructure, the query planner does not have inherent knowledge of available service instances, but instead receives this information externally from the *Search Orchestrator*. This favours both extensibility, by adding/removing service instances, and flexibility, by changing existing instances.

It is a fact that, due to the plethora of resources, a single user query can be served by more than one execution plan, with semantic equivalence yet significant diversion in terms of resource requirements. Under this observation, the Query Planner, and more specifically its optimisation component, is responsible not only to construct a semantically and operationally valid execution plan, but also to achieve minimal resource consumption while maintaining a certain quality of service level. Yet, this *optimisation* has to accomplished within a reasonable time limit, since searching for the best execution plan is generally a computationally intractable problem and involves enumerating and checking a potentially huge number of alternative options.

Query optimisation is managed with optimisation techniques borrowed from distributed databases [16,17]. It traverses through the solution space of alternative execution plans, estimates their costs and chooses the best candidate. This involves not only selecting the best set of services that can compute a user query, but also choosing the best hosting nodes of these service instances. Optimisation takes place in two-steps [18]. First, an abstract execution plan is produced and then site selection is performed.

A mathematical cost formula, tailored to the DILIGENT service oriented architecture, is employed. It takes into consideration factors like data source statistics, service operational complexity, intermediate results size, cost of messages among service invocations, communication initialization/termination overheads, intermediate result fragmentation, etc. Cost estimation is constantly enhanced by an active component that monitors the plan execution and refines both the formula and the stored statistics [19].

Moving Large DataSets. Throughout the execution of a search workflow, the need to transfer potentially large amounts of data between services is evident. Given the particular hosting environment of the Grid, enriched by the possibilities provided by the dynamic deployment features of DILIGENT, it is essential to utilise a common framework for data transferring.

The separation of concerns achieved by extracting relevant concepts out of the main functional logic of the services, allows them to be easily and uniformly reused for all search elements (i.e. Services). This lead to the DILIGENT ResultSet framework, i.e. the leveraging system data transfer mechanism be comprised of the *ResultSet* service and client elements. Its utilisation aims at hiding the complexities of underlying protocols and data locations. Yet, benefits rising from their exploitation are offered to consumer / producer services, which are able to take advantage of them with the minimum cost and complexity.

The encapsulated logic allows on-the-spot processing of data, eliminating unnecessary data movements, usually avoiding protocol stack and network engagement.

Furthermore, pipelining of execution is enabled through paged data transfer facilities, integrated in the framework. Based on this feature, the ResultSet can also act as a flow control mechanism, freeing component services of unnecessary resource consumption in a uniform manner.

2.2 Index Generation and Management

The role of the Index service in the Search framework is to facilitate fast and scalable information retrieval from a number heterogeneous information sources over the distributed and unstable Grid environment. This is achieved by generating and maintaining a number of different indices, deeply integrated in the DILIGENT infrastructure. In collaboration with the Planner and the other Search services, both low response time services and complex search operators are made available.

The main obstacle to be overcome by the design of the Index service, was to be able to ensure both stability and low response times on a highly distributed and heterogeneous system. Clearly replication, both concerning files and services, was needed. As an indices might grow very big, replicating the full index is potentially a slow and bandwidth heavy process. With this in mind, it was decided to represent indices by way of *delta files*[3], which can both easily be replicated through DILIGENT services and be used to keep service replications up to date. In order to manage the delta files and replication process the Index service has been designed as service oriented framework characterised by services playing three distinct roles: (*i*) *Manager service*, i.e. a service managing and representing one specific index in terms of delta files used to build it; (*ii*) *Updater service*, i.e. a service responsible for consuming content from a content source, transforming this into delta files, and updating the Manager service of a specific index. Any number of Updater instances may be connected to a single Manager instance, allowing for highly distributed feeding of an index; and (*iii*) *Lookup service*, i.e. a service that will use the delta files maintained by a Manager in order to build a replication of the index locally on a node. Any number of Lookup instances can be connected to one logical index representations (Manager instances), thereby providing replication of the Lookup Service and the actual physical index, adding both stability, fault tolerance and query performance.

In order to ensure that the Manager-Updater-Lookup framework is easily and uniformly implemented current and future Index service implementations, a library handling delta files storage, management and retrieval in addition to providing needed Web Service operations for the different roles was implemented. Using the library, the three roles can be implemented in a single Service, or as distinctly separate Services. In this manner, four different index distribution configurations can be implemented: (*i*) *All-in-one*, all roles are implemented through the same Service thus ensuring low latency between document feeding and searchability; (*ii*) *Lookup separated*, promoting any number of lookup instances thus supporting query intensive environments even if it might not be applicable for large indices or indices with a large number of information

[3] Delta files contain information on how to transform each version of the index to the next a.k.a. the difference between the versions.

sources; (*iii*) *Updater separated*, keeps the Updater separated from the rest thus being able to handle a more intense feeding process for large indices or indices with a number of information sources where a low query frequency is expected; (*iv*) *One service per role*, promotes one service per role on diverse nodes thus offering replication both at the updater and lookup level.

Three standard index implementations have been created in the current DILIGENT implementation supporting three different indexing scenarios with distinct data types. A *Full Text Index* providing the functionality of retrieving entries based on text queries against the full text contents of the entries. By manipulating the index profile it is possible to customize this index, e.g. specify the index structure, the query processing supported and the result sets including advanced linguistic processing. The full text index is implemented using the one-service-per-role distribution. A *Forward Index* supporting simple and fast key-value lookups. It is implemented using the one-service-per-role distribution. A *Geographical Index*, supporting geospatial and spatio-temporal search over a very large set of objects described by their location in a geographical system. In expectation of highly distributed content sources, intense feeding process, and high query frequencies, it was decided to use the one-service-per-role index distribution. This lead to the Geographical index being implemented by way of the following three Web Services: GeoIndexManagementService, GeoIndexUpdaterService and GeoIndexLookupService. The functionality of the latter Web Service in respect to Earth Science will be further described in Section 3.

2.3 DIR Services

Complementing search and indexing services, three service classes provide further support for content-based retrieval within the framework: namely, *Content Source Selection* (CSS), *Content Source Description* (CSD), and *Data Fusion* (DF). Collectively, CSD, CSS, and DF services perform the tasks which characterise content-based *Distributed Information Retrieval* [3], an active field of research which has had limited uptake in the practice of information services so far [20]. In more detail: (*i*) CSD services generate and maintain summary descriptions of content sources, such as partial indices, collection-level term statistics, or result traces from training or past queries; (*ii*) CSS services limit the routing of queries to the sources which appear to be the best targets for their execution, where 'goodness' criteria include the relevance of content, the sophistication of retrieval engines, and the monetary costs associated with query execution; and (*iii*) DF services derive a total order of the result sets produced by target sources with respect to different scoring functions and content statistics.

The framework sets out to support a wide range of DIR strategies. For example, a CSD service may base source descriptions on term statistics derived from full-text content indices, while another may do so using partial indices derived directly from the content through query-based sampling techniques [21]. Similarly, a DF service may rely on a round-robin algorithm to merge results, another may be biased by the output of a CSS service, and yet another may employ non-heuristic techniques and leverage the output of a CSD service to 'consistently' re-rank results with respect to global content statistics.

Though pairwise different, strategies of description, selection, and fusion share a common architecture which the framework attempts to capture within an extensible design. In it, services are stateful and the state of their RIs is comprised of source descriptions (CSD) or sets thereof (CSS, DF) which are generated, accessed, and updated through distinguished web services. In particular:

- *access services* expose the state of RIs to clients, or otherwise consume it on their behalf. CSS *selectors* and DF *mergers* consume sets of descriptions to select over content sources and merge results which emanate from them, respectively. CSD *descriptors* expose descriptions through fine-grained interfaces suitable for selective access, or through file-transfer facilities suitable for coarse-grained access. Selectors choose sources based on cut-off points within rankings of their descriptions, where cut-offs are either specified by the client or else are derived from upper bounds on the number of results to be retrieved, also indicated by clients; in the latter case, selectors return an estimate of the number of results to be retrieved from selected sources. To promote responsiveness and optimal resource consumption, mergers process streams of results, using facilities provided the ResultSet service. Streaming is also supported in output, if the merging strategy allows it; in this case, a callback mechanism allows result merging on demand within configurable timeouts.
- *monitor services* observe the external environment for changes which may trigger an update to the state of RIs. CSD monitors react to changes to indices of content sources, for which they subscribe with instances of Index services; the regeneration of a description is governed by *update policies* based on a configurable combination of time and space criteria (i.e. every so often and/or whenever indices have changed of a given proportion). CSS and DF monitors react instead to changes to descriptions, for which they subscribe with CSD descriptors. In all cases, subscriptions are brokered by services in the CL, so as to achieve resilience to the redeployment of notification producers.
- *factory services* generate the state of RIs. The separation of factories and access services distinguishes two phases in the lifetime of RIs: in the *operative phase*, clients interact with access services to act upon state; in the *generative phase*, state is created, derived, updated or otherwise materialised locally to the instances. While the two phases may interleave during the lifetime of instances, their exact time of occurrence is ultimately determined by client strategies. Further, state generation may occur in either a passive or a proactive mode: in the *passive mode*, clients trigger generation by interacting with factories at any point in the lifetime of RIs; in the *proactive mode*, the instances create resources autonomously by reacting to the observation of key events in the environment, starting from their very deployment of the instance on a node (bootstrapping).

State persistence, service publication, Grid-based file exchange mechanisms, streamed processing, lifetime management, and other forms of interactions with the infrastructure are handled transparently. Specialisation is supported by: (*i*) extensive use of declarative configurations; (*ii*) domain-specific libraries for inverted index management, update policy, and best-effort discovery strategies; (*iii*) design patterns which allow pluggable algorithms for selection, fusion, and object bindings of XML serialisations of descriptions and results. Specific CSD, CSS, and DF services which make use of these facilities are described in Section 3.

3 The Search Framework in Action: Searching the Earth Science Information Space

Earth Science is a discipline that well represents the complex nature of e-Science activities and may thus gain tremendous benefits from the DILIGENT infrastructure. Earth Science scientists need to access data and tools within a multi-institutional, heterogeneous and large-scale context. The analysis and the generation of objective facts on the Earth status, i.e. Earth Observation (EO), require integration of specific data products, handling of information in multiple forms and use of storage and computing resources in a seamless, dynamic and cost effective way. The typical desiderata about the retrieval paradigm consists in mixing bugs of keywords, either free terms or ontology extracted, with geo-location features aiming to capture the area of pertinence.

The building of *periodical environmental reports*, for example, is a typical EO activity where the DILIGENT search infrastructure proves its appropriateness. These complex information objects, mostly built as aggregation of other information objects, require a lot of existing information, coming from worldwide distributed heterogeneous sources. This information has to be properly discovered and uniformly accessed. The so collected information has often to be coherently integrated with pertinent information generated on-demand through procedures that often need to access and process huge amount of data. This scenario has been termed *Implementation of Environmental Conventions* (IMPECT) and details on its implementation are provided in the follow.

The DILIGENT infrastructure to serve IMPECT consist of "external" content providers, such as the NASA CEOS IDN initiative[4], the European Environment Agency[5], and Medspiration[6], plus a pool of three community specific data sources, all placed at the ESA's European Space Research Institute (ESRIN), namely: the EO ESA web portal[7] documents and data, the EO Grid on demand system[8], and EO catalogue together with relevant databases and archives.

The resulting information space is tremendously heterogeneous, it contains classic documents like research studies and meteorological papers, satellite images, EO products like Chlorophyll-1 measure or vegetation indexes. To process such data effectively and efficiently appropriate customisation and instantiations of the DILIGENT Search framework have been needed but easy thanks to the possibility to plug-in new search operators in the search procedure.

With respect to the indexing facilities, the Geographical index is intended for such use. The web services used to implement this index use innovative techniques providing a highly dynamic search experience and allowing for post-index-creation addition of ad hoc query and sorting algorithms.

The Geographical index can be queried through an "index replication" represented by an instance of a GeoIndexLookupService. As these replications are based on a two dimensional R-Tree [22], the two step query processing normally used with R-Trees

[4] http://idn.ceos.org

[5] http://www.eea.eu.int/

[6] http://www.medspiration.org/products/

[7] http://www.eoportal.org

[8] http://giserver.esrin.esa.int/

[23] is also used in the Geographical index. This scheme calls for a filter step and a refinement step. In the filter step, standard MBR (Minimal Bounding Rectangle) queries are performed against the R-Tree producing a candidate set based on entries MBRs, which may have a number of false hits when considering the actual detailed geometry of both the query and entries [23]. In order to eliminate false hits, the candidate set is refined based on additional parameters, often but not necessarily relating to the actual geometry of the objects or queries. In between the standard two R-Tree query processing steps, the GeoIndexLookupService also implements a third step in order to rank and sort the refined results. The algorithms used in both the refinement and ranking steps greatly affect the functionality of the application and will vary for different use cases. By relying on the openness of the whole framework and on the Index, it is possible to introduce other refinement and sorting algorithms making the Geographical index adaptable to potentially any use case.

Two refinement operators and two ranking operators have been implemented. The TemporalRefiner and PolygonalRefiner refinement operators allow the user to refine the search results based on their timestamp or a specified polygonal shape. The TemporalRankEvaluator and ArealOverlapRankEvaluator ranking operators allow the results to be ranked based on their timestamp or based on the amount of overlap between their MBR and the query.

In case the refinement algorithm is very computing intensive and the candidate set returned from the filter step is large, low response times are upheld by exploiting the ResultSet Service mechanism. By only doing partial filtering [24] and ranking steps, and synchronising these with requests to the ResultSet Service, these steps are only performed for the entries returned to the user, saving a vast amount of computing cycles, and greatly lowering the GeoIndexLookupService's response time.

With respect to the Distributed Information Retrieval, the CSD service generates and maintains *term histograms* of textual sources, a coarse-grained form of index where containment relationships between terms and documents is intentionally abstracted over. The service interacts with the Index services to derive the histograms from full-text content indices and also to subscribe for point-to-point notifications of changes to such indices. The CSS service selects sources based on rankings produced with the standard CORI algorithm [25]; rankings are based on estimated relevance of content, and rely on term histograms staged from the CSD service prior to query submission. In particular, the service subscribes with the CSD service for changes to the staged histograms and updates them upon notification of such changes. Finally, the DF service merges query results based on either one of three techniques: a plain round-robin algorithm, a consistent merging algorithm, and a linear regression method based on source selection scores. The first offers the least effectiveness but acts as an upper bound on performance (results remain unparsed, output can be streamed). The second uses global statistics to give the best effectiveness but also the highest overhead (results are fully parsed, output cannot be streamed); in this case, the service interacts with the reference CSD service to gather histograms in advance of result submission. The third explores middle ground between the first two, and uses the output of the reference CSS service to heuristically normalise inconsistent result scores; as interaction with the CSS service must necessarily occur during query execution, deployment services in the CL layer are instructed to co-deploy both services on the same node.

4 Conclusion and Future Works

We have outlined the design of a service-based framework for large-scale distributed retrieval, built atop the computational facilities of a European Grid platform. While initial experience in the Earth Observation domain has built up some confidence around the capacity of the framework to accommodate the requirements of e-Science applications, there are a number of implementation and design improvements which are to be addressed in the immediate future, some of which we outline next.

Further abstraction over some particular service types, such as the information sources (e.g. indices, external search engines), will enhance opportunities for integration in search operations. Experimentation on query planning and optimisation by utilisation of domain-specific heuristics and content distribution statistics, based on non-linear regression techniques [26] is expected to yield faster and higher quality results. Improvements on the performance of the ResultSet transport mechanism are expected to be achieved through further exploitation of facilities provided by the underlying platform, such as GridFTP's parallel striped transfers. Partitioning of indices across DHNs, so as to exploit the resource pooling of the Grid for the distributed storage of very large indices, will improve availability on extremely large datasets. Finally, the support of uncooperative DIR strategies, such as query-based sampling techniques for generating term histograms or partial indices of external content sources, would allow us to support more advanced techniques of selection and fusion (e.g. the Semisupervised Learning method of data fusion [27] and the Unified Utility Maximisation method of resource selection [28]).

Acknowledgments. This work is partially funded by the European Commission in the context of the DILIGENT project, under the 2nd call of FP6 IST priority.

References

1. Blair, D.C.: The data-document distinction revisited. SIGMIS Database 37, 77–96 (2006)
2. Sanderson, R.: Srw: Search/retrieve webservice. Public Draft (2003)
3. Callan, J.: 5 Distributed Information Retrieval. In: Advances in Information Retrieval, pp. 127–150. Kluwer Academic Publishers, Hingham, MA (2000)
4. Kobayashi, M., Takeda, K.: Information retrieval on the web. ACM Comput. Surv. 32, 144–173 (2000)
5. Risson, J., Moors, T.: Survey of research towards robust peer-to-peer networks: search methods. Comput. Networks 50, 3485–3521 (2006)
6. Atkinson, M., Crowcroft, J., Goble, C., Gurd, J., Rodden, T., Shadbolt, N., Sloman, M., Sommerville, I., Storey, T.: Computer Challenges to emerge from eScience (e-Science vision document)
7. Foster, I., Kesselman, C., Tuecke, S.: The Anatomy of the Grid: Enabling Scalable Virtual Organization. The International Journal of High Performance Computing Applications 15, 200–222 (2001)
8. Foster, I., Kesselman, C., Nick, J., Tuecke, S.: The Physiology of the Grid: An Open Grid Services Architecture for Distributed Systems Integration. Open Grid Service Infrastructure WG, Global Grid Forum (2002)
9. Globus Alliance: The Globus Alliance Website, `http://www.globus.org/`

10. EGEE: Enabling Grids for E-sciencE. INFSO 508833, http://public.eu-egee.org/
11. Atkins, D.E., Droegemeier, K.K., Feldman, S.I., Garcia-Molina, H., Klein, M.L., Messerschmitt, D.G., Messina, P., Ostriker, J.P., Wright, M.H.: Revolutionizing science and engineering through cyberinfrastructure. Report of the National Science Foundation Blue-Ribbon Advisory Panel on Cyberinfrastructure (2003)
12. Larson, R.R., Sanderson, R.: Grid-based digital libraries: Cheshire3 and distributed retrieval. In: JCDL '05: Proceedings of the 5th ACM/IEEE-CS Joint Conference on Digital Libraries, pp. 112–113. ACM Press, New York (2005)
13. GRACE: GRid seArch & Categorization Engine (2005), http://www.grace-ist.org
14. Banks, T.: Web Services Resource Framework (WSRF) - Primer. Committee draft 01, OASIS (2005), http://docs.oasis-open.org/wsrf/wsrf-primer-1.2-primer-cd-01.pdf
15. Niblett, P., Graham, S.: Events and service-oriented architecture: The oasis web services notification specification. IBM Systems Journal 44, 869–886 (2005)
16. Kossmann, D.: The state of the art in distributed query processing. ACM Computing Surveys 32, 422–469 (2000)
17. Ioannidis, Y.E.: Query optimization. ACM Computing Surveys 28, 121–123 (1996)
18. Stonebraker, M., Aoki, P., Litwin, W., Pfeffer, A., Sah, A., Sidell, J., Staelin, C., Yu, A.: Mariposa: A Wide-Area Distributed Database System. The VLDB Journal 5, 48–63 (1996)
19. Chen, C., Roussopoulos, N.: Adaptive selectivity estimation using query feedback. In: 1994 ACM SIGMOD International Conference on Management of data, pp. 161–172 (1994)
20. Simeoni, F., Azzopardi, L., Crestani, F.: An application framework for distributed information retrieval. In: Sugimoto, S., Hunter, J., Rauber, A., Morishima, A. (eds.) ICADL 2006. LNCS, vol. 4312, pp. 192–201. Springer, Heidelberg (2006)
21. Callan, J.P., Connell, M.E.: Query-based sampling of text databases. Information Systems 19, 97–130 (2001)
22. Guttman, A.: R-trees: a dynamic index structure for spatial searching. In: SIGMOD '84: Proceedings of the 1984 ACM SIGMOD international conference on Management of data, pp. 47–57. ACM Press, New York (1984)
23. Manolopoulos, Y., Nanopoulos, A., Papadopoulos, A., Theodoridis, Y.: R-Trees: Theory and Applications. In: Advanced Information and Knowledge Processing, Springer, Heidelberg (2006)
24. Martínez, C.: Partial Quicksort. In: The First Workshop on Analytic Algorithmics and Combinatorics (ANALCO04), New Orleans (2004)
25. Callan, J.P., Lu, Z., Croft, W.B.: Searching distributed collections with inference networks. In: SIGIR '95: Proceedings of the 18th annual international ACM SIGIR conference on Research and development in information retrieval, pp. 21–28. ACM Press, New York (1995)
26. Sun, W., Ling, Y., Rishe, N., Deng, Y.: An instant and accurate size estimation method for joins and selections in a retrieval-intensive environment. In: SIGMOD '93: Proceedings of the 1993 ACM SIGMOD international conference on Management of data, pp. 79–88. ACM Press, New York (1993)
27. Si, L., Callan, J.: A semisupervised learning method to merge search engine results. ACM Trans. Inf. Syst. 21, 457–491 (2003)
28. Si, L., Callan, J.P.: Unified utility maximization framework for resource selection. In: Grossman, D., Gravano, L., Zhai, C., Herzog, O., Evans, D.A. (eds.) CIKM, pp. 32–41. ACM, New York (2004)

VIRGIL – Providing Institutional Access to a Repository of Access Grid Sessions

Ron Chernich, Jane Hunter, and Alex Davies

The University of Queensland, St Lucia, Queensland, Australia
{chernich, jane}@itee.uq.edu.au
and
Australian National University, Canberra, ACT, Australia
u4313969@anu.edu.au

Abstract. This paper describes the VIRGIL (Virtual Meeting Archival) system which was developed to provide a simple, practical, easy-to-use method for recording, indexing and archiving large scale distributed videoconferences held over Access Grid nodes. Institutional libraries are coming under increasing pressure to support the storage, access and retrieval of such mixed-media complex digital objects in their institutional repositories. Although systems have been developed to record access grid sessions, they don't provide simple mechanisms for repository ingestion, search and retrieval; and they require the installation and understanding of complex Access Grid tools to record and replay the virtual meetings. Our system has been specifically designed to enable both: the easy construction and maintenance of an archive of Access Grid sessions by managers; and easy search and retrieval of recorded sessions by users. This paper describes the underlying architecture, tools and Web interface we developed to enable the recording, storage, search, retrieval and replay of collaborative Access Grid sessions within a Fedora repository.

1 Introduction

Access Grids [1, 2] have become widely established in universities and institutions globally to enable collaboration between large scale distributed teams. They support scalable group to group (G2G) communication over network connections. The deployment and usage of Access Grid Nodes has grown despite the difficulties, complexities, performance problems and instability associated with the underlying IP Multicast technology and the associated Vic [3] and Rat [4] tools. Vic and Rat were originally developed by the University College London, for IT researchers to hold multi-way videoconferences over MBone [5] (multicast backbone for the Internet), and weren't designed for general use by the public.

As the use of Access Grid nodes has grown, so has the demand for tools to enable the recording of Access Grid sessions so they can be replayed at a later date. This is of particular value when applied to online collaborative teaching sessions that consist of lectures or seminars involving multiple speakers at distributed sites.

L. Kovács, N. Fuhr, and C. Meghini (Eds.): ECDL 2007, LNCS 4675, pp. 174–185, 2007.

Two previous projects have specifically developed systems to support such functionality – AGVCR [6] and Memetic [7]. Both of these systems are described in detail in Section 2.2. They provide user interfaces for recording and replaying the Vic and Rat streams separately. There are two critical limitations with these systems. Firstly they do not provide simple tools to enable Access Grid sessions to be recorded in platform-independent formats that can be easily replayed without the need to install Vic and Rat. Secondly they do not provide tools to enable recordings to be archived by uploading to an institutional repository (as a composite synchronized multimedia object) with associated metadata description(s).

This paper describes the VIRGIL (Virtual meeting Archival) system [8] which was developed to provide a simple, practical, easy-to-use method for recording, indexing and archiving large scale distributed videoconferences held over Access Grid nodes. In addition, we describe the Web search interface we developed to enable the ingest, search, retrieval and replay of the collaborative Access Grid sessions stored in the archive. VIRGIL achieves this through four specific capabilities that distinguish our system from other Access Grid recording tools:

1. Sessions are recorded in formats suitable for embedding in web pages that can be played through widely available plug-ins for platform-independent Web browsers.
2. Metadata describing each session recording (and each of the embedded streams) is generated automatically. This provides the search terms for the web-based search and retrieval interface.
3. An interface is provided to upload the indexed composite digital objects to an underlying Fedora repository [9].
4. A web-based search, browse, retrieval and replay interface is provided that requires no specific software downloads.

2 Background

2.1 Access Grid Nodes

The Access Grid is a project initiated by Argonne National Laboratories, Maths and Computer Science, Futures Laboratory in the USA [1, 2]. It is essentially an open global project to develop a large scale collaborative environment, similar to video-conferencing rooms but scaled up to allow multi-site G2G communication via high speed networks. There are over 200 Access Grid nodes established worldwide primarily at research universities, national laboratories, and corporate research divisions.

A typical Access Grid node is normally a room with 8-100 seats, a very large-scale display and associated computing and audio/video hardware that includes cameras, projectors, recorders, and electronic whiteboards.

Although Access Grid nodes are still being widely deployed, the user-interface to the supporting software is less than friendly, the protocol standards are still very basic, and their overall robustness is suspect. In addition, most access grid nodes require one or more dedicated operational staff to help users set up and maintain communication and tolerable audio/video quality throughout a session. Access Grids use IP multicast for the underlying network transport protocol. Various solutions exist for "tunneling" the traffic over normal links, but they are neither scalable nor user-friendly at either end of the tunnel [9].

Access Grid software is almost exclusively open source multi-platform software. In particular it revolves around two pieces of software:

- Vic [3] the video conferencing tool, which is intended to link multiple sites with multiple simultaneous video streams over a multicast infrastructure.
- Rat [4] the robust audio tool, which allows multiple users to engage in a audio conference over the Internet in multicast mode.

Vic and Rat were developed as part of the Internet Multicast backbone, or MBone [5], which provided multicast services over the unicast Internet backbone. They were designed for use by collaborating researchers. They were not designed for use by the general public, who require robustness, minimal packet loss, low latency, high quality video and audio, precise synchronization and streamlined user friendly interfaces.

Despite this, there is an increasing demand to record access grid sessions, so they can be retrieved and replayed by users unfamiliar with Access Grid technologies. The recordings of such sessions should be able to be uploaded into institutional repositories (such as Fedora [9] or DSpace [10]), described using metadata, and then discovered, retrieved and replayed by users with little or no knowledge of Access Grid technologies.

2.2 Related Activities and Previous Work

A number of research groups have developed tools in the past for recording access grid sessions.

AGVCR [6] is a relatively mature, well-designed and easy-to-use tool for recording Access Grid sessions. It was written by Derek Piper at the Indiana University School of Informatics. AGVCR records RTP and RTCP from multiple unicast or multicast streams and provides the ability to replay the conference to multicast or unicast addresses. Replayed conferences are almost indistinguishable from a live session. Alternatively playback can be to a localhost by using Vic and Rat in a standalone manner from the AG toolkit.

Argonne National Laboratory to provide a scalable multi-stream record and playback engine for recording and retrieving collaborative MBone sessions. It has subsequently been extended to support the recording and playback of both Access Grid and Virtual Reality sessions such as the CAVE[12].

The MBone VCR on Demand Service [13] is a Java application that enables recording and playback of MBone sessions and the associated Vic and Rat streams. MBone VCR doesn't provide a search interface to recorded sessions.

Memetic [7] is a more recent development from the University of Southampton, that began in 2005. It focuses on the capture and replay of Access Grid sessions, but with enhanced annotation functionality – primarily manual collaborative annotation tools which allow participants to create 'nodes' that record notes, issues, ideas, decisions or links to documents or websites associated with the events within a meeting. Memetic is an extension of the Access Grid tools developed within the CoAKTinG [14] (Collaborative Advanced Knowledge Technologies) project.

All of these prior systems rely on recording and replay of separate Vic (video) and Rat (audio) streams. The existing *rtpdump* approach does not scale well, often drops packets and does not record all of the potential material. In addition, precise synchronization of these multiple streams at playback time is extremely difficult so it is frequently a challenge to determine who is speaking at any one time, due to poor lip-synchronization.

None of the previous systems enables recording in platform independent formats. None provide the ability to upload sessions to standard institutional repositories, nor provide a Web interface to search across the metadata descriptions to discover, retrieve and replay relevant sessions. Apart from *Memetic* (which relies on the manual attachment of semantic annotations), current tools only support the recording and non-interactive playback of entire Access Grid streams – our aim is to provide a tool to support richer, more interactive and fine-grained, discovery and navigation of pre-recorded access grid sessions based on the automatically generated metadata.

2.3 Objectives of VIRGIL

The objectives of the VIRGIL project were to develop a robust, efficient and interoperable system which provides:

- An easy-to-use utility based on the VCR paradigm that can be replayed via widely available Web plug-ins for desktop environments;
- Automatic generation of high quality, fine-grained metadata;
- Interactive editing and augmentation of metadata descriptions;
- Uploading of the session and associated metadata into an institutional repository;
- A sophisticated web-based search, browse and retrieval interface based on the underlying metadata schema;
- Presentation of selected results as dynamic HTML with an embedded link to the "movie" providing platform independent replay;
- An interactive replay which does not require the installation of Vic and Rat.

3 Design and Implementation

The VIRGIL system comprises three main components:

1. The Access Grid Recording tool – Virgil Video Recorder (VVR).
2. The Metadata Editor and Repository Ingest tool.
3. The Search, Browse, Retrieval and Replay interface.

The key design challenges were to leverage the existing technology to provide a user friendly, host-neutral design with a minimal change footprint.

3.1 The Virgil Video Recorder (VVR)

VVR differs from other tools such as AGVCR [6] in two significant ways:

1. It generates simple output in "movie" file formats (.mov and .avi) suitable for embedding in web pages that can be played through plug-ins for platform independent web browsers.
2. It generates metadata for the recording suitable for use in searchable metadata repositories that can reference the "movie" as dynamic HTML.

The VVR tool provides a rich, portable GUI environment. Written in Perl and PerlTK for portability, it interacts with modified versions of Vic and Rat used by the Access Grid Toolkit using socket based Inter-Process Communication. The use of "hacked" versions of Vic and Rat is not ideal, but significant effort has gone into making the extent of the modifications and the process of implementing these modifications as simple as possible. Figure 1 shows the user interface to VVR.

VVR controls Vic and Rat through inter-process communication (IPC) based on the passive file transfer protocol model for communications port exchange. When they initialize, Vic and Rat read a user defined socket value from the VVR properties file. They then attempt to communicate with VVR using this port. If successful, each opens a random, system-selected socket and sends that port number to VVR. VVR is then able to send commands individually to the two utilities and query them for status, record start and stop times, and stream metadata using a simple text based request/response protocol.

Once Vic and Rat have performed their port exchange with VVR, the *record* button records the Access Grid audio and video streams separately. To minimise the real-time processing overhead, these are later multiplexed on selection of the VVR *Create Movie* button. This operation also generates XML metadata that may be edited after the event to include user supplied documentation such as the agenda, minutes etc., that will augment the envisaged search and retrieval capabilities.

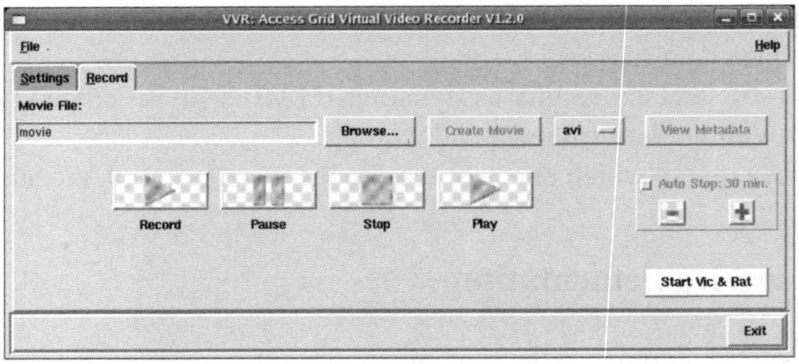

Fig. 1. VVR User Interface

The Rat utility has an existing facility to write the combined audio output to a file when given appropriate command line arguments. The modified version takes advantage of this capability by sending the file name with start/pause/finish commands via IPC from VVR.

The modified Vic utility also receives IPC commands and is responsible for extracting the metadata from un-muted video feeds. While recording, it composes a "tiled" video image in real-time from all the un-muted video streams being received. Each video stream window is labelled with the most appropriate name extracted from the stream metadata. The composite window matrix is labelled with a dynamic date/time stamp, plus an elapsed time counter to assist viewers with the location of sections of interest.

The overall movie frame size is fixed, so as more video streams join the selected venue, the individual images are resized and fitted into the best-fit matrix. Should a feed disappear, or be muted via the Vic GUI, the space occupied may be blanked, or the matrix and image sizes re-computed. The action is specified by the user through a VVR checkbox choice.

Recording may be paused at any time. While in this mode, the network connections will be read and packets parsed for participant information, but nothing will be written to the files. When the *Stop* button is pressed, the audio and video output files are closed in preparation for post-recording processing and conversion to the selected movie format. The user must provide a filename to store the "processed" output (ie, combined audio and video streams). The same file name but with an "xml" extension is used to store the session's metadata. The raw audio and video files may be retained, or automatically deleted when VVR terminates as specified by a checkbox item on the Settings page.

Like a physical VCR, the Virgil VVR may be "programmed" to automatically terminate recording after a specific time period elapses. Post-recording processing however still requires user interaction and input.

Fig. 2. Tiled Access Grid Session Recording

3.2 The Metadata Editor and Repository Ingest Tool

The metadata captured during recording is confined to that provided with the audio and video streams that identifies the participants, plus data that can be derived from the environment such as date, time and duration. To facilitate archiving and later search and retrieve operations, a step that allows additional data to be entered by a cataloguer is inserted ahead of the final storage process following upload to the repository. This metadata is arbitrary. In the prototype, we have provided elements for title, subject, agenda, and minutes of the conference. All are optional.

The Metadata Editing/Input form is generated from the underlying XML-based metadata schema which was developed following a review of related efforts which included a survey report by the Terena TF-Netcast taskforce on metadata models for video-on-demand assets in academic communities [15, 16].

The metadata values in the majority of the elements are automatically generated by the VVR tool. Other may be manually input by the person responsible for uploading the recording to the repository.

The *participants* section of the metadata contains elements derived from the Vic and Rat metadata received with the streams. The VVR program employs a heuristic that attempts to aggregate the audio (A) and video (V) stream data originating from an individual Access Grid node. The stream attribute of the participant elements indicates whether the source is audio only, video only, or combined *AV*. This latter condition is detected by searching for matching user-name@IP-address element values in the separate Vic and Rat generated metadata.

This aggregation process is not straight forward. A session participant may not be sending video, or the session host computer may be *dual-homed* (ie, have two network cards). This is not uncommon. It is employed in large Access Grid rooms to increase the effective stream bandwidth by streaming the audio and video data over separate TCP/IP connections. In this case, the VVR heuristic will be unable to aggregate the AV metadata reliably, so the Access Grid node will appear as two separate participants.

Once the metadata has been appropriately edited, merged and corrected, the associated XML file is uploaded to the Fedora repository along with the recording of the session and a snap-shot image from the recording. After a new recording is uploaded to the Fedora repository, an RSS feed announcing the availability and details of the new Session is sent to registered subscribers. This service could easily be personalized, so only the details of new Sessions on specified topics are sent to subscribers.

3.3 The Search, Browse, Retrieval and Replay Interface

The aim of the search interface is to provide a simple, efficient search interface and high speed access and retrieval of stored Access Grid sessions – by searching on available metadata. Figure 3 illustrates the "simple" search functionality.

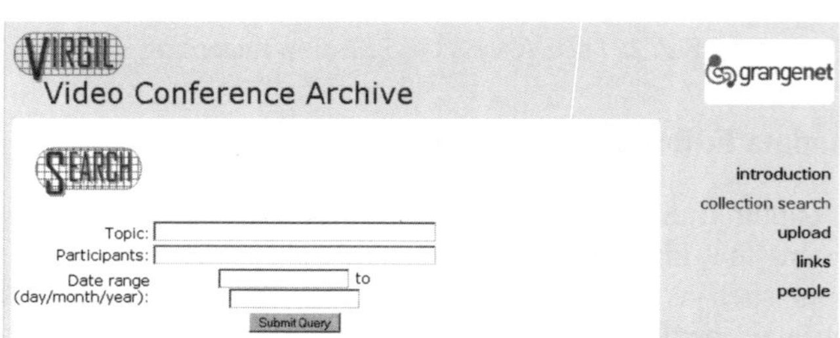

Fig. 3. Simple Search Interface

The search interface was implemented as a web-based PHP interface to the underlying Fedora database. The search is implemented using iTQL which is an RDF query language. This allows the database to be searched on any of the metadata fields in the underlying schema.

The Search Results summary page displays basic metadata - Title, Subject, Date, Duration and Participants. This is useful for further identifying the relevant sessions. The title for each retrieved result contains a hyperlink to a dynamically generated HTML page containing the full record.

The full metadata page displays all of the metadata recorded for the given session, as well as a screen shot and a link to the recording. This is implemented in PHP/Fedora. Figure 4 illustrates the complete Web search results for a retrieved recording. Clicking on the screen shot opens up the plug-in which enables replay and navigation of the recording, as illustrated in Figure 2.

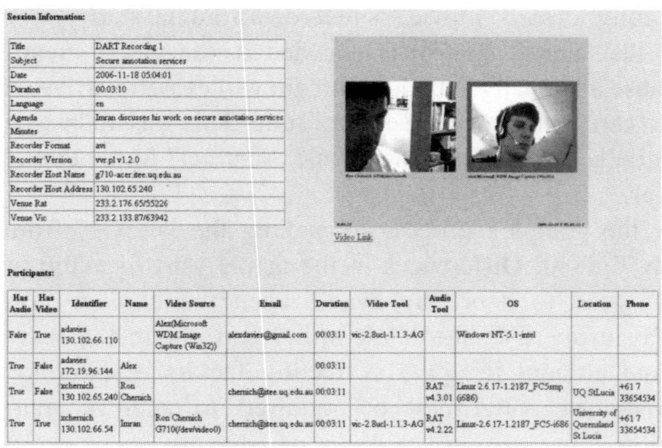

Fig. 4. Session Information Retrieval

4 Evaluation, Future Work and Conclusions

4.1 Discussion and Evaluation

Usability tests were carried out by four different groups selected for their lack of prior knowledge or experience of the Access Grid toolkit. Feedback from user testing was generally positive. However specific requests and comments from the test users led to the following improvements:

- Selected audio/video streams were able to be "muted" (ie, not appear in the movie). This request was addressed by allowing users to either blank-out or totally remove muted streams. Muting of a currently active stream, may cause a sudden rearrangement and resizing of the tiled frames. This can confuse a viewer as the location of a participant suddenly shifts in a disconcerting manner. On the other hand, simply blanking a stream may result in a sparse matrix of windows that is equally disconcerting to the viewer.

- When Vic connects to a venue with a large number of video streams active, there will be a significant delay before the "full" visual matrix is built. This is due to the way that Vic conserves bandwidth by sending 8x8 pixel blocks based on a "most recently changed" algorithm. Early tests indicated that a delay of well over one minute before all block pixel groups had been sent at least once was typical for a venue with six live Vic streams. Until this is achieved, the matrix has missing blocks that adversely affect the image quality.

There were a number of additional significant challenges encountered during the development of the VIRGIL system:

- Reducing this initial period of poor video quality is not possible, but by participant agreement, the VVR operator can indicate verbally when the picture build-up at the recorder location has completed and recording of the session may commence to ensure that a fully formed "movie" is recorded from the start.
- The state of the "mute" control is encoded in the video stream. This causes a problem because a "muted" Vic video stream will cease to arrive. Hence there is no data stream to carry the new mute control state. This was addressed by trapping the Vic mute button action and sending a final "sentinel" frame that could be detected by the recorder.
- Control over the complex process of making the "movie" from the streams is comparatively limited. Differences in the actual start of audio and video stream recording can lead to poor "lip sync" when the two are combined in post-processing. By using IPC, the VVR utility can obtain the individual recording start times and attempt to apply correcting factors. Experience to date shows further heuristic tailoring may be required to achieve more "natural" lip synchronization.
- Modification of Vic and Rat source code requires advanced C/C++ ability on the part of the user. To reduce the complexity of this step, an installation script was written in Perl that identifies the locations of changes in the standard distributions of the Vic and Rat source code and build scripts are generated. If the script is able to locate all points with confidence, the changes are made automatically and the results checked. If unverifiable, all changes are removed and the user must attempt manual modification from the supplied documentation.
- Significant effort was spent minimizing the footprint of the modifications (the number of changes to Rat and Vic). All the required IPC functionality was written into a common C++ base class that is extended for Vic and Rat. Modification of the two utilities requires a one line reference to the derived class that will initiate an exchange of port numbers with the VVR utility. In the case of Rat, the derived class is then able to initiate all the required control for the recording process through calls to the existing Rat functions. Unlike Rat, Vic has no native ability to write aggregate video data to a disk file. This capability is provided by an additional module that is referenced from the derived IPC controller object and fed data by a one line insertion into the Vic codebase. Mute button control requires an additional conditional statement to be inserted into the

Vic source, making the overall source level changes required extremely small and simple.

- Difficulties were experienced with the calling conventions in the Rat codebase. Vic uses C++ throughout whilst Rat uses a combination of C and C++. This unpleasant surprise was discovered after the C++ base class for IPC had been written. It required some additional gymnastics in the Rat codebase and distributed Rat "makefile" script.

In addition, feedback from test users on the search and retrieval interface, led to slight modifications and extensions to the metadata schema. Two new metadata fields were added: a "type" field and a "rights" field. The "type" field is a pull-down list of access grid session types including: *meeting, workshop, conference, seminar, lecture, tutorial, discussion*. The "rights" field points to the scanned and signed permissions forms, granting permission from the participants for the session to be recorded, archived and made available either to the public or a specified user group.

4.2 Future Work

The current system could be further improved and enhanced by applying additional effort to the following issues:

- Currently we only consider the recording, description, synchronization and replay of video and audio streams. Access Grids often include other shared application events such as shared browsers, chat, whiteboards or visualizations. These data streams also need to be identified, recorded, indexed, displayed and replayed in synchronization with the audiovisual streams;
- Temporal alignment of the agenda and minutes with segments of the recorded session would enable much more precise, fine-grained search and retrieval;
- Scope exists for fine-tuning the audio and video post-recording processing to improve lip synchronization;
- The VVR recorder together with the Vic and Rat modifications were designed for cross-platform portability. However at this time, they have only been validated under Linux. For wider use, they should be validated on Microsoft Windows and Apple Mac environments. Note that while the recording must currently be made under Linux, the session participants can use standard Access Grid toolkit installations on any supported platform.
- Although the recorder tool is simple to use, building the modified versions of the Vic and Rat utilities requires skills at source code compiling. Opportunity exists to move the project to the next level by creating Install Wizards with pre-built and tested binary code for the popular target platforms.

4.3 Conclusions

This paper describes a system we have developed to enable collections managers with little or no knowledge of Access Grid technologies to quickly and easily build an archive of recordings of such collaborative virtual meetings. VIRGIL has achieved all of the objectives that were listed in Section 2.3. More specifically it enables users to:

- Record and combine all of the audio and video streams associated with an Access Grid session into a single file in a de facto format (.avi and .mov);
- Automatically generate and validate fine-grained precise metadata (conformant with an underlying XML Schema);
- Replay the recordings and edit both the recording and associated metadata descriptions for quality control purposes;
- Augment the metadata before uploading the recording to a searchable repository.

Acknowledgements

This project was funded by GrangeNet (Grid and Next Generation Network), the Australian Broadband Research Network under the Australian Government's BITS Advanced Network program.

References

[1] Childers, L., Disz, T., Olson, R., Papka, M.E., Stevens, R., Udeshi, T.: Access Grid: Immersive Group-to-Group Collaborative Visualization. In: Proc. 4th International Immersive Projection Technology Workshop (2000)

[2] Access Grid Homepage, www.accessgrid.org

[3] McCanne, S., Jacobson, V.: vic: A Flexible Framework for Packet Video. ACM Multimedia 95, 511–522 (1995)

[4] Hardman, V., Sasse, A., Handley, M., Watson, A.: Reliable Audio for Use over the Internet. In: INET'95, Honolulu, Hawaii (1995)

[5] Eriksson, H.: MBONE: the multicast backbone. Communications of the ACM 37, 54–60 (1994)

[6] Piper, D.: AccessGrid Video (Cassette) Recorder, http://iri.informatics.indiana.edu/~dcpiper/agvcr/

[7] Buckingham Shum, S., Slack, R., Daw, M., Juby, B., Rowley, A., Bachler, M., Mancini, C., Michaelides, D., Procter, R., De Roure, D.: Memetic: An Infrastructure for Meeting Memory. In: Proceedings 7th International Conference on the Design of Cooperative Systems, Carrey-le-Rouet, France (2006)

[8] VIRGIL project Home Page, http://www.itee.uq.edu.au/~eresearch/projects/virgil/index.html

[9] Fedora, www.fedora.info

[10] DSpace, www.dspace.org

[11] Disz, T., Judson, I., Olson, R., Stevens, R.: The Argonne Voyager multimedia server, High Performance Distributed Computing, 1997. In: Proceedings. The Sixth IEEE International Symposium on, pp. 71–80 (1997)

[12] Cruz-Neira, C., Sandin, D.J., DeFanti, T.A.: Surround-screen projection-based virtual reality: the design and implementation of the CAVE. In: Proceedings of the 20th annual conference on Computer graphics and interactive techniques, pp. 135–142 (1993)

[13] Holfelder, W.: MBone VCR: video conference recording on the MBone. In: Proceedings of the third ACM international conference on Multimedia, pp. 237–238 (1995)
[14] CoAKTinG Project, http://www.aktors.org/coakting/
[15] Salminen, H.K.: Metadata survey report (April 2003), http://www.terena.org/activities/tf-netcast/deliverables/deliverable-a.html
[16] Salminen, H.K.: TF-netcast: Final Report (September 2004), http://www.terena.org/activities/tf-vvc/docs/Deliverable_I.pdf

Opening Schrödingers Library: Semi-automatic QA Reduces Uncertainty in Object Transformation

Lars R. Clausen

The State and University Library
Århus
Denmark

Abstract. Object transformation for preservation purposes is currently a hit-or-miss affair, where errors in transformation may go unnoticed for years since manual quality assurance is too resource-intensive for large collections of digital objects. We propose an approach of semi-automatic quality assurance (QA), where numerous separate automatic checks of "aspects" of the objects, combined with manual inspection, provides greater assurance that objects are transformed with little or no loss of quality. We present an example of using this approach to appraise the quality of OpenOffice's import of Word documents.

1 Introduction

Libraries are central players in the long-term preservation business. While commercial businesses may think of 5 years as long-term, and public institutions might be happy to keep objects around for a few decades, libraries must think in terms of centuries when we plan for preservation. One central pillar of preserving digital objects is the ability to understand the way their information is encoded in a series of bits. This encoding, loosely known as a "file format", is typically a highly complex system, but frequently taken for granted because they "just work". Current file formats, which at present seem ubiquitious and easy to access, will one day be things of the past, or at the very least will be heavily modified. The PDF format exists in eight official versions[4] as well as several derivations, and the wide-spread JPEG format has two worthy successors lined up already[6,1].

To preserve access to the wealth of information currently stored in digital objects, two complementary methods are commonly suggested: Emulation and object transformation. In this article, we shall not try to determine which of the two is better, but will assume that object transformation will be the strategy of choice for a significant amount of objects now and in the future.

Once the decision to perform object transformation has been made, the question of "how do we preserve our information" becomes "how do we ensure that the information from the old objects also exists in the new objects". The prevalent way of answering this question at the moment is to take a (hopefully representative) sample of objects and examine before-and-after versions manually for differences. This method has several fundamental flaws:

1. We have no idea if the objects picked are representative, or particularly good or bad examples.

L. Kovács, N. Fuhr, and C. Meghini (Eds.): ECDL 2007, LNCS 4675, pp. 186–197, 2007.

2. We have little idea if the differences seen are caused by the transformation, or are merely an artifact of the tools used to examine the objects.
3. We may overlook errors in some significant properties in the examination if the errors are not obvious with the tools used.
4. For those objects left unexamined, we have only a statistical assurance that the information is intact.

These flaws together put us in the situation of ending up with a “Schrödingers Library”: a large number of unopened boxes of information, where only the act of opening the boxes some day in the future will tell us if the information is alive, or has been dead for decades.

In order to collapse this digital superposition of states to certainly alive or certainly dead, quantum mechanics teaches us that we need to observe the objects, for instance by measuring them. Each measurement we make will collapse one or more dimensions of uncertainty, hopefully allowing us to notice transformation failures early enough to make another attempt. By combining the quality measures of a number of smaller tools, rather than attempting one big, complex check, we average out the shortcomings of each tool and gain a more detailed, yet more reliable, view of the quality of the transformation.

In the next section, we discuss some prior work and the state of the art. We then give a more detailed description of the concept of “aspects” in section 3 and use them as a mental framework for semi-automatic quality assurance in section 4. Section 5 shows an example where semi-automatic QA is applied to importing of Word documents in OpenOffice 2.0. Finally, in section 6 we conclude and look at future work.

2 Related Work

Jeff Rothenberg describes a number of the problems with object transformation[8] and argues that emulation is a more viable way of preserving access. While we do not agree that emulation is always the better solution for digital preservation, he eloquently describes many of the problems that we seek to solve.

Rauber and Rauch describes in [7] how to use Utility Analysis to decide on the best preservation strategy. They present a method for analyzing file formats and goals for preservation which could possibly be adopted for our purposes.

Most current transformations happen on an ad-hoc basis, using whatever tools happen to be available for the purpose. There is some work being done on a more systematic approach, creating generic frameworks for describing file formats and file contents. One such framework is the XCEL/XCDL system[2], which uses XML descriptions of the structure of a file plus an automatically generated extractor to turn current files into a more durable format. A similar approach is that of persistent objects[3], where a description of the encoding format, including structures and relationships, is preserved. Both these approaches require a deep understanding of the formats in question, a formidable task for complex objects like PDF. Additionally, they do not provide any guarantee that the understanding is correct. The approach described in this article could complement these approaches by providing some assurance that their understanding of the old format is actually in line with reality.

Our method is related to factor analysis[10], in that we use multiple measureable factors (aspects) to investigate what can be seen as a single unmeasurable cause (quality of transformation). In our case, the causes are errors in the transformation, either caused by problems with the transformation system or due to errors in the original documents. We may consider using factor analysis techniques to determine which underlying errors cause the most problems, indicating where to apply improvements to the transformation system. However, the main use of our analysis is to point out which documents are poorly transformed, such that these can be used to investigate the underlying errors.

Surowiecki describes in [11] examples of how averaging multiple independent guesses gives significantly better answers than trying to agree on one single answer. His examples come from areas as different as trivia shows, stock markets and the finding of lost submarines, but all show that a multitude of independent, diverse guess are better than even the most expert single guess. Even if each of the guessers only have access to a very limited amount of information, the combined estimate averages out errors to such a degree that the combined guess is surprisingly precise. Our work can be seen as applying this principle to the realm of digital preservation, where for practical reasons we cannot find the most poorly transformed objects ourselves, but must rely on an educated guess to find the problematic objects.

3 Aspects

First proposed by Anders Johansen in connection with the PLANETS project[5], aspects are an abstraction of the information stored in digital objects. Originally envisioned as a replacement for the concept of file formats, we now view it as a complementary way to discuss digital aspects and how to access the information in them.

An *aspect* is an abstract view of (a subset of the) information in one or more digital objects. Example aspects could be ICC profiles in JPEG images, metadata in MP3 files, or page breaks in Word documents. Aspects commonly correspond to certain parts of files, but they don't have to. *Implicit aspects* are aspects that require some processing of the data in the objects to be found, e.g. word counts of text files, histograms of image colors or bounding boxes of CAD objects. While explicit aspects normally can be found at a specific place in a digital object, and thus should be present in both the source and target files of a transformation, implicit aspects are mostly useful for quality control. An implicit aspect may be easier or more meaningful to compare than the raw information.

Aspects are not constrained to a given file format. An aspect like "creator metadata" may be found in all manner of formats, sometimes under different names. It is important to be specific about the meaning of aspects when using them across different formats or even when considering the same format written by different systems that may have different interpretations of the specifications.

We can fruitfully consider hierarchies of aspects or overlapping aspects. For instance, the five significant properties – content, context, appearance, functionality and structure – defined in [9] can be considered major aspects that in turn encompass numerous smaller aspects like those described earlier. As such, people have been discussing aspects in various ways before, but by unifiying these views and thinking of them all as aspects, we promote novel approaches to existing problems.

4 Semi-automatic Quality Assurance

Approaching QA from an aspect point of view suggests doing QA on each aspect separately. As part of the preservation planning, repository administrators should enumerate which aspects are to be preserved and which, if any, can be considered irrelevant. It is useful to start this by thinking about the five significant properties (content, context, appearance, behaviour and structure), but any information present in the file should be considered to belong to some aspect. Rauber and Rauch describes in [7] how to use Utility Analysis to identify important parts of a format, each of which can be seen as an aspect.

Most explicit aspects that one can come up with are likely to be worthy of preservation, especially in a library context, but some might be considered artifacts of the old format or are simply internal housekeeping. Examples of such could be a separate list of page breaks when page break markers exist in the text (a sort of non-normalized data), or a table of colors in an indexed pixmap when the target format uses full RGB representation. Such irrelevant aspects should be noted in transformation metadata.

For all other aspects, we need one or more checks to ensure that they are preserved in the transformed object. While some transformation tools may have built-in checks of the transformation quality, it is the exception rather than the rule, and would share implementation deficiencies with the transformation tool. It is preferable to use external tools to extract the aspects and compare them, and the more the better. Particularly useful are tools that don't share the same code base, since they will be less susceptible to systematic errors.

4.1 Finding Tools

The easiest way to get such tools is if somebody has already made them. Most file formats in active use will have their own ecosystem of tools available for various uses: Checking conformity, extracting information for display or debugging, automatic cataloguing etc. While they may be written for other purposes, they can frequently be used with little or no modification to extract or compare aspects. They can range from something as simple as the Unix `grep(1)` command to advanced signal processing systems. The simplest possible tool may just show the file size, for cases where the sizes of the source and target files can be easily correlated (e.g. audio and video).

Any tool that can read either the source or the target format is potentially useful, too. Even if no output is given, error messages can be used to indicate encoding problems or semantic errors. Tools that can read a format and write a radically different one can allow different kinds of comparisons than those that can just give the same kinds of format. For instance, reducing a CAD diagram to a low-resolution bitmap may allow one to check the overall positioning of objects without interference from finer details (see section 5.6 for an example).

4.2 Making Tools

Once the existing tools have been examined, if there are still some aspects that are not sufficiently checked, it is time to consider making new tools. One approach to this is using a generic file format abstraction framework like XCEL/XCDL[2] or persistent objects[3]. These allow a system-independent description of the layout of a file and a way to automatically extract the information thus encoded. While creating a full machine-readable description of complex formats like PDF may be an insurmountable task, it should be quite feasible to make one to, say, extract metadata information or list embedded hyperlinks.

If source code is available for a program that can read either format, it may be a minor task to make from it a tool that emits a certain aspect in a form amenable to comparison. While it may be tempting to check all aspects this way if a complete reader is available, it cannot be recommended as it leaves one open to systematic error. Diversity in error checking leads to higher quality.

4.3 Comparing Measurements

Once tools for extracting aspects are assembled, one should look to how to compare them. This may be as easy as comparing two numbers or running `diff`, or could involve complex comparison algorithms and further conversions. Each comparison should yield but a single quality number on some given scale. One should not try to check too many things at a time; it is better to have many local but precise measurements than a few larger but muddled ones.

Let us consider for example a diagram format like the one used by Microsoft Visio. The appearance could be checked by converting to a high-resolution bitmap and comparing those. However, that would be less informative than if we separately compared object placements, object size, fonts used and other more detailed features. Doing a single comparison would not only leave us with only one measurement, it would also be conflating a number of different possible errors. Comparing low-resolution bitmaps would still be useful as one of several checks, as it can be a check of the overall layout that does not get affected by font rendering details or the shapes of arrowheads, but it cannot stand alone.

The output of each comparison should be a quality index of some sort. It doesn't matter if the output has no obvious units or even an identifiable meaning — as long as there is a correspondence between the output and some possible conversion error, the measurement is useful (though it is more useful if you can reason about it). The measure will be combined with a number of other measurements to pin-point the bad transformations. If the individual measures on occasion gives high marks to a bad transformation or vice versa, it need not be a disaster, as combining it with the other measurements will average out the occasional error. Having measures that overlap somewhat, or that measure the same thing in different ways, gives extra insurance against measurement errors. If an aspect is considered particularly critical, one would want to be extra careful that it gets measured accurately, and multiple measures help with that.

Once all the measurements are taken on a particular object, they should be normalized to a uniform scale. The obvious choice for normalizing is to use the average error as the midpoint of the scale, and use the standard deviation to determine the endpoints. Thus if the quality (inverted error) for a measure m of an object o is $Q_m(o)$, and the average and standard deviations of the measure for all objects is E_m and σ_m, the *normalized quality* of the object for that measure is $\frac{Q_m(o)-\max(0,E_m-\sigma_m)}{2\sigma_m}$ capped to the range $[0,1]$. The normalized quality of the transformation of an object is the average of the normalized qualities of that object for all measures.

The normalized quality will tell how overall well the transformation of that object went compared to the other ones. Manually examining objects with the highest and lowest normalized quality will give an indication of the quality range of the transformation, and plotting the averages can tell something about the overall quality distribution. When the transformation is performed on a large number of objects, the outliers should be manually checked to see if they are still within the bounds of acceptable quality. Also, objects with non-normalized measurements far outside the range of the standard deviation should be examined to see what caused such abberations.

Rauber and Rauch[7] uses a separate value "Not Acceptable" in their quality assessments. Such a value could also be used in this context, for characteristics that are critical and accurately checked by a single measurement. If this value is assigned for an object, all other measurements are overruled and the conversion is considered of unacceptable quality. This approach should probably be reserved for cases where resources become virtually unusable without a specific aspect correctly transformed, but could provide a shortcut to finding critical failures.

Objects measured as being of very low quality will have to be checked manually. A manual check can be aided both by the individual measurements that went into the normalized quality rating (possibly before capping to the normalized range) and by specialized or modified tools to compare originals and converted objects. Details of how to implement such aids are beyond the scope of this paper.

5 An Example: Reading Word Files in OpenOffice

As a proof of concept, we took a semi-random selection of 46 Word files from the Danish archive site vaerkarkivet.dk and investigated how well OpenOffice 2.0 could understand them. To facilitate comparison, we exported the documents to PDF using Adobe Acrobat in Word and OpenOffice's native PDF exporter. Various features of the resulting PDF files were then compared.

5.1 Setup

50 Microsoft Office files were downloaded at random from Værkarkivet, a Danish public archive of digital objects (`http://pligt.kb.dk`. Of these, 2 turned out to be Excel files rather than Word files, 1 was removed since OpenOffice could not convert it, and 2 were removed later when one of the tools failed to process it, leaving us with 45 files. These were first converted with Adobe Acrobat 7.0 Professional (Danish version) into one group of PDFs (the Acrobat conversions), and then loaded one at a time into OpenOffice 2.0.3 (Danish version), where they were exported into PDF (the OpenOffice conversions). All this was done on the same Windows XP machine.

5.2 Measure 1: Number of Pages

The first measure was the number of pages in the PDFs. The `pdftodsc` tool was used to extract this from both sets of PDFs. Only 25 of the files had exactly the same number

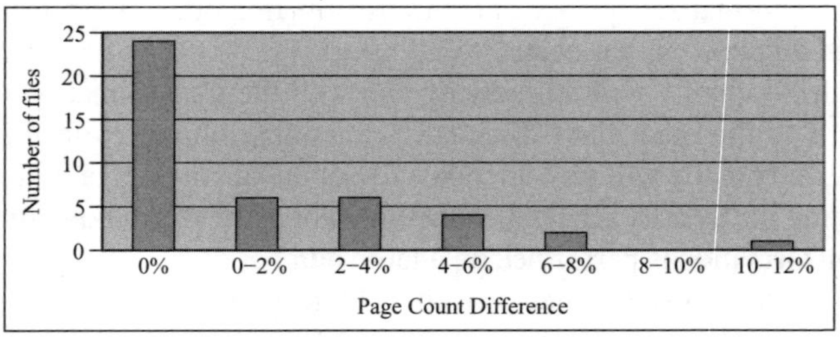

Fig. 1. Count of differences in page count

of pages. The remaining files had differences of mostly less than 5%, with a few going as high as 10%. Figure 1 shows the distribution of differences in page counts.

5.3 Measure 2: Metadata Similarity

The second measure was of the metadata found in PDF files. Using the `pdfinfo` tool, various metadata fields could be extracted, of which three (Title, Author and Page Size) could reasonably be expected to be taken from the original document. The measurement was simplistic: We measured how many of the metadata fields were the same. Only twelve differences were found, and only for one file did two of the three fields differ. Most differences were either encoding errors or fields that had been truncated. Figure 2 shows the distribution of number of metadata fields that differed.

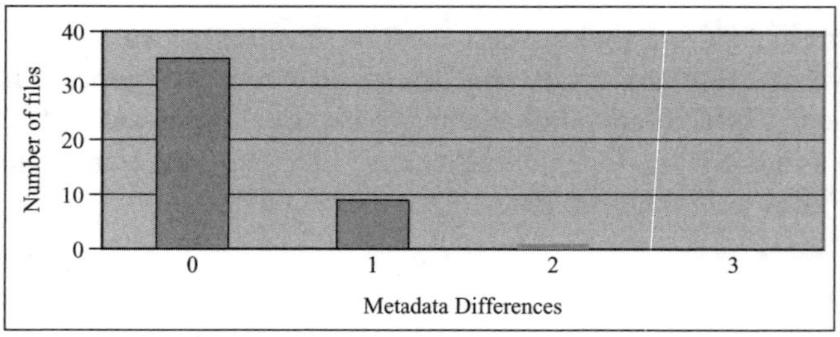

Fig. 2. Errors in metadata fields

5.4 Measure 3: Font Substitutions

The `pdffonts` utility extracts a table of which fonts are used. For this example, we merely compared the names of the fonts to see how many fonts were missing or added. It is interesting here to notice that pdffonts consistently complained that the Acrobat conversions did not embed TrueType fonts as required by Adobe's specifications. On average, the 58% of the fonts were the same in the original and the converted PDFs, with only 6 files having exactly the same set of fonts. It is unclear how much influence this has on the actual rendering, but it can still be used as a measure of difference. Figure 3 shows the distribution of number of fonts added or removed.

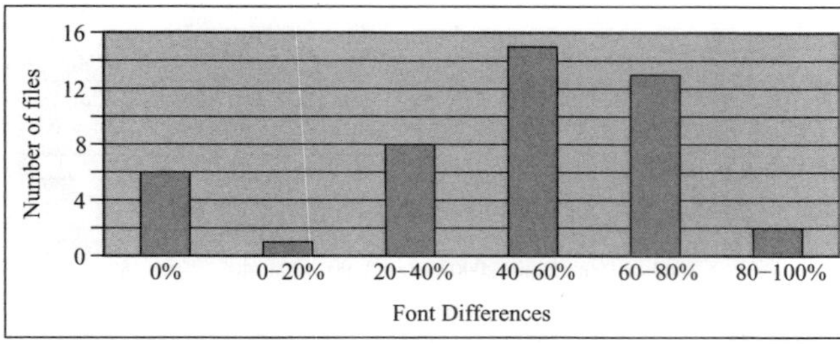

Fig. 3. Differences in included fonts

5.5 Measure 4: Text Similarity

One would hope that the text is preserved reasonably intact when transforming a text document. To check this, we used the `pdftotext` utility, which extracts into plain UTF-8. We then sorted the words and ran `diff` on them to see the number of words added or removed.

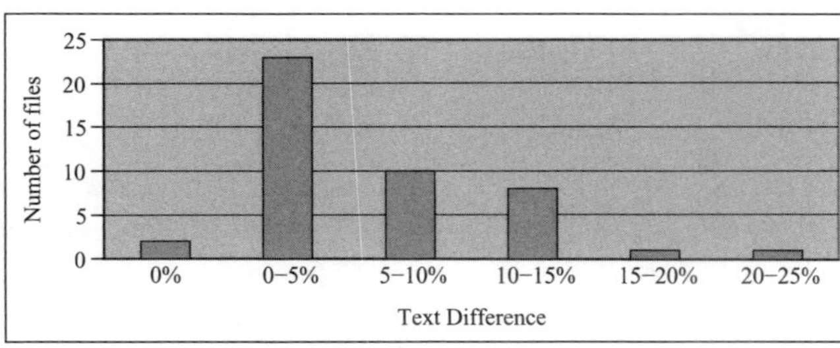

Fig. 4. Differences in words in text

On the average, 5.5% of the words had changed. Most of the changes were either due to differences in hyphenation or different layout of the titles, table of contents or index. Figure 4 shows the distribution of the percentage of words added or removed.

5.6 Measure 5: Layout Similarity

As a final measurement, we converted each page into a 40x40 pixmap with the `convert` program from ImageMagick, and then compared these using `compare` from the same package using the Mean Average Error metric. Two files from the OpenOffice set could not be converted, but caused the `convert` program to die with "unrecoverable error". Of the rest, none were exactly the same, but some exhibited significantly larger differences than others. Figure 5 shows the distribution of differences in layout

A main reason for layout changes is that lines and paragraphs get broken in different ways. If this happens near the end of a section, extra pages may be added or removed, causing the layout of pages to go out of sync. There is a correlation (0.51) between the layout similary and page count similarity.

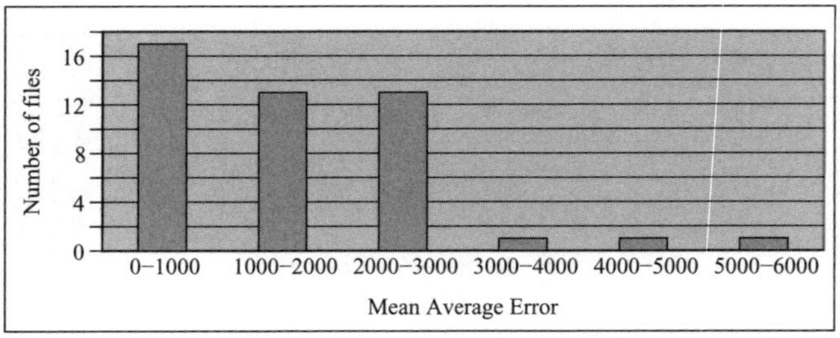

Fig. 5. Differences in low-resolution versions of pages

5.7 Combining the Measures

As described in section 4.3 above, the quality measurements are normalized based on the standard deviation. The normalized quality is then the average of the five normalized measurements. Figure 6 shows the combined error rates (inverse quality) for all documents, sorted by overall quality.

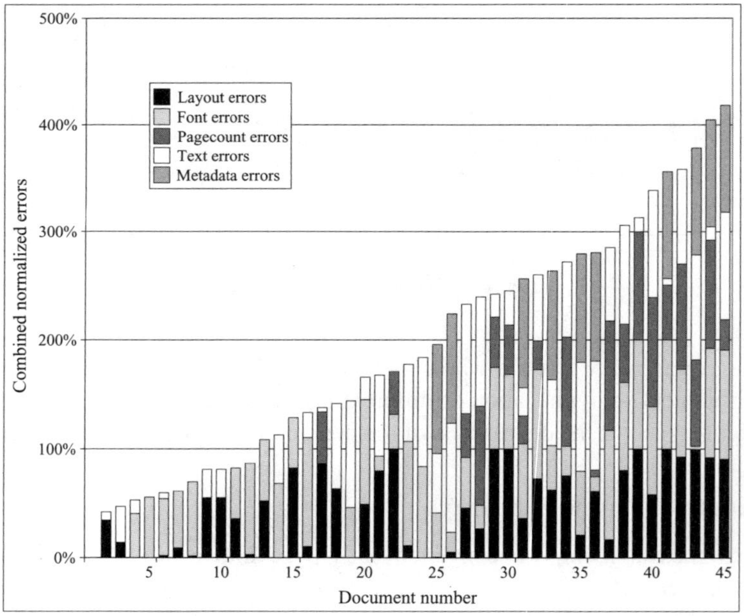

Fig. 6. Combined errors rates for all documents, sorted by total error

Correlation testing shows that the largest correlation between measurements is between the layout measurement and the pagecount measurement, with a correlation coefficient of 0.51. This is not surprising, as changes in page count must lead to some amount of change in the layout when different pages are compared. Other than that, there are correlations of between 0.2 and 0.3 between the layout and the metadata measures, between the fonts and the pagecount measurements, between the fonts and the metadata measurements, and between the pagecount and text measurements. Outside of the correlations with metadata, these may be the result of different hyphenation systems and font substitutions causing layout changes.

5.8 Result

Based on the combined results from above, we manually examined the original Word files in Microsoft Office 2003 and OpenOffice 2.0.3 by displaying them next to each other and looking for visible differences. We examined a random sample of 10 documents as well as the 5 highest-quality and 5 lowest-quality documents.

The most common problem was changes in line breaks and page breaks, partly due to differences in font rendering, hyphenation and spacing. This would have a marked effect on the bitmap and page count measures and some effect on the text measure. Almost all the documents examined had some amount of difference in page breaks.

The manual inspection did, as expected, not give a perfect match to the calculated quality. However, the 5 highest quality documents did turn out to have very high quality conversions, with only two having any significant shifts in page breaks, and all having markup, foot notes, table of contents etc. essentially the same.

Among the five conversions with the lowest quality, all had significant to major shifts in layout, and each displayed one or more other errors, including graphics superimposed on text, table contents fused together, images missing, spontaneously appearing elements or major additions in table of contents.

It was obvious from the inspection that in this example, differences in word- and line-breaking had too much weight in the overall quality measure. The presence of a correlation of over 0.5 indicates that two of the measures measure the same error to some degree. Extra tools to extract diagrams, table of contents and other features would have pinpointed errors more accurately, as would extraction of text in a way that disregarded hyphentation. 5 measures is not enough to give a reliable quality indication, but does give strong hints.

It is particularly noteworthy that the quality measures worked given the chain of processing the data went through. Rather than comparing Word files and OpenOffice files, both were converted to PDF and in one case further converted to PNG. If used for preservation, such a chain of conversions is normally expected to accumulate errors from each transformation. However, since these transformations are allowed to drop information not relevant to the measurement being taken, such error accumulation is limited enough to vanish in the measurement errors. Thus, we can use a plethora of tools to perform our measurements without worrying overmuch about whether each tool makes a perfect transformation.

6 Conclusion and Future Work

Quality assurance is a critical part of transforming digital objects from one file format to another or to a newer version of the same format. There are numerous things that can go wrong in such a process, and on the scale of a digital library, manual inspection of all transformed objects is a Herculean task. Thus in many cases, we inspect only a small number of objects and hope that they give enough indication of errors for the transformation process to be sufficiently debugged. This leaves us with a majority of objects in an uncertain state of accessibility until somebody in the future attempts to access them, by when it may be too late to correct the errors.

To avoid this uncertainty, we have proposed a method called *semi-automatic QA*, in which a multitude of separate quality measurements are taken and their results combined to give an overall quality rating. We base this approach on the concept of *aspects*, in which we view digital objects not as specific file formats but through a prism of smaller parts, ranging from the five significant properties of [9] over very specific aspects such as "creator metadata" or "color profile name" to implicit aspects calculated from the data in the objects.

We have given an example of using semi-automated QA to assess the quality of reading Word files in OpenOffice 2.0. In order to facilitate the comparison, we converted the documents to PDF from both Word and OpenOffice, and subsequently compared the PDF files. Despite having a small number of measures and a long chain of conversions, the highest-rated objects were indeed well transformed, while the lowest-rated objects turned out to have transformation errors of types that we had not checked explicitly for. We conclude that semi-automated QA can give a higher degree of confidence in the quality of digital object transformations by allowing practical, early pin-pointing of errors. We also make note that for measurement purposes, a longer chain of conversion programs does not necessarily accumulate errors impeding the measurements.

The concept of semi-automatic QA holds promise as a part of a digital preservation strategy, however more research needs to be done on it. Methods for defining aspects and the measures based on them needs to be developed and collected, and a firmer statistical founding needs to be incorporated. In particular, there is a need for ways to help identify the desired aspects and to analyze whether the measures in place cover all desired aspects with sufficient overlap and in a sufficiently independent manner. Methods from factor analysis can surely be applied to some of these problems, while other parts of them are a problem for preservation planning systems more than for the actual transformation systems.

It may be possible to use the approach described herein for object characterization as well. For instance, one could use fine-grained aspects to determine properties that all or nearly all objects in a collection has, either for validation of expected properties or for improving the description of the collection.

Another intriguing notion suggested by one of the anonymous reviewers is to apply entropy minimization principles to determine that all quantifiable information has been characterized. If this is feasible, it would provide guarantees that the aspects cover everything. However, it should be kept in mind that the semi-automatic QA method does not infer anything about the format of the digital objects being investigated, only about the information content.

The connection between the aspect approach and the "definitive description" approaches [2,3] has yet to be investigated. Besides aspect providing a complementary view of the objects, partial definitive descriptions could be used to extract aspects as well: even if no complete description of a format is available, making an automatable description of the aspects that no other tools can easily extract could be much more feasible. As mentioned earlier, aspect-based investigations can also be used to verify the validity of definitive descriptions.

There is also an open area of methods to assist manual checking of quality. Several approaches can be envisioned, such as automatic side-by-side viewing, flipping back and forth between images, or highlighting automatically detected differences. The opportunities and problems in this area needs investigation, and in particular methods for data other than images need to be developed.

The methods discussed herein can also be used to extend the work of Rauber and Rauch[7], whose tests methods for transformation tools do not include anything equivalent to our implicit aspects.

References

1. Hd photo specification v1.0. Technical report, Microsoft (2006)
2. Heydegger, V., Neumann, J., Schnasse, J., Thaller, M.: Basic design for the extensible characterisation languages. Technical report, Universität zu Köln (October 2006)
3. Moore, R.: The san diego project: Persistent objects. In: Proceedings of the Workshop on XML for Digital Preservation, Urbino, Italy (October 2002)
4. Pdf reference: Technical report, Adobe Systems Incorporated (November 2006)
5. Planets: Preservation and long-term access through networked services (2006), URL `http://www.planets-project.eu`
6. Rabbani, M., Joshi, R.: An overview of the jpeg 2000 still image compression standard. Signal Processing: Image Communication 17(1), 3–48 (2002)
7. Rauch, C., Rauber, A.: Preserving Digital Media: Towards a Preservation Solution Evaluation Metric. In: Chen, Z., Chen, H., Miao, Q., Fu, Y., Fox, E., Lim, E.-p. (eds.) ICADL 2004. LNCS, vol. 3334, pp. 203–212. Springer, Heidelberg (2004)
8. Rothenberg, J.: Avoiding technological quicksand: Finding a viable technical foundation for digital preservation. Council on LIbrary and Information Resources (CLIR) (January 1999)
9. Rothenberg, J.: Carrying Authentic, Understandable and Usable Digital Records Through Time. RAND Europe, Leiden, The Netherlands (1999)
10. Rummel, R.J.: Applied Factor Analysis. Northwestern University Press, Evanston (1979)
11. Surowiecki, J.: The Wisdom of Crowds: Why the Many Are Smarter Than the Few and How Collective Wisdom Shapes Business, Economies, Societies and Nations. DoubleDay (May 2004)

Texts, Illustrations, and Physical Objects: The Case of Ancient Shipbuilding Treatises

Carlos Monroy[1], Richard Furuta[1], and Filipe Castro[2]

[1] Center for the Study of Digital Libraries and Department of Computer Science
Texas A&M University
College Station, TX 77843-3112, USA
{cmonroy, furuta}@csdl.tamu.edu
[2] Center for Maritime Archaeology and Conservation
Texas A&M University
College Station, TX 77843-4352, USA
fvcastro@tamu.edu

Abstract. One of the main goals of the Nautical Archaeology Digital Library (NADL) is to assist nautical archaeologists in the reconstruction of ancient ships and the study of shipbuilding techniques. Ship reconstruction is a specialized task that requires supporting materials such as reference to fragments and timbers recovered from other excavations and consultation of shipbuilding treatises. The latter are manuscripts written in a variety of languages and spanning several centuries. Due to their diverse provenance, technical content, and time of writing, shipbuilding treatises are complex written sources. In this paper we discuss a digital library approach to handle these manuscripts and their multilingual properties (often including unknown terms and concepts), and how scholars in different countries are collaborating in this endeavor. Our collection of treatises raises interesting challenges and provides a glimpse of the relationship between texts and illustrations, and their mapping to physical objects.

Keywords: Nautical archaeology, ancient technical manuscripts, shipbuilding treatises, ship reconstruction.

1 Introduction

The Nautical Archaeology Digital Library (NADL) [39] is a collaborative effort between the Center for the Study of Digital Libraries and the Center for Maritime Archaeology and Conservation at Texas A&M University. Our effort includes the design, implementation, and evaluation of a framework for supporting research in nautical archaeology with these goals: a) to efficiently catalog, store, and manage artifacts and ship remains along with the associated data and information produced by an underwater archeological excavation; b) to integrate heterogeneous data sources from different media to facilitate research work; c) to incorporate historic sources to help in the study of current artifacts; d) to develop visualization tools to help

L. Kovács, N. Fuhr, and C. Meghini (Eds.): ECDL 2007, LNCS 4675, pp. 198–209, 2007.

researchers manipulate, study, and analyze artifacts and their relationships; and e) to develop algorithms and visualization-based mechanisms for ship reconstruction.

The life cycle of an underwater excavation begins with the discovery of a shipwreck. Once permissions with the local government are cleared and funding is available, a survey is carried out, which gives a preliminary assessment of the site, ship, and artifacts. Teams of archaeologists carry out field work at the site over several years. Ship cargo (artifacts) and timbers (ship remains and fragments) are recorded, and are later recovered, carefully documented, and sent to specialized laboratories for conservation. This process generates a large amount of material in photographs, diver notes, drawings, video, and digital representations.

Once ship remains and fragments are measured and their properties and conditions documented, researchers begin the time consuming task of reassembling the ship. Due to exposure to underwater conditions, ship remains are quite often damaged and incomplete; thus, scholars have to relay on evidence recovered from other excavations and information in the written literature provided by shipbuilding treatises.

Ship reconstruction is a broad area of research; our goal in this paper is to focus on a subset—the use of shipbuilding treatises by scholars for ship reconstruction after timbers are recovered. In the paper, we discuss the application of a scalable architecture we have developed that enables scholars to edit/access a multilingual glossary of nautical terms, and an image-tagging interface to link terms from the glossary and to structure the contents of the treatises. We also show how the architecture can be extended for mapping physical ship remains recovered from underwater excavations with their corresponding illustrations and relevant texts.

Documents written in multiple languages are source materials that researchers in other disciplines, such as literature, poetry, history, and art need to access for their scholarly work. Therefore, we expect that our approach will help other multilingual digital library repositories. Similarly, our work has been informed by projects from other domains in the humanities, although the specific characteristics of Nautical Archaeology provide us with additional opportunities.

2 Related Work

Techniques, tools, and software in Digital Libraries have made it possible to digitize, preserve, and disseminate priceless historic, scientific, literary, artistic, and archaeological information and collections. Despite the use of computers and software tools by archeologists, current practices in certain areas of Nautical Archaeology either do not exploit the potential that information technology can offer, or use the tools in a very limited way—a common phenomenon also present in other humanities fields.

Recently archaeologists have started using a variety of computing technologies to speed up research and make information much easier to access, manipulate, and analyze. Archaeology however is a complex area, mainly because of the heterogeneity of the data, the large number of artifacts and source materials, and the time required to study and publish archaeological findings. The ETANA-DL initiative [25, 26, 31] provides an archaeology digital library for assisting archaeologists in collecting and recording their data, as well as in disseminating their findings to the public. ETANA-DL uses the 5S framework [11] for modeling archaeological data and procedures.

The Alexandria Archive Institute in association with the University of Chicago's OCHRE project [16], assists archaeologists in documenting surveys and excavations. In order to preserve and disseminate cultural heritage, they have created ArchaeoML—the Archaeological Markup Language—an XML schema that enables the mapping of XML documents with relational databases.

The Perseus Project [6, 7] is a digital library in the context of cultural and historical heritage material, focused originally on ancient Greek culture and currently including Roman and Renaissance collections, it provides a variety of visualization tools for its contents, as well as several access mechanisms to its collection of texts and images. Crane [8] states that cultural digital libraries often have to handle multilingual documents—an important issue in our collection of manuscripts. The Digital Atheneum [3, 4] hosted at the University of Kentucky has developed new techniques for restoring and editing humanities collections with special emphasis on technical approaches to restoring severely damaged manuscripts, along image-text linking [5].

The Petra Great Temple excavations [15, 33], a joint Brown University and the Jordanian Department of Antiquities archeological excavation shows the development of new technologies based on the archaeologist needs. The Digital Imprint [37] at the Institute of Archaeology (UCLA) proposes a project to design standards for the electronic publication of archaeological site reports. Helling, et al. [13], describe the creation of an interactive virtual reality exhibit of archaeological artifacts from the Port Royal excavation (Jamaica); one of several archaeological projects conducted by the Institute for Advanced Technology in the Humanities.

The Brown University SHAPE Laboratory [1, 2, 12, 34] has developed several techniques and tools that can be applied to Archaeology; their multidisciplinary team designed software that enables archeologists to model and reconstruct columns, buildings, statues, and other complex shapes from photos and video. The Theban Mapping Project [27, 28, 35] based at the American University in Cairo, Egypt provides a comprehensive archaeological detailed map and database of every archaeological, geological, and ethnographic feature in Thebes.

Related to digital texts and their linkage to images, The Society of Early English and Norse Electronic Texts (SEENET), uses the Elwood Viewer [38] for displaying TEI-compliant documentary and critical editions of medieval texts, the viewer presents readers with parallel text and image displays, and allows for multiple regular expression-based text search. Fekete, et al. [9], show the use of Compus, a visualization tool for analyzing a corpus of 16th century French manuscript letters. The tool requires XML-encoded documents. Plaisant, et al. [24], integrate text mining and a graphical user interface in the interpretation of literary works; their system assumes documents to be XML-encoded. Spiro, et al. [29], integrate TEI-encoded text and digital images in the Travelers in the Middle East Archive.

Text encoding—such as TEI or XML—allows structuring and indexing documents (especially old manuscripts), an intermediate step for making them available to scholars and the public. This process however, requires term disambiguation and thesauri. Medelyan and Witten [18] propose a method for enhancing automatic key phrase extraction. Perrow and Barber [23] on the other hand, propose a method for parsing unstructured textual records of the archives at the Abbaye de Saint-Maurice,

Switzerland, a collection of manuscripts dating from the 11th century, noting that one of the challenges with old manuscripts is the one of disambiguation.

With the use of computer-based tools, The Canterbury Tales Project [36] has collated several of Geoffrey Chaucer's manuscripts for reconstructing the history of the text. Related to ancient written documents and artifacts, The InscriptiFact Project [40] makes accessible to scholars a database of high-resolution images of ancient inscriptions—the focus is on some of the earliest written records.

3 Shipbuilding Treatises

Shipbuilding treatises are ancient technical manuscripts that describe the characteristics of a ship or ships, properties of the wood and materials used, and the steps to be followed in their construction. Due to provenance and time of writing, their content varies. For scholars, they are a rich source of information in the reconstruction of sunken ships, as well as in the understanding of the evolution of shipbuilding techniques. For Nautical Archaeology students who as part of their curriculum are required to take a course on Books and Treatises on Shipbuilding, they provide information about naval concepts and techniques, as well as history of ship construction in different traditions.

From the Renaissance until the 19th century, the development of shipbuilding techniques experienced a tremendous advancement. From an early oral tradition, their evolution eventually led to sophisticated documents that included illustrations, detailed descriptions, glossaries, proportions, curves, designs, and finally, geometric algorithms and physics. To have a general idea of shipbuilding treatises and better understand the challenges they pose to nautical archaeologists, we briefly discuss three of the most significant late 16th and early 17th-century Portuguese treatises.

3.1 16th and 17th-Century Portuguese Shipbuilding Treatises

O Livro da Fabrica das Naus [22] composed by Father Fernando Oliveira in 1580 illustrates the need to create formal guidelines in the construction of ships. This manuscript begins describing the characteristics of the wood, based on its function and stresses they have to endure; as well as properties of other materials used in assembling timbers, sealing, and caulking. Eventually, the manuscript makes a transition from a descriptive approach into a more technical one. Oliveira describes the proportions of the ship with good degree of detail, including illustrations to demonstrate the use of proportions.

Joao Baptista Lavanha, c. 1610, begins his manuscript *Livro Primeiro da Architectura Naval* [17] with an introduction on architecture, and its related disciplines. Geometric descriptions are used throughout the manuscript. Given the importance Lavanha gives to architecture, he insists on the importance of making drawings and physical models to correct imperfections in the design prior to the building of the ship. The author mentions the importance of the quality of the materials to be used suggesting what kind of woods should be used for different parts of the ship and when they should be cut. The following sections describe along their corresponding illustrations, the proportions, and steps in the construction of ships. As stated earlier, Lavahna's manuscript is rich in the usage of geometric descriptions.

Livro de Tracas de Carpinteria [10], written by Manoel Fernandez and dated 1616, provides a comprehensive list of dimensions for different vessels, calculations, and assembling guidelines for ships of different tonnage. The second section contains illustrations depicting the construction of the ships. It also provides a detailed index of contents and tables listing quantities and characteristics of components to be used in the construction of a variety of ships. Illustrations provide a great degree of detail for a variety of vessels, of the way pieces have to be placed, how they should be assembled, distances that need to be kept, and in some instances providing the rationale and practical reasons. The final section is devoted to masts and sails.

3.2 How Treatises Are Used

Our initial experience working with shipbuilding treatises shows that users can be grouped into three categories: a) nautical archaeologists and scholars, b) Nautical Archaeology students, and c) the general public, who are non-experts but curious about the history of naval construction, seafaring, and the cultures where they flourished. Based on these groups of users, we had to first understand what the characteristics, structure, and contents of the treatises are. As briefly discussed in the previous section, treatises' contents vary. However they share some important similarities. In a broader sense, shipbuilding treatises can be seen as technical manuals that describe the parts (ship components) required to build a composite object (ship), and provide instructions on how they have to be assembled.

The reconstruction of an incomplete and damaged ancient ship—a complex composite object—is a task that requires the use of supporting materials such as treatises and timbers recovered from other excavations. An archaeologist analyzing a recovered timber or fragment from a shipwreck, searches the treatises to find information about the properties of those pieces, what part of the ship they belong to, and how they were assembled. With incomplete and damaged components, treatises can help to project their original dimensions. Ship construction obviously follows a sequence of steps. At each step it is necessary to know how pieces are joined and what material is used (nails, clamps). At a macro-level, treatises contain information about proportions of the vessels. In general they indicate how wide, and high they should be in terms of the length of the keel.

Typically, contents of digital libraries have been related to literary works, such as novels or poetry, legal records, letters, and historical narratives. Collections of ancient scientific and technical manuscripts are more rare. However, they are important for understanding the history of science and technology. Due to their own particular structure and use, they can be a great source for the creation and advancement of algorithms and techniques that can be applied to other digital collections.

Given their technical contents and their use in the reconstruction of ships, shipbuilding treatises require a different approach from general literary works. There are two main problems when scholars study and analyze what construction techniques, or what treatise—if any—were used in a particular vessel. The first problem is to determine the origin of the ship—sometimes the provenance of the ship is still subject to debate. The second problem is when a ship has been properly identified but the time of construction is not well known. In the latter, it is difficult to determine if a particular treatise was used in its construction.

4 Our Architecture

Our architecture [21] has been designed based on the use and properties of technical manuscripts, which extends the notion of a text that describes and illustrates a composite physical object, namely a shipbuilding treatise describing a ship. It also reflects the characteristics of physical timbers and fragments recovered from underwater excavations. From the ship construction point of view we have identified three main ways to structure the content of shipbuilding treatises: temporal, spatial, and functional. Temporal refers to the steps in the construction sequence (keel, framing, planking, or rigging). Spatial refers to a physical section of the ship they describe (lower deck, upper deck, bow, stern, or cargo section). Functional refers to the role that sections and components in the text play in the ship (structural, transversal, longitudinal, joints, or ornamental). This approach can be extended to any "composite object," because in order to build it: a) a series of steps are required for its completion (temporal property), b) sub-components have to be assembled (spatial property), and c) components play different roles in the whole (functional property).

Other literary works such as novels, poetry, or historical narratives can be seen to certain degree as a text related to a "composite object." For example, our work on the iconography of *Don Quixote* [30] aims at exploring the relationship between illustrations and the novel. In this case, an illustration depicting an episode or adventure in the novel can be related to a section or sections in the text. In the case of the historical narrative of the life of Pablo Picasso (the On-line Picasso Project) [19], the artist's life could be considered a composite object, formed by events in his life. However, in contrast to a "real physical object" such as a ship, the history told in a novel or the narrative in a historical text does not have a tangible physical equivalent.

4.1 Handling Objects in Multiple Languages

Nautical Archaeology is a field where language introduces another layer in the relationship between a physical object and relevant references in sections and illustrations in written and printed materials, since treatises: a) are written in different languages, and b) may contain unknown technical nautical terms. Therefore, the content of technical manuscripts used in understanding a composite real object establishes a direct link between the description in the text, relevant illustrations, and the physical object and its subcomponents. This is an important property because it plays a key role for archeologists searching for relevant images and texts when analyzing a particular timber based on spatial, temporal, or functional roles, thus constraining the design of our architecture.

Based on these properties we can formalize the relationship between physical objects and manuscripts as follows: **TC** is a collection of treatises, $\mathbf{O}_j$ is a physical object recovered from the excavation, $\mathbf{T}_j$ is a treatise in the collection of treatises, $\boldsymbol{\sigma}_j$ is a section within a treatise, $\boldsymbol{\delta}_j$ is an illustration in a treatise, and $\boldsymbol{\Gamma}_j$ is a language a treatise in the collection is written. Thus,

$$\mathrm{O}_i \Rightarrow \mathrm{T}_1[\sigma_1 \dots \sigma_j], \mathrm{T}_2[\sigma_1 \dots \sigma_j], \dots \mathrm{T}_m[\sigma_1 \dots \sigma_j] \tag{1}$$

$$\mathrm{O}_i \Rightarrow \mathrm{T}_1[\delta_1 \dots \delta_j], \mathrm{T}_2[\delta_1 \dots \delta_j], \dots \mathrm{T}_m[\delta_1 \dots \delta_j] \tag{2}$$

Expression (1) states that information relevant to the physical object $\mathbf{O}_i$ recovered from the excavation can be found in sections $[\boldsymbol{\sigma}_1 \ldots \boldsymbol{\sigma}_j]$ of a subset of treatises $\{\mathbf{T}_1 \ldots \mathbf{T}_m\}$. Conversely, $[\boldsymbol{\delta}_1 \ldots \boldsymbol{\delta}_j]$ are relevant illustrations to object $\mathbf{O}_i$ (2). We can also state that a given section of a treatise can be related to a subset of illustrations,

$$\sigma_i \Rightarrow \{\delta_1, \delta_2 \cdots \delta_j\} \tag{3}$$

and that references to and explanations about an illustration can be found in a subset of sections of a treatise,

$$\delta_i \Rightarrow \{\sigma_1, \sigma_2 \cdots \sigma_j\} \tag{4}$$

Because of the technical contents of the manuscripts, a section in one treatise can be relevant to illustrations in other treatises, $\{\delta_1, \delta_2 \cdots \delta_j\} \Rightarrow \mathrm{T}_1, \mathrm{T}_2 \cdots \mathrm{T}_j$ conversely, illustrations in one treatise can be related to the contents of other treatises, $\{\sigma_1, \sigma_2 \cdots \sigma_i\} \Rightarrow \mathrm{T}_1, \mathrm{T}_2 \cdots \mathrm{T}_j$.

Our architecture extends the basic functions of a dictionary in two ways. First, it is not limited to a certain number of languages. This is important for our collection when incorporating new treatises from a particular naval tradition written in a language that was not originally included. Second, it allows multiple spellings, synonyms, and other *roles* that can be required. Spellings are very useful for archaeologists because technical terms in the manuscripts tend to have multiple spellings as well as synonyms.

To enable scalability, our architecture is based on the concept of an entity with multiple properties and roles. Therefore, a *term* can be seen as an entity where every language corresponds to a property's value, and *synonyms* and *spellings* correspond to *roles*. An entity **E** (term) can have *n properties and m roles*; a property can be a characteristic, attribute, or feature (in the present case languages). Roles on the other hand, describe functions related to the entity (in the present case, the *term itself*, *spellings*, and *synonyms*). Therefore, each term can be seen as a matrix $\mathbf{E}_{\mathbf{n,m}}$, where $\boldsymbol{n}$ is the number of properties, $\boldsymbol{m}$ the number of roles, and each cell $\rho_{i,j}$ in **E**—with the exception of the base role (first column)—can be denoted as a vector of values $\rho_{i,j} = \{v_1 \quad v_2 \quad \cdots \quad v_k\}$.

4.2 Structuring Treatises

As stated earlier, there are at least three well defined ways to structure the content of shipbuilding treatises: spatial, temporal, and functional. This is accomplished in two steps: first, scholars using the multilingual glossary editing interface— based on the previously described architecture—(figure 1) can assign categories and taxa to the terms. Second, using a parser—adapted from the one developed for a collection of 17th-century poems by John Donne [32, 20]—terms from the treatises can be extracted, and based on the taxonomy and categories assigned to them, sections in the ship, assembling sequences, or functions in their construction can be assigned. The problem is how can illustrations be segmented and associated to the texts?

Using an image tagging interface, scholars can associate terms to either areas or points in the images. The latter is useful for components with irregular shapes. Figure 2 shows the image tagging interface. Editors are presented with images of

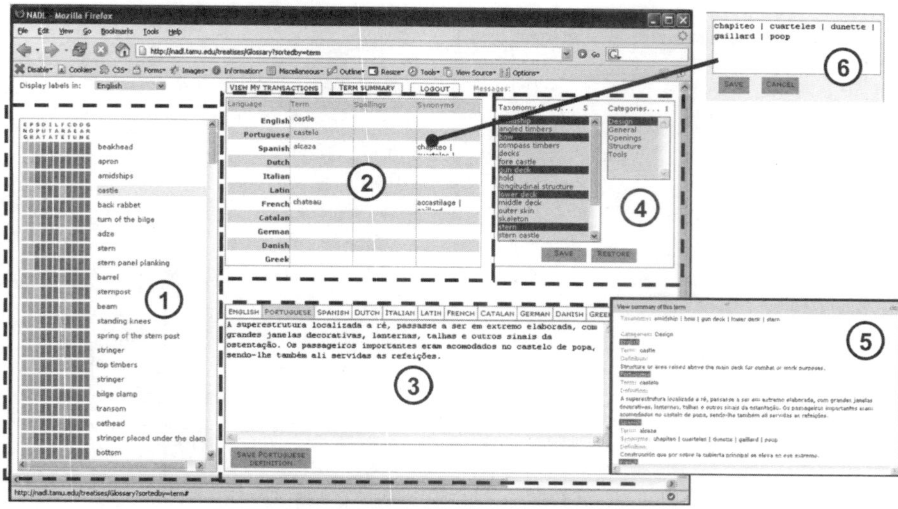

Fig. 1. Multilingual glossary interface: 1) term list, 2) terms, synonyms, and spellings area, 3) definitions editing area, 4) taxonomy, and category editing area, 5) a preview of a term, and 6) term editing area

illustrations from the treatises. Terms from the glossary can be assigned to an area or a set of points, which are then saved into a database. Since terms are associated with a taxonomy and categories it is straightforward to search for images in the collection.

Our architecture can be easily adapted and extended to fragments and timbers recovered from archaeological excavations based on the fact that physical objects correspond to terms and concepts in the multilingual glossary.

4.3 Mapping Composite Objects

One of the main characteristics of ships is that individual components assembled together form a particular section of the ship. In technical manuscripts—as is the case with shipbuilding treatises—physical characteristics, properties, and dimensions of objects are carefully described. This is a major difference with literary works, thus requires a special approach. The main reason is the role they play in the context of the "narrative." They are after all required in the construction of a composite physical object. A composite object CO can be expressed as **CO =** $\{C_1, C_2 \cdots C_k\}$ where each $\mathbf{C}_i$ is a subcomponent, which in turn can be composed of other subcomponents—reminiscent of a recursive property until atomic components are reached. Furthermore, a component $\mathbf{C}_i$ can have particular relationships with other components $\{\mathbf{C}_k, \ldots \mathbf{C}_m\}$. For instance, sub-component $\mathbf{C}_1$ has to be fastened to component $\mathbf{C}_2$, this intermediate component called $\mathbf{C}_{1,2}$ can in turn be attached to other component $\mathbf{C}_3$, a process that can be repeated until the whole physical object is completed.

The problem faced by archaeologists looking for relevant information in the manuscripts is first, finding components he or she might be analyzing. Second, a subset of components can play spatial, temporal, or functional roles in the ship, thus

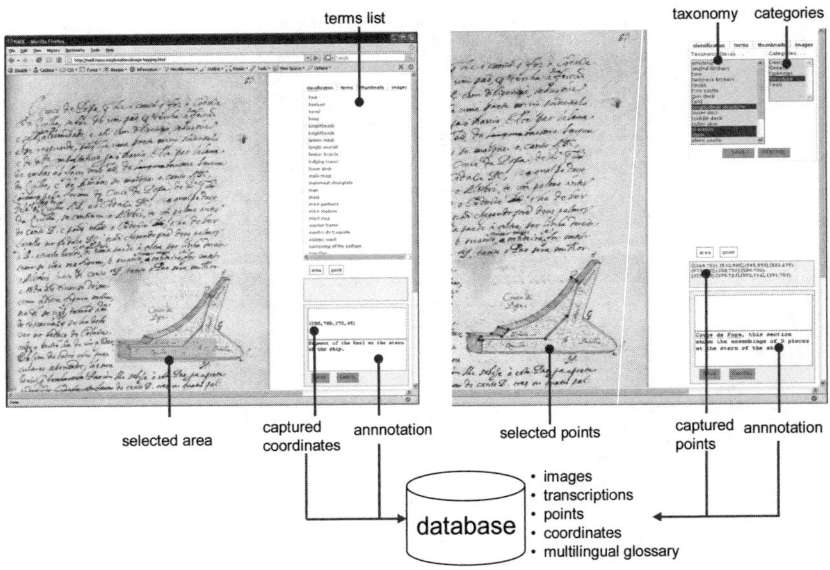

Fig. 2. Web-based image-tagging interface. On the left a selected area in the image (green rectangle) is associated to terms in the glossary. On the right, the association of series of points (red dots) with the taxonomy and categories. In both cases annotations can be entered.

the need for associating them based on these categories. Additionally, in technical manuals, the building of a composite object **CO** involves a series of steps $\mathbf{S_i}$, $\mathbf{CO} = \{ S_1, S_2 \cdots S_k \}$ each one requiring a set of components $\{ \mathbf{C_1}, \mathbf{C_2} \ ... \ \mathbf{C_i} \}$. Thus, components required in a particular construction step can be expressed as $\mathbf{S_i} = \{ C_1, C_2 \cdots C_k \}$. We can then define that assemblage steps can be mapped to both illustrations as $S_i \Rightarrow \{\delta_1, \delta_2 \cdots \delta_j\}$ and text $S_i \Rightarrow \{\sigma_1, \sigma_2 \cdots \sigma_j\}$ in the treatises.

Since ship timbers and fragments are physical objects, we have adapted our architecture to handle them and their properties, For example, auxiliary components of a ship can be seen as *roles*. Fastening, type of wood, and dimensions, on the other hand can be considered *properties*. Further, in the case of dimensions, a timber can have more than one value as generally measurements are taken at different intervals along the piece. Similarly more than one technique can be used to fasten two pieces together. These issues can be handled applying expressions (3) and (4). The table below shows a partial list of properties and their values of a timber.

Property	Values
attachment	{ nailed to keel, bolted to keel, treenailed to keel, treenailed to frame, treenailed, bolted to keel, bolted to frame and keel }
joins	{ diagonal, hook, butt }
material	{ wood, iron, cooper cedar, acacia, cypress, pine, oak, maple, elm, walnut }

5 Conclusions

This initiative illustrates how digital libraries enable a group of archaeologists, historians, and naval experts in different geographical sites to work collaboratively on a collection of ancient technical materials from a diverse provenance. Due to the location of the excavations and archaeological research centers, our web-based interface allows the creation and constant update of a multilingual glossary of nautical terms and concepts, extending the properties of a traditional multilingual dictionary.

Our architecture is based on the concept of *roles* and *properties* associated to an entity (term). Our findings are based on the needs of archaeologists accessing shipbuilding treatises working primarily in the reconstruction of ships, as well as Nautical Archaeology students learning diverse shipbuilding traditions.

Because of their contents, shipbuilding treatises are in fact technical manuals, as such they provide interesting challenges and problems given their technical contents as well as the way they are used. At a high level their contents can be seen as text and images; thus techniques and algorithms from other digital libraries initiatives can be adapted to suit to some extent certain needs. However, a major difference with traditional literary works is the fact that shipbuilding treatises map a composite physical object (ship), hence the need to develop new approaches.

During our preliminary work with treatises, we discovered that characteristics and properties of timbers and ship remains recovered from underwater excavations could be represented and described with the architecture we developed for the glossary. In both cases—terms and physical objects—our model is scalable, which enables the addition of new properties and roles as they are required.

Since our architecture handles physical composite objects and their components, adapting it to work on other domains sharing similar characteristics is an interesting area to explore. For instance, literary works such as a novel can be divided into chapters and paragraphs. An anthology of poems which is made up of poems, and then segmented into stanzas. However, in contrast to the problem we address in nautical archaeology neither an anthology nor a novel are tied to physical objects in the way that the treatises are tied to ships.

The creation of a concordance of terms can be useful for establishing correlations among terms. For instance, one could argue that an unknown term in one language could have been taken from another language based on their similarity.

Given the contents, date, and provenance of shipbuilding treatises, linguistic analysis on nautical terms and their context can help scholars to understand unknown or uncertain terms. For example, working with an Italian scholar we have encountered cases of unknown terms in the translation of naval terms into 14th and 15th-century Venetian. Also, linguistic similarities of a term and its translations into other languages can help to determine whether a particular construction technique was adopted from a different tradition. In combination with the time the treatises were written, it could be used to estimate when the techniques were introduced.

Acknowledgments. This material is based upon work supported by the National Science Foundation under Grant No. IIS-0534314. Special thanks to Wendy van Duivenvoorde for her perspective on Nautical Archaeology, to Mr. Richard Steffy for providing a collection of information about timbers recovered from underwater excavations, and to the Academia de Marinha (Lisbon, Portugal) for granting permission to digitize facsimiles of Portuguese shipbuilding treatises.

References

1. Acevedo, D., Vote, E., Laidlaw, D., Joukowsky, M.: ARCHAVE: A Virtual Environment for Archaeological Research. Proceedings of IEEE Visualization (2000)
2. Acevedo, D., Vote, E., Laidlaw, D., Joukowsky, M.: Archaeological Data Visualization in VR: Analysis of Lamp Finds at the Great Temple of Petra. a Case Study. Proceedings of IEEE Visualization (2001)
3. Brown, M., Seales, W.: The Digital Atheneum: New Approaches for Preserving, Restoring and Analyzing Damaged Manuscripts. In: Proceedings of the First ACM/IEEE-CS Joint Conference on Digital Libraries, 2001, pp. 437–443. ACM Press, NY (2001)
4. Brown, M., Seales, W.: Beyond 2D Images: Effective 3D Imaging for Library Materials. In: Proceedings of the 5th ACM Conference on Digital Libraries, pp. 27–36 (2000)
5. Cheng, J., Seales, B.: Guided Linking: Efficiently Making Image-to-Transcript Correspondence. In: 1st ACM/IEEE-JCDL, Roanoke, VA (2001)
6. Crane, G.: The Perseus Project: An Interactive Curriculum on Classical Greek Civilization. Educational Technology 28(11), 25–32 (1988)
7. Crane, G.: Building a Digital Library: The Perseus Project as a Case Study in the Humanities. In: Proceedings of the First ACM Conf. on Digital Libraries, pp. 3–10 (1996)
8. Crane, G., Wulfman, C.: Towards a Cultural Heritage Digital Library. In: Proceedings of the 2003 Joint Conference on Digital Libraries, pp. 75–86 (2003)
9. Fekete, J., Dufournaud, N.: Compus: visualization and analysis of structured documents for understanding social life in the 16th century. In: Proceedings of the fifth ACM Conference on Digital Libraries, San Antonio, Texas, June 2-7, pp. 47–55 (2000)
10. Fernandez, M.: Livro da Tracas de Carpintaria. Transcription and Translation. Barros, E., Leitao, M., Academia de Marinha (1995)
11. Goncalves, M.A., Fox, E.A., Watson, L.T., Kipp, N.A.: Streams, Structures, Spaces, Scenarios, Societies (5S): A Formal Model for Digital Libraries. ACM Transactions on Information Systems (TOIS) 22(2), 270–312 (2004)
12. Hadingham, E.: Secrets of a Desert Metropolis: The hidden Wonders of Petra's Ancient Engineers. Scientific American Discovering Arch. 2(4), 70–74 (2000)
13. Helling, H., Steinmetz, C., Solomon, E., Frischer, B.: The Port Royal Project. A Case Study in the Use of VR Technology for the Recontextualization of Archaeological Artifacts and Building Remains in a Museum Setting. In: Proceedings of the Computer Applications and Quantitative Methods in Archaeology, Prato, Italy (April 13-16, 2004)
14. Hu, S., Furuta, R., Urbina, R.: An Electronic Edition of Don Quixote for Humanities Scholars. Document Numerique (Paris: Editions Hermes), spécial Documents anciens 3(12), 75–91 (1999)
15. Joukowsky, M.: Archaeological Excavations and Survey of the Southern Temple at Petra. Jordan, in Annual of the Dept. of Antiquities of Jordan 38, 293–322 (1993)
16. Kansa, E.: A community approach to data integration: Authorship and building meaningful links across diverse archaeological data sets. Geosphere 1(2), 97–109 (2005)
17. Lavanha, J.B.: Livro Primeiro Da Architectura Naval. Facsimile, Transcription, Translation, and Commentary. In: Pimentel, J., Baker, R., Domingues, F. (eds.) Academia de Marinha, Lisbon Portugal (1996)
18. Medelyan, O., Witten, I.: Thesaurus Based Automatic Keyprhase Indexing. In: Proc. of the 6th ACM/IEEE-CS JCDL, Chapel Hill, NC., USA, June 11-15, pp. 296–297 (2006)

19. Monroy, C., Furuta, R., Urbina, E., Mallen, E.: Texts, Images, Knowledge: Visualizing Cervantes and Picasso. In: Visual Knowledges Conference, University of Edinburgh, Scotland (September 2003)
20. Monroy, C., Stringer, G., Furuta, R.: Digital Donne: Workflow, Editing Tools, and the Reader's Interface of a Collection of 17th-century English Poetry. In: Forthcoming on Proceedings of JCDL 2007, Vancouver, B.C. Canada (June 18-23, 2007)
21. Monroy, C., Furuta, R., Castro, F.: A Multilingual Approach to Technical Manuscripts: 16th and 17th-century Portuguese Shipbuilding Treatises. In: Proceedings of JCDL 2007, Vancouver, B.C. Canada (June 18-23, 2007) (Forthcoming)
22. Oliveira, F.: O Livro da Fábrica das Naus. In: Domingues, F., Baker, R., Leitao, M. (eds.) Academia de Marinha, Lisbon, Portugal (1991)
23. Perrow, M., Barber, D.: Tagging of Name Records for Genealogical Data Browsing. In: Proc. of the 6th ACM/IEEE-JCDL, Chapel Hill, NC., USA, June 11-15 2006, pp. 316–325 (2006)
24. Plaisant, C., Rose, J., Yu, B., Auvil, L., Kirschenbaum, M., Smith, M., Clement, T., Lord, G.: Exploring Erotics in Emily Dickinson's Correspondence With Text Mining and Visual Interfaces. In: 6th JCDL, Chapel Hill, NC, USA, June 11-15 2006, pp. 141–150 (2006)
25. Ravindranathan, U., Shen, R., Goncalves, M.A., Fan, W., Fox, E.A., Flanagan, J.W.: Prototyping Digital Libraries Handling Heterogeneous Data Sources - The ETANA-DL Case Study. In: Heery, R., Lyon, L. (eds.) ECDL 2004. LNCS, vol. 3232, pp. 12–17. Springer, Heidelberg (2004)
26. Ravindranathan, U., Shen, R., Goncalves, M.A., Fan, W., Fox, E.A., Flanagan, J.W.: ETANA-DL: A Digital Library for Integrated Handling of Heterogeneous Archaeological Data. ACM-IEEE (JCDL 2004), Tucson, AZ (June 7-11, 2004)
27. Reeves, N., Wilkinson, R.: The Complete Valley of the Kings: Tombs and Treasures of Egypt's Greatest Pharaohs. London: Thames and Hudson (1996)
28. Reeves, C. (ed.): After Tut'ankhamun: Research and Excavation in the Royal Necropolis at Thebes. Kegan Paul International, London (1992)
29. Spiro, L., Wise, M., Henry, G., Bearden, C., Byrds, S., Garza, E., Decker, M.: Enabling Exploration: Travelers in the Middle East Archive. In: Proceedings of the 6th ACM/IEEE-JCDL, Chapel Hill, NC., USA, pp. 163–164 (June 11-15, 2006)
30. Urbina, E., Furuta, R., Smith, S., Audenaert, N., Deng, J., Monroy, C.: Visual Knowledge: Textual Iconography of the Quixote, a Hypertextual Archive. Literary and Linguistic Computing (Oxford UP) 21(2), 247–258 (2006)
31. Vemuri, N., Shen, R., Tupe, S., Fan, W., Fox, E.: ETANA-ADD: An Interactive Tool for Integrating Archaeological DL Collections. In: Proceedings of the 6th ACM/IEEE-JCDL, Chapel Hill, NC, USA, pp. 161–162 (June 11-15, 2006)
32. Donne Variorum (accessed on January 2007), http://donnevariorum.tamu.edu/
33. Petra: The Great Temple. American Journal of Archaeology 103(3), Egan, V., Bikai, P. (eds.), pp. 504–506 (July 1999)
34. SHAPE Lab. at Brown University, http://www.lems.brown.edu/vision/extra/SHAPE/
35. Theban Mapping Project, http://www.thebanmappingproject.com/about/
36. The Canterbury Tales Project: http://www.cta.dmu.ac.uk/projects/ctp/index.html
37. The Digital Imprint. Institute of Archeology. University of California at Los Angeles, http://www.sscnet.ucla.edu/ioa/labs/digital/imprint/proposal.html
38. The Elwood Viewer: The Society for Early English & Norse Electronic Texts (Accessed on January 2007), http://jefferson.village.virginia.edu/seenet/elwoodinfo.htm
39. The Nautical Archaeology Digital Library (NADL) (accessed on January 2007), http://nadl.tamu.edu
40. The InscriptiFact Project (accessed on May 2007), http://www.inscriptifact.com/

Trustworthy Digital Long-Term Repositories: The *nestor* Approach in the Context of International Developments

Susanne Dobratz[1] and Astrid Schoger[2]

[1] Humboldt-University Berlin, University Library, 10099 Berlin, Germany
dobratz@cms.hu-berlin.de
[2] Bavarian State Library, 80328 München, Germany
astrid.schoger@bsb-muenchen.de

Abstract. This paper describes the general approach *nestor – the German "Network of Expertise in Long-Term Storage of Digital Resources"* has taken in designing a catalogue of criteria for trustworthy digital repositories for long-term preservation and how this approach relates to internationalisation and standardisation of criteria and developments of evaluation methods to facilitate the audit and certification process.

Keywords: Digital Repositories, Long-Term Preservation, Certification, Trustworthiness, Auditing, Standardisation.

1 Introduction

One of the central challenges to long-term preservation in a digital repository is the ability to guarantee the authenticity and interpretability (understandability) of digital objects for users across time. This is endangered by the aging of storage media, the obsolescence of the underlying system and application software as well as changes in the technical and organisational infrastructure. Malicious or erroneous human actions also put digital objects at risk. Trustworthy long-term preservation in digital repositories requires technical, as well as organisational provisions. A trustworthy digital repository for long-term preservation has to operate according to the repository's aims and specifications.

Already in 1996, the Task Force on Archiving of Digital Information by *The Commission on Preservation and Access* and the *Research Libraries Group* called for a certification programme for long-term preservation repositories: *"... repositories claiming to serve an archival function must be able to prove that they are who they say they are by meeting or exceeding the standards and criteria of an independently-administered program for archival certification .."*, [11]. Some investigations in creating criteria and measuring the risk for a long-term preservation of digital objects have been carried out by several stakeholders, like the *"Cornell Library Virtual*

L. Kovács, N. Fuhr, and C. Meghini (Eds.): ECDL 2007, LNCS 4675, pp. 210–222, 2007.

Remote Control Tool "project of Cornell University [5], the ERPANET project [4] and most recently by the Digital Repository Certification Task Force of the Research Libraries Group (RLG) and OCLC, the Digital Curation Centre (DCC) in cooperation with the European Commission funded project Digital Preservation Europe (DPE) and the German *nestor* project. The latter approach and it's relation to international work is described in this paper.

2 Recent Research on Trustworthy Digital Repositories

The ideas discussed in this paper are based on early developments on a framework describing requirements and functionalities for operating systems that focus on the long-term preservation of digital materials, the Open Archival Information System (OAIS), [2].

From that work the Digital Repository Certification Task Force of the Research Libraries Group (RLG) and OCLC derived attributes and responsibilities for so called trusted digital repositories in 2002, [10].

As those basic recommendations are hardly applicable to any organisation setting up a long-term preservation repository, the need for more detailed criteria and practical guidance became apparent.

In 2003 RLG and the National Archives and Records Administration (NARA) created a joint task force, the RLG-NARA Task Force on Digital Repository Certification. This task force together with the Auditing and Certification of Digital Archives project run by the Center for Research Libraries (CRL) worked on the development of certification criteria applicable to a range of digital repositories and archives and on a checklist useable to conduct audits, first draft from August 2005, [9], finally released in February 2007, under the title: *"Trustworthy Repositories Audit and Certification Checklist" (TRAC)* [7].

In Germany, *nestor – the German "Network of Expertise in Long-Term Storage of Digital Resources"* in 2004 has started efforts in designing a catalogue of criteria for trustworthy digital repositories for long-term preservation, based on the work of the RLG/OCLC and RLG/NARA task force and CRL project following a different approach, which can be interpreted as more community based approach intended for use in Germany.. It began with a survey for existing standards and approaches used for storing digital materials in libraries, archives, museums, universities and data centers and derived a state of the art in digital preservation in Germany from that. Based on the survey findings criteria have been formulated and examples generated in order to support the setup of digital long-term preservation repositories in Germany, [6].

Meanwhile, the Digital Curation Centre (DCC) in cooperation with the European Commission funded project Digital Preservation Europe (DPE) conducted some test audits based on the first draft of the RLG-NARA/CRL checklist. Their investigations led to the development of an auditing tool for trusted digital long-term repositories, called *"Digital Repository Audit Method Based on Risk Assessment" (DRAMBORA)*, based upon common ideas of risk management. The first draft version was published February 2007.

Within the PLANETS project [12], the development of a Preservation Test Bed to provide a consistent and coherent evidence-base for the objective evaluation of different preservation protocols, tools and services and for the validation of the effectiveness of preservation plans will take place.

In January 2007 the OCLC/RLG-NARA Task Force, CRL, DCC, DPE and *nestor* agreed upon a set of so called common principles, ten basic characteristics of digital preservation repositories [8].

The current TRAC checklist together with the *nestor* catalogue are the basis for an ISO standardisation effort carried out under the umbrella of the OAIS standards family by the Consultative Committee for Space Data Systems (CCSDS) via ISO TC20/SC13 and led by David Giaretta (DCC).

2.1 Trustworthiness

Trustworthiness (German: Vertrauenswürdigkeit) of a system means that it operates according to its objectives and specifications (it does exactly what it claims to do). From an information technology (IT) security perspective, integrity, authenticity, confidentiality and availability are important building blocks of trustworthy digital preservation repositories. Integrity refers to the completeness and exclusion of unintended modifications to repository objects. Unintended modifications could arise, due to malicious or erroneous human behavior, or from technical imperfection, damage, or loss of technical infrastructure. Authenticity here means that the object actually contains what it claims to contain. This is provided by documentation of the provenience and of all changes to the object. Availability is a guarantee (1) of access to the repository by potential users and (2) that the objects within the repository are interpretable. Availability of objects is a central objective, which must be fulfilled in relation to the designated community and its requirements. Confidentiality means that information objects can only be accessed by permitted users.

Potential interest groups for trustworthiness are:

- repository users who want to access trustworthy information – today and in the future,
- data producers and content providers for whom trustworthiness provides a means of quality assurance when choosing potential service providers,
- resource allocators, funding agencies and other institutions that need to make funding and granting decisions, and
- long-term digital repositories that want to gain trustworthiness and demonstrate this to the public either to fulfill legal requirements or to survive in the market.

There is a wide range of preservation repositories that exist or are under development: from national and state libraries and archives with deposit laws; to media centres having to preserve e-learning applications; to archives for smaller institutions; to world data centres in charge of "raw" data.

Trustworthiness can be assessed and demonstrated on the basis of a criteria catalogue.

3 *nestor*- Catalogue of Criteria for Trusted Digital Repositories

The catalogue primarily addresses cultural heritage organisations - archives, libraries, and museums - and is designed as guidance for the planning and setup of long-term digital repositories. Furthermore this catalogue is intended as an orientation guide for commercial and non-commercial service providers, software developers, and third party vendors.

3.1 Concepts Central to the Derivation and Application of the Criteria for Trustworthy Digital Long-Term Repositories

3.1.1 Accordance to OAIS Terminology

The Reference Model for an Open Archival Information System (OAIS) [2] serves - where possible - as the basis for terminology and structure of the catalogue. The OAIS is used to define the core concepts of digital repository and digital objects, describe core processes, from ingest via archival storage to access. The OAIS also helps to describe the life cycle of digital objects within the repository.

3.1.2 Abstraction

The catalogue's overall aim is to introduce stable criteria for a wide variety of long-term digital repositories and to maintain the criteria over a long period. For this reason, the catalogue criteria have been formulated at a very abstract level. They are enriched by detailed explanations and concrete examples. The latter conform to the current state-of-the-art in terms of technology and organisation. In some cases, they only make sense within the context of a very special preservation task.

3.1.3 Documentation

The goals, concepts, specifications and implementation of a long-term digital repository should be documented adequately. The documentation demonstrates the development status internally and externally. Early evaluation based on documentation may also prevent mistakes and inappropriate implementations. Adequate documentation can help to prove the completeness of the design and architecture of the long-term digital repository at all steps. In addition, quality and security standards require adequate documentation.

3.1.4 Transparency

Transparency is achieved by publishing appropriate parts of the documentation, which allows users and partners to gauge the degree of trustworthiness for themselves. Producers and suppliers are given the opportunity to assess to whom they wish to entrust their digital objects. Internal transparency ensures that any measures can be traced, and it provides documentation of digital repository quality to operators, backers, management and employees. Parts of the documentation which are not suitable for the general public (e.g. company secrets, security-related information) can be restricted to a specified circle (e.g. certification agency). Transparency establishes trust, because it allows interested parties a direct assessment of the quality of the long-term digital repository.

3.1.5 Adequacy

According to the principle of adequacy, absolute standards cannot be given. Instead, evaluation is based on the objectives and tasks of the long-term digital repository in question. The criteria have to be seen within the context of the special archiving tasks of the long-term digital repository. Some criteria may therefore prove irrelevant in certain cases. Depending on the objectives and tasks of the long-term digital repository, the required degree of fulfilment for a particular criterion may also differ.

3.1.6 Measurability

In some cases - especially regarding long-term aspects - there are no objectively assessable (measurable) features. In such cases we must rely on indicators showing the degree of trustworthiness. As the fulfillment of a certain criteria depends always on the designated community, it is not possible to create "hard" criteria for some of them, e.g. how can be measured, what adequate metadata is? Transparency also makes the indicators accessible for evaluation.

3.2 Structure of the *nestor*-Catalogue, Example Criterias

Based on the initial *nestor* survey and similar to the approach taken by the CRL project, the *nestor* working group used abstract criteria in the main catalogue instead of asking very detailed and specific questions (e.g. which metadata is used). The *nestor* catalogue includes best practice values and provides examples and specific literature references for the listed criteria, despite the need to update such examples regularly. The intention is that this criteria catalogue, and its planned revisions, will help customers to share information and expectations. The criteria composed in this catalogue are seen as a sufficient set to demonstrate the trustworthiness of a digital long-term repository.

3.2.1 Overview of the Criteria

Within the following table the term "repository" is taken as abbreviation for "long-term digital repository".

A	**Organisational Framework**
1	**The repository has defined its goals.** 1.1 selection criteria 1.2 responsibility for the long-term preservation of the information represented by the digital objects 1.3 designated community
2	**The repository grants its designated community an adequate usage of the information represented by the digital objects.** 2.1 access for the designated community 2.2 interpretability of the digital objects by the designated community
3	**Legal and contractual rules are being observed.** 3.1 existence of legal contracts between producers and the repository 3.2 operation on a legal basis regarding archiving 3.3 operation on a legal basis regarding usage
4	**The organisational form is adequate for the digital repository.** 4.1 adequate funding 4.2 sufficient numbers of qualified staff 4.3 organisational structure 4.4 repository engages in long-term planning 4.5 continuation of preservation tasks even beyond the existence of the repository
5	**Adequate quality management is conducted.** 5.1 definition of processes and responsibilities 5.2 documentation of elements and processes 5.3 reaction to substantial changes

B	**Object Management**
6	**The repository ensures integrity of digital objects during all processing stages:** 6.1 ingest 6.2 archival storage 6.3 access
7	**The repository ensures authenticity of digital objects during all processing stages:** 6.1 ingest 6.2 archival storage 6.3 access
8	**The repository has a strategic plan for its technical preservation measures.**
9	**The repository accepts digital objects from its producers based on defined criteria.**

	9.1 specification of SIPs[1] 9.2 identification of relevant features of the digital objects for the information preservation 9.3 technical control over its digital objects in order to execute preservation methods
10	**The archival storage of the digital objects is undertaken to defined specifications.** 10.1 definition of AIPs[2] 10.2 transformation of the SIPs into AIPs 10.3 storage and readability of the AIPs 10.4 implementation of preservation strategies for AIPs
11	**The repository permits usage of the digital objects based on defined criteria** 11.1 definition of DIPs[3] 11.2 transformation of AIPs into DIPs
12	**The data management system is capable of providing the necessary digital repository function.** 12.1. persistent identification of objects and their relations 12.2. metadata for content and formal description and identification of the digital objects 12.3 metadata for structural description of the digital objects 12.4 metadata for documenting changes made on the digital objects 12.5 metadata for the technical description of the digital objects 12.6 metadata for the usage rights and terms of the digital objects 12.7 The assignment of metadata to the digital objects is guaranteed every time

C	Infrastructure and Security
13	**The IT infrastructure is adequate** 13.1 The IT infrastructure implements the demands from the object management 13.2 The IT infrastructure implements the security demands of the IT-security system.
14	**The infrastructure protects the digital repository and its digital objects..**

3.2.2 Example Criteria

A criterion consists of 4 parts: the criterion itself, an explanation, possible examples and citations.

[1] SIP: submission information package (cf. OAIS), information unit submitted by the producer to the repository.

[2] AIP: archival information package (cf OAIS), an information unit stored by the repository.

[3] DIP: dissemination information package (cf. OAIS), an information unit that a user receives in response to an request to the repository.

8 **The digital repository has a strategic plan for its technical preservation measures.**

In order to fulfil its responsibility for preserving information, the DR should have a strategic plan covering all outstanding or expected tasks, and the timetable for their completion. This strategic planning (cf. 4.4) should be specified at the object level. Such measures should keep pace with ongoing technical developments (such as changes to data carriers, data formats, and user demands).

Measures for physical data preservation (integrity, authenticity), its accessibility and the preservation of its interpretability should be conceived to provide long-term preservation functionality. Long-term preservation measures cover both content and metadata.

See 10.4 regarding implementation of the long-term preservation measures.

Output onto analogue media (e.g. microfilm) and redigitisation may be appropriate for certain digital objects.

The following are the main methods used to preserve interpretability:

Conversion to a current format or a current format version (migration)

Recreation of the old application environment within a new technical infrastructure (emulation).

Long-term planning of the tasks arising from the formats can be based e.g. on a format register. Format registers are currently being developed by e.g. Harvard (Global Digital Format Registry: http://hul.harvard.edu/gdfr/) and the National Archives, Kew (PRONOM: http://www.nationalarchives.gov.uk/pronom/).

[DigiCULT: Technology Watch Reports, 2006]

[Rauch, Carl und Rauber, Andreas: Anwendung der Nutzwertanalyse zur Bewertung von Strategien zur langfristigen Erhaltung digitale Objekte, 2006]

4 The *nestor*-Catalogue in International Comparison

Although the *nestor* catalogue is focused on application in Germany, and it is crucial to analyze generally accepted criteria with regard to the situation in Germany, it must be discussed internationally and should adhere to international standards. In evaluating repositories, various components must be considered such as specific judicial constraints, the setup of public institutions (financially and with respect to human resources), national organisational decisions, and the status of development in Germany as a whole.

nestor, the Digital Curation Centre and the Project Digital Preservation Europe (DPE) as well the Centre for Reseach Libraries have been interchanging information about the current status of their work regularly and in January 2007 have come up with 10 basic common principles for the trustworthiness of digital repositories, on the basis of the TRAC-checklist and the *nestor* catalogue.

The *nesto*r catalogue as well as the TRAC-Checklist could both be seen as national instances of the formulated common principles, [8]. Taking only the first headings of the criteria they would fit into the general picture as follows. Further work has to be done, producing a detailed crosswalk between the criteria, the following list just lists three examples:

1. The repository commits to continuing maintenance of digital objects for identified community(ies).
2. Demonstrates organizational fitness (including financial, staffing structure, and processes) to fulfill its commitment. This criteria could be compared with the *nestor* criteria *A.4" The organisational form is adequate for the digital repository"* and the TRAC criteria section *A2. "Organizational structure & staffing"*.
3. Acquires and maintains requisite contractual and legal rights and fulfills responsibilities.
   In *nestor* criteria *A.3 "Legal and contractual rules are observed"* would be useable, for the TRAC catalogue it would be *A5. "Contracts, licenses, & liabilities"*
4. Has an effective and efficient policy framework..
5. Acquires and ingests digital objects based upon stated criteria that correspond to its commitments and capabilities.
6. Maintains/ensures the integrity, authenticity and usability of digital objects it holds over time.
7. Creates and maintains requisite metadata about actions taken on digital objects during preservation as well as about the relevant production, access support, and usage process context before preservation.
8. Fulfills requisite dissemination requirements.
9. Has a strategic program for preservation planning and action. This idea applies to *nestor* section *B.8 "The digital repository has a strategic plan for its technical preservation measures."* In TRAC it would be section *B3. "Preservation planning"*
10. Has technical infrastructure adequate to continuing maintenance and security of digital objects.

Concluding this initial survey we can state, that a conclusive mapping of the national approaches to the agreed international principles is possible.

5 Coaching – Self-audit – Certification

Currently, no method has been developed for the formal certification of long-term digital repositories according to the *nestor*-catalogue. For many of the abstract criteria expressed in the catalogue, it is not yet possible to define accepted standards on which auditing processes could be based. Therefore, *nestor* has for the moment focused on presenting the paper as a set of guidelines for setting up a trustworthy digital repository. We are convinced that this will be helpful for many institutions and will stimulate the development of trustworthy digital repositories. The catalogue can be used as an instrument for self-evaluation on all steps of development, from the concept and specification to implementation. We regard that as the first step.

Next steps will be the participation in a national/international standardisation process via the German Standardisation Organisation (Deutsches Institut für Normung, DIN) and the International Standardization Organization (ISO) and the establishment of a formal certification process, in which the catalogue will function as auditing tool.

Certification supports repositories that need to provide objective evidence, and it encourages competition even in the public sector. Competition is meant in those fields, where no formal or legal requirements exist to deliver digital materials to a particular long-term repository. A "user" will than decide independently where his digital materials will be archived. He will take the decision based upon the services, the quality and prize offered. In such a scenario, certification provides a quality label to the repository and therefore supports the quality management and assurance of public administration. Whenever data have to be archived, certification can be very important.

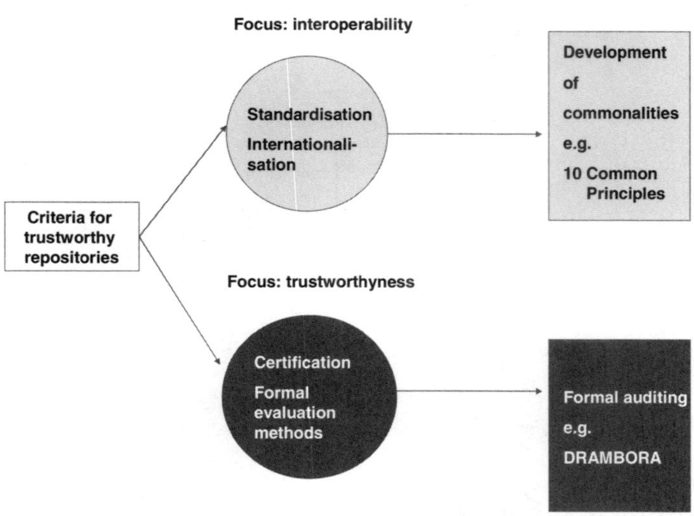

Fig. 1. The role of standardisation and certification

The work done by the DCC/DPC is based on common risk management ideas. Those always interprete measures as prevention of risks, see [1]. The self-auditing tool DRAMBORA is a next step towards formal evaluation and certification. *"It is intended to facilitate internal audit by providing repository administrators with a means to assess their capabilities, identify their weaknesses, and recognize their strength."… "Rather than representing a straightforward alternative (and therefore competitive) means for repository assessment, the DCC/DPE work aims to provide a complementary approach that can be used in association with efforts of both TRAC and nestor"* [3]. It takes the principle of adequacy into account, starts with identifying the goals of a repository and derives actions from those. It than identifies the risks and advises how those are to be handled. Trustworthiness can be interpreted as assurance that the owners have taken countermeasures minimize the risks to the valuable assets.

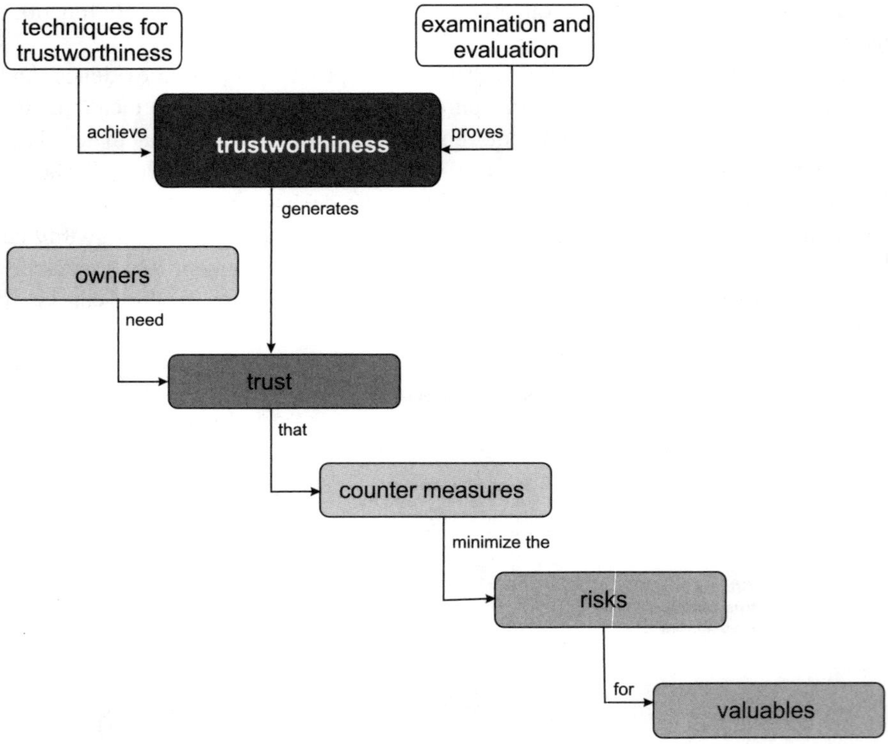

Fig. 2. Trustworthiness as risk management method, derived from [1]

6 Conclusion and Further Work

The common goal is to come to internationally agreed and accepted formal evaluations and audits taking into account national laws and conditions. Due to the formulation of the ten core requirements on one hand and the start of an ISO standardisation process on the other hand, we have a good chance finally to meet those expectations.

Furthermore there have been agreements on ideas for further cooperation and collaboration between CRL, DCC, DPE and *nestor*, such as consistently and openly sharing results, joining test audits and developing a common training for managers and staff of digital repositories. International agreements ensure the interoperability of long-term repositories, their quality and their services offered on an international level.

Nevertheless all partners also see the urgent necessity to provide guidelines and tools to their own national heritage institutions and to make repositories work according to local conditions and national laws. *nestor* plans to use the existing criteria to implement a multi-step training tool for repository managers, technicians, archival, library and museums staff. Within that task, *nestor* plans to augment the concrete criteria in the actual catalogue with examples of best practise scenarios. Test audits within Germany using the *nestor* criteria as well as the risk management tool provided by the DPE project are planned.

Acknowledgements

We greatly acknowledge the whole *nestor Working Group Trusted Repositories - Certification*, see http://www.longtermpreservation.de/ag-repositories, especially the following colleagues: Dr. Andrea Hänger, Karsten Huth, Max Kaiser, Dr. Christian Keitel, Dr. Jens Klump, Dr. Nikola Korb, Peter Rödig, Dr. Stefan Rohde-Enslin, Kathrin Schroeder, Stefan Strathmann and Heidrun Wiesenmüller.

We also thank Robin Dale (Research Libraries Group) and Bernard Reilly (Centre for Research Libraries), Seamus Ross and Andrew McHugh (Digital Curation Centre), Raivo Rusaalep (Digital Preservation Europe) for the fruitful discussions.

References

[1] Bundesamt für Sicherheit in der Informationstechnik: Common Criteria V 2.3 (2005), URL http://www.bsi.bund.de/cc/index.htm

[2] CCSDS (Consultative Committee for Space Data Systems): Reference Model for an Open Archival Information System (OAIS). Blue Book ISO 14721:2003 Issue 1 (2002), URL http://www.ccsds.org/docu/dscgi/ds.py/Get/File-143/650x0b1.pdf

[3] Digital Curation Centre und DigitalPreservationEurope: DCC and DPE Digital Repository Audit Method Based on Risk Assessment, V1.0 (2007) (retrieved 28.02.2007), URL: from http://repositoryaudit.eu/download

[4] Erpanet Project: Risk Communication Tool (2003), URL http://www.erpanet.org/guidance/docs/ERPANETRiskTool.pdf

[5] McGovern, N.Y., Kenney, A.R., Entlich, R., Kehoe, W.R., Buckley, E.: Virtual Remote Control: Building a Preservation Risk Management Toolbox for Web Resources, D-Lib Magazine 10 [4] (2004), URL http://www.dlib.org/dlib/april04/mcgovern/04mcgovern.html

[6] *nestor* Working Group on Trusted Repositories Certification: Criteria for Trusted Digital Long-Term Preservation Repositories – Version 1 (Request for Public Comment) English Version, Frankfurt am Main (2006), URL http://nbn-resolving.de/urn:nbn:de:0008-2006060703

[7] OCLC und Center for Research Libraries: Trustworthy Repositories Audit and Certification: Criteria and Checklist (2007), URL http://www.crl.edu/PDF/trac.pdf

[8] OCLC/RLG-NARA Task Force on Digital Repository Certification; CLR; DCC; DPE und *nestor*: Core Requirements for digital Archives (Common Principles) (2007), URL http://www.crl.edu/content.asp?l1=13&l2=58&l3=162&l4=92

[9] RLG NARA Task Force on Digital Repository Certification: Audit Checklist for Certifying Digital Repositories, RLG, NARA Task Force on Digital Repository Certification, Mountain View, CA (2005), URL http://www.rlg.org/en/pfds/rlgnara-repositorychecklist.pdf

[10] RLG Working Group on Digital Archive Attributes,: Trusted Digital Repositories: Attributes and Responsibilities, RLG; OCLC, Mountain View CA (2002), URL http://www.rlg.org/longterm/repositories.pdf

[11] Task Force on Archiving Digital Information: Preserving Digital Information, Commission on Preservation and Access, Washington, D.C. (1996), URL ftp://ftp.rlg.org/pub/archtf/final-report.pdf

[12] http://www.planets-project.eu/

Providing Context-Sensitive Access to the Earth Observation Product Library

Stephan Kiemle[1] and Burkhard Freitag[2]

[1] German Aerospace Center (DLR), German Remote Sensing Data Center (DFD)
Oberpfaffenhofen, D-82234 Weßling, Germany
Stephan.Kiemle@dlr.de

[2] University of Passau, Department of Computer Science and Mathematics
D-94030 Passau, Germany
Burkhard.Freitag@uni-passau.de

Abstract. The German Remote Sensing Data Center (DFD) has developed a digital library for the long-term management of earth observation data products. This Product Library is a central part of DFD's multi-mission ground segment Data and Information Management System (DIMS) currently hosting one million digital products, corresponding to 150 Terabyte of data. Its data model is regularly extended to support products of upcoming earth observation missions. The ever increasing complexity led to the development of operating interfaces which use a-priori and context knowledge, allowing efficient management of the dynamic library content. This paper presents the development and operating of context-sensitive library access tools based on meta modeling and online grammar interpretation.

Keywords: context sensitivity, meta modeling, earth observation, object query language, information management.

1 Introduction

The Product Library developed and operated at the German Aerospace Center DLR manages ever increasing amounts of digital earth observation products. The data growth rates are challenging, and even more so the increasing diversity of data structures and formats. Currently the Product Library already hosts about 80 different product types.

To be able to efficiently manage the huge amount of heterogeneous data, comprehensive human-machine interfaces and tools have been developed at DLR. This paper addresses the development of context-sensitive, interactive operating interfaces and presents operational experiences in the domain of earth observation data management. In particular, we describe an interactive query editor that makes intensive use of static a-priori information and meta information about the dynamic library data model to help the user formulating his or her queries and ensure valid interactions.

L. Kovács, N. Fuhr, and C. Meghini (Eds.): ECDL 2007, LNCS 4675, pp. 223–234, 2007.

The following two sections give an overview of the architecture of the DIMS system and describe the problem to be solved by providing context-sensitive access to the Product Library. We will then discuss the underlying data model. Next, the interactive query editor supporting ad-hoc metadata queries is presented, followed by an evaluation section and a conclusion.

2 The Data and Information Management System DIMS

The Data and Information Management System (DIMS) has been developed as a distributed multi-mission infrastructure for production, cataloguing, archiving, ordering, accounting and distribution of earth observation products [1]. Fig. 1 shows an overview of the system architecture with the main service components EOWEB® user services, ordering control for the processing of user orders, production control for the organization of production workflows, different flavors of processing systems for the ingestion, value adding and publishing of earth observation data, the Product Library, the product generation and delivery component and components for monitoring and control.

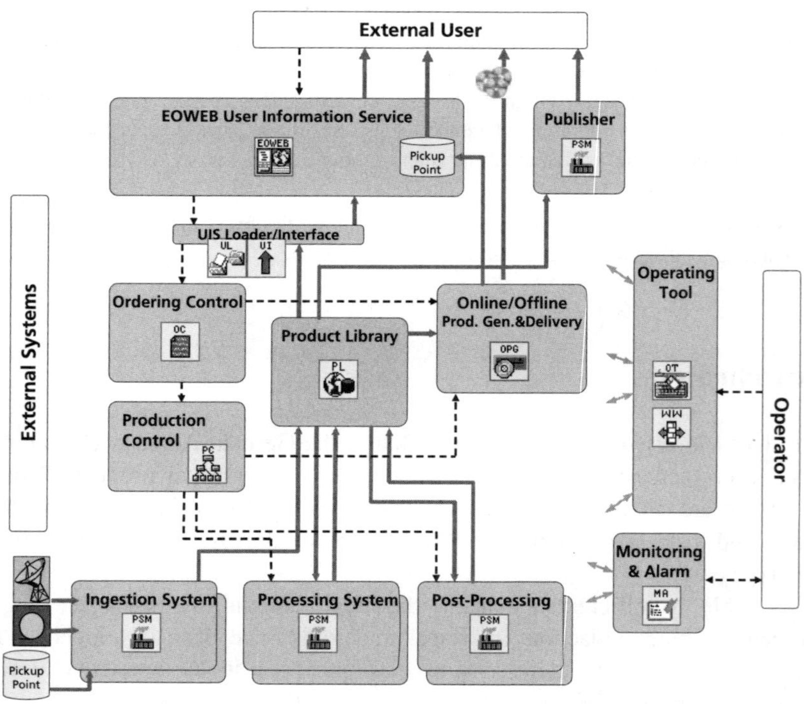

Fig. 1. Data and Information Management System Overview

As a central component the Product Library is responsible for the consistent long-term preservation of digital data products. It consists of an archive for the long-term storage of primary data and an inventory for efficient storage of metadata. A middleware encapsulates these components providing a comprehensive library interface for the consistent management of digital data products. This middleware decouples high-level information modeling and evolving low-level storage structures such as the robot-driven media library and hierarchical storage management for primary data and a relational database management system for metadata [2].

All product data can be accessed via the object oriented query language, extending the OQL standard [3]. The Product Library provides several functions required for data management. The Operating Tool (Fig. 2) is used to access these functions. All items of a collection can be listed using the incremental query mechanism, individual items can be searched by entering object query language conditions (including spatial operators) and item details (metadata, component structure, browse images) can be viewed. Items can be inserted, updated, retrieved and destroyed. Items can be registered and unregistered (manipulating only the metadata but not the data files), items can be re-located and un-archived (manipulating only the data files but not the metadata).

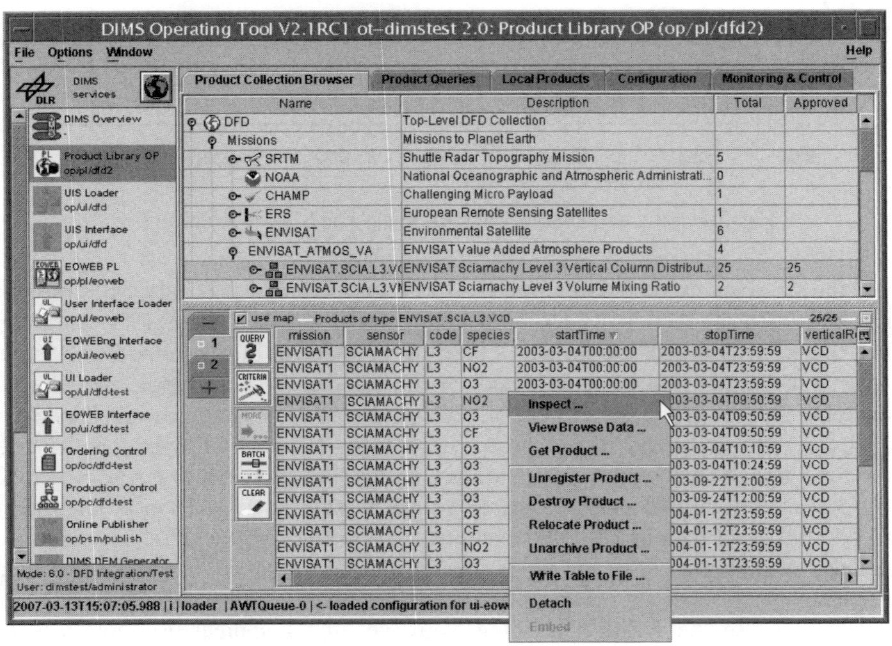

Fig. 2. DIMS Operating Tool, Product Library Collection Browser with Menu of Product Management Functions

The Operating Tool also provides configuration views allowing to manage the data collection hierarchy, the item spaces used for modular data modeling in the inventory and the archiving rules used to organize the file directory structure within the archive.

3 Problem Description

The tasks of product management include different operating use cases requiring interactive access to the library content. Knowledge about the evolving information model is absolutely essential e.g. when placing ad-hoc queries to the inventory or when browsing the library content and generating population reports.

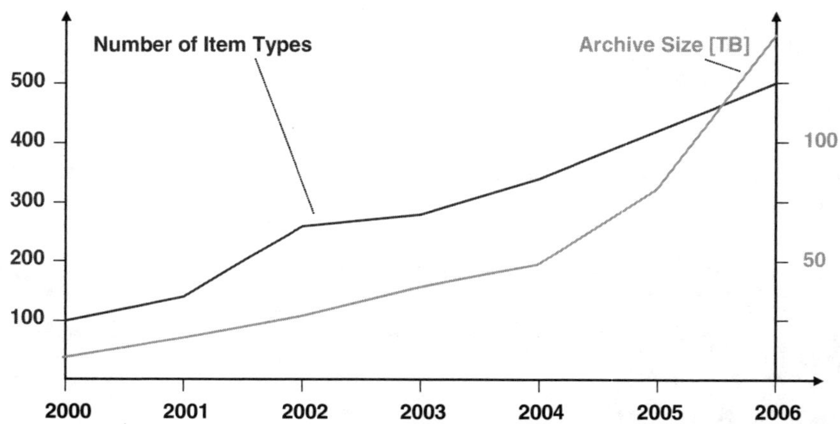

Fig. 3. Evolution of Number of Item Types and Library Archive Size

In the six years of operation of the DIMS Product Library, 500 item types (product and component collections) have been configured using a total of 1970 attributes. Growth and evolution of the Product Library is permanent. Fig. 3 shows how the size of the information model, represented by the number of item types, increased in parallel to the size of the library. The new German remote sensing mission TerraSAR-X [4], for example, added 30 new product item types and will multiply, together with other upcoming missions the current volume of the library by six in terms of number of products and archive size, leading to a total number of 10 million product items and 840 TByte of data in 2012. The variety of collections will significantly increase, making the management of the huge amount of heterogeneous data more and more difficult.

Operators use the DIMS Operating Tool, i.e., the graphical user interface for unified operating of all DIMS services, to browse the library content and place ad-hoc queries. Besides a hierarchical collection tree operators can view a textual documentation to get orientation in the bits and pieces of the information model and to get help on the use of the query language.

The librarian, i.e. one of the operators using the DIMS Operating Tool, is responsible for the management of the earth observation data in the Product Library. In this function he or she

- decides what products to store for the long term
- defines and maintains the data model
- configures the library according to the data model
- grants library access to users
- supervises data ingestion and access activity
- monitors library operations
- decides about data expiration and removal
- reports about library operations and use

Therefore the librarian needs comprehensive tools to access and monitor the Product Library. The librarian has to be able to browse the library content, retrieve individual items and perform actions on single or a set of identified products.

However, the available support for library operations and access turned out to be insufficient. Operators require aware client applications with knowledge about the underlying data model in order to cope with the increasing complexity in this dynamic application environment. Operating clients should also give support in the formulation of correct ad-hoc query expressions and take into account individual operator preferences, habits and the activity history.

As one consequence, the DIMS Operating Tool had to be extended by a context-sensitive interactive OQL query editor for ad-hoc queries as presented in this paper.

4 Data Model

In the following we will focus on the product data model to show how this knowledge can be used for context-sensitive management tools supporting the librarian.

4.1 Object Model

Object orientation as it can be defined with the Unified Modeling Language (UML 2.0) is particularly well suited for the domain of earth observation data products. Products are independent identifiable objects composed of other objects such as browse images, primary data, processing logs and quality maps. Different products of the same mission can inherit common properties. Higher level information products derived from raw data products are associated to their “predecessors”. Beyond the features described above there exist of course more properties of earth observation products which can also be represented very well using an object model.

In its upper part Fig. 4 shows the basic product model underlying the Product Library. Specific mission collections, products and product components are added by extending the classes *Collection*, *ProductGroup*, *Product*, *PrimaryData* and *BrowseData*,

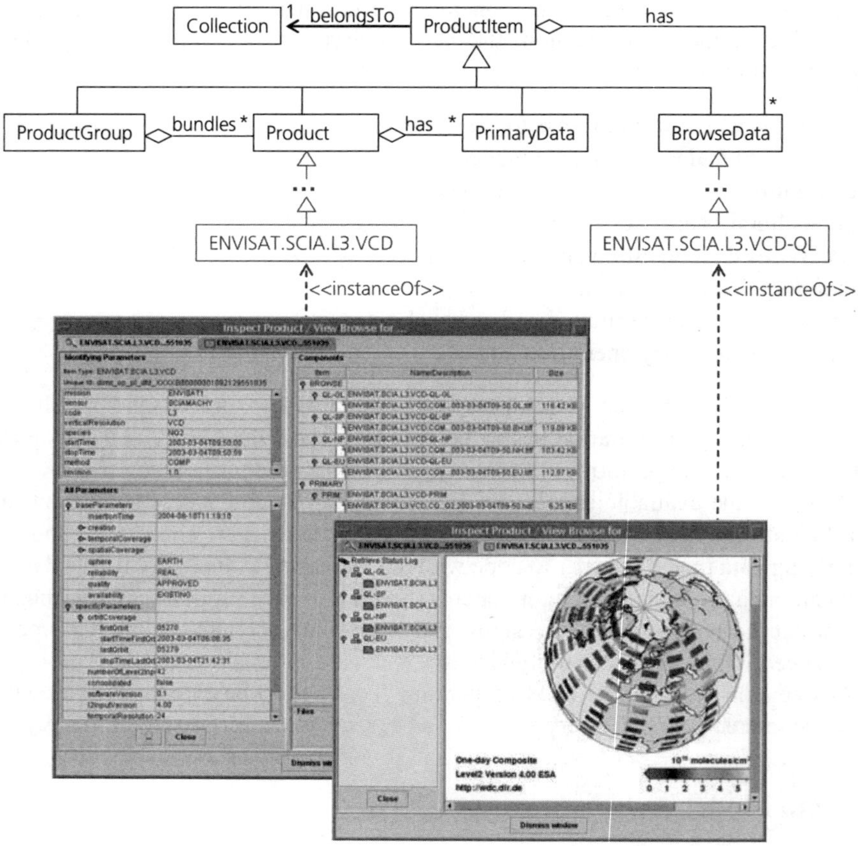

Fig. 4. Basic Product Model (Extract) and Extension Example with Instances Symbolized by Operating Tool Product Inspection and Browse Views

4.2 Data Model Evolution

In the dynamic environment of the Product Library the data management task of configuring new product types for new missions is a nominal use case which has to be supported without interruption of operations. By configuring the library it is possible to define additional archiving rules extending the archive system as well as to extend the product metadata model in the inventory system.

The inventory of the Product Library allows to configure object data models. *Collections* are used to define the component structure of a product and to place products in a freely configurable collection hierarchy allowing easy navigation e.g. by mission, sensor or application domain. *Item types* are used to define product and component types by specifying name, meaning, a list of identifying attributes and describing attributes. Types can be set in a single-inheritance hierarchy, inheriting properties of parent types. *Attributes* are defined by specifying name, meaning, data type and other basic properties such as valids, value ranges and value constraints. Attributes can be structured, meaning that their data type is not primitive but a *structure* itself defining a list of slot attributes. Associations, aggregations and composition *references* can be defined to link item types.

In a huge digital library system like the DIMS continuous change at various levels has to be anticipated. In by far the most cases an existing data model will be extended. One way to achieve this is to extend already defined item types (see Fig. 4). Of course, also new item types can be defined as well. They can reuse already defined attributes, structures and references if the meaning matches. This simplifies modeling and leads to easier manageable data models.

4.3 Meta Model

The entities introduced above to define data models are called modeling elements. Of course these elements can again be modeled and managed within the library. The Product Library inventory therefore maintains the *meta item space*, a repository of all modeling elements ever defined to build application data models.

The advantages of managing modeling elements in a distinct repository are obvious: the modeling tools use this repository for safe persistence of configured data models and they can browse already defined modeling elements to allow their reuse.

In the OMG meta model architecture [5], different levels of modeling are defined. The M0 level represents the real world, in our case the earth observation products in the Product Library.

The M1 level represents the data models of M0, here the product data model consisting of types, attributes and references as described above. The M1 level of modeling gives a common formal view on reality, allowing to describe, compare, reuse and exchange application data items.

The M2 level represents the data models of M1, i.e., the meta model used to define application data models. The M2 level of modeling gives a standard and formal view on application data models, allowing to describe, compare, reuse and exchange application data model elements.

The OMG meta model architecture also defines a M3 level again abstracting the M2 level and intended to give an ubiquitous, generally applicable representation of meta models to be able to even represent and formally define different ways of defining meta models.

In practice, the Product Library uses the M0 level (product instances stored in the library), the M1 level (product data model) and the M2 level (repository of modeling elements). The M3 level is not used, since there is no need for different meta models and thus not need to further abstraction. However, the repository containing the modeling elements is self-contained, meaning the structures of the meta model are themselves defined as instances in the meta model. Thus the repository of modeling elements corresponds to both the M2 and the M3 level. This allows e.g. to access the repository of modeling elements using the same tools and interfaces (such as the object query language) as for accessing the product data models.

Fig. 5 shows an extract of the Product Library meta model hosting the modeling elements. Based on this meta information on the configured data models, the inventory is able to configure the physical storage layer, namely the underlying relational database management system. The inventory middleware maps all access to the product metadata such as object queries and insertions to corresponding statements to the database systems, thereby decoupling application level interfaces from the relational storage model. This allows an independent physical design, e.g. choosing normalization to save space or de-normalization to save access time.

In addition, client applications can access the repository of modeling elements to add model awareness and guide the user through the library data model.

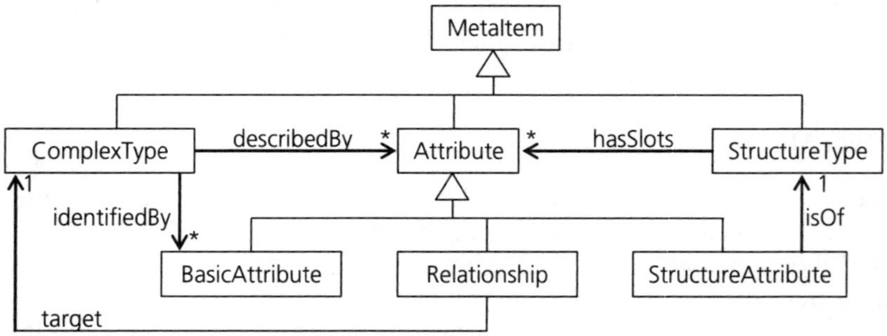

Fig. 5. Product Library Meta Model (Extract)

5 The Interactive OQL Query Editor

5.1 Requirements

To support users in formulating ad-hoc queries, a context-sensitive OQL editor had to be developed supporting

- query completion at an arbitrary input position
- error marking
- special token evaluation.

  If the proposal list includes special tokens which can be replaced with model elements, this will be done. For example the special token <CT> will be replaced with a list of available ComplexTypes stored in the repository.
- usage of meta model information
- template selection for the `select` or the `where` clauses of a OQL query.

5.2 Grammatical Context

The online interpretation of the query language grammar, i.e. the analysis of expressions during the editing process, allows the evaluation and validation of human inputs on three information levels.

Lexical correctness means that the query consists of valid tokens whereas syntactical correctness guarantees that it is valid with respect to the rules defining the grammar. Finally, semantical correctness ensures that the types, conditions and expressions are consistent and match the data model. For instance, in semantically correct queries comparisons of attributes with literal values use the same data type, and the attributes used in conditions refer to an object type which has actually been specified in the `from` clause.

The OQL query editor has been developed based on an EBNF definition of the query language and using the parser generator JavaCC [7]. The generated lexer and parser classes allow the addition of semantic actions required to distinguish equally defined identifier tokens in different contexts and to connect the repository of modeling elements in order to compute sensitive suggestions for the next inputs in the given context. Depending of the current position, the suggestions may include grammar terminals such as keywords, brackets or comparators, as well as names of types and attributes as defined in the data model. If the input is syntactically incorrect, the parser issues an error message listing the expected tokens, even if the input is still incomplete.

The following example shows a valid OQL query where **syntactical** and semantical correctness is highlighted.

```
select    min sceneIndex, max sceneIndex
from      SRTM1.X-SAR.IFDS
where
 (dataTakeOrbit = 61 and availability = 'PRELIMINARY'
  and there exists no corresponding SRTM1.X-SAR.IFDS
  with equal dataTakeOrbit and equal sceneIndex
  where availability = 'EXISTING')
```

This query computes the scene index range of the interferometric dataset products (Shuttle Radar Topography Mission) on orbit number 61, which have not been processed yet and therefore are catalogued only with a preliminary status.

5.3 Repository-Related Context

Interactive editors supporting input completion based on a static information model are common in human machine interfaces. Less common is the capability to determine the correctness of partial expressions. Rather infrequent, however, is the capability to validate inputs against the dynamic data model.

To be able to give suggestions for elements of the data model and to check semantical correctness, the query editor retrieves information from the repository of modeling elements. The first information retrieved is the list of available object types which can be specified in the `from` clause of the query. Each object type is defined by its name and a list of identifying and describing attributes. In subsequent actions, the query editor retrieves meta information about selected attributes, such as data type, valid values, value ranges and structure slots.

Depending on the selected object type, the specific attributes describing this type are suggested to be included after `select` or within the condition of the query. Structured attributes can be expanded to their slot attributes. As each attribute has a well-defined data type, the editor can ensure the correct choice of operations, comparators and literals within expressions, e.g. not allowing the comparison of a numeric attribute with a date literal. The editor is able to recognise specified set attributes and references via properties of the corresponding modeling elements and is able to suggest appropriate conditions on the set elements or referenced object types.

Fig. 6 shows the context-sensitive OQL editor with a partial query. The object type has already been selected and a `where` condition has been partially specified. On typing a control key, the editor shows a pop-up menu with a collection of suggested valid language tokens or data model elements to be entered next. When the query has been completely specified this way, it is again validated and then sent to the inventory for execution. The Operating Tool displays the results in a table and on the map.

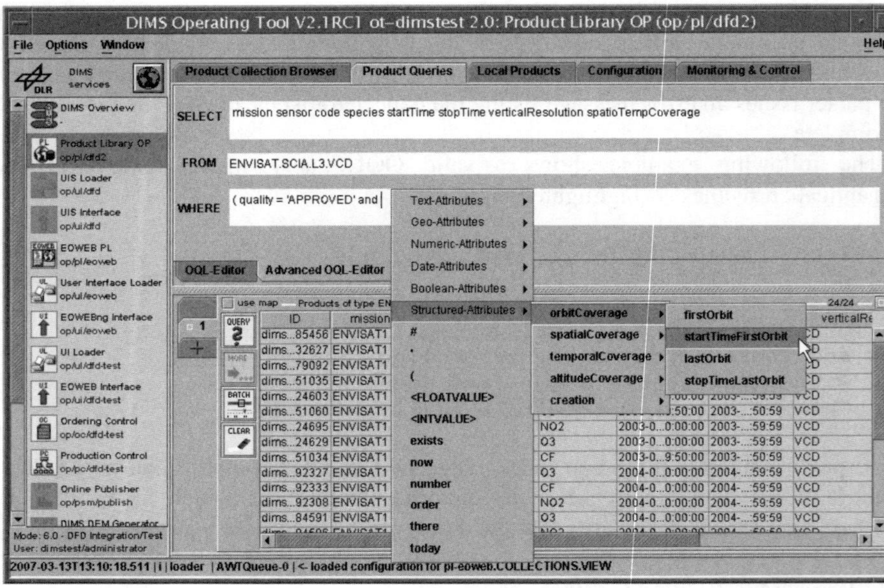

Fig. 6. Context-sensitive OQL Editor Embedded in the DIMS Operating Tool

6 Evaluation

The object query language editor of the Product Library illustrates the benefits of context-sensitivity in interactive library applications. This editor supports an easy ad-hoc specification of complex search queries which are syntactically correct and semantically meaningful. The knowledge exploited for context-sensitivity consists of the static grammar of the query language and the dynamic data model of the library. Therefore the editor goes beyond classical language-directed or syntax-directed editors based on common compiler design [6].

The approach to develop a language based editor using a parser generator is very effective. One of its features is its declarative approach as opposed to developing a dedicated imperative program which of course would depend tightly on the grammar. It turned out in practice that grammar changes - which are more frequent than one would assume at first sight - could indeed be implemented in a more straight forward way as compared to a pure programmatic approach.

The general procedure to generate code with the aid of the parser generator instead of writing it by hand is helpful and prevents code failures. The usage of context information and metadata, especially data provided by the meta model, makes it possible to develop an editor which provides the user with information matching at the current position of the query. As mentioned above, the editor is able to validate the input not only syntactically but also semantically. Our evaluation showed that the number of erroneous or unreasonable queries has decreased significantly. Users report that they found that the error messages produced by the syntax checker are well understandable and helpful. On the semantical level the type checks for literals, operators and attributes help constructing a valid query. Very good acceptance received the context-aware automatic suggestion of valid attributes that takes into account the current product type and other content-related contextual properties.

As the editor is based on a parser, it provides the possibility to support the user at every position of the query. Taking a look at very powerful IDEs like Eclipse, it can be seen that this is not the case in every IDE. The approach entails a lot of possible features that can be implemented to provide the user with more help and information. The editor turned out to be useful for both kinds of users, beginners and professionals. The former one gets help in any situation. The latter one, already knowing the syntax of the language, only takes the assistant to get metadata information, especially from the available models. In most cases the usage of meta model information takes place in the background. In any case there is no need to look up the documentation of the data model or the OQL syntax as in former days. Moreover, OQL features that have seldom been used are now more frequently "detected" by the users.

The query example provided in section 5.2 illustrates the power and expressiveness of OQL compared to some SQL catalogue look-up in a pure relational system: This query can easily be formulated with the help of the context-sensitive editor, but it corresponds to the following translated SQL code, which is quite hard to be specified and understood:

```
SELECT
  MIN(t.intermediateSceneI), MAX(t.intermediateSceneI)
FROM M_SRTM1XSARIFDS t
WHERE (
  t.dataTakeOrbit = '61' AND
  t.availability = 'PRELIMINARY' AND
  NOT EXISTS (
    SELECT unique_id
    FROM M_SRTM1XSARIFDS r
    WHERE (
      r.availability = 'EXISTING' AND
      r.dataTakeOrbit = t.dataTakeOrbit AND
      r.intermediateSceneI = t.intermediateSceneI ) ) )
```

Therefore the interactive query editor allows operators and library users to specify ad-hoc queries without requiring detailed knowledge about the data model and without being an expert on SQL.

The context-sensitive interactive query editor is an important constituent of the sustainability of the DIMS Product Library, which has not only to cope with a permanently growing amount of data and diversity of information, but also to integrate existing digital archives and provide application-level interfaces for other services to cover all earth observation ground system tasks of product processing, monitoring, long-term storage, ordering and delivery.

7 Conclusion

This paper addresses the problem of user support in a very large digital library system. In particular, extensions of the data model and dynamic library content put a heavy burden on the user who has to extract application-specific data using a standard query language. We have shown how a context-sensitive editor can be constructed and integrated into the system that supports the user in formulating his or her queries. The editor is aware of the underlying data model as well as (part of) the dynamic content of the library and thus is able to propose syntactically correct and semantically meaningful continuations of a query. An evaluation has shown that the context-aware editor significantly improves user-friendliness und usability of the DIMS digital library system.

Acknowledgments. Special thanks to our student Ulrich Frank who significantly supported this work by investigation, assessment and prototyping. We also thank Sven Kröger, DLR, for his support during prototyping and integration.

References

1. Mikusch, E., Diedrich, E., Göhmann, M., Kiemle, S., Reck, C., Reißig, R., Schmidt, K., Wildegger, W., Wolfmüller, M.: Data Information and Management System for the Production, Archiving and Distribution of Earth Observation Products. Data Systems in Aerospace 2000, EUROSPACE. ESA Publications Division, SP-457, Noordwijk (2000)
2. Kiemle, S.: From Digital Archive to Digital Library – a Middleware for Earth-Observation Data Management. In: Agosti, M., Thanos, C. (eds.) ECDL 2002. LNCS, vol. 2458, Springer, Heidelberg (2002)
3. Cluet, S.: Designing OQL: Allowing objects to be queried. Information Systems 23(5), 279–305 (1998)
4. German TerraSAR-X Radar Satellite Mission homepage at the German Aerospace Center, Available in the WWW at http://www.dlr.de/tsx/start_en.htm
5. Object Management Group (OMG): Common Warehouse Metamodel (CWM) Specification. Version 1.1, volume 1 (March 2003), Available in the WWW at http://www.omg.org/docs/formal/03-03-02.pdf
6. Grune, D., Bal, H., Jacobs, C., Langendoen, K.: Modern Compiler Design. John Wiley, Chichester (2002)
7. javaCC project home (last visited 13/03/2007), Available in the WWW at https://javacc.dev.java.net/

T-Scroll: Visualizing Trends in a Time-Series of Documents for Interactive User Exploration

Yoshiharu Ishikawa[1,2] and Mikine Hasegawa[3,⋆]

[1] Information Technology Center, Nagoya University
[2] Nagoya University Library Study
[3] Department of Information Engineering, School of Engineering, Nagoya University
ishikawa@itc.nagoya-u.ac.jp

Abstract. On the Internet, a large number of documents such as news articles and online journals are delivered everyday. We often have to review major topics and topic transitions from a large time-series of documents, but it requires much time and effort to browse and analyze the target documents. We have therefore developed an information visualization system called *T-Scroll* (Trend/Topic-Scroll) to visualize the transition of topics extracted from those documents. The system takes periodical outputs of the underlying clustering system for a time-series of documents then visualizes the relationships between clusters as a scroll. Using its interaction facility, users can grasp the topic transitions and the details of topics for the target time period. This paper describes the idea, the functions, the implementation, and the evaluation of the T-Scroll system.

1 Introduction

Due to the evolution of information services on the Internet, various kinds of documents, such as news articles and online journals, are delivered everyday. Since a large amount of textual information is obtained continually, research aimed at summarizing huge text information and detecting trends becomes an important issue today [1,2]. Although we can reduce the efforts of users by using clustering and information extraction techniques, users still have to make the effort to capture overall trends from the documents. For this purpose, the user needs an intuitive tool to see which kind of major topics appear and how topics change as time passes.

Based on this background, we have developed an information visualization interface called *T-Scroll* (Topic/Trend-Scroll) to visualize the overall trend of a time-series of documents based on their contents and timestamps. T-Scroll is constructed over a document clustering system and visualizes periodical clustering results. It organizes the clustering result for each time period along the time axis and displays links between clusters. Links are generated to represent related clusters and the system presents the topic flow in a scroll-like style. The

⋆ Current affiliation: Nihon Seifun Co. Ltd.

L. Kovács, N. Fuhr, and C. Meghini (Eds.): ECDL 2007, LNCS 4675, pp. 235–246, 2007.

user can browse the T-Scroll interface using Web browsers and can select and explore more detailed information if they need it.

The organization of the paper is as follows. Section 2 introduces related work. Section 3 describes the novelty-based clustering method for a time-series of documents, which is the basis of the T-Scroll system. Section 4 presents the features and functions of T-Scroll. Section 5 describes the implementation techniques then Section 6 shows the evaluation results. Finally, Section 7 concludes the paper and indicates future work.

2 Related Work

2.1 Visualization of a Time-Series of Documents

Müller et al. [3] provides a short survey of visualization techniques for time dependent data. There are few proposals of the visualization of a time-series of documents except for the following two systems.

ThemeRiver [4] is an information visualization system which visualizes topic streams like a *river*. The displayed image resembles a river that flows from left to right along the time axis. The river contains several streams in different colors and they correspond to the selected topics (themes). For each topic stream, phrases are displayed on the screen to help users' interpretation. The width of a stream changes depending on time and reflects the number of documents for each time period. ThemeRiver shares similar ideas with T-Scroll since they utilize a scroll-based interface, but it does not use clustering. ThemeRiver is a system that focuses on providing visual impact and cannot represent topic transitions. Although it may be useful to see an overview of the trend, the system is not a powerful tool for analyzing and browsing a time-series of documents. In contrast, T-Scroll provides facilities so that users can view document titles and contents if they need.

TimeMine [5] is a system that extracts topics from a time-series of documents then displays *timelines* to represent topics on the screen. It analyzes a time-series of documents over the specified time period using a statistics-based method and extracts topics which are represented by groups of documents. Based on the analysis, the system displays rectangular regions representing timelines on the screen in which time flows from left to right. In addition, the system displays keywords along the corresponding timelines. The main focus of TimeMine is to select major topics and their time periods. Although the proposed techniques are quite interesting, the system does not provide functionalities for more detailed analysis.

2.2 Analysis of Time-Dependent Clusters

There are some proposals for tracking and analyzing clusters changing in time, but they do not aim for visualization. Mei and Zhai [6] propose a statistical approach for discovering major topics from a time-series of documents. In this scheme, a theme is represented as a probability distribution over a time period and can be seen as a cluster. Relationships between consecutive time instants are determined based on probabilistic criteria. The derived theme transition graph resembles the graph generated by the cluster relationships of T-Scroll. In [6], they also provide a global method for analyzing the whole graph to mine meaningful patterns.

MONIC [7] proposes an approach for detecting various types of patterns from cluster transitions such as the splitting and merging of clusters, cluster size change, etc. MONIC discovers events based on historical snapshots of clusters. Its underlying idea is related with our approach.

3 Novelty-Based Clustering Method for a Time-Series of Documents

T-Scroll is based on the *novelty-based document clustering method* [8,9,10]. The target of the method is a *time-series of documents* such as news articles and online journals. Such documents have the general property that additional documents with new timestamps are continually delivered over the network.

The clustering method focuses on the clustering of a time-series of documents and has the following features:

1. To calculate similarity, it considers not only document contents but also the *novelty* of each document. It incorporates a similarity function that considers the novelty of documents then puts high weights on recent documents.
2. When a new document is delivered, clustering should be performed to acquire the new clustering result. To alleviate the processing cost, the method uses incremental processing as much as possible.
3. Since the method puts high weights on novel documents, old documents tend to have low effect on the clustering result and become outliers. Therefore, old documents are deleted from the clustering targets automatically so we can reduce the processing cost.

Based on this approach, the method clusters a time-series of documents in an online manner and provides clustering results focusing on current major topics.

We now introduce the similarity function used in the clustering method. In a time-series of documents, such as news articles and online journals, the value of a document generally decreases over time. The novelty-based clustering method for a time-series of documents [8,9,10] proposes the *document forgetting model* and derives the document similarity based on that.

The forgetting model assumes that the importance (weight) of a document declines in an exponential manner as time passes, and defines the weight of document d_i as follows:

$$dw_i = \lambda^{\tau - T_i} \qquad (0 < \lambda < 1), \tag{1}$$

where τ is the current time and T_i is the timestamp of d_i. The parameter λ represents how fast the weight declines. The model inherits the idea from *aging* or *obsolescence* in library information science and infometrics [11]. Now we define the total weight of a document set with n documents $d_1, \ldots, d_n$ as $tdw = \sum_{l=1}^{n} dw_l$ and define the occurrence probability of d_i within a document set as a subjective probability $\Pr(d_i) = dw_i/tdw$. Since old documents have small probabilities, this represents the idea of forgetting old documents.

Document similarity is defined based on a probabilistic approach [8,9,10]. Its general form is given by

$$sim(d_i, d_j) = \Pr(d_i)\Pr(d_j)\frac{\boldsymbol{d}_i \cdot \boldsymbol{d}_j}{len_i \times len_j}, \tag{2}$$

where "·" is the inner product of document vectors and len_i is the vector length of $\boldsymbol{d}_i$. Thus, document similarity considers not only how documents are similar, but also whether two documents are old or not. Very old documents tend to be dissimilar to other documents and become outliers. By using the similarity in the clustering procedure, we can achieve a novelty-based clustering that has a bias toward recent documents.

The clustering method actually used in [9,10] is an extended version of the k-means method [12]. When new documents are obtained, we need to perform a new clustering to reflect them. Since clustering from scratch is quite costly, our approach utilizes k cluster representatives from the previous clustering result as initial cluster representatives. Based on this approach, the clustering procedure converges faster than the naive approach. Moreover, it can improve the clustering quality [10].

As described above, the novelty-based clustering method periodically performs incremental clustering for continually delivered documents then outputs the clustering results. Each clustering result represents major topics for the period when the clustering was performed. By storing such clusters permanently, we can use them for analyses to be performed later. T-Scroll is based on such an idea and can be used as a visual interface for analyzing retrospective document collections.

4 Overview of the T-Scroll System

4.1 System Features

The main features of the *T-Scroll* system are summarized as follows:

1. It displays the clustering result for each time period along the time axis with topic labels so the user can grasp overall topics for the target time interval.
2. The user can select the cluster in which he or she is interested in, then the user can obtain more detailed information such as the keyword list or can refer to the original articles in an interactive way.
3. For clusters obtained in a period, it creates *links* from the clusters of the previous time period based on the cluster similarity; the user can observe the relationships between clusters.
4. The user can select an appropriate interval to visualize clusters on the screen then the user can perform analysis depending on his or her requirement with different veles of detail. The approach corresponds to *roll-up* and *drill-down* facilities in *OLAP* (*On-Line Analytical Processing*) [12].

Based on these features, the flow of topics and trends are represented as a scroll and we call the system *T-Scroll*.

4.2 System Functionalities

Figure 1 shows a screenshot of T-Scroll. The figure represents news articles from the TDT2 Corpus [2]. The corpus contains news broadcasts on TV and radio in 1998. On the interface, the time flows from left to right. Using the slide bar on the screen, we can move to the previous time period. Ellipses shown on the same vertical line are clusters obtained in the same clustering process. In this figure, $k = 20$ clusters are generated for each time period. The interval between two consecutive clusterings is set to one day.

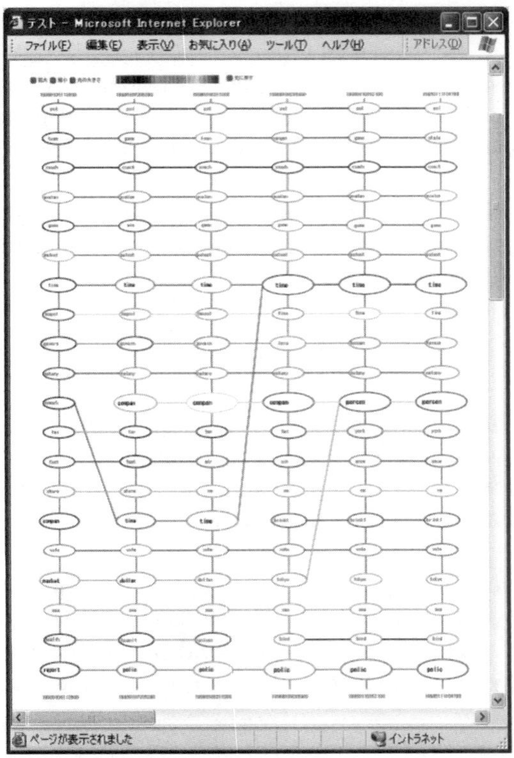

Fig. 1. Screenshot of T-Scroll (one day basis)

The vertical order of clusters is not very meaningful: clusters are displayed in order of their increasing cluster ID. However, the novelty-based clustering method [10] is able to generate the "regular" graph structure as shown in the figure. When a new clustering is performed, the method reuses the previous cluster representatives then performs a clustering process based on the k-means method. Therefore, the previous cluster IDs are retained for the new clustering result. Such situations occur quite often, especially when we utilize a short period for the display interval such as "one day" for Fig. 1.

Cluster labels. For each cluster, we select a feature term that has the highest score within the terms contained in its documents as a *cluster label*. After trials of several scoring methods, we have decided to assign the score for term t_j in cluster C_p as

$$score(t_j) = \sum_{d_i \in C_p} \Pr(d_i) \cdot tf_{ij}. \tag{3}$$

Namely, for each document d_i in the cluster, the term frequency tf_{ij} for term t_j is multiplied with the document weight $\Pr(d_i)$ then the summation is taken. Although we have tried to display multiple terms on a cluster, our impression was that it is too complicated. So we select only one term in the current implementation.

Cluster sizes. The area of a cluster ellipse corresponds to the number of documents in the cluster. To represent the cluster size, we select an appropriate size from several size levels. Thus, the user can be made aware of topic sizes.

Cluster links. As shown in Fig. 1, links are generated between selected clusters. Each link means that those clusters are related. The cluster relationship score is defined as a probability:

$$score(C_i \to C_j) = \Pr(C_j|C_i) = \frac{|C_i \cap C_j|}{|C_i|}. \tag{4}$$

The formula measures the degree to which the documents in cluster C_i are contained within cluster C_j. We allow zero or multiple links to emerge from one cluster so that the system can represent topic expiration (represented by zero link) and topic separation (represented by multiple links).

Cluster qualities. To help the user to capture the quality of a cluster, T-Scroll visualizes cluster quality using different colors for the cluster border lines. Red represents the highest cluster quality and purple means the lowest cluster quality. The quality score of cluster C is defined as follows [10]:

$$quality(C) = |C| \cdot avg\_sim(C), \tag{5}$$

where $|C|$ means the number of documents in C, and $avg\_sim(C)$ represents the average similarity of all the document pairs in the cluster which is defined as follows:

$$avg\_sim(C) = \frac{1}{|C|(|C|-1)} \sum_{d_i, d_j \in C, d_i \neq d_j} sim(d_i, d_j). \tag{6}$$

Note that $quality(C)$ takes a large score not only when the cluster size is large but also documents in a cluster are similar each other.

Drill-down/roll-up functions. T-Scroll supports drill-down and roll-up functions. For example, Fig. 1 is an example with a one day basis, but we can utilize more coarse values (e.g., three days, one week). In the actual implementation, we periodically perform clustering then determine whether to create links between clusters based on Eq. (4). Then we store the result as a graph structure. When a visualization request is issued to T-Scroll, the system extracts the required subgraph from the stored graph.

Displaying a keyword list. As shown in Fig. 1, T-Scroll displays one keyword as a label for each cluster, but the user often needs more keywords to understand the cluster content. Therefore, T-Scroll also provides a facility for seeing the cluster contents. When the user moves the mouse cursor over a cluster ellipse, the system displays a keyword list for the cluster on the screen as shown in Fig. 2. The figure shows the situation when we move the mouse cursor over the "iraq" cluster. The system displays top-ranked keywords for the cluster.

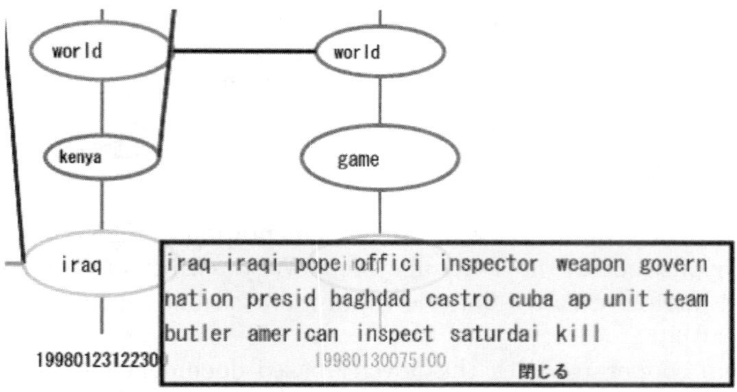

Fig. 2. Displaying keyword list

Access to original documents. Although we can see the overall contents of clusters using the above functions, it is difficult to know which documents are contained in the cluster. Therefore, the system provides a facility for displaying documents in a cluster by clicking the mouse on the cluster ellipse. Figure 3 shows this situation. The system displays the titles of recent documents in the cluster. In addition, if the user clicks on a document title, its content appears on the display (the figure is omitted here).

Keyword-based emphasis. We can perform keyword-based queries by entering keywords in the keyword query field on the T-Scroll interface. The system emphasizes the clusters if their top-20 keywords contain the given keyword. Figure 4 shows the situtaion. The figure shows the result when we provide the keyword "olympic" (a Winter Olympic was held in the display period). The emphasized clusters are matched ones. In addition, the system can receive multiple keywords. In this case, if either of the given keywords is contained in the keyword list, the cluster is matched. Based on this functionality, the user can see topic transition more easily.

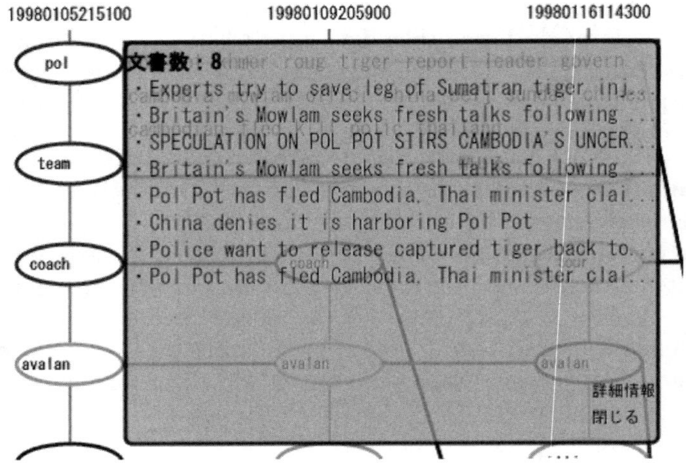

Fig. 3. Displaying document titles

5 System Implementation

This section provides an overview of the implementation of the system. Figure 5 shows the organization of the T-Scroll system. We describe each system component. A solid line represents a data flow and a dotted line means a control flow (procedure call).

The system cooperates with the novelty-based document clustering system [9,10] and uses its outputs. A new clustering result is obtained by giving a newly acquired document set to the clustering program. The clustering result is output as an XML file.

The T-Scroll system reads the XML files output from the clustering system. Selected XML files are incorporated and used according to the period and the parameters specified by the user. The main module of T-Scroll is written in JavaScript and runs within a Web browser. Some part of processing concerning the user interface is implemented by JavaScript and AJAX.

Given the target period and other parameters, T-Scroll displays the interface on a Web browser. For this purpose, a submodule written in Perl is called from the main module. This submodule analyzes the XML files and generates an SVG file to be displayed on the interface. The SVG file is read in the Web browser then the interface appears as shown in Fig. 1. JavaScript codes are embedded in the SVG file and modules written in Perl are called on as necessary.

6 System Evaluation

This section summarizes the results of the evaluation experiments. The evaluation experiments were conducted by 10 users. The data set used was articles collected from Japanese news web sites from September 2006 to February 2007.

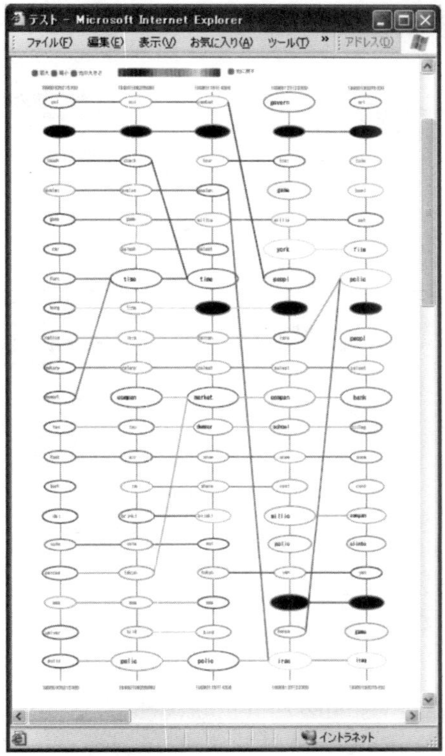

Fig. 4. Emphasized cluster display based on keywords

On average, 100 articles were collected and clustering was performed at six-hour intervals.

Overall impressions. First, we asked for a general impression of the T-scroll user interface. The scores were selected from five levels: 1 (very bad) to 5 (very good). Four evaluation categories (usability, understandability, usefulness, and design) were used.

Figure 6 shows the evaluation result. The averaged scores with standard errors are plotted. Although the usefulness score is 3.7 on average, the usability score is 2.5, which means that further system improvement is necessary. Scores for understandability and design are 3.1 and 2.8, respectively, but the design score has large variance. We conducted user interviews and collected valuable comments. The major problems are 1) the response time of the system and 2) the label for a cluster is not necessarily an intuitive one. The first problem can be solved by revised implementation. The second problem is more important and we will consider it later.

Evaluation of each function. The evaluation results for the individual system functions are shown in Fig. 7. The evaluation criteria are as follows:

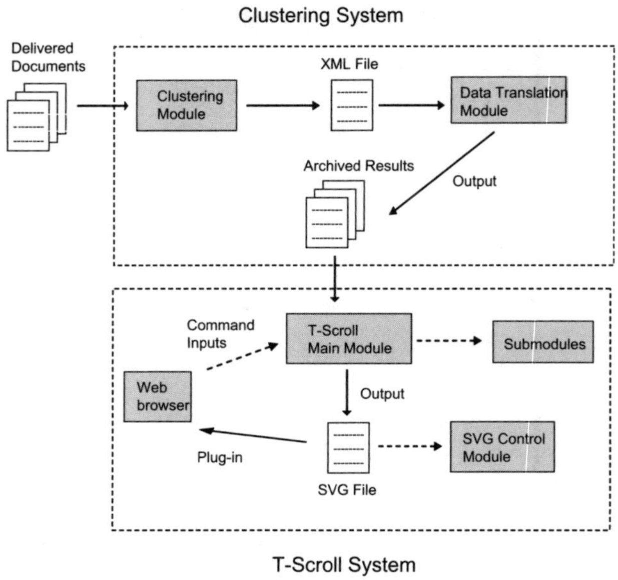

Fig. 5. System organization of T-Scroll system

- Scroll: The scroll-like visualization approach
- DocNum: The appropriateness of associating the number of documents of a cluster with the size of its corresponding ellipsoid
- Label: The label display facility
- Quality: The method of showing the quality of clusters by colors
- Keyword: The keyword list display function (Fig. 2)
- TitleList: The function for displaying document titles (Fig. 3)
- Emphasis: The keyword-based emphasis function (Figure 4)
- Interval: The function for allowing multiple interval settings

All the average scores are over three except for the "Label" facility. The reasons for the "Label" problem are as follows: 1) We have used Japanese morphological analysis tool to extract feature terms (e.g., noun terms). Since we did not tune the dictionary of the tool for the experiment, the quality of the extracted terms is not satisfactory. Expansion of dictionary would improve the quality of terms. 2) The automatic label selection method based on Eq. (3) does not necessarily select comprehensible terms. It may be better to use a controlled vocabulary for labels. Next, we consider the "Score" criteria. One of the reasons that it has relatively low score 3.1 would be that there is no candidate to compare with T-Scroll in this experiment. Finally, consider the "TitleList" facility. The experimental result says displaying document titles is quite useful for the users.

Observability of topics. We conducted another experiment to see whether the users could observe the major five topics in Japan in November 2006. The five topics include big events and accidents such as "damage by big tornado on

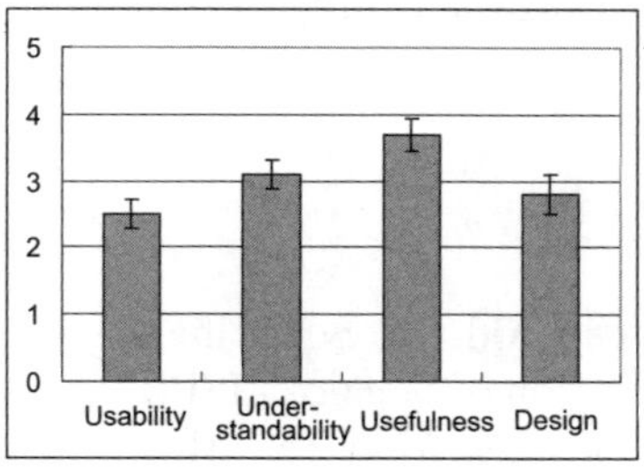

Fig. 6. Overall evaluation scores

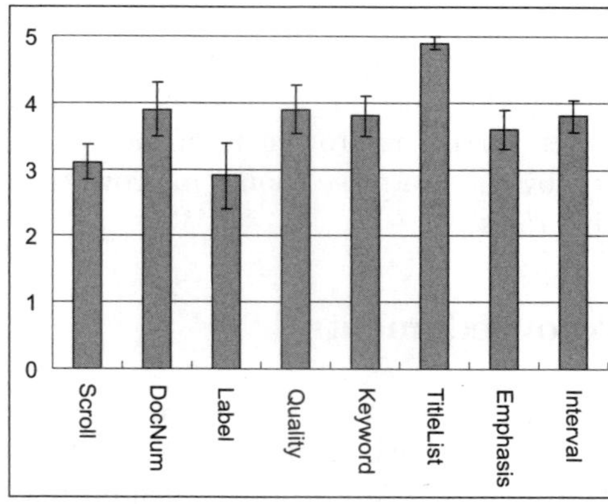

Fig. 7. Evaluation score for each function

November 7th", but their details are omitted. Figure 8 shows the evaluation result by ten users. We have asked the users whether they can actually observe each topic. We can say that all the average scores are successful. The reason for the relatively low score on Topic 3 is that the topic was a big issue for this period and it contains subtopics. Since subtopics have appeared in some periods as multiple topic threads, the users might find it difficult to make a judgment.

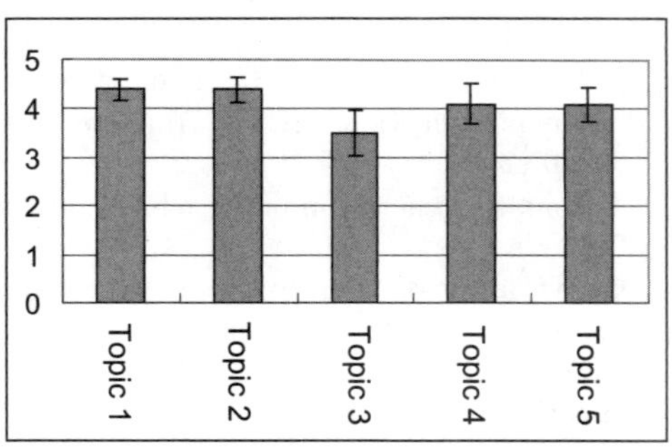

Fig. 8. Observability of topics

7 Conclusions and Future Work

In this paper, we have described the idea, the functions, the implementation, and the evaluation of the T-Scroll system, a visual interface for analyzing the transition of topics from a time-series of documents. This system is based on the novelty-based clustering method for time-series of documents and uses the clustering results for the visualization. T-Scroll supports interactive processing facilities and has several functions such as keyword list display, document title display, and so on.

Based on evaluation by users, it was shown that they can observe major topics that actually happened using the system. We can say that the objective of capturing the trends in a time-series of documents is achieved by the system. However, further improvement of the system is necessary. As shown in the evaluation by the users, we should improve the usefulness and understandability of the interface.

Acknowledgments

This research is partly supported by a Grant-in-Aid for Scientific Research (19300027) from the Japan Society for the Promotion of Science (JSPS), Japan. In addition, this research was supported by grants from the Hoso Bunka Foundation.

References

1. Kontostathis, A., Galitsky, L.M., Pottenger, W.M., Roy, S., Phelps, D.J.: A survey of emerging trend detection in textual data mining. In: Berry, M.W. (ed.) Survey of Text Mining: Clustering, Classification, and Retrieval, pp. 185–224. Springer, Heidelberg (2003)
2. Allan, J. (ed.): Topic Detection and Tracking: Event-based Information Organization. Kluwer, Dordrecht (2002)
3. Müller, W., Schumann, H.: Visualization methods for time-dependent data: An overview. In: Proc. of 2003 Winter Simulation Conf., pp. 737–745 (2003)
4. Havre, S., Hetzler, E., Whitney, P., Nowell, L.: ThemeRiver: Visualizing thematic challenges in large document collections. IEEE Trans. on Visualization and Computer Graphics 8(1), 9–20 (2002)
5. Swan, R., Allan, J.: Automatic generation of overview timelines. In: Proc. of ACM SIGIR, pp. 49–56 (2000)
6. Mei, Q., Zhai, C.: Discovering evolutionary theme patterns from text: An exploration of temporal text mining. In: Proc. of ACM KDD, pp. 198–207 (2005)
7. Spiliopoulou, M., Ntoutsi, I., Theodoridis, Y., Schult, R.: MONIC: Modeling and monitoring cluster transitions. In: Proc. of ACM KDD, pp. 706–711 (2006)
8. Ishikawa, Y., Chen, Y., Kitagawa, H.: An on-line document clustering method based on forgetting factors. In: Constantopoulos, P., Sølvberg, I.T. (eds.) ECDL 2001. LNCS, vol. 2163, pp. 332–339. Springer, Heidelberg (2001)
9. Khy, S., Ishikawa, Y., Kitagawa, H.: Novelty-based incremental document clustering for on-line documents. In: Proc. of International Workshop on Challenges in Web Information Retrieval and Integration (WIRI 2006) (2006)
10. Khy, S., Ishikawa, Y., Kitagawa, H.: A novelty-based clustering method for on-line documents. World Wide Web Journal (2007) (in press)
11. Egghe, L., Rousseau, R.: Introduction to Informetrics: Quantitative Methods in Library, Documentation and Information Science. Elsevier, Amsterdam (1990)
12. Han, J., Kamber, M.: Data Mining: Concepts and Techniques, 2nd edn. Morgan Kaufmann, San Francisco (2005)

Thesaurus-Based Feedback to Support Mixed Search and Browsing Environments

Edgar Meij and Maarten de Rijke

ISLA, University of Amsterdam,
Kruislaan 403, 1098 SJ Amsterdam, The Netherlands
{emeij, mdr}@science.uva.nl

Abstract. We propose and evaluate a query expansion mechanism that supports searching and browsing in collections of annotated documents. Based on generative language models, our feedback mechanism uses document-level annotations to bias the generation of expansion terms and to generate browsing suggestions in the form of concepts selected from a controlled vocabulary (as typically used in digital library settings). We provide a detailed formalization of our feedback mechanism and evaluate its effectiveness using the TREC 2006 Genomics track test set. As to the retrieval effectiveness, we find a 20% improvement in mean average precision over a query-likelihood baseline, whilst increasing precision at 10. When we base the parameter estimation and feedback generation of our algorithm on a large corpus, we also find an improvement over state-of-the-art relevance models. The browsing suggestions are assessed along two dimensions: relevancy and specifity. We present an account of per-topic results, which helps understand for what type of queries our feedback mechanism is particularly helpful.

1 Introduction

A query that is used to express the information need of a digital library user may fail to match the relevant words in the domain being explored. Even if the query terms do match terms and documents from the domain, they may not be used by all authors of relevant articles. Authors working in different areas may use different terms for a single concept or may even denote different concepts with the same term. Several methods exist for overcoming this vocabulary mismatch problem, many of which are based on *query expansion*. Query expansion adds terms and possibly reweighs original query terms, so as to more effectively express the original information need. Automatic approaches to query expansion have been studied extensively in information retrieval (IR). Most of these operate by using some initial set of retrieved documents to look for additional, significant terms. Much work has been dedicated to these kinds of techniques and, over time, various methods have been proposed. One class of solutions looks at the problem from a data-driven perspective, e.g., by generating expansion terms from entire documents [17], document summaries [15], or the context in which the original query terms appear [21]. Other, more knowledge-based apporaches look at "external" resources, such as ontologies, thesauri, co-occurence tables, or synonym lists [20].

L. Kovács, N. Fuhr, and C. Meghini (Eds.): ECDL 2007, LNCS 4675, pp. 247–258, 2007.

In this paper, we consider query expansion in the setting of a digital library, where information access is usually a mixture of two tasks: *searching* and *browsing* [10, 13, 18]. While query expansion is typically aimed at increasing the effectiveness of the search component, we are interested in expansion techniques that can also help to improve browsing support. In particular, our goal is to achieve effective query expansion (at least as effective as state-of-the-art data-driven approaches) which, at the same time, incorporates explicit knowledge inherent in a digital library to facilitate browsing and exploring. More specifically, we aim to enhance a user's search by facilitating this kind of browsing directly and transparently from the searching process, by suggesting controlled vocabulary terms and integrating them into the retrieval model.

The research questions we address are fourfold. First, how can we use a language modeling framework to incorporate thesaurus information for generating terms to facilitate browsing? Second, can this be done in such a way that the feedback mechanism achieves state-of-the-art performance? Third, and inspired by recent work on document expansion [8, 19], what is the impact of the size of the corpus from which feedback terms are being generated? Fourth, how can we assess the quality of the thesaurus terms being proposed for browsing?

Our main contribution is the introduction of a thesaurus-biased feedback algorithm that uses generative language modeling to not only generate expansion terms to improve retrieval results, but also to propose thesaurus terms to facilitate browsing. Our algorithm, which achieves state-of-the-art performance, consists of three steps: First, we determine the controlled vocabulary terms most closely associated with a query. We then search the documents associated with these terms, in conjunction with the query, and look for additional terms to describe the query. Finally, we weigh these proposed expansion terms, again using the document-level annotations. For evaluation purposes we use the TREC 2006 Genomics track test set [9]. Specifically, we use and compare this collection and the contents of the entire PubMed database for estimation purposes.

The remainder of this paper is organized as follows. In Section 2 we describe the background of our work, as well as our proposed query expansion algorithm. In Section 3 we detail our experimental setup, and in Section 4 we present our experimental results. Related work is discussed in Section 5 and Section 6 contains our conclusions.

2 Thesaurus-Biased Query Models

Within the field of IR, language modeling is a relatively novel framework. It originates from speech recognition, where the modeling of speech utterances is mapped onto textual representations. The ideas behind it are intuitive and theoretically well-motivated, thus making it an attractive framework of choice. It provides us with an easily extendible setting for incorporating the information captured in document annotations. Before introducing our novel feedback mechanism we recall some general facts about language models for IR.

2.1 Generative Language Modeling

Language modeling for IR is centered around the assumption that a query, as issued by a user, is a sample generated from some underlying term distribution. The documents in the collection are modeled in a similar fashion, and also regarded as samples from an unseen term distribution—a generative language model.

At retrieval time, the language usage in documents is compared with that of the query and the documents are ranked according to the likelihood of generating the query. Assuming independence between query terms, the probability of a document given a query can be more formally stated using Bayes' rule:

$$P(Q|\theta_d) \propto P(d) \cdot \prod_{q \in Q} P(q|\theta_d), \tag{1}$$

where θ_d is a language model of document d, and q the individual query terms in query Q. The term $P(d)$ captures the prior belief in a document being relevant, which is usually assumed to be uniform. $P(\cdot|\theta_d)$ is estimated using maximum-likelihood estimates which, in this case, means using the frequency of a query term in a document: $P(q|\theta_d) = c(q,d)/|d|$. Here, $c(q,d)$ indicates the count of term q in document d and $|d|$ the length of the particular document. This captures the notion that $P(q|\theta_d)$ is the relative frequency with which we expect to see the term q when we repeatedly and randomly sample terms from this document. The higher this frequency, the more likely it is that this document will be relevant to the query.

2.2 Smoothing

It is clear from Eq. 1, that taking the product of term frequencies has a risk of resulting in a probability of zero: "unseen" terms will produce a probability of zero for that particular document. To tackle this problem, *smoothing* is usually applied, which assigns a very small (non-zero) probability to unseen words. One way of smoothing is called Dirichlet smoothing [4, 22], which is formulated as:

$$P(Q|\theta_d) = P(d) \cdot \prod_{q \in Q} \frac{c(q,d) + \mu P(q|\theta_C)}{|d| + \mu},$$

where θ_C is the language model of a large reference corpus C (such as the collection) and μ a constant by which to tune the influence of the reference model. When comparing the language modeling framework for IR with more well-known TF.IDF schemes, the application of smoothing has an IDF like effect [11, 22].

2.3 Relevance Models

Relevance models are a special class of language models, which are used to estimate a probability distribution θ_Q over terms in a query's vocabulary [16]. The underlying intuition is that the query and the set of relevant documents are both sampled from the same (relevant) term distribution. They differ, however, in the way these distributions are modeled. While general language modeling assumes that queries are generated from documents, relevance models assume that both are generated from an unseen source—the relevance model.

So, how to create such a relevance model? A set of documents R, which has been judged to be relevant to a specific query, can be used as a model from which the terms are sampled. In the absence of such relevance information, an initial retrieval run is performed and the top-ranked documents are assumed to be relevant. Bayes' rule is then applied to determine the probabilities of the terms given this document set. This approach normally assumes the document prior to be uniform and we obtain:

$$P(w|\hat{\theta}_Q) \propto \sum_{d \in R} P(w|\theta_d) \cdot P(Q|\theta_d). \tag{2}$$

The term $P(w|\theta_d)$ is again estimated using maximum-likelihood techniques. To obtain an estimate of $P(Q|\theta_d)$—the probability of a query, given a document model, i.e., the confidence in a particular document being relevant to the original query—Bayes' rule is applied again, together with Dirichlet smoothing. Eq. 2 thus essentially estimates the "confidence" of translating the original query Q into a particular term w, based on some set of relevant documents R.

2.4 Biasing Relevance Models

We now introduce a new latent variable into Eq. 2, which is derived from documents categorized with thesaurus terms m. Through this model we bias the generation of a relevance model towards terms associated with the thesaurus terms. For any given query we take the l thesaurus terms that are most likely to generate the query, based on some corpus of annotated documents, and then condition the generation of a relevance model on these terms:

$$P(w|\hat{\theta}_Q) \propto \sum_{d \in R} P(w|\theta_d) \cdot P(d|m_1, \ldots, m_l) \cdot P(Q|\theta_d). \tag{3}$$

We assume the thesaurus terms to be independent, so we can express their joint probability $P(d|m_1, \ldots, m_l)$ as the product of the marginals: $\prod_{i=1,\ldots,l} P(d|m_i)$. Each term $P(d|m_i)$ can be estimated using Bayes' rule, by determining the following posterior distribution, based on documents annotated with that particular term:

$$P(d|m) = \frac{P(m|d) \cdot P(d)}{P(m)},$$

where $P(d)$ is again assumed to be uniform. We estimate the prior probability of seeing a thesaurus term as $P(m) = c(m) \cdot |M|^{-1}$ for any given thesaurus term m, where $c(m)$ is the total number of times this thesaurus term is used to categorize a document and $|M| = \sum_{m \in M} c(m)$. Doing so ensures that frequently occuring, more general (and thus less discriminative thesaurus terms) receive a relatively lower probability mass. $P(m|d)$ is estimated in a similar fashion: it is 0 if m is not associated with d, and the reciprocal of the number of thesaurus terms associated with document d otherwise.

2.5 Clipped Relevance Model

Relevance models generally perform better when they are linearly interpolated with the original query estimate—the so-called "clipped relevance model" [14]—using a mixing weight λ:

$$P(w|\theta_Q) = \lambda \cdot \frac{c(w,Q)}{|Q|} + (1-\lambda) \cdot P(w|\hat{\theta}_Q). \tag{4}$$

The final query is thus composed of an initial and an expanded query part, with terms and weights in the latter chosen according to either Eq. 2 or 3. When λ is set to 1, the ranking function reduces to the regular query-likelihood ranking algorithm.

3 Experimental Setup

Now that we have put forward our proposed thesaurus-biased expansion algorithm, we turn to answering our research questions. In this section we detail the test collection and experimental setup and in the next we present our findings.

3.1 Test Collection

As our test collection we take the TREC 2006 Genomics test set [9]. The 2006 edition of the TREC Genomics track provides a set of queries (topics), a document collection of full-text biomedical articles, and relevance assessments. The task put forward by the organizers of this particular year's track was to identify relevant documents given a topic and to extract the relevant passages from these documents. The topics themselves were based on four distinct topic templates, and instantiated with specific genes, diseases or biological processes. Relevance was measured at three levels: the document, passage and aspect level. For our experiments, we use the judgments at the document level and those at the aspect level.

All of the documents in this collection are also accessible through PubMed, a bibliographic database maintained by the National Library of Medicine (NLM). It contains bibliographical records of almost all publications from the major biomedical research areas, conferences, and journals and uses controlled vocabulary terms to index the documents. This vocabulary, called MeSH (Medical Subject Headings), is a thesaurus containing 22,997 hierarchically structured concepts, and is used by trained annotators from the NLM to assign one or more MeSH terms to every document indexed in PubMed. These terms can then later be used to restrict, refine, or focus a query, much in the same way a regular library categorization system does.

We base our estimations of the relevance models and the thesaurus-biased models either on the TREC Genomics 2006 document collection or on all the abstracts as found in PubMed. The former collection contains 162,259 full-text documents, whereas the entire PubMed database contains 15,806,221 abstracts. Both have document-level MeSH terms categorizing their content, with an average of around 10 MeSH terms per publication.

3.2 Runs

We created five runs. As a baseline, we perform a regular query-likelihood run (QL) based on Eq. 4 with λ set to 1. We will refer to the run implementing our thesaurus-biased relevance models as MeSH-biased models (MM); it uses Eq. 4 in conjunction with Eq. 3. We compare the results with standard relevance models (RM) which are also estimated using Eq. 4, but with the expanded query portion based on Eq.2. As stated before, we estimate the expanded part of the query either on the TREC Genomics

Table 1. Comparison between different query models and a query-likelihood baseline (best scores in boldface.)

	λ	$\|R\|$	k	l	MAP	Change	P10	Change
QL	1	-	-	-	0.359		0.45	
RM (collection)	0.10	10	50	-	0.426	+19%	0.48	+7%
RM (PubMed)	0.35	1	50	-	0.425	+18%	0.48	+7%
MM (collection)	0.05	10	10	20	0.424	+18%	0.48	+7%
MM (PubMed)	0.45	1	30	20	**0.429**	+20%	**0.49**	+9%

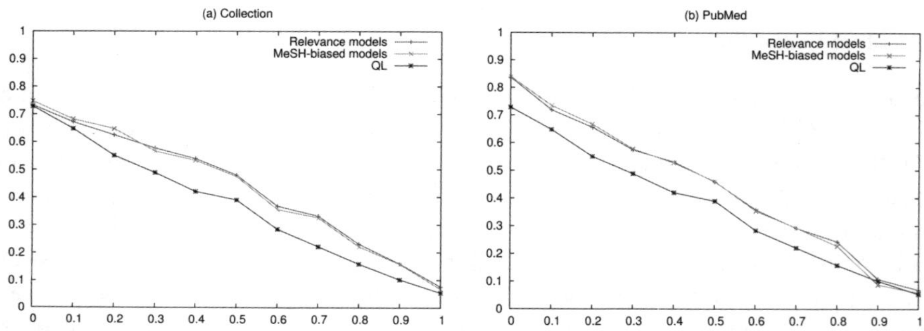

Fig. 1. Precision-recall graphs comparing relevance models and MeSH-biased models, estimated on (a) the collection or (b) PubMed. The results of the baseline are included as reference.

2006 document collection (MM/RM (collection)), or on the contents of the much larger PubMed collection (MM/RM (PubMed)). All runs are morphologically normalized as described by **(author?)** [12] and stemmed using a Porter stemmer .

3.3 Parameters and Optimization

Based on earlier experiments, we fix $\mu = 100$ and focus on the following dimensions; the number of documents used to construct the relevance model ($|R|$), the number of expansion terms (k), the number of MeSH terms used to describe the query (l), and the value of λ. We have compared an exhaustive range of values and, for the sake of conciseness, we only report the optimal ones found.

3.4 Evaluation Measures

We compare the five runs (QL, RM (collection/PubMed), MM (collection/Pubmed)) in terms of retrieval effectivess, using precision at 10 (P@10) and mean average precision (MAP). In addition, we look at the thesaurus terms returned by the MM runs, and determine their relevancy as follows. We do not have the resources to recruit domain experts capable of assessing the broad range of topics included in the TREC 2006 Genomics track test collection. Instead, we created "pseudo-relevance judgments." from

Table 2. Comparison of top expansion terms for topic 173: "How do alpha7 nicotinic receptor subunits affect ethanol metabolism?", using estimations from the collection and PubMed. The terms associated with MeSH-biased models, were based on the MeSH terms as described in Table 4. Terms specific to a method are marked in boldface.

Relevance models		MeSH-biased models	
Collection terms	PubMed terms	Collection terms	PubMed terms
receptor	ethanol	receptor	ethanol
nicotin	nicotinic	nicotin	nicotinic
subunit	nicotine	of	nicotine
of	chronic	the	chronic
acetylcholin	cells	subunit	cells
the	treatment	**humans**	treatment
alpha7	receptor	acetylcholin	receptor
abstract	mrna	**animals**	mrna
alpha	nachr	**icotinic**	nachr
medlin	m10	**study**	m10
2003	**levels**	alpha7	subunit

the additional assessments provided by TREC Genomics. Besides judging document-level relevance, the assessors for the 2006 Genomics track also used MeSH terms to categorize each relevant passage (the so-called "aspects" [9]). So, for each topic we have a list of MeSH terms which the assessors judged as being descriptive of the relevant passages. We compare this list (per topic) with the top-10 MeSH terms found by the MM runs.

4 Results and Discussion

We present our experimental results in two sets. First, we focus on the retrieval effectiveness of our thesaurus-biased query expansion method. After that we zoom in on the browsing suggestions being generated.

4.1 Thesaurus-Biased Relevance Models

Table 1 displays the results of the evaluated runs (best scores in boldface). We note that the MAP score of our baseline is well above the median score achieved by participants of the TREC 2006 Genomics track [9] (which was 0.279). Our first two research questions asked for an effective query expansion method that combines feedback term generation with browsing term generation. We observe that the retrieval effectiveness of our thesaurus-biased models is in the same range as that of relevance models, both when using the collection and when using PubMed as the source for feedback terms, in terms of MAP and P@10 scores—RM and MM statistically significantly outperform the baseline.

We see a mixed picture when the size of the feedback corpus is changed (our third research question). Let us look at the precision-recall graphs. Figure 1 clearly shows

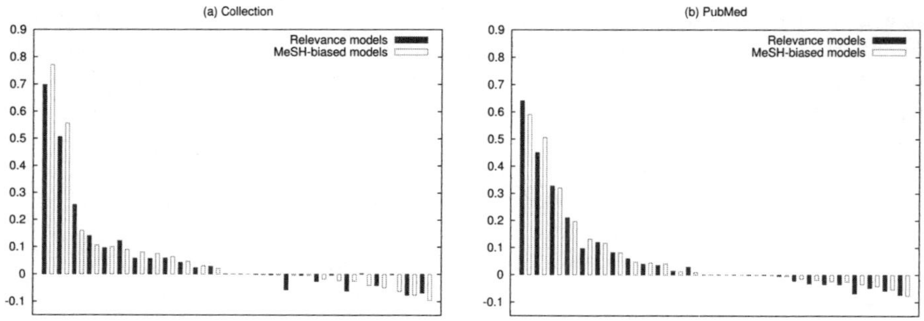

Fig. 2. Sorted difference in per-topic MAP values when comparing MeSH-biased models and relevance models with the query-likelihood baseline, estimated on either (a) the collection or (b) PubMed

that both models succeed in exceeding the baseline on almost all levels of recall and that estimating on a larger collection mostly helps to improve early precision, i.e., precision at lower recall levels. The improvement of MeSH-biased models over relevance models is marginal, however, and visible only at the lower recall levels.

A Closer Look: Feedback Terms. Next, we look at the specific expansion terms which each model finds from the vocabulary. Table 2 provides a detailed example of the top-10 vocabulary terms which are found for the same topic. While the terms themselves change little (viz. the second and last column of Table 2), the assigned term weights do, which is the main cause of the increase in performance. The effect of basing the estimations on PubMed are visible in the specificity of the expansion terms. This is witnessed, for example, in the addition of low content-bearing terms such as "the" and "of" using the collection.

Topic Details. Figure 2 displays the per-topic change in MAP scores for the baseline run and the MeSH-biased model over the baseline. When zooming in on these individual topics, we find that applying MeSH-biased relevance models only helps in half of the cases (13 out of 26). Our model performs slightly better than relevance models, but this result is not significant (when tested with a Wilcoxon signrank test at $p = 0.05$)—an effect which is probably due to the small size of the topic set. Put more positively, the performance of the models is at a comparable level, while our approach readily facilitates browsing activities through the found thesaurus terms.

We observe that some queries benefit from applying thesaurus-biased relevance models, whilst others are helped by the estimation of a traditional relevance model. Because these models perform differently on different topics, we investigate possible ways of predicting which model to use on which topic. There are several methods of predicting and classifying a priori classes of query difficulty. One of these is through determining the *query clarity*, which is a way of quantifying the possible ambiguity in a query [1, 3, 7]. According to **(author?)** [7], it correlates at a significant level with the resulting retrieval performance of that query. However in our case, we find no signifi-

Table 3. Generic topic types on which each topic is based together with the number of topics which were created with it

Bin	Topic type	Topics
1.	Find articles describing the role of a gene involved in a given disease.	6
2.	Find articles describing the role of a gene in a specific biological process.	8
3.	Find articles describing interactions between two or more genes in the function of an organ or disease.	7
4.	Find articles describing one or more mutations of a given gene and its biological impact.	7

cant correlation between the query clarity scores and the resulting performance for the current topic set.

A specific feature of the current topic set is that the topics are generated based on four templates, or so-called "generic topic types" [9], which are represented in Table 3. The table shows each template, as well as the actual number of topics based on it. The topic templates emphasize different search tasks, which may in turn influence the effectiveness of the various approaches. If this is the case, then that would indicate that this particular "class" of topics is sensitive to the chosen model. To understand the issue, we bin the topics per topic type and determine the means of all the results per model (and bin). We test if the differences between the means of MAP of all runs, grouped by the four combinations of models and collections, are significantly different for each topic type. We use a Newman-Keuls test [6] to do a pair-wise comparison and test the null hypothesis that the means of a group is equal to that of another group.

When tested, we find that only topic type 1 and 2 have a significantly different performance for each model ($p < 0.01$) and only when estimation is done using PubMed. In these case, the mean of the MeSH-biased model is higher than the mean of the relevance model. We conclude that our proposed algorithm does a better job at finding relevant documents for these topic types. We argue that they have a more "open" nature than the other two, suggesting that our method favors more open queries. Whether this is the case and whether it holds for a larger topic set remains as future work.

4.2 Thesaurus Terms Generated

Finally, we turn to another aspect of our algorithm's output: the MeSH terms being generated for browsing purposes. Table 4 shows the MeSH terms found for topic 173 (the first topic in the topic set has number 160), using our proposed approach. Estimating $P(m)$ on a smaller corpus (first column) has the effect of introducing slightly more general terms, e.g., "Research support" and "Humans," which might account for the slightly lower scores for this particular method of estimation. The MeSH terms estimated from PubMed are more specific, e.g., "Bungarotoxins" and "Nicotinic (ant)agonists." We can quantify this observation (thesaurus terms generated by MM(collection) tend to be somewhat more general than thesaurus terms generated by MM(PubMed)), by computing for every topic the average distance to the root of the MeSH thesaurus of the suggested thesaurus; so, the lower distance, the more abstract the terms. For MM(collection) the average distance to the root was 4.46 while for MM(medline) it was 4.78.

Table 4. Comparison of top MeSH terms for topic 173: "How do alpha7 nicotinic receptor subunits affect ethanol metabolism?", using estimations from the collection and PubMed

MeSH-biased models	
Collection MeSH terms	PubMed MeSH terms
Animals	Receptors, Nicotinic
Humans	Ethanol
Research Support, Non-U.S. Gov't	Nicotinic Agonists
Receptors, Nicotinic	Animals
Research Support, U.S. Gov't, P.H.S.	Central Nervous System Depressants
Brain	Nicotine
Mice	Mice
Comparative Study	Bungarotoxins
Ion Channels	Nicotinic Antagonists
Membrane Proteins	Rats
Immunohistochemistry	Receptors, Serotonin

Finally, what is the quality of the generated thesaurus terms, using the evaluation criteria put forward in Section 3? When we estimate the MeSH-biased model on the collection, on average 2.3 MeSH terms per topic match. When we look at the estimation from PubMed, 3 out of the 10 MeSH terms match. The difference between these two is significant at the $p < 0.05$ level, using a Wilcoxon signrank test.

5 Related Work

Besides earlier mentioned query expansion work, most other related work can be found among language modeling approaches to information retrieval. **(author?)** [19] describe a method to create augmented language models, based on the documents in a collection. The authors assume, in a similar fashion as with relevence models, that a document is itself generated from an unseen language model. So, instead of expanding queries, they expand the documents to better describe this underling generative model. The authors argue that such an *enlarged* document is a better representation, which is reflected in the reported increases in retrieval performance.

The method most closely in line with the current work, however, is described by **(author?)** [5]. The authors describe a way of combining multiple sources of evidence to predict relationships between query and vocabulary terms, which uses a Markov chain framework to integrate semantic and lexical features into a relevance model. The semantic features they investigate are general word associations and synonymy relations as defined in WordNet. **(author?)** [2] describe a more principled way of integrating WordNet term relationships into statistical language models, but they do not use relevance models. Both methods are evaluated on "general" corpora—viz. news collections—and result in consistent improvements. We, however, place our work in a digital library setting, where document-level annotations play an important role. Our work differs from these approaches in the fact that we particularly focus on, and utilize. the knowledge that has gone into the construction and assignment of controlled vocabulary terms to documents. Doing so enables our approach to assist the user in browsing a collection, while keeping end-to-end retrieval performance comparable with other state-of-the-art approaches.

6 Conclusion

We have described a transparent method to integrate document-level annotations in a retrieval model based on statistical language models. Our goal was to incorporate the information and semantics stored in a document categorization system to achieve effective query expansion, while at the same time facilitating browsing.

We evaluated our algorithm in a biomedical setting, using the TREC 2006 Genomics track test set and the MeSH thesaurus. We used the terms from this thesaurus and the documents annotated with them to bias the estimation of a relevance model—a special class of statistical language models. We determined the impact of increasing the size of the document set on which we base our estimations on the quality of the found thesaurus terms, and found a significant difference in favour of the larger PubMed database.

We have found a 20% improvement in mean average precision when comparing the end-to-end retrieval results of our model with a query-likelihood baseline. When we look at estimating our model from the much smaller evaluation collection, we find a 19% increase in mean average precision over the same query-likelihood baseline. These results would have put these runs in the top segment of the runs submitted to the TREC 2006 Genomics track. We have looked at ways to determine, which type of topic benefits from which approach. When we group the topics together based on the topic template, we find a statistically significant difference in favour of our method for two out of four particular topic "classes."

Future work includes an analysis on a larger set of topics, as well as incorporating the tree-like structure inherent in a thesaurus—we have assumed thesaurus terms to be independent, while in fact they may not be. Finally, we will look for additional ways to predict if and when biased query modeling is beneficial.

Acknowledgements

This work was carried out in the context of the Virtual Laboratory for e-Science project (http://www.vl-e.nl), which is supported by a BSIK grant from the Dutch Ministry of Education, Culture and Science (OC&W) and is part of the ICT innovation program of the Ministry of Economic Affairs (EZ). Maarten de Rijke was supported by the Netherlands Organization for Scientific Research (NWO) under project number 220-80-001.

References

[1] Allan, J., Raghavan, H.: Using part-of-speech patterns to reduce query ambiguity. In: SIGIR '02, pp. 307–314 (2002)

[2] Cao, G., Nie, J.-Y., Bai, J.: Integrating word relationships into language models. In: SIGIR '05, pp. 298–305 (2005)

[3] Carmel, D., Yom-Tov, E., Darlow, A., Pelleg, D.: What makes a query difficult? In: SIGIR '06, pp. 390–397 (2006)
[4] Chen, S.F., Goodman, J.: An empirical study of smoothing techniques for language modeling. In: ACL, pp. 310–318 (1996)
[5] Collins-Thompson, K., Callan, J.: Query expansion using random walk models. In: CIKM '05, pp. 704–711 (2005)
[6] Cooley, W., Lohnes, R.: Multivariate data analysis. Wiley, Chichester (1971)
[7] Cronen-Townsend, S., Zhou, Y., Croft, W.B.: Predicting query performance. In: SIGIR '02, pp. 299–306 (2002)
[8] Diaz, F., Metzler, D.: Improving the estimation of relevance models using large external corpora. In: SIGIR '06, pp. 154–161 (2006)
[9] Hersh, W., Cohen, A.M., Roberts, P., Rekapalli, H.K.: TREC 2006 Genomics track overview. In: TREC Notebook. NIST (2006)
[10] Herskovic, J.R., Tanaka, L.Y., Hersh, W., Bernstam, E.V.: A Day in the Life of PubMed: Analysis of a Typical Day's Query Log. J. Am Med. Inform. Assoc. 14(2), 212–220 (2007)
[11] Hiemstra, D.: A linguistically motivated probabilistic model of information retrieval. In: Nikolaou, C., Stephanidis, C. (eds.) ECDL 1998. LNCS, vol. 1513, pp. 569–584. Springer, Heidelberg (1998)
[12] Huang, X., Ming, Z., Si, L.: York University at TREC 2005 Genomics track. In: Proceedings of the 14th Text Retrieval Conference (2005)
[13] Koch, T., Ardö, A., Golub, K.: Browsing and searching behavior in the renardus web service a study based on log analysis. In: JCDL '04, pp. 378–378 (2004)
[14] Kurland, O., Lee, L., Domshlak, C.: Better than the real thing?: Iterative pseudo-query processing using cluster-based language models. In: SIGIR '05, pp. 19–26 (2005)
[15] Lam-Adesina, A.M., Jones, G.J.F.: Applying summarization techniques for term selection in relevance feedback. In: SIGIR '01, pp. 1–9 (2001)
[16] Lavrenko, V., Croft, W.B.: Relevance based language models. In: SIGIR '01, pp. 120–127 (2001)
[17] Mitra, M., Singhal, A., Buckley, C.: Improving automatic query expansion. In: SIGIR '98, pp. 206–214 (1998)
[18] Tan, K.F., Wing, M., Revell, N., Marsden, G., Baldwin, C., MacIntyre, R., Apps, A., Eason, K.D., Promfett, S.: Facts and myths of browsing and searching in a digital library. In: Nikolaou, C., Stephanidis, C. (eds.) ECDL 1998. LNCS, vol. 1513, pp. 669–670. Springer, Heidelberg (1998)
[19] Tao, T., Wang, X., Mei, Q., Zhai, C.: Accurate language model estimation with document expansion. In: CIKM '05, pp. 273–274 (2005)
[20] Voorhees, E.M.: Using wordnet to disambiguate word senses for text retrieval. In: SIGIR '93, pp. 171–180 (1993)
[21] Xu, J., Croft, W.B.: Query expansion using local and global document analysis. In: SIGIR '96: Proceedings of the 19th ACM SIGIR conference, pp. 4–11 (1996)
[22] Zhai, C., Lafferty, J.: A study of smoothing methods for language models applied to ad hoc information retrieval. In: SIGIR '01, pp. 334–342 (2001)

Named Entity Identification and Cyberinfrastructure

Alison Babeu, David Bamman, Gregory Crane, Robert Kummer, and Gabriel Weaver

Perseus Project, Tufts University

Abstract. Well-established instruments such as authority files and a growing set of data structures such as CIDOC CRM, FRBRoo, and MODS provide the foundation for emerging, new digital services. While solid, these instruments alone neither capture the essential data on which traditional scholarship depends nor enable the services which we can already identify as fundamental to any eResearch, cyberinfrastructure or virtual research environment for intellectual discourse. This paper describes a general model for primary sources, entities and thematic topics, the gap between this model and emerging infrastructure, and the tasks necessary to bridge it.

1 Introduction

New terms such as eScience and eScholarship have emerged to describe the qualitatively distinctive processes of intellectual life possible in a digital age. We have begun debating what underlying cyberinfrastructure will be necessary to support virtual research environments (VRE) that support scholars in various disciplines [11,19]. This paper describes work towards a VRE for the humanities in general, with a current pragmatic focus on Greco-Roman studies.

As we explore Greco-Roman research within a digital library we find three general and complementary challenges. First, we need to be able to integrate broad interdisciplinary and deep domain knowledge. Libraries have developed vast, general classification schemes and authority lists to structure all academic knowledge, but humanists, like their colleagues in the sciences, have created their own authority lists that go beyond, and are often unconnected with, library data. Second, we need to be able to customize general services. Google, for example, has produced a service that identifies and maps place names in its digitized books, but this service will not reach its full potential until scholarly communities have integrated into it their expert knowledge about people, places, etc. Third, we need scalable methods to absorb decentralized contributions, large and small. The general public is very good at disambiguating references to people, places, and other entities, as witnessed by the millions of accurate disambiguating links (links between ambiguous names and their articles) in Wikipedia[23].

All three of these problems rely on a single underlying infrastructure: the ability to canonically refer to people, places, and objects in a text, and to integrate knowledge about those entities from disparate sources. Data structures

L. Kovács, N. Fuhr, and C. Meghini (Eds.): ECDL 2007, LNCS 4675, pp. 259–270, 2007.

such as CIDOC CRM[7], FRBRoo[9], and MODS/MADS[17,16] provide a foundation for this infrastructure, but we must still build on top of them to create useful services. This paper reports on the extent to which we have had to supplement existing resources (data structure, content, and algorithms) as we develop a VRE. We offer a general logical model of the system and then report on the issues that have arisen at three distinct layers within this system. While we focus upon the Greco-Roman cultural heritage that all Europe shares, the specific issues are relevant to other cultural heritage domains and the underlying model supports much intellectual activity beyond the humanities.

2 Semantic Classification and Named Entities

Our work with cultural heritage materials has led us to identify five layers of scholarship, as illustrated in Figure 1. Surrogates in the library include critical editions reconstructing literary texts, documentary editions that reconstruct particular written artifacts such as manuscripts or papyri, archaeological surveys, descriptions of buildings, and catalogues of artifacts. These sources generally strive for transparency, documenting the current evidence and reconstructing the original text or site as it appeared at some point in the past. Secondary sources include reference works, articles and monographs that explore original ideas. Reference works and secondary sources, however, both supplement observational and reconstructive data as reported in library surrogates with direct observation (where places or artifacts survive).

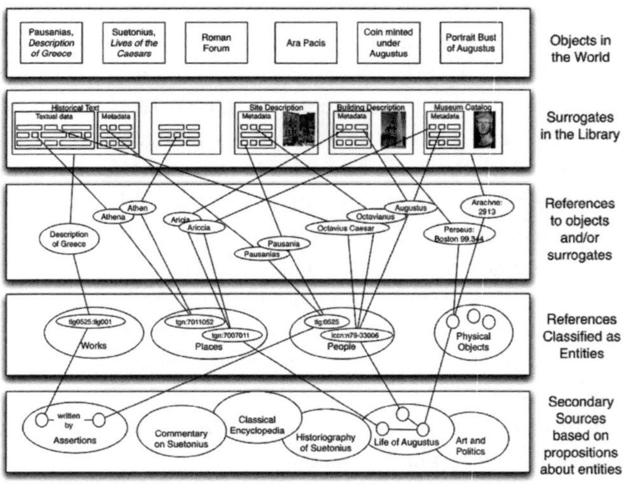

Fig. 1. Model of digital scholarship

Our model emphasizes two layers between surrogates and secondary sources. In the first we find references with some semantic classification - in this level, we are populating ontologies such as the CIDOC CRM or FRBRoo. In the simplest case, we have subsets of objects: any arbitrary chunk of text extracted for discussion is a quotation; any subset of an object is a detail. Insofar as quotations or details are meaningful, they advance some particular point. Articles of daily life - cooking implements, furniture, jewelry - may form hierarchical classes of object on which we base analysis of social history. In many cases, however, we need to go beyond this kind of semantic classification and associate specific references with entities from the world. We want to associate a reference to a temple of Apollo to a particular archaeological site; to determine not only that Alexandria is a place but which of the many Alexandrias is meant; and to establish whether a given Antonius was the son, grandson, father - or some other person with this name. We are not simply interested in altars but in the monumental Ara Pacis constructed to memorialize the peace which Augustus brought to the Roman world.

In our view, annotating and aggregating references, whether classified by semantic class or as particular entities, are the fundamental processes of scholarship in the humanities – the degree to which an argument bases itself on such annotations defines the degree to which it qualifies as serious intellectual discourse, whether the author holds an endowed chair or is an amateur contributing to Wikipedia. We and others in the field of classics have needed to extend the pre-existing metadata from libraries and general services from information science.

3 Extending Metadata

In twenty years of continuous development, we have attempted, with varying success, to integrate first-class publications of art and archaeological data with first-class textual sources. Most collections will focus on one or the other. Textual collections may include a few illustrative images but lack professional cataloguing information and metadata; while the art and archaeology collections will quote primary sources, often translated and without machine-actionable citations. To address both issues we build upon the foundations of FRBR and CIDOC CRM.

3.1 Managing Primary Texts: FRBR and Canonical Text Services

While we may discover previously unknown documents on inscriptions or in archives, primary sources are by definition finite in number. Every historical document – whether a canonical work or a private contract preserved on papyrus – may appear in multiple editions, multiple translations, and as the subject of commentaries that annotate well-defined extracts of the document as a whole.

Serious users of historical documents need two classes of service. First, they need structured reports about multiple editions and/or translations of, commentaries on, and secondary texts about their historical sources – not just the major canonical works such as the *Aeneid* but every historical document in the public record. Second, they need better tools with which to understand how these versions of a single work are different. Print editions, for example, only occasionally note where they differ from a previous edition. In a digital library, we can and should be able to see how each edition compares to those previously published and to visualize the relationships between these editions over time. We should also be able to identify translations of any given document, even when these are embedded in unusual places (e.g., translations of short poems from the *Greek Anthology* in a 19th-century magazine). We should be able to compare translations with each other and with their sources. Parallel text analysis not only can help readers of a particular text but provides the foundation for multilingual services such as cross-langage information retrieval and machine translation.

While we need automated methods to track everything published about the Greek tragedian Sophocles, we can create careful metadata about Sophocles, his surviving plays and the numerous fragments of his lost works. Well-curated data about a finite set of documents becomes, in effect, a classification scheme that can be applied to an open set of editions, translations and commentaries.

In 2006, with the rise of Google Book Search and other large scale projects, we realized that we needed to expand our coverage of Greek and Latin source texts. In particular, we needed better data to manage multiple editions of works that were available not only in our collections but as components of image books published by Google and others. In this ongoing work, we have catalogued roughly 585 primary source texts containing 842 distinct authors and at least 1588 individual works. This collection also contains many reference works, including bibliographies, grammars, histories and lexicons. While we found disparate elements with which to create a catalog for Greek and Latin source texts, none was adequate in itself.

MODS records. As reported in [15], our catalog utilizs MODS records downloaded from the LC web service[18] and bibliographic records found in OCLC's WorldCat (used to create MODS records for works not found within the LC Catalog.) Perhaps the greatest challenge is the fact that the majority of our collection can be described as "container works" according to the FRBRoo: a class that "comprises Individual Works whose essence is the selection and/or arrangement of expressions of other works"[9]. A number of our texts fall into this category, such as the *Greek Anthology* (a five-volume series of Greek epigrams with over 100 different authors) or the *Historicorum Romanorum Reliquiae* (a multi-olume set of fragmentary Roman historians, with "works" as short as a paragraph). A large number of volumes contain multiple works by multiple authors, such as a work with selected poems from Vergil, Ovid, and Catullus, or the Greek military histories of Aeneas Tacticus, Asclepiodotus and Onasander. Similarly, even when many books contain only one author, they often have multiple works by that one author, such as the collected orations of Antiphon or the collected plays of Euripides.

Comprehensive domain-specific bibliographies of Greek and Latin. Classicists have long created exhaustive checklists of classical authors – major dictionaries traditionally provide bibliographies of the editions which they used, outlining broad surveys of Greek and Latin. The Thesaurus Linguae Graecae, Packard Humanities Institute (PHI) and Stoa Consortium have created comprehensive electronic checklists which provide numerical identifiers for a wider range of authors and works than the LC NAF. Unfortunately, none of these lists uses the standard names for authors or works that are already in the LC NAF. Thus, Cicero may be "Marcus Tullius Cicero" in the domain list rather than "Cicero, Marcus Tullius," and Cicero's letters to Atticus may be "Epistulae ad Atticum" rather than "ad Atticum." We combine the LC NAF uniform name with one or more domain specific identifiers: the PHI lists Cicero as author 474, his "Letters to Atticus" as work 57. Neither the MODS records nor the domain specific lists provide a structure within which we can manage multiple editions, much less translations, commentaries, etc. For this we turn to FRBR.

Functional Requirements for Bibliographic Records (FRBR). FRBR is an important data model without which we cannot accomplish the most basic functions on which our user community depends: we need to be able to identify multiple instantiations of primary texts[12]. We wanted to know precisely how many editions, translations, and commentaries of canonical works such as the *Iliad* are in our collection at any one time. We use the FRBR object hierarchy of work, expression and manifestation to represent the *Iliad* as a general work, its various editions, translations and commentaries (which we treat as subclasses of expression) and the various instantiations of these publications such as page images and uncorrected OCR vs. various XML transcriptions (which we treat as manifestations). Related experiments with FRBR and how it might benefit current cataloging practices and digital libraries have proved informative in our efforts reported here[1,2].

Canonical Text Services (CTS). FRBR is, however, not sufficient for classical studies. Scholars have developed elaborate citation schemes with unique identifiers for particular chunks of text. Strings such as "Il. 3.44" and "Thuc. 3.21" describe book 3, line 44 of Homer's *Iliad* and book 3, chapter 21 of Thucydides. While the precise wording of these chunks will vary from one edition to another and some editors will occasionally redefine the boundaries of particular chunks, canonical citations generally point to the same text in multiple editions. Our digital infrastructure already depends on this foundational knowledge structure that classicists have inherited from earlier centuries. To this end, the CTS protocol has been developed to support more sophisticated querying, organizing, and referencing of texts. The CTS extends the FRBR hierarchy both upwards and downwards, upwards by "grouping Works under a notional entity called 'TextGroup' " and "downwards, allowing identification and abstraction of citeable chunks of text (Homer, *Iliad* Book 1, Line 123), or ranges of citeable chunks (Hom. Il. 1.123-2.22)"[20]. FRBR's "manifestation" may not be relevant for scholarly citation. Therefore CTS focuses more on the semantics of citation practice traditional in fields like classics or biblical studies. We plan to exploit both FRBRoo and CTS as we continue work on our developing catalog.

Our work has thus been fourfold. First, for each "container work" we have created one XML file, which contains both the bibliographic information for that manifestation and component records for each individual work contained within that manifestation (which include any relevant work identifiers, links to author's online authority records, language information, translator/editor information, etc.) Second, we are creating expression-level XML records for each of these component works within a manifestation (this work is ongoing as we explore means automating this process). The hierarchical nature of XML is quite useful for this kind of bibliographic entity. Third, we are assigning identifiers from standard canons such as the TLG, PHI, the LC NAF, and other relevant bibliographies in order to support the most granular level of text identification possible, a goal of the FRBR-CIDOC harmonization[8]. Where identifiers are not available, we are exploring means of creating them. Fourth, we encode the citation schemes whereby we can extract canonical chunks of text from online documents.

3.2 Managing References by Semantic Class: CIDOC CRM

We have published results from our own work on semantic classification elsewhere[4,21] (and, of course, the FRBR/CTS work described above entails classification). In this section, we describe one fundamental classification task: mapping fields from two substantial and somewhat overlapping collections on Greco-Roman art and archaeology. This task documents both the importance of semantic classification and the need for entity identification, the fourth layer of Figure 1. For our interchange format, we have chosen the CIDOC CRM, a network-like data structure initiated by the International Council of Museums[7] and accepted as an official ISO standard in 2006.

The CIDOC CRM has evolved over ten years and provides a blueprint for describing concepts and relationships used in cultural heritage documentation. CIDOC CRM can provide an interlingua with which to connect existing data models as well as provide a foundation for new ones. While CIDOC CRM was developed to represent information about objects – especially those managed by museums – a new version of FRBR, FRBRoo, is being developed as an ontology aligned to the CIDOC CRM[9]. FRBRoo provides the means to express the IFLA FRBR data model with the same mechanisms and notations provided by the CIDOC CRM. From our perspective this is a major advance, providing the first third-party integrated data model for textual and art and archaeological collections in twenty years of collection development.

Integration of different cultural heritage vocabularies and descriptive systems is an ongoing research challenge[22]. The CIDOC CRM and FRBR harmonization – especially when extended with the CTS protocol – will allow collections to integrate complex textual materials with rich metadata about objects. Figure 2 shows how two resources – an ancient text passage and a museum catalog object– can be linked together.

As a test case, Perseus has begun collaborating with the German Arachne, the central object database of the German Archaeological institute[10], to create CIDOC CRM records for our art and archaeological collections (5,900 objects and 36,500 images in Perseus, 100,000 objects and 165,000 images in Arachne).

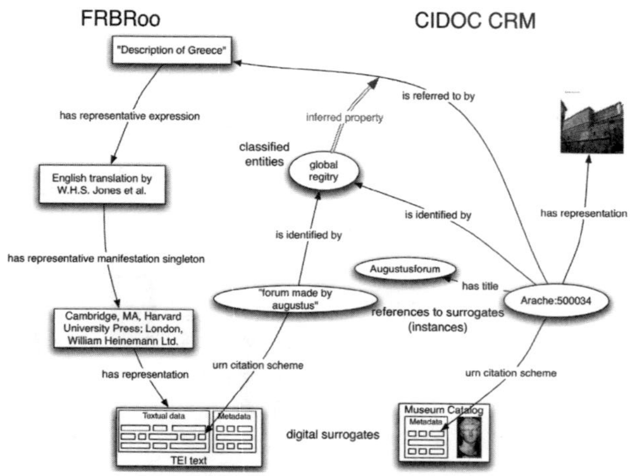

Fig. 2. Entities are linked by using terms of CIDOC CRM and FRBRoo

This will not only produce a unified database but will link the Greek and Latin collections in Perseus to the same materials in Arachne. Creating CIDOC CRM records from existing metadata is fundamentally a semantic classification task. We map fields labeled x and y in Perseus and a and b in Arachne to m and n in CIDOC CRM. Both Perseus and Archne implement specialized data models that have been refined to meet the needs of a specific perspective. They do not directly conform with standard metadata schemas and therefore have to be manually mapped to a data model that conforms to the classes and properties of the CIDOC CRM[14].

While the complexity of the CIDOC CRM data model poses difficulties for conversion, Figure 3 illustrates the even deeper challenges that we face. In this case where we have two records for the same object, we can see where semantic alignment introduces questions of data analysis and fusion. The problem of language appears at once – we need to establish that "bust" and "Portraitkopf" are English and German equivalents. We also need to address variations where language is not a factor. For example, we need to match "H 44 cm" in Arachne with "H . 0433 m" in Perseus – two comparable but not quite equivalent figures for the height of the bust. Augustus is the same in German and English but none of the data presented unambiguously indicates that this is "Augustus, Emperor of Rome, 63 B.C.-14 A.D." We find variant spellings of the placename Aricia/Ariccia in each record. More significantly, the Perseus record "Aricia, near Rome" provides a clue that a named entity system could use to establish that this Aricia corresponds to tgn,7007011[1] in the Getty Thesaurus of Geographic Names[13]. We want to be able to recognize that "Boschung 1993" in Perseus and "D . Boschung, Die Bildnisse des Augustus" refer to the same bibliographic entity.

[1] "Ariccia [12.683,41.717] (inhabited place), Roma, Lazio, Italia, Europe."

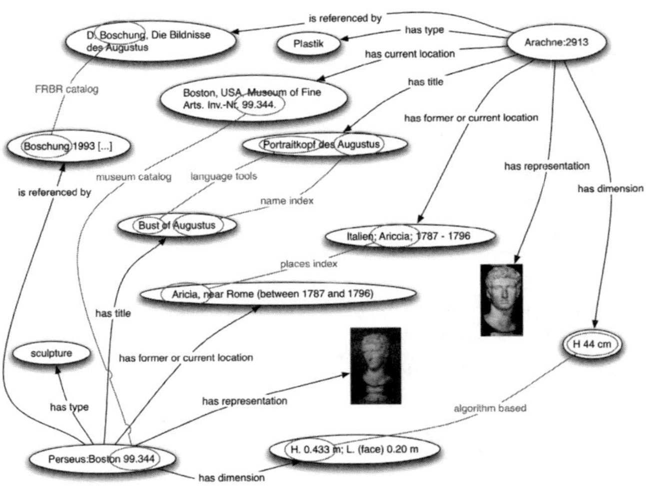

Fig. 3. Identification of instances that refer to the same entity

Semantic classification thus raises the problem of entity identification. Knowing Alexandria is a place is useful, but not nearly as useful as knowing that a particular Alexandria refers to the famous Egyptian city (tgn,7001188).

4 Named Entity Identification

In twenty years of digital collection development, we have consistently stressed developing knowledge sources that not only enumerate but provide machine-actionable descriptions of domain-specific entities. Many comprehensive knowledge sources exist in print form that can be converted into machine-actionable resources to provide new services for users. Our own group has focused on creating such machine-actionable knowledge sources and accompanying services[5,6]. As we move towards a VRE for Greco-Roman studies, we have focused on three sources.

1. *Markup of primary sources:* Multiple editions of the same work can be aligned against one another, collated and used to correct each other. Careful markup from one edition of an author, however, can be projected onto other editions as well. Thus, while the number of editions for any historical work may be an open set, a single well-structured version can become a template to structure many other editions. In a field such as classics, primary source citations are probably the most important single entity – if we can recognize and decode strings such as "Thuc. 1.38" as references to Thucydides' book one, chapter thirty eight, we can generate links between many different works and analyze scholarly trends. If we have one full text marked up, we can then often identify floating quotations even when there are no recognizable citations nearby.

2. *Author indices:* Multiple indices exist for most classical authors – thousands of indices with hundreds of thousands of entries and millions of references. These indices store the judgments of experts as to which Alexander or which Alexandria is meant in a given passage. A baseline name identification strategy based on document indices produces good results because most names are unambiguous in a given document – real ambiguity occurs as documents grow in size or are combined. If we simply connect every ambiguous entity to the most common entity with that name, we are successful 97.4%, 95.3%, 93.5% and 91.7% of the time for Thucydides, Herodotus, Pausanias and Apollodorus, respectively. Thucydides has the most well-defined subject and it is thus not surprising that this baseline method performs best with his work and worst with the much more heterogeneous Apollodorus. However, if we combine Herodotus, Pausanias and Apollodorus into one large document, the overall accuracy of this baseline technique for those authors falls to 91.4%. This reinforces the intuitive assumption that this baseline method becomes less accurate as documents increase in size (thus increasing the probability that ambiguous names will appear).
3. *Reference works:* In fields where canonical citation schemes map source texts, we find not only the usual textual descriptions of people and places, but citations that associate passages of particular texts with the current article. Such encyclopedias thus constitute broad indices of major entities across a specific domain. We concentrated on two reference works: Smith's *Dictionary of Greek and Roman Geography* for place names (which contains 11,564 entries and has yielded 25,748 citations) and Smith's *Dictionary of Greek and Roman Biography and Mythology* for personal names (which contains 20,336 entries and has yielded 37,549 citations). Together, they provide a broad framework for the field.

In the 300-volume Perseus American collection, roughly 25% of the books have indices – as very large collections include millions of books we will need to consider how best to mine the information from millions of indices as well as many thousands of reference materials[3]. In a field such as classics, however, the canonical citation schemes available for most authors provides citations that are not only useful in themselves but that contribute to a major development challenge: we need to integrate the deep information available in individual author indices with broad resources such as the Smith's dictionaries.

Figure 4 shows a personal name entry in the Perseus Encyclopedia (PE), that for Abderus, a son of Hermes, identified by "abderus-1,' while Figure 5 shows a similar entry from the Smith *Dictionary of Greek and Roman Biography and Mythology*, where the identifier for the same Abderus is "abderus-bio-1." Using the context of both entries, our automatic system was able to correctly map the entries from these two resources to each other, identifying PE "abderus-1" as the Smith "abderus-bio-1." While this example is far more straightforward than most, it serves to illustrate the type of matching being performed.

The system achieved an overall accuracy of 78.6% when aligning these two resources. Table 1 provides an overview of the tagging accuracy of the system

```
<div1 type="entry" id="abderus">
  <head>Abderus</head>
  <div2 type="subentry" id="abderus-1">
    <head><persName>
    <surname>Abderus</surname> </persName>,son of <persName><surname>Hermes</surname>
    </persName></head>
      <div3 type="index"><list type="index">
      <item>killed by the mares of Diomedes: <bibl n="Apollod. 2.5.7">Apollod.2.5.7</bibl></item>
      <item>the city of Abdera founded by Herakles beside his grave: <bibl n="Apollod.
            2.5.7">Apollod. 2.5.7</bibl></item>
        </list></div3></div2></div1>
```

Fig. 4. Personal Name Entry in PE XML file

```
<div2 type="entry" id="abderus-bio-1" org="uniform" sample="complete">
    <head><label>ABDE´RUS</label></head>
    <p>(<label lang="greek">*)/Abdhros</label> ), a son of Hermes, or according to others of
      Thromius the Locrian. (<bibl n="Apollod. 2.5.8" default="NO" valid="yes">Apollod.
      2.5.8</bibl>; Strab. 7. p. 331.) He was a favourite of Heracles, and was torn to pieces by
      the mares of Diomedes, which Heracles had given him to pursue the Bistones. Heracles is said
      to have built the town of Abdera to honour him. According to Hyginus, (<bibl n="Hyg. Fab. 30" default="NO"
      valid="yes">Hyg. Fab. 30 </bibl>,) Abderus was a servant of Diomedes, the king of the Thracian Bistones, and was killed by
      Heracles together with his master and his four men-devouring horses. (Compare Philostrat. <hi rend="ital">Heroic.</hi>
      3. &sect; 1; 19. &sect; 2.)</p>
    <byline>[<ref target="author.L.S" targOrder="U">L.S</ref>]</byline></div2>
```

Fig. 5. Personal Name Entry in Smith

Table 1. Alignment Accuracy by Entity Type

Category	Total	Ethnic	Place	Personal	Other
Corr. found no match	3065	111	356	1421	1178
Error	14	1	10	3	0
Uncertain	5	0	5	0	0
Incor. matched	1880	217	423	1156	83
Corr. matched	3950	65	1221	2660	4
Tot. entities	8914	394	2015	5240	1265
Accuracy	**78.69%**	44.89%	78.26%	77.86%	93.44%

across all entity types. The system achieved similar results for personal and place names with significantly lower performance for ethnic groups. When the system correctly found no match it meant that the PE entity had no relevant match in Smith. The category of errors reflects when either an error in the PE or in the Smith XML file caused a tagging or other type of error. Occasionally, a match had to be marked as uncertain, due to insufficient textual content. It required 1,000 hours of labor to align 9,000 entities but the resulting unified database of disambiguated reference to entities in texts is c. 100,000. We should emphasize that these 100,000 disproportionately identify less common entities: our indices contain a far larger percentage of references to the lesser Alexandrias than to the famous city of that name in Egypt. The bias of these 100,000 entries provides broader coverage than a random sampling of 100,000 entries would contain, since a random sampling would contain more references to very common (and less frequently indexed) names such as Alexandria. In real work, users need help finding these obscure entities - they want to find references to one of the smaller cities that Alexander founded and named after himself. If 95% of our Alexandria references point to Egypt, digital libraries only begin to add value insofar as they help us locate the ten ancient Alexandrias that make up most of the remaining 5%.

5 Conclusion

Recent steps towards a VRE for Greco-Roman antiquity strengthens our long-term belief that any effective digital infrastructure must address the entity problem at various levels. First, library catalogue records in classics not only need to include more authors and works but they need to incorporate canonical citation schemes – new classes of entity – if they are to provide the foundations for serious digital libraries. In the first generation of digital collections, classicists for the most part ignored catalogue records as being incomplete and, from their perspective, static. Second, using the CIDOC CRM to unify large collections of data provides an important and useful first step but immediately raises the problem of entity identification: we need to be able not only to recognize that English Athens and German Athen are equivalent but to distinguish Athens, Greece, from Athens, Georgia. Third, document indices, encyclopedias, gazetteers and other reference tools contain vast amounts of named entity identification data of the form "entity-X occurs at location-Y." These sources provide information of immediate value to human readers and potential training data for machine learning. Improved tools with which to merge this data should be a major priority of cyberinfastructure. While these conclusions reflect work on a particular domain within the humanities and stress textual materials, all intellectual discourse bases its arguments on meaningful entities extracted from raw data. We need to move towards a generalized architecture that supports named entity services for engineering and the social and natural sciences as well as the humanities.

References

1. Aalberg, T., Haugen, F.B., Husby, O.: A tool for converting from MARC to FRBR. In: Gonzalo, J., Thanos, C., Verdejo, M.F., Carrasco, R.C. (eds.) ECDL 2006. LNCS, vol. 4172, pp. 453–456. Springer, Heidelberg (2006)
2. Buchanan, G.: FRBR: enriching and integrating digital libraries. In: JCDL '06: Proc. of the 6th ACM/IEEE-CS Joint Conf. on DLs, pp. 260–269. ACM Press, New York (2006)
3. Crane, G., Jones, A.: Perseus American Collection 1.0. Tufts DL (2005), `http://dl.tufts.edu//view_pdf.jsp?urn=tufts:facpubs:gcrane-2006.00001`
4. Crane, G., Jones, A.: The challenge of Virginia Banks: an evaluation of named entity analysis in a 19th-century newspaper collection. In: JCDL '06: Proc. of the 6th ACM/IEEE-CS Joint Conf. on DLs, pp. 31–40. ACM Press, New York (2006)
5. Crane, G., Jones, A.: Text, information, knowledge and the evolving record of humanity. D-Lib Magazine 12(3) (2006)
6. Crane, G., et al.: Towards a cultural heritage digital library. In: JCDL' 03: Proc. of the 3rd ACM/IEEE-CS Joint Conf. on DLs, pp. 75–86, Houston, TX

7. Crofts, N., et al.: Definition of the CIDOC object-oriented conceptual reference model. Technical report, http://cidoc.ics.forth.gr/docs/cidoc_crm_version_4.2.pdf
8. Doerr, M., Le Bouef, P.: Modelling intellectual processes: the FRBR-CRM harmonization. In: DELOS Conf. on DLs, Tirennia, Pisa, Italy (02/2007)
9. Doerr, M., LeBouef, P.: FRBR: Object-Oriented definition and mapping to the FRBR-ER (02/2007), http://cidoc.ics.forth.gr/docs/frbr_oo/frbr_docs/FRBR_oo_V0.7.0.pdf
10. Förtsch, R.: ARACHNE - Datenbank und kulturelle Archive des Forschungsarchivs für Antike Plastik Köln und des Deutschen Archäologischen Instituts (2007), http://arachne.uni-koeln.de/inhalt_text.html
11. Gietz, P., et al.: TextGrid and eHumanities. In: E-SCIENCE '06: Proc. of the Second IEEE International Conf. on e-Science and Grid Computing, pp. 133–141. IEEE, Wash., D.C. (2006)
12. IFLA: Functional Requirements for Bibliographic Records: Final Report. UBCIM Publications-New Series. Saur, K.G., München, vol. 19 (1998), http://www.ifla.org/VII/s13/frbr/frbr.pdf
13. Getty TGN, http://www.getty.edu/research/tools/vocabulary/tgn/
14. Kummer, R.: Integrating data from the Perseus Project and Arachne using the CIDOC CRM: An examination from a software developer's perspective. In: Exploring the Limits of Global Models for Integration and Use of Historical and Scientific Information-ICS Forth Workshop, Heraklion, Crete (10/2006), http://www.perseus.tufts.edu/~rokummer/KummerCIDOC2006.pdf
15. Mimno, D., Crane, G., Jones, A.: Hierarchical catalog records: Implementing a FRBR catalog. D-Lib Magazine, 11(10) (2005)
16. Library of Congress. MADS, http://www.loc.gov/standards/mads/
17. Library of Congress MODS, http://www.loc.gov/standards/mods/
18. Library of Congress, http://z3950.loc.gov:7090/voyager?
19. ACLS Commission on Cyberinfrastructure. Our cultural commonwealth: The final report of the ACLS Commission on Cyberinfrastructure for the Humanities and Social Sciences (2006), http://www.acls.org/cyberinfrastructure/OurCulturalCommonwealth.pdf
20. Porter, D., et al.: Creating CTS collections. In: Digital Humanities, pp. 269–274 (2006)
21. Smith, D.A.: Detecting events with date and place information in unstructured text. In: JCDL '02: Proc. of the 2nd ACM/IEEE-CS Joint Conf. on DLs, pp. 191–196. ACM Press, New York (2002)
22. van Gendt, M., et al.: Semantic Web techniques for multiple views on heterogeneous collections: A case study. In: Gonzalo, J., Thanos, C., Verdejo, M.F., Carrasco, R.C. (eds.) ECDL 2006. LNCS, vol. 4172, pp. 426–437. Springer, Heidelberg (2006)
23. Weaver, G., Strickland, B., Crane, G.: Quantifying the accuracy of relational statements in Wikipedia: a methodology. In: JCDL '06: Proc. of the 6th ACM/IEEE-CS Joint Conf. on DLs, p. 358. ACM Press, New York (2006)

Finding Related Papers in Literature Digital Libraries

Nattakarn Ratprasartporn and Gultekin Ozsoyoglu

Department of Electrical Engineering and Computer Science
Case Western Reserve University, Cleveland, OH 44106 USA
{nattakarn, tekin}@case.edu

Abstract. This paper is about searching literature digital libraries to find "related" publications of a given publication. Existing approaches do not take into account publication topics in the relatedness computation, allowing topic diffusion across query output publications. In this paper, we propose a new way to measure "relatedness" by incorporating "contexts" (representing topics) of publications. We utilize existing ontology terms as contexts for publications, i.e., publications are assigned to their relevant contexts, where a context characterizes one or more publication topics. We define three ways of context-based relatedness, namely, (a) relatedness between two contexts (*context-to-context* relatedness) by using publications that are assigned to the contexts and the context structures in the context hierarchy, (b) relatedness between a context and a paper (*paper-to-context* relatedness), which is used to rank the relatedness of contexts with respect to a paper, and (c) relatedness between two papers (*paper-to-paper* relatedness) by using both paper-to-context and context-to-context relatedness measurements.

Using existing biomedical ontology terms as contexts for genomics-oriented publications, our experiments indicate that the context-based approach is accurate, and solves the topic diffusion problem by effectively classifying and ranking related papers of a given paper based on the selected contexts of the paper.

1 Introduction

In searching literature digital libraries, three main issues arise: (1) how to provide an efficient and effective keyword-based search technique, (2) how to effectively rank search results, and (3) how to find "related" publications of a given publication. Towards an answer for the first two issues, recently [1], we proposed a new literature digital library search paradigm, *context-based search*, which provides controlled ways of eliminating search output topic diffusion, and effectively ranks keyword-based query output publications. More specifically, we propose to employ as a context hierarchy an existing ontology hierarchy, i.e., an ontology term constitutes a context. Before any user query sessions, we perform two query-independent pre-processing steps: automatically assign publications into pre-specified ontology-based contexts; and compute *prestige scores* for papers *with respect to their assigned contexts* [1, 2]. Hence, in a given context, only papers that are relevant to the context reside. For a keyword-based search, at search time, (a) contexts of interest are selected, and only papers in the selected contexts are involved in the search, and (b) search results are

L. Kovács, N. Fuhr, and C. Meghini (Eds.): ECDL 2007, LNCS 4675, pp. 271–284, 2007.

ranked separately within contexts. We have found that the context-based search effectively ranks query outputs, controls topic diffusion, and reduces output sizes [1, 2].

For a given paper *p*, we define *related papers* of *p* as a set of papers that are connected to *p* in some manner. The notion of "relatedness" is broader than the notion of "similarity" in the sense that "similarity" is a specific type of "relatedness", i.e., two similar papers are related to each other using a certain similarity metric involving the two papers; on the other hand, two papers, even without a high similarity score based on a similarity metric, may be related because their "contexts" are related. A number of existing approaches have been developed to compute the "relatedness" between two papers, with different approaches employing different interpretations of relatedness. Examples of paper relatedness are:

- Text-based relatedness: two papers are considered *related* if the components of both papers are textually similar.
- Link (Citation) -based relatedness: co-citation [7] and bibliographic coupling [6] are widely used in measuring relatedness between two papers. Co-citation score of papers p_1 and p_2 is higher if p_1 and p_2 are co-cited by larger numbers of papers, and bibliographic coupling score of p_1 and p_2 is higher when p_1 and p_2 have larger numbers of common citations. Using the complete citation graph of publications, relative importance of a paper to a given paper (e.g., citation path or modified PageRank [8]) can also be used as a measure of relatedness between two papers.

Although both text- and link-based approaches are well-studied, they have limitations. In the text-based approach, two papers that are topically related, but do not share a large number of common terms are not considered related. In the link-based approach, two papers are considered related only when they are "close" to each other in the citation graph with sufficient connections to each other. However, different citations of a paper are related to that paper in different ways, e.g., two citations of a paper may refer to two different topics, one of which is more related to the paper than the other. We argue that the topics of papers need to be taken into account when computing the relatedness between papers. Thus, there is a need to revisit the notion of relatedness, and classify the relatedness between two papers based on the topics that they belong to.

In the context-based environment, a paper is assigned to its relevant contexts, where a context characterizes one or more topics. Therefore, two papers appearing in the same or related contexts are potentially related to each other through the topics that they belong to. Hence, we propose the notion of context as a vehicle to refine the notion of relatedness between two papers.

The primary contribution of this paper is to propose and evaluate different empirical ways to compute the degree of relatedness between two papers by incorporating papers' context information as follows:

- We define three notions of relatedness measurements:
  1. *Context-to-Context* relatedness between two contexts is defined by using different approaches involving paper sets and context structures in the context hierarchy of the two contexts.
  2. *Paper-to-Context* relatedness computes and ranks the relatedness of the contexts to the paper. This is useful since a paper may be assigned to multiple contexts.

3. *Paper-to-Paper* relatedness: by using the context-to-context and the paper-to-context relatedness measures, we define the relatedness between two papers as the relatedness between two sets of selected contexts that represent the papers.

- A paper may be assigned to multiple contexts due to the variety in its content, and a user may be interested in only a few contexts. To better suit the user's needs, we add user interaction to our context-based approach. When searching for related papers of a given paper *p*, the user is allowed to choose contexts of interest from a list of all contexts assigned to *p*. Then, context-based paper-to-paper relatedness is computed based on the user-selected contexts, and only papers that are most relevant to the selected contexts are returned.

For evaluation, a digital library database is populated with 72,027 PubMed papers, and papers with prestige scores are assigned to their relevant ontology-based contexts [1, 2, 22]. We compare the proposed context-based relatedness approaches with existing approaches as well as illustrate the approach through several examples.

Experimental results show that:

- The context-based approach gives high relatedness scores (~ 0.6 on the average in [0, 1] range) to paper pairs with high text- and citation-based scores, and provides low scores (~ 0.2 on the average) to paper pairs with low text- and citation-based scores. Thus, our approach distinguishes highly-related papers from unrelated ones, and is accurate.
- The context-based approach is more effective than the existing approaches in the sense that it effectively classifies and ranks related papers based on selected contexts (topics) of interest, thus eliminating the problem of topic diffusion across related paper outputs.

In section 2, we define context-to-context relatedness. Section 3 describes a method to compute paper-to-context relatedness. In section 4, we present context-based paper-to-paper relatedness. Section 5 describes ways to include user interaction to the context-based approach for locating related papers. Sections 6 and 7 present experimental setup and experimental results. Section 8 summarizes the related work, and section 9 concludes.

2 Relatedness Between Two Contexts

In this section, we present three approaches to define relatedness between two contexts with each approach interpreting the notion of relatedness in different ways.

2.1 Count-Based Context Relatedness

One measure of context-relatedness is the number of common papers between two contexts. "Paper-count relatedness" between contexts c_1 and c_2 is defined as follows:

$$CC\text{-}Relatedness_{Paper\_Count}(c_1, c_2) = \frac{|P_{c1} \cap P_{c2}|}{min(|P_{c1}|, |P_{c2}|)} \tag{2.1}$$

where P_{c1} and P_{c2} are paper sets of contexts c_1 and c_2, respectively.

The problem of using only the context paper sets is that two related contexts may not share a large number of common papers, but the papers in both contexts are nevertheless related. To adjust the relatedness score, citations of a paper ("citation papers") for each context can also be used since a paper usually cites or is cited by other relevant papers. However, the number of citation papers in a context can be large, and not all citation papers are relevant to the context. Thus, we use the following criteria to determine a citation paper's relevancy to context c: (i) A citation paper that cites or is cited by a large number of papers in c is highly relevant to c, and (ii) A citation paper that cites or is cited by a paper in most of the contexts is less relevant to c.

Based on the above criteria, the *citation score* of a citation paper p for context c, which we adapt from the notion of Term Frequency-Inverse Document Frequency (TF-IDF) of information retrieval [9], is defined as:

$$Citation\_Score(p, c) = log(CF_{p,c} + 1) * log(ICF_p) \tag{2.2}$$

where p is a paper that cites or is cited by a paper in context c, *citation frequency* ($CF_{p,c}$) *of* p *in* c is the number of papers in c that cite or are cited by p, and *inverse context frequency* (ICF_p) *of* p is defined as N/N_p, N is the total number of contexts, and N_p is the number of contexts containing a paper that cites or is cited by p.

For each context, the citation score of each citation paper as defined in (2.2) is computed, and top-k scored citation papers are selected as *context citation paper set* of c. By combining paper and citation paper counts, we define the count-based relatedness between contexts c_1 and c_2 as:

$$CC\text{-}Relatedness_{Count}(c_1, c_2) = max\left(\frac{|P_{c1} \cap P_{c2}|}{min(|P_{c1}|,|P_{c2}|)}, \frac{|C_{c1} \cap C_{c2}|}{min(|C_{c1}|,|C_{c2}|)}, \frac{|C_{c1} \cap P_{c2}|}{min(|C_{c1}|,|P_{c2}|)}, \frac{|P_{c1} \cap C_{c2}|}{min(|P_{c1}|,|C_{c2}|)}\right) \tag{2.3}$$

where C_{ci} is the context citation paper set of context c_i, and P_{ci} is the paper set of c_i.

2.2 Text-Similarity-Based Context Relatedness

In this section, we define the relatedness between two contexts as the text similarity between the contexts. The simplest way is to compute the text-based similarity between the context terms representing the two contexts. However, a context term is represented as a short phrase, and two related contexts may not share common terms. One way to solve this problem is to view a context as a document containing a large set of selected *context keywords*. The relatedness between two contexts is then defined as text-based similarity between two keyword vectors representing the two contexts. We select context keywords from papers in a context as follows. Each paper in a context is represented by a vector of terms, where each term is represented by the TF-IDF [9] score. We compute the centroid of all paper vectors in the context, and select terms with k highest centroid TF-IDF scores as the context keywords. The value of k is chosen as the average number of terms in all papers. The motivation behind this approach is that, in order for a term in a context to have a high centroid TF-IDF score, that term must appear in a number of papers in the context with high TF-IDF scores, and, thus, is important in characterizing the context.

Text-similarity-based relatedness of two contexts c_1 and c_2 is defined as the cosine similarity [9] between vectors v representing c_1 and w representing c_2 as follows:

$$CC\text{-}Relatedness_{Text}(c_1, c_2) = \frac{\sum_{i=1}^{|T|} f(v_i) \cdot f(w_i)}{\sqrt{\sum_{i=1}^{|T|} f(v_i)^2} \cdot \sqrt{\sum_{i=1}^{|T|} f(w_i)^2}} \tag{2.4}$$

where *f()* is a damping function, which may be the square-root or logarithm function, and |T| is the number of terms.

2.3 Structure-Based Context Relatedness

Since contexts are defined via a context hierarchy, structural information within the hierarchy is useful as a measure as to how related two contexts are. Several works have used the minimum path length connecting the two contexts in the context hierarchy to define the relatedness or the semantic similarity between them [11]. The problem with using only the path length is that all edges in the hierarchy are assumed to be equally important, which may negatively affect the relatedness computation [13].

Another way to compute structure-based relatedness between two contexts is to utilize the information shared between the two contexts, i.e., the informativeness of their common ancestor contexts. If the common ancestor context is highly informative, the two contexts are considered highly related. One existing measure is the *information content* of a concept [10], which is computed by counting the number of objects that are assigned to the concept. When a concept is mapped to a large set of objects, it is more general and less informative. Applying the notion of information content to our context-based environment, we define the information content (IC) of a context c as follows [10]:

$$IC(c) = -log(N_c / N) \tag{2.5}$$

where N_c is the number of papers in context c, and N is the total number of papers.

Information content has been successfully used to measure the semantic similarity between two contexts [10, 15]. Next, we use this semantic similarity measurement to define the relatedness between two contexts. The simplest way to define semantic similarity is to compute the information content of the lowest common ancestor of the two contexts [10]. The problem with this approach is that any two contexts that share the same common ancestor receive the same semantic similarity score regardless of their information contents. Thus, a modification of the above approach is to scale the information content of the lowest common ancestor context by the individual information contents of the two contexts [15]. This modified approach [15] can be used to compute the relatedness between two contexts c_1 and c_2, which is defined as:

$$CC - Relatedness_{Structure}(c_1, c_2) = \max_{c \in S(c_1, c_2)} \frac{2 * IC(c)}{IC(c_1) + IC(c_2)} \tag{2.6}$$

where S is the set of common ancestors of c_1 and c_2, and $IC(c_i)$ is the information content of context c_i as defined in equation 2.5.

3 Relatedness Between Paper and Context

There are two natural queries regarding the relatedness between a paper and a context: (1) Find top-k most-related papers of a given context, and (2) Find top-k most-related contexts of a given paper.

Since a paper in each context is assigned its prestige (context) score with respect to the context, a reasonable answer to the first query is to return the set of top-k papers with highest prestige scores within the given context.

For the second query, we select the top-k most-related contexts of a given paper from the set of contexts that the paper resides in. We use the following criteria to determine the relatedness of context *c* to a given paper *p*:

1. *p* is highly important with respect to *c*, i.e., the prestige score of *p* in *c* is high.
2. *c* is informative and specific. Generally, contexts at the upper levels in the hierarchy are more general. The problem with using only the context depth is that two contexts at the same depth may not be equally semantically precise [13]. For example, in the GO hierarchy, the depths of terms "sodium channel auxiliary protein activity" and "cellular metabolism" are both 4, but the first term is more specific. Moreover, the first term is a leaf node, while the height of the subtree with the second term as the root of the subtree is 11. Intuitively, when a context is closer to the leaf level, as a term, it is generally more precise. Therefore, we use both context depth and subtree height with context as the root to define the specificity of context *c*, called *context level specificity* (*LS*), as follows:

$$LS(c)= \frac{Depth(c)}{Depth(c)+SubtreeHeight(c)} \tag{3.1}$$

where *Depth(c)* is the depth of the node representing *c*, and *SubtreeHeight(c)* is the height of the subtree starting at *c*.

In addition to the context level, a context *c* is more general and less informative if *c* contains a large set of papers. We define the *specificity-based informativeness* of context *c* by combining the context level specificity and the information content of *c* as follows:

$$Specificity\text{-}based\_Informativeness(c)= \frac{LS(c)+\frac{IC(c)}{MaxIC}}{2} \tag{3.2}$$

where *LS(c)* is the context level specificity of *c* (see equation 3.1), *IC(c)* is the information content of *c* (see equation 2.5), and *MaxIC* is the maximum *IC* of any context.

Finally, we define the top-k most related contexts of a given paper as a set of k contexts that most satisfy the above two criteria. However, criterion one is more important since it involves the prestige scores of papers based on contexts, while criterion two considers only context structures. Taking the above consideration into account, we define the relatedness of context *c* to paper *p* as follows:

$$PC\text{-}Relatedness(c,p)= \alpha \cdot Score(p,c) + \beta \cdot Informativeness(c) \tag{3.3}$$

where *Score(p, c)* is a pre-computed prestige score of *p* in *c*, *Informativeness* (of *c*) is defined in equation 3.2, and α and β are weights of prestige and informativeness scores. As described above, the first criterion involving prestige scores is more important than the second criterion; thus, we have $\alpha > \beta$ (i.e., $\alpha = 0.7$ and $\beta = 0.3$).

Given a paper *p*, we locate its top-k related contexts as follows. First, we select only contexts that the paper *p* resides in, say C_p. Then, we compute the relatedness scores of each context in C_p with respect to p. Finally, the top-k related contexts of p are those k contexts with highest PC-relatedness scores.

4 Context-Based Relatedness Between Two Papers

As described in the introduction, the relatedness between two papers is measured by different approaches, where different techniques within each approach define relatedness in different ways. In our context-based environment, a paper is represented by its relevant contexts. Thus, papers that are assigned to the same or related contexts are potentially related to each other. In this section, we define the relatedness between two papers using only their assigned contexts. We do not use other direct measures involving paper contents, authors, and citations in the relatedness computation.

If papers were assigned to only one context, the relatedness between two papers could easily be computed as the relatedness between the two contexts that both papers are in. Since a paper may reside in multiple contexts, the problem here is how to compute the relatedness between two sets of contexts. One way to measure the context-based relatedness between two papers is to compute the average of the relatedness scores between every pair of contexts that both papers are in. However, the number of contexts that each paper resides in may be large, and computing the relatedness between every pair of contexts may be less accurate. Also, due to low specificity, some contexts may not be highly related to their papers as described in section 3.

In order to eliminate contexts that are not highly relevant to a paper, we introduce the notion of *representative contexts* as a set of contexts that best characterize the paper. Representative contexts of a paper are selected as the top-k most-related contexts of the paper (as described in section 3). Note that the value of k defines a compromise: as the value of k gets higher, the set of representative contexts include contexts that are less related to the paper; on the other hand, when k is too small, some relevant contexts may be excluded. As a compromise, (1) k should be small (e.g., < 10) enough to include only relevant contexts, and (2) contexts with paper-to-context relatedness scores higher than a given threshold t (e.g., $t = 0.5$ for [0, 1] score range) should be included to ensure that all relevant contexts are selected.

Representative contexts are chosen as contexts that are highly related to the paper. Thus, if all contexts in a set of representative contexts of p_1 are closely related to at least one of the representative contexts of p_2 and vice versa, p_1 and p_2 should be considered closely related, and receive a high context-based relatedness score. Using the above reasoning, we define the context-based relatedness of papers p_1 and p_2 as:

$$PP\text{-}Relatedness(p_1, p_2) = \frac{\sum_{c_i \in C_1} \max_{c_j \in C_2}\left(CC\text{-}Relatedness(c_i, c_j)\right) + \sum_{c_j \in C_2} \max_{c_i \in C_1}\left(CC\text{-}Relatedness(c_i, c_j)\right)}{|C_1| + |C_2|} \tag{4.1}$$

where C_1 and C_2 are sets of representative contexts of p_1 and p_2, and *CC-Relatedness* is the degree of relatedness between two contexts as described in section 2.

5 Context-Based Relatedness with User Interaction

Since a paper may belong to multiple contexts, a user may only be interested in a few specific contexts. Therefore, it is useful to add user interaction in locating related papers so that the user specifies which contexts he/she is most interested in, and only papers that are highly related to the selected contexts are returned. Context-based Paper-to-Paper (PP)-relatedness is modified to incorporate user interaction as follows:

1) From a given paper *p*, the list of all contexts that *p* resides is presented to the user.
2) The user manually selects the set of contexts *C* that he/she is interested in.
3) Context-based PP-relatedness (see equation 4.1) between *p* and *every paper* in the database is computed with respect to *C* as the set of representative contexts of *p*. For other papers, representative contexts are selected as described in section 4.
4) Search results are ranked by PP-relatedness scores and returned to the user.

With this new approach, we return only papers that are related to a given paper based on the set of manually-selected contexts. Hence, the located related papers highly satisfy the user's needs. Note that this capability does not exist, and not possible to implement using the existing relatedness measures. Several examples illustrating this approach are presented in section 7.2.

In the case that the user does not want to select contexts, default representative contexts (as described in section 4) are used in PP-relatedness computation.

As a variation of the above proposed approach, step 3 can be changed from "*every paper* in the database" to "a set of *interesting papers*". That is, the user may want to rank a set of papers based on the degree of relatedness to the selected contexts. E.g., given a set of citations on a citation path of length 3 starting or ending at paper *p*, the user may want to rank the citations based on their relevancy to the selected contexts since different citations refer to different topics and are related to *p* in different ways.

6 Experimental Setup

We downloaded, parsed, and populated a literature digital library database with information from 72,027 full-text PubMed papers [22, 23]. These papers were assigned to contexts using both automated and manual approaches [1, 2].

- **Automatically-Generated Context Paper Set**

For this paper set, we utilized the Gene Ontology (GO) hierarchy as a context hierarchy [4, 14]. A paper was automatically assigned to its relevant GO contexts using a detailed (and independently verified) process [1, 2]. Briefly, a context is represented by its identifying elements (e.g., the relevant paper set, constructed phrases, etc.), and a paper is assigned to contexts whose identifying elements match well to the paper. More details about the automated context paper set construction can be found elsewhere [1, 2].

- **Manually-Generated Context Paper Set**

In this set, a context refers to a Medical Subject Headings (MeSH) [5] term. In PubMed [3], MeSH terms are assigned to each paper by expert subject analysts. If a MeSH term *m* is assigned to paper *p*, *p* is included in the paper set of the context *m*, i.e., each MeSH context's paper set includes all papers that are marked up with that context term and all papers of its descendant contexts.

7 Experimental Results

This section evaluates our proposed context-based approach. First, we compare the context-based paper-to-paper (PP-)relatedness approach to existing approaches. Then, we present several examples to illustrate the results when applying user interaction.

We tested our context-based approach using both automatically- and manually-generated context paper sets, and experimental results for both sets were quite similar. Thus, we present here only the results involving the automatically-generated set.

7.1 Comparison with Existing Approaches

In this section, we compare the context-based PP-relatedness approach with two existing approaches: PubMed relatedness and bibliographic coupling relatedness.

7.1.1 Comparison with PubMed Related Papers

PubMed [3] computes the relatedness between two papers using text-based similarities between paper titles, abstracts, and assigned MeSH terms [5]. Given a paper, PubMed provides a list of related papers with relatedness scores.

We created two test sets as follows.

- *Highly-related PubMed paper pairs*: we randomly selected 200 pairs of papers with very high PubMed relatedness scores (i.e., PubMed (non-normalized) scores higher than 90000000). For a selected paper pair (p_i, p_j), p_i is usually ranked in the top-5 most related papers of p_j by PubMed. Thus, two papers in each selected paper pair in this test set are highly related in terms of the text-based relatedness approach.
- *Unrelated PubMed paper pairs*: we randomly generated 200 paper pairs. For each pair (p_i, p_j) in this test set, p_i is not in the PubMed related paper list of p_j, i.e., a paper in each paper pair is not considered related to the other paper by PubMed.

Steps to compute the context-based PP-relatedness score of every selected pair of papers (p_i, p_j) in the experiment are as follows:

1) Select top-k most-related contexts of p_i (and p_j) as well as contexts with paper-to-context-relatedness scores (see equation 3.3) higher than a threshold t as representative contexts of p_i (and p_j). For the choice of k, we present only the results when $k = 5$. We tested different values of k, and the results were not significantly different. For the threshold t, we manually verified the results and chose $t = 0.5$.
2) Compute the three PP-relatedness scores between p_i and p_j using equation 4.1 with the three different CC-relatedness approaches (i.e., count-, text-similarity-, and structure-based approaches as described in section 2)

Average PP-relatedness scores of all paper pairs in each test set are shown in figure 1.

Observations

- For highly-related PubMed paper pairs, the average context-based PP-relatedness scores are higher than 0.5 for all three CC-relatedness approaches (Figure 1).
- The average context-based PP-relatedness scores for unrelated PubMed paper pairs are much lower (i.e., the difference is approximately 0.4) than highly-related PubMed paper pairs for all three CC-relatedness approaches.

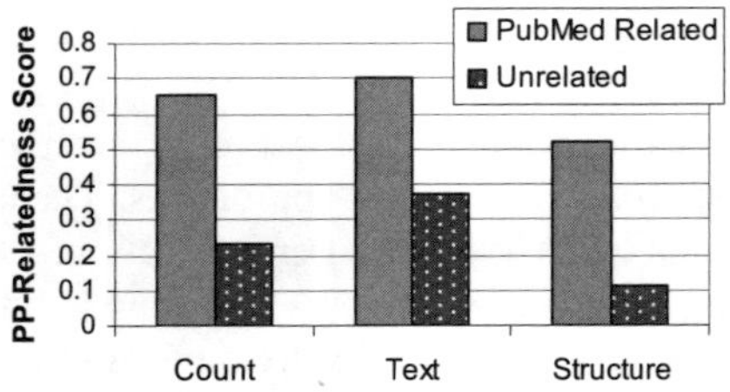

Fig. 1. Average context-based PP-relatedness scores of highly-related PubMed paper pairs (PubMed Related) versus unrelated PubMed paper pairs (Unrelated)

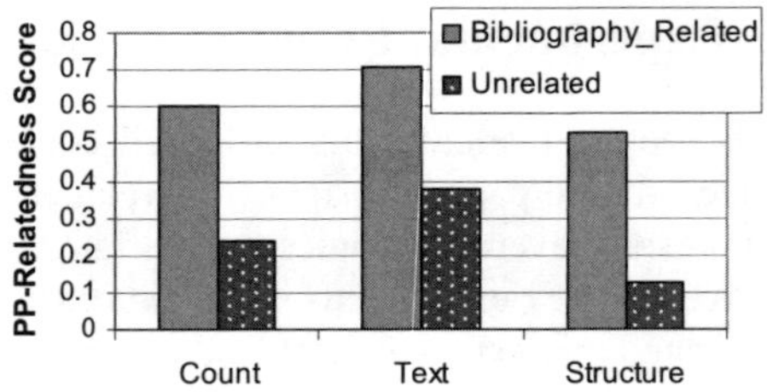

Fig. 2. Average context-based PP-relatedness scores of highly-related bibliographic coupling paper pairs (Bibliography Related) versus unrelated bibliographic coupling paper pairs (Unrelated)

Thus, from these experimental results, the context-based relatedness approach does distinguish highly-related paper pairs from unrelated paper pairs as compared to the PubMed text-based measurement.

7.1.2 Comparison with Bibliographic Coupling Related Papers

As stated in the introduction, two widely-used citation-based approaches are co-citation [7] and bibliographic coupling [6]. Since our database contains only a subset of PubMed papers, information regarding papers outside of our database citing a paper in the database is missing. As a result, we do not have complete citation information for computing co-citation scores between papers for our data set. Therefore, we used only the bibliographic coupling approach for comparison in this section. More specifically, we use the following formula to compute the bibliographic coupling score between two papers p_1 and p_2 in the database.

$$Bib\_Coupling(p_1, p_2) = common\ citation\ count\ between\ p_1\ and\ p_2 / MaxB \quad (7.1)$$

where *MaxB* is the maximum number of common citations between any two papers.

Similar to previous experiments, we created two paper sets: *highly-related bibliographic coupling* and *unrelated bibliographic coupling* paper pairs. Highly-related bibliographic coupling paper pairs include only paper pairs with high bibliographic coupling scores (i.e., we chose scores > 0.3). Unrelated bibliographic coupling paper pairs were created randomly from the paper pairs with 0 or very small bibliographic coupling scores. An average score for each paper set is shown in figure 2.

Observations

- For highly-related paper pairs, the average context-based relatedness scores are higher than 0.5 for all three CC-relatedness approaches (Figure 2).
- The average context-based PP-relatedness scores of the paper pairs in the highly-related set are much higher than the average scores for unrelated paper set for all three CC-relatedness approaches.

Thus, from these experimental results, the context-based relatedness approaches distinguish highly-related paper pairs from unrelated paper pairs as compared to bibliographic coupling measurement. From both experimental results in section 7.1.1 and in this section, we conclude that the context-based relatedness approach is accurate.

7.2 Results When Adding User Interaction

As described in section 5, we refine the context-based approach by adding user interaction so that only related papers in contexts of interest are included. In this section, we give several examples to illustrate how this feature works.

Table 1 displays all MeSH terms that are marked up with the "example paper": "K-ary clustering with optimal leaf ordering for gene expression data" [21] in PubMed service. In the context paper set, this paper is assigned to all the MeSH terms in Table 1 as well as their ancestor contexts (omitted here).

Table 1. MeSH terms of the example paper

Mesh Terms
Algorithms, Animals, Bursa of Fabricius, Chickens, Cluster Analysis, Decision Trees, Gene Expression Profiling, Gene Expression Regulation, Genes, myc, Lymphoma, B-Cell, Oligonucleotide Array Sequence Analysis, Pattern Recognition, Quality Control, Sequence Alignment, Sequence Analysis, DNA, Sequence Homology, Stochastic Processes, User-Computer Interface

From Table 1, the example paper belongs to various topics from computer science to genomics areas. When searching for related papers of this paper, a user may want to see a set of papers with more in-depth study in computer science-related areas (e.g., various clustering algorithms), or the user may want to find only papers in the genomics domain (e.g., gene expression).

Applying the approach presented in Section 5, Table 2 shows the top-5 most related papers with respect to three sets of contexts: set 1: "algorithms" and "cluster analysis", set 2: "gene expression profiling", "genes, myc", and "sequence alignment", and set 3: "animals" and "lymphoma, B-cell".

Observations

- We have found that all of the results returned from Table 2 are related to the example paper in some manner since they are all related to one or more contexts (topics) assigned to the example paper.
- Related papers returned for each context set are strongly relevant to the context set. For example, all of the results for context set 1 are about clustering techniques in bioinformatics while the results for context set 3 are all strongly related to lymphoma.

The above examples illustrate the capabilities of the context-based approach in ranking and classifying related papers of a given paper. By manually selecting interesting contexts, the user retrieves only papers that are really relevant to what he/she is looking for. If the user is not satisfied with the results, he/she can modify the selected contexts and re-submit the revised query. Thus, we conclude that our context-based approach satisfactorily handles the problem of topic diffusion problem that frequently occurs in other approaches.

Table 2. Top-5 most related papers of the example paper based on context sets 1, 2, 3

Context Set 1: "algorithms" and "cluster analysis"
1. Strong-association-rule mining for large-scale gene-expression data analysis: a case study on human sage data (Becquet et al.) 2. Excavator: a computer program for efficiently mining gene expression data (Xu et al.) 3. Click and expander: a system for clustering and visualizing gene expression data (Sharan et al.) 4. Kernel hierarchical gene clustering from microarray expression data (Qin et al.) 5. Prediction of saccharomyces cerevisiae protein functional class from functional domain composition (Cai et al.)
Context Set 2: "gene expression profiling", "genes, myc", and "sequence alignment"
1. Rash, a rapid subtraction hybridization approach for identifying and cloning differentially expressed genes (Jiang et al.) 2. Identification of c-myc as a down-stream target for pituitary tumor-transforming gene (Pei, L.) 3. Project normal: defining normal variance in mouse gene expression (Pritchard et al.) 4. Analysis of gene expression in the developing mouse retina (Diaz et al.) 5. Mouse chromosome 17a3.3 contains 13 genes that encode functional tryptic-like serine proteases with distinct tissue and cell expression patterns (Wong et al.)
Context Set 3: "animals" and "lymphoma, B-cell"
1. The c-mer gene is induced by epstein-barr virus immediate-early protein brlf1 (Li et al.) 2. Cloning and sequence analysis of an ig lambda light chain mrna expressed in the burkitt's lymphoma cell line eb4 (Anderson et al.) 3. Relation of burkitt's tumor-associated herpes-ytpe virus to infectious mononucleosis (Henle et al.) 4. Human c-myc onc gene is located on the region of chromosome 8 that is translocated in burkitt lymphoma cells (Dalla-Favera et al.) 5. A mammalian dna-binding protein that contains a chromodomain and an snf2/swi2-like helicase domain (Delmas et al.)

8 Related Work

A number of existing works are proposed to measure the relatedness and/or similarity of two objects by using relevant information of the two objects. Many measures are developed using objects' structures in a tree or graph representation. Early approaches used path distances between nodes [11], and assumed that two objects are highly semantically similar if they are close in the graph. Li et al. [12] proposed a measure of semantic similarity between two words in a hierarchy by using a non-linear combination of both shortest path length and subsumer depth. The notion of *information content* is used in information theory to measure semantic similarity between two objects in an "is-a" hierarchy [10, 15, 16]. Pedersen et al. [17] adapted both path length and information content approaches to measure the similarity and relatedness between concepts in the biomedical domain. The information content method was successfully applied to measure semantic similarity of two proteins based on their Gene Ontology annotations [13]. Maguitman et al. [19] adapted the information content technique to compute the semantic similarity between two documents stored in the Open Directory Project (ODP) ontology [20]. However, only one non-hierarchical link is allowed in the computation of Maguitman's measure. Moreover, the algorithm is computationally very expensive and not practical for large ontologies since many matrix operations are involved in the computation. Stepping Stones and Pathways (SSP) [18] created a network of additionally related topics and involved documents of given two queries, where each query represents an endpoint topic.

9 Conclusions

To efficiently and effectively locate a set of related papers of a given paper and to solve the topic diffusion problem of returned papers, we have proposed a new context-based measure to compute the degree of relatedness between two papers. A paper is represented by its most relevant contexts, and the relatedness between any two papers is computed from the relatedness between the two context sets representing the two papers. We also provide user interaction in our approach so that the user selects interesting contexts of a given paper, and only papers that are related to the selected contexts are returned. We show that the context-based approach efficiently and effectively ranks and classifies related papers of a given paper based on all or selected contexts of the paper. Moreover, the context-based approach solves the problem of topic diffusion that occurs in other approaches.

Acknowledgments

This research is supported by the US National Science Foundation grants ITR-0312200 and CNS-0551603.

References

1. Ratprasartporn, N., Po, J., Cakmak, A., Bani-Ahmad, S., Ozsoyoglu, G.: Context-Based Literature Digital Library Search. Technical Report, CWRU (2006)
2. Ratprasartporn, N., Bani-Ahmad, S., Cakmak, A., Po, J., Ozsoyoglu, G.: Evaluating Different Ranking Functions for Context-Based Literature Search. In: DBRank workshop. In Conjunction with ICDE (2007)
3. PubMed, http://www.ncbi.nih.gov/entrez/query.fcgi
4. Gene Ontology, for a visualization of the Gene Ontology, see [14], http://geneontology.org
5. Medical Subject Headings (MeSH), http://www.nlm.nih.gov/mesh/
6. Kessler, M.M.: Bibliographic Coupling between Scientific Papers. American Documentation 14, 10–25 (1963)
7. Small, H.: Co-citation in the Scientific Literature: A New Measure of the Relationship between Two Documents. Journal of the American Society for Information Science 24(4), 28–31 (1973)
8. White, S., Smyth, P.: Algorithms for Estimating Relative Importance in Networks. In: SIGKDD (2003)
9. Salton, G.: Automatic Text Processing. Addison-Wesley, Reading (1989)
10. Resnik, P.: Using Information Content to Evaluate Semantic Similarity in a Taxonomy. In: International Joint Conference on Artificial Intelligence (1995)
11. Rada, R., Mili, H., Bichnell, E., Blettner, M.: Development and Application of a Metric on Semantic Nets. IEEE Trans. Systems, Man, and Cybernetics 9(1), 17–30 (1989)

12. Li, Y., Bandar, Z., McLean, D.: An Approach for Measuring Semantic Similarity between Words Using Multiple Information Sources. IEEE Transactions on Knowledge and Data Engineering 15(4) (2003)
13. Lord, P.W., Stevens, R.D., Brass, A., Goble, C.A.: Investigating Semantic Similarity Measures across the Gene Ontology: the Relationship between Sequence and Annotation. Bioinformatics 19(10) (2003)
14. CaseMed Ontology Viewer, CWRU, http://nashuatest.case.edu/termvisualizer/
15. Lin, D.: An Information-Theoretic Definition of Similarity. In: Proceedings of the Fifteenth International Conference on Machine Learning, pp. 296–304. Morgan Kaufmann Publishers Inc., San Francisco (1998)
16. Jiang, J., Conrath, D.: Semantic Similarity Based on Corpus Statistics and Lexical Taxonom. In: The 10th International Conference on Research in Computational Linguistics (1997)
17. Pedersen, T., Pakhomov, S., Patwardhan, S., Chute, C.: Measures of Semantic Similarity and Relatedness in the Biomedical Domain. Journal of Biomedical Informatics (2006)
18. Das-Neves, F., Fox, E.A., Yu, X.: Connecting Topics in Document Collections with Stepping Stones and Pathways. In: CIKM (2005)
19. Maguitman, A.G., Menczer, F., Roinestad, H., Vespignani, A.: Algorithmic Detection of Semantic Similarity, WWW (2005)
20. Open Directory Project, http://dmoz.org/
21. Bar-Joseph, Z., Demaine, E.D., Gifford, D.K., Srebro, N., Hamel, A.M., Jaakkola, T.S.: K-ary Clustering with Optimal Leaf Ordering for Gene Expression Data. Bioinformatics 19(9), 1070–1078 (2003)
22. Po, J.: Context-Based Search in Literature Digital Libraries, MS Thesis, CWRU (2006)
23. Pan, F.: Comparative Evaluation of Publication Characteristics in Computer Science and Life Sciences, MS Thesis, CWRU (2006)

Extending Semantic Matching Towards Digital Library Contexts

László Kovács and András Micsik

MTA SZTAKI, Computer and Automation Research Institute
of the Hungarian Academy of Sciences, Department of Distributed Systems,
Budapest, Hungary
{laszlo.kovacs, micsik}@sztaki.hu

Abstract. Matching users' goals with available offers is a traditional research topic for electronic market places and service-oriented architectures. The new area of Semantic Web Services introduced the possibility of semantic matching between user goals and services. Authors show in the paper what kind of benefits semantic matching may provide for digital libraries. Various practical examples are given for the usefulness of semantic matching, and a novel algorithm is introduced for computing semantic matches. The implementation and operation of matching are explained using a digital document search scenario.

Keywords: Semantic matchmaking, discovery.

1 Introduction

Libraries have a rich and old tradition of describing, cataloguing and finding content. Library catalogues and digital library systems traditionally use non-semantic, keyword-based search techniques. Current digital library systems are mostly available as distributed, Internet-based applications, and we think that the new technologies of the Semantic Web has much to offer for them as well.

Semantic description of library content and user profiles helps the creation of new user interfaces and information visualization techniques, and it also enhances ways for personalization. Semantic description of system capabilities and service-oriented architecture enables the creation of more flexible and dynamic digital library systems. With the application of Semantic Web Services not only the content, but also the library services can be discovered and selected on-demand.

Most of the previously listed use cases rely on the primitive operation of semantic matching or matchmaking, which associate semantically described artifacts with a semantically described goal or desire. This is parallel to the query and the query result in traditional IR systems, but it is clear that IR techniques cannot be used for semantic matching. Semantic matching needs new methods and new base infrastructure, which is currently under intensive research. In this paper we investigate the possibilities and benefits of semantic matchmaking within digital libraries and describe a working environment for semantic matching.

L. Kovács, N. Fuhr, and C. Meghini (Eds.): ECDL 2007, LNCS 4675, pp. 285–296, 2007.

2 Semantic Matching

Semantic matching is often used in the areas of Grid and Web Services, where relevant resources, hosts or services have to be found for given purposes. The Web Services glossary [9] gives a basic definition of service discovery:

"The act of locating a machine-processable description of a Web service-related resource that may have been previously unknown and that meets certain functional criteria. It involves matching a set of functional and other criteria with a set of resource descriptions. The goal is to find an appropriate Web service-related resource."

Preist gives a profound analysis of the complex scenario when semantically described services have to be matched with given requirements [20]. There are numerous efforts for Semantic Web Service frameworks, such as OWL-S, WSMO, SAWSDL, and SWSF. In WSDL and OWL-S a service is most typically specified with inputs and outputs, where these inputs and outputs are matched to relevant ontology concepts. Another approach is to specify the precondition and the postcondition of a service, i.e. the criteria to use the service, and the expectable outcome.

In our work, we use the Web Service Modeling Ontology (WSMO) framework [6], and we explain the meaning of semantic matching on the basis of WSMO. In WSMO the user specifies a goal, which is matched against services. Both goals and web services provide capability descriptions consisting of precondition, assumption, postcondition and effect in the format of Web Service Modeling Language (WSML). WSML is a layered logical language on the basis of Description Logics, First-Order Logic and Logic Programming [2]. A simple textual description of web service capability is given as example:

- Precondition: the user provides a text in Hungarian language using UTF-8 encoding and her credit card number.
- Postcondition: the service returns a text in English language, which is the translation of the text provided by the user, and the price of the translation is charged to the given credit card.

WSMO deliverable D5.1 [12] defines semantic matching as:

$$W, G, O \models \exists x(g(x) \wedge ws(x))$$

where W is the definition of the web service, G is the definition of the goal, O is a set of ontologies to which both descriptions refer, $g(x)$ and $ws(x)$ are the first-order formulae describing the effects of the goal and web service, respectively. The logical expression guarantees that there exists an outcome offered by the service, which is requested by the user.

Based on this definition a classification of matches can be built:

- *Exact match*: the possible outcomes of the service and the goal are equivalent; the service does exactly what the user desires.

- *Subsumption match*: each possible outcome of the service is accepted by the goal, i.e. all service offers are acceptable by the user, though there might be desires not covered by the service.
- *Plug-in match*: each possible outcome requested by the goal can be produced by the service, i.e. all user requests can be satisfied by the service, although the service may provide additional, non-matching outcomes as well.
- *Intersection match*: there is at least one service outcome accepted by the user (goal).

The list of matching services and the types of match are computed by discovery engines, which apply reasoners such as Prolog, Fact++ or Pellet.

It is important to distinguish logical queries and logical (semantic) matching. Logical queries return all solutions for a given query. This broadly corresponds to exact and plug-in matches. The logical matching depends on the computed possible common solutions, which creates a broader and different sense of match.

2.1 Semantic Matching in Digital Libraries

In the following, the notion of semantic matching is brought to the area of digital libraries.

According to the DL conceptual model worked out by the DELOS Working Group on Evaluation [8], a digital library model falls into three non-orthogonal components: the users, the data/collection and the technology used. The joint scenario of these three aspects determines the fourth aspect: usage.

Examining these aspects, one can realize that all of them contain possibilities for semantic matching. Matching in the area of technology can be used to find services with given capabilities, which returns us to the area of Semantic Web Services. Digital library systems built on a service-oriented architecture can incorporate various services, including services to find, arrange and manipulate digital objects.

Matching of users is the basis of collaborative filtering and recommendations. User profiles are usually compared using statistical approaches, which leads to the formulation of user proximity or user clusters. If statistical user profiles are replaced with semantic user descriptions, it can enable more focused and thematic user queries.

Matching can also be applied to user interfaces, which also belong to the area of technology in the DL model. Each user interface has certain preconditions (access rights, bandwidth and visibility issues, etc.) and capabilities (speed, graphic resolution, navigation paradigms, etc.). These can be matched semantically to the current environment of the user and to the capabilities of the user's device.

In the aspect of content, most of the currently applied matching techniques are non-semantic and rely on text-based browsing and searching. Recently, the use of structured metadata, controlled vocabularies and ontologies enhance the semantics of catalogue entries. Metadata elements are related to each other using ontologies such as CIDOC CRM [5]. The Dublin Core metadata set is also described as an RDF schema [10], and thus DC metadata can be connected with the tools for RDF and OWL. The possible values for certain metadata elements (e.g. format, subject) can also be related to ontologies. These are important prerequisites for semantic interoperability of digital collections, which facilitates unified or transparent queries.

The traditional meaning of semantic matching can be easily converted to the task of searching digital content. In this case, the user's goal describes the kind of document or digital object she would like to have, while the services are replaced with the semantic descriptions of the available digital objects. The task of semantic matching is to find relevant objects for the user. This seems to be the same as traditional IR, but IR provides non-semantic matches, and therefore it cannot exploit the meanings and inter-relations inside the matched objects.

Some examples are given for queries, which are more suitable for semantic matching:

- Find novels where the lead's wife is an actress,
- Find reviews of mobile phones with UMTS support,
- Find a book with the short biography of Liszt, the Hungarian composer,
- Find a book containing the proof of X mathematical theorem,
- Find books criticizing the relativity theory,
- Find books with illustrations copyrighted by Swiss photographers,
- Find books which are annotated as 'worth reading' by my friends.

These examples show that semantic matching provides richer facilities for querying. With an everyday searching experience, we feel that it would not be easy to find the results for such queries using keyword search, and most probably our real results would be hidden in a longer list of useless documents. The prerequisite of these benefits is that we need semantic descriptions of the searched items. In the next subsection, we show some solutions to obtain semantic descriptions for digital objects. A further problem is that the query expression also has to be in a semantic format. Visual axiom editors, such as the one implemented in the INFRAWEBS project [1], may provide easy ways in the near future for non-expert users to compile logical queries.

A short overview was given on the benefits and use of semantic matching in the field of digital libraries. There are more key concepts of digital libraries, as for example collected in [13], and many of these are good targets for semantic matching.

2.2 The Creation of Semantic Descriptions

One possible barrier to use semantic matching in digital libraries is the lack of semantic descriptions and the cost of creating them. This can be viewed as three options:

- *Lifting existing data on the semantic level*: the contents of existing SQL databases can be easily converted into the form of Prolog predicates or RDF graphs. However, with this approach, one often does not get richer descriptions than the original ones, and thus one cannot exceed the quality of results provided by traditional IR techniques. A much more futuristic method is the automatic conversion of textual descriptions into logical facts using NLP techniques.
- *Incorporation of emerging semantic approaches*: the RDF-based annotation protocol of Annotea is the best example of this option [11]. There are also initiatives for semantic description of rights metadata (e.g. Creative Commons at http://creativecommons.org/). Annotations are usually collected in separate

databases, but connecting them to the catalogue data extends the available semantic information.

- *Generation of new semantic descriptions*: the previously mentioned visual editors coupled with case-based reasoning provide a productive workbench for state-of-the-art semantic catalogues [1]. In simpler scenarios, the metadata editor itself can support the creation of simple facts.

3 Implementation of Semantic Matching

Within the EU-funded INFRAWEBS project the authors implemented a discovery engine for Semantic Web Services [19]. However, we found that the engine and the algorithm is more general, and can be used in the previously described DL-focused scenarios as well. In the following, the discovery engine is described, and an example for semantic matching is given.

3.1 The Two-Step Approach

The INFRAWEBS discovery engine combines the keyword-based and the logic-based aspect of matching. The main reason is that current logic-based matching techniques are significantly slower than traditional keyword-based techniques. Therefore, in the first, pre-filtering step a keyword search is used to generate a smaller initial set for the logic-based matching. This two-step approach is in harmony with the task of searching in digital catalogues, where keyword-based search facilities are usually available.

Initially, the goal, the capability of expressing the user's desire is compiled. In case of services this can be a full-blown capability with preconditions, assumptions, postconditions and effects, while in case of digital objects the goal contains a single "postcondition" describing the desired digital object.

In parallel or based on the goal, the keyword-based query expression is generated, and the query is executed. The list of results is passed on to the next step of logical matching, which will attempt to match the listed objects to the goal semantically.

Although, the query generation process contains further interesting details and sets several problems [17], the focus of the current paper is on the next step, which is logical matching.

3.2 Prolog-Based Matching

Our solution applies the unification facility of Prolog engines. If we find matching terms within the goal and the digital object, we can use this information to decide on the matching. A schematic explanation of unification can be found in Fig. 1. Let us assume that we met a researcher at a conference who talked to us about a new, refereed publication citing him. We would like to find this paper, but we forgot the name of the researcher, we only remember that he was from London. This desire is expressed on the left side of Fig. 1, while the right side of the figure describes the paper we search for. The first logical terms in both columns are identical, so they match. The second pair of terms has the same signature, so they can be unified yielding *X=Y* where *Y works for Lab Z.* After these unifications, we see that the fact

"*X is from London*" became true (here we also use a knowledge base stating that Lab Z is in London). Then, we again unify the next terms from both sides, getting *J*=*K*. However, it is not known yet whether *K* is a refereed journal or not, because of missing data. The last fact in the goal generates no contradiction, and the document is accepted as a match for the goal.

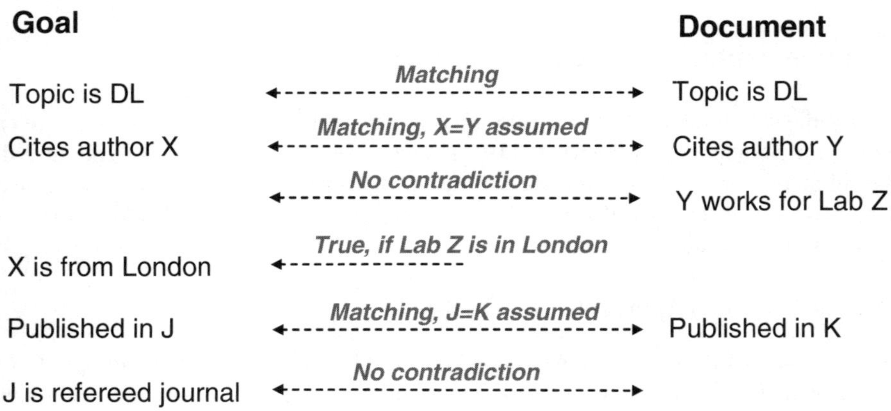

Fig. 1. Example for semantic matching of a document and the user's goal

It is worth to note that by using a plain logical query we would not get this document, because of missing data about the publishing journal. If we omitted the criterion for the refereed journal, we could get many irrelevant results mixed with the desired document. When using our matching approach, both refereed and non-refereed publications are found, but the refereed ones are ranked higher than others.

In the following, we describe the matching algorithm. In order to reach a comparable list of terms some kind of normalized form is needed, of which the Disjunctive Normal Form (DNF) was the most suitable. The DNF consists of clause sets in the form of *(*C_{11} *and* C_{12} *and …) or… (*C_{m1} *and* C_{m2} *and …)*, where C_{ij} are atomic terms. We call C_{ij} a clause, and *(*C_{11} *and* C_{12} *and …* C_{1n}*)* a clause set. A DNF is true if at least one clause set is true. A DNF clause set is true if all its clauses are true. This means that a true clause set provides a complete solution for the matching in itself.

Before any semantic matching, the matching environment has to be set up:

- Ontologies used in semantic document descriptions are converted to Prolog. Special predicates are used to represent subconcept, attribute and attribute type relationships within concepts. Instances are converted to Prolog using the *type/2* and *attr/3* predicates, which describe the concept of the instance and the attribute values of the instance, respectively.
- Then all document descriptions are converted into DNF clause sets. The conversion process applies the usual steps found in logic handbooks:
  - Logical constructs, such as implication or equivalence, are replaced with an equivalent form using only conjunction, disjunction and negation,

  - Negations are moved inwards to reach Negation Normal Form (NNF),
  - *Forall* and *exists* constructs are eliminated with the help of skolemization,
  - Disjunctions are moved to the outermost level to reach DNF.
- DNF clause sets are converted to Prolog. Membership molecules of WSML are converted to *type/2* predicates and attribute molecules are represented with *attr/3* predicates.

An excerpt of generated Prolog clauses is given for the document in Fig. 1:

```
type(Paper, paper),
attr(Paper, cites, Y),
attr(Y, worksFor, labZ),
attr(Paper, publishedIn, K).
```

When the environment is initialized, the following steps are needed for semantic matching with a given goal:

- The goal is converted first to DNF and then to Prolog clause sets the same way as semantic document descriptions,
- The clause sets are optimized for the matching (e.g. order of clauses is changed),
- The matching algorithm is run: an attempt is made to match each document with the goal,
- The result is a list of matching documents with ranking.

As part of the matching algorithm, we need to find a matching between the DNF clause sets representing the goal and a digital object. The steps to be performed for each pair of clause sets (one from the goal and one from the digital object) are:

- Unification of clauses in the clause sets: two clauses are unified if they have the same signature, then corresponding variables in the two clauses are unified,
- Labeling each clause: matched, failed or ignored,
- Decision of match or failure.

The detailed description of the matching algorithm is given in [14], here only a summary of the algorithm is given. First, all possible unifications are made. Second, the algorithm has to examine all clauses in the clause set with the effects of unifications made. During this examination, all clauses are labeled with one of the labels: 'matched', 'ignored', and 'failed'. The label 'failed' means that a contradiction arose, which prohibits the match between the goal and the digital object. The label 'matched' means that the clause yields true in this match, which means that the fact represented by that clause is fulfilled. The label 'ignored' means that the clause did not match, but it does not create any contradiction, so it can be silently ignored in the matching process.

Finally, the algorithm has to decide whether the goal and the digital object match with each other. If there is a failed clause, it means a disagreement of the goal and service, so there is no match. If there are only matched and ignored clauses, then further heuristics are needed to decide about the match. We implemented two types of heuristics for our experiments:

- A rough heuristics says there is a match if the number of matched clauses is greater than the number of ignored clauses.
- A more elaborate heuristics automatically distinguishes features that are required by the user and features that are optional, based on special marking applied in the underlying ontologies. In this case, all required features must match, while any number of optional features may be ignored.

We demonstrate the outcome of the algorithm based on the example of Fig. 1. After the unifications shown in the figure are made, it is seen that no contradictions were found. The number of matched clauses is 4, both in the goal and in the document. The number of ignored clauses in the goal is 1 (refereed journal), and this number in the document is also 1 (has date 2007). Based on these numbers, the algorithm declares the match. The result of the matching algorithm is given in a summary, where each fact is followed by its matching label:

Goal:	*Document:*
P has topic DL (M)	*D has topic DL (M)*
P cites X (M)	*D cites Y (M)*
X is from London (M)	*Y works for Lab Z (M)*
P was published in J (M)	*D was published in K (M)*
J is a refereed journal (I)	*D has date 2007 (I)*

The main advantage of the algorithm is finding intersection matches. Finding intersection matches is equally problematic when using traditional logical querying or Description Logic. Another benefit of the algorithm is that the goal may be composed somewhat superfluously. If these extra clauses cannot be matched against the documents because the semantic descriptions contain no such details, then they will be silently ignored. If there is such information in the semantic descriptions, then the user will get a more accurate answer.

In addition to that, the matching process has exact knowledge about the cause of each match or non-match. During the matching, the clauses labeled as failed in the goal provide an explanation why the document could not be matched. In case of a match, the clauses labeled as ignored may explain the difference or added value of the matched document.

The ability to ignore some clauses may lead to an overhead of matches. This is compensated with the ranking of the result list. The algorithm provides a new possibility to rank matched objects based on the available simple metrics:

- Number of clauses matched in the object
- Number of clauses matched in the goal
- Number of clauses ignored in the object
- Number of clauses ignored in the goal

Based on these metrics various rank orders can be implemented. A higher number of matched clauses in the goal in general mean a more precise fulfillment of user desires. A practical approach for example is to rank matches first by the number of matched clauses in the goal (in descending order), and then by the number of ignored clauses in the document (in ascending order).

3.3 Implementation of the Matching Engine

The matching algorithm was implemented in Prolog, and was tested with SWI-Prolog. The matching engine is written in Java, which initializes the Prolog implementation and feeds the WSML descriptions for ontologies and digital objects into it. Then, for each discovery request only the goal is converted into Prolog and the matching algorithm is run.

The use of WSML is not restricting: the algorithm is also able to work with semantic descriptions in OWL or RDF. The WSML-DL variant is very close to OWL, and a partial mapping from OWL to WSML exists [2]. Furthermore, RDF can be directly converted into Prolog terms by SWI-Prolog.

The matching algorithm has the following costs for each step (where goal has L clauses and the object has M clauses):

- Unification of clauses: at most $L*M$ operations,
- Checking each clause: $L+M$ operations,
- Decision of match or failure: constant number of operations.

So the matching of one goal clause set with one service clause set takes approximately $(L+1)*(M+1)$ operations. If we assume that the number of clauses for a service or goal has an upper limit in the system (an upper limit for L and M), we get the estimation that the order of complexity of the discovery algorithm is linear with respect to the number of services in the system.

For our internal experiments and performance tests we created 25 different book descriptions about food based on basic food ontology. Unfortunately, we did not find any collection of digital objects with semantic descriptions available and suitable for our tests. In order to get more digital objects for the tests, multiple copies were generated from each book description.

The Prolog matcher on a 1.6 GHz P4 desktop PC provided the following response times:

250 objects:	1.82s	(.00728s/object)
1000 objects:	7.47s	(.00747s/object)
4000 objects:	32.94s	(.00823s/object)
8000 objects:	65.63s	(.00820s/object)

The tests therefore verify the linearity of the algorithm. This is naturally worse than the cost of some keyword-based query techniques, but as we saw the expressive power of semantic matching may compensate for the slower response. In general, we believe that the two techniques of querying should be used together.

4 Related Work

In the previous sections, we have shown how the presented semantic matching algorithm works for digital documents. In [14] and [17], we have shown that the same algorithm works for the matchmaking of Semantic Web Services.

While the last years produced several results in the area of Semantic Web Service discovery, these results have not found their ways into the field of digital library systems yet. We would refer to [16] as one of the most influential general papers in this area.

In the field of digital libraries, the thorough application of semantic descriptions and semantic search is infrequent. JeromeDL [15] is one example, which uses Semantic Web technologies. JeromeDL is an open-source digital library system, which applies semantic description of resources and integrates remote semantic metadata such as RDF annotations and FOAF into its database. Based on this architecture, JeromeDL can improve the text-based queries using semantically enabled query expansion and extrapolating user profiles.

The Semantic Content Organization and Retrieval Engine (SCORE) extracts ontology-driven metadata from structured and semi-structured content [21]. The aggregated information goes through the steps of metadata extraction, semantic normalization and semantic association or clustering. By using SCORE it is possible to search for typed entities (e.g. director Redford), and it can automatically collect documents in given topics.

Probabilistic queries, such as probabilistic Datalog, were studied in the IR community. For example, the DOLORES system [7] is able to perform logical queries in databases where the stored documents are described also with uncertain information, characterized with probability values. The result of such queries can be ranked according to their matching probability, which can be similar to the result of our approach. However, processing "overspecified" queries and the possibility of ignoring facts in the matching process is supported more clearly in our approach.

Research on semantic methods in digital libraries so far focused mostly on supporting unified search across collections with different metadata schemas [3,3]. This usually means that text-based query mechanisms are enriched with semantics. Usually, queries are automatically translated to different metadata schemas, or the queries are enhanced with synonyms and other related keyword terms. However, in our suggestion, the query is performed on the semantic level, and therefore the match itself has different meaning.

The advantage of the suggested approach is revealed only when sufficiently sophisticated semantic descriptions of digital objects are available. The lack of semantic test data was a significant difficulty in this research. In order to reach better results with this approach, a sufficient knowledge base is required and several levels of depth in the chains of terms of type "X has property Y". The traditional object descriptions containing facts in the form of "metadata element has value X" may be queried efficiently using OPAC-style keyword search.

5 Conclusion

It was shown in this paper that semantic matching has much to offer in the area of digital libraries. Semantic matching can be applied not only to DL services, but also to digital objects and users. Semantic matching has greater costs than IR techniques, but the examples in the paper demonstrate that it can perform queries that are very hard to implement using text-based information retrieval.

A semantic matching algorithm was introduced in the paper using a novel technique based on Prolog-style unification of terms. This approach has linear cost and it provides possibilities to compare, rank and explain semantic matches (or non-matches). The presented working implementation of a semantic matching engine may accelerate the application of semantic matching techniques in digital library systems.

References

1. Agre, G., Kormushev, P., Dilov, I.: INFRAWEBS Axiom Editor - A Graphical Ontology-Driven Tool for Creating Complex Logical Expressions. International Journal Information Theories and Applications 13(2), 169–178
2. de Bruijn, J., Lausen, H., Krummenacher, H., Polleres, A., Predoiu, L., Kifer, M., Fensel, D.: The Web Service Modeling Language WSML. WSML Deliverable D16.1v0.2, http://www.wsmo.org/TR/d16/d16.1/v0.2/
3. Cinque, L., Malizia, A., Navigli, R.: A Semantic-Based System for Querying Personal Digital Libraries. In: Marinai, S., Dengel, A. (eds.) DAS 2004. LNCS, vol. 3163, pp. 8–10. Springer, Heidelberg (2004)
4. Ding, H., Solvberg, I.T., Lin, Y.: A Vision on Semantic Retrieval in P2P Network. In: 18th International Conference on Advanced Information Networking and Applications (AINA'04), March 29-31 2004, Fukuoka, Japan, vol. 1, p. 177 (2004)
5. Doerr, M., Hunter, J., Lagoze, C.: Towards a Core Ontology for Information Integration. Journal of Digital Information 4(1) (April 2003), http://journals.tdl.org/jodi/article/view/jodi-109/91
6. Feier, C., Domingue, J.: WSMO Primer. WSMO Deliverable D3.1v0.1 (April 2005), http://www.wsmo.org/TR/d3/d3.1/v0.1/
7. Fuhr, N., Gövert, N., Rölleke, Th.: DOLORES: A System for Logic-Based Retrieval of Multimedia Objects. In: Proceedings of the 21st Annual International ACM SIGIR Conference on Research and Development in Information Retrieval, pp. 257–265
8. Fuhr, N., Hansen, P., Mabe, M., Micsik, A., Sølvberg, I.: Digital Libraries: A Generic Classification and Evaluation Scheme. In: Constantopoulos, P., Sølvberg, I.T. (eds.) ECDL 2001. LNCS, vol. 2163, pp. 187–199. Springer, Heidelberg (2001)
9. Haas, H., Brown, A. (eds.): Web Services Glossary. W3C Working Group Note (February 11, 2004), http://www.w3.org/TR/ws-gloss/
10. Heery, R., Johnston, P., Fülöp, Cs., Micsik, A.: Metadata schema registries in the partially Semantic Web: the CORES experience. In: 2003 Dublin Core Conference, DC-2003, September 28 - October 2, 2003, Seattle, Washington USA (2003)
11. Kahan, J., Koivunen, M-R., Prud'Hommeaux, E., Swick, R.R.: Annotea: An Open RDF Infrastructure for Shared Web Annotations. In: Proceedings of the WWW10 International Conference, Hong Kong (May 2001)
12. Keller, U., Lara, R., Polleres, A. (eds.): WSMO Web Service Discovery. WSMO deliverable D5.1 version 0.1 (2004), http://www.wsmo.org/, /d5/d5.1/v0.1/
13. Kovács, L., Micsik, A.: An Ontology-Based Model of Digital Libraries. In: Fox, E.A., Neuhold, E.J., Premsmit, P., Wuwongse, V. (eds.) ICADL 2005. LNCS, vol. 3815, pp. 38–43. Springer, Heidelberg (2005)
14. Kovács, L., Micsik, A., Pallinger, P.: Two-phase Semantic Web Service Discovery Method for Finding Intersection Matches using Logic Programming. In: Workshop on Semantics for Web Services (SemWS'06) in conjunction with ECOWS'06, Zurich, Switzerland (December 4-6, 2006)

15. Kruk, S.R., Decker, S., Zieborak, L.: JeromeDL - Adding Semantic Web Technologies to Digital Libraries. In: Andersen, K.V., Debenham, J., Wagner, R. (eds.) DEXA 2005. LNCS, vol. 3588, pp. 716–725. Springer, Heidelberg (2005)
16. Li, L., Horrocks, I.: A software framework for matchmaking based on semantic web technology. In: Proceedings of the 12th International Conference on the World Wide Web, Budapest, Hungary (May 2003)
17. Micsik, A., Kovács, L., Tóth, Z., Pallinger, P., Scicluna, J.: INFRAWEBS Deliverable D6.2.2 – Specification & Realisation of the Discovery Component, Available at http://www.infrawebs.eu
18. Nern, H.J.: INFRAWEBS - Open development platform for web service applications. In: FRCSS 2006, 1st International EASST-EU Workshop on Future Research Challenges for Software and Services, Vienna, Austria (2006)
19. Nern, H.J., Atanasova, T., Agre, G., Micsik, A., Kovacs, L., Saarela, J.: Semantic Web Service Development on the Base of Knowledge Management Layer - INFRAWEBS Approach. In: i.TECH, Third International Conference Information Research, Applications and Education, Varna, Bulgaria (June 27-30, 2005) ISBN 954-16-0034-4, 217-223
20. Preist, C.: A conceptual architecture for semantic web services. In: McIlraith, S.A., Plexousakis, D., van Harmelen, F. (eds.) ISWC 2004. LNCS, vol. 3298, Springer, Heidelberg (2004)
21. Sheth, A., Bertram, C., Avant, D., Hammond, B., Kochut, K., Warke, Y.: Managing semantic content for the Web. IEEE Internet Computing 6(4), 80–87

Towards a Unified Approach Based on Affinity Graph to Various Multi-document Summarizations

Xiaojun Wan and Jianguo Xiao

Institute of Computer Science and Technology,
Peking University, Beijing 100871, China
{wanxiaojun, xiaojianguo}@icst.pku.edu.cn

Abstract. This paper proposes a unified extractive approach based on affinity graph to both generic and topic-focused multi-document summarizations. By using an asymmetric similarity measure, the relationships between sentences are reflected in a directed affinity graph for generic summarization. For topic-focused summarization, the topic information is incorporated into the affinity graph using a topic-sensitive affinity measure. Based on the affinity graph, the information richness of sentences is computed by the graph-ranking algorithm on differentiated intra-document links and inter-document links between sentences. Lastly, the greedy algorithm is employed to impose diversity penalty on sentences and the sentences with both high information richness and high information novelty are chosen into the summary. Experimental results on the tasks of DUC 2002-2005 demonstrate the excellent performances of the proposed approaches to both generic and topic-focused multi-document summarization tasks.

1 Introduction

Generic multi-document summarization aims to produce a summary delivering the majority of information content from a set of documents about an explicit or implicit main topic. Given a specified topic description (i.e. user profile, user query), topic-focused multi-document summarization aims to create from the documents a summary which either answers the information need expressed in the topic or explains the topic. Generic multi-document summary can be used to concisely describe the information contained in a cluster of documents and facilitate the users to understand the document cluster (e.g. Google News and NewsBlaster). Topic-focused summary can be used to provide personalized services for users after the user profiles are created manually or automatically. In the communities of natural language processing and information retrieval, a series of workshops and conferences on automatic text summarization (e.g. NTCIR, DUC), special topic sessions in ACL, COLING, and SIGIR have advanced the summarization techniques and produced a couple of experimental online systems.

A particular challenge for multi-document summarization is that a document set might contain much information unrelated to the main topic, and hence we need effective summarization methods to analyze the information stored in different

L. Kovács, N. Fuhr, and C. Meghini (Eds.): ECDL 2007, LNCS 4675, pp. 297–308, 2007.

documents and extract the globally important information to reflect the main topic. Another challenge for multi-document summarization is that the information stored in different documents inevitably overlaps with each other, and hence we need effective summarization methods to merge information stored in different documents, and if possible, contrast their differences. In one word, a good summary is expected to preserve the globally important information in the documents as much as possible, and at the same time keep the information as novel as possible. For topic-focused multi-document summarization, a particular challenge is that the information in the summary needs to be both globally important over the document set and biased to the given topic.

The graph-ranking based methods [5, 15, 16] have recently been proposed for multi-document summarization based on sentence relationships. All these methods make use of the relationships between sentences and select sentences according to the "votes" or "recommendations" from their neighboring sentences, which is similar to PageRank [2] and HITS [12]. In this study, we propose a unified extractive approach based on affinity graph to both generic and topic-focused multi-document summarizations by extending previous graph-ranking algorithms by 1) using asymmetric similarity measures to build directed affinity graphs in order to further measure the significance of the similarity between each sentence pair; 2) incorporating the topic information in the affinity graph for topic-focused multi-document summarization in order to extract both generic and topic-focused summaries in a unified way; 3) differentiating the intra-document links and inter-document links between sentences in the graph-ranking algorithm in order to attach more importance to inter-document links; 4) integrating the diversity penalty process based on the affinity graph in order to remove redundancy.

Intensive experiments have been performed on the tasks of DUC 2002-2005 and the results show that the proposed approach can much outperform the top performing systems and the baseline systems for both generic and topic-focused multi-document summarizations.

The rest of this paper is organized as follows: Section 2 briefly introduces the related works about extractive multi-document summarization. The unified approach based on affinity graph is proposed in Section 3. In Section 4, we describe the experiments and results on DUC tasks. Lastly we conclude this paper in Section 5.

2 Related Works

A variety of multi-document summarization methods have been developed recently. Generally speaking, those methods can be either extractive summarization or abstractive summarization. Extractive summarization is a simple but robust method for text summarization and it involves assigning salience scores to some units (e.g. sentences, paragraphs) of the documents and extracting those with highest scores, while abstractive summarization (e.g. NewsBlaster) usually needs information fusion, sentence compression and reformulation. In this study, we focus on extractive summarization.

The centroid-based method [19] is one of the most popular extractive summarization methods. MEAD [18] is an implementation of the centroid-based method that scores sentences based on sentence-level and inter-sentence features, including cluster centroids, position, TF*IDF, etc. NeATS [14] uses sentence position, term frequency, topic signature and term clustering to select important content, and use MMR [9] to remove redundancy. XDoX [11] is a cross document summarizer designed specifically to summarize large document sets by identifying the most salient themes within the set by passage clustering and then composes an extraction summary, which reflects these main themes. The passages are clustered based on n-gram matching. Much other work also explores to find topic themes in the documents for summarization, e.g. Harabagiu and Lacatusu [10] investigate five different topic representations and introduce a novel representation of topics based on topic themes.

Most recently, the graph-ranking based methods have been proposed to rank sentences or passages based on the "votes" or "recommendations" between each other. Websumm [15] uses a graph-connectivity model and operates under the assumption that nodes which are connected to many other nodes are likely to carry salient information. LexPageRank [5] is an approach for computing sentence importance based on the concept of eigenvector centrality. It constructs a sentence connectivity matrix and computes sentence importance based on an algorithm similar to PageRank. Mihalcea and Tarau [16] also propose a similar algorithm based on PageRank and HITS to compute sentence importance for single document summarization, and for multi-document summarization, they use a meta-summarization process to summarize the meta-document produced by assembling all the single summary of each document. Our work in this study extends the above graph-ranking methods from four aspects as mentioned in Section 1 and the unified approach can be applied to both generic and topic-focused multi-document summarizations. More related works can be found on DUC 2002 and DUC 2004 publications.

Most methods for topic-focused document summarization incorporate the information of the given topic or query into generic summarizers and extracts sentences suiting the user's information need. In [20], a simple query-based scorer by computing the similarity value between each sentence and the query is incorporated into a generic summarizer to produce the query-based summary. The query words and named entities in the topic description are investigated in [8] and CLASSY [3] for event-focused/query-based multi-document summarization. CATS [6] is a topic-oriented multi-document summarizer which first performs a thematic analysis of the documents, and then matches these themes with the ones identified in the topic. BAYESUM [4] is proposed to extract sentences by comparing query models against sentence models the language modeling for IR framework. More related work can be found on DUC 2003 and DUC 2005 publications. To the best of our knowledge, there are few works on using the graph-ranking based methods for topic-focused multi-document summarization.

3 The Unified Summarization Approach

The unified summarization approach consists of the following three steps: (1) A directed affinity graph is built to reflect the relationships between the sentences in the document set to be summarized. For topic-focused summarization, the edges (links) in the graph are topic-sensitive (i.e. topic-oriented, topic-based); (2) The information richness of each sentence is computed based on the affinity graph; (3) Based on the affinity graph and the information richness scores, the diversity penalty is imposed on each sentence and the affinity rank score of each sentence is obtained to reflect both the information richness and the information novelty of the sentence. The sentences with high affinity rank scores are chosen into the summary. The aim of the proposed approach is to include the sentences with both high information richness and high information novelty in the summary, and the included sentences need to be relevant to or biased towards the given topic for topic-focused summarization.

3.1 Affinity Graph Building

In the proposed approach, the affinity graphs for generic and topic-focused multi-document summarizations need to be built using different similarity measures in order to make use of different information, which are presented respectively as follows.

3.1.1 Generic Affinity Graph Building

Given a sentence collection $S=\{s_i \mid 1\leq i\leq n\}$, according to the vector space model, each sentence s_i can be represented by an vector $\vec{s}_i$ containing a number of terms with associated weights. The weight associated with term t is calculated with the tf_t*isf_t formula, where tf_t is the frequency of term t in sentence s_i and isf_t is the inverse sentence frequency of term t, i.e. $1+\log(N/n_t)$, where N is the total number of the sentences in a background corpus and n_t is the number of the sentences containing term t. Then the affinity weight between a sentence pair of s_i and s_j can be calculated using the following affinity measure:

$$aff(s_i,s_j)=\frac{\vec{s}_i \cdot \vec{s}_j}{\left\|\vec{s}_i\right\|} \tag{1}$$

Note that the above affinity measure is asymmetric and usually we have $aff(s_i, s_j)\neq aff(s_j,s_i)$. We adopt this measure instead of the standard Cosine measure [1] in order to further measure the significance of the similarity between each sentence pair by taking into account the length normalization of each sentence separately, as in [22].

If sentences are considered as nodes, the sentence collection can be modeled as a directed graph by generating a link between two sentences if the corresponding affinity weight exceeds 0, i.e. a directed link from s_i to s_j ($i\neq j$) is created if $aff(s_i,s_j)>0$; otherwise no link is constructed.

Thus, we construct a directed graph G reflecting the affinity relationship between the sentences according to their affinity values. The graph is called as *Affinity Graph*, and because it is built for generic summarization, we call it as *Generic Affinity Graph*.

3.1.2 Topic-Focused Affinity Graph Building

The main difference between topic-focused summarization and generic summarization lies in that topic-focused summarization is tailored to suit the user's information need in a specified topic, so we adopt a topic-sensitive affinity measure to exhibit the inherent similarity dictated by the given topic itself for topic-focused summarization. The topic-sensitive affinity measure biases inter-sentence relationships towards pairs of sentences that jointly possess attributes (i.e. terms) that are expressed in the given topic. In this way, the topic description is considered to be salient features that define the context under which the affinity of any two sentences is judged. Similar to [21], the topic-sensitive affinity measure is given as follows:

$$aff(s_i, s_j | q) = \vartheta_1 \frac{\vec{s}_i \cdot \vec{s}_j}{\|\vec{s}_i\|} + \vartheta_2 \frac{\vec{c}_{ij} \cdot \vec{q}}{\|\vec{q}\|} \tag{2}$$

where q is the given topic. $\vec{c}_{ij} = \vec{s}_i \cap \vec{s}_j$ is a vector which contains the common terms of the sentences s_i and s_j. The weight of each term t in $\vec{c}_{ij}$ is the average value of the associated weights of t in $\vec{s}_i$ and $\vec{s}_j$. The above affinity measure is a linear combination of two sources: the original sentence affinity and the topic-biased affinity. θ_1 and θ_2 are parameters specifying different weights to the two sources and we haveθ_1+θ_2=1.

In addition to the linear combination, we can also use a product combination of the two sources as follows:

$$aff(s_i, s_j | q) = \left(\frac{\vec{s}_i \cdot \vec{s}_j}{\|\vec{s}_i\|} \right)^p \cdot \left(\frac{\vec{c}_{ij} \cdot \vec{q}}{\|\vec{q}\|} \right)^{\frac{1}{p}} \tag{3}$$

where p>0 is a parameter specifying different weights to the two sources in the left hand of the equation.

With the above topic-sensitive affinity measures, the affinity graph can be constructed in the same way as the generic affinity graph building. The affinity graph built for topic-focused summarization is called as *Topic-Focused Affinity graph*. The two topic-sensitive affinity measures will be investigated in the experiments.

3.2 Information Richness Computation

The computation of the information richness of sentences is based on the following three intuitions: 1) The more neighbors a sentence has, the more informative it is; 2) The more informative a sentence's neighbors are, the more informative it is; 3) The more heavily a sentence is linked to by other informative sentences, the more informative it is. Based on the above intuitions, we apply the graph-ranking algorithm to compute the information richness for each node in the affinity graph. The proposed algorithm is similar to PageRank [2]. First, we use an affinity matrix **M** to describe the affinity graph with each entry corresponding to the weight of an edge in the graph. **M** = $(M_{i,j})_{n\times n}$ is defined as follows:

$$M_{i,j} = \begin{cases} aff(s_i, s_j), & if\ i \neq j \\ 0 & , otherwise \end{cases} \tag{4}$$

Note that $M_{i,j} \neq M_{j,i}$. Then **M** is normalized as follows to make the sum of each row equal to 1:

$$\widetilde{M}_{i,j} = \begin{cases} M_{i,j} \Big/ \sum_{j=1}^{n} M_{i,j}\ , & if\ \sum_{j=1}^{n} M_{i,j} \neq 0 \\ 0 & , otherwise \end{cases} \tag{5}$$

Based on the normalized affinity matrix $\tilde{\mathbf{M}} = (\tilde{M}_{i,j})_{n\times n}$, the information richness score *InfoRich(s$_i$)* for sentence s_i can be deduced from those of all other nodes linked to it and it can be formulated in a recursive form as follows:

$$InfoRich(s_i) = d \cdot \sum_{all\ j\neq i} InfoRich(s_j) \cdot \tilde{M}_{j,i} + \frac{(1-d)}{n} \tag{6}$$

And the matrix form is:

$$\vec{\boldsymbol{\lambda}} = d\tilde{\mathbf{M}}^{\mathrm{T}}\vec{\boldsymbol{\lambda}} + \frac{(1-d)}{n}\vec{\mathbf{e}} \tag{7}$$

where $\vec{\boldsymbol{\lambda}} = [InfoRich(s_i)]_{n\times 1}$ is the vector containing the information richness of all the sentences. $\vec{\mathbf{e}}$ is a unit vector with all elements equaling to 1. d is the damping factor set to 0.85.

In the context of multi-document summarization, the links in the affinity graph can be classified into the following two categories: intra-document link and inter-document link. Given a link from sentence s_i to sentence s_j, if s_i and s_j come from the same document, the link is an intra-document link; if s_i and s_j come from different documents, the link is an inter-document link. We believe that the intra-document links and the inter-document links have unequal contributions for the computation of the information richness. In order to investigate this intuition, different weights are specified to the two kinds of links respectively. The recursive computation form is then as follows:

$$InfoRich(s_i) = d \cdot \sum_{\substack{all\ j\neq i \\ doc(j)=doc(i)}} \alpha \cdot InfoRich(s_j) \cdot \tilde{M}_{j,i} + d \cdot \sum_{\substack{all\ j\neq i \\ doc(j)\neq doc(i)}} \beta \cdot InfoRich(s_j) \cdot \tilde{M}_{j,i} + \frac{(1-d)}{n} \tag{8}$$

where α, β are parameters for specifying different contribution weights to the intra-document links and the inter-document links, respectively. In the experiments, we let $0\leq\alpha, \beta\leq 1$. In Equation (8), *doc*(*j*)=*doc*(*i*) means that the link from s_j to s_i is an intra-document link and *doc*(*j*)≠*doc*(*i*) means that the link from s_j to s_i is an inter-document link.

And the matrix form is:

$$\vec{\boldsymbol{\lambda}} = d(\alpha\tilde{\mathbf{M}}_{\text{intra}}{}^{\mathrm{T}}\vec{\boldsymbol{\lambda}} + \beta\tilde{\mathbf{M}}_{\text{inter}}{}^{T}\vec{\boldsymbol{\lambda}}) + \frac{(1-d)}{n}\vec{\mathbf{e}} \tag{9}$$

where $\tilde{\mathbf{M}}_{\text{intra}}$ is the affinity matrix containing only the intra-document links (the entries of inter-document links are set to 0) and $\tilde{\mathbf{M}}_{\text{inter}}$ is the affinity matrix containing only the inter-document links (the entries of intra-document links are set to 0). Note that if α=β=1, Equations (8) and (9) reduce to Equations (6) and (7).

3.3 Diversity Penalty Imposition

Based on the affinity graph and the information richness scores, the greedy algorithm is applied to impose the diversity penalty and compute the final affinity rank scores of the sentences. The algorithm goes as follows [22]:

1. Initialize two sets $A=\phi$, $B=\{s_i \mid i=1,2,\ldots,n\}$, and each sentence's affinity rank score is initialized to its information richness score, i.e. $ARScore(s_i) = InfoRich(s_i)$, $i=1,2,\ldots n$.
2. Sort the sentences in B by their current affinity rank scores in descending order.
3. Suppose s_i is the highest ranked sentence, i.e. the first sentence in the ranked list. Move the sentence s_i from B to A, and then the diversity penalty is imposed on the affinity rank score of each sentence linked with s_i as follows:

   For each sentence s_j in B, $j \neq i$

   $ARScore(s_j) = ARScore(s_j) - \omega \cdot \tilde{M}_{j,i} \cdot InfoRich(s_i)$

   Where $\omega>0$ is the penalty degree factor. The larger ω is, the greater penalty is imposed on the affinity rank score. If $\omega=0$, no diversity penalty is imposed at all.
4. Go to step 2 and iterate until $B=\phi$ or the iteration count reaches a predefined maximum number.

In the above algorithm, the third step is the crucial step and its basic idea is to decrease the affinity rank score of less informative sentences by the part conveyed from the most informative one. After the affinity rank scores are obtained for all the sentences, several sentences with highest affinity rank scores are chosen to produce the summary according to the summary length limit.

In contrast to the MMR [9] for removing redundancy, the above algorithm is based on the affinity graph and can be seamlessly and conveniently integrated in the proposed approach.

4 Experiments and Results

4.1 Experimental Setup

Generic multi-document summarization has been evaluated on task 2 of DUC 2001, task 2 of DUC 2002 and task 2 of DUC 2004, and topic-focused multi-document summarization has been evaluated on tasks 2 and 3 of DUC 2003 and the only task of DUC 2005. We use task 2 of DUC 2001 and task 2 of DUC 2003 for training and parameter tuning, and use other DUC tasks for test. Note that the topic representations of the three topic-focused summarization tasks are different: task 2 of DUC 2003 is to produce summaries focused by *events*; task 3 of DUC 2003 is to produce summaries focused by *viewpoints*; the task of DUC 2005 is to produce summaries focused by *DUC Topics*. Table 1 gives a short summary of the test sets.

As a preprocessing step, the dialog sentences (sentences in quotation marks) have been removed. In the process of affinity graph building, the stop words are removed and Porter's stemmer [17] is used for word stemming.

Table 1. Summary of data sets

	Generic summarization		Topic-focused summarization	
	DUC 2002	**DUC 2004**	**DUC 2003**	**DUC 2005**
Task	Task 2	Task 2	Task 3	the only task
Number of clusters	60	50	30	50
Data source	TREC-9	TDT-2	TREC	TREC
Summary length	100 words	665 bytes	100 words	250 words

We use the ROUGE [13] toolkit 1.4.2 (http://haydn.isi.edu/ROUGE/) for evaluation, which has been widely adopted by DUC for automatic summarization evaluation. It measures summary quality by counting overlapping units such as the n-gram, word sequences and word pairs between the candidate summary and the reference summary.

ROUGE toolkit reports separate scores for 1, 2, 3 and 4-gram, and also for longest common subsequence co-occurrences. Among these different scores, unigram-based ROUGE score (ROUGE-1) has been shown to agree with human judgment most [13]. We show three of the ROUGE metrics in the experimental results: ROUGE-1 (unigram-based), ROUGE-2 (bigram-based), and ROUGE-W (based on weighted longest common subsequence, weight=1.2). Note that we mainly show the ROUGE-1 results due to page limit.

In order to truncate summaries longer than length limit, we use the "-l" or "-b" option in ROUGE toolkit and we also use the "-m" option for word stemming.

4.2 Experimental Results

4.2.1 Generic Multi-document Summarization

The systems based on the proposed approach are compared with top three performing systems and two baseline systems on task 2 of DUC 2002 and task 2 of DUC 2004 respectively. The top three systems are the performing systems with highest ROUGE scores, shown in the tables as S26, S19, etc. The *lead baseline* and the *coverage baseline* are two baselines employed in the multi-document summarization tasks of DUC. Tables 2 and 3 show the system comparison results on the two tasks respectively. The *AffinityRank* is based on the proposed approach using the affinity measure in Equation (1). Instead of the asymmetric affinity measure in Equation (1), the *SimRank* uses the standard Cosine measure to build an undirected affinity graph. The performances of the *AffinityRank* and the *SimRank* in the tables are achieved when the parameters are set as follows: ω=10, α=0.3 and β=1.

Seen from Tables 2 and 3, the proposed systems, including the *AffinityRank* and the *SimRank*, outperform the top performing systems and the baseline systems on both tasks over ROUGE-1 and ROUGE-W[1]. The *AffinityRank* outperforms the *SimRank* on task 2 of DUC 2002 and has a trivially different performance with the *SimRank* on task 2 of DUC 2004. These observations demonstrate that the proposed summarization approach is robust for both the asymmetric affinity measure and the symmetric

Table 2. System comparison on Task 2 of DUC 2002

System	ROUGE-1	ROUGE-2	ROUGE-W
AffinityRank	**0.38111**	0.08163	**0.12292**
SimRank	0.37721	**0.08183**	0.12250
S26	0.35151	0.07642	0.11448
S19	0.34504	0.07936	0.11332
S28	0.34355	0.07521	0.10956
Coverage	0.32894	0.07148	0.10847
Lead	0.28684	0.05283	0.09525

Table 3. System comparison on Task 2 of DUC 2004

System	ROUGE-1	ROUGE-2	ROUGE-W
SimRank	**0.40026**	0.09080	**0.12303**
AffinityRank	0.39926	0.08793	0.12228
S65	0.38232	**0.09219**	0.11528
S104	0.37436	0.08544	0.11305
S35	0.37427	0.08364	0.11561
Coverage	0.34882	0.07189	0.10622
Lead	0.32420	0.06409	0.09905

[1] The flag indicates that the difference is significant at the 95% confidence level.

Cosine measure. We report only the detailed experimental results of the *AffnityRank* in this section and similar trends and conclusions for the *SimRank* have been obtained in our study.

The parameters of the proposed *AffinityRank* are investigated and the results on the tasks of DUC 2002 and DUC 2004 are shown in Figures 1 and 2.

Figure 1 demonstrates the influence of the penalty factor ω when α=0.3 and β=1. ω varies from 0 to 20. We can see that on both tasks the performances are the worst when no diversity penalty is imposed (i.e. ω=0).

Figure 2 demonstrates the influence of the intra-document and inter-document link differentiation weights α and β when ω=10. α and β range from 0 to 1 and α: β denotes the real values α and β are set to. It is observed that when more importance is attached to the intra-document links (i.e. α=1 and β<0.7), the performances decrease sharply on both tasks. It is the worst case when the inter-document links are not taken into account (i.e. α: β=1:0), while the performances are still very well when the intra-document links are not taken into account (i.e. α: β=0:1). This demonstrates that the inter-document links are much more important than the intra-document links for sentence "recommendation" in the graph-ranking algorithm.

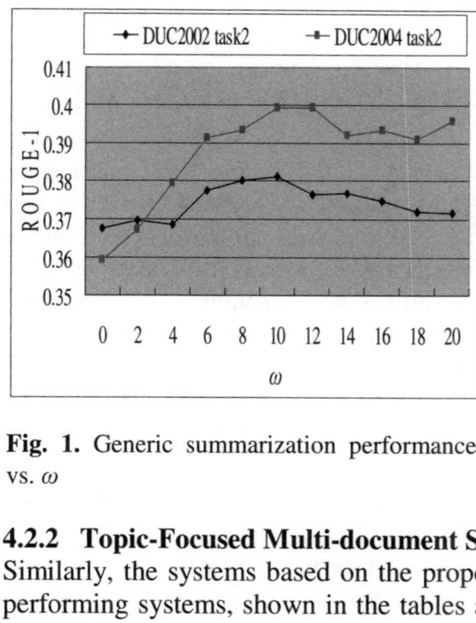

Fig. 1. Generic summarization performance vs. ω

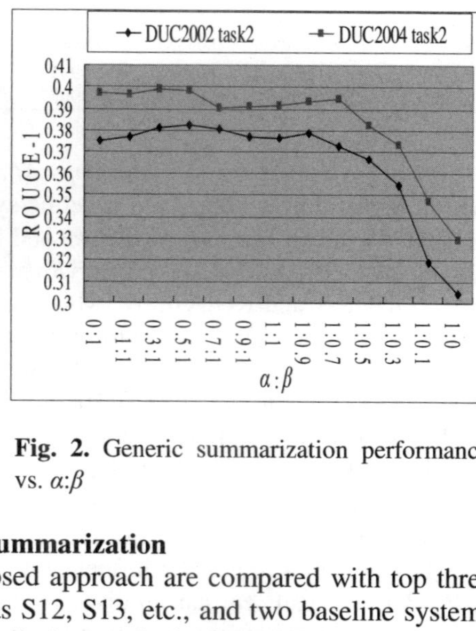

Fig. 2. Generic summarization performance vs. α:β

4.2.2 Topic-Focused Multi-document Summarization

Similarly, the systems based on the proposed approach are compared with top three performing systems, shown in the tables as S12, S13, etc., and two baseline systems (i.e. the lead baseline and the coverage baseline) on tasks 3 of DUC 2003 and the only task of DUC 2005 respectively. Tables 4 and 5 show the comparison results on the two tasks respectively. The *TopicAffinityRank1* is based on the proposed approach using the linear form of the topic-sensitive affinity measure in Equation (2); the *TopicAffinityRank2* uses the product form of the topic-sensitive affinity measure in Equation (3), and the *TopicSimRank1* and *TopicSimRank2* use the following symmetric topic-sensitive measures based on the Cosine metric respectively:

$$aff'(s_i,s_j|q)=\vartheta_1 \frac{\vec{s}_i \cdot \vec{s}_j}{\|\vec{s}_i\| \cdot \|\vec{s}_j\|}+\vartheta_2 \frac{\vec{c}_{ij} \cdot \vec{q}}{\|\vec{c}_{ij}\| \cdot \|\vec{q}\|} \tag{10}$$

$$aff'(s_i, s_j | q) = \left(\frac{\vec{s}_i \cdot \vec{s}_j}{\|\vec{s}_i\| \cdot \|\vec{s}_j\|} \right)^p \cdot \left(\frac{\vec{c}_{ij} \cdot \vec{q}}{\|\vec{c}_{ij}\| \cdot \|\vec{q}\|} \right)^{\frac{1}{p}} \tag{11}$$

The performances of the proposed systems are achieved when the parameters are set as follows: ω=10, α=0.3 and β=1, θ_1=0.75, θ_2=0.25 (i.e. θ_1: θ_2 =3:1) and p=1.

Table 4. System comparison on Task 3 of DUC 2003

System	ROUGE-1	ROUGE-2	ROUGE-W
TopicAffinityRank1	**0.36187**	0.07114	**0.11464**
TopicSimRank1	0.36011	0.07141	0.11311
TopicAffinityRank2	0.35311	0.06897	0.11282
TopicSimRank2	0.35282	0.06885	0.11482
S16	0.35001	**0.07305**	0.10969
S13	0.31986	0.05831	0.10016
S17	0.31809	0.04981	0.09887
Coverage	0.30290	0.05968	0.09678
Lead	0.28200	0.04468	0.09077

Table 5. System comparison on the task of DUC 2005

System	ROUGE-1	ROUGE-2	ROUGE-W
TopicAffinityRank1	**0.38354**	0.07069	**0.10080**
TopicSimRank1	0.38101	0.07103	0.09884
S4	0.37396	0.06842	0.09867
S15	0.37383	**0.07244**	0.09842
S17	0.36901	0.07165	0.09751
TopicAffinityRank2	0.36284	0.06082	0.09547
TopicSimRank2	0.35329	0.05576	0.09466
Coverage	0.34568	0.05915	0.09103
Lead	0.30470	0.04764	0.08084

Seen from Tables 4 and 5, the *TopicAffinityRank1* and *TopicSimRank1* outperform the top performing systems and baseline systems on both tasks over ROUGE-1* and ROUGE-W*. The *TopicAffinityRank2* and *TopicSimRank2* do not perform well on the task of DUC 2005. The *TopicAffiniyRank1* performs better than the *TopicSimRank1* over ROUGE-1 and ROUGE-W, which demonstrates the advantage of the asymmetric topic-sensitive affinity measure in Equation (2) over the symmetric topic-sensitive measure in Equation (10). We can also see that the linear forms of the topic-sensitive measures in Equations (2) and (10) always perform better than the corresponding product forms in Equations (3) and (11). In next section, we report only the detailed experimental results of the *TopicAffinityRank1*.

The penalty factor ω, the link differentiation weights α and β of the *TopicAffinityRank1* are investigated and the results are shown in Figures 3-4 respectively.

Figure 3 demonstrates the influence of the penalty factor ω when α=0.3 and β=1, θ_1:θ_2 =3:1. We can see that no diversity penalty and too much diversity penalty will both deteriorate the summarization performances.

Figure 4 demonstrates the influence of the intra-document and inter-document link differentiation weights α and β when ω=10 and θ_1:θ_2 =3:1. It is also observed that when more importance is attached to the intra-document links (i.e. α=1 and β<0.7), the performances decrease sharply on all the three tasks. It is the worst case when the inter-document links are not taken into account (i.e. α: β=1:0), however, when the intra-document links are not taken into account (i.e. α: β=0:1), the performances are still very well, which also demonstrates that the inter-document links are much more important than the intra-document links for topic-focused summarization.

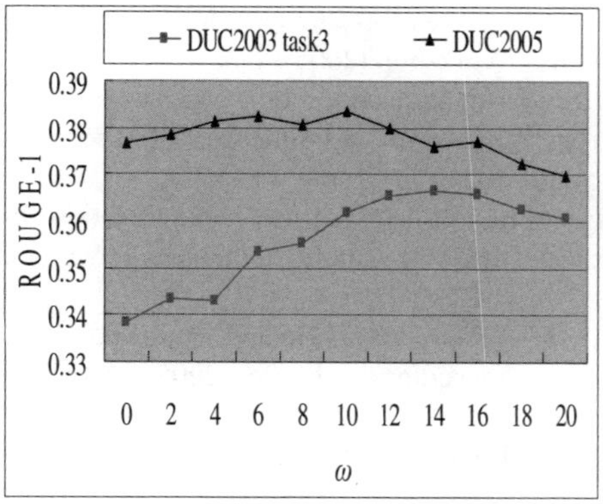

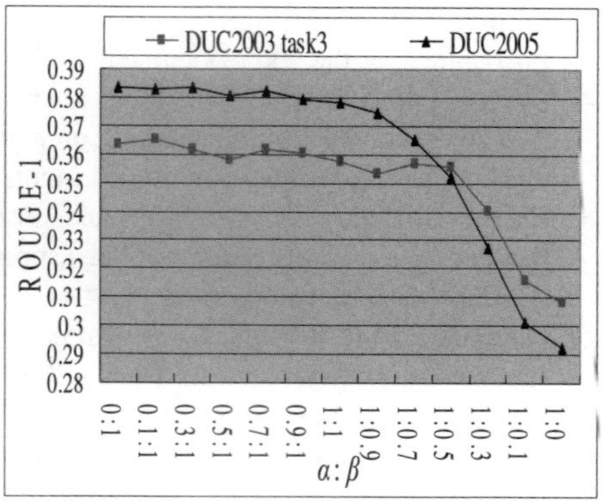

Fig. 3. Topic-focused summarization performance vs. ω

Fig. 4. Topic-focused summarization performance vs. α:β

The experimental results demonstrate the great importance of the inter-document links between sentences for both generic and topic-focused multi-document summarizations. We explain the results with the essence of multi-document summarization. The aim of multi-document summarization is to extract important information form the whole document set, in other words, the information in the summary should be globally important on the whole document set. So the information contained in a globally informative sentence will be also expressed in the sentences of other documents and the votes or recommendations of neighbors nodes in other documents are more important than the votes or recommendations of neighbors in the same document.

5 Conclusion and Future Work

In this paper we propose a unified approach based on affinity graph for both generic and topic-focused multi-document summarizations. The idea is to extract the sentences with both high information richness and information novelty based on affinity graph. Experimental results on DUC tasks demonstrate the excellent performances of the proposed approach.

In future work, we will incorporate the semantic relationship between words into the affinity graph to better reflect the true semantics between sentences. In current approaches, words are assumed to be independent with each other, however, different words have weak or strong semantic relationships with each other, as shown in WordNet [7]. We believe that the appropriate incorporation of the semantic relationships between words into the affinity graph will benefit the summarization tasks.

References

1. Baeza-Yates, R., Ribeiro-Neto, B.: Modern Information Retrival. ACM Press and Addison Wesley (1999)
2. Brin, S., Page, L.: The anatomy of a large-scale hypertextual Web search engine. Computer Networks and ISDN Systems 30, 1–7 (1984)

3. Conroy, J.M., Schlesinger, J.D.: CLASSY query-based multi-document summarization. In: Proceedings of the 2005 Document Understanding Workshop (2005)
4. Daumé., H., Marcu, D.: Bayesian query-focused summarization. In: Proceedings of the 21st International Conference on Computational Linguistics and 44th Annual Meeting of the Association for Computational Linguistics, pp. 305–312 (2006)
5. Erkan, G., Radev, D.: LexPageRank: prestige in multi-document text summarization. In: Proceedings of the Conference on Empirical Methods in Natural Language Processing (EMNLP'04), Barcelona, Spain (2004)
6. Farzindar, A., Rozon, F., Lapalme, G.: CATS a topic-oriented multi-document summarization system at DUC 2005. In: Proceedings of the 2005 Document Understanding Workshop (2005)
7. Fellbaum, C.: WordNet: An Electronic Lexical Database. The MIT Press, Cambridge (1998)
8. Ge, J., Huang, X., Wu, L.: Approaches to event-focused summarization based on named entities and query words. In: Proceedings of the 2003 Document Understanding Workshop (2003)
9. Goldstein, J., Kantrowitz, M., Mittal, V., Carbonell, J.: Summarizing Text Documents: Sentence Selection and Evaluation Metrics. In: Proceedings of ACM SIGIR-99, Berkeley, CA, pp. 121–128 (1999)
10. Harabagiu, S., Lacatusu, F.: Topic themes for multi-document summarization. In: Proceedings of SIGIR'05, Salvador, Brazil, pp. 202–209 (2005)
11. Hardy, H., Shimizu, N., Strzalkowski, T., Ting, L., Wise, G.B., Zhang, X.: Cross-document summarization by concept classification. In: Proceedings of SIGIR'02, Tampere, Finland (2002)
12. Kleinberg, J.M.: Authoritative sources in a hyperlinked environment. Journal of the ACM 46(5), 604–632 (1999)
13. Lin, C.-Y., Hovy, E.H.: Automatic Evaluation of Summaries Using N-gram Co-occurrence Statistics. In: Proceedings of 2003 Language Technology Conference (HLT-NAACL 2003), Edmonton, Canada (2003)
14. Lin, C.-Y., Hovy, E.H.: From Single to Multi-document Summarization: A Prototype System and its Evaluation. In: Proceedings of ACL-02, Philadelphia, PA, U.S.A. (July 7-12, 2002)
15. Mani, I., Bloedorn, E.: Summarizing Similarities and Differences Among Related Documents. Information Retrieval 1(1) (2000)
16. Mihalcea, R., Tarau, P.: A language independent algorithm for single and multiple document summarization. In: Dale, R., Wong, K.-F., Su, J., Kwong, O.Y. (eds.) IJCNLP 2005. LNCS (LNAI), vol. 3651, pp. 19–24. Springer, Heidelberg (2005)
17. Porter, M.F.: An algorithm for suffix stripping. Program 14(3), 130–137 (1980)
18. Radev, D., Allison, T., Blair-Goldensohn, S., Blitzer, J., et al.: The Mead multi-document summarizer (2003), http://www.summarization.com/mead/
19. Radev, D.R., Jing, H.Y., Stys, M., Tam, D.: Centroid-based summarization of multiple documents. Information Processing and Management 40, 919–938 (2004)
20. Saggion, H., Bontcheva, K., Cunningham, H.: Robust generic and query-based summarization. In: Proceedings of EACL-2003 (2003)
21. Tombros, A., van Rijsbergen, C.J.: Query-sensitive similarity measures for information retrieval. Knowledge and Information Systems 6(5), 617–642 (2004)
22. Zhang, B., Li, H., Liu, Y., Ji, L., Xi, W., Fan, W., Chen, Z., Ma, W.-Y.: Improving web search results using affinity graph. In: Proceedings of SIGIR'05, Salvador, Brazil (2005)

Large-Scale Clustering and Complete Facet and Tag Calculation

Bolette Ammitzbøll Madsen

The Digital Resources and Web Group,
The State and University Library of Denmark
bam@statsbiblioteket.dk
http://www.statsbiblioteket.dk

Abstract. The State and University Library of Denmark is developing an integrated search system called Summa, and as part of the Summa project a clustering module and a facet module. Simple clusters have been created for a collection of more than six and a half million library metadata records using a linear clustering algorithm. The created clusters are used to enrich the metadata records, and search results are presented to the user using a faceted browsing interface alongside a ranked result list. The most frequent tags in the different facets in the search result can be calculated and presented at a rate of approximately three million records per second per machine.

Keywords: Library Metadata, Large Data Sets, Clustering, Categorisation, Faceted Browsing.

1 Introduction

The State and University Library of Denmark is currently developing an integrated search system called Summa [9]. The Summa system simultaneously searches across metadata records from a number of different library databases and other relevant data sources. Integrating a number of different data sources into one index inevitably leads to a larger set of data and to larger search results. Larger as well as more heterogeneous search results suggest increased focus on a clear and well-arranged presentation of the results, which also means increased focus on good ranking and on some kind of similarity grouping. The ranking is an important part of the Summa search module, and similarity grouping is handled by the two modules described in this paper.

Similarity grouping is usually a choice between classifications and clustering. Given the heterogeneous data in the Summa index, we have chosen to use both. We have records which contain different classifications and records which contain abstracts or descriptions but no classifications. We have chosen to create (non-exclusive) clusters both to introduce groups to the items without classifications and to introduce groups across the data from different sources. We have chosen to use faceted browsing [3] to utilise all the groups in the data and present them in a well-arranged manner. When presenting a search result, we present a number

L. Kovács, N. Fuhr, and C. Meghini (Eds.): ECDL 2007, LNCS 4675, pp. 309–320, 2007.

of chosen facets including *authors*, *material types*, a number of classifications and the created clusters. In each facet the tags, such as *Orhan Pamuk* or *Sound on DVD*, occurring most frequently in the search result are presented as links to limiting the search to this group.

The *cluster module* is responsible for creating clusters offline, and the created clusters are used to enrich the index. The module currently offers three clustering or grouping methods, which are all linear, but only the simple categorisation method scales to the size of the current index.[1] The simple method takes descriptive words from existing classifications and for each word joins records containing this word in large clusters. The simple method can create clusters and enrich the index in approximately four hours on an office pc for an index of six and a half million library metadata records.

The *facet module* handles calculation of the present tags in all the different facets in a search result. This module is the necessary source for providing a faceted browsing interface. Given a query with a result set of three million records, the facet module calculates a complete *facet and tag result* in a second on a single pc. A facet and tag result is a list of facets, where each facet contains a list of tags present in the result set. A *complete* facet and tag result means that *all* tags in the result set are counted. The list of tags can either be a list of the most popular tags, i.e. the tags occurring most frequently in the result, or an alphabetical list of tags present in the result.

1.1 Related Work

Little has been written about clustering large library metadata databases or other large structured data sets. Some work has been done on clustering full-text documents [1,12], but few report results on large collections, and even fewer aim for non-hierarchical and non-exclusive clusters. The American West Project[2] have determined a topic decomposition of 360000 metadata records using probabilistic latent semantic analysis [15,10]. Franke and Geyer-Schulz [5] worked on clustering large collections based on usage histories. They report that *some* million documents can be clustered on a standard pc.

Complete facet result calculation used for faceted browsing is done by for instance Scopus (`www.scopus.com`) [8]. The facet result is presented under the heading *Refine Results*. Scopus and probably most other faceted browsing library sites use the facets inherent in their data sources. The Scopus data set contains hundreds of millions of records, but their facet calculation method has not been published.

1.2 Outline

The basic Summa system is described in section 2. The data collection used in the Summa project is described in section 3. The cluster module is described in

[1] The index of the 19th of February (2007) contained 6572841 records.

[2] Project homepage: `www.cdlib.org/inside/projects/amwest/`

section 4 and the facet module in section 5. Results are discussed in section 6 and further work in section 7.

2 Summa

The Summa search system consists of a set of independent modules all developed in Java. The Summa architecture overview is presented in figure 1. The heart of the search system is the indexing module, which builds the Summa index (based on Lucene [7]) and the search module, which provides the search functionality. The indexing module depends on access to a storage, and it uses the DICE (DIstributed Computing Environment) module, which is a simplified implementation of the MapReduce model [2].

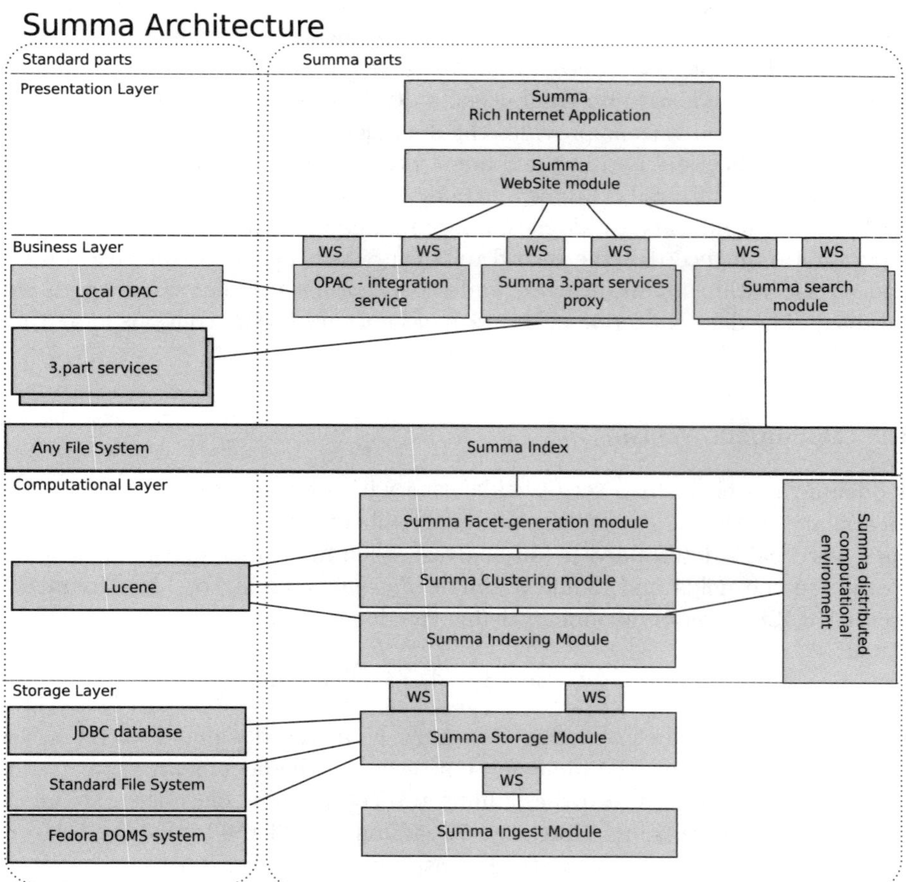

Fig. 1. The Summa architecture is basically modular as illustrated by this figure from the Summa presentation [13] given at Göttingen State and University Library in January 2007 by Hans Lund, Summa project manager

The storage can be developed separately, but Summa also includes storage modules[3] and an ingest module, which can ingest data from multiple sources. A website can be developed using the search module services directly. Summa also includes a website module build on top of the search functionality.

The Summa search system is currently used as the primary search functionality offered by the State and University Library of Denmark. The system can be tested at `www.statsbiblioteket.dk/search/` and a list of Summa features is available at `www.statsbiblioteket.dk/summa/summa_english.jsp`. The Summa search system is being stabilised and distributed to a number of Danish libraries in 2007 and is planned to be open sourced in 2008.

3 Data

A digital bibliographic item or library metadata element or *record* usually contains authors, title, a number of classifications, location, language and perhaps abstract or description or other *fields*. We assume that all records have a unique record id. Once indexed into the Lucene index, the record is usually referred to as a *document*, and Lucene provides the document with a document id.

The data collection used in the Summa project consists of local records from the State and University Library catalogue, records from five University of Aarhus institute library catalogues, a large number of oai records[4], some 'field expert librarian records' (the record tells you which librarian can give you the best advise within a certain field) and records from a danish commercial-film database. The data collection of the 19th of February (2007) contains more than six and a half million very diverse records.

3.1 Document Vectors

A document is basically a set of fields, each with a set of terms. Terms are the vocabulary of the index, i.e. the words, numbers, abbreviations and in some cases word pairs determined by an analyser when first indexing the documents. We ignore the fields and define a simple *document vector* or term frequency vector [16,12]. Given a document, define the document vector

$$a = [a_1 a_2 \cdots a_m] \in \mathbb{N}^m, \tag{1}$$

where m is the number of terms. An entry a_i in the document vector is the number of occurrences (the frequency) of term i in the document.

The current index used in the Summa project contains more than six and a half million documents and more than 70 million (70093009) terms. We however use a limited vocabulary, i.e. instead of using the 70 million terms occurring in

[3] Summa offers a storage module implemented against a JDBC database, a storage module implemented against a standard file system and a storage module implemented against a local Fedora [4] DOMS (Digital Object Management System).

[4] Open Archives Initiative records harvested from a large number of selected sites.

the index, we restrict the vocabulary to terms occurring in certain fields and we filter out stop words.[5] This means that we have just less than ten million (9996835) rather than 70 million terms in our further calculations.

Our implementation of sparse document vectors optimises object size and includes a possibility for normalisation. Currently we use Euclidean distance when comparing document vectors, but Cosine similarity has been reported to be more appropriate for text documents (e.g. in the survey by Berry [6]), and this is certainly something we will look at.

4 Clustering and Index Enrichment

The clustering methods developed for Summa were developed ad hoc, and in some aspects the methods are better described as categorisation methods. We note that many library metadata records already contain good classifications, and the facet module can retrieve these as well as the new clusters. One reason for creating new clusters is that many of the records in our data set contain abstracts but not classifications. Another reason is uniting existing classifications.

The clustering and index enrichment is done in two steps. The first step is creating the clusters using one of the three methods described below. We note that the created clusters are non-exclusive, non-exhaustive and non-hierarchical, i.e. a record can belong to two clusters or to none, and all the clusters are on the same level. The second step is enriching the index. This is currently done by building a parallel cluster index, which can be read by the search module.

4.1 Grouping Methods

We have implemented three clustering or grouping methods: a simple search based method, a search and centroid based method and a distance based method. Each of these methods have been tested, but only the simple method scales to the current index size. The Summa stabilisation work will include work on scalability and optimisation of clustering methods and possibly developing new methods.

In all three methods, we start by finding terms, which can be used in a search and provide search results which are good candidates for initial clusters. A good cluster candidate is defined by a candidate term, which occurs in a reasonable number of records and in different fields. The terms occurring in the index can be obtained from an index reader, and a reasonable number is provided as minimum and maximum occurrence properties. As we are aiming for topic clusters, some fields do not contain suitable terms, and the initial set of fields in which to look as well as a set of stop words are also provided as properties. This initial step is linear in the number of terms in the index and determines the number of clusters, which the documents can be assigned to in the following steps. Currently the number of clusters used for the full index is only 2775; this number can be regulated by regulating the above mentioned properties.

[5] Stop words are non-descriptive words such as *the*, *in*, *of* and in our implementation numbers are also removed.

Simple Search Based Method. In the simple search based method, the found terms are simply used in a new search in an extended set of fields (also supplied as a property). The search results are saved in a *cluster map* from document ids to sets of cluster names using the search terms as cluster names.

We have tested the simple method on an index of six and a half million records with the number of clusters restricted to less than 3000. The size of the cluster map kept in memory during this test is over one gigabyte. This means that even the simple method needs a scalability update.

The result of the simple method is basically collecting documents containing the same word. Documents classified using different classifications and documents with descriptive title words or notes are joined. This means that the quality of the clusters (and the names of the clusters) are more or less guarantied by the data quality. It however also means that no new information is discovered; thus the method is hardly a clustering method, but rather a categorisation method.

Search Based Method Using Centroids. In this method we start by finding the candidate terms, and for each term, a search is performed and a cluster candidate retrieved as above. Given such a cluster candidate, which is a set of documents, we retrieve the document vectors from the set of documents and treat the vectors as a set of points in m-dimensional space. We then build a *centroid* incrementally.

We define a centroid or a mean for a set of points (a definition also used for the k-means and many other algorithms [14,16]). Given a set S of points, the centroid of the set is

$$c = \frac{1}{|S|} \sum_{x \in S} x \ . \tag{2}$$

In our module the calculation of the centroid is done incrementally, but leaving division till the end. Our implementation of the incremental centroid also allows for trimming [1], i.e. removing the least significant entries. This is a reasonable approximation in itself, but we also allow trimming along the way which is not a nice approximation as the order in which the points are added influences which dimensions are removed, however given the amount of data, we decided to allow this option.

We now have a set of centroid candidates, which can be used as a seed selection [12] for any clustering algorithm. In this search based method we use the centroids to create new queries. The queries are created using the most significant centroid dimensions weighted with the dimension coordinates. The queries are then used in a new search, and the top search results are saved as clusters in a cluster map using the original search terms as cluster names. This method does not scale to the size of the current index at present.

Distance Based Method. In this method initial cluster candidates are retrieved and centroids are build as above. Close clusters are joined based on proximity of centroids, as done by the Join refinement operator in the Scatter/Gather approach [1]. Then every document in the index is translated to a document vector and for each document vector the distance to each centroid is calculated to determine which clusters this document belongs to. The last part of this method is basically equivalent to the final step of the k-means algorithm by MacQueen [14] or to the Centroid-based Classification Algorithm by Park, Jeon and Rosen [16] with the exception that the documents are allowed to belong to any number of close clusters rather than only the closest one. Again the result is saved in a cluster map using the original search terms as cluster names. This method also does not scale to the size of the index currently used by Summa.

4.2 Building the Parallel Cluster Index

Both a cluster map (with around six and a half million entries) and an index writer (with the same number of additions) use a lot of memory. To reduce memory requirements, we divide the map into smaller maps and save the small maps before building the new index. The small maps can then be loaded one at a time when building the parallel cluster index. This further makes it possible to resume building the index, if the work should be interrupted.

The parallel cluster index contains only one field, which is the cluster field. The index is built by looping through all document ids in the original index, and for each id looking up the clusters in the cluster map, and adding a document with this id and a cluster field with the looked up clusters to the new index. Now we can use a parallel reader to look up records across the two indexes.

Building the parallel index is linear in the number of documents in index, which means that all three methods are linear in the number of terms plus the number of documents.

5 Facet Calculation

Ranganathan [11] introduced the idea of faceted subject classification, and today faceted browsing is becoming increasingly popular. Out of all the fields occurring in the document set, we choose the *facets*, which we wish to retrieve information from. In the facet context we call the terms occurring in these fields *tags* (facets are also sometimes called grouped tags).

The facet module offers an online service, which given a query, retrieves a result set and counts the number of occurrences of all tags in the specified facets. The service returns either the tags occurring most frequently or an alphabetical list of tags. The service can calculate the 15 most popular tags in each of 20 facets in one second on a single pc for a search result of three million records. The fields to use as facets as well as the number of top tags to return are provided as properties.

5.1 Facet Internal Data Structure

The trick to fast calculation is preprocessing and memory. Our module first creates an internal facet map or facet data structure for the look-up operations to avoid expensive online read operations from the index. To facilitate fast look-ups the facet map is kept in memory. This means that we do not want any redundant information and we do not want any more object memory overhead than necessary.

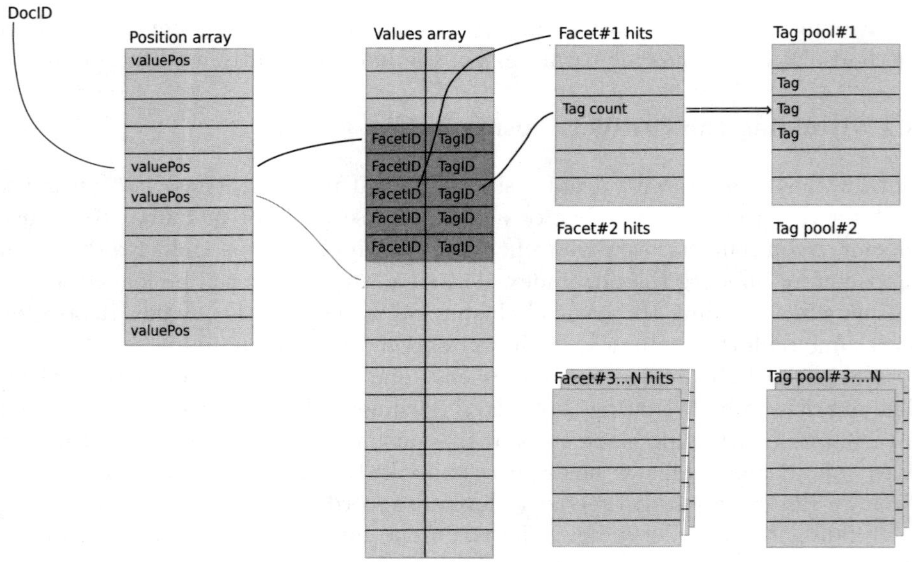

Fig. 2. The facet data structure consists of a number of integer arrays

The facet map is constructed as a number of integer arrays and a tag pool as shown in figure 2. We use the nice property that the document ids in an optimised Lucene index are consecutive integers from zero to the number of documents in the index. The first (left most) integer array has an entry for each document id, and this entry is simply a position in the second *values* integer array. The values of the document can be found in the second array from the given position to the position of the next document id. The values are a list of integers, which can each be divided into two positions: one for the facet and one for the tag. If the number of facets or tags exceeds the available space in integers, the values array is not integer, but long.

Then we have a two-dimensional integer *hits* array. For each possible tag in each facet the array contains a position, and this position is used to count the number of occurrences of this tag in this facet in a given search result.

Finally we have a (two-dimensional) *tag pool*. The pool can either be a string pool, which is the fastest but also the most memory expensive solution, or it can be another integer array, which holds the addresses to the strings in the disc space string pool.

The positions of the values array are valid both in the hits arrays and in the pool array. The data structure is build in a preprocessing step by running through all the documents in the index. The data structure is probably best understood through an example of its use.

5.2 Given a Query

Given a query, the facet module first retrieves a slim search result from the Summa index. The slim result is basically a list of document ids and we use it to update the hits arrays with the tag counts of this result as follows:

```
for each document id
  read values position
  for each value
    split value into facet array position and tag position
    look up facet array
    in this array increment counter at tag position by one
```

When we have counted the total number of tags occurring in the search result, we need to construct the facet and tag result. In the current website we ask for the most popular tags. These are found by for each facet running through the hits array and collecting the top tag counts or rather the positions of the top tag counts. These positions are the same in the tag pool and the actual tags can be looked up. Finally the result is transformed into a nice xml version and returned. The hits array is reset to zero in a separate thread. By ensuring that the strings in the pool are sorted alphanumerically when the map is build, it is possible to return alphanumerically sorted tags instead without a performance hit.

6 Performance

The two clustering methods using document vectors and centroids do not scale to the size of the current index and we will not present tests for these methods (they currently scale to a three million document (13 GB) test index).

The simple categorisation method has been tested using different size indexes. The categorisation can currently be done in a few hours on an office pc. The test results are shown in table 1. Most of the time spent by the method is spent on building the new parallel index rather than on creating clusters. In the test with the largest index of 27 GB, the extra disc space used to store the new parallel index is 334 MB, which is not much compared to the size of the original index (the space used to save the cluster map temporarily is even less).

Note that there is quite a jump in time from the 13 GB index to the 27 GB index. The time complexity is linear, and the unexpected increase is caused by the memory complexity, which is also linear. The pc used for testing has only 1.5 gigabytes of memory, which means swapping was necessary in the test of the largest index, and this caused the jump. We are working on saving the cluster map or parts of the map at regular intervals (based on the size of the map).

Table 1. Simple method time and space. The tests were run on a 2 processor, 3 GHz, 1.5 GB RAM pc. The memory used by the method is roughly linear as is the time if we leave aside the result for the largest index. The reason for this seemingly long time for the largest index is that the memory use exceeds the available RAM and swapping is necessary.

Index Size	906 MB	1.8 GB	3.5 GB	7 GB	13 GB	27 GB
# docs	205402	410803	821606	1643211	3286421	6572841
# terms	4252133	7434324	13026680	22854818	40084960	70093009
Time	2 min.	5 min.	12 min.	27 min.	1 hour, 6 min.	4 hours, 4 min.
Memory	103 MB	242 MB	348 MB	458 MB	817 MB	1808 MB

This should limit the memory complexity to a constant (the space complexity will of course still be linear), and the time complexity should then remain linear regardless of available RAM.

Building the internal data structure for the facet module is a linear time algorithm and one million documents can be added to the structure in approximately ten minutes. The space usage is also linear, and the structure is currently build in memory and holds one million documents in approximately 0.5 GB RAM on a 64-bit pc. This means that the structure can be built for the current index of approximately six million documents in an hour and requires approximately three gigabytes of random access memory.

For now, we require 0.5GB per million documents for building the map. If we want a build-algorithm which uses less memory, it is not a problem to build the map with a disc-based pool. The performance is however a challenge as we for each tag occurrence have to determine whether this tag is in the pool by searching for the string (tag) rather than look it up in a map. For the facet and tag calculation service, we can then either keep the string pool on disc or read the pool into memory if wanted, but again we have to look at performance.

Table 2. The facet and tag calculation times in this table include search time. The test runs were performed on a hyper-threaded dual-CPU, 64-bit pc with four gigabytes parallel access RAM using two concurrent threads. The index used in these tests was a 6281659 document index from October 2006.

Search Result Size	6281659 docs	3771901 docs	1928047 docs	1 document
Time	1 second, 356 ms	790 ms	533 ms	73 ms

Keeping the string pool on disc reduces the memory used to around 50 MB per million documents, but adds around 300 ms to the calculation time. Calculation times have been measured for the version with the string pool in memory for different result set sizes and are shown in table 2. We note that facet and tag calculation is near-trivial to run in parallel between different machines, with expected near-perfect increase in performance. The bottleneck for facet and tag calculation is memory speed, which means that multiple CPUs but shared memory does not give much performance increase.

7 Conclusion and Further Work

It is possible to calculate full facet and tag information for a query with a three million document result set in less than one second. This makes faceted browsing a possibility, and we certainly consider the facet module a success. The facet and tag structure is used at the current State and University Library website `www.statsbiblioteket.dk/search/` to facilitate exploratory searching.

It is possible to create simple clusters for a data set of more than six and a half million library metadata elements within a few hours. To create better clusters or better clustering algorithms, we need better scaling. We want our clustering algorithms to scale to datasets of hundreds of millions of elements. We also want to investigate lexical analysis, stemming and dimension reduction to improve cluster quality and avoid an explosion in the number of dimensions.

Currently indexing into Summa is distributed, but the actual index is centralised. The Summa stabilisation work includes introducing a distributed index and an incremental update work flow. The cluster module will be changed to fit into the new environment. We will create clusters based on the full distributed index, and we will develop a new cluster data structure, which can be used in an incremental update work flow.

Besides the general and continuing improvement to the indexing work flow and to the clusters themselves, the perceived quality of the clusters and the faceted browsing is of major importance. A large part of this is the visual presentation on a web page, concretely on the webpage of the State and University Library. A large-scale Summa user study is planned in 2007. This will hopefully give us some input on the quality of the clusters and the facet and tag structure.

Acknowledgements. The Summa project group is also Jens Hofman Hansen, Michael Poltorak Nielsen, Hans Lund, Jørn Thøgersen, Mads Villadsen, Hans Lauridsen, Mikkel Kamstrup Erlandsen, Toke Eskildsen, Dorete Bøving Larsen, Gitte Behrens and Birte Christensen-Dalsgaard. A special thanks to Toke Eskildsen, Mads Villadsen and Hans Lund for help on this paper.

References

1. Cutting, D.R., Karger, D.R., Pedersen, J.O., Tukey, J.W.: Scatter/gather: a cluster-based approach to browsing large document collections. In: SIGIR '92: Proceedings of the 15th annual international ACM SIGIR conference on Research and development in information retrieval, pp. 318–329. ACM Press, New York (1992)
2. Dean, J., Ghemawat, S.: MapReduce: Simplified data processing on large clusters. In: OSDI, pp. 137–150 (2004)
3. English, J., Hearst, M., Sinha, R., Swearingen, K., Yee, K.-P.: Hierarchical faceted metadata in site search interfaces. In: CHI '02: CHI '02 extended abstracts on Human factors in computing systems, pp. 628–639. ACM Press, New York (2002)

4. Fedora Development Team: Fedora open source repository software: White paper (October 2005), Available from http://www.fedora.info/documents/WhitePaper/FedoraWhitePaper.pdf
5. Franke, M., Geyer-Schulz, A.: Automated indexing with restricted random walks on large document sets. In: Heery, R., Lyon, L. (eds.) ECDL 2004. LNCS, vol. 3232, pp. 232–243. Springer, Heidelberg (2004)
6. Frigui, H., Nasraoui, O.: Simultaneous clustering and dynamic keyword weighting for text documents. In: Berry, M.W. (ed.) Survey of Text Mining, pp. 45–72. Springer-Verlag New York, Inc, Secaucus, NJ (2003)
7. Gospodnetić, O., Hatcher, E.: Lucene in Action. Manning Publications (2005), See also http://lucene.apache.org/java/
8. Griffiths, G.: The value of structure in searching scientific literature (July 2004), Available from http://www.info.scopus.com/docs/wp2_structure_search.pdf
9. Hansen, J.H., Lund, H., Lauridsen, H.: Summa – integrated search (2006), Available from http://www.statsbiblioteket.dk/publ/summaenglish.pdf
10. Hofmann, T.: Probabilistic latent semantic indexing. In: SIGIR, pp. 50–57. ACM, New York (1999)
11. Kabir, A.M.F.: Ranganathan: A universal librarian. Journal of Educational Media & Library Sciences 40(4), 453–459 (2003)
12. Larsen, B., Aone, C.: Fast and effective text mining using linear-time document clustering. In: KDD '99: Proceedings of the fifth ACM SIGKDD international conference on Knowledge discovery and data mining, pp. 16–22. ACM Press, New York (1999)
13. Lund, H.: Summa: integrated search. Presentation given at Göttingen State and University Library (January 2007), Available from http://www.statsbiblioteket.dk/publ/summa-presentation.pdf
14. MacQueen, J.: Some methods for classification and analysis of multivariate observations. In: Le Cam, L.M., Neyman, J. (eds.) Proceedings of the Fifth Berkeley Symposium on Mathematical Statistics and Probability (June 21-July 18, 1965 and December 27, 1965-January 7, 1966), University of California Press, vol. 1, pp. 281–297 (1967)
15. David, J.: Newman and Sharon Block Probabilistic topic decomposition of an eighteenth-century american newspaper. J. Am. Soc. Inf. Sci. Technol. 57(6), 753–767 (2006)
16. Park, H., Jeon, M., Rosen, J.B.: Lower dimensional representation of text data based on centroids and least squares. BIT Numerical Mathematics 43(2), 427–448 (2003)

Annotation-Based Document Retrieval with Probabilistic Logics

Ingo Frommholz

University of Duisburg-Essen
Duisburg, Germany
ingo.frommholz@uni-due.de

Abstract. Annotations are an important part in today's digital libraries and Web information systems as an instrument for interactive knowledge creation. Annotation-based document retrieval aims at exploiting annotations as a rich source of evidence for document search. The POLAR framework supports annotation-based document search by translating POLAR programs into four-valued probabilistic datalog and applying a retrieval strategy called knowledge augmentation, where the content of a document is augmented with the content of its attached annotations. In order to evaluate this approach and POLAR's performance in document search, we set up a test collection based on a snapshot of ZDNet News, containing IT-related articles and attached discussion threads. Our evaluation shows that knowledge augmentation has the potential to increase retrieval effectiveness when applied in a moderate way.

1 Introduction

In today's digital libraries and Web information systems, annotations are an important instrument for interactive knowledge sharing. By annotating a document, users change their role from passive readers to active content providers. Annotations can be used to establish annotation-based collaborative discussion when they can be annotated again, or they can appear as private notes or remarks. Depending on their role as content-level or meta-level annotations [2], they are an extension to the document content or convey interesting information about documents. In any case, annotations are an important adjunct to the primary material a digital library deals with [11]. Examples for annotation-based discussion can be found in newswire systems on the Web like ZDNet News (`http://news.zdnet.com/`), where users can write comments to the published articles, which in turn can be commented again. We also find annotation-based discussion in several digital libraries (see, e.g., [6]). Annotations are an important source for satisfying users' information needs, which is the reason why we evaluated some annotation-based discussion search approaches recently [7]. But annotations can also play an important part in document search as an additional source of evidence for the decision whether a document is relevant w.r.t. a query or not. It is thus a straightforward step to seek for effective methods for *annotation-based document retrieval.*

L. Kovács, N. Fuhr, and C. Meghini (Eds.): ECDL 2007, LNCS 4675, pp. 321–332, 2007.

While classical retrieval tools enable us to search for documents as an atomic unit without any context, systems like POOL [14] are able to model and exploit the document structure and nested documents. But in order to consider the special nature of annotations for retrieval, we proposed POLAR (Probabilistic Object-oriented Logics for Annotation-based Retrieval) as a framework for annotation-based document retrieval and discussion search [8]. POLAR cannot only cope with structured documents like POOL, but also with annotations to help satisfying various information needs in an annotation environment. Although some of the POLAR concepts like knowledge and relevance augmentation with so-called context and highlight quotations were already evaluated for discussion search [7], there has been no evaluation of annotation-based document search so far. In this paper, we are thus going to present the results of further experiments applying knowledge augmentation for document search with a prototype of the POLAR system. We start with a brief description of POLAR and its implementation before discussing our test collection and the evaluation.

2 POLAR

POLAR is a framework targeted at annotation-based retrieval, i.e. document, annotation and discussion search [8]. With POLAR, developers of digital libraries can integrate methods for document search (exploiting annotations), annotation search and discussion search (considering the structural context in threads) into their systems. It supports annotation types and is able to distinguish between annotations made on the content- or meta-level. In this paper, we assume that our collection consists of main documents and, attached to them, annotation threads establishing a discussion about their corresponding root document. This is the typical annotation scenario we find on the Web and in many digital libraries (e.g., [6] and many others).

In POLAR, documents, annotations and their content, categorisations, attributes and relationships are modeled as *probabilistic propositions* in a given *context*. A context, in our case, is a document or an annotation. Figure 1 shows an example knowledge base modeled in POLAR. Line 1 describes the document `d` as a *context*. `d` is indexed with the terms 'information' and 'retrieval'; their term weights are the probabilities of the corresponding term propositions and can be derived, e.g., based on their term frequency within the given context. `d` is annotated by the content annotation `a` (also described as a context), which

```
1  d[ 0.5 information  0.6 retrieval 0.6 *a ]
2  a[ 0.7 search  0.7 *b ]         b[...]
3  document(d). annotation(a). annotation(b)
4  0.5 °search   0.4 °information
```

Fig. 1. An example POLAR knowledge base

contains the term 'search' (l. 2). `a` in turn is annotated by `b`. Line 3 categorises `d`, `a` and `b` as documents and annotations, respectively. If a context c_1 relates to another context c_2 (e.g. if c_2 annotates c_1), we define the *access probability* that c_2 is entered from c_1. As an example, `b` is accessed from `a` with probability 0.7. Access probabilities can be given directly, for example as a global value valid for all contexts accessed by other contexts, or individually for every entered context. They can also be derived via rules, e.g. to reflect users' preferences for or against certain authors of annotations. In our experiments in Section 4.2, we assume global values for access probabilities and provide these values directly. Line 4 shows some global term probabilities for 'search' and 'information'; these probabilities can be based on, e.g. the inverse document frequency. To allow for annotation-based retrieval, POLAR supports rules and queries like

```
rel(D) :-  D^q[search]
rel(D) :-  D^q[information]
?- rel(D) & document(D)
```

which return all documents relevant to a query `q` = "information OR search" (capital letters denote variables).

The core concept of annotation-based retrieval in POLAR is *augmentation* [7]. Augmentation in our scenario means that we extend a context with its corresponding annotation (sub-)threads. In *radius-1 augmentation*, each context is augmented only with its direct annotations, whereas in *full augmentation*, it is augmented with the whole annotation (sub-)threads. Figure 2 shows the augmented context for document `d` in our example. The solid line shows the augmented context `d(a)` for radius-1 augmentation, whereas the dotted line shows the augmented context `d(a(b))` of `d` when applying full augmentation. In the latter case, `a` and `b` are subcontexts of the supercontext `d(a(b))`, whereas in radius-1 augmentation, only `a` is a subcontext of `d(a)`. It is clear that full augmentation, where we traverse whole annotation threads, is more resource-consuming than radius-1 augmentation where we only consider direct comments. We recently proposed two basic augmentation strategies for annotation-based

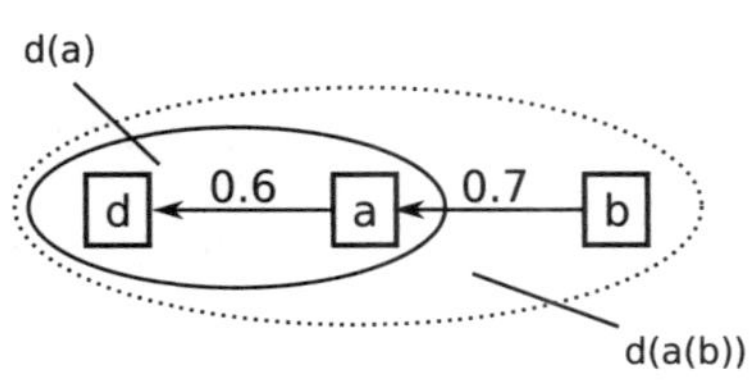

Fig. 2. Augmented contexts for radius-1 and full knowledge augmentation

retrieval: *knowledge augmentation*, where the knowledge contained in contexts is propagated to its corresponding supercontext, and *relevance augmentation*, where we propagate relevance probabilities (see [7] for a further discussion). We focus on knowledge augmentation only. Without augmentation, the above POLAR query would calculate a retrieval status value (RSV) of $0.5 \cdot 0.4 = 0.2$ for d, based on the term 'information' alone (its weight within the context d and the global term probability), since d does not know about 'search'. The POLAR program

```
rel(D) :- //D^q[search]
rel(D) :- //D^q[information]
?- rel(D) & document(D)
```

applies knowledge augmentation (indicated by the '//' prefix). The term 'search' is propagated from a to d according to the access probability of 0.6 and thus has the term weight $0.6 \cdot 0.7 = 0.42$ in the augmented context d(a). For d, the RSV is 0.368 now, based on both terms 'information' and 'search' in the augmented context d(a) (the calculation of this value is explained in the following section). Note that POLAR not only supports the augmentation of term propositions, but also, like POOL [14], of classifications and attributes. We focus our further considerations on term augmentation as this is applied in our experiments reported later.

3 POLAR Implementation and Translation into FVPD

POLAR is implemented on top of four-valued probabilistic Datalog (FVPD) [9] by translating POLAR programs into FVPD ones and executing these with an FVPD engine. FVPD allows for dealing with inconsistent and contradicting knowledge and the open world assumption, which are important features for annotation-based discussion or semantic annotation where annotators might have different opinions about things or how to tag a document. After being parsed and translated into FVPD, each POLAR program is executed by Hyspirit[1] [9], a probabilistic Datalog implementation. Besides translation methods, the implemented POLAR prototype offers classes for creating an index for the required datastructures.

Our prototype realises certain translation methods which we call `trans` here, to translate POLAR propositions, rules and queries into FVPD. As an example, `trans("rel(D) :- D^q[search]")` creates the FVPD rule

```
instance_of(D,rel,this) :- term(search,D) & termspace(search)
```

(`this` denotes the global database context) with, e.g.,

```
trans("a[0.7 search]") = "0.7 term(search,a)"
trans("0.5 °search") = "0.5 termspace(search)".
```

as a translation of probabilistic POLAR propositions into FVPD ones. For knowledge augmentation, the POLAR rule `rel(D) :- //D^q[search]` is translated into

[1] http://qmir.dcs.qmul.ac.uk/hyspirit.php

```
term_augm(T,D) :- term(T,D)
!term_augm(T,D) :- !term(T,D)
term_augm(T,D) :- acc_contentanno(D,A) & term_augm(T,A)
!term_augm(T,D) :- acc_contentanno(D,A) & !term_augm(T,A)
instance_of(D,rel,this) :- term_augm(search,D) &
                           termspace(search)
```

if full knowledge augmentation is applied; for radius-1 knowledge augmentation, the third and fourth `term_augm` rules are non-recursive and formulated as

```
term_augm(T,D) :- acc_contentanno(D,A) & term(T,A).
!term_augm(T,D) :- acc_contentanno(D,A) & !term(T,A).
```

It is, e.g., `trans("d[0.6 *a]") = "0.6 acc_contentanno(d,a)"`.

To execute the translated knowledge augmentation rules in Section 2, the FVPD engine combines the probabilistic evidence using the inclusion-exclusion formula. If $e_1, \ldots, e_n$ are joint independent probabilistic events, the engine computes

$$P(e_1 \wedge \ldots \wedge e_n) = P(e_1) \cdot \ldots \cdot P(e_n)$$

$$P(e_1 \vee \ldots \vee e_n) = \sum_{i=1}^{n} (-1)^{i-1} \left(\sum_{\substack{1 \le j_1 < \\ \ldots < j_i \le n}} P(e_{j_1} \wedge \ldots \wedge e_{j_i}) \right)$$

In our example, this yields

$$\begin{aligned} P(\texttt{term\_augm(search,d)}) &= P(\texttt{acc\_contentanno(d,a)} \wedge \texttt{term(search,a)}) \\ &= 0.6 \cdot 0.7 = 0.42 \\ P(\texttt{term\_augm(information,d)}) &= P(\texttt{term(information,d)}) = 0.5 \\ P(\texttt{instance\_of(d,rel,this)}) &= P((\texttt{term\_augm(search,d)} \wedge \\ &\quad \texttt{termspace(search)}) \vee \\ &\quad (\texttt{term\_augm(information,d)} \wedge \\ &\quad \texttt{termspace(information)})) \\ &= 0.42 \cdot 0.5 + 0.5 \cdot 0.4 - 0.42 \cdot 0.5 \cdot 0.5 \cdot 0.4 \\ &= 0.368 \end{aligned}$$

4 Evaluation

Previous experiments showed that knowledge augmentation using context and highlight quotations can be beneficial for discussion search [7]. In contrast to these experiments, we are now going to show the effectiveness of our full and radius-1 knowledge augmentation approaches on document search. Another difference to the experiments in [7] is that we do not consider any highlight or context quotations for augmentation when determining the RSV of an annotated object, but propagate the content of its annotations instead. As many content providers on the Web let users comment delivered articles in order to discuss their content, we apply this scenario in our experiments as well: we are searching for documents and augment our knowledge about their content with the discussion threads attached to them. As far as we know, no such experiment has been performed before, so we had to create a suitable test collection first.

4.1 Test Collection Creation

We downloaded a snapshot of ZDNet News and set up a testbed for our experiments based on this collection. ZDNet News provides news and some background information about developments in information technology (IT). Figure 3 shows an example thread of comments belonging to an article. Our ZDNet snapshot

Fig. 3. ZDNet article and discussion thread

consists of 4,704 articles and 91,617 annotations, from which 26,107 are direct comments to the articles. The collection was harvested from December 2004 to July 2005. We categorise all comments as being content-level annotations to the object they refer to, although some of them might be better regarded as meta-level annotations.

To create our testbed, we defined 20 topics and queries[2] Since relevance assessments could not be achieved within an evaluation initiative like INEX or TREC, we only had limited resources for the assessments – we asked colleagues, students and IT experts outside our institute to assess the topics. As our assessors volunteered for working on the topics in their spare time, we asked them to assess 150 documents (articles) per topic. To create an initial ranking we applied a simple approach for annotation-based document search: articles and

[2] We plan to make the testbed available on the POLAR web site, `http://www.is.inf.uni-due.de/projects/polar/index.html.en`

their direct annotations were merged and regarded as one atomic document[3]. We defined a 3-tier ranking system. The assessment procedure was as follows: after reading an article, the assessor looks if it is *relevant* w.r.t. the given topic. If so, it is judged like that. If not, the assessor looks at the direct annotations to see if there are relevant comments. If the assessor finds any relevant comment, the article is judged as being *not relevant but having relevant annotations*. If there are no relevant comments, the article is judged as *not relevant*. Non-relevant articles might nevertheless be interesting to users when there are annotations which contain the information the users seek (and the system is able to point them to these). From all documents judged, our accessors classified 679 documents as being relevant and 113 as not relevant but having relevant annotations.

4.2 Experiments and Results

Our experiments targeted the following questions: can knowledge augmentation, where the content of an article is augmented with the content of the connected discussion threads, enhance retrieval effectiveness? Furthermore, do we need to consider all comments in the discussion threads or is it sufficient to consider the direct comments only for knowledge augmentation? When annotating, annotators might use a different vocabulary to express the same issues as found in the annotated object. This would possibly increase recall as the searcher might use a vocabulary which is closer to the one used by the annotator than to the one used by the author of the annotated object. On the other hand, if an annotator uses the same terms as in the annotated object, we might conclude with higher certainty that these terms, found both in annotations and the annotated object, can be used to index the latter. This might have a positive effect on precision (which is the main target of our evaluation).

We indexed all articles and annotations in our testbed by applying stemming and stopword elimination and calculated the probabilities of tuples in our `term` relation as

$$P(\texttt{term(t,d)}) = \frac{tf(t,d)}{avgtf(d) + tf(t,d)} \tag{1}$$

with $tf(t,d)$ as the frequency of term t in article or annotation d and $avgtf(d)$ as the average term frequency of d, calculated as $avgtf(d) = \sum_{t \in d^T} tf(t,d)/|d^T|$ and d^T being the set of terms occurring in document d. For a term t, we calculate $P(\texttt{termspace(t)}) = \mathit{idf}(t)/\mathit{maxidf}$ with $\mathit{idf}(t) = -\log(\mathit{df}(t)/\mathit{numdoc})$, $\mathit{df}(t)$ as the number of documents in which t appears and numdoc as the number of documents in the collection, and maxidf being the maximum inverse document frequency. For a topic T, let `qterm_1`, ..., `qterm_n` be the corresponding query terms. For our baseline run (denoted `baseline`), where no augmentation is applied, we created the following POLAR program

[3] Since our POLAR prototype was not available to the date the assessments started, we did not apply a pooling procedure. The initial ranking was produced directly with HySpirit.

```
rel(D) :- D[qterm_1]   ...   rel(D) :- D[qterm_n]
?- rel(D) & document(D)
```

to express the query "`qterm_1 OR ... OR qterm_n`". We made experiments with both full and radius-1 knowledge augmentation and different global access probabilities ranging from 0.1 to 1 in 0.1 steps. The experiments with full knowledge augmentation are denoted `knowlaug-<accProb>` with `accProb` being the access probability (e.g, `knowlaug-0.1` means full knowledge augmentation with $P(\texttt{acc\_contentanno(o1,o2)}) = 0.1$ for two objects `o1` and `o2` and `o1` accesses `o2`). Similarly, we tested radius-1 knowledge augmentation with the same different access probabilities as above (denoted `knowlaug-r1-<accProb>`). For all knowledge augmentation runs, we executed the POLAR program

```
rel(D) :- //D[qterm_1] ... rel(D) :- //D[qterm_n]
?- rel(D) & document(D)
```

providing different POLAR translations for full and radius-1 knowledge augmentation (as discussed in Section 3). The simple approach described in Section 4.1 is called `merged`.

Table 1 shows the results[4] of some selected runs where we assumed an article as being relevant only if it was actually judged as relevant. In contrast, for the results in Table 2 we assumed an article as being relevant if it was actually judged relevant or had relevant annotations. Listed are the result of the experiments which gained better results than the baseline. In the other experiments (not listed here) we noticed that performance decreases with increasing access probabilities, leading to the conclusion that the bias coming from the discussion thread should not be too strong. But we also see that a slight bias, when the access probability is 0.1, is beneficial w.r.t. retrieval effectiveness. We also discover that the difference between performing full knowledge augmentation vs. radius-1 knowledge augmentation is only marginal, so it seems fine to apply radius-1 knowledge augmentation instead of traversing whole annotation threads. In fact, as we can see in the recall-precision graph in Figure 4, for high access probabilities full knowledge augmentation has a more destructive effect. This can be explained by topic changes occurring in a discussion thread. If the terms describing a new topic after a topic change are propagated with a high access probability to the root document, the algorithm assumes this document to be relevant to the new topic, which it is most probably not. With low access probability, this effect vanishes, and with radius-1 knowledge augmentation, the probability of a topic change is small as we regard only direct annotations here.

Table 2 shows the results of selected runs where we assume a document to be relevant when it itself is judged relevant or has relevant annotations. We can see an even bigger gain in retrieval effectiveness w.r.t. the baseline for access probabilities 0.1 and 0.2, and the `merged` run. This is of course not a big surprise, as our baseline run does not consider the additional knowledge coming

[4] All results were generated with the TREC tool `trec_eval`; t-tests with confidence $p \leq 0.05$ were applied for determining statistical significance [15].

Table 1. Mean average precision (MAP) and precision at 5, 10, 15, 20 and 30 documents retrieved for some selected runs. Best results are printed in bold, '*' denotes statistical significance (compared to the baseline).

Run	MAP	P@5	P@10	P@15	P@20	P@30
baseline	0.5609	0.77	0.7	0.66	0.615	0.5467
merged	0.5511	0.77	0.66	0.59	0.5625*	0.51
knowlaug-0.1	**0.5773**	**0.78**	0.705	**0.6867**	**0.63**	**0.5517**
knowlaug-0.2	0.5627	0.74	0.705	0.67	0.62	0.5383
knowlaug-r1-0.1	0.5768	**0.78**	**0.71**	**0.6867**	0.6275	**0.5517**
knowlaug-r1-0.2	0.567	0.75	0.705	0.6733	0.6275	0.5417

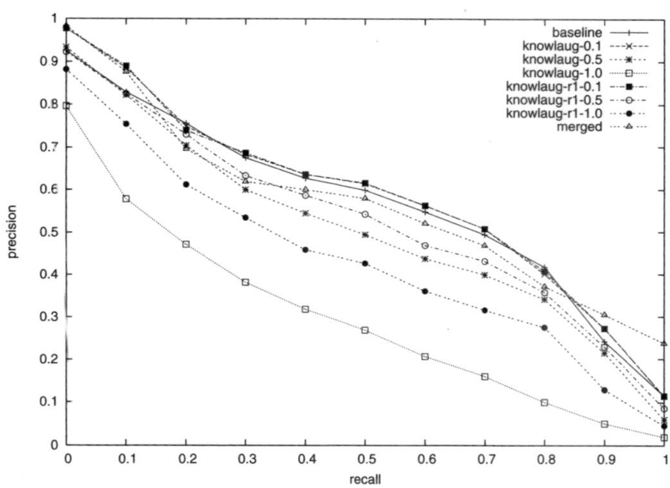

Fig. 4. Interpolated recall-precision graph of selected runs

from (relevant) annotations. We also observe the tendency to worse results with increasing access probabilities (Fig. 5).

In our experiments, we regarded documents as relevant only if they were judged so in one case, and additionally when they had relevant annotations in another case. What difference this makes can be observed in one certain topic about "Firefox security". Here, the difference between the `baseline` MAP and the `knowlaug-0.1` MAP is 0.09 in the first case and -0.14 in the second, so knowledge augmentation performed much better in the second and worse in the first case. In this particular topic, many non-relevant articles are judged as having relevant annotations. As an example, in an article about Microsoft's Internet Explorer (IE) being divorced from Windows, also some Firefox security issues were mentioned in the annotations (in fact, in this particular article, many discussions arose about Firefox vs. IE in general, which led this article to be ranked 2nd place for the query about Firefox security). Topics like this, having many documents with relevant annotations, thus benefit from our knowledge

Table 2. Mean average precision (MAP) and precision at 5, 10, 15, 20 and 30 documents retrieved for some selected runs. Relevant articles are relevant itself or have relevant annotations. Best results are printed in bold, '*' denotes statistical significance (compared to the baseline).

Run	MAP	P@5	P@10	P@15	P@20	P@30
baseline	0.5257	0.78	0.71	0.6667	0.6225	0.555
merged	**0.5828**	**0.81**	0.71	0.64	0.6075	0.56
knowlaug-0.1	0.5605*	**0.81**	0.72	0.7*	0.645	0.5667
knowlaug-0.2	0.5596*	0.77	**0.725**	0.69	0.6375	0.565
knowlaug-r1-0.1	0.5595*	**0.81**	**0.725**	**0.7033***	0.6425	**0.5683***
knowlaug-r1-0.2	0.5616*	0.78	**0.725**	0.69	**0.645**	**0.5683**

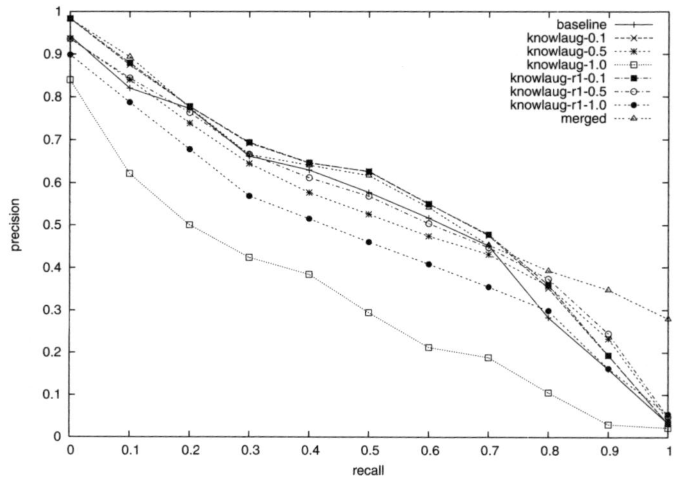

Fig. 5. Interpolated recall-precision graph of selected runs. Relevant articles are relevant itself or have relevant annotations.

augmentation as well as from the merged approach. This is again no big surprise as the baseline does not consider annotations at all.

We are aware that, due to our limited resources, our testbed with 20 topics and 150 documents judged per topic, and the fact that some results are not statistically significant has an effect on the reliability of our results [15]. However, we conclude that in essence there is an improvement in retrieval effectiveness for the given settings by applying knowledge augmentation in a very moderate way (global access probabilities around 0.1 and 0.2), especially in cases where it is sufficient that non-relevant articles have relevant annotations (many of our results are significant here). But we have to keep in mind that the ZDNet collection contains a very special kind of annotation, namely user comments and discussion about articles. While we find such annotations in various news portals on the web, we cannot necessarily expect that our results are valid for other kinds of annotations (like personal notes or annotations in scholar environments or humanities) or subject areas, as the type and quality of annotations might differ. Further experiments certainly need to be performed to learn if and how the types and subject areas of annotations affect results.

5 Related Work

Related and important work for our annotation-based retrieval approach has many different sources. Marshall et *al.* thoroughly studied annotations in the context of digital libraries (see, e.g., [12,13]). Annotation-based document search is used by Golovchinsky et *al.* in a relevance feedback approach where only highlighted terms instead of whole documents are considered [10]. Another annotation-based document retrieval method is introduced by Agosti and Ferro in [1], where the evidence coming from a document and its attached annotation threads is combined using data fusioning. This interesting approach was never evaluated yet, due to the lack of a suitable test collection (like the ZDNet snapshot) so far. The idea of using the thread structure as a context for retrieval is also applied in several discussion search approaches [16,17]. Other related areas, especially when it comes to exploiting the link context of a document, are hypertext IR (see, e.g., [3]) and topic distillation [5]. The idea of knowledge augmentation has its roots in structured document retrieval and is discussed thoroughly by Rölleke in [14].

6 Conclusion

After giving an outline of the POLAR framework, we discussed full and radius-1 knowledge augmentation. POLAR programs are translated into FVPD ones and executed by an FVPD engine. To evaluate the integrated knowledge augmentation approach for document search, we set up a test collection based on ZDNet News. The results show that applying knowledge augmentation with a low global access probability can be beneficial for retrieval effectiveness. Future work will concentrate on enhancing the POLAR prototype in order to perform further experiments for document and discussion search, and on the integration of POLAR into an existing digital library system supporting annotations.

Acknowledgements

Our work was funded by the German Research Foundation (DFG) as part of the project "Classification and Intelligent Search on Information in XML (CLASSIX)". We thank our assessors for sacrificing their valuable spare time for relevance judgements. We also like to thank CNet for giving us permission to use the harvested ZDNet snapshot for our experiments.

References

1. Agosti, M., Ferro, N.: Annotations as context for searching documents. In: Crestani, F., Ruthven, I. (eds.) CoLIS 2005. LNCS, vol. 3507, pp. 155–170. Springer, Heidelberg (2005)
2. Agosti, M., Ferro, N., Frommholz, I., Thiel, U.: Annotations in digital libraries and collaboratories – facets, models and usage. In: Heery, R., Lyon, L. (eds.) ECDL 2004. LNCS, vol. 3232, pp. 244–255. Springer, Heidelberg (2004)
3. Agosti, M., Smeaton, A.F. (eds.): Information Retrieval and Hypertext. Kluwer Academic Publishers, Boston (1996)
4. Koch, T., Sølvberg, I.T. (eds.): ECDL 2003. LNCS, vol. 2769. Springer, Heidelberg (2003)
5. Craswell, N., Hawking, D.: Overview of the TREC-2004 web track. In: The Thirteenth Text Retrieval Conference (TREC 2004). NIST (2004)
6. Frommholz, I., Brocks, H., Thiel, U., Neuhold, E., Iannone, L., Semeraro, G., Berardi, M., Ceci, M.: Document-centered collaboration for scholars in the humanities – the COLLATE system. In: Constantopoulos and Sølvberg [4], pp. 434–445
7. Frommholz, I., Fuhr, N.: Evaluation of relevance and knowledge augmentation in discussion search. In: Gonzalo, J., Thanos, C., Verdejo, M.F., Carrasco, R.C. (eds.) ECDL 2006. LNCS, vol. 4172, pp. 279–290. Springer, Heidelberg (2006)
8. Frommholz, I., Fuhr, N.: Probabilistic, object-oriented logics for annotation-based retrieval in digital libraries. In: Nelson, M., Marshall, C., Marchionini, G. (eds.) Proc. JCDL 2006, pp. 55–64. ACM, New York (2006)
9. Fuhr, N., Rölleke, T.: HySpirit – a probabilistic inference engine for hypermedia retrieval in large databases. In: Schek, H.-J., Saltor, F., Ramos, I., Alonso, G. (eds.) EDBT 1998. LNCS, vol. 1377, pp. 24–38. Springer, Heidelberg (1998)
10. Golovchinsky, G., Price, M.N., Schilit, B.N.: From reading to retrieval: freeform ink annotations as queries. In: Proceedings of SIGIR 1999, pp. 19–25. ACM, New York (1999)
11. Marshall, C.C.: Annotation: From paper books to the digital library. In: Proceedings of the ACM Digital Libraries '97 Conference, pp. 131–140 (July 1997)
12. Marshall, C.C.: Toward an ecology of hypertext annotation. In: Proceedings of the ninth ACM conference on hypertext and hypermedia, pp. 40–49 (1998)
13. Marshall, C.C., Brush, A.J.: Exploring the relationship between personal and public annotations. In: Proc. JCDL 2004, pp. 349–357. ACM Press, New York (2004)
14. Rölleke, T.: POOL: Probabilistic Object-Oriented Logical Representation and Retrieval of Complex Objects. PhD thesis, University of Dortmund, Germany (1998)
15. Sanderson, M., Zobel, J.: Information retrieval system evaluation: effort, sensitivity and reliability. In: Marchionini, G., Moffat, A., Tait, J. (eds.) Proceedings of SIGIR 2005, ACM, New York (2005)
16. Voorhees, E.M., Buckland, L.P. (eds.): The Fourteenth Text REtrieval Conference (TREC 2005), Gaithersburg, MD, USA, NIST (2005)
17. Voorhees, E.M., Buckland, L.P. (eds.): The Fifteenth Text REtrieval Conference (TREC 2006), Gaithersburg, MD, USA, NIST (2006)

Evaluation of Visual Aid Suite for Desktop Searching

Schubert Foo and Douglas Hendry

Division of Information Studies, School of Communication and Information
Nanyang Technological University, Singapore 637718
{assfoo, hend0007}@ntu.edu.sg

Abstract. The task of searching for documents is becoming more challenging as the volumes of data stored continues to increase, and retrieval systems produce longer results list. Graphical visualisations can assist users to more efficiently and effectively understand large volumes of information. This work investigates the use of multiple visualisations in a desktop search tool. These visualisations include a List View, Tree View, Map View, Bubble View, Tile View and Cloud View. A preliminary evaluation was undertaken by 94 participants to gauge its potential usefulness and to detect usability issues with its interface and graphical presentations. The evaluation results show that these visualisations made it easier and quicker for them to find relevant documents. All of the evaluators found at least one of the visualisations useful and over half of them found at least three of the visualisations to be useful. The evaluation results support the research premise that a combination of integrated visualisations will result in a more effective search tool. The next stage of work is to improve the current views in light of the evaluation findings in preparation for the scalability and longitudinal tests for a series of increasingly larger result sets of documents.

Keywords: Query result processing, query reformulation, tree view, map view, bubble view, tile view, cloud view, evaluation, search engine, user interface.

1 Introduction

The worldwide explosion in digital information due to rapidly increasing computer usage and the development of the Internet has been widely noted and documented [1]. As the volume of information stored electronically has grown, so has the need to be able to search this information resource in order to be able to answer individual information needs [2]. This has led to the dramatic increase in the development of search tools to meet the growing demand to locate information more easily.

The dramatic growth in web search technology, pioneered since 1998 by Google, has led to the widespread use of such tools by most computer users. Mainstream development to-date has concentrated on providing tools for searching the World Wide Web. Desktop search tools, for searching documents held on local computers hard drives, have been slower to develop. It is notable that these tools are now being incorporated into the latest desktop Operating Systems - Spotlight in Apple's OSX

L. Kovács, N. Fuhr, and C. Meghini (Eds.): ECDL 2007, LNCS 4675, pp. 333–344, 2007.

and Microsoft's Vista also incorporates similar functionality. Therefore, these desktop tools are starting to reach a much larger user base.

In a classic search engine, the users enter their search terms and then request the system to search for matching results. These are then returned as a list of resources that best matches the users' queries. Typically, a large text-based list of ranked results is returned to the users who scan through them to identify deemed relevant documents, and read through the contents to extract information to satisfy their information needs. As the volumes of data to be searched increase and result lists becomes increasingly longer, the challenge is now to maintain the efficiency and effectiveness of the search and result selection process.

Well-presented graphical views can convey large amounts of complex information in a simple and easy to understand manner [3]. It is, therefore, not surprising that graphical visualisations have been employed in search engines to assist users in the searching process.

2 Related Work

Much research in Information Retrieval Systems (IRS) has been focused on the algorithms used for searching and relevance ranking. This includes work on augmenting search results by the use of metadata such as thesauri for aggregating results. However, most of the deployed systems (including search engines) are based on returning textual list of results for users to review.

Some graphical tools have been developed to visually assist the user in formulating their query. These include the use of Venn Diagrams, Filter-Flow Visualisations and Block Orientated Visualisations, which have been documented elsewhere.

However, the principal area where visualisation techniques have been applied is in the results review process. Here a visualisation is used to replace or augment the results list and/or the document preview functions. A number of tools have been created that use a variety of 2D and 3D graphical visualisations in order to allow the user to explore and understand the results of their query.

In order to support query reformulation visualisations usually present terms that are related to the query terms being used. These related terms often come from a controlled dictionary, thesaurus or other metadata held in the system. The user can review these new terms and use them to modify their query. One such tool is the AquaBrowser Library [4] which shows a visual word cloud that suggests words similar or related to the users query terms.

Established online search engines such as Google have a very traditional user interface. While the search and ranking algorithms behind these search engines are very sophisticated their interfaces have remained traditional and text based. However, a number of new online search engines have started to offer more graphical interfaces to assist users. Grokker and Ujiko are examples of visualisations being used to present the results of web searches.

Whilst some evaluation studies have reported mixed results [5] many have found positive support that the visualisations have aided user performance [6, 7]. Even in cases where performance has not improved users often report better satisfaction with tools incorporating visualisations [8]. Visualisations seem to be particularly effective where the complexity of the task and volumes of data are at their highest [9, 10]. They also seem to work well when they are kept as simple as possible [11].

3 Design

A Java based lightweight desktop search engine was developed that could index and search content on a desktop computer. The indexing and searching sub-systems were designed based on traditional IRS principles and incorporates stop word removal, stemming and is based on Boolean logic.

The design of the user interface was based on the following research premises: -

- Visualisations can assist users to search for documents [7, 10]
- Different visualisations can be used to support different elements of the searching process (results review and query reformulation)
- Different graphical techniques can be used to assist users to visualise different kinds of information
- Visualisations work best when they are kept simple [11].

The search engine GUI has a plug-in view architecture that allows different views to be created independent of the searching mechanism. Six views were constructed for use and evaluation. While most of the individual views have been used elsewhere as standalone views in different forms of IRS, the novelty in our work lies in the bubble view, and the provision of a suite of related views thereby providing synergy through flexibility to switch views to visualise, infer and process the result sets differently.

3.1 List View

The List View (see Fig 1) is the classic search results view. It contains a list of files that, based on Boolean logic, match the users query. Each file name is shown along with the number of "hits" from the query. A hit is defined as one occurrence of one query term in the file contents. The files are listed in descending order of the total number of hits found.

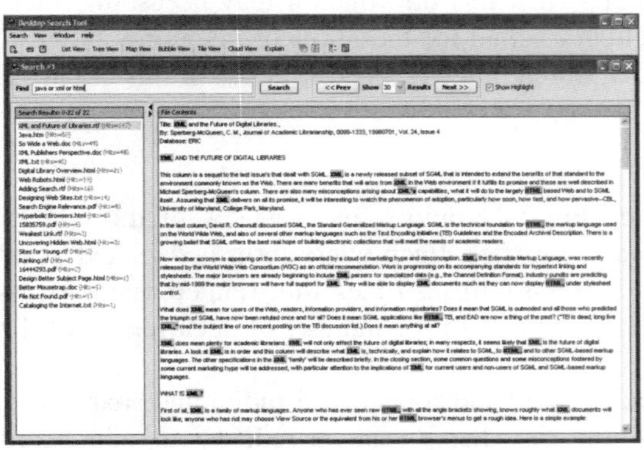

Fig. 1. List View

This view also contains a File Viewer window. This window will display the textual contents of a selected file in order to allow quick review of the file contents. Any non-textual content, such as images etc. in a Word or PDF document, are not displayed. Similarly, some of the source document formatting will be lost as only line and paragraph breaks are preserved in the text extraction process.

3.2 Tree View

The Tree View is similar to the List View (see Fig 2). The files are organised based on their underlying folder structure. For each file in the results list, all of its parent folders are added to the folder hierarchy (avoiding duplicates). The Result files are then added into the tree at the appropriate folder for their physical location.

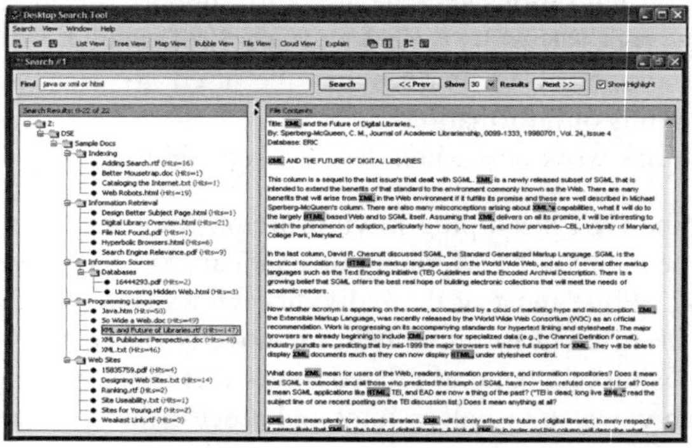

Fig. 2. Tree View

This view is very similar to the Microsoft Windows Explorer view. However, only files that match the query string are displayed and only the parent folders of these files are included in the tree.

The purpose of this view is to use the physical file structure as part of the results display. If users have taken the time to organise their documents into meaningful folders and hierarchies then this information may be useful when reviewing results. This view is particularly suited for thesaurus or taxonomy based folder organisations where documents are stored in the respective nodes of this organisation scheme.

3.3 Map View

The Map View (see Fig 3) provides an overview of the relationship between the query terms and the result files. Each query term is depicted as a blue rectangle and each result file as a green ellipse. Lines link related query terms and results files. These are annotated (in red) with the number of occurrences of the query term in the result file.

The view can be zoomed and rotated and individual shapes can be moved around on screen. In addition, the shapes can be reduced to mini icons if the display is overcrowded.

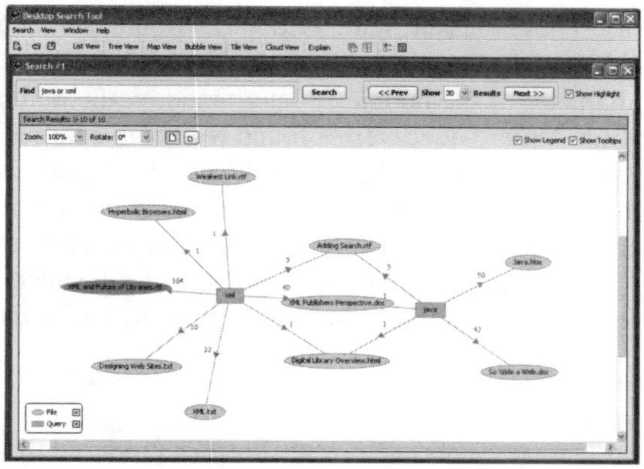

Fig. 3. Map View

The purpose of this view is to provide an overview of the query and how the individual query terms are influencing the results. Therefore, this bird's eye view can be used to detect problems in the query specification if the required results are not as expected. It will clearly show the relative influence of each query term in producing the result files and therefore help the user in deciding whether the query needs to be reformulated and how to do so.

3.4 Bubble View

Boolean logic systems make it difficult to judge the relevance of a result file. The total number of hits may not be a good guide to relevance especially when document length is taken into consideration. Therefore, it is desirable to normalise this measure to take into account document size. In this work, this is done by calculating a hit density for each result file expressed as the number of hits per 1,000 searchable terms (non stopwords) in the document.

The intention of the Bubble View (see Fig 4) is to help the user better assess the relevance of different documents. The axes of the graph are the number of hits and the

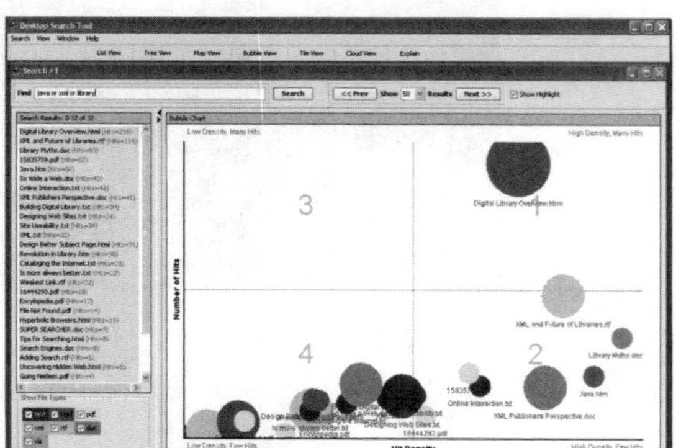

Fig. 4. Bubble View

calculated hit density. These measures are used to distribute the documents along each axis as they provide good document discrimination in order to achieve a better visualisation. The diameter of the bubble is determined by the number of query terms present in the result file – more query terms found results in a larger bubble diameter.

Quadrant 1 is expected to contain the most relevant documents as both the number and density of hits is greatest. Correspondingly, quadrant 4 will be expected to contain the least relevant documents, as both the hit count and density are smallest.

The Bubble View provides an overview of document relevance for a given query and aids the review of documents most likely to be relevant to the query.

3.5 Tile View

The Tile View (see Fig 5) presents each result file as a coloured tile using a Treemap. A Treemap is "a space-constrained visualization of hierarchical structures" [12]. The size of each tile is determined by a measure such as Total Number of Hits, File Size, and Hit Density (Hits per 1,000 searchable terms). Using the control panel the user can change the measure used to determine the size of a tile.

In addition, the colour of a tile is determined by its file type. The display can be restricted to certain file types or all can be shown.

The Tile View can optionally include the folder hierarchy of the results files. In this variant, all the result files in a specific folder are grouped together in a "super tile". Each folder is enclosed within a tile representing its parent so that the entire folder structure of the results files can be displayed.

The purpose of the Tile View is to allow users to review the results visually and judge their relevance based on different criteria with larger tiles denoting the most relevant documents. They can then decide which files to review in detail by looking at their contents.

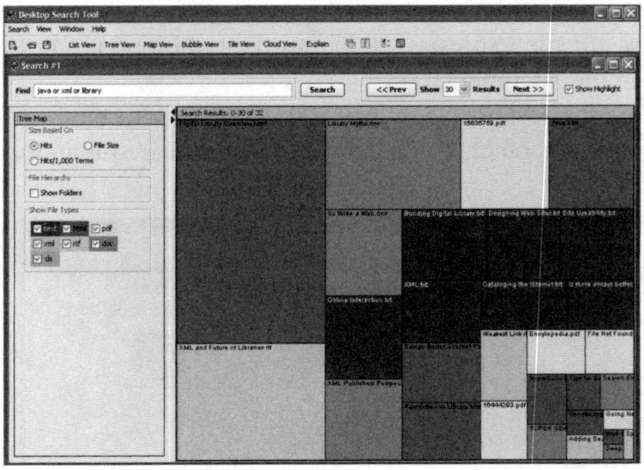

Fig. 5. Tile View

3.6 Cloud View

The Cloud View (see Figure 6) is adapted from the Tag Clouds popular on social networking sites such as Flickr [13]. A Tag Cloud is a weighted list which contains the most popular tags used on that site and the relative popularity of each tag is indicated by changing its font. It is thus easy to see the most popular tags.

The Cloud View creates a Word Cloud based on the (indexable) content of the result files. The contents of these files are examined and stop words and non-indexable terms are removed. The words are then stemmed and a simple term count made of all the terms in the documents. The top 300 terms are then displayed in a Word Cloud as they represent the most common indexable terms in the documents.

Only files selected in the Results List (in the left hand window) have their contents included in the Word Cloud. If the user changes the selection of files, the Word Cloud is dynamically refreshed with information based on the new selection of files.

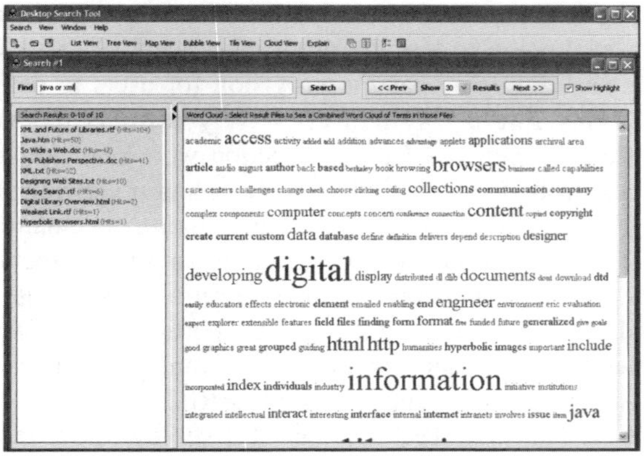

Fig. 6. Cloud View

When the user clicks on a word in the Word Cloud a popup menu appears offering the choice to expand, restrict or exclude the word from the current query or to create a new search using the selected word.

The purpose of the Cloud View is to help users to reformulate their queries based on the searchable terms found in the results documents. This could be used to expand or restrict the search in order to better refine the results set.

4 Evaluation

The next stage was to undertake a preliminary system evaluation in order to determine the usefulness of the views in the system. The principal aim was to determine if the availability of such visualisations was useful and which of them would be worth developing further. As such, the work reported in this study is mainly intended as a proof of concept and to have a first gauge of usability and usefulness of the views.

The evaluation was carried out through a user survey based on the questionnaire technique. A questionnaire comprising 51 questions was developed to gather user opinion about the visualisations and their usefulness. The evaluation was split into five tasks – each task required the user to perform a search in support of a given information need and the participants worked through these in sequence. For each task they were given five minutes to interact with an interface to find the most relevant documents to satisfy the information need. Following this, they were asked to complete a series of questions pertaining to the interface used.

Prior to the evaluation, a handout describing the search engine and views was provided to the evaluators, followed by a briefing and demonstration. Evaluators were also invited to download the search engine to familiarise themselves with it and the various views. Each evaluator had a minimum of one week of familiarity prior to the evaluation, and each spent 45 to 60 minutes in completing the evaluation.

Since the purpose of this evaluation was to review the visualisation aspects of the search tool, it was important to remove other factors that could influence user responses. Therefore, for each task the search terms to be used were pre-specified.

The evaluation system was based on a small collection of 30 documents since this was a preliminary evaluation to test the proof of concept of these visualisations. At the same time, the search engine has the provision for users to define and show the top ***n*** documents. This filtering system effectively restricts the volume of results displayed to the user, so even if a larger collection were used for indexing, the user would only see a controlled subset of documents when reviewing the results. Based on the results of this evaluation, we expect future evaluations to be more comprehensive and extended to test for scalability to larger document collections.

The documents covered topics on information retrieval systems, the World Wide Web, indexing and programming languages and a portion of the ERIC thesaurus was used to create a hierarchical folder structure. The sample documents were then stored into the folders based upon their categorisation in ERIC.

The students of the Nanyang Technological University M.Sc. Information Studies class of 2006/07 participated in the evaluation. There were a total of 94 participants – 57% were female and 43% were male.

4.1 List View Results

This is the classic search engine results view with no additional visualisation. The responses received (see Table 1) showed strong support that the List View is both easy to use and useful in reviewing the results. These results confirm that the basic design and operation of the desktop search engine is effective and useful.

Table 1. List View Results

#	Question	% Who Agree / Strongly Agree
1	The List View was easy to use.	89%
2	The List View was useful in reviewing my results.	86%

4.2 Tree View Results

The results strongly indicate that the Tree View (see Table 2) was easy to use and useful in reviewing the results. The results are very similar to those of the List View. As would be expected from these results a large majority (93%) of the evaluators found the function of the Tree View clear and obvious.

The evaluators also indicated that they organise and structure their own folders so most of them could potentially benefit from a search engine that uses the folder structure to present search results. This confirms the design premise that the user's folder structure would be a useful aid to presenting the results documents as well as a means to logically organise information in thesaurus/taxonomy-like structures that can support browsing as well as searching in this instance.

Table 2. Tree View Results

#	Question	% Agree / Strongly Agree
6	The function of the Tree View in the left hand window was clear and obvious.	93%
7	The Tree View was easy to use.	91%
8	The Tree View was useful in reviewing my results.	85%
9	I organise my documents logically in folders so this view would be useful to me.	87%

4.3 Map View Results

The evaluation results for the Map View (see Table 3) showed that slightly over half of the evaluators (51%) agreed or strongly agreed that the Map View was useful in reviewing their query results and reformulating their query. The distribution of responses for ease of use and usefulness are very similar.

Table 3. Map View Results

#	**Question**	**% Agree / Strongly Agree**
13	The Map View was easy to understand.	53%
14	The popup windows were useful.	75%
15	The Map View was easy to use.	58%
16	The Map View was useful in reviewing my query results and reformulating my query.	51%

Comment analysis indicated that the most useful aspect noted by the evaluators (33) was the ability to see an overview of the relationship between the query terms and the results files. This was the design premise for the Map View – to provide a clear overview of the query. However, the view can become very crowded when a large number of items are displayed resulting in overlapping of the graphic objects. A significant number of evaluators (34) indicated that this caused confusion.

4.4 Bubble View Results

The evaluation results for the Bubble View (see Table 4) show that around half the evaluators (46%) found this view useful in reviewing their query results. The majority of evaluators found the position (65%) and size (59%) of the bubbles gave them useful information, which supports the concept of this view as a means to convey several dimensions about the relevance of the results documents.

The comments analysis showed that useful features were the ability to get a quick and easy overview of the relevancy of the results and the ability to see the hit density.

The major confusion factors reported were related to the display of a large number of result documents. In this case, the document titles overlap and become unreadable and the evaluators found the display to be very cluttered and messy. Some evaluators

(10) did not understand that the size of the bubble related to the number of different query terms found in the result document.

Table 4. Bubble View Results

#	Question	% Agree / Strongly Agree
20	The position of a Bubble on the Chart gave me useful information.	65%
21	The different sizes of the Bubbles made sense and was useful.	59%
22	The Bubble View was easy to use.	51%
23	The Bubble View was useful in reviewing my query results.	46%

4.5 Tile View Results

The results of the evaluation of the Tile View (see Table 5) show over half the evaluators (59%) agreed or strongly agreed that the Tile View was useful in reviewing their results. Over two thirds found the tiles to be obvious and easy to understand (68%) and the ability to use different criteria to control their sizing was found to be useful (69%). This supports the design objective for this view to easily support the use of different criteria for judging the relevance of the results documents.

The ability to group files by folders also received strong support with 75% of evaluators agreeing or strongly agreeing that this was useful.

The comments analysis indicated that useful features were the ability to change tile size based on different criteria, the ability to group files by folder and the use of colour to distinguish file types.

Table 5. Tile View Results

#	Question	% Agree / Strongly Agree
27	The purpose of the Tiles and the Information they display was obvious and easy to understand.	68%
28	The ability to change Tile Size based on different criteria was useful.	69%
29	The ability to group files by Folders was useful.	75%
30	The Tile View was useful in reviewing my query results.	59%

4.6 Cloud View Results

The results for the Cloud View (see Table 6) showed that nearly two thirds of the evaluators found the Cloud View useful in reformulating their query (63%) and easy to use (61%). However, the distribution profile for question 37 (usefulness of Cloud View) is different– it has a bi-polar distribution, with a peak for disagree and agree. This implies that the evaluators were split into two groups.

A review of the comments strongly supported this conclusion. Those evaluators who scored the usefulness of the Cloud View very low (strongly disagree or disagree) reported a lot of confusion as to the contents of the Cloud. In other words, they did not find the view useful because they did not understand what it does.

In order to support this conclusion, the responses to question 34 (about understanding the contents of the view) were compared to those of question 37 (usefulness of the view). Of those who found the view difficult to understand (disagree or strongly disagree with Q34) only 29% found it useful. However, 85% of those who found the view easy to understand (agree or strongly agree with question 34) found it useful. Therefore, it is reasonable to conclude that the reported usefulness of the Cloud View would increase if the users better understood what it does. The comments imply that some users had not seen this type of visualisation before.

Table 6. Cloud View Results

#	Question	% Agree/ Strongly Agree
34	The contents of the Word Cloud were obvious to me and easy to understand.	56%
35	The popup menu on the Word Cloud was easy to use.	66%
36	The Cloud View made it easy to reformulate my query.	61%
37	The Cloud View was useful in reformulating my query results.	63%

4.7 General Results

After evaluating each of the views, the evaluators were asked for feedback that was more general about the search engine and its visualisations. There was strong support that they made it easier (83%) and quicker (86%) to find relevant documents.

4.8 Limitations of Evaluation

As this was intended to be a preliminary evaluation, we did not address the issue of scalability in terms of document collection sizes (hence result list sizes), as the main aim was to obtain a first set of evaluation results to validate the ease of use and usefulness of the various views to display and aid users to effectively use the search results. As such, we have left the testing of scalability for future evaluation. Along with this, we expect to carry out a series of longitudinal studies as research has found that complex interfaces summarising lots of data in comparison with simple interfaces will invariably fall short of users' satisfaction metrics initially but stand to have the potential to be gradually accepted when used for longer periods of time [14]. Another potential limitation is in the form of learning effects in using a small document set in the evaluation. In order to minimise this, we have used different scenarios in each of the 5 tasks with different queries resulting in different relevant documents. With hindsight, we might have used a larger set of documents in different domains for the evaluation to ensure that this effect is eliminated. Nonetheless, we do not view this as a serious limitation due to the context of our current evaluation objectives.

5 Conclusion

The results of the evaluation indicate that overall the users found the visualisations useful and easy to use. They also felt that it would help them find their desired results quicker. In particular, the Tree View and Cloud View were rated highly by the evaluators. The Tree View takes advantage of the users own defined hierarchies (their folder structures) to present the search results in a format that significant numbers of the evaluators found useful.

The Cloud View is a much more novel interface and some of the evaluators had difficulty understanding its principle of operation. A large majority of those users who understood the concept found the view to be very useful.

In conclusion, this work has shown that the inclusion of multiple visualisations would be likely to increase the usefulness and ease of use of a search tool and that different visualisations can be integrated together to provide support for different elements of the search process.

References

1. Moore, F.: Digital Data's Future - You Ain't Seen Nothin' Yet! Computer Technology Review 20(10), 1–2 (2000)
2. Mostafa, J.: Seeking Better Web Searches. Scientific American 292(2), 66–73 (2005)
3. Tufte, E.R.: The visual display of quantitative information, Cheshire, Conn. (Box 430, Cheshire 06410): Graphics Press. 197 (1983)
4. Kaizer, J., Hodge, A.: AquaBrowser Library: Search, Discover, Refine. Library Hi Tech News 22(10), 9–12 (2005)
5. Heo, M., Hirtle, S.C.: An empirical comparison of visualization tools to assist information retrieval on the Web. Journal of the American Society for Information Science and Technology 52(8), 666 (2001)
6. Sebrechts, M.M., et al.: Visualization of search results: a comparative evaluation of text, 2D, and 3D interfaces. In: Proceedings of SIGIR: International Conference on R&D in Information Retrieval, vol. 22, pp. 3–10 (1999)
7. Veerasamy, A., Heikes, R.: Effectiveness of a graphical display of retrieval results. In: Veerasamy, A. (ed.) Proceedings of the 20th annual international ACM SIGIR conference on Research and development in information retrieval, ACM Press, Philadelphia, Pennsylvania (1997)
8. Heflin, J., et al.: WebTOC: Evaluation of a Hierarchical Browsing Interface for the World Wide Web, [cited 7-Nov-2006] (1997), Available from http://www.otal.umd.edu/SHORE/bs11/
9. Morse, E., Lewis, M., Olsen, K.A.: Testing visual information retrieval methodologies case study: comparative analysis of textual, icon, graphical, and spring displays. J. Am. Soc. Inf. Sci. Technol. 53(1), 28–40 (2002)
10. Wingyan, C., Chen, H., Nunamaker, Jr., J.F.: A Visual Framework for Knowledge Discovery on the Web: An Empirical Study of Business Intelligence Exploration. Journal of Management Information Systems 21(4), 57–84 (2005)
11. Chen, C., Yu, Y.: Empirical studies of information visualization: A meta-analysis. International Journal of Human-Computer Studies 53(5), 851–866 (2000)
12. Bederson, B.B., Shneiderman, B., Wattenberg, M.: Ordered and Quantum Treemaps: Making Effective Use of 2D Space to Display Hierarchies. ACM Transactions on Graphics (TOG) 21(4), 833–854 (2002)
13. Yahoo Inc.: Popular tags on Flickr photo sharing, [cited 11-Nov-2006] (2006), Available from http://www.flickr.com/photos/tags/
14. Shneiderman, B., Plaisant, C.: Strategies for Evaluating Information Visualization Tools: Multi-dimensional In-depth Long-term Case Studies. In: AVI workshop on Beyond time and errors: Novel evaluation methods for information visualisation, Venice (2006)

Personal Environment Management

Anna Zacchi and Frank Shipman

Texas A&M University, Texas, USA
{zacchia, shipman}@cs.tamu.edu

Abstract. We report on a study of the practices people employ to organize resources for their activities on their computers. Today the computer is the main working environment for many people. People use computers to do an increasing number of tasks. We observed different patterns of organization of resources across the desktop and the folder structure. We describe several strategies that people employ to customize the environment in order to easily perform their activities, access their resources, and overview their current tasks.

Keywords: PIM, Document Management, Project Management.

1 Introduction

The computer is the primary work environment for a lot of people. People perform an increasing number of activities on their computer, and at the same time they accumulate an increasing number of documents. While the literature reports many studies on how people organize documents on their computers, the number of studies on how people organize resources and set the environment for their activities is limited.

The resources needed to accomplish tasks or projects include not only documents but also applications. People need an environment in which to organize those resources in ways that support their projects and activities. Today's computer systems offer an environment mainly based on a file storage paradigm. The hierarchical directories of the file system were developed for storing and retrieving files and not really as an environment for carrying out activities.

This paper presents a study on how people organize resources on their computer in order to accomplish tasks. We observed how people structured their environment, how they made use of the desktop, of the folder structure, and of the other characteristics and tools that computer systems offer. We observed how and where they gather resources for projects, how they access them, and which type of resources and structures are common among several projects and people. These insights will inform the development of digital library systems that integrate the organizational strategies that people use.

The next section describes prior studies of file and resource organization as well as system designs for better supporting people's work practices. After this is the description of the study method and its results. This is followed by a presentation and discussion of the results.

L. Kovács, N. Fuhr, and C. Meghini (Eds.): ECDL 2007, LNCS 4675, pp. 345–356, 2007.

2 Previous Work

A number of previous studies have analyzed how people organize paper [4; 14; 16] and electronic [1; 3; 9; 10; 15] documents. The focus of prior research was on strategies used for archiving and organizing, on the type of classification or categorization of documents, on retrieval strategies, on relationships among job and type of organization, and on the influence of context. Other strands of research focused on the integration between document management and email management.

Malone [14] studied how people organize paper documents in their office. He distinguished between two organization strategies: files and piles. He wrote that a very important role of the desk organization is to remind users of things to do, not just to help users find desired information. Bondarenko [4] finds that document management is strongly related to task management and that context is a very important aspect of information handling. Whittaker [16] observed paper handling strategies and in particular user habits in filing and piling and the reasons why people keep documents and duplication of documents on private and group collections. Barreau and Nardi [1] studied document organization in electronic systems. They distinguished among three types of information: ephemeral, working, and archived. Boardman et al. [3] tracked personal information handling across different type of data: files, email, and bookmarks. Ravasio et al. [15] detailed practices of document classification and retrieval. They analyzed average age of archival documents, number of files in folder, details of the hierarchical structures etc.

Different solutions to the management of documents have also been proposed. Karger et al. [12; 13] propose to unify different kinds of information, such as files and emails, in a single structure. Dumais et al. [6] propose a search interface, SIS (Stuff I've Seen) as a tool to integrate different data that has been previously viewed. Bellotti et al. [2] propose to use email as the center for organizing personal information.

Much of the above research indicates that how people organize information is heavily influenced by their current activities. There are a few studies of environment organization in computer systems aimed at understanding its relation to task accomplishment or project management. Jones [9] explored the way people organize information in support of projects. He wrote that folders frequently reflect basic problem decomposition or a plan for project completion. Kaptelinin [10] studied strategies people use in customizing their workspace and the typical problems people encounter in creating and using their virtual workspace.

The connection between activities and resource management has motivated the development of tools for supporting projects. ROOMS [7] was an early tool to manage windows. The Universal Labeler (UL) [8] unites different types of information in a common project outline structure. UMEA [11] collects interaction histories that it uses to automatically add resources to a project space.

This study focuses on resources and workspace organization in relation to people's activities. This study observes broader system use in creating a project space. This broader context includes the use of shortcuts, the desktop, the taskbar, and the start menu and the role of applications (e.g. Excel or MathLab) in project organization.

3 Study

This study looks at the strategies people use to set up their personal environment. Our main focus is in how documents and the environment are configured in relation to users' activities. Which strategies do users apply regarding document management in order to accomplish their tasks? We are interested in seeing what characteristics of the file system and operating system interface people use to organize resources around tasks and projects. The study also investigates users' motivations behind their resource organization. Several studies [2] highlighted the importance of emails to organize tasks and to-do lists. In this study the focus is on the organization of documents and tasks outside of the email environment.

3.1 Participants

30 people took part in the study. They were faculty, staff, and Ph.D. Students at a USA university. They belonged to different disciplines ranging across computer science, engineering, horticulture and the humanities. They included 12 women and 18 men. They all had more than 5 years experience with computers, with 26 of them having more than 10 years of experience. There were 3 Mac OS X, 4 Linux and 23 Windows XP users. Among the people willing to participate in the study we gave preference to people that dealt with several different activities so that they faced more complex resource organization. We were also interested in people with several years of experience since we wanted to record strategies established with time.

3.2 Method

The study took place either at the participant's office or, in case he or she worked on a laptop, at the place of choice of the participant. We asked each participant to walk us through the file organization on their computer. The beginning of the walk through was guided by questions such as: 1) Which kind of activities do you do on your computer? 2) Can you show us where you keep all of your documents? The interview proceeded with more questions according to the way each participant was dealing with the documents. The study included the common questions 3) Can you tell us about those files on your the desktop? 4) Is there a special organization for files and why? 5) How do you access your documents? 6) How would you like to organize your documents differently? While the questions focused on documents and their organization, participants' rationales and follow up questions provided information about how participants accomplished their tasks within this context. As the study progressed, we noticed the importance of some aspects and we began to ask more detailed questions regarding those aspects, such as taking notes and organization relative to projects. Each study lasted between 20 and 60 minutes. The interviews were recorded using a video camera pointed towards the screen. Analyzing the videos we identified several characteristics of workspace organization.

4 Results

Today's operating systems offer a rich environment that users can customize in order to work and organize their resources. We observed how participants put together various elements to create their own personal work environment.

We first identify participants' main work space. Then, we characterize their use of the desktop. We then look at the way they set access to their documents and applications. Next we describe the use of resources and the setting of the environment while working on a task. These include details of the role of temporary organization, file names and metadata, and notes.

4.1 Work Environment / Portal

Each participant had a preferred place used as the starting point for his activities. Using a web nomenclature we can call it the portal or home. For 50% of the participants this place was the desktop, for the others it was a folder or a directory.

One participant used the desktop as her main work environment. She put items related to current activities in the center of the desktop and items related to next day tasks in the top left corner: "Every time I switch on my laptop I check the top left corner. Like in a book the left top corner is the first spot I would look at."

When participants used folders as their main context, those were either "My Documents" or the equivalent folder in Mac or Linux, a home directory created under the local "C:\" disk, or a folder on a network drive. Many considered their main folder as their own personal environment. They complained that applications create folders inside "My Documents" or in the Linux "Home" directory. They regarded it as an intrusion of the system in their own space. Some, to avoid this intrusion, created their main folder under the root directory "C:\".

In the following paragraphs we describe how the participants used the desktop and the folder structure as their work environment.

4.2 Desktop Use

87% of the participants used the desktop to some extent. They placed documents and shortcuts on it for either a short (few days) or long term and gave it a structure.

Most of the participants (80%) used the desktop as a temporary place for documents before moving them into the folder structure, or to get them ready to transfer to another device (for example to a PDA), or to send as an attachment by email. While only one participant used the desktop exclusively for transient files, all others also used it to organize more long term resources. We can characterize the use of the desktop according to the following classification.

1) **Information Workspace.** A group of users (50%) used the desktop as an information workspace with actual files and folders, not only shortcuts. For example, one researcher kept the files that she was currently working on at the center of the screen. On the left of the screen she had a couple of folders related to projects she has been working on during the last two months. When she completes this work, she will archive the files into "My Documents". Another professor had a similar strategy. He kept several clusters of documents on his desktop: one cluster related to the classes he

was teaching, one related to the proposals he was writing, one for papers, and another cluster for documents that he would like to read eventually. All of the documents in the clusters will be either thrown away or archived once processed. In particular he cleaned up the desktop at the end of every academic semester. Another participant cleaned up the desktop regularly at the end of every day.

2) **Dashboard.** One group (13%) had a lot of shortcuts to applications and folders, but not the real files. They often put some effort in creating an organization for those shortcuts on the desktop. They also used the desktop as a temporary space for documents that they did not intend to put into their folder structure but that they eventually wanted to take a look at. The position of those documents on the desktop also served as a reminder that they eventually wanted to take a look at them. One user in this group said he didn't want to place files that he intended to keep on the desktop because he could not back up the desktop easily. Another user put shortcuts to folders that she was using frequently and that were deep in the tree structure of her network drive. She had about 40 shortcuts to applications and folders.

3) **Minimum.** A group of participant (20%) used the desktop only for a few basic shortcuts to applications and folders. One participant only had links to "My Documents", Internet Explorer and MS Word. He said he liked to have a clean desktop. He used those links to access his main work environment that was the folder "My Documents".

Four participants did not use the desktop at all. Three Linux users didn't use the desktop because they used the command line to invoke applications on files (Emacs or MatLab for example); for them the graphic environment was useless. A XP user didn't like to have the files on desktop always covered by open windows.

4.3 Resources Access

Participants expressed the importance of having the resources currently used on hand. Besides arranging shortcuts and documents on the desktop and in the folder structure, participants also customized the XP start menu, the XP quick launch bar, or the Mac OS X dock. They used the menu bar and the launch bar not only for applications, but also for shortcuts to the most frequently used folders.

33% of participants added application and folder shortcuts to the quick launch bar. One professor used a green arrow icon for the folder containing the material of the class that he was currently teaching. He added this icon to the quick launch bar. A student had an icon on the quick launch bar with the image of a gear pointing to the folder for an engineering class.

13% of participants modified the XP start menu to find frequently used applications more easily. They grouped similar programs, added shortcuts, or changed the names of the shortcuts. One participant modified the organization of links in the XP startup button menu "All programs". Another participant created folders on the top left column of the XP start menu. He grouped similar applications such as MS office programs, graphics applications, or internet applications. A couple of users preferred to place their list of shortcuts to applications in a folder on the desktop.

4.4 File Identification

Participants employed a variety of strategies to aid their identification of files inside folders and to make the files they are interested in stand out. They often used the system's sorting capabilities to locate files. In addition participants used naming schemes, color, and modified icons to support identification. They extended file names with comments about the content of the file.

Most participants had a preferred type of sorting inside a directory, most often alphabetical or by date. 50% left the default sorting, i.e. the alphabetical one. At least 33% switch sorting methods, such as between by "last modified" and by name, when looking for a file. One user preferred sorting by type in folders containing her papers so she could visually isolate the pictures from the text. Another user used sorting by type on the desktop to separate real files from links.

33% of participants occasionally used a date in the name of the file in order to force a chronological sort. For example a professor called the folders with classes taught with names such as "2005_CPSC333 (HCI)" using date, class name, and class title in the same filename. The date was the order he wanted his files to appear. This order doesn't depend by the date the file was last modified or created. The same user created folders for classes that he will teach in two years.

Only one participant used a spatial layout inside a directory. She was writing a book and she had a file for each chapter. She had to correct all the chapters. Therefore she put on the left of the window all the chapters that she had already corrected, and on the right side the ones she still had to process.

13% of the participants, one Mac and three XP users, changed the icons for the most frequently accessed folders. One participant said, "I used it [the modified icon] to distinguish between folders that I tend to use a lot. It gives me a better idea of what is going on with them." Another participant was not satisfied with the standard icons provided by her system, and so she created new ones using the graphic program Paint. For example, she used the image of an airplane for her travel folder.

One Mac user colorized files to make them distinguishable. She used red or green for important documents.

Occasionally participants added comments to file names indicating the document characteristics. One participant used the following convention for paper names, "Paper-name, version, date, collaborators, notes". She had comments such as "No images", and so on. An example name is "genetic 5-15 gb lb mj no_images" where gb and the following initials are people who contributed to that version of the paper.

4.5 Temporary Organization

There are files that are neither archived in the folder structure; neither do they belong to current activities. Participants may want to do something with them, but for lack of time or other reasons they put them aside.

These files may be divided in three categories:

1. *To Process.* Files they intend to look at and then throw away. They will throw them away anyway if they do not get to them for long time.
2. *To Keep.* Files they need to file away in an archival structure.
3. *To Throw.* Files they need to throw away but they have not got to them yet. They may never get to them.

Different participants had different strategies for dealing with potentially temporary documents. Some kept "To Process" files on the desktop, either scattered on the desktop surface or in a folder. Others used a temporary directory in the folder structure. One user had a "temp" directory on every network and local disks she was working on "I'm a big fan of the temp directory. I use it a lot but nothing there is really important. Everything in the temp directory can be deleted."

"To Keep" files were either files that participants didn't know where to file or files that had not been filed yet due to time constraints or for other reasons. A Mac user kept all the documents that she didn't know where to file on the desktop in a folder called "Untitled". Other users kept them in the main folder outside of other subfolders. A user said, "You have to have a mess somewhere, right? A fundamental rule of organizing things is you have to have one place where you put things that don't fit anywhere else. In my computer it is the desktop. There is no inherent structure on the desktop. The structure is in My Document."

"To Throw" files were often kept in the root of the main folder, for example in My Documents. One user kept all temporary documents under "My documents". He had 30 folders under My Documents and hundreds of loose files: "The folders are what is really important, but the documents under the root directory are not. They end up there and I don't use them anymore." Others users had a similar organization: they dumped everything in the root directory and then forgot about them.

"To Keep" and "To Throw" documents often were mixed together. Users said that that among the tens of files to throw away in their main directory there were files they intended to keep, but they didn't want to spend time sifting them out.

4.6 Notes

People working on projects or tasks typically maintain notes or to-do lists. We therefore observed our participants' practices regarding notes. They took notes in either paper or electronic form. They had both general notes and notes specific to projects. The note files were often given the same name, "notes" for example, across different locations.

30% of the participants reported writing notes on paper. One user sometimes wrote a to-do list in an email that she then sent to herself, but she prefered to write them on paper so that when she completes an item she feels satisfied as she marks it off.

67% of the participants used an electronic form of notes at some time. One Mac user used sticky notes in a dashboard (a Mac application), an XP user uses MS OneNote, and others wrote them in text files or Word. Many participants reported using two types of files for notes: one general, that contains a to do list, and that is maintained in their main directory, often on the desktop, and other note files that are relative to projects and are maintained in the folder relative to the project. One user kept a file called "notes" in every project directory. One user kept a sort of diary that he called "log" on the desktop in Word format. He organized the notes by date, and at the top of the document there was the list of items to do. Another user wrote note on paper, then she scanned them and stores them in PDF format in project directories.

4.7 Project Context and Work Environment

Previously we observed that each user has a portal, we described how participants use the desktop and how they personalize the start menu and launch bar. We now step back and present an overview of how all those ingredients combine to form a working environment. It is useful to distinguish between the organization of resources around a single project (*project context*) and the organization of groups of projects (*work environment*.)

The *work environment* is the general space that participants use to carry out activities, to work and manage their projects and other tasks. The work environment is the place that users personalize in order to work on their current projects. It is also the place where the user gets an overview of all the activities in which they are involved. The desktop is an example of a work environment.

Project Contexts are elements of a work environment which provide context for individual projects or tasks. A folder or a cluster of documents on the desktop are examples of project spaces. Kaptelinin [11] writes that "To carry out a higher-level task (or project) the user typically has to set up and manage a project-specific work context, that is, organize necessary resources to make them readily available when working on the project".

The standard environments used by our participants (Windows XP, Mac OS X, and Linux) offer little support for managing individual projects or groups of projects. Users may gather resources related to a single project inside a folder or may cluster them in an area of the desktop. Beyond surveying the desktop or user's main directory, there are no facilities that provide an overview of the user's projects.

There are systems dedicated to the management of projects. Kaptelinin [11] surveys systems that provide specific support for high-level user activities. Among them he includes Personal Information Management systems (PIM) such as Microsoft Outlook alongside dedicated project spaces such as ROOMS [7], the X Windows Manager, and non hierarchical file systems such as Presto [5].

None of our participants used any dedicated software for managing resources. Some of our Windows XP users made use of Outlook. Applications such as Outlook provide elements useful for supporting activities, such as calendars, address books, to-do lists, and notepads; but they do not provide any support for the management of the resources related to those activities.

The following explores how our participants set up their resources and environment to keep track of their projects' activities.

4.8 Practices for Project Context …

The project context is achieved by organizing resources and by creating the space that is used as the working space. Typically participants collected the resources needed in a folder, or in a cluster of documents on the desktop. Besides collecting resources, people also set the space by facilitating access to some resources and by creating an organization functional to the project.

Our participants used various strategies to create a context. For some participants the project context was a folder. For others it was a cluster of documents on the screen. For others it was a specific location on the desktop. For one participant the current project was in the center space of the desktop while for another it was in the right area of the desktop.

For participants using Linux, the context was often represented by a Linux workspace. Linux has the possibility to create multiple workspaces; it shows a map of them in the taskbar from where it is possible to select the workspace to make current. Participants used different workspaces for different contexts. One professor kept one workspace for her research and one to work with students. One student used a workspace for emails, and a workspace for each network machine he was working on.

For other participants the context was the set of open programs and documents. Some participants, in order to keep the current context, never switched off their computer. One Mac Laptop user said she switched it off a couple of times in the last three years. She wanted to keep open all the documents she was working on.

For a participant a system based on projects instead of folders better characterizes her working practices. "When I save a file, I would like the system to ask me not the folder but the name of the project. Then the system should file the document using the convention for that project."

A substantial number of documents do not fit in any particular project. Examples among the study participants were media files, such as music and photos. General purpose documents such as to-do lists, frequently used forms, and department phone lists also did not fit the participants' project specific organizations. These files often ended up on the desktop, or loose in the user's main directory. It is difficult for users to find an appropriate location to archive these files as they do not belong to any projects but are part of the general working environment.

4.9 … and Work Environment

The borders between project context and work environment are often blurred. Since current systems do not offer projects facilities, it is difficult sometimes to distinguish between the setting of a project context and of a work environment. Spaces can be shared between the current project and the set of all projects. People place resources belonging to separate projects along with general resources on the desktop and in the quick launch bar.

In setting the environment participants looked for ways to overview all projects, to highlight the current project among all the others, to show a priority among projects.

For a technical assistant in an engineering department the desktop was both his work environment and the space for his current project. He worked on tasks assigned to him by a pool of twenty professors. He kept folders relative to tasks on the desktop. He named the folders with the date followed by the professor name. He said that this convention helped him "keep the context". If he were to create a folder with a professor name and inside it subfolders with the date for each task, or vice versa, he would loose the context when he had to move subfolders to other locations. For him the professor name and date represented the task context. The set of all tasks on the desktop represented the work environment. He kept the tasks he was currently working on and those he recently worked on the desktop. He moved folders off the desktop and to an archival location under "My Documents" only when the desktop was ¾ full. He always kept ¼ of the desktop free to drag the folder for the current task to that location. That was the place to work on his current task.

The blurring between project and environment was problematic for some people. One professor used two screens and both were completely covered by icons. Documents belonging to different projects were mixed together on the desktop. "All my documents are organized by activities. On the desktop I use a chronological order, but then different activities overlap and it is a problem."

The overview of multiple tasks and their priorities is an important part of the context. One user had folders on the desktop called "Burning" and "In progress" to visualize priorities.

The setting of the work environment shows an interesting characterization of areas on the computer. 46% of the participants distinguished file locations on their computer as working context and archival. The working context being the desktop or the root of the main directory, while the archive the deeper folder structure. Interestingly though, the others 54% do not separate locations between current and archival: they keep all their documents in the same folder structure, but they create access to the current context by using shortcuts on the desktop. Therefore archived and current documents are all mixed together in the same location. What distinguishes archival and current documents is not the location but the structures people build to access them. For example, a professor with one folder for each class taught had about 20 folders in a subdirectory called "Classes" under "My Documents" folder. Present, past and even future classes were in the same location, in the same structure. But he had a shortcut on the desktop and in the launch bar to the folder with the class that he was currently teaching. Those shortcuts made current working folders and documents easily accessible.

Users that separated archival and working files express the geographical concept of "close" location. They filed archival documents in the directory structure and placed current documents in a "closer" position. The close position was the desktop, the root of the main directory, or the upper folder structure. For example, one user had three levels: the desktop for current files, the folder structure for archival documents, such as "Home\classes\HCI\2004", and an intermediate location, the folder "Home\classes\HCI", for the documents related to the most recently taught HCI class. Another user kept all current and recently completed tasks on the desktop, and moved them in the archival section only when the desktop was too full.

To summarize, users construct an environment using a combination of document organization and access features. Some users rely heavily on access features while others use different locations.

4.10 Issues or Motives

It is normal to think that people organize resource on their own computer in order to work with them efficiently. But several of our participants reported that they chose a particular organization in order to deal with a technical issue.

54% of participants indicated that **backup** influenced their document organization. A couple of users put all documents in a single folder structure under "C:\", so they could backup them with a single mouse click. One user was very concerned with the backup. He kept all files in a directory under "C:\" and he would frequently back it up. He wouldn't trust the standard folder "My Documents" because "all applications know about the existence of that folder and who knows what they may do". Other participants avoided putting documents on the desktop because they considered the desktop as a path difficult to reach and that meant extra steps for backup. Conversely other users avoided putting files where they were automatically backed up. They created two parallel structures: a set of files that they wanted to back up under "My Documents" and another set of files outside of the area designated for automatic backup. The main reason for these behaviors was either space or time. Some reported that the backup was to a disk with limited storage and they did not want to cause a problem with lots of media files.

Another common technical issue (33%) influencing resource organization was **synchronization** with other computers, either with a laptop, a home desktop, or a network disk. A couple of users used versioning software (CVS). Others organized documents in such a way to make synchronization with other computers easier. A few users solved the problem by keeping all their files on a machine accessible both by home and by the office, usually a network disk.

4.11 Changing Practices (or Not)

Participants reported that the way they organized their files was not necessarily the best one or an optimized one. Sometimes the organization had a long history. A couple of users said they have been using the same file structure for more than 10 years and had become used to it. "It is organized [tree structure] in a way that I have gotten used to over the years". They knew where to put and find everything.

Other people started organizing resources in a certain way and after a while they changed their strategy. One participant initially saved all the attachments she received by email in folders with the name of the sender. After a while she realized that the documents of some users belonged to different projects and, at the same time, the documents related to one project were spread in different folders. She changed strategies and began to organize everything by project.

Other users were not happy with their organization but they simply had not thought about changing it or were avoiding the effort of converting their organization.

5 Conclusion

When talking about a computer environment there is much more entailed than just document organization. The customization of a work environment includes organization of documents and applications and the creation of ways to easily access these resources.

The focus of this study was on customization of the personal computer environment in order to work and to perform tasks. Our participants used a variety of strategies to set up their working environment, to highlight current projects, to let stand out currently used documents, to overview the whole set of activities, and to visualize the different phases of a project. This study looked at people's strategies for resources organization for working on a computer. The study helps in understanding people's needs for a working environment that supports activities as opposed to an archival environment. Understanding these strategies will help in the design of digital library systems that support the strategies people actually employ.

References

1. Barreau, D., Nardi, B.A.: Finding and reminding: file organization from the desktop. SIGCHI Bull. 27, 39–43 (1995)
2. Bellotti, V., Ducheneaut, N., Howard, M., Smith, I.: Taking email to task: the design and evaluation of a task management centered email tool. In: Proc. of the SIGCHI conference on Human Factors in Computing Systems, ACM Press, New York (2003)
3. Boardman, R., Sasse, M.A.: Stuff goes into the computer and doesn't come out: a cross-tool study of personal information management. In: Proc. of the SIGCHI conference on Human Factors in Computing Systems, pp. 583–590. ACM Press, New York (2004)
4. Bondarenko, O., Janssen, R.: Documents at Hand: Learning from Paper to Improve Digital Technologies. In: Proc. of the SIGCHI conference on Human Factors in Computing Systems, pp. 121–130. ACM Press, New York (2005)
5. Dourish, P., Edwards, W.K., Lamarca, A., Salisbury, M.: Presto: an experimental architecture for fluid interactive document spaces. ACM Trans. on Computer-Human Interaction 6, 133–161 (1999)
6. Dumais, S., Cutrell, E., Cadiz, J.J., Jancke, G., Sarin, R., Robbins, D.C.: Stuff I've seen: a system for personal information retrieval and re-use. In: Proceedings of the 26th annual international ACM SIGIR conference on Research and development in information retrieval, ACM Press, New York (2003)
7. Henderson, Jr., D.A., Card, S.: Rooms: the use of multiple virtual workspaces to reduce space contention in a window-based graphical user interface. ACM Trans. Graph. 5, 211–243 (1986)
8. Jones, W., Munat, C., Bruce, H.: The Universal Labeler: Plan the project and let your information follow. In: 68th Annual Meeting of the American Society for Information Science and Technology. American Society for Information Science & Technology (2005)
9. Jones, W., Phuwanartnurak, A.J., Gill, R., Bruce, H.: Don't take my folders away!: organizing personal information to get things done. In: Ext. abstracts CHI 2005, pp. 1505–1508. ACM Press, New York (2005)
10. Kaptelinin, V.: Creating computer-based work environments: an empirical study of Macintosh users. In: Proc. of the 1996 ACM SIGCPR/SIGMIS conf. on Computer personnel research, pp. 360–366. ACM Press, New York (1996)
11. Kaptelinin, V.: UMEA: translating interaction histories into project contexts. In: Proc. of the SIGCHI conference on Human Factors in Computing Systems, pp. 353–360. ACM Press, New York (2003)
12. Karger, D.R., Quan, D.: Haystack: a user interface for creating, browsing, and organizing arbitrary semistructured information. In: Ex. abs. CHI 2004, pp. 777–778. ACM Press, New York (2004)
13. Karger, D.R., Jones, W.: Data unification in personal information management. Commun. ACM 49, 77–82 (2006)
14. Malone, T.W.: How do people organize their desks?: Implications for the design of office information systems. ACM Trans. Inf. Syst. 1, 99–112 (1983)
15. Ravasio, P., Schär, S.G., Krueger, H.: In pursuit of desktop evolution: User problems and practices with modern desktop systems. ACM TOCHI 11, 156–180 (2004)
16. Whittaker, S., Hirschberg, J.: The character, value, and management of personal paper archives. ACM Trans. on Computer-Human Interaction 8, 150–170 (2001)

Empirical Evaluation of Semi-automated XML Annotation of Text Documents with the GoldenGATE Editor*

Guido Sautter, Klemens Böhm, Frank Padberg, and Walter Tichy

Department of Computer Science, Universität Karlsruhe (TH)
Am Fasanengarten 5, 76128 Karlsruhe, Germany
{sautter,boehm,padberg,tichy}@ira.uka.de

Abstract. Digitized scientific documents should be marked up according to domain-specific XML schemas, to make maximum use of their content. Such markup allows for advanced, semantics-based access to the document collection. Many NLP applications have been developed to support automated annotation. But NLP results often are not accurate enough; and manual corrections are indispensable. We therefore have developed the GoldenGATE editor, a tool that integrates NLP applications and assistance features for manual XML editing. Plain XML editors do not feature such a tight integration: Users have to create the markup manually or move the documents back and forth between the editor and (mostly command line) NLP tools. This paper features the first empirical evaluation of how users benefit from such a tight integration when creating semantically rich digital libraries. We have conducted experiments with humans who had to perform markup tasks on a document collection from a generic domain. The results show clearly that markup editing assistance in tight combination with NLP functionality significantly reduces the user effort in annotating documents.

1 Introduction

The digitization of printed literature currently makes significant progress. The Google Libraries Project, for instance, aims at creating digital representations of the entire printed inventory of libraries. Other initiatives specialize on the legacy literature of specific domains, such as medicine, engineering, or biology. While some projects only aim at creating digital versions of the text documents, domain-specific efforts often have more ambitious goals: To make maximum use of the content, text documents are annotated according to domain-specific XML schemas. The XML markup is necessary to access the document collection with techniques that are more sophisticated than keyword search and provide richer semantics. It enables fine-grained searching via XPath or XQuery, mining the document content, and linking the documents.

* Work partially supported by grant BIB47 of the DFG.

L. Kovács, N. Fuhr, and C. Meghini (Eds.): ECDL 2007, LNCS 4675, pp. 357–367, 2007.

Manually creating markup for digitized documents is a cumbersome task. While the advances in NLP (Natural Language Processing) help automate the markup process, fully automated markup solely relying on NLP is not feasible, for several reasons: First, if markup quality is a hard requirement, the accuracy of 95-98% provided by up-to-date NLP applications [1] tends to be insufficient. Second, NLP accuracy decreases heavily if the data is noisy [2]. However, noise is common in raw OCR output. Third, if the markup process involves more than one NLP application, errors add up. When five NLP components arranged in serial order build on the output of each other, the overall estimated accuracy is $98\%^5 \approx 90\%$ at best. Only intermediate manual corrections can mitigate this effect. To date, no existing NLP toolkit allows manual editing of the documents. To achieve high markup quality, a user has to save the document after each NLP step and correct it in an XML editor, then apply the next NLP step, and so on. This back and forth incurs considerable effort. In addition, many NLP components do not produce XML, but other formats. Such output becomes editable only after expensive conversions. These problems call for tools that allow users to deploy NLP components and edit NLP output manually. To this end, we have developed the GoldenGATE editor [3]. It provides a slim API for the seamless integration of NLP components, such as automated taggers for locations or taxonomic names [4]. GoldenGATE offers useful features for editing markup that is the output of NLP, e.g., annotating all occurrences of a given phrase in one step. It also provides functions for cleaning up OCR artifacts and for restoring the structure of the original document.

To quantify the benefit of editing assistance and NLP integration, we conducted a *controlled experiment* [5, 6] in which participants were asked to annotate generic documents using GoldenGATE or XMLSpy, a standard pure XML editor. We measured the task completion times and performed a statistical analysis of the time differences between the editors. The experiment shows that a tight integration of editing assistance and NLP reduces the effort for marking up documents. This finding is of interest to a broader audience: In almost any application domain, large document collections need to be digitized and enhanced with semantic annotations.

Paper outline: Section 2 discusses XML editors and relevant NLP tools. Section 3 describes the features and design of GoldenGATE. Section 4 presents the setup and results of our experiment. Section 5 concludes.

2 Related Work

General-purpose text editors like UltraEdit [7] or Emacs provide little XML-specific support, e.g., for inserting tags. Specialized XML editors, like Oxygen [8] or XMLSpy [9], are tailored to handling XML data. They include document validation against DTDs and XML schemas, interpreters for the XPath and XQuery query languages and XSLT, etc. They also alleviate the creation of markup to some extent, but do not give way to any automation. They are not designed to integrate NLP applications either, since NLP has not been a usual part of XML data handling so far.

The OpenNLP [10] project encompasses a multitude of mostly open-source projects concerned with the development of NLP tools, which are heterogeneous regarding purpose, programming platform, and quality. LingPipe [11] is a professional NLP library. Except for the rule-based tokenization, the analysis functions apply statistical models such as Hidden Markov Models [12]. While its functionality is powerful, LingPipe lacks a user interface: It has to be integrated in other programs to be accessible in ways other than the command line.

The NLP framework GATE [13] offers functionality comparable to OpenNLP, but allows for more complex applications and is capable of producing XML output. It includes Apache Lucene [14] for information retrieval and a GUI for visualization. It is relatively easy to extend with additional components. GATE is dedicated to NLP research and evaluation, rather than document markup and management: It provides functions for assessing markup results obtained with test corpora, but lacks any facility for manual correction of text or markup. Applications similar to GATE are WordFreak [15] and Knowtator [16].

3 The GoldenGATE Editor

In this section, we describe the GoldenGATE editor, which we have designed and built to support annotating text documents. This includes assistance for manual editing (Section 3.1) as well as the seamless integration of NLP components and functionality for correcting NLP output manually (Section 3.2). The development of GoldenGATE is part of a research effort which aims at creating a digital library of biosystematics literature by scanning and marking up the huge body of legacy articles from this domain.

3.1 The Document Editor

In GoldenGATE, a document is displayed and edited in its own document editor (Figure 1), which is a tab in the main window. The editor provides all the functionality required for manually editing both text and markup.

Controlled XML Syntax Generation: If the user has to handle the XML syntax manually – character-wise – this is unnecessarily cumbersome and gives way to syntax errors. Thus, the document editor only allows editing the tag content (i.e., the XML element name, and the names and values of attributes). It generates the syntax (e.g., the angle brackets) automatically and shields it from manual editing. It arranges the tags automatically to enforce wellformedness.

Markup Creation: To mark up a sequence of words with an XML tag, the user can simply select the words in the document and use the *Annotate* function in the context menu. The editor then prompts for the element name and does the rest automatically. To reduce the editing effort further, the context menu pro-vides the most recent element names for instant reuse. Changing the name of an element works similarly, the user does not need to modify start and end tag separately. The same is true for removing the markup around some text, or removing a marked up document fragment, i.e., both the tags and the text enclosed.

Global Markup Editing: Creating, modifying, and removing XML tags often applies to all elements of a certain type. The editor offers support for this, e.g., renaming all XML tags with a certain name, or removing them with or without the text enclosed.

For instance, this is useful for removing the `font` tags from HTML-formatted OCR output. Only when marking up a piece of text with an XML tag, the functionality is slightly different: The user can choose to mark up all occurrences of the selected phrase throughout the document instead of just one. This facilitates marking up, say, all the mentions of a person or location in a document with just a single action.

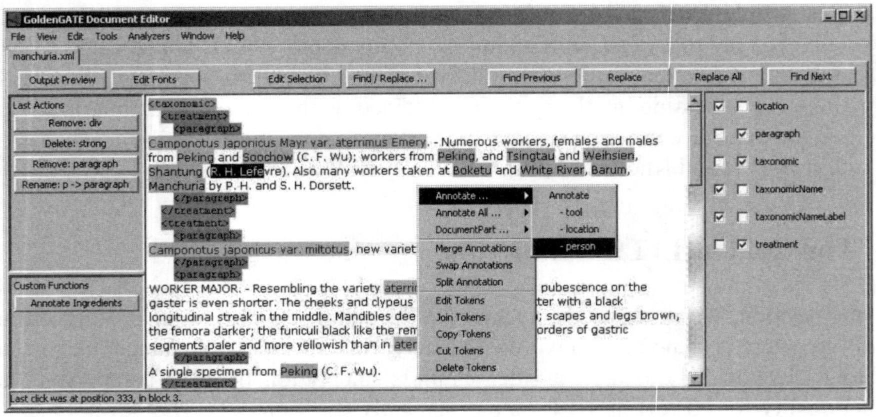

Fig. 1. The annotation editor

Advanced Search Functionality: In many situations, a user needs to access just certain XML elements, which are spread out over the document. With existing editors, this requires a search for each element. In order to simplify this form of element-specific access, the document editor allows displaying and editing elements with a certain name only. This is useful for, say, checking if the section titles in a document are in the correct case.

Flexible Document Display: If the number of tags becomes too large, the document will not be concise any more, and readability is reduced. Thus, the presentation of the document in the editor is flexible to provide the appropriate level of detail for the current editing activity. In the display control (see Figure 1, to the right of the document), a user may choose to highlight text enclosed by certain tags instead of displaying the tags, or not to show the markup at all.

OCR Cleanup: OCR output documents often contain artifacts that were recognized correctly, but do not belong to the text itself. They rather originate from the print layout, like page numbers and titles. Another problem are line breaks that do not mark the end of a paragraph, but also originate from the print layout. Related to the latter are hyphenated words. These artifacts may compromise NLP result quality se-verely, and removing them manually is cumbersome. Therefore, the document editor provides a function for resolving hyphenation and removing erroneous line breaks. In particular, resolving hyphenation automatically is far from trivial, since one has to pay attention not to destroy enumerations that use pre- or postfixes as abbreviations.

3.2 Integration of NLP Tools and NLP Correction

As mentioned in Section 2, powerful NLP tools exist. A major difficulty when implementing such a tool is that XML editors work on characters, while NLP components usually work at the word level: NLP regards text as a sequence of tokens, which are atomic units. This results in data models of different granularities, and the mapping between these models is complex. GoldenGATE hardly includes any hard coded NLP functionality, but lets users add arbitrary NLP functionality without difficulty. We have paid much attention to ensuring that the interface to the NLP components is slim.

To facilitate correction of NLP errors, the editor provides specific views on the NLP results. In particular, it can display a list of all XML elements of a certain name. The user can then review all these annotations without having to search them. He can choose which ones to keep, and which ones to remove. This facilitates finding parts of a text that have erroneously been marked as locations by a Named Entity Recognition component, for instance. On the other hand, if the component failed to recognize some location names, one can easily correct this using the function for annotating all occurrences of a phrase at once.

Another type of markup error is that two distinct entities have been marked as one, e.g., `<loc>Jamaica and Haiti</loc>`, or vice versa, e.g., `<loc>Trinidad</loc> and <loc>Tobago</loc>`. For correcting this type of error and similar ones at the structure level, e.g., paragraphs, the document editor includes functions for both splitting an XML element at a position between its tags and for merging XML elements of the same name. Within this step, attributes are copied or coalesced, respectively.

3.3 Further Functionality

The GoldenGATE editor natively provides basic NLP functionality like gazetteer **Lists** and **Regular Expression** patterns. Both can be applied for annotating a text document automatically. This is to overcome the need for integrating heavyweight external components for lightweight markup tasks.

All facilities for automated markup can be configured to be one-click accessible in the editor. This saves time when accessing the functions most important for the current task. Besides the ones named here, GoldenGATE pro-vides various further features, which we cannot describe here due to space limitations. New features integrate easily through a **resource manager** interface.

4 Controlled Experiment

To find out empirically whether GoldenGATE supports document mark-up tasks better than existing XML editors, we conducted a controlled experiment. In the experiment, participants were asked to annotate documents according to some XML schema (see 4.5). The independent variable ("experimental condition") was the editor in use, either GoldenGATE configured with certain custom functions (see 4.5), or XMLSpy. The measured, dependent variable was the completion time for the mark-up task. All other variables which might affect the mark-up performance had to be controlled by experimental techniques.

4.1 Experimental Design

To achieve sufficient statistical power (see 4.6), we needed about 10 data points for *each* editor. We expected to attract no more than 15 volunteers for the experiment; experience shows, though, that not all volunteers actually show up. Hence, it was necessary to choose an experimental design in which every participant would contribute *two* data points, one for each editor.

In our experiment, every participant worked on two different tasks, using XMLSpy for one task and GoldenGATE for the other. We made sure that the tasks were equivalent (see 4.5). When exposing each participant to both experimental conditions (i.e., usage of both editors), there is a general risk that an observed effect is not caused by the variation of the independent variable alone, but also by the order in which the conditions were applied (sequencing effect). Two important sequencing effects might affect our experiment: An increased familiarity with the mark-up task, the structure of the documents, and the experimental environment after completing the first task might have a positive impact on the performance in the second task (learning effect). Being asked to use the "old" XMLSpy editor in the second task after using the "more comfortable" GoldenGATE editor in the first task might have a negative impact on motivation and performance (motivation effect).

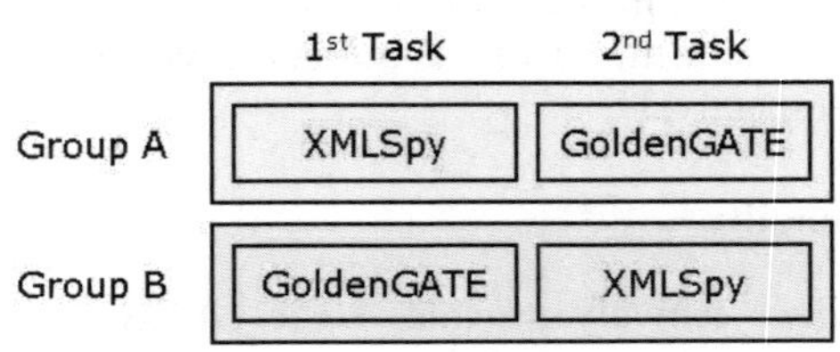

Fig. 2. Counterbalanced experimental design

To make sure that conclusions about performance advantages of the GoldenGATE editor are valid, selecting a proper design which controls for sequencing effects is mandatory. We applied a *counterbalanced* design [18]: half of the participants used XMLSpy for the first task and GoldenGATE for the second one (Group A); the other participants used the editors in the opposite order (Group B), see Figure 2. To even out differences in individual abilities of participants we *randomized* the assignment of participants to groups.

4.2 Pilot Study

A pilot study serves the purpose of validating the experimental material and environment. A pilot study also helps to estimate the size of the effect to be observed in the experiment, a number which is needed to determine the number of data points required for the experiment (see 4.6). In February, we conducted a pilot study with about half a dozen student volunteers as participants. We used excerpts from biosystematics documents (3, 4) in the tasks for the pilot study. A half-day tutorial was offered the day before the pilot study. It covered the features of XMLSpy and GoldenGATE, but also the structure of biosystematics documents. The emphasis in the tutorial was on hands-on work with the editors.

In the experimental tasks, some participants used XMLSpy to mark up their document, others used GoldenGATE. The pilot study revealed several problems with setup and material. Despite the training, the participants showed a lack of proficiency using the more advanced features of Golden-GATE. They did not have sufficient domain knowledge regarding the structure and contents of the biosystematics articles; hence, they needed considerable time to recognize the relevant parts of the documents. Finally, the experimental tasks were too long, and participants became tired before the tasks were finished. As a consequence, we adjusted the tutorial contents and the material for the main experiment.

4.3 Tutorial

In March, we offered an extended tutorial on one day and carried out the experiment on the next day. Given the insights from the pilot study, we included more and longer practical exercises covering the features of the GoldenGATE editor in the tutorial. We still covered XMLSpy to make sure that the participants had the same degree of familiarity with both editors.

For the tutorial and experimental tasks, we let go of the biosystematics documents and used documents from generic domains which are immediately understood by everyone, such as sports news and recipes for Italian dishes. We held a "competition" at the end of the tutorial where the participants had to mark up a document as quickly as possible using GoldenGATE. The rationale was to see how individuals use the tools when working under pressure. The competition showed that the participants were sufficiently familiar with GoldenGATE.

4.4 Participants

12 graduate students in computer science volunteered for the tutorial and experiment. We had 2 no-shows who attended the tutorial, but did not show up for the experiment, and 1 dropout who gave up after having worked on the first task for more than 2.5 hours. Therefore, we had a total of 9 participants in the experiment. The majority of these students were in their 7th semester; the others were more senior, up to their 13th semester. All of them had taken a graduate level database class this semester, which also covered XML.

At the beginning of the tutorial, we handed out a pre-test questionnaire that asked for the students' knowledge of XML, their practical experience with editing XML documents using an XML editor, and their practical experience with correcting errors in digitized documents by hand. Except for two students who had used XMLSpy on and off in the past, the pre-test did not reveal any capabilities of the participants relevant for the experiment.

4.5 Tasks

For the experimental tasks, we used sets of recipes as documents, mainly pasta dishes. We made sure that the two documents had about the same length (12 pages), number of recipes (20), and difficulty. The participants easily understood the structure and contents of the recipes. This was important as we wanted to measure the speed advantages resulting from the features of GoldenGATE and not the time needed to understand the problem domain or document content.

The descriptions of the two experimental tasks were identical, except for the name of the document and editor to use. The participants were asked to add suitable tags to structure the document in recipes, preparation sections, and preparation steps. They had to mark up recipe titles, ingredient lists, individual ingredients, and cooking tools. In addition, the participants had to correct errors which are typical left-overs from a previous OCR phase, including extra page titles, incorrect line and page breaks, and misspelled words. This last requirement is particularly tedious when using XMLSpy, hence it was relaxed during the experiment for the XMLSpy users.

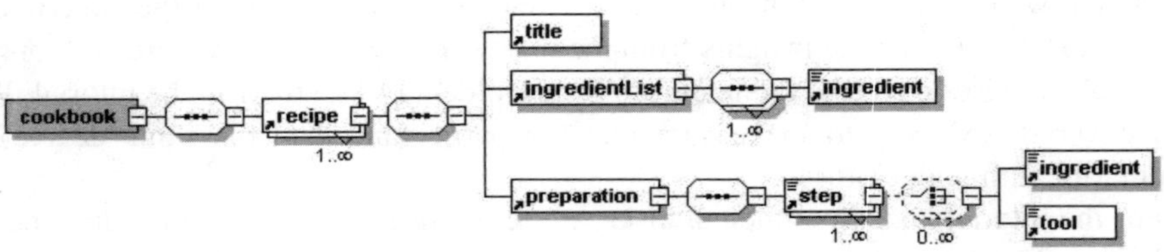

Fig. 3. XML schema for the experiment

XMLSpy users were given a schema (Figure 3) to help them with the markup. The only NLP functionality that was part of the GoldenGATE configuration used in the experiment was an ingredient tagger and a function for normalizing paragraphs. Thus, if GoldenGATE is superior in this current setup already, we can expect it to be better in 'real' settings with more NLP functionality as well. Other GoldenGATE features that we expected to be particularly useful for the experimental task are the list of most recently used annotations and the function for global annotations.

4.6 Sample Size

When planning the experiment, we performed a *power analysis* [17] to estimate the number of data points required to achieve statistically meaningful results. We first chose a significance level of 5 per cent and a desired power [17] of 80 per cent. Then we estimated the effect size for a t-test by considering the expected overlap of the completion time distributions for XMLSpy and GoldenGATE. Based on the data from the pilot study, we expected a large performance advantage of GoldenGATE; hence, we assumed a small overlap of the time distributions of just 10 per cent. This expected overlap maps to an effect size [17] of 1.3 for the t-test. Given a significance level of 5 per cent and an effect size of 1.3, a power of 80 per cent maps to a requirement of 8.3 data points in each experimental condition (i.e., for each editor) for a one-sided t-test [17]. Similarly, the desired power maps to a requirement of 9.6 data points for each editor for a one-sided Wilcoxon test. As a result, we needed to collect between 8 and 10 data points for each editor in the experiment.

4.7 Document Quality

When measuring task completion times as the dependent variable, it is important to make sure that the output of the experimental tasks has a uniform (and minimum) quality; otherwise, short completion times might simply correlate with low or even unacceptable output quality. We defined thresholds for the correctness of the final document: We required 100% correct structural mark-up (recipe, title, ingredientList, preparation, step) and 85% correctness of the semantic markup (ingredients, tools).

We installed a test server in the local intranet which compares the quality of uploaded documents against "gold documents." As testing had very low overhead, we encouraged the participants to upload their intermediate documents to the test server for acceptance testing at will during the experiment. Participants were finished with their task only after having passed the full acceptance test. This required meeting all thresholds and implied having worked on all parts of the task successfully.

4.8 Results

We have 9 valid data points for each editor. For all but one participant, the task completion time when using GoldenGATE was *significantly smaller* than the task completion time when using XMLSpy (Figure 4). The mean of the XMLSpy task completion times is 107 minutes; the mean for GoldenGATE is 77 minutes. The average relative speed-up was 25 per cent with GoldenGATE.

The performance advantage of GoldenGATE over XMLSpy is statistically significant at the 2 per cent level, with a p-value < 0.013 for the paired t-test and a p-value < 0.004 for the paired Wilcoxon test. Our experiment provides strong empirical evidence that the GoldenGATE editor supports document mark-up tasks better than a standard XML editor, such as XMLSpy.

On average, the time needed to complete the first task (102 minutes) was longer than for the second task (82 minutes). Obviously, there was a *learning effect* between the two tasks. This effect does *not* invalidate our findings, though, because the learning effect applied uniformly to both editors: For XMLSpy, the mean task completion time decreased from 117 (Group A) to 97 (Group B) minutes between the two tasks; for GoldenGATE, it decreased from 84 (Group B) to 72 (Group A) minutes. (These differences were visible, but not statistically significant, with p-values larger than 0.11 and 0.19, respectively). Note that this analysis would not have been possible without a counterbalanced design.

When comparing XMLSpy with GoldenGATE for the first task only, the performance difference is significant at the 6 per cent level; similarly, when comparing the editors for the second task only, the difference is significant at the 2 per cent level. Hence, the performance advantage of GoldenGATE over XMLSpy is independent of the order in which the editors were used.

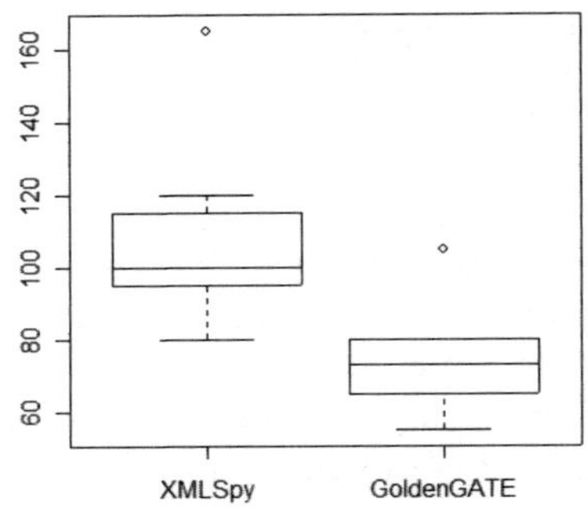

Fig. 4. Boxplot of the completion time distributions

In one exceptional case, the participant was slightly faster using XMLSpy than using GoldenGATE. As a possible explanation, this participant stated in the pre-test questionnaire that he had used XMLSpy on and off prior to the tutorial. In addition, he used GoldenGATE in the first task; hence, the learning effect between the two tasks is likely to have aggravated the observed effect.

From the means and variances of the completion time distributions, we compute [17] an observed effect size of 1.43. Given a significance level of 5 per cent, the experiment has a post-hoc power of 89 per cent for the t-test and of 77 per cent for the Wilcoxon test. Thus, even with fewer data points than originally planned our experiment had a satisfactory power.

5 Conclusions

Integrating assisted manual XML editing and automated markup via NLP applications is promising to efficiently create semantically rich digital libraries. We have implemented this integration in the GoldenGATE editor. In this paper, we have reported on a thorough empirical assessment of this approach. Our study provides strong evidence that a user can perform markup tasks much faster when he can conveniently use NLP functions and does not have to pay attention to the XML syntax, as he would have to in a conventional XML editor. GoldenGATE shows a strong performance because of its easy-to-integrate task-specific NLP functions and its sophisticated assistance for manual XML editing. Users do not need to worry about the wellformedness of the markup because the editor enforces it with each editing step.

In our controlled experiment, the performance advantage of GoldenGATE configured with moderate NLP-functionality was 25% over XMLSpy. When fully customized for a class of documents, NLP can automate the annotation task to a large degree. Thus, we expect a much larger performance advantage of GoldenGATE in domains where the documents have a richer semantic structure, for instance, in biosystematics legacy literature.

The current version of GoldenGATE is available for download at http://idaho.ipd.uka.de/GoldenGATE/.

References

1. Mikheev, A., Moens, M., Grover, C.: Named Entity Recognition without Gazetteers. In: Proceedings of EACL, Bergen, Norway (1999)
2. Miller, D., Boisen, S., Schwartz, R., Stone, R., Weischedel, R.: Named Entity Extraction from Noisy Input: Speech and OCR. In: Christodoulakis, D.N. (ed.) NLP 2000. LNCS (LNAI), vol. 1835, Springer, Heidelberg (2000)
3. Sautter, G., Agosti, D., Böhm, K.: Semi-automated XML Markup of Biosystematics Legacy Literature with the GoldenGATE Editor. In: Proceedings of PSB, Weilea, HI, USA (2007)
4. Sautter, G., Agosti, D., Böhm, K.: A Combining Approach to Find All Taxon Names (FAT) in Legacy Biosystematics Literature, Biodiversity Informatics Journal 3 (2006)
5. Tichy, W.: Hints for Reviewing Empirical Work in Software Engineering. Journal of Empirical Softw. Eng. 5, 309–312 (2000)
6. Müller, M., Padberg, F.: An Empirical Study about the Feelgood Factor in Pair Programming. Int. Symp. on Softw. Metr. 10, 151–158 (2004)
7. IDM Computer Solutions Inc., www.ultraedit.com
8. oxygen/, www.oxygenxml.com
9. Altova GmbH, www.altova.com
10. The OpenNLP project, www.opennlp.org
11. LingPipe, www.alias-i.com/lingpipe
12. Rabiner, L., Juang, B.: An Introduction to Hidden Markov Models. IEEE ASSP Magazine 3(1), 4–16 (1986)
13. GATE, General Architecture for Text Engineering, gate.ac.uk
14. Lucene, A.: lucene.apache.org/java/docs
15. WordFreak, http://wordfreak.sourceforge.net/
16. Knowtator, http://bionlp.sourceforge.net/Knowtator/index.shtml
17. Cohen, J.: Statistical Power Analysis for the Behavioral Sciences, 2nd edn., Erlbaum, Hillsdale, NJ. (1988)
18. Christensen, L.: Experimental Methodology, 10th edn. Pearson, Boston, MA (2007)

Exploring Digital Libraries with Document Image Retrieval

Simone Marinai, Emanuele Marino, and Giovanni Soda

Dipartimento di Sistemi e Informatica - Università di Firenze
Via S.Marta, 3 - 50139 Firenze - Italy
marinai@dsi.unifi.it

Abstract. In this paper, we describe a system to perform Document Image Retrieval in Digital Libraries. The system allows users to retrieve digitized pages on the basis of layout similarities and to make textual searches on the documents without relying on OCR. The system is discussed in the context of recent applications of document image retrieval in the field of Digital Libraries. We present the different techniques in a single framework in which the emphasis is put on the representation level at which the similarity between the query and the indexed documents is computed. We also report the results of some recent experiments on the use of layout-based document image retrieval.

1 Introduction

Document Image Retrieval (DIR) aims at identifying relevant documents relying on image features only. Until today, the largest portion of documents belonging to libraries is made by printed books and journals. The electronic counterparts of these physical objects are scanned documents that are traditionally the main subject of Document Image Analysis and Recognition research, which includes DIR. In this paper, we first review the current research in DIR with special interest in applications to digital libraries. Through this brief analysis we show how DIR techniques can offer new ways to explore large document collections. To support this view, we describe in the rest of the paper a document image retrieval system that has been developed by our research group. The system integrates tools aimed at performing the word indexing at the image level with layout-based retrieval components.

The paper is organized as follows. In Section 2 we review the recent work on Document Image Retrieval. The proposed system is sketched in Section 3, whereas sections 4 and 5 analyze the word indexing and layout retrieval, respectively. Our final remarks are drawn in Section 6.

2 Document Image Retrieval

From a broad point of view, the document retrieval from digital libraries relies on three main components: document storage (or indexing), query formulation, and

L. Kovács, N. Fuhr, and C. Meghini (Eds.): ECDL 2007, LNCS 4675, pp. 368–379, 2007.

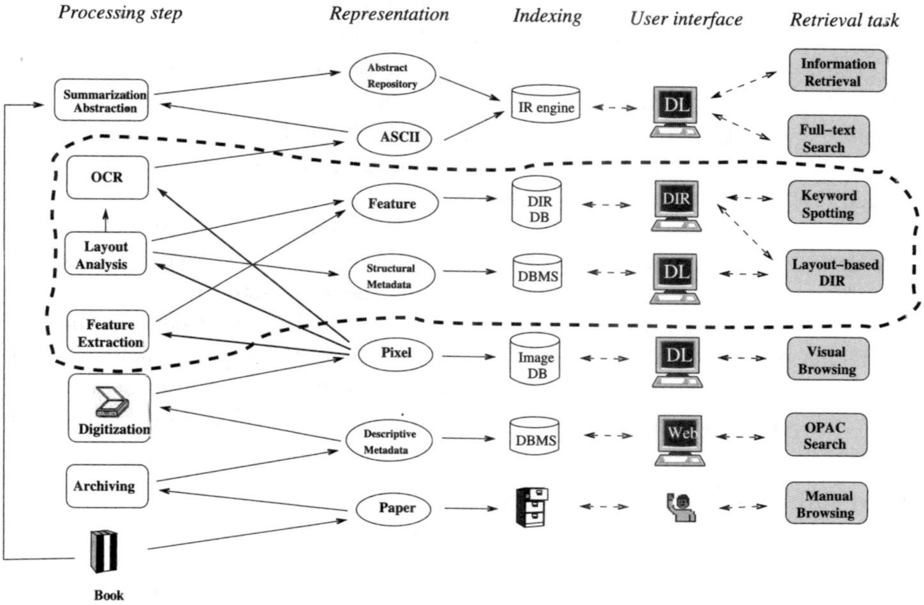

Fig. 1. User interaction in retrieval from libraries. Left: the operations performed during the indexing. Right: user interfaces (**DL**: Digital Library, **Web**: a web interface to the library catalog, **DIR**: Document Image Retrieval interface). The part enclosed in the dashed line is addressed by document image retrieval.

similarity computation with subsequent ranking of the indexed documents. All the retrieval approaches proposed so far can be described on the basis of these three components and the main difference is the "level" at which the similarity computation occurs. To explain this point of view, in Figure 1 we summarize the main steps performed during indexing (either manually or automatically) as well as some typical user interactions with the retrieval system.

Search in libraries has been performed for a long time by using catalog cards and manually encoded information such as printed bibliographies or collections of abstracts ("Manual Browsing" in Fig.1). The direct evolution of this approach was the electronic storage of descriptive meta-data collected with a manual process. From the user point of view the interface with this information is made through "OPAC search".

One key service of current digital libraries is the ability to browse collections by looking at individual pages, stored in appropriate image databases, with the help of customized user interfaces ("Visual Browsing"). One of the most significant services of these DLs is the use of IR techniques associated with full-text search. However, the cost of the text encoding bounds the size of collections that can be accessed in this way. Therefore, the full-text search can be performed only on few documents. To allow the full-text search from large collections, Optical Character Recognition (OCR) packages have used in approaches that follow the recognition-based framework [1,2]. These methods assume that a recognition engine can extract all the information from the digitized documents and possible errors will not affect too much the retrieval performance. The recognition-based approach has some limitations when dealing with documents having a high level of noise, a variable layout, or containing multi-lingual text printed with non-standard fonts. The latter problems are peculiar to ancient and early modern printed documents that populate most libraries.

Several recognition-free approaches have been proposed recently to tackle these problems. Two factors pushed this research: the increased performance of modern computers, and a new interest for the processing of historical documents. In the recognition-free approaches, the similarity between the indexed documents and the query is computed at the raw data or at the feature level, avoiding the explicit recognition during the indexing (see the interfaces "DIR" in Fig. 1). This approach has been exploited for several tasks as outlined in the following.

Word indexing and keyword spotting
Keyword spotting, whose goal is to locate user defined words from an information flow (e.g. audio streams or sequences of digitized pages, such as faxes) [3,4], is one of the first examples of the recognition-free paradigm. In the earlier approaches the similarity computation took place considering the image or low level features and demonstrated the feasibility of the general idea with low expectations concerning the scalability towards large datasets. Some recent applications addressed the processing of larger and heterogeneous collections [5,6] or the integration of word image matching at feature level into an existing DL framework (Greenstone) [7]. The literature on this domain is very large, and we invite interested readers to refer to [1,2,6].

Graphical items
The retrieval of graphical items allows the user to identify interesting documents from a new perspective. Retrieval techniques seem to be appropriate since graphical symbols can have different sizes and are prone to segmentation problems being frequently connected with other parts of the documents. Examples of applications are the logo retrieval [8] and the retrieval of architectural symbols [9]. A related problem is the retrieval of graphical drop-caps from historical documents (e.g. [10]).

Handwriting
The design of systems for the retrieval of handwritten documents working at the image or feature level is still at the beginning. Interesting approaches have dealt with single writer manuscripts. For instance, in [11] the manuscripts of George Washington collection are used as test-bed. Other applications address the processing of on-line handwritten documents [12] and the signature-based document retrieval [13].

Layout retrieval
Document image retrieval based on layout similarity offers to users a new retrieval strategy that was possible before only by manually browsing documents

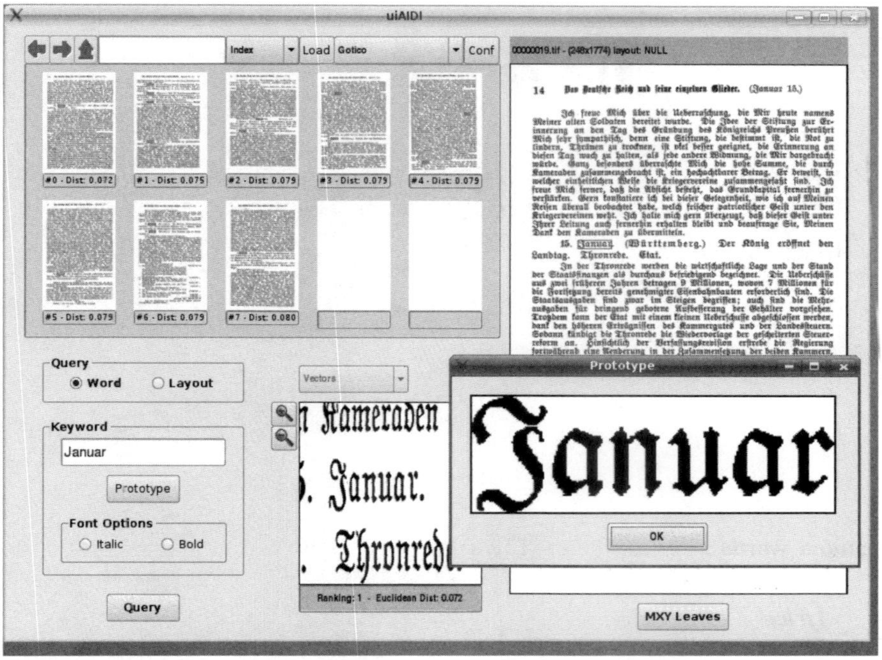

Fig. 2. The user interface of the AIDI system

(either by interacting with physical books/journals or dealing with on-line images on DLs). From the user point of view the retrieval by layout similarity is similar Content Based Image Retrieval (CBIR). In most cases, a fixed-size feature vector is obtained by computing some features in the regions defined by a grid superimposed to the page [14,15]. To overcome the problems due to the choice of a fixed grid size, hierarchical representations of the page layout have been considered as well [16,17]. In the system proposed in [18] the document layout is described by means of relationships between pairs of text lines. A similar approach has been proposed to retrieve documents with different resolutions, different formats and multiple languages [19]. At the crossroad between classification and retrieval are some methods devoted to the slide retrieval in the domain of E-learning [20].

3 The AIDI System

In this section we describe the Automatic Indexing of Document Images (AIDI) system that has been developed by our research group. The system integrates a font-independent word indexing and a layout-based document retrieval into a unique framework.

Figure 2 shows a snapshot of the user interface. On the top-left there are 10 thumbnails that contain either the browsed pages or the retrieval results. The

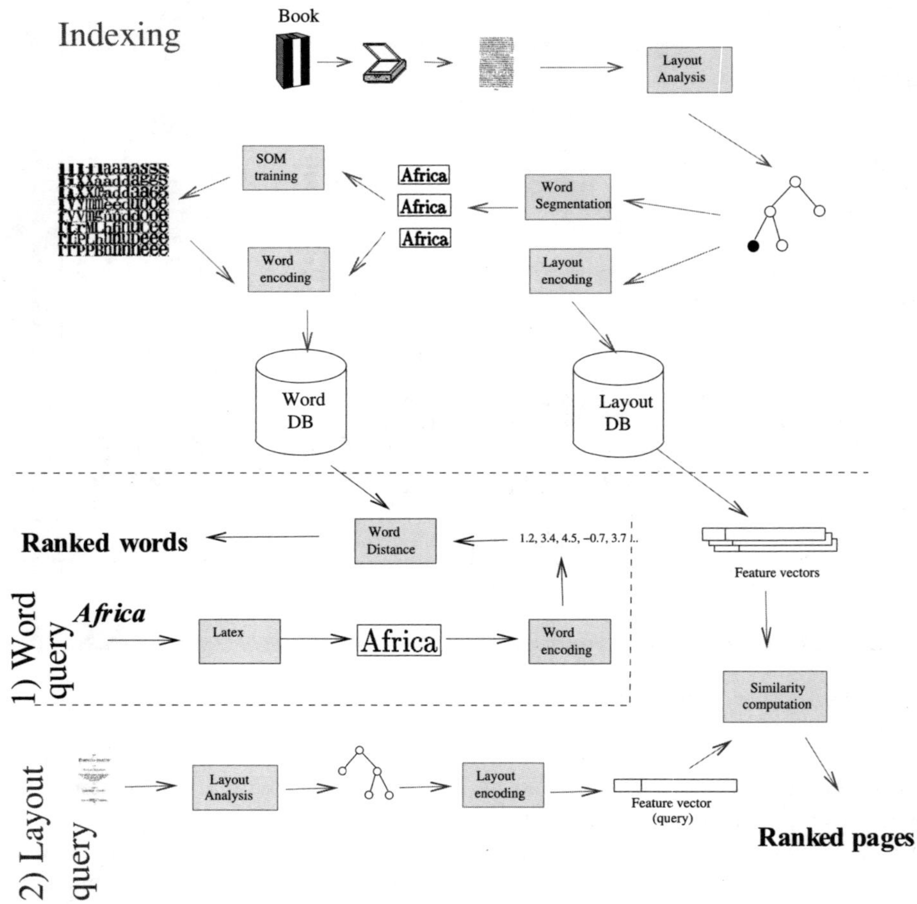

Fig. 3. The AIDI system architecture

image on the right is one selected page that can be further enlarged in the zoom area. The bottom-left part contains the buttons used to perform the queries. In the case of textual queries the user enters the query word in the appropriate field. The figure contains also a window displaying the generated prototype (in this case it is a word printed with the Gothic font). Layout-based queries are made with a query by example approach. Therefore, the user selects a page of interest from the list of thumbnails and performs the query by pressing the appropriate button.

Figure 3 summarizes the AIDI system architecture. During the indexing, the pages are first processed by a layout analysis tools that extracts homogeneous regions. Textual regions are subsequently analyzed so as to extract the words, that are encoded with appropriate character labels. At the same time the layout is encoded in order to obtain a page-level representation of the documents. The pages can be retrieved by taking into account both textual and layout queries. In the first case, a query prototype is obtained by rendering the word entered by the user with the LaTeX package (see the small window in Figure 2). The prototype is encoded similarly to the indexed words that are lastly ranked according to their similarity with the query. Analogously, a query page can be represented in the same way of indexed pages that can be ranked according to their layout similarity.

In the next sections we summarize the main peculiarities of the word indexing and of the layout retrieval, respectively.

4 Word Indexing

Word indexing, that aims at a fast retrieval of words in a document collection, can either process the output of OCR engines or directly work on the document image (e.g. [21]). With few remarkable exceptions, OCR packages are customized on contemporary office documents. The difficulties when processing modern printed documents are of two main categories. First, the fonts evolved in the centuries: some symbols are no longer used, (e.g. specific abbreviations) or are used in different ways (e.g. up to the 18th C. the "s" character was written like an "f"). Second, it should be reminded that a significant contribution to the OCR performance is provided by suitable dictionaries that help disambiguate potential mistakes. If the dictionaries are not aligned with the text to be read, then worst recognition results can be expected.

When the use of OCR is not advisable, either due to the low quality of images or to the presence of non-standard fonts, then image-based word retrieval is a viable alternative. Two main strategies have been considered: holistic word representation and character-like coding.

In holistic word representation each word image is encoded by means of some of its most salient features (e.g. the number of characters or the number of ascenders/descenders) [22]. Most keyword spotting methods are based on a holistic representation (e.g. [23]). In methods based on character-like coding, some objects (that potentially correspond to characters) are extracted from each word. The word is then represented by concatenating the codes assigned to the objects so that similar shapes share the same code.

In our research we deal with modern printed documents that frequently contain text printed with legacy fonts. We use a character clustering by means of Self Organizing Map (SOM) [24] for performing the word indexing with a character-based approach.

During the indexing each document image is first processed with a layout analysis tool that identifies the text regions and extracts the words. The words are then processed to identify their Character Objects (*CO*) by merging overlapping connected components [25]. One *CO* is a part of the word image that generally corresponds to a character (in most cases the *CO* is made of a single connected component). The *CO*s extracted from a few random pages are used to compute appropriate collection-specific character prototypes with the SOM clustering. Labels assigned to characters are used to represent each indexed word.

Fig. 4. Examples of character prototypes computed with SOM clustering. Left: map for the Gothic alphabet; Right: map obtained with the Devanagari Indian script.

One important peculiarity of this approach is the adaptation to different fonts and scripts that is achieved with SOM clustering. In Figure 4 we show two examples of SOMs computed from two collections: a collection of German documents of the 19th Century printed in Gothic and some Indian documents printed with the Devanagari font. In both cases we can see a peculiarity of SOM clustering: more similar clusters are usually put together in the map.

In the retrieval, we take advantage of the cluster proximity. The user enters a query word by means of a textual interface. This word is then processed with the LaTeX software and one word image prototype is generated (Figure 2). From this query image a suitable word representation based on character clustering is computed. The indexed words are then sorted on the basis of their similarity to the query as detailed in [6]. Basically the distance between words is computed taking into account the distance between clusters corresponding to *CO*s so as to reduce the distance between most similar words. In the experimental results discussed in [6] we compared the precision-recall plots obtained with the proposed method with those computed by means of an OCR-based retrieval approach. When dealing with clean documents printed with current technology, then the OCR-based retrieval had slightly better results. However, the proposed method was significantly better than the OCR-based when we addressed documents printed in Gothic font, and Italian and Spanish documents printed in the 18th and 17th Centuries, respectively.

5 Layout Retrieval

In this section we analyze the page retrieval computed on the basis of layout similarity. The layout of a page conveys some semantics that is important for both scholars and general readers, but it's often neglected by DL's indexing approaches. For instance, users could be interested on identifying the pages having a *marginalia* in the right side, or wish to retrieve a page containing a figure on some specific position in the leftmost of the two columns in the page. Another

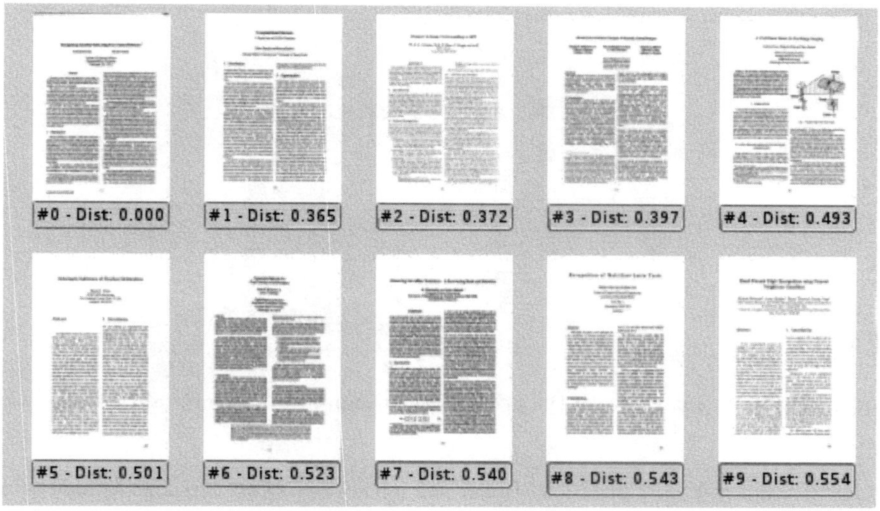

Fig. 5. Example of layout-based page retrieval. The query page is the top-left one.

example is the retrieval of the title page of scientific papers that, starting from a general structure, can have different actual layouts (Figure 5).

The page layout can be represented with a hierarchical description (e.g. the XY tree [26]) that is appropriate when dealing with documents having a layout of average complexity such as digitized books and journals. In particular, MXY trees have been demonstrated to be useful when dealing with documents containing ruling lines and can deal with multi-column pages as well as with pages where the pictures partially cover some text columns [27]. Leaves of the tree correspond to homogeneous regions in the page. To perform the page retrieval, the MXY trees are encoded into a fixed-size representation that is subsequently used to rank the pages. Several approaches can be adopted to compute this vectorial representation as discussed in the following.

In [27] we proposed the use of the *vector model* to describe the page layout. The basic idea that is behind this encoding is the observation that similar layouts frequently contain similar sub-trees in the corresponding MXY tree. Each tree is described by counting the occurrences of tree-patterns composed by three nodes. Trees composed by three nodes can have two basic structures: the first one is composed by a root and two children, the second one is composed by a root, a child, and a child of the second node. To use the vector model the occurrences of *tree-patterns* are considered instead of word-based index terms. These occurrences are weighted with the *tf-idf* approach, and the page similarity is computed by means of the *cosine of the angle* between the query vector and the indexed pages. The choice of this similarity measure is quite natural since the *cosine* is traditionally adopted together with the *tf-idf* weighting in text-retrieval. In analogy with the methods described below we tested also the comparison of these representations with the Euclidean distance, however the results that we

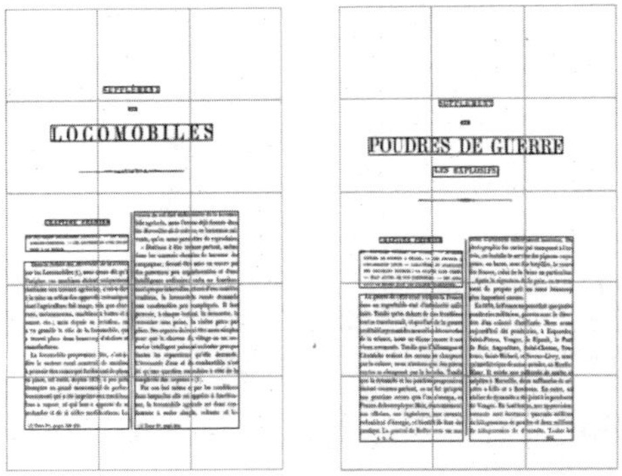

Fig. 6. Two issue2 pages with the grids used to compute the vectorial representation

achieved were worst than those obtained with the *cosine*. In the following we refer to this approach as method "D".

A second approach (method "B") is based on the use of the vectorial representation obtained by computing appropriate features in the regions defined by a grid superimposed to the page [14,15]. Basically, we superimpose a uniformly spaced grid over the page (Figure 6) and we compute, for each cell, the percentage of its area that is covered by text, image and line regions.

The third method (method "C") still starts from the vectorial encoding of the MXY tree based on the occurrences of tree-patterns. However, instead of computing the *tf-idf* weights it uses the occurrences of the patterns as features. In order to select the most significant patterns, a feature selection step is performed, computing the *information gain* provided by each pattern on the basis of a labeled training set.

The last approach (method "A" below) gives more importance to the leaves of the MXY tree (regions in the page) and adds four features corresponding to the percentage of area in the page covered by image and text regions as well by horizontal and vertical lines.

In the latter three cases we take into account the Euclidean distance between feature vectors to compute the vector similarity.

5.1 Experimental Results

To compare the previous methods we made some experiments with a data set is composed by 6 books (containing a total of 4029 pages) belonging to an Encyclopedia of the 19th Century. The pages belong to seven main classes (see Figure 7 for some examples). In addition, there are some pages belonging to other classes, with few pages each, that are not used as query pages. In the experiments we considered one book to perform the feature selection and the others books to compute the precision-recall plots for the four methods described above. These methods have been selected among various alternatives since they are the most interesting and shown the best results. We use each page (belonging to the seven

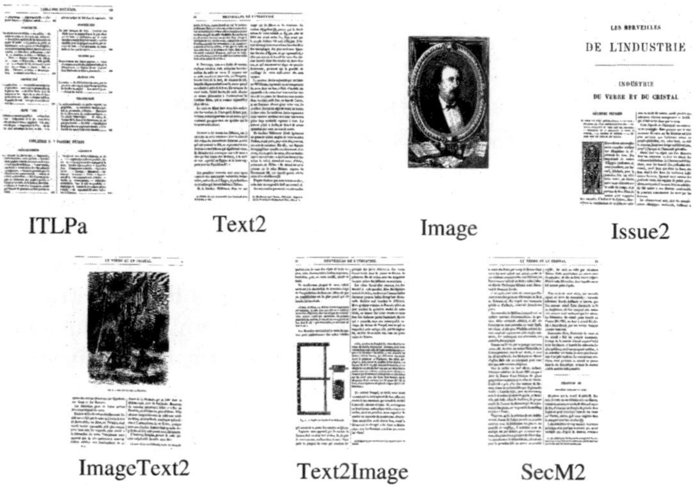

Fig. 7. Examples of pages of the seven classes considered in the experiments

main classes) in the 5 remaining books as query page and compute a precision-recall plot for this query. The plot is computed through an interpolation ([28] page 76) and therefore we have some values of Precision at 0% Recall. All the plots are then averaged in order to compute the graphs shown in Figure 8. From the plots it is clear that for this kind of collection, having regular pages,

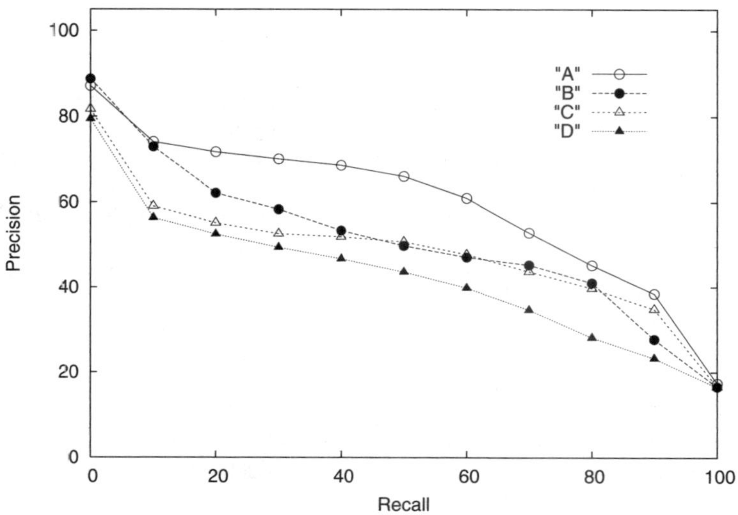

Fig. 8. Comparison of precision-recall plots with four approaches for layout-based retrieval. "A" contribution of leaves; "B" grid-based representation; "C" feature selection with information gain; "D" original approach.

the methods taking into account the information related to the layout regions (methods "A" and "B") are the best ones, since these similarities favour pages having exactly the same layout.

When dealing with other collections, then the generalization capabilities of the MXY-tree based representations (methods "C" and "D") can be more useful since pages of the same class can have quite different layouts. With these methods two pages are estimated to be similar if they share some tree-patterns regardless of their position in the page. An example of this effect has been shown in Figure 5 where a query page corresponding to a "Title" page allows to retrieve pages having various appearances. Choosing among different retrieval strategies is somehow subjective and depends on the user expectations from a given search. We therefore included in the AIDI interface a selector to use either the method "A" or the method "C".

6 Conclusions

In this paper we described a new approach for the analysis of digital collection using document image retrieval techniques. The AIDI system, developed by our research group in the last few years, allows users to retrieve information from documents that are not recognized by current OCR packages. Moreover, layout-based document image retrieval is possible. Future work concerns the evaluation of the text retrieval approach with non-Latin scripts (e.g. the Indians), and the integration into existing DL frameworks, such as Greenstone. Another important improvement is a closer integration of the two retrieval strategies allowing users to perform queries involving both strategies together.

References

1. Doermann, D.: The indexing and retrieval of document images: A survey. Computer Vision and Image Understanding 70(3), 287–298 (1998)
2. Mitra, M., Chaudhuri, B.: Information retrieval from documents: A survey. Information Retrieval 2(2/3), 141–163 (2000)
3. Curtis, J.D., Chen, E.: Keyword spotting via word shape recognition. In: Proceedings of the SPIE - Document Recognition II, pp. 270–277 (1995)
4. Williams, W., Zalubas, E., Hero, A.: Word spotting in bitmapped fax documents. Information Retrieval 2(2/3), 207–226 (2000)
5. Tan, C.L., Huang, W., Yu, Z., Xu, Y.: Imaged document text retrieval without OCR. IEEE Transactions on PAMI 24(6), 838–844 (2002)
6. Marinai, S., Marino, E., Soda, G.: Font adaptive word indexing of modern printed documents. IEEE Transactions on PAMI 28(8), 1187–1199 (2006)
7. Balasubramanian, A., Meshesha, M., Jawahar, C.: Retrieval from document image collections. In: Bunke, H., Spitz, A.L. (eds.) DAS 2006. LNCS, vol. 3872, pp. 1–12. Springer, Heidelberg (2006)
8. Jain, A., Vailaya, A.: Shape-based retrieval: a case study with trademark image databases. Pattern Recognition 31(9), 1369–1390 (1998)
9. Terrades, O.R., Valveny, E.: Radon transform for linear symbol representation. In: Proc. 7th Int.l. Conf. Document Analysis and Recognition, pp. 700–704 (2003)

10. Pareti, R., Uttama, S., Salmon, J., Ogier, J.M., Tabbone, S., Wendling, L., Adam, S., Vincent, N.: On defining signatures for the retrieval and the classification of graphical drop caps. In: Proc. Int.l. Workshop Document Image Analysis for Libraries, pp. 220–231. IEEE press, Los Alamitos (2006)
11. Rath, T., Manmatha, R.: Features for word spotting in historical manuscripts. In: Proc. 7th Int.l. Conf. Document Analysis and Recognition, pp. 218–222 (2003)
12. Jain, A.K., Namboodiri, A.M.: Indexing and retrieval of on-line handwritten documents. In: Proc. 7th Int.l. Conf. Document Analysis and Recognition, pp. 655–659 (2003)
13. Srihari, S.N., Shetty, S., Chen, S., Srinivasan, H., Huang, C., Adam, G., Frieder, O.: Document image retrieval using signatures as queries. In: Proc. Int.l. Workshop Document Image Analysis for Libraries, pp. 198–203. IEEE press, Los Alamitos (2006)
14. Hu, J., Kashi, R., Wilfong, G.: Comparision and classification of documents based on layout similarity. Information Retrieval 2(2/3), 227–243 (2000)
15. Tzacheva, A., El-Sonbaty, Y., El-Kwae, E.A.: Document image matching using a maximal grid approach. In: Proceedings of the SPIE Document Recognition and Retrieval IX, pp. 121–128 (2002)
16. Marinai, S., Marino, E., Soda, G.: Layout based document image retrieval by means of XY tree reduction. In: Proc. 8th Int.l. Conf. Document Analysis and Recognition, pp. 432–436 (2005)
17. Duygulu, P., Atalay, V.: A hierarchical representation of form documents for identification and retrieval. International Journal on Document Analysis and Recognition 5(1), 17–27 (2002)
18. Huang, M., DeMenthon, D., Doermann, D., Golebiowski, L.: Document ranking by layout relevance. In: Proc. 8th Int.l. Conf. Document Analysis and Recognition, pp. 362–366 (2005)
19. Liu, H., Feng, S., Zha, H., Liu, X.: Document image retrieval based on density distribution feature and key block feature. In: Proc. 8th Int.l. Conf. Document Analysis and Recognition, pp. 1040–1044 (2005)
20. Behera, A., Lalanne, D., Ingold, R.: Enhancement of layout-based identification of low-resolution documents using geometric color distribution. In: Proc. 8th Int.l. Conf. Document Analysis and Recognition, pp. 468–472 (2005)
21. Marukawa, K., Hu, T., Fujisawa, H., Shima, Y.: Document retrieval tolerating character recognition errors - evaluation and application. Pattern Recognition 30(8), 1361–1371 (1997)
22. Madhvanath, S., Govindaraju, V.: The role of holistic paradigms in handwritten word recognition. IEEE Transactions on PAMI 23(2), 149–164 (2001)
23. Rath, T.M., Manmatha, R., Lavrenko, V.: A search engine for historical manuscript images. In: SIGIR04, pp. 369–376 (2004)
24. Kohonen, T.: Self-organizing maps. Springer Series in Information Sciences (2001)
25. Marinai, S., Marino, E., Soda, G.: Indexing and retrieval of words in old documents. In: Proc. 7th Int.l. Conf. Document Analysis and Recognition, pp. 223–227 (2003)
26. Nagy, G., Seth, S.: Hierarchical representation of optically scanned documents. In: Proc. 7th ICPR, pp. 347–349 (1984)
27. Marinai, S., Marino, E., Cesarini, F., Soda, G.: A general system for the retrieval of document images from digital libraries. In: Proc. Int.l. Workshop Document Image Analysis for Libraries, pp. 150–173. IEEE press, Los Alamitos (2004)
28. Baeza-Yates, R., Ribeiro-Neto, B.: Modern Information Retrieval. Addison-Wesley, Reading (1999)

Know Thy Sensor: Trust, Data Quality, and Data Integrity in Scientific Digital Libraries

Jillian C. Wallis[1], Christine L. Borgman[2], Matthew S. Mayernik[2], Alberto Pepe[2], Nithya Ramanathan[3], and Mark Hansen[4]

[1] Center for Embedded Networked Sensing, UCLA
jwallisi@ucla.edu
[2] Department of Information Studies
Graduate School of Education & Information Studies, UCLA
borgman@gseis.ucla.edu, mattmayernik@ucla.edu, apepe@ucla.edu
[3] Department of Computer Science
Henry Samueli School of Engineering & Applied Science, UCLA
nithya@cs.ucla.edu
[4] Department of Statistics
College of Letters & Science, UCLA
cocteau@stat.ucla.edu

Abstract. For users to trust and interpret the data in scientific digital libraries, they must be able to assess the integrity of those data. Criteria for data integrity vary by context, by scientific problem, by individual, and a variety of other factors. This paper compares technical approaches to data integrity with scientific practices, as a case study in the Center for Embedded Networked Sensing (CENS) in the use of wireless, in-situ sensing for the collection of large scientific data sets. The goal of this research is to identify functional requirements for digital libraries of scientific data that will serve to bridge the gap between current technical approaches to data integrity and existing scientific practices.

Keywords: data integrity, data quality, trust, user centered design, user experience, scientific data.

1 Introduction

Digital libraries of scientific data are only as valuable as the data they contain. Users need to trust the data, which in turn depends on notions such as data integrity and data quality. Users also need the means to assess the quality of data. Scholarly publications are vetted through peer review processes, but comparable mechanisms to evaluate data have yet to emerge. Data that are reported in publications are evaluated in the context of those publications, but that is not the same as evaluating the data *per se* for reuse. When data are submitted to repositories such as the Protein Data Bank [1], they are evaluated rigorously. When data are made available through local websites or local repositories, mechanisms for data authentication are less consistent. Scientific researchers often prefer to use their own data because they are intimately familiar

L. Kovács, N. Fuhr, and C. Meghini (Eds.): ECDL 2007, LNCS 4675, pp. 380–391, 2007.

with how those data were collected, the actions that were taken in the field to collect them, what went wrong and what was done to fix those problems, the context in which the data were collected, and local subtleties and quirks. Such knowledge of data integrity is difficult to obtain for data collected by other researchers. Researchers (or teachers or students) who wish to reuse data rely on a variety of indicators such as reputation of the data collector and the institution, quality of papers reporting the data, and documentation. Standardized criteria and methods that users can apply to assess data quality are essential to the design of digital libraries for eScience [2].

Enabling reuse of scientific data can be of tremendous future value as such data are often expensive to produce or impossible to reproduce. Data associated with specific times and places, such as ecological observations, are irreplaceable. They are valuable to multiple communities of scientists, to students, and to nonscientists such as public policy makers. Research on scientific data practices has concentrated on big science such as physics [3, 4] or on large collaborations in areas such as biodiversity [5-7]. Equally important in understanding scientific data practices is to study small teams that produce observations of long-term, multi-disciplinary, and international value, such as those in the environmental sciences. The emergence of technology such as wireless sensing systems has contributed to an increase in the volume of data that can be generated by small research teams. Scientists can perform much more comprehensive spatial and temporal in situ sensing of environments than is possible with manual field methods. The "data deluge" resulting from these new forms of instrumentation is among the main drivers of e-Science and cyberinfrastructure [8]. Data produced at these rates can be captured and managed only with the use of information technology. If these data can be stored in reusable forms, they can be shared over distributed networks.

Research reported here is affiliated with the *Center for Embedded Networked Sensing* (CENS), a National Science Foundation Science and Technology Center established in 2002 [http://www.cens.ucla.edu/]. CENS supports multi-disciplinary collaborations among faculty, students, and staff of five partner universities across disciplines ranging from computer science to biology. The Center's goals are to develop and implement wireless sensing systems as described above, and to apply this technology to address questions in four scientific areas: habitat ecology, marine microbiology, environmental contaminant transport, and seismology. Application of this technology already has been shown to reveal patterns and phenomena that were not previously observable. CENS' immediate concerns for data management, its commitment to sharing research data, and its interdisciplinary collaborations make it an ideal environment in which to study scientific data practices and to construct digital library architecture to support the use and reuse of research data.

Digital library tools and services will be important mechanisms to facilitate the capture, maintenance, use, reuse, and interpretation of scientific data. This paper draws together studies of data practices of CENS researchers and analyses of technical approaches to managing data integrity and quality, with the goal of establishing functional requirements for digital libraries of scientific data that will serve this community. Two of the authors of this paper are involved primarily in studies of data practices, two primarily in systems design for data integrity, and two primarily in the development of digital libraries.

Section 2 discusses the characteristics of scientific sensor data collected by CENS. Section 3 presents the research methods used to study data integrity practices of CENS researchers. Research results are presented in Section 4 and discussed in Section 5. Our findings address ways in which digital libraries can assist in improving the integrity of scientific data and in facilitating their reuse.

2 The Data Integrity Problem Redefined

CENS' scientific sensor deployments are generating far more data than can be managed by the traditional methods used for field research. CENS researchers are committed in principle to making their data available for reuse by others. However, they are finding that substantial effort is required to capture and maintain these large volumes of data for their own use, and that even more effort appears to be required to make them available for reuse by others. These data are an important end product of scientific research. They can be leveraged for future analyses by the same or other investigators, whether for comparative or longitudinal research or for new research questions. The ability to interpret data collected by others depends, at least in part, on the ability to assess the integrity and quality of those data. Criteria for data integrity vary by context and by individual, however.

As data production becomes an end unto itself, instead of solely another step towards a publication, and researchers use data produced by others in their own publication, consistent methods are needed to document data integrity and quality criteria in ways that will facilitate data interpretation. The variety of practices associated with data management and range of understanding of what constitutes "data," which are well known issues in social studies of science [9], present practical problems in the design of digital libraries for wireless sensing data.

2.1 Static vs. Dynamic Embedded Sensor Networks

Sensing systems are not a new technology, *per se*. Common applications of sensing networks in the environmental sciences include monitoring of water flow and quality, for example. Most applications of wireless sensing systems in the environmental sciences are static deployments: sensors are placed in appropriate positions to report data continuously on local conditions. Sensors are monitored, both by humans and by computers, to determine changes in conditions. Autonomous networks can rely on machine actuation to capture scientifically relevant data, to alter data collection (e.g., capture data more frequently if excessive pollution is suspected), or to report emergencies that require intervention (e.g., faults in dams, water contamination).

While the initial framework for CENS was based on autonomous networks, early scientific results revealed the difficulty of specifying field requirements in advance well enough to operate systems remotely. Most CENS' research is now based on dynamic "human in the loop" deployments where investigators can adjust monitoring conditions in real time. In addition to conducting extended "static" sensor deployments, where sensing systems are installed and left for weeks or months at a time with only intermittent physical monitoring, CENS teams regularly conduct short term "campaigns" to collect data, in which they deploy a wireless sensing system in the field for a few hours or a few days with constant human presence. They may return to the same site, or a similar site, repeatedly, each time with slightly different equipment or research questions.

Discrete field deployments offer several advantages to the scientific researchers, allowing the deployment of prototype, delicate, or expensive equipment. Scientists also can alter the position of their sensors and the frequency of sampling while in the field, and collect samples for in-field verification. However, the dynamic nature of these deployments poses additional challenges to data integrity, as the conditions, context, and sensor technology may vary by deployment.

2.2 Data Diversity

One of the biggest challenges in developing effective digital libraries in areas such as habitat ecology is the "data diversity" that accompanies biodiversity [5]. Habitat ecologists observe phenomena at a local scale using relatively ad hoc methods [10]. Observations that are research findings for one scientist may be background context to another. Data that are adequate evidence for one purpose (e.g., determining whether water quality is safe for surfing) are inadequate for others (e.g., government standards for testing drinking water). Similarly, data that are synthesized for one purpose may be "raw" for another [2, 9]. For example, CENS technology researchers may view the presence or absence of data as an indicator of the functionality of the equipment, whereas the application science researchers may require data that accurately reflect the environment being measured [11].

2.3 Wireless Sensing Data

While researchers in process control have studied faults, failures, and malfunctions of sensors for many years [12], the problem is significantly harder in the case of wireless sensing systems. First, the scale is larger in wireless sensing systems in terms of number of sensors and areas of coverage. Second, the phenomena being observed in many applications of wireless sensing systems are far more complex and unknown than the manufacturing and fabrication plants studied in classical process control. Consequently, model uncertainty is higher, and often the model is unknown. Third, the sensors used in scientific experiments are often in nascent stages of development and not yet designed for robust field use. Frequent calibration and sensor damage are among the faults that affect the quality of sensor data. Fourth, whereas sensors in factories obtain power and connectivity over wires, resulting in a robust data-delivery infrastructure, wireless sensing systems rely on batteries and wireless channels. Even well planned deployments experience high rates of packet loss [13], resulting in largely incomplete datasets. Lastly, in process control, inputs to the plant are controlled and measured, which is not the case with many phenomena observed by wireless sensing systems (e.g., environmental phenomena; inhabited buildings or other structures). Together, these differences make the problems of detecting, isolating, diagnosing, and remediating faults and failures, and being resilient to their occurrence, more difficult in wireless sensing systems than in traditional plant control.

2.4 Digitizing the Oral Culture

CENS has relied on a largely oral culture for the exchange of information about how data are collected, the equipment used, and the state of the equipment. As the Center has grown, an oral culture is no longer sufficient to capture and retain institutional memory. The student research population turns over rapidly and tacit knowledge needs to be exchanged within and between a larger number of research teams. These are but two reasons for communication breakdowns to occur in the data lifecycle. Research deployment practices were identified as a critical area that required more consistent documentation and better means of information exchange.

Data sharing is often an interpersonal exchange between data collectors and data requestors. This can be a time- and labor-intensive process to describe and document data appropriately for use by others. Interpersonal exchanges do not scale well to large research centers and frequent data requests [2]. Much of our research is devoted to developing tools, services, and policies that will facilitate data capture, management, use, and sharing, while respecting rights and preferences of researchers in determining what data to release to whom, in what formats, and under what conditions [11, 14, 15].

3 Research Methods

The goal of our research initiative within CENS is to provide researchers with a transparent framework of tools that will allow them to create, describe, store, and share data resources efficiently. The design of these tools, and associated digital library services and policies, is based on studies of data practices. We have applied a variety of research methods over a five-year period, including survey studies, field observation, and documentary analyses [11, 14].

In this paper we compare technical approaches to data integrity with scientists' practices associated with data integrity. We draw upon multiple sources to identify functional requirements for digital libraries, including analysis of documents produced by the CENS data integrity group, interviews with members of that group, interviews with domain scientists, computer scientists, and engineering researchers in CENS, and analysis of existing data sets and data archives.

3.1 Studies of Scientific Data Practices

The interview data reported here are drawn from a study of five environmental science projects within CENS. For each project we interviewed a complementary set of science and technology participants, including faculty, post-doctoral fellows, graduate students and research staff. We interviewed 22 participants, each for 45 minutes to two hours; interviews averaged 60 minutes [14, 15]. Results from interviews with computer science and engineering researchers are included in the section on technical approaches to data integrity; results from interviews with the scientists are reported in the section on scientific practices.

Interviews were audiotaped, transcribed, and complemented by the interviewers' memos on topics and themes [16]. Initial analysis identified emergent themes. A full coding process, using NVIVO, was used to test and refine themes in the interview transcripts. With each refinement, the remaining corpus was searched for confirming or contradictory evidence, using the methods of grounded theory [17]. Interview questions were grouped into four categories: data characteristics, data sharing, data policy, and data architecture. In this paper we report only responses that discussed data integrity, quality, trust, or related issues about data interpretation. Most of the responses reported here were elicited by questions about data characteristics or data architecture.

3.2 Integrity Research Group

As CENS research has matured and many basic technical challenges of sensor systems have been addressed, data integrity and quality have become driving concerns of all parties in this multidisciplinary collaboration. The Integrity Group, consisting of ten students and three faculty from computer science, engineering, and statistics, addresses technical approaches to data integrity. This group has surveyed existing approaches to data integrity, implemented both rule-based and statistical learning algorithms, and initiated data integrity experiments, either leveraging existing CENS field deployments or designing original experiments. Members of this group are routinely included in pre-deployment design discussions and consulted during post-deployment analysis, for applications as diverse as aquatic sensing [18], a soil observing system for examining CO2 flux [19], and a short-term deployment in a rice paddy in Bangladesh to study groundwater arsenic content [20].

4 Results

Results are reported in two sections. First we summarize current scientific practices to ensure data integrity. Evidence of these practices is drawn from the interviews with domain scientists within CENS; most of these respondents are faculty or doctoral students in the biological sciences. Second we present technical approaches to ensuring data integrity, drawing upon the observations and expertise of CENS researchers in computer science, engineering, and statistics. Of the many systems approaches being pursued at CENS, we have identified these as having the most direct impact on digital library design for CENS research.

4.1 Needs of CENS Application Scientists

"We have to have confidence...in what the measurements are collecting for information." This simple statement by a CENS scientist belies the complexity of achieving trust in one's own data. Many factors influence a researcher's confidence in data, most of which arise from the complexities of generating and capturing data. Confidence in data depends upon trust in the entire data life cycle, from the selection and calibration of equipment, to in-field setups and equipment tests, to equipment reliability once it is in the field, to human reliability. Trust can be enhanced by documentation of each step in the process and by recording of tacit knowledge that may be exchanged orally in the field. Lab and field notebooks also are essential forms of documentation, whether in paper or digital form. Results reported in this section

address questions of what scientists need to know about the data collection process to interpret and trust the data, which in turn depends upon data integrity and quality.

Equipment Selection. As with any task, the equipment used must be able to perform the task adequately. Thus it is necessary to understand the capabilities or limitations of a given sensor to determine whether it is appropriate to capture the desired observations. As one scientist put it, *"you really need to know what its limitations are, what are its confounding factors, so that you can be relatively confident that your reading is correct."* Each model of sensor has a level or range of sensitivity, and some applications require a very fine level of sensitivity and others require a more gross reading. Understanding where and how the sensor is to be used informs the choice and use of equipment.

Sensors can measure variables in multiple ways. Some sensing methods are direct and others are proxy-based. The method chosen will influence both the interpretation of the resulting data and one's trust in them, as illustrated by the following comment of a biologist:

> *"There are hundreds of different ways of measuring temperature. If you just say, 'The temperature is...,' then that's really low-value compared to, 'The temperature of the surface measured by the infrared thermal pile, model number XYZ, is...'. From this I know that it is measuring a proxy for a temperature, rather than being in contact with a probe. And it is measuring it from a distance. I know that its accuracy is plus or minus .05 of a degree based on the instrument itself. I want to know that it was taken outside versus inside in a controlled environment."*

Equipment Calibration. Off-the-shelf sensors presumably have been tested for quality before being sold. Such testing normally includes calibration against the standards described in the technical specifications. The majority of off-the-shelf sensing equipment used by CENS researchers are also calibrated by the investigators and their technical staff. Sensing equipment that can only be calibrated by the manufacturer must be returned periodically for recalibration, as described by this researcher:

> *"We calibrate against a standard. So it depends on the instrument. If it's something simple we can calibrate it here. If it's a more high-tech instrument, like a lot of what we use are infrared gas analyzers for measuring photosynthesis and they're factory calibrated. We've got to send it back to the factory... once or twice a year to get it calibrated... the complicated things we definitely send back."*

Each sensor model has a specific process for calibration and specific standards for calibration, as reflected in this comment:

> *"The [four] parameters that we collect for each sensor [are] the upper and lower detection limit...and the slope and the Y-intercept for the calibration equation...the calibration equation is just a linear Y = MX + B."*

Calibration information for sensors such as these can be captured in a succinct manner. Other important information to capture is the date of the most recent calibration, because once calibrated, equipment does not necessarily remain calibrated. As another scientist said, *"there is no way to measure in laboratory conditions and have it apply to the field."* Thus an important part of interpreting the data includes knowledge of how the calibration parameters change over time. One approach to capturing changing calibration parameters is periodically to calibrate the sensor in-situ (i.e., without extracting it from the soil or water) by providing a known input and recording the reported output.

Ground-truthing. Unfortunately data from many sensors cannot be blindly trusted. This is partly due to the uncertainty of field conditions and partly to frailty of equipment. Calibration accuracy is known to degrade over time. When possible, scientists periodically validate sensor data by applying a known perturbation to a sensor, over-sampling the phenomena, and capturing physical samples (e.g., water, dirt, leaves, plankton) to validate measures.

4.2 Technical Approaches to Data Integrity

The Integrity Group has led two significant development efforts within CENS that influence the design of digital libraries. First is a move toward in-field analysis of data to support both system design and monitoring. This project is diffuse, branching across several Ph.D. projects and not yet producing a unified platform, but essential because methods to access models and data in the field are becoming part of most CENS systems. Second is SensorBase.org, a database platform for data from short-term, rapidly deployed experiments and from longer-lived, continuously operating installations [21, 22]. SensorBase.org is a central component of CENS' data ecology.

Real-Time, Adaptive Fault Detection. Fault detection is an important technical component of data integrity for embedded networked sensing systems. Often fault detection is viewed solely as a component of post-deployment analysis. Instead of identifying faults in real-time, many users assume they can wait until all the data have been collected, discarding faulty data later. This assumption is flawed for two reasons. First, it is not always easy to tell which data are faulty once the collection process is complete. Researchers may need specific information about the context (e.g., an irrigation event occurred at 3PM during the data collection), or need to take physical measurements (e.g., extracting physical samples to validate the sensor data) to determine if the sensor data are faulty. If scientists interact with the network while in the field to perform data analysis and modeling, data quality can be improved significantly. For example, physical soil samples taken at specific times were useful in validating questionable chloride and nitrate data collected by the network of sensors in Bangladesh. Second, especially for soil sensor deployments, where sensors are short-lived and require frequent calibration, the amount of data available is so small that none can be spared. For example, during one deployment, 40% of the data had to be discarded, limiting the amount of scientific analysis possible.

In addition to detecting faults in real-time, systems must be dynamic. Simple fault detection includes applying statically defined thresholds to data in order to separate good and bad data. This approach is not ideal because environments are dynamic, and notions of what it means to be faulty change over time, both as the sensor ages and as environmental processes develop. Further, notions of faults vary by deployment, so users often must set their own thresholds for each new sensor and environment.

Tools to Improve Data Quality. The above lessons are being incorporated into the design of *Confidence*, a system to improve the quality of data collected from large sensor networks. *Confidence* enables field researchers to administer sensors more effectively by automating key tasks and intelligently guiding a user to take actions that demonstrably improve the data quality. The system uses a carefully chosen set of features to group similar data points and to identify actions a user can take to improve system quality. As users take actions and manually validate sensor data, the system adjusts how data are grouped, thus learning to modify parameters for good and faulty data.

Confidence includes tools to annotate data with actions users have taken and to perform other types of data validation. However, this approach is a primitive implementation of a more complete documentation system; much more information is needed to document the context of sensor data collection adequately.

Building an Information Ecology. A set of complimentary tools and services is being developed by CENS to capture sensor data and metadata, which together form a CENS information ecology. These include *Confidence*, described above, to improve the initial data capture in the field, SensorBase to capture, analyze, and visualize data, the CENS Deployment Center (CENSDC) to capture and share information about deployments, and a bibliographic database of CENS publications.

SensorBase provides the sensing research community with a framework for sharing data and for experimenting with models and computation to support data integrity. SensorBase allows for the "slogging" of sensor data directly from the field into the database. Many of its diagnostics and alerting capabilities, leveraging RSS and email, facilitate research by the Integrity Group. Sensorbase acts as a data digital library, but currently lacks metadata crucial for the interpretation of CENS data. SensorBase will rely on in-field tools such as fault detection to increase the quality of data as they enter the database, and will provide other tools to add necessary metadata.

The CENS Deployment Center is a planning tool for documenting field deployments. It attempts to supplement the "oral culture" of deployments through simple interfaces to record equipment requirements, calibration requirements, personnel requirements, and other contextual information, as well as lessons learned from individual field deployments.

The bibliographic database of CENS publications complements SensorBase and CENSDC. Publications traditionally have served as access points to data and as wrappers containing descriptions of equipment, data collection methods, and other information necessary to interpret results. The internal CENS bibliographic database has been ported over to the University of California eScholarship Repository with its own home page [http://repositories.cdlib.org/cens/], greatly improving public access.

Our goal is a tight integration of SensorBase, CENSDC, and the CENS eScholarship repository. CENSDC will document the SensorBase datasets such that deployment records will link to resulting datasets and vice versa. As research results are published, links can be established between the publication, dataset, and deployment records. This tight coupling will establish a rich value chain through the life cycle of CENS data, documentation, and publications [2].

5 Discussion and Conclusions

The early years of wireless sensing research were focused largely on the problems associated with resource-constrained communications, processing of sensed data, and metrics such as quantity and timelines of data collected. Not much attention was paid to the quality of information returned by the system or the integrity of the system itself. As deployment experience increases, data integrity has become a core concern. Researchers now recognize that data and system integrity are limiting factors in scaling these technologies. The focus of data integrity activities has shifted from post-deployment to concurrent processes within deployments. By capturing cleaner data upstream, later problems in identifying potentially errant data are minimized. These techniques facilitate greater trust in those data and enable scientists to analyze data with the assurance that data are complete and of high quality.

A set of complimentary tools and services are being developed to capture sensor data, metadata, and publications, which together form a CENS information ecology. The information ecology described here can be leveraged before, during, and after deployments to collect contextual information, to provide access to an array of information about CENS research, and to follow the life cycle of a research project.

In sum, we are developing an architecture for data integrity and quality in wireless sensing systems. Through interviews, observation, consultation, and systems development, we are learning enough about scientific data practices to build digital libraries that will facilitate data integrity and will improve the ability of current and future researchers to interpret and trust those data. Wireless sensing systems have advanced to the point where the technology is producing data of real scientific value. Data integrity problems must be addressed if these data are to be useful to the larger scientific community.

Digital libraries can facilitate data integrity by recognizing and accounting for the scientific practices and requirements identified here. Scientists have established methods for describing the network, sensors, and calibrations, but often this information is documented separately from the data, if it is documented at all. Among the many research questions provoked by our research are how digital libraries can store essential contextual information and associate it with relevant data points. Sensor faults have a huge impact on the quality and quantity of data generated by wireless sensing system deployments. Similarly, we are concerned with how sensor fault detection can be reflected in digital libraries. Calibration information is essential to post-deployment data analysis, but calibration information varies for each type of sensor, and in some circumstances even between sensors of the same type on the same deployment. Issues arise such as what level of granularity in the calibration information needs to be associated with each data set. Future architecture for wireless sensing systems must address capturing, organizing, and accessing this information.

Acknowledgements. CENS is funded by National Science Foundation Cooperative Agreement #CCR-0120778, Deborah L. Estrin, UCLA, Principal Investigator; Christine L. Borgman is a co-Principal Investigator. CENSEI, under which much of this research was conducted, is funded by National Science Foundation grant #ESI-0352572, William A. Sandoval, Principal Investigator and Christine L. Borgman, co-Principal Investigator. Alberto Pepe's participation in this research is supported by a gift from the Microsoft Technical Computing Initiative. The CENS Integrity Group is supported by NeTS-NOSS seed funding. SensorBase research in CENS is led by Mark Hansen and Nathan Yau. Support for CENSDC development is provided by Christina Patterson and Margo Reveil of UCLA Academic Technology Services.

References

1. Protein Data Bank. Visited: (October 4, 2006), http://www.rcsb.org/pdb/
2. Borgman, C.L.: Scholarship in the Digital Age: Information, Infrastructure, and the Internet. MIT Press, Cambridge, MA (2007)
3. Traweek, S.: Beamtimes and lifetimes: the world of high energy physicists. 1st Harvard University Press pbk. xv, p. 187. Harvard University Press, Cambridge, Mass (1992)
4. Galison, P.: Image and Logic: A Material Culture of Microphysics. University of Chicago Press, Chicago (1997)
5. Bowker, G.C.: Biodiversity datadiversity. Social Studies of Science 30(5), 643–683 (2000)
6. Bowker, G.C.: Mapping biodiversity. International Journal of Geographical Information Science 14(8), 739–754 (2000)
7. Bowker, G.C.: Work and information practices in the sciences of biodiversity. In: VLDB 2000, Proceedings of 26th international conference on very large data bases. El Abbadi, A., et al. Cairo, Egypt Kaufmann, pp. 693–696 (2000)
8. Hey, T., Trefethen, A.: The Data Deluge: An e-Science Perspective. In: Grid Computing -- Making the Global Infrastructure a Reality Wiley, Chichester (Visited January 20, 2005), http://www.rcuk.ac.uk/escience/documents/report_datadeluge.pdf
9. Bowker, G.C.: Memory Practices in the Sciences. MIT Press, Cambridge, MA (2005)
10. Zimmerman, A.S.: New Knowledge from Old Data: The Role of Standards in the Sharing and Reuse of Ecological Data. Science, Technology, & Human Values (in press)
11. Borgman, C.L., Wallis, J.C., Enyedy, N.: Little Science confronts the data deluge: Habitat ecology, embedded sensor networks, and digital libraries. International Journal on Digital Libraries (in press)
12. Isermann, R.: Fault diagnosis and fault tolerance. Springer, Heidelberg (2005)
13. Tolle, G., et al.: A macroscope in the redwoods. In: Sensys, San Diego, CA (2005)
14. Borgman, C.L, Wallis, J.C., Enyedy, N.: Building Digital Libraries for Scientific Data: An exploratory study of data practices in habitat ecology. In: Gonzalo, J., Thanos, C., Verdejo, M.F., Carrasco, R.C. (eds.) ECDL 2006. LNCS, vol. 4172, pp. 170–183. Springer, Heidelberg (2006)
15. Borgman, C.L., et al.: Drowning in Data: Digital Library Architecture to Support Scientists' Use of Embedded Sensor Networks. In: JCDL '07: Proceedings of the 7th ACM/IEEE-CS Joint Conference on Digital Libraries. Vancouver, BC. Association for Computing Machinery (in press)
16. Lofland, J., et al.: Analyzing Social Settings: A Guide to Qualitative Observation and Analysis, Wadsworth/Thomson Learning, Belmont, CA(2006)
17. Glaser, B.G., Strauss, A.L.: The discovery of grounded theory; strategies for qualitative research. Observations, Aldine Pub. Co., Chicago (1967)
18. Singh, A., et al.: IDEA: Iterative experiment Design for Environmental Applications. CENS Technical Report (Visited January 28, 2007) (2006), http://research.cens.ucla.edu/pls/portal/docs/page/cens_resources/tech_report_repository/spots07_idea.pdf

19. Ramanathan, N., et al.: Investigation of hydrologic and biogeochemical controls on arsenic mobilization using distributed sensing at a field site in Munshiganj, Bangladesh. in American Geophysical Union, Fall Meeting. (Visited June 6, 2007) (2006), http://adsabs.harvard.edu/abs/2006AGUFM.U41B0823R
20. Ramanathan, N., et al.: Designing Wireless Sensor Networks as a Shared Resource for Sustainable Development. In: Information and Communication Technologies and Development (2006)
21. Chen, G., et al.: Sharing Sensor Network Data. CENS Technical Report. (Visited January 28, 2007) (2007), http://research.cens.ucla.edu/pls/portal/docs/page/cens_resources/tech_report_repository/share_sn_data.g.chen.pdf
22. Chang, K., et al.: SensorBase.org - A Centralized Repository to Slog Sensor Network Data. In: International Conference on Distributed Networks (DCOSS)/EAWMS (2006)

Digital Libraries Without Databases: The Bleek and Lloyd Collection

Hussein Suleman

Department of Computer Science, University of Cape Town
Private Bag, Rondebosch, 7701, South Africa
hussein@cs.uct.ac.za

Abstract. Digital library systems are frequently defined with a focus on data collections, traditionally implemented as databases. However, when preservation and widespread access are most critical, some curators are considering how best to build digital library systems without databases. In many instances, XML-based formats are recommended because of many known advantages. This paper discusses the Bleek and Lloyd Collection, where such a solution was adopted. The Bleek and Lloyd Collection is a set of books and drawings that document the language and culture of some Bushman groups in Southern Africa, arguably one of the oldest yet most vulnerable and fragile cultures in the world. Databases were avoided because of the need for multi-OS support, long-term preservation and the use of large collections in remote locations with limited Internet access. While there are many advantages in using XML, scalability concerns are a limiting factor. This paper discusses how many of the scalability problems were overcome, resulting in a viable XML-centric solution for both greater preservation and access.

1 Introduction and Motivation

Digital Library Systems (DLSes) have shared a close relationship with database systems as such databases are often the underlying data storage fabric of the DLS. The almost inseparable nature of this relationship is clear in popular tools such as EPrints [10] and DSpace [9], that nominally use mySQL and Postgres respectively to hold their primary metadata repositories. The databases provide an efficient mechanism to add, update and retrieve items from a collection. Alternatives to databases that fulfil the same needs may be feasible replacements.

It can be argued that in some situations a database may not be the most desirable or effective storage mechanism and that efficient solutions can be crafted from other structured data storage technologies. In the digital preservation arena, it has already been suggested and demonstrated that XML and its sister technologies may be better suited for aspects of digital preservation [2] [11].

A convergence of factors provides additional support for this hypothesis. Firstly, there is a growing acceptance that managing large quantities of data is one of the key challenges for digital libraries. The Storage Resource Broker [8] abstracts the details of data access in dealing with scalability, thus creating

L. Kovács, N. Fuhr, and C. Meghini (Eds.): ECDL 2007, LNCS 4675, pp. 392–403, 2007.

middleware that is independent of actual underlying databases or filesystems. Secondly, most modern DLSes have accepted the importance of interoperability. This is usually achieved by supporting DL standards such as the Open Archives Initiative Protocol for Metadata Harvesting [5] and/or Web standards such as Really Simple Syndication (RSS) [14]. In both cases, metadata is transferred from one collection to another without any notion of how the source or destination metadata is stored or processed. Finally, archival storage mechanisms such as the OAI Static Repository Gateway Specification [6] are being defined at the level of structured data in XML, rather than database-centric tables. All of these factors indicate a higher abstraction for structured data, that is increasingly making it possible to connect and architect systems without knowing about the underlying database used for storage, or even not using an underlying database at all.

In comparing database-centric solutions to XML-centric solutions, databases have a clear advantage in some areas, including:

- the efficiency of insertion and retrieval operations;
- a well-established and standardised query language;
- and existing installations of the software on most servers.

There are, however, a few challenges in using databases, and most of these are in fact addressed by XML data stores and XML-specific data manipulation tools. Some key issues are enumerated in Table 1.

Based on this comparison of data representation approaches, it does appear that XML-based solutions may be more appropriate for some problems. However, efficiency and scalability are still concerns that must be addressed.

This paper discusses how an XML-centric solution was devised for the Bleek and Lloyd Collection; and how the scalability and efficiency concerns were addressed for this project.

2 The Bleek and LLoyd Collection

The Bleek and Lloyd Collection [13] is a collection of paper-based artefacts that document the culture and language of the `|Xam` and !Kun groups of Bushman people. It is widely held that the Bushman people are among the oldest known ethnic groups in the world. Alas, the Bushman way of life - including oral traditions, language, morality and relationship with the natural environment - has been largely subsumed by the onslaught of Western civilization, and the `|Xam` and !Kun languages are already extinct. In general, it is estimated that within only a few years the last generation of Bushman people who are knowledgable in the ancient customs will have passed away. This impending loss of an entire ancient culture underscores the importance of any and all preservation activities. Digital preservation of the Bleek and Lloyd Collection is currently underway in this context.

The books and drawings that constitute the bulk of the Bleek and LLoyd Collection are jointly owned by the National Library of South Africa, the Iziko

Table 1. Challenges in using database systems and how these map to XML-centric solutions

Issue	Database Systems	XML Systems
Installation	Needs to be installed and running, and on multi-user systems is often owned by the administrator	No need for daemon or administrator privileges, and many tools are commonly embedded in Web browsers
Platform	Systems are not usually platform-independent because of performance tuning	There are many tools to manipulate XML and modern Web browsers integrate some of them, e.g., DOM parsers
Processing	Data must be extracted before it can be processed	Backups, data transformations, etc. require only handling of flat files so can be conducted at the OS level
Long-term preservation and access	Databases are usually stored in binary formats for efficiency, therefore their data is not human-readable	XML data is always human-readable

National South African Museum and the University of Cape Town. The books record information obtained by Wilhelm Bleek and Lucy Lloyd in the 19th century from prisoners interned at the Breakwater Prison in Cape Town. Drawings done by these same individuals supplement the narratives in the notebooks. Figures 1 and 2 provide examples of the book page images and drawing images respectively.

In 1997, these artefacts were added to the UNESCO Memory of the World register. This stresses the need for them to be preserved at all costs. At the same time access needs to be granted to researchers and scholars around the world, including in Africa, where Internet bandwidth is often poor or non-existent.

In 2003, the Lucy Lloyd Archive and Research Centre at the Michaelis School of Fine Art arranged for all artefacts to be scanned at high resolution and then generated metadata and re-keyed the text for each granular object [7]. These images and metadata were then used as the basis for this digital library system.

There are a total of 157 notebooks, containing a sum of 14128 page images. The page images correspond primarily to pairs of facing pages, but they also include inserts, covers and spines. The average size of image files is approximately 172 kilobytes - these are low-resolution versions of the images that are to be made available on a DVD-ROM version of the collection. The page images are in JPEG format.

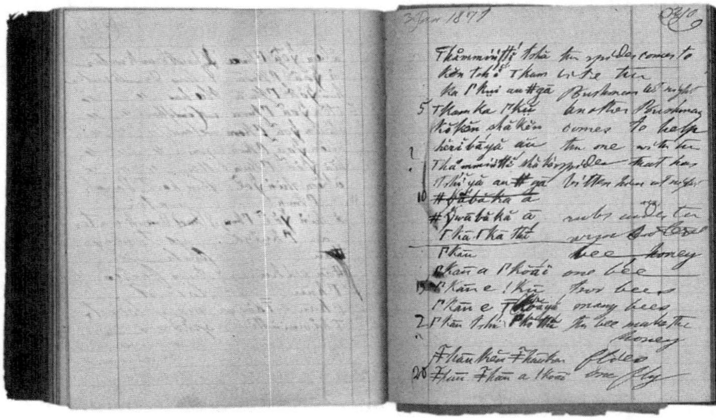

Fig. 1. Page image from notebook

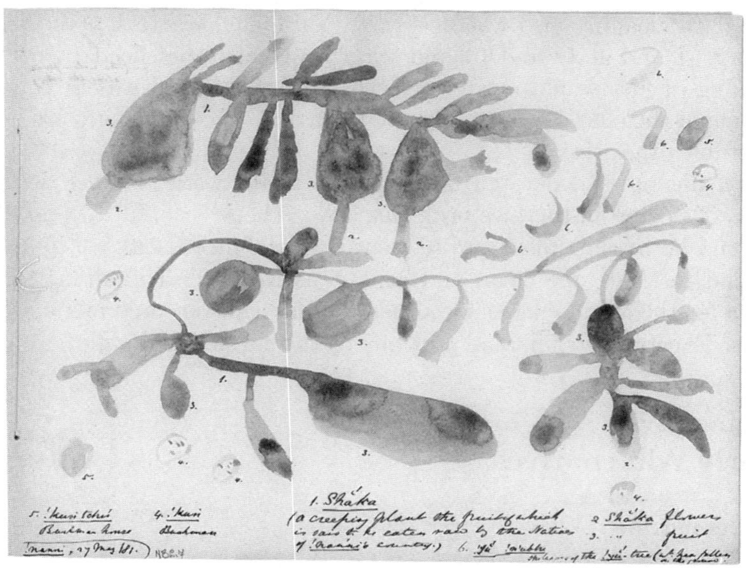

Fig. 2. Image from drawing

There are a total of 752 drawings. These are scanned versions of single pages. The average size of each drawing file is approximately 15 kilobytes and these images also are stored in JPEG format.

Each image filename is unique and the images are arranged into a few high-level directories corresponding to notebook number or source of images.

In both cases, Excel spreadsheets contained all metadata. The spreadsheets for drawings contained one row of fields per drawing. The spreadsheets for notebooks contained one row of fields for each story. These stories were manually determined from the notebooks and each is associated with a list of page ranges, possibly across notebooks. All spreadsheets were exported to XML as a first step in processing the information therein.

3 Data Pre-processing

A usable meta-structure was first built by pre-processing the source datasets. For this and further data transformation, the notebooks were dealt with separately from the drawings, using similar techniques.

As a starting point, the Excel-generated XML documents were interpreted, cleaned and checked for correspondence with the image files.

The source data contained inconsistences introduced by human editors. For example, a page range was indicated in many different ways (e.g., from `A1_1 - A1_10`, `A1_1` to `A1_10`) as was a single page (e.g., `A1_1.JPG`, `A1_1`). In both instances, the pre-processor determines which is intended (using pattern matching) and includes the appropriate individual pages.

Some data cleaning also was necessary. Various characters were used incorrectly (e.g., I and 1, O and 0) and typographical errors need to be fixed so that linking of files would occur correctly. All source data was in Unicode because some of the characters used in the !Kun and `|Xam` languages are not easily representable otherwise.

Finally, filenames generated from the metadata were matched with actual filenames of images in the filestore. This 2-way check ensured that no files were left out and no missing files were referenced in the metadata.

The end result is one clean and consistent XML file containing structured metadata for the notebooks and another containing structured metadata for the drawings. Excerpts of different portions of the former XML file are shown in Figure 3.

4 Early Alternatives

4.1 Greenstone

Initially, Greenstone was considered to be the ideal solution for the Bleek and Lloyd Collection because it is one of the rare DLSes that will export a collection to CD-ROM for wide distribution and offline viewing [15]. However, Greenstone requires some basic software installation and this creates a portability problem if the system is meant to work on arbitrary operating systems.

4.2 Single PDF

As a prototype, a single PDF was created to store the notebooks. An XSLT transformation first mapped the internal XML format to XSL-FO [1], a page layout language, then the XSL-FO data was converted into PDF output.

```
<data>
   <stories>
      <story><id>1</id><collection>Wilhelm Bleek
       Notebooks</collection><title>Covers and first
       pages of Bleek&apos;s Book I or BC151_A1_4_001
       </title></story>
      ...
   </stories>
   <categories>
      <category><id>2</id><name>Words and sentences
       </name></category>
      ...
   </categories>
   <authors>
      <author><id>2</id><name>Adam Kleinhardt</name>
       </author>
      ...
   </authors>
   <keywords>
      <keyword><id>2</id><kw>vocabulary</kw>
       <subkw>|xam</subkw></keyword>
      ...
   </keywords>
   <pages>
      <story id="6">
         <page>A1_4_1_00160.JPG</page>
         <page>A1_4_1_00161.JPG</page>
         ...
      </story>
      ...
   </pages>
   <books>
      <collection name="Wilhelm Bleek Notebooks"
       source="images/bleek_nb_lowres">
         <book name="BC_151_A1_4_001">
            <page>A1_4_1_FUCOV.JPG</page>
            ...
         </book>
      </collection>
   </books>
</data>
```

Fig. 3. Excerpts from source XML data file

This solution had very poor scalability. The PDF file for just 20% of the notebooks was approximately 182MB in size and took approximately 30 seconds to load on an average Pentium 4 PC (circa 2003). This PDF file included only thumbnails of the page images, with links to the local directory for the full versions. The advantage of a single PDF file was its self-contained search, browse and linking capability. However, this solution led to slow response times as well as low-quality presentation of information. In addition, as PDF sizes increase, accessibility to the collection is compromised even over reasonably fast Internet connections (whereas linked XHTML pages can be accessed easily and quickly from a local drive or online).

PDF was thus abandoned at an early stage in favour of an XHTML rendering. Separate PDF files could be created for each book, but indices across book boundaries will require other techniques.

5 Scalable Hyperlinked XHTML

5.1 Overview

XHTML pages were pre-generated from the XML source data using XSLT stylesheets. A better alternative may be to generate these client-side on demand, but some major browsers (e.g., Opera) do not support client-side XSLT.

The collection can be browsed and individual items accessed using hyperlinks. An Ajax-based search system was integrated into the XHTML pages - pre-generated inverted files were stored in an XML format and a Javascript routine performed the query operation. Thus searching can be conducted completely within the browser, with no server-side search engine necessary.

The following discussion focuses on scalability concerns addressed in the generation of hyperlinked XHTML files from XML. Searching is discussed elsewhere.

Given a source XML document, an XSLT transformation was created to generate either an index page or a list of individual pages for each subsection of the navigation. For notebooks, the page images can be listed by author, keyword, category, book or story. Thus, for example, the stylesheet can generate a list of authors and the stories attributed to each or a set of pages corresponding to each of the stories with full details on that story. The entire collection was represented in the source XML document so that it is possible to generate next/previous links in some places and also to perform iteration over subsets of the collection within the XSLT. Figure 4 displays a listing of authors and their stories, as generated by this process while Figure 5 displays a single page corresponding to one story.

5.2 Memory

XSLT v1.0 only creates a single output document for each transformation. Thus, in order to create multiple files, these were structured into subsets of a single large tree which was interpreted externally to create the actual files. The ability to output multiple files is available as extensions and in XSLT v2.0. However,

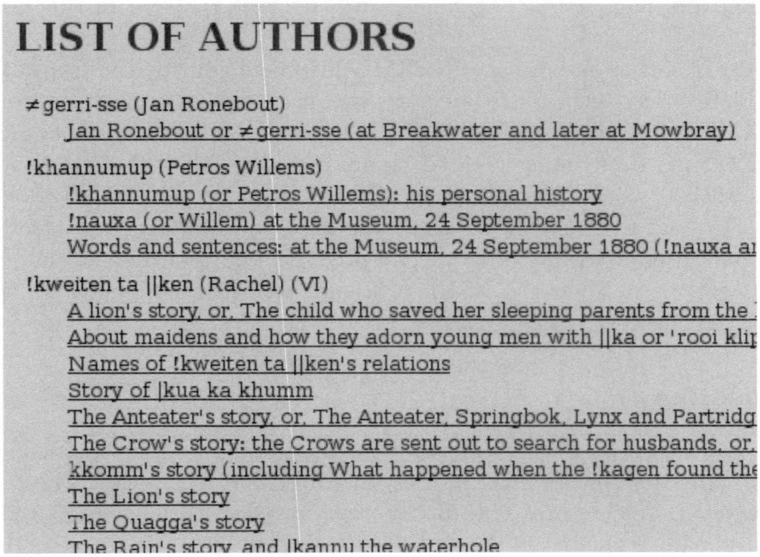

Fig. 4. List of authors and stories from each author

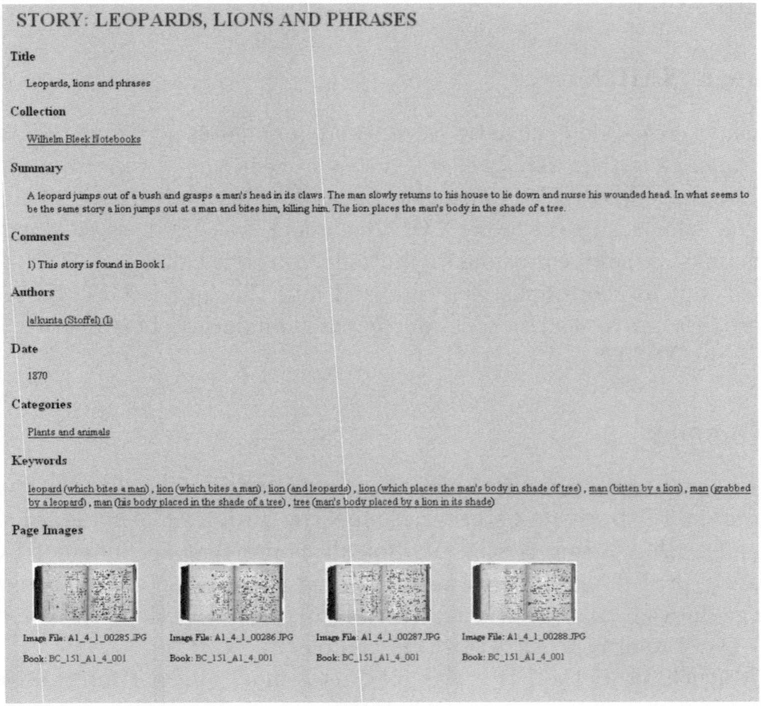

Fig. 5. Story listing with metadata and thumbnails of page images

portability and memory management were concerns that led to this not being pursued.

The size of source and destination XML documents during the transformation process determined how much memory was used during transformations. The source XML is fixed but the destination XML depends on the number of subsets of the XHTML data being created simultaneously. All XSLT transformation engines crashed when trying to generate the entire set of XHTML documents at once. To deal with this scale issue, the external application controlling the process passed in a parameter to specify precisely which subsets of the XHTML pages to generate. Then the XSLT processor was executed multiple times to generate the entire set of pages.

5.3 Indexing

XPath expressions were used to locate matching nodes and automatically insert extensive cross-referenced links in the generated XHTML pages. These expressions, however, quickly proved to be too slow for practical reasons as they often seemed to be implemented in the XSLT processors as linear time scans. To alleviate this, XSLT keys were used to create indices for particular complex structures. This is akin to database indices and the search performance increased substantially, as expected. Multiple keys also were used just as they would serve the same purpose in databases.

5.4 Single XML Source

Keys used to cross-reference data also crossed boundaries across metadata fields. For example, an author may be indexed to a story in one instance but elsewhere the author may need to be indexed to a book. This high degree of linking is the reason why a single source XML document was used, even when XSLT supports multiple source documents. Initially, multiple smaller XML documents were used, but as more links were inserted into the target XHTML, some indices needed to cross source XML document boundaries. This is not currently supported by XSLT.

5.5 Grouping

While the source data contained many authors in arbitrary order, the generated pages contain a listing of all stories, grouped by author. The standard solution to generate such a listing is to search for all names that are different from the immediately preceding name. However, finding a preceding sibling is expensive for a large dataset (algorithm complexity $O(n)$) and very slow if this has to be done for every item in a list (algorithm complexity $O(n^2)$).

The Muenchian Method [12] was used as a more efficient alternative. This technique involves using keys to order the names. Then, for each name, the current node can be combined with the first result found from a key search to create a nodeset. If the nodeset contains only a single node it means that the current node is in fact the first one found during a key search. Thus, unique names can be found with algorithm time complexity $O(n)$, which was sufficiently efficient for the datasets in this project.

This technique was extended to other indices. The keyword index (keyword to subkeyword to list of pages) used multi-level grouping, also with linear time complexity.

5.6 Performance

The 2 steps of the process were individually timed on a dual-CPU 3GHz Xeon 2GB RAM machine running FreeBSD 5.

Generation of the source XML document took 13.14 seconds for notebooks and 2.67 seconds for drawings.

Generation of 15426 XHTML documents related to the notebooks took 1 minute and 3.73 seconds. Generation of 1059 XHTML documents related to the drawings took 3.53 seconds. Given that this collection corresponds to the contents of a complete DVD-ROM, and the collection is not expected to grow in size, this is an acceptable processing rate.

Any alternative that did not reuse images or included embedded images in document formats (such as PDF by default) would not have been feasible.

Navigating through the collection is near-instantaneous. This was tested off a local drive, a network shared drive, a local and remote website and a DVD. Viewing the collection smoothly across multiple technologies is a distinct advantage over popular DLSes and database-driven approaches.

6 Conclusions

This paper has demonstrated how XML+XSLT+XHTML can be used to generate a usable and useful static and portable digital library.

XML-centric solutions have been recommended for heritage-based digital collections because of the expected long-term preservation of data. This paper has illustrated how such a solution was implemented for a real-world collection, addressing scalability and efficiency concerns in both generation of and access to the collection.

Databases may be most suitable for some problems, such as institutional repositories; but XML-centric solutions surely offer greater advantages for other problems, such as heritage preservation.

7 Future Work

Probably the most interesting future project would be to create tools for the automatic generation of XML-based collections and renderings thereof without having to hand-craft either data formats or transformations. This is similar to the Greenstone approach and one solution may be to have Greenstone generate static XML collections instead of or in addition to its own internal collection formats.

An alternative is to transform Greenstone so that a user can access a collection without any installation of software.

Scalability is a major current concern in digital preservation/libraries [3] [4]. While current XML technology is reasonably scalable, as shown in this paper, it is necessary to devise similarly portable techniques to deal with arbitrary and massive quantities of information.

As more tools are generated to deal with static DL collections, it may be necessary to formalise how such collections are represented and include support for import and export of such collections in keeping with current content packaging and representation standards, such as VRA-Core and METS.

Acknowledgements

This project was made possible by funding from University of Cape Town, NRF (Grant number: GUN2073203) and the Lucy Lloyd Archive Resource and Exhibition Centre.

References

1. Berglund, A.: Extensible Stylesheet Language (XSL) Version 1.1, W3C Recommendation, W3C (December 5, 2006) Available `http://www.w3.org/TR/2006/REC-xsl11-20061205/`
2. Digitale Bewaring: XML Digital Preservation: Digital Preservation Testbed White Paper, Dutch National Archive (2002), Available `http://www.digitaleduurzaamheid.nl/bibliotheek/docs/white-paper_xml-en.pdf`
3. Haedstrom, M.: Research Challenges in Digital Archiving and Long-term Preservation. In: NSF Post Digital Library Futures Workshop, June 15-17, 2003, Cape Cod (2003), Available `http://www.sis.pitt.edu/~dlwkshop/paper_hedstrom.html`
4. Imafouo, A.: A Scalability Survey in IR and DL. TCDL Bulletin, 2(2) (2006), Available `http://www.ieee-tcdl.org/Bulletin/v2n2/imafouo/imafouo.html`
5. Carl, L., Van de Sompel, H., Nelson, M., Warner, S.: The Open Archives Initiative Protocol for Metadata Harvesting – Version 2.0, Open Archives Initiative (June 2002), Available `http://www.openarchives.org/OAI/2.0/openarchivesprotocol.htm`
6. Carl, L., Van de Sompel, H., Nelson, M., Warner, S., Hochstenbach, P., Jerez, H.: Specification for an OAI Static Repository and an OAI Static Repository Gateway, Open Archives Initiative (April 2004), Available `http://www.openarchives.org/OAI/2.0/guidelines-static-repository.htm`
7. Lucy Lloyd Archive and Resource and Exhibition Centre: Lloyd Bleek Collection, University of Cape Town (2007), Available `http://www.lloydbleekcollection.uct.ac.za/index.jsp`
8. Moore, R., Baru, C., Rajasekar, A., Ludascher, B., Marciano, R., Wan, M., Schroeder, W., Gupta, A.: Collection-Based Persistent Digital Archives Parts 1 and 2, D-Lib Magazine, April/March 2000 (2002), Available `http://www.dlib.org/dlib/march00/moore/03moore-pt1.html` `http://www.dlib.org/dlib/april00/moore/04moore-pt2.html`

9. Mackenzie, S., Bass, M., McClellan, G., Tansley, R., Barton, M., Branchofsky, M., Stuve, D., Walker, J.H.: DSpace: An Open Source Dynamic Digital Repository, D-Lib Magazine, 9(1) (January 2003), Available http://www.dlib.org/dlib/january03/smith/01smith.html
10. Sponsler, E., Van de Velde, E.F.: Eprints.org Software: A Review, Sparc E-News (August-September 2001), Available http://resolver.library.caltech.edu/caltechLIB:2001.004
11. Stefan, S., Rauber, A., Rauch, C., Hofman, H., Debole, F., Amato, G.: The DELOS Testbed for Choosing a Digital Preservation Strategy. In: Sugimoto, S., Hunter, J., Rauber, A., Morishima, A. (eds.) ICADL 2006. LNCS, vol. 4312, pp. 81–90. Springer, Heidelberg (2006)
12. Tennison, J.: Grouping Using the Muenchian Method (2007), Available http://www.jenitennison.com/xslt/grouping/muenchian.html
13. University of Cape Town: Jewel in UCT's crown to be digitised for world's scholars, Monday Paper (March 31, 2003), Available http://www.uct.ac.za/print/newsroom/mondaypaper/?paper=114
14. Winer, D.: RSS 2.0 Specification, Berkman Centre for Internet and Society (2002), Available http://blogs.law.harvard.edu/tech/rss
15. Ian, W., Cunningham, S.-J., Rogers, B., McNab, R., Boddie, S.: Distributing Digital Libraries on the Web, CD-ROMs, and Intranets: Same information, same look-and-feel, different media. In: Yen, J., Yang, C.C. (eds.) Proc First Asia Digital Library Workshop: East Meets West, Hong Kong, pp. 98–105 (1998), Available http://nzdl.sadl.uleth.ca/gsdl/collect/publicat/index/assoc/HASH0199/95cc7f7f.dir/doc.pdf

A Study of Citations in Users' Online Personal Collections

Nishikant Kapoor[1], John T. Butler[2], Sean M. McNee[1], Gary C. Fouty[2], James A. Stemper[2], and Joseph A. Konstan[1]

[1] GroupLens Research, Department of Computer Science and Engineering, University of Minnesota, Minneapolis, MN 55455, USA
{nkapoor,mcnee,konstan}@cs.umn.edu

[2] University Libraries, 117 Pleasant St SE, University of Minnesota, Minneapolis, MN 55455, USA
{j-butl,g-fout,stemp003}@umn.edu

Abstract. Users' personal citation collections reflect users' interests and thus offer great potential for personalized digital services. We studied 18,120 citations in the personal collections of 96 users of RefWorks citation management system to understand these in terms of their resolvability i.e. how well these citations can be resolved to a unique identifier and to their online sources. While fewer than 4% of citations to articles in Journals and Conferences included a DOI, we were able to increase this resolvability to 50% by using a citation resolver. A much greater percentage of book citations included an ISBN (53%), but using an online resolver found ISBNs for an additional 20% of the book citations. Considering all citation types, we were able to resolve approximately 47% of all citations to either an online source or a unique identifier.

1 Introduction

Library users increasingly have access to integrated, online tools for managing personal citation collections. These tools help users to maintain a personal citation collection, to annotate the citations, and to produce formatted bibliographies and reference lists. While the first generation of these tools were largely disconnected from library search systems - in essence they were computerized versions of index cards with citations on them - newer versions can import citations directly from such library systems, and allow users to navigate directly from their citation to the document itself in an online collection or to the library's record for that document.

We are interested in understanding how these personal citation collections can be used to personalize the services provided to library users. Personalized library services have mostly evolved around published literature, and are therefore oriented towards serving the interests of the authors with publishing history. For example, TechLens from GroupLens [1,10], TalkMine and @ApWeb from APR [2], MyLibrary[1], use keywords and the citation index in the documents to generate recommendations for the user. If you have published any articles, and the

[1] http://dewey.library.nd.edu/mylibrary/

L. Kovács, N. Fuhr, and C. Meghini (Eds.): ECDL 2007, LNCS 4675, pp. 404–415, 2007.

system knows about at least some of them, the keywords and references in those documents would serve as a representation of your profile, which can then be used to generate more relevant or matching documents.

However, for users who are not authors of any published work, and do not have a history of publications from which to build their profile, personalized recommendations are often generated using one of the techniques like, keyword searching, explicit listing of preferred documents for the user, past searches, and descriptive profiling. We believe that personal citation collections of such users are representative of their interests, and possess a great potential for offering them personalized services. In particular, we have experience building recommender systems [3] for research articles [1,4], and wondered whether personal citation collections could be used to construct such a recommender system.

In this work we examined 18,120 citations from the personal collections of 96 users of an online citation management system, RefWorks[2]. Our goal was to empirically measure how frequently we could resolve the citations in these collections to a unique identifier (which is useful for collaborative filtering recommender systems) or to an online source for the content or content metadata (which is useful for content filtering recommender systems). Specifically, we examined the following two research questions:

- **What percentage of citations in users' personal collections can be resolved to a unique identifier?** What percentage of items in the collections is of a type that even has a unique identifier? For those that do, how many include the unique identifier in the citation? How many can be found using existing citation resolvers?
- **From what percentage of citations in users' personal collections can we navigate to an online source for the content or content metadata?** Are there citations that have an online source but not a unique identifier?

The rest of this paper is organized as follows. Section 2 provides background and related work on personalized services in digital libraries. Section 3 reports on the nature of the citation collections, breaking down citations by type and users by discipline and status. Section 4 reports on citation resolvability, looking first at resolving citations to a unique identifier, and then at resolving citations to an online source. Finally, Section 5 discusses the implications of this work for future library services as well as the privacy issues raised by such services.

2 Related Work

Digital libraries have been growing rapidly since early 1990s. They have been in extensive use in various sectors ranging from academics (University of Minnesota Libraries) to public (TEL-ME-MOR - The European Library: Modular Extensions for Mediating Online Resources) to government (NLM - U.S. National Library of Medicine).

[2] http://www.refworks.com/

There are number of applications that attempt to provide enhanced, and personalized library services to users, for example, MyLibrary creates a personalized web page listing information resources available from the Libraries based on user info. TalkMine and @ApWeb from the Active Recommendation Project (ARP) [2] use prior knowledge about the user to generate useful recommendations. TalkMine uses keywords, and @ApWeb uses association between the documents authored (or co-authored) by the user to learn about the user. TechLens [1,10] uses citation co-occurrence in published literature to generate personalized recommendations. The Quickstep and Foxtrot [5] systems recommended on-line research papers to academic researchers. PYTHIA-II [6] provides recommendations to scientists trying to identify the appropriate software for their research needs. The Ilumina project [7] provides recommendations based on document metadata, available subject expert analysis of documents, resource use as discovered in logs, and user profiles for those users who are registered with the system. The Melvyl Recommender project [8] analyzed server logs captured when users chose to view detailed information about certain documents, and used those as the user profile when generating recommendations.

Most of the research in providing such personalized services in digital libraries has focused on mining the content of the papers authored by the user, or the implicitly rated citations in the reference section of those papers (i.e., public collections of rated citations). Our work focuses on citations in users' personal collections. Users' personal citation collections are an implicit means to learn about their interests, and are representative profiles. These collections, therefore, offer a great potential for systems such as a citation recommender system to offer personalized tools and services in digital libraries [9]. However, in order to build such personalized library services, we first need to be able to link the citations in these collections to their unique IDs, i.e., evaluate their resolvability. Resolvability of citations enables us to match users' collections (a) with public repositories - to help users get customized selections, (b) with metadata - to build their profile, and (c) between the users to form correlations between them. Unique identification of identical citations in different users' collections is the key to building similarities between the users. It opens the door to matching citations between collections, and to obtaining additional metadata from which to generate recommendations.

3 Citation Data

We conducted this study in April and May 2006 using the RefWorks web-based personal citation management tool installed at the University of Minnesota. Subjects who met all of the following eligibility criteria were sent an email invitation:

- Had at least 10 citations in their RefWorks citation collection.
- Had actively used their RefWorks accounts at least once within the preceding six months (i.e., added, deleted, or modified at least one citation).
- Had logged on to their RefWorks accounts at least twice within the preceding six months.

Of the 1,253 users invited, only 96 accepted the invitation (7.67%), completed informed consent, and shared their personal citation collections with us. Limitations of our dataset are further discussed in the Discussion section.

Figure 1 shows the logarithmic distribution of citations for the 96 users. Each point on the line graph represents a user. The distribution is highly skewed, with an average number of citations of 316, a median of 99, and a mode of 37. 50 users had 100 or fewer citations in their collections, and only 19 had 300 or more citations.

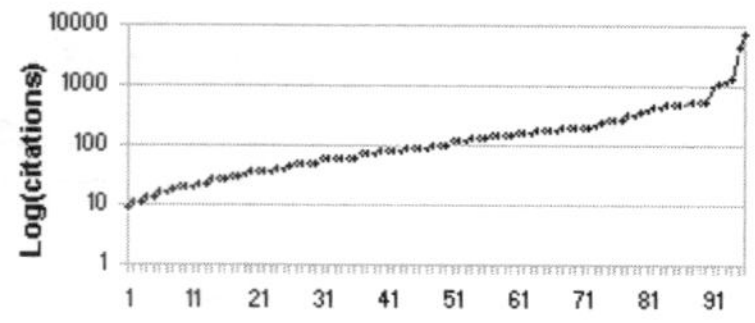

Fig. 1. Distribution of citation collection size

The collected data totaled 30,336 citations. There were, however, two high-end outliers with 7,777 and 4,439 citations in their collections respectively. Since the two outliers contained atypical data (not necessarily bad data), we conducted the data analysis with, and without the two outliers. However, due to space considerations, we are presenting only the results that do not contain the outlier data. Thus, the rest of our analysis is based on 94 users and 18,120 citations.

Figure 2 shows the distribution of citation types across our dataset of 18, 120 citations. A vast majority of citations (82.74%) are to articles in Journals and in Conference Proceedings. The high number of these citations is not surprising, given that articles in journals and conference proceedings are among the most easily found in online bibliographic search tools, and are the primary literature in many fields. Citations to books are a distant second with just over 7% of total citations.

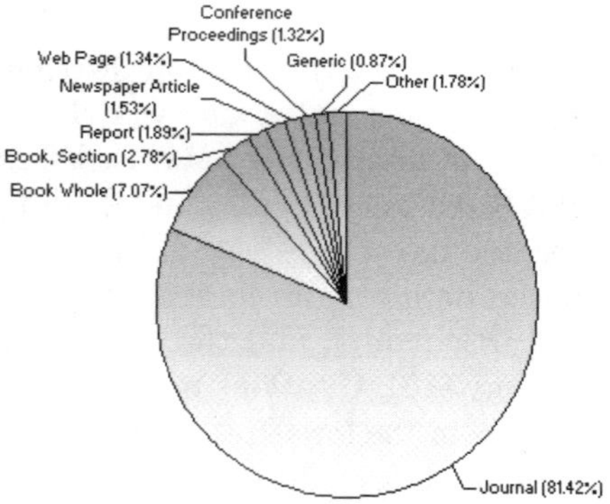

Fig. 2. Distribution of citation types

We should note that "citation type" is a property of the RefWorks citation. We were concerned that the citation type might be inaccurate if non-journal articles (e.g., book chapters or monographs) were mistakenly entered as journal articles, either because of manual entry errors or because of import filters that might improperly classify some references. To check for this possibility, we hand-validated a random sample of 100 citations classified as journal articles. We found that 98% of these citations were clearly journals, and the other two were to a university symposium series (which is published as if it were a serial) and Dissertation Abstracts International (which is a serial, if not a journal per se). Hence, we can conclude that we don't have a high percentage of mistaken classifications of non-journal entries as journal-type citations.

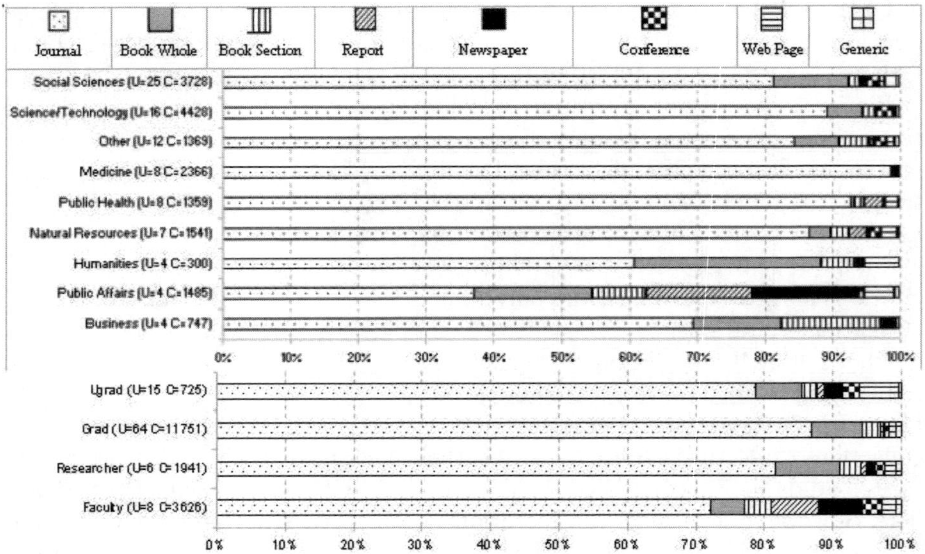

Fig. 3. Distribution of citations by (a) discipline (b) status

Figure 3 shows the citation distribution of the user disciplines and statuses, along with the number of users (U), and the number of citations (C) for the users in the discipline or status. Disciplines with fewer than four participants are not listed in the figure (and in all the subsequent tables and figures), but are aggregated into the totals.

In the dataset, the largest groups represented were graduate students (64 of 94 participants), and the disciplines of social sciences (25) and science and technology (16). Citations to Journal articles form the majority of the citations, ranging from the lowest at about 37% for Public Affairs, to the highest at about 98% for Medicine. Public Affairs has the most diverse collection - citations to Books, Newspaper articles and Reports, all hovering at about 17% of its total citations. Humanities is the largest consumer of citations to whole books at 28%.

For user statuses, the average number of citations to Journal articles is about 83% of their citations, ranging from a low of 72% for Faculty, to a high of about 87% for Graduate students. After Journal citations, whole books at about 9% form the next major share of their collections for Researchers. Within a collection, Faculty had the largest share of citations to Newspaper articles and to Reports at 7% and 6% respectively.

We analyzed the dataset by status, and found that the differences are statistically significant ($p <= .01$), except between Graduate and Researcher groups, and between Faculty and Researcher groups. Faculty had the highest number of citations per participant at 453, followed by Researchers, Graduates and Undergraduates. We carried out the similar analysis across the disciplines but there are not enough participants per discipline to generate results with confidence.

4 Citation Resolvability

When we look at citation resolvability, we are actually exploring two different questions. First we are asking whether the citation can be mapped to a unique identifier. This identifier serves as a means for determining whether different citations refer to the same underlying entity. Second, we are asking whether we can use the citation to find the entity being referenced online. Because of the different nature of books, articles, etc., we consider this type of resolvability to succeed if we can find either metadata for the entity cited, or the contents of the entity itself.

Neither of these types of resolvability automatically implies the other. A book's ISBN may serve as a unique identifier, yet we may be unable to find any online contents or metadata for that book. A technical report citation may come with a URL that leads us to the content online, yet lack any unique identifier to match it against other citations to the same report. The field as a whole, however, is moving quickly towards a greater percentage of unique IDs that also serve as pointers to online content. The DOI (Digital Object Identifier) for a journal or conference article serves both roles. We specifically explore three ways in which a citation may be resolved.

DOI: Citations to articles in Journals and in Conference Proceedings can potentially have a valid unique identifier, called Digital Object Identifier (DOI). DOIs, by their nature, serve as both unique identifiers and pointers to online content. There are three ways in which we can obtain a DOI for a citation: (a) the DOI may already be in the citation, stored in either the DOI field or the URL field; (b) we can use a DOI query at CrossRef[3], a service of the Publishers International Linking Association, which requires a journal title and author or page number, and uses other fields as provided, to look up a DOI; (c) we can construct an OpenURL - a URL to represent a reference in compliance with ANSI/NISO Standard Z39.88 and sending that OpenURL to a resolver to obtain a DOI (we used the resolver at CrossRef, which requires certain fields including author last name, title, year, volume, and issue).

ISBN: Book citations (which include whole books, monographs, and edited books) can potentially have a unique ID (a ten or thirteen digit long) called the International Standard Book Number (ISBN). There are two ways in which we can obtain an ISBN for a citations: (a) the ISBN may already be present in the ISBN field of the citation; or (b) we may be able to look up the ISBN using a resolver such as the one at WorldCat[4], a service of OCLC[5]. For this study, we did not include citations of type "Book Section" in our analysis because the ISBN uniquely identifies only a book, not a specific chapter or section.

URL: Any cited entity that is online may be found through a URL. We therefore separately examine all citations that include a value for the URL field, and validate that the URL points to an actual web page.

[3] http://www.crossref.org/
[4] http://www.worldcat.org/
[5] http://www.oclc.org/

For all the citation types in the dataset, we separated out the ones that could potentially include, or be resolved to a unique identifier, and analyzed each one of them separately to assess its resolvability. Since citations of other types such as Reports, Newspaper Articles, etc. do not necessarily have a unique ID (even though they might have an online source), they were not considered for resolvability analyses.

4.1 DOI Resolvability

Figure 4 shows the DOI resolvability breakdown by user discipline, and by user status (shaded portion). The last row of the table shows the cumulative statistics for the entire collection. The column headers for the table need some explanation before we get into detailed discussion of its contents.

	Citations	Resolved	RW only	Both	CR only
Science/Technology	4,027	2,637 (65%)	10	100	2,527
Natural Resources	1,346	754 (56%)	4	76	674
Business	518	283 (55%)			283
Public Health	1,229	562 (46%)	2	58	502
Medicine	2,326	1,033 (44%)	2	109	922
Other	1,158	487 (42%)	12	81	394
Social Sciences	3,015	1,216 (40%)	1	59	1,156
Humanities	189	73 (39%)	2	14	57
Public Affairs	552	158 (29%)			158
Faculty	2,694	1,718 (64%)	1	39	1,678
Researcher	1,584	798 (50%)	14	92	692
Graduate	10,170	4,716 (46%)	18	388	4,310
Undergraduate	562	234 (42%)		11	223
Totals	**15,010**	**7,466 (50%)**	**33**	**530**	**6,903**

Fig. 4. DOI resolvability breakdown

Citations: Total number of citations for the discipline (or status) that could potentially have a DOI. These are citations to articles in Journals and Conference Proceedings.

Resolved: Total number of citations that resolved at CrossRef using either DOI, or OpenURL resolver. This column also shows the percentage resolvability of total citations in the discipline or the status.

RW only: Number of citations that had a valid DOI in the RefWorks record, but the CrossRef DOI resolver failed to find these. These DOIs were already available in the citations when we harvested the citation collections. These DOIs could either have been entered manually by the user at the time of building the collection, or automatically inserted by RefWorks citation management tool during import of the citation.

CR only: Number of additional DOIs that we were able to fetch from CrossRef using the DOI and OpenURL resolvers. These DOIs were either not present in the original RefWorks record, or were invalid.

Both: Number of citations where the fetched DOI from CrossRef matched with the DOI already available in the RefWorks record. These DOIs already existed in the citations, and were valid.

The listing in the Figure 4 is sorted by the percentage of citations resolved for the discipline/ status. As shown, the citations from Science/ Technology have the highest resolvability at about 65%. The highest number of new DOIs (2,527) was fetched for citations from Science/ Technology; which is a clear indication that Science/ Technology is embracing the DOI standardization much faster than other disciplines. Business and Public Affairs, collectively had 441 resolved citations, but no resolvable citations in their RefWorks records. All of the 441 DOIs were resolved by CrossRef.

The impact of DOI resolvability is clearly visible from Figure 4. Out of 15,010 potentially resolvable citations, only 566 citations (3.77%) had a valid DOI in their RefWorks account. Using CrossRef resolved another 6,903 DOIs, increasing the total resolvability to 7,466 citations (approximately 50%) - a significant improvement over the initial resolvability.

4.2 ISBN Resolvability

Figure 5 summarizes the resolvability of book and monograph citations to ISBNs. The columns in the table represent data similar to the DOI resolvability presentation, except for the following differences:

Citations: Total number of citations for the discipline (or status) that could potentially have an ISBN. These are citations to whole books, edited books and monographs.

Resolved: Total number of citations that resolved at WorldCat Libraries using the ISBN resolver.

RW only: Number of citations that had a valid ISBN in the RefWorks record when the collection data was harvested.

WC only: Number of additional ISBNs that we were able to fetch from WorldCat Libraries using the ISBN resolver.

	Citations	Resolved	RW only	Both	WC only
Other	98	83 (85%)	23	42	18
Business	97	81 (84%)	13	38	30
Public Affairs	258	215 (83%)	24	121	70
Social Sciences	414	301 (73%)	70	173	58
Science/Technology	236	164 (69%)	23	84	57
Humanities	78	53 (68%)	10	37	6
Medicine	16	10 (63%)		4	6
Natural Resources	51	22 (43%)	5	8	9
Public Health	36	7 (19%)		1	6
Graduate	916	713 (78%)	144	419	150
Faculty	180	126 (70%)	11	31	84
Undergrad	53	36 (68%)	9	11	16
Researcher	183	102 (56%)	19	68	15
Totals	**1,332**	**977 (73%)**	**183**	**529**	**265**

Fig. 5. ISBN resolvability breakdown

Both: Number of citations where the fetched ISBN from WorldCat matched with the ISBN already available in the RefWorks record.

The data in Figure 5 is sorted by the percentage of resolved citations for the discipline/ status. Each row can be interpreted in terms of its original resolvability and enhanced resolvability. For example, the total number of resolved citations for Science/ Technology is 164, of which 107 ISBNs (23 RW only + 84 Both) were already available in the original RefWorks record; and an additional 57 citations were resolved by the WorldCat ISBN resolver.

Overall, we were able to resolve 977 of 1,332 citations (73%). 183 of these citations had an ISBN in the record but were not found otherwise by the WorldCat Libraries ISBN resolver; 265 had no ISBN in the record but were found by the resolver; and 529 were found both in the record and by the resolver.

4.3 URL Resolvability

Figure 6 shows the URL validity breakdown by user discipline and user status. The data is sorted by the number of citations with a valid URL. The two columns are:

Citations: Total number of citations for the discipline (or status) that had a value in the URL field. These citations included all citations with a URL value, regardless of type.

Valid: Total number of citations that had a valid URL and were successfully traced to the web page they pointed to.

All citations that contained a value in the URL field were validated by following them to determine whether they point to a live web page. We examined 20 random URLs and found that 18 of them pointed to the correct content, the article. We did not attempt to find URLs for citations that did not have them, except in the case of DOIs discussed above. 613 citations had a value in the URL field, of which 7 were DOI-formatted. However, none of those 7 citations resolved using the DOI and/or OpenUrl citation resolvers at CrossRef. Of the total 613 citations, 542 were valid (about 88%). The high percentage is encouraging, given concerns that citations to web pages are likely to "go bad" over time.

	Citations	Valid
Humanities	13	13 (100%)
Public Health	8	8 (100%)
Medicine	2	2 (100%)
Social Sciences	178	175 (98%)
Natural Resources	71	69 (97%)
Business	174	160 (92%)
Public Affairs	95	77 (81%)
Other	10	7 (70%)
Science/Technology	62	31 (50%)
Graduate	441	417 (95%)
Faculty	105	89 (85%)
Researcher	63	34 (54%)
Undergraduate	4	2 (50%)
Totals	**613**	**542 (88%)**

Fig. 6. URL validity breakdown

At the same time, we note that faculty URLs are less likely to be valid than graduate student ones, which may be an indication that URLs go bad over time (e.g., pages go away or change address). Of particular note is the fact that science and technology URLs were the least resolvable, perhaps suggesting that they refer to more rapidly-changing and ephemeral content.

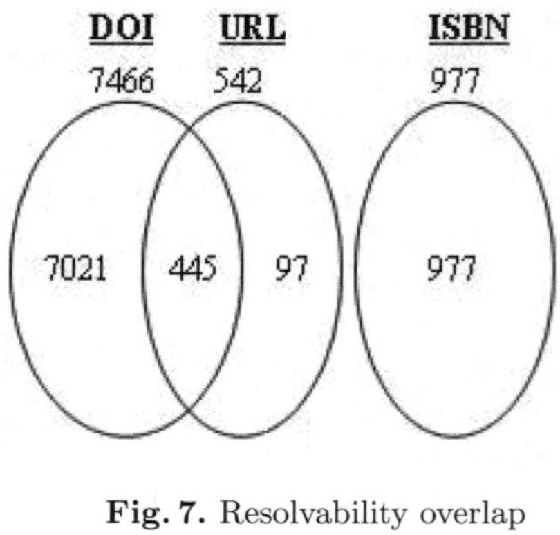

Fig. 7. Resolvability overlap

4.4 Resolvability into Multiple Identifiers

We addressed the issue of identifying citations by exploring the collections in three ways: (a) DOI resolvability, (b) ISBN resolvability, and (c) URL validity. Since DOI resolvability only looked at citations that could have a DOI, i.e., citations to articles in Journals and Conference Proceedings, and ISBN resolvability examined only the citations that could have an ISBN, i.e., citations to whole books, edited books, and monographs, there was no possibility for citation resolvability overlap between DOI-resolved citations and ISBN-resolved citations.

However, all citations could contain a URL. Accordingly, to understand the total resolvability of the dataset, we need to identify those cases where a single citation was resolved through both a URL and another mechanism. Figure 7 summarizes the resolvability overlap among the three IDs.

4.5 Cumulative Resolvability

DOI resolvers enhanced the resolvability of citations to articles in Journals and Conference Proceedings from less than 4% to about 50% (Figure 4). Figure 5 shows that using ISBN resolver enhanced ISBN resolvability from about 53% to about 73%. Figure 8 summarizes the overall resolvability of all the 18,120 citations of 94 citation collections. Using the DOI and ISBN resolvers, we were able to enhance the overall resolvability from under 13% to about 47%, gaining an impressive additional 34%. Since we did not retrieve any URLs for the citations, their resolvability remains unchanged.

5 Discussion

What percentage of citations in users' personal collections can be resolved to a unique identifier? Of all the citations that could be resolved to either a unique identifier or to an online source, we only were able to resolve certain citation types. Journal and conference papers have a unique online identifier (the DOI) (50%). Books have an ISBN, which can be used to find metadata and is a unique ID (73%). For other types of citation, the only possibility was a URL (88%), but their incidence is low (613). Citations to articles in Science and Technology have the highest resolvability at about 65%, and all 100% of citations to books resolved in Nursing. The citation collections of Faculty members are likely to be more resolvable than Researchers, Graduate and Undergraduate students.

	Number of resolved citations		
	Before	After	Gain
DOI	1,083 (7%)	7,466 (50%)	6,383 (43%)
ISBN	712 (53%)	977 (73%)	265 (20%)
URL	542 (88%)	542 (88%)	n/a
Totals	**2,337 (13%)**	**8,540 (47%)**	**6,203 (34%)**

Fig. 8. Resolvability summary

From what percentage of citations in users' personal collections can we navigate to an online source for the content or content metadata? The original dataset of users' personal citation collections was only 13% resolvable, i.e., only 2,337 citations out of the total 18,120 had either have a valid

DOI, ISBN, or URL. We found that many citations in users' personal collections were not well formed. Some were bad citations which we examined and could not resolve by hand and some were duplicate citations. We speculate that some users may bulk import the results of queries, not examine and select each citation individually. Such a practice would call into question whether the citation collections are indeed good sources of user preference information.

In this study, we analyzed resolvability of users' citation collections. There are, however, other necessary criteria that we are still studying such as, whether the resolved citations are representative of the user's interests, and how much of an overlap is there between these collections.

Privacy Concerns. Most invited subjects failed to respond at all, but 14 replied and actively declined to participate in this study, citing various concerns including privacy. This is a serious issue. While many people seem happy to share citation collections (and do so online in many venues from citeUlike to ACM DL binders), others have legitimate concerns about revealing too much information about their current interests or pursuits to possible competitors. Even if the citation collections themselves are not public, we recognize that there are scenarios in which a recommender system might compromise a user's private citations by recommending them to another user. Understanding how to protect this data is critical if recommender-enhanced library services are to gain wide acceptance. We suspect that personal collections may be used to generate profiles, but that only public citations (e.g., references in published papers) can be used to recommend citations to users.

Limitations. There are several limitations to this work. Our dataset came from volunteer participants (who may not be representative of the entire user base) and had too few representatives of some disciplines to adequately draw conclusions about those fields. We used only a single source for resolving each type of citations (CrossRef and WorldCat); while we generated significant improvements in resolvability, we believe that adding additional services for lookup (for example, Citation Matcher from PubMed) could further enhance resolvability. Other tools (e.g., Google, Google Scholar) are capable of finding unofficial copies of articles that may not be easily found through a resolver. Finally, due to the size of our dataset, we were unable to hand-validate the resolved citations. We did random spot-checks, but it is possible that some of the DOIs, ISBNs, and URLs we validated did not match the user's intended citation.

6 Conclusion

We studied 18,120 citations in the personal collections of 96 users of RefWorks citation management system. These users included graduates, undergraduates, researchers, and faculty - graduates being the majority (64). We believed that such personal collections represent users' interests and have a tremendous potential in guiding and supporting personalized services in digital libraries, such as a citation recommender system. The primary objective of this study was to evaluate the resolvability of users' personal citation collections. While fewer than 4% of citations to articles in Journals and Conferences included a DOI, we were able to increase this resolvability to 50% by using a citation resolver. A greater percentage of book citations included an ISBN (53%), but using an online resolver found ISBNs for an additional 20% of the books. All together, we were able to resolve approximately 47% of all citations to either an online source or a unique identifier.

Acknowledgements

We are grateful to RefWorks for their assistance in carrying out this experiment. This research was funded in part by a grant from the University of Minnesota Libraries, and in part by grant IIS-0534939 from the National Science Foundation.

References

1. McNee, S., Albert, I., Cosley, D., Gopalkrishnan, P., Lam, S.K., Rashid, A.M., Konstan, J.A., Riedl, J.: On the Recommending of Citations for Research Papers. In: Proceedings of ACM 2002 Conference on Computer Supported Cooperative Work (CSCW2002), New Orleans, LA, pp. 116–125 (2002)
2. Rocha, L.M.: TalkMine: a soft computing approach to adaptive knowledge recommendation. In: Loia, V., Sessa, S. (eds.) Soft Computing Agents: New Trends For Designing Autonomous Systems, Springer Studies In Fuzziness And Soft Computing, pp. 89–116. Physica-Verlag GmbH, Heidelberg (2002)
3. Resnick, P., Varian, H.R.: Recommender systems. Commun. ACM 40(3), 56–58 (1997)
4. Torres, R., McNee, S.M., Abel, M., Konstan, J.A., Riedl, J.: Enhancing digital libraries with TechLens+. In: Proceedings of the 4th ACM/IEEE-CS Joint Conference on Digital Libraries, JCDL '04, Tuscon, AZ, USA, June 07 - 11, 2004, pp. 228–236. ACM Press, New York (2004)
5. Middleton, S.E., Shadbolt, N.R., De Roure, D.C.: Ontological user profiling in recommender systems. ACM Trans. Inf. Syst. 22(1), 54–88 (2004)
6. Houstis, E.N., Catlin, A.C., Rice, J.R., Verykios, V.S., Ramakrishnan, N., Houstis, C.E.: PYTHIA-II: a knowledge/database system for managing performance data and recommending scientific software. ACM Trans. Math. Softw. 26(2), 227–253 (2000)
7. Geisler, G., McArthur, D., Giersch, S.: Developing recommendation services for a digital library with uncertain and changing data. In: Proceedings of the 1st ACM/IEEE-CS joint conference on Digital libraries, Roanoke, Virginia, United States, pp. 199–200 (January 2001)
8. Geyer-Schulz, A., Neumann, A., Thede, A.: Others Also Use: A Robust Recommender System for Scientific Libraries. In: Koch, T., Sølvberg, I.T. (eds.) ECDL 2003. LNCS, vol. 2769, pp. 113–125. Springer, Heidelberg (2003)
9. Renda, M.E., Straccia, U.: A personalized collaborative digital library environment: a model and an application. Inf. Process. Manage 41(1), 5–21 (2005)
10. Konstan, J.A., Kapoor, N., McNee, S.M., Butler, J.T.: TechLens: Exploring the Use of Recommenders to Support Users of Digital Libraries. CNI Fall Task Force Meeting Project Briefing. Coalition for Networked Information. Phoenix, AZ (2005)

Investigating Document Triage on Paper and Electronic Media

George Buchanan and Fernando Loizides

Future Interaction Technology Laboratory
University of Wales, Swansea
{g.r.buchanan,csfernando}@swansea.ac.uk

Abstract. Document triage is the critical point in the information seeking process when the user first decides the relevance of a document to their information need. This complex process is not yet well understood, and subsequently we have undertaken a comparison of this task in both electronic and paper media. The results reveal that in each medium human judgement is influenced by different factors, and confirm some unproven hypotheses. How users claim they perform triage, and what they actually do, are often not the same.

Keywords: Digital Libraries, Interaction Design, Document Triage.

1 Introduction

The activity of information seeking drives the use of digital libraries. Better understanding of the information seeking process unveils new aspects of user behaviour that can subsequently be used to improve the function and interaction of digital library services. This paper investigates the critical stage of information seeking called *document triage*. During document triage, a user examines a document and determines its relevance to their information need. This initial decision may subsequently revised: the perceived relevance may rise or fall as the user comes to a fuller understanding of the piece. Our focus is purely upon the initial relevance decision that determines if this subsequent reading will occur.

Previous studies (e.g.[12,13]) have identified which elements of documents are used to make relevance judgements during interactive information retrieval. These experiments have elicited subjective information from users as to which document properties they use when making relevance judgements. The findings of this foundational research have gradually accumulated to give us a consistent set of document features that play a key role in relevance decision–making: e.g., when searching academic papers, users often first refer to the document's abstract [12]. Researchers have also studied many differences between paper and electronic texts, particularly in the case of reading (e.g.[11], and how users scan search result lists [16] but document triage has received little attention.

Our goal is to improve the effectiveness of relevance decision–making in electronic environments. We already know what document properties provide the key features for document triage. However, users explore documents interactively,

L. Kovács, N. Fuhr, and C. Meghini (Eds.): ECDL 2007, LNCS 4675, pp. 416–427, 2007.

not simply as passive abstractions with particular properties. During triage, documents are explored and evaluated in a short timespan, and we do not yet understand *how* users encounter and *process* this data.

There is good reason to scrutinise these interactive issues, particularly in digital systems. Experiments have explored the use of scrolling and interaction data for relevance feedback[6]. Further progress requires that we better understand the interaction itself to provide a foundation for progress with that approach. Likewise, users are increasingly using digital documents and computer–based reading[7]. Improvements to the document reader software through which this reading and judgement is being made can increase the total efficiency of digital information retrieval, by enhancing the human performance just as information retrieval research advances search engine capability.

This paper reports on the experimental investigation of the differences between the document triage process on paper and electronic media. By providing a contrast of the two forms, we gain a deeper knowledge both of what users do during information triage, and how they interact with the documents that they evaluate. The paper proceeds in five parts: first, we briefly examine some key features of the existing literature; second, we describe the experiment itself, before proceeding to a discussion of our findings, qualitative and quantitative; subsequently, we reflect on the findings in the light of existing work, before concluding wth a summary of the key findings and their impact for future research.

2 Related Work

Information triage is the activity where a user determines the relevance of a piece of information for a particular information task [8]. This decision can be made at various stages of the information process: e.g. on first encounter, when it is selected for detailed reading; on review after closer reading; or subsequently when it is considered for long–term retention or re–interpreted in the light of other material. Document triage is encapsulated in the early stages of triage, when basic relevance is assessed. Though later reflection may result in its later omission from a user's final repertoire of documents, all this later activity is contingent upon the document's initial acceptance.

Models of document relevance have been considered, contested and discussed over many years, focussing on the properties of documents: for instance, the relative significance of titles or abstracts [12]. Such studies have been focussed upon relevance as a property of a document, to be assessed, rather than upon the method and means of that assessment. Likewise, many studies, such as [3], have viewed relevance and related document features within the framework of information retrieval: namely, how to operationalise relevance computationally.

Only recently has attention within computer science moved from document properties and information retrieval mechanisms to the corresponding human processes. Recent papers by Badi[1] and Bae[2], Wacholder[15] and others have pointed the way to a more detailed consideration of the interaction that occurs during document triage, in electronic and physical information media.

3 User Study

In order to uncover the gaps in existing understanding, we undertook a user–study to explore the differences between document triage behaviour in electronic and physical environments. Recent research[7] demonstrates that significant shifts in user behaviour emerge with a move from physical to digital media, thus a better understanding of the current differences is timely. Existing research provides triangulation data for new findings. This section first describes the experimental design, before discussing the quantitative and qualitative results.

3.1 Experimental Design

Information triage is a multi-stage process, as is the even more specific task of document triage. One common distinction in the digital environment is between reviewing the document through: its full–text; a descriptive overview page with title, abstract, etc.; or at the result list of document titles. We subsequently studied two electronic conditions: the first requiring the user to open the full document; the second giving a descriptive page that listed title, abstract, author and publication information. In all conditions, including paper, a printed list of document titles was given, and in both electronic forms a result–list format of document titles appeared at the commencement of the experiment.

The experiment was conducted in three conditions: first, paper–based with each participant being given a list of document titles and a set of printed documents; second, digital documents accessed via a results list and overview page; third, digital documents accessed as PDFs from a single file folder. In the digital folder condition, the files appeared with their titles, rather than filenames.

The study was conducted on a standardised task: judging the relevance of 20 documents from the ACM Digital Library on a set topic. The search for this study was standardised, and thus every partipant viewed the same twenty documents. For the paper condition, these papers were printed double–sided on A4 paper. Digital documents were presented as PDFs, read using Adobe Acrobat.

Thirty participants were recruited: 10 for each condition. Participants completed a pre–study questionnaire, and a post–experimental interview was used to elicit particular details of their interaction with the documents. Video recordings were taken of all participants' sessions, and the on–screen activity captured by Blackberry Flashback for the digital sessions. Each participant was asked to score each of the twenty documents for relevance to the task, giving a rating out of 10 (completely relevant) to 0 (non-relevant).

Participants were computer science staff and post– and under–graduate students, aged from 18 to 52. Of the thirty participants, twenty one were in their final undergraduate year or were postgraduate. Participants were assigned to each condition to ensure balance between the different modes. The task topic was of variable familiarity to the participants: from two who were research active in the area, to four first–year undergraduates with only limited knowledge.

A panel of three domain experts examined each paper in detail and rated each as relevant, part–relevant or non–relevant, and scored out of ten for relevance.

Where disagreement occurred (re. two papers), a discussion was engaged with until consensus was found. This basic deisgn reflects the common practice for assessing relevance for experimental corpora in the TREC conference series[14].

3.2 Findings: Process

Before studying the interaction of users with individual documents, we will first review the behaviour of users during their relevance judgement as a whole. Though there were some common patterns, in fact there were a number of critical divergences in the process followed by participants in the three different modes.

One key difference was total time taken for document triage: the ten paper–mode participants taking a mean of 23m 42s, overview–page mode 17m 11 s, and folder–mode 28m 12s. A t–test of these differences was significant at the 10% level for all cases, except between the two electronic modes, which was significant at the 5% level (p=0.021). One reason for the low times of overview–page participants was that few papers were read in their full–text form. Only two participants opened more than three papers for full viewing. In contrast, in both paper and folder modes 96% of all papers were read as full documents.

Process Strategy. The most common approach to the triage process was a linear process of reading the first document and then reading and scoring every document in turn. This is the dominant case both with the participants in the paper and electronic groups (25 of 30 participants). Those five participants using a non–linear method were all found to be in the eleven participants who took the longest total time. One potential weakness of the linear approach, identified by six participants, is that an individual's use of relevance scores can change as further documents are read. On paper, however, the eight linear–method participants often paused to reconsider their current scoring, whilst this was not observed at all in the two electronic modes: one participant commenting that "I realised at some point that the titles are kinda wrong sometimes in the meaning, so some of my scores in the beginning might be wrong but there we go".

Organising Documents. Our paper–mode participants frequently used the available deskspace to organise the scored documents in piles. One participant organised tthe documents at the start of the process, spreading them over the desk in order to gain an overview of the whole list: "If I can see the titles all at once, then I can judge more relevant documents and save time". Most participants, however, categorised documents as they were read in turn, reflecting the perceived relevance (see Figure 1, left). Seven out of ten participants divided the (tentatively) scored documents into piles, each pile being a set of documents with the same ranking category. The most common practice (5 users) was three piles: relevant, non-relevant and part-relevant documents. Six participants used these piles at the end of the task, placed across the desk as they confirmed their final relevance scores. Four of these reviewed all documents at this stage, and subsequently gave each a revised score in light of the scores given to other papers. One participant used a notable fanning effect (see Fig.1, inset) produced by the

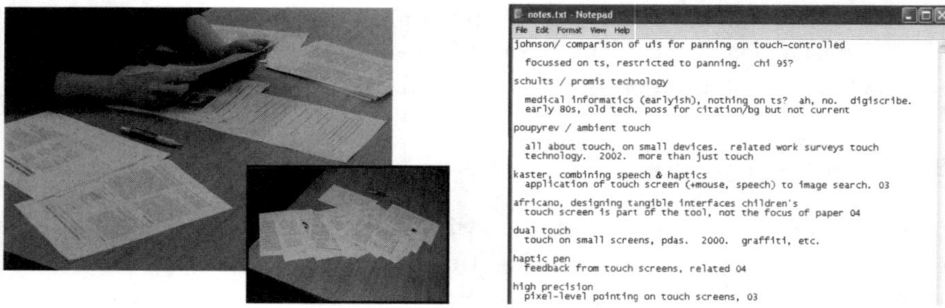

Fig. 1. Users organising pages for triage (left), fanning document (inset left) and electronic note taking (right)

relevance of the documents. When asked why he did it he commented that "they sort of fanned out without me realising". This fanning effect was not reproduced in any way by any of the electronic or folder participants.

The same set–creating activity was seen in two participants in the electronic modes. One marked potential relevance by placing a mark next to the paper title on the scoring sheet, whilst another kept score on a Notepad document (Fig.1, right). These participant thus created virtual document sets and proceeded to go back to the relevant documents in more depth to verify their judgements.

Average relevance scores were very similar across the different modes (6.356 and 6.512 in the digital and physical conditions respectively), and show no statistically significant difference (p=0.74).

Triage Effectiveness. The 20 documents used in the experiment were rated by our expert panel as containing 7 relevant, 5 partially relevant and 8 non-relevant documents. We evaluated the performance of our participants by considering the number of relevant documents in their 7 most highly ranked choices. This score showed little deviation across all modes, with 128 of the 210 documents (61%) in question being considered relevant by our experts. Paper and folder modes scored a little higher (63% each) and the overview–page mode lower (57%). These differences are not statistically significant within our sample size.

However, this picture hides considerable variation between modes, and we shall meet a number of these differences as we study how users viewed and evaluated the document content. Overview–page users highly rated short papers: three their four top–rated papers were 4 pages or less, whilst all top–ranked document in folder or paper modes were more than four pages long. Folder participants favoured documents with more statistical tables and technical diagrams.

3.3 Document Content

Abstracts and Titles. Previous research has indicated that document abstracts and titles play a key role in the relevance judgement of human readers[12]. This was true of all participants, particularly those in the two electronic modes.

Overview–page participants frequently (157 of 200 documents) viewed *only* the overview page of document title, abstract etc. provided after clicking on a document in the list. One participant opened all 20 documents, another ten, five opened documents that did not provide an abstract on the overview page, and the remaining three viewed no full documents at all. When documents were opened, the users performed only limited scrolling: suggesting that only the abstract and title from the top of the documents was read in detail, even with two page documents. Folder–mode participants also spent a high proportion of their time on the first page of the document, as we shall see below. Differences also appeared regarding the conclusion pages of documents: electronic participants rarely displaying them (total 17 of 243 opened documents), whilst reading was common in the paper mode (89 from 173 read documents).

Subjective feedback reinforced this observational data: e.g. twenty six participants reported that the title was important, and they favoured a "title including the search words". Imprecise abstracts were criticised by most of these participants, but this was not always acted on: eight overview–page participants noted specific abstracts that they found vague, but we observed that subsequently they did not chose to open any of these documents in question for reading.

Headings and Emphasis. Existing literature reports a common focus upon section heading text, which we also observed in all modes. However. participants reported seeking all emphasised text: e.g. italicised paragraphs, bullet points and figure captions. Participants commented that though they first look for key words in titles, later attention is given to headings in general. Post–experimental feedback and talk–aloud comments revealed that though title text was an initial attractor during triage, in all participating groups the initial importance of titles declined as heading and caption text was scrutinised. Participants from every group observed that titles can be misleading, and as the task progressed they therefore stopped relying so heavily on the titles alone. Yet again, few participants subsequently reconsidered the documents that were already ranked. Only two paper–mode participants who made this observation returned to review the score they had given earlier documents. Participants frequently paused at length on pages containing large amounts of bold text, whilst few pauses of over half a second were recorded on pages with no emphasised content.

Images. Images and figures play a very important role in general to both the paper and the electronic folder participants. Sixteen of these twenty participants rated images as "useful" or "extremely useful" when deciding the relevance of a document. One participant commented that "A picture is a thousand words they say. I think it is much more". Subjective feedback also revealed a favourable emphasis on concise, easy to read diagrams, when these support the relevance–judgement decision: e.g "Pictures are the main thing I look at. You can pick up the meaning and get the general idea of the paper I think from them". Participants also reported scanning neighbouring and caption text. In contrast, the seven of the ten overview-page participants rated images "not important" for relevance judgements. This difference in reaction could well be a product of the readers' behaviour or received stimuli from the different experimental modes.

We subsequently evaluated the relationships between images, tables and technical figures and users' relevance judgements. Photographic images seem to have no discernable effect: indeed, there is a moderate negative correlation (r=-0.31) between the number of images in a document and its relevance score. This relationship is explicable by document length effects (see below). Technical figures and tables, on the other hand, have a positive correlation between the number of figures and relevance rating (r=0.34), which is particularly noticable in the case of those in the electronic folder mode (r=0.57), and statistically significant at the 5% level in both cases. Statistical analysis thus concurs with the subjective feedback: when reading full– electronic documents, technical illustrations and tabulated data play significant roles in relevance judgement.

Document Length. Document length played an important part in document review. Even in the paper mode, where participants would often glance at most, if not all, document pages there was a declining likelihood of text being read when it fell later in the document. For example, in the case of one 24–page document, only one reader was observed as having viewed every page in paper mode, whilst not one reader in the electronic mode read beyond the second page.

A comparison of the paper–only against the two digital–mode groups illuminates differences in relevance judgements. From our experimental data, there are statistically significant effects from document length: shorter papers being favoured in the digital domain, when compared to paper (p=0.05). Further scrutiny between the two digital conditions reveals further detail: those using the overview–page interface were most likely to score longer documents lower – often without actually reading them. Individual papers demonstrate these general differences: e.g. paper no. 16 (4 pages) moved from rank 13 (paper) to 4 (digital), and its mean score average rose from 5.4 to 7.5.

Within–Document Navigation. Document navigation methods varied notably between the physical and electronic modes. In electronic modes, many documents (34%) were never scrolled, and 64% not read beyond the first page. Subsequent to this initial view, users would often rapidly scrolling the document downwards before unpredictably and apparently randomly skimming the document. Our participants explained that they were searching for relevant–looking headings. In contrast, those searching on paper repeated a superficially similar pattern, reading the first page in some detail, before skimming linearly through the document, often with a particular pause on the page containing the paper's conclusions. This repeated the emphasis on the beginning and end of the document, with the modification that the body was typically read before the conclusions.

One method of within–document navigation only available to electronic documents is the search function. Subjectively, this feature was rated highly by all our participants, twenty four of whom cited "Ctrl-F" as a key advantage of reading on the PC. The search facility of a reader application could be used to identify the specific parts of the document that contained the search terms used in the original query. Fifteen digital–mode users reported the advantages of search, and all claimed to use it. However, the observational data is at odds with these claims. Out of a total of 243 documents read in full PDF form, search was only used on 11 occasions by 4 users. Furthermore, on the majority (8) of these occasions, the first match only was inspected.

Differences also appear if we evaluate the amount of time spent in different parts of the document. Taking data from the screen–captures for the participants in the electronic folder mode, and the video capture of the paper mode, we can compare the displayed time for different parts of the document. Those in the electronic mode spent 68% of their viewing time on the first page of the PDF, without scrolling (i.e. on the top, visible portion of the first page). In contrast, only 32% of their time was spent on the remainder of the document, nearly equally divided between scrolling activity (15%) and the stationary reading of content (17%). Interviews revealed that most of the content time was focussed on larger visible elements such as headings and images. This contrasts markedly with the user behaviour when interacting with paper, with an average of 47% of time spent on the entire first page, with the remainder spent on the rest of the document. However, between–page movement accounted for a small percentage of time ($< 5\%$) and reading for nearly 50% of total document viewing time.

Users in overview–page and folder modes often continually scrolled documents up and down without pausing. It is hard to compare this mode of reading with the serial reading of pages seen in our paper–based participants, but the data above shows that the paper mode participants spent longer on the second and subsequent pages of documents. The conclusion page of papers was a common navigational destination in full–text reading; however, this was viewed for 52% of read papers in the paper mode, and for only 17% in the folder mode. Of the twenty participants in these two modes, only five stated that the conclusion played a notable part in their relevance judgement. In the overview–page mode only 43 papers were read, and only six were navigated to their conclusion page.

In electronic modes, following the skimming review of a document, users usually (72% of documents) return again to the top of the document. On the other hand, paper participants pause at several points in a document. Pages containing diagrams or illustrations are viewed for a longer period of time (average per viewed image page of 10.3s compared to 4.8s in electronic modes). Users' subjective feedback reported stopping to read the text relating to the images, headings, and sentences from paragraphs that are considered important. Readers seldom returned to the abstract page (24% of papers) at the conclusion of reading. Four paper participants reported that they would even stop to read something of interest that is not necessarily related to what they were looking for. Twenty two of all participants reported that recalling location of material within a document was easier on paper, and reading within documents seems more systematic (linear) in our observations of participants' reading.

Subjective Feedback. Participants were asked whether they would prefer to use the other medium (e.g. electronic/PDF for paper participants) to perform a search, or if they would prefer to use both physical paper and electronic media simultaneously. Only 3 (10%) of participants would chose to swap medium, whilst 10 (33.3%) would choose to use both media at the same time.

In order to discover the different affordances of the two media, participants were asked to list the features of each medium they find useful. In addition to those already mentioned, 14 participants reported greater comfort for paper, 11 noted annotation was easier, 10 said it was easy to organise (e.g. into piles) and nine cited it as being more portable. In comparison, few advantages were cited for electronic media did not have so many points in its favour – the only advantage reported by more than two people was the search facility.

When asked specifically about annotations twenty three participants considered them very important for triage but only one of the twenty digital participants took annotations of any kind. Participants commented that they could "write their own annotations for future searches" and that annotations help in organisation or, as one participant put it, "collecting my thoughts".

4 Discussion

As noted in Section 2, there is a gathering body of evidence on user behaviour in document triage. Some of our findings strongly triangulate with this existing literature: e.g. the significance of titles and the dependence of readers upon abstracts of academic texts is already well documents [12,4]. Our participants were entirely consistent with this recorded focus upon these key document features.

Digital document triage has also been reviewed, often in the context of web searching[13]. However, such studies have either focussed upon generalised web searching, or validated electronic information seeking criteria against the previous literature. This paper has focussed upon how these known items are actually used during the triage process itself.

Document length is one property that carries across physical and electronic environments, if experienced in differing ways: e.g. download times – a known concern on the web – does not translate to paper. Reviews of relevance literature[9] make clear that longer documents are less likely to be accepted for casual information seeking, whilst shorter documents are less likely to be accepted when "authorative" data is being sought. Overview–page participants scored longer documents lower than participants using paper. Given that the participants were given the same task in both modes, and the experiment balanced for experience and other effects, it is reasonable to assert that this difference is a property of the electronic environment.

Other recent work (e.g. [7]) suggests that electronic reading is associated with more casual styles of reading, when compared to paper. Our results suggest a similar difference in terms of triage: a preference for shorter documents, and a high proportion of skimming activity are more commonplace in the digital domain. When given a summary page of a document, readers in the digital domain seldom move beyond it, and even when reading full–texts, readers seldom scroll beyond the first screen of text. In comparison, over 80% of paper documents were read beyond the first page. What is not clear is the cause of this variance: is it a direct consequence of the interactive affordances of reader software, or indirectly caused by different expectation of digital resources?

4.1 Factors Affecting Relevance Choices

Users in the electronic modes made lower relevance decisions for longer documents. Whilst classic relevance ratings have viewed relevance in purely semantic terms, it would appear that in practice users adjust their relevance judgements when considering other factors. One model for this is to consider that a user's perceived relevance for a document is factored by the perceived cost of reading the document. In our case, wider navigation of paper documents suggests a lower cost than in electronic modes. In line with other research[5], our participants behaved as if electronic reading were a higher cost than reading on paper. Our earlier research has demonstrated that interactive costs for within–document navigation and reading can be reduced through changes to interaction design[5], though triage reading is substantially different to deep reading[1].

Our experiment confirms again the importance of document abstract and titles, but adds that interaction affects the impact of these elements. Participants, even when obliged to download the document, spent a high proportion of their time on first view provided by the document reader, and additional reading had little impact on user's relevance precision. Janes[4] used different presentations to evaluate the significance of abstracts and other elements of documents for relevance judgements. His conclusion was that abstracts formed the most important element of a user's decision, but his experiment used pre–defined formats, rather than allowing users to explore at will. What we observed during the interactive retrieval process was that when insufficient data was gleaned from an abstract, a higher volume of detailed reading proceeded. Furthermore, readers would often refer back to the abstract after linearly reading the paper for further detail. User confidence in the abstract is therefore tested by interaction, and doubt in the abstract drives users to higher interaction.

Time is also critical: initial response to a document (e.g. of the abstract or images) appears to be dominant. Our folder–mode participants were strongly influenced by images, but we have no evidence that this judgment is any more open to revision than the enduring impact of abstracts.

Paper–based participants showed more annotational and organisational behaviour than our overview–page and folder users – suggesting that these activities are easier on paper than in Acrobat.

Nicholas et al[10] observed, through a deep log analysis of major online journal repositories, that when an abstract webpage was accessed before the document itself could be downloaded, users often did not continue to the download stage. Their observation was clouded by issues of subscription – i.e. not all visitors *could* download full documents, and many could only view the abstract page. We can confirm Nicholas et al's hypothesis.

4.2 Future Work

Our experiment identified further details regarding user interaction with documents during document triage. However, there are some natural limitations to the experiment that mean many issues require future study. First, we were not able to track the actual parts of the screen used by the users. Eye-tracking may uncover further details that give a more certain insight into the fine–grained viewing processes of readers. Secondly, the focussed task used here is clearly only one of a nearly infinite range of tasks that could be used. Other tasks on different topics, using different user groups, and studying different stages of the information seeking process – from initial topic investigation to the double–checking of fine detail – may reveal different patterns and behaviours.

In particular, this experiment suggests that full–document review is more time consuming in electronic forms than on paper, and that any electronic form yields a lower level of precision than is the case for paper. Further experimentation is certainly required to identify where these differences do and do not apply. The experimental design also meant that we did not gain any insight into the effect upon the number of documents selected in any mode, and this is clearly an issue deserving of further study. The long history of research into relevance judgements[9] clearly demonstrates that this complex and important task cannot hope to be resolved by any one study.

5 Conclusion

This study revealed that many stages of the triage process differ between paper and electronic environments. Annotation and organising behaviour is rare during the electronic triage process, yet is commonplace in the medium of paper. Navigational behaviours also vary, with those reading on paper showing a broader reading of the content of papers, evidenced by a longer viewing time of content beyond the first page. In contrast, where a summative page of basic information is given in an electronic environment, document content is seldom used to shape the initial relevance decision. When full documents are read in an electronic environment, the larger proportion of time is spent on the first page, and much less on viewing of the subsequent content. This had significant impacts on the relevance judgments of our users, with certain features, such as greater length, leading to erroneously low relevance ratings. Users also seem to place high value on their first impression of a document, and further reading of the wider text has limited impact. For effective triage, initial reading needs to be concentrated on the most salient parts of the document.

Acknowledgements

This research is supported by EPSRC Grant GR/S84798.

References

1. Badi, R., Bae, S., Moore, J.M., Meintanis, K., Zacchi, A., Hsieh, H., Shipman, F., Marshall, C.C.: Recognizing user interest and document value from reading and organizing activities in document triage. In: Procs. IUI '06, pp. 218–225. ACM Press, New York (2006)
2. Bae, S., Badi, R., Meintanis, K., Moore, J.M., Zacchi, A., Hsieh, H., Marshall, C.C., Shipman, F.M.: Effects of display configurations on document triage. In: Costabile, M.F., Paternó, F. (eds.) INTERACT 2005. LNCS, vol. 3585, pp. 130–143. Springer, Heidelberg (2005)
3. Cool, C., Belkin, N.J., Kantor, P.B.: Characteristics of text affecting relevance judgments. In: Procs. 14th National Online Meeting, Learned Society, pp. 77–84 (1993)
4. Janes, J.W.: Relevance judgments and the incremental presentation of document representations. Information Processing & Management 27, 629–646 (1991)
5. Jones, M., Buchanan, G., Mohd-Nasir, N.: An evaluation of webtwig - a site outliner for handheld web access. In: Gellersen, H.-W. (ed.) HUC 1999. LNCS, vol. 1707, pp. 343–345. Springer, Heidelberg (1999)
6. Kelly, D., Belkin, N.J.: Reading time, scrolling and interaction: exploring implicit sources of user preferences for relevance feedback. In: Procs. 24th ACM SIGIR Conference, pp. 408–409. ACM Press, New York (2001)
7. Liu, Z.: Reading behavior in the digital environment. Journal of Documentation 60, 700–712 (2005)
8. Marshall, C.C., Shipman, I.F.M.: Spatial hypertext and the practice of information triage. In: HYPERTEXT '97: Proceedings of the eighth ACM conference on Hypertext, pp. 124–133. ACM Press, New York (1997)
9. Mizzaro, S.: Relevance: The whole history. Journal of the American Society of Information Science 48(9), 810–832 (1997)
10. Nicholas, D., Huntington, P., Jamali, H.R., Watkinson, A.: The information seeking behaviour of the users of digital scholarly journals. Inf. Process. Manage. 42(5), 1345–1365 (2006)
11. O'Hara, K., Sellen, A.: A comparison of reading paper and on-line documents. In: CHI '97: Proceedings of the SIGCHI conference on Human factors in computing systems, pp. 335–342. ACM Press, New York (1997)
12. Saracevic, T.: Comparative effects of titles, abstracts and full text on relevance judgments. Journal of the American Society for Inf. Science 22, 126–139 (1969)
13. Tombros, A., Ruthven, I., Jose, J.M.: How users assess web pages for information seeking. Journal of the American Society for Information Science and Technology 56(4), 327–344 (2005)
14. Voorhees, E.M, Harman, D.K: TREC: Experiment and Evaluation in Information Retrieval. MIT Press, Cambridge (2005)
15. Wacholder, N., Liu, L., Liu, Y.-H.: Selecting books: a performance-based study. In: Procs. 6th ACM/IEEE-CS Joint Conference on Digital libraries, pp. 337–337. ACM Press, New York (2006)
16. Woodruff, A., Rosenholtz, R., Morrison, J.B., Faulring, A., Pirolli, P.: A comparison of the use of text summaries, plain thumbnails, and enhanced thumbnails for web search tasks. JASIST 53(2), 172–185 (2002)

Motivating and Supporting User Interaction with Recommender Systems

Andreas W. Neumann

Institute of Information Systems and Management,
Universität Karlsruhe (TH), 76128 Karlsruhe, Germany
a.neumann@iism.uni-karlsruhe.de
http://www.iism.uni-karlsruhe.de/a.neumann

Abstract. This contribution reports on the introduction of explicit recommender systems at the University Library of Karlsruhe. In March 2006, a rating service and a review service were added to the already existing behavior-based recommender system. Logged-in users can write reviews and rate all library documents (books, journals, multimedia, etc.); reading reviews and inspecting ratings are open to the general public. A role system is implemented that supports the submission of different reviews for the same document from one user to different user groups (students, scientists, etc.). Mechanism design problems like bias and free riding are discussed, to address these problems the introduction of incentive systems is described. Usage statistics are given and the question, which recommender system supports which user needs best, is covered. Summing up, recommender systems are a way to combine the support of library user interaction with information access beyond catalog searches.

Keywords: Recommender system, rating service, review service, mechanism design, incentive system.

1 Introduction

The general public is lately becoming accustomed with recommender systems of different kinds at various online stores. But scientific libraries, where the profit contribution of a product (library document) is not the first concern and the costumers (library users) are coming due to very different incentives, are definitively a not less promising application area. Due to the supply complexity or the evaluation of the quality, scientists and students are more and more incapable of efficiently finding relevant literature in conventional database oriented catalog systems and search engines. A common solution to this problem lies in asking peers (see e. g. [10]). Recommender systems aggregate knowledge from many peer groups to the level of expert advice services. They bear the potential to significantly reduce transaction costs for literature searches by means of their aggregation capabilities. Scientific libraries are in a good strategic position to become (even more than now) the information centers of the future [7]. Turning library online public access catalogs (OPAC) into customer oriented service portals supporting the interaction of the customers is one step to this

L. Kovács, N. Fuhr, and C. Meghini (Eds.): ECDL 2007, LNCS 4675, pp. 428–439, 2007.

goal. Valid and credible information is a scarce resource [20]. Information consumes the attention of its recipients. "Hence a wealth of information creates a poverty of attention and a need to allocate that attention efficiently among the overabundance of information sources that might consume it." [21]

The more general term "recommender system" was coined by Resnick and Varian to better describe the action than the more narrow "collaborative filtering" [16]. A recommender system reads observed user behavior or opinions from users as input, then aggregates and directs the resulting recommendations to appropriate recipients. Recommender systems can be classified into two different main categories. An implicit recommender system is based on behavioral usage data like purchases, digital library catalog inspections, or lending data. An explicit recommender system directly asks the users for their opinions on certain objects. A more technical classification with a focus on applications in e-commerce can be found in [18] and [19]. For a more up-to-date overview on recommender systems e. g. see Adomavicius and Tuzhilin [1]. In Geyer-Schulz et al. [5] an early application of recommender systems including group-specific services in e-learning is presented. Herlocker et al. [9] deals with the technical evaluation of recommender systems.

The focus of this paper lies on the experiences with motivation and support of interaction between library users at the University Library of Karlsruhe. First, the introduced recommender systems are described, then mechanism design is discussed to address motivational problems. Finally, general lessons learned from integrating different recommender systems into large existing legacy library applications are summarized and the evaluation of such systems is discussed.

All in this paper presented recommender systems are fully operational services accessible by the general public. For further information on how to use these see "Participate!" at `http://reckvk.em.uni-karlsruhe.de/`. In answer to strong privacy concerns among students and scientists all portrayed recommender services are object-centered. They do not classify the users by observation or asking them for their interest, but they classify and gather data on the documents of a library. Figure 1 shows a cutout of the detailed document inspection page of [13] in the OPAC of the University Library of Karlsruhe. The behavior-based service is accessibly by clicking on "Empfehlungen" (Recommendations), the rating service by "Bewertung abgeben" (Submit rating) or direct inspection of "Bewertung des Titels nach Nutzergruppen" (Ratings of the titles by user group), and finally the review service by "Rezension schreiben" (Write review), "Rezensionen anzeigen" (Inspect reviews), and "Meine Rezensionen" (My reviews). All systems are programmed in Perl or PHP (or a combination of both), use PostgreSQL databases, and are running on Linux servers.

2 Behavior-Based Recommender Service

Behavior-based recommender services are observing the behavior of users and thereby implicitly collecting information about the objects the users are inspecting. The necessary homogeneity of a group of users in this case is granted by

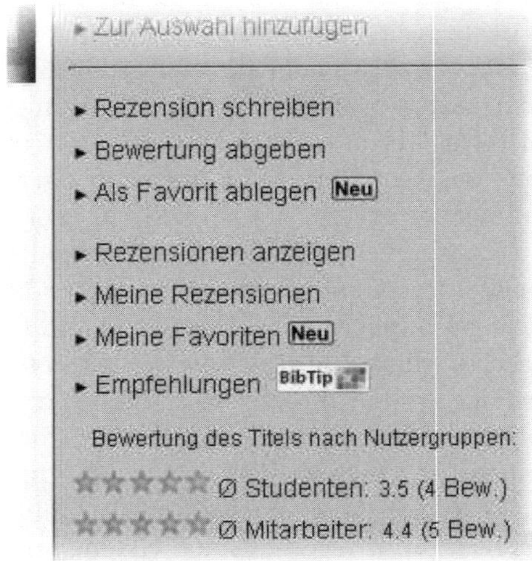

Fig. 1. Recommender start interface on a document's detailed inspection page. Rezension schreiben – Write review; Bewertung abgeben – Submit rating; Rezensionen anzeigen – Inspect reviews; Meine Rezensionen – My reviews; Empfehlungen – Recommendations; Bewertung des Titels nach Nutzergruppen – Ratings of the titles by user group.

the principle of self-selection [17,22]. In a library setting usage behavior can be observed at different stages: detailed inspections of documents in the OPAC, ordering paper documents from the magazine, ordering paper documents that are currently lent, and finally picking-up a paper document or downloading a file from the digital library. The main concern for the data selection is bias. It can be shown that lending and ordering data is highly biased, since e. g. students very often do not order the book they are mostly interested in, because most likely it is already lent, but actually their consideration-set only includes documents that they will be able to obtain timely before the corresponding examination. In marketing several conceptual models which describe a sequence of sets (e. g. total set $\supseteq$ awareness set $\supseteq$ consideration set $\supseteq$ choice set ([11], p. 153)) have been developed to describe such situations [14,23]. For this reason the behavior-based recommender service at the University Library of Karlsruhe is based on anonymized OPAC searches (hits on document inspection pages) and not on lending data. Due to transaction costs the detailed inspection of documents in the OPAC of a library can be put on a par with a purchase incidence in a consumer store setting. A market basket consists of all documents that have been co-inspected by one anonymous user within one session. To answer the question, which co-inspections occur non-random, an algorithm based on calculating inspection frequency distribution functions following a logarithmic series distribution (LSD) is applied [6]. Such a recommender system is operational at the OPAC of the University Library of Karlsruhe in a first version since

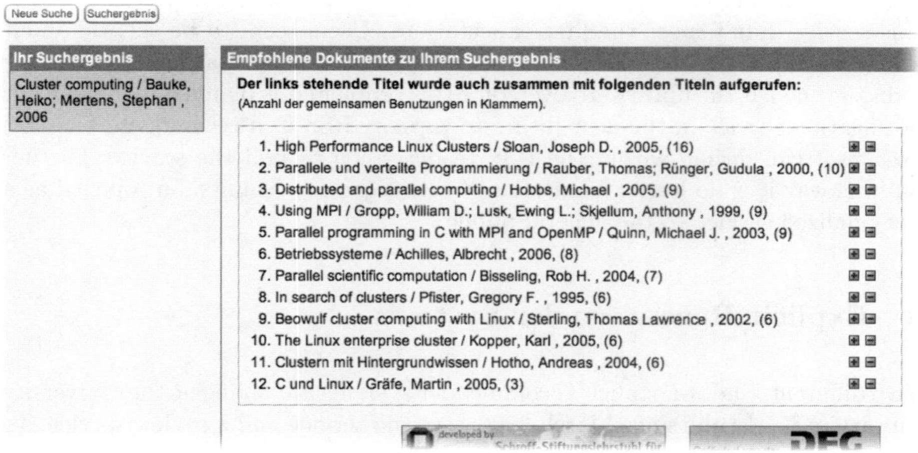

Fig. 2. Recommendation list of "Cluster computing" by Bauke and Mertens. The number of co-inspections is given in brackets after each title.

June 2002 [8] and in the current web service version (facilitating WSDL, XML and SOAP) since January 2006.

Figure 2 shows the recommendation list of "Cluster computing" by Bauke and Mertens (cut-out from the web page). The number of co-inspections is given in brackets after each title. Documents with less than three co-inspections have been rated by the LSD test to be not significantly related to this book. Since the usage distribution of documents in nearly every library is highly skewed (newer documents, or documents to topics that interest a large part of the overall library users, in general are more requested), many recommendations will be generated for documents that are used often while seldom used documents have fewer or no recommendations. Recommendations are updated daily. Of the 929 637 documents in the catalog, 192 647 documents have lists with recommendations, a total of 2 843 017 recommendations exist. Because of the skewness, the coverage of actual detailed document inspections is 74.9% (much higher than the coverage of the complete catalog). So the probability that recommendations exist for a document a user is currently interested in is 0.749 (status of 2007-03-19). A user survey asking the library users "I consider the recommendation service in general" on a Likert scale from 1 (very bad) to 5 (very good) yielded a mean of 4.1 from 484 votes between 2005-03-21 and 2006-03-06. This type of recommender service is best suited to users trying to find standard literature or further standard readings of a field corresponding to the document they are currently inspecting. Although it does not support the direct interaction (communication) between customers, everybody using the service profits from the actions of other library users.

An e-mail notification service was added at a later stage. Users with a library account receive an e-mail including a direct link to the recommendation page if new recommendations appear for a previously specified document. The usage of this service didn't meet the first expectations. Users seem to be skeptic about any service that tries to grab their attention (like spam mails) at times when they didn't even visit the library. To overcome this problem it is planned to extend this notification service in the near future to support RSS feed techniques. Thereby, each user can decide within the RSS reader when to poll the service. Further on, this way it is no longer connected to existing user accounts, but opened as a personalized service to the general public

3 Explicit Recommender Systems

Two different kinds of explicit recommender systems are online at the University Library of Karlsruhe since March 2006, a rating service and a review service. To prevent fraudulent use, submitting ratings and reviews is possible only for logged-in users. These services differ from most other systems (e. g. Amazon.com's) by means of user and target groups and strict separation of ratings and reviews. Currently three different user groups exist: students (Studenten), university staff (Mitarbeiter), and others (Externe) not directly associated with the university. While one could easily come up with more elaborate user classifications, these three groups have been used by the library for many years preceding these services. They are checked (and afterwards tracked over time) by the library for each user before handing out the library card. The guarantee of correctness made this user classification the (pragmatic) choice of approach for a library with an existing base of approximately 24 400 active users.

3.1 Rating Service

This service allows logged-in users so submit a numerical rating for a document on a Likert scale from 1 (very bad) to 5 (very good). Every user can submit only one rating per document. The ratings are aggregated for each user group separately and are shown in numerical form (average rating, number of ratings) as well as an enlightened-star-graphic on the detailed document inspection page. In figure 1 we see 4 ratings from students (Studenten) with an average of 3.5 and 5 ratings from university staff (Mitarbeiter) with an average 4.4. Thus, at a first glance [13] seems to be an overall good book, even more praised by scientists than by students.

Figure 3 shows the overall number of ratings online from 2006-03-03 to 2007-03-19. One large drawback of the current setup is known. Users searching the catalog are normally not logged-in until they want to order a paper copy of a document not freely available right now. To submit ratings they have to first log-in. This hurdle seems to have a huge influence on the number or submitted ratings, although it should have a very positive influence on the quality of the ratings. This service is best suited to get a first quick estimation of the overall quality of a document within certain user groups.

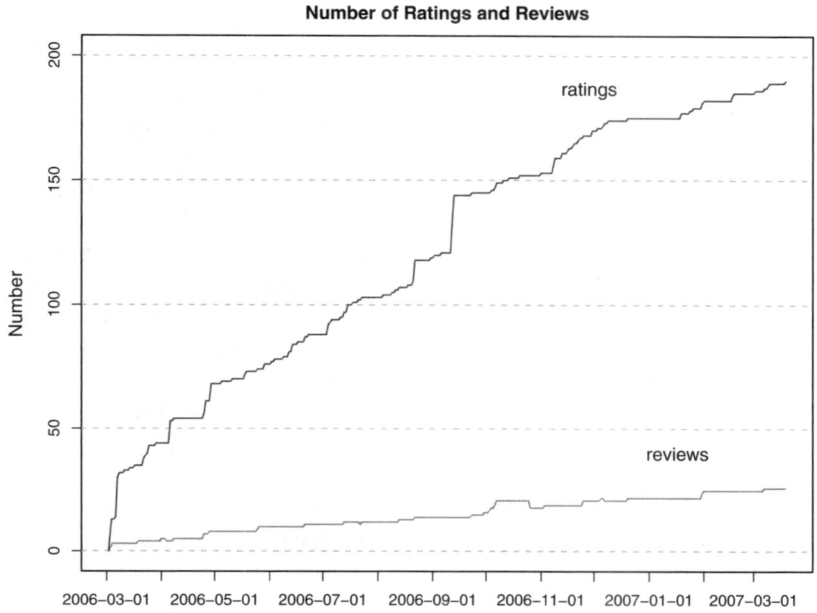

Fig. 3. Number of ratings and reviews online for the general public in the OPAC from 2006-03-03 to 2007-03-19

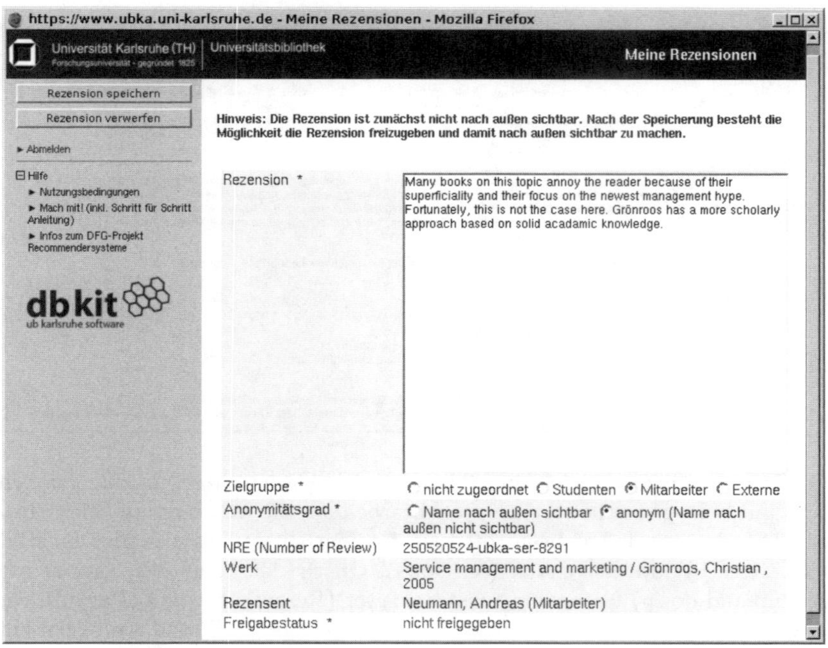

Fig. 4. Editing page for reviews. The author has to choose a target group (Zielgruppe) and his own degree of anonymity (Anonymitätsgrad).

3.2 Review Service

The review service manages document reviews written by library users. Figure 4 shows the editing page for reviews. Every logged-in user is allowed to submit four different reviews for each of the library's documents, one addressed to each of the three user groups (Zielgruppe – the target groups of the review) and a fourth one not assigned to any user group. This offers the possibility to focus the reviews on the specific needs of the target groups. Parts of a book may be suited very well for a specific course (target group of students), while other aspects e. g. the cited literature are mostly valued by scientists. Reviews can be written and saved within the system over several sessions, only after explicitly releasing a review, it shows up in the OPAC. The user can choose for each review, if it is published anonymously or under his real name. Writers are informed about guidelines for reviews, but no further checks from library staff is included in the workflow of submitting a review. Offending reviews can be reported to the library by every user. Since the writer of every review is known at least to the library, such reviews could be deleted and the writers contacted. No such case has been reported so far, although some users have deleted some of their own reviews (confer figure 3).

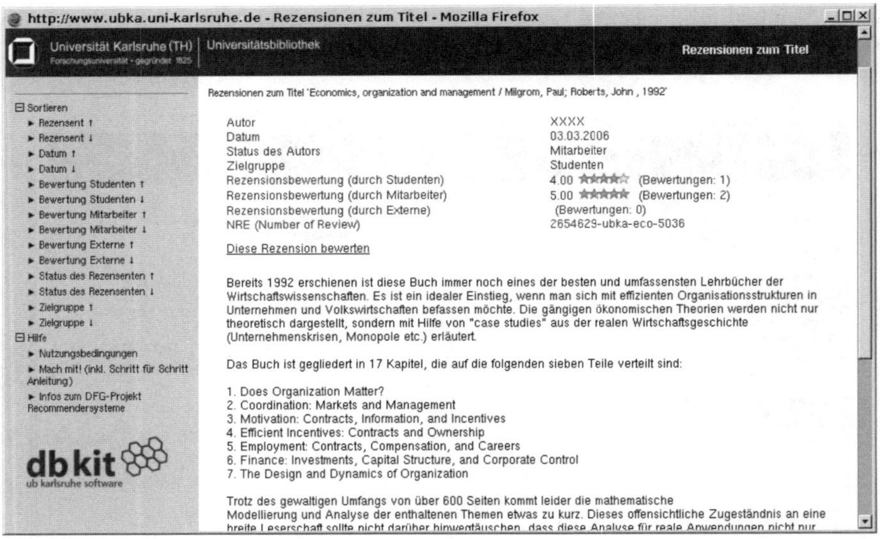

Fig. 5. Browsing page for reviews. The author (Autor) chose to stay anonymous (XXXX) but belongs to the staff group (Mitarbeiter), the target group (Zielgruppe) is students (Studenten), it has been rated (Rezensionsbewertung) one time by students and two times by university staff (see stars). On the left hand side various sorting criteria (up and down) for reviews exist: reviewer (Rezensent), date (Datum), ratings (Bewertung) from the different user groups, reviewer group (Status des Rezensenten), as well as target group.

Figure 5 shows the browsing page for reviews. A rating service analog to the one described in section 3.1 is available on the level of reviews. By means of this a first impression of the quality of certain reviews can be assessed without reading them. Reviews can be browsed and sorted by different criteria: reviewer, date, average ratings of the three user groups respectively, user group of the reviewer, and target group. By means of this service more detailed information about the content, the quality and the adequacy of a document for certain tasks (like preparation for an examination) can be assessed, even if the full text of the document is not available online. Inspection of this information on the other hand takes significantly longer than with the previously described systems. When searching the full text of all reviews for keywords, it can be used as a user generated indexing of the library catalog. At 2007-03-19 26 reviews (see figure 3) and 11 ratings of reviews are online. The reasons behind these numbers are discussed in the following sections.

4 Mechanism Design Problems ... and Solutions

Motivating users to write reviews or rate documents in a digital library is a game of (static) mechanism design, a special class of games of incomplete information. See e.g. "Game Theory" by Fudenberg and Tirole [4] pp. 243–318 for an introduction. By determining the structure of the digital library and the corresponding recommender services the operator of the library chooses the mechanism that maximizes his desired outcome. Here, the players are all library users and the desired outcome is a large number of high quality (implicit and explicit) recommendations. The following mechanism design problems are most dominant in the described applications:

Free-riding. Observing recommendations is highly valued, but due to transaction costs few users actually are willing to produce them.

Bias. Conscious or unconscious prejudice. E.g. a book author favors his product to the ones of competitors.

Credibility. Are recommendations mixed with sales promotion or advertisements?

Privacy vs. recognition of good cooperation. To laud users with exemplary cooperation you need their allowance to recognize them.

Positive/Negative feedback effects. The first good or bad recommendation may lead to further good or bad recommendations respectively (path dependency).

Economies of scale. The more contributing users (and thus recommendations) a system has, the more useful it is and thereby attracting even more users.

To solve these problems a suited incentive systems has to be implemented. Recommendations are no standard consumer goods thus needing a special user motivation approach [2]. Motivation can be intrinsic or extrinsic. Extrinsic motivation is generated e.g. by payments or public commendation. Compensations not only fulfill the purpose of inducing effort on the existing user group but also aiding the selection of appropriate new users [15]. On the other hand, when offering compensations, intrinsic motivation is often displaced by extrinsic motivation. So, once you offer compensations e. g. in form of free book donations to the best reviewers, you scare away some users, that were willing to contribute out of altruism or their implicit membership to the scientific community before. Unfortunately, it has been shown that experiments to measure these motivations correctly are very hard to accomplish [12].

In e-commerce applications shilling of recommender systems is often a motivation. The possibility to submit anonymously (or with fake accounts only requiring an e-mail address) ratings and reviews for one's own products to boost sales leads to significantly more submissions. This mechanism is less dominant in a library setting. The more restrictive the submission process is handled, the less submissions can be expected. The recommender systems at the University Library of Karlsruhe in the current first implementation are very restrictive in the area of the accepted user group and the anonymity towards the system administrator. Lessening the restrictions may lead to more submissions with the drawback of a higher rate of biased ratings and reviews.

In general, mechanism design problems are of less concern with behavior-based recommender systems. Free-riding is almost not possible, to create bias consciously in a well implemented system (including web robot prevention) has very high transaction costs and therefore is mostly unattractive in a library setting, and finally all users of the OPAC (regardless of their interest in recommendations) contribute to the recommender system and thereby helping to scale it up. Achieving the critical mass is the most important goal for stand-alone recommender systems (cold start problem) but is less indispensable to life for systems that are placed as value-added services to already high frequented information centers like digital library OPACs. The credibility in the academic environment comes to a large part from the institution to which the library belongs. If promotions or advertisements of any kind within the OPAC exist, a user should perceive a clear separation between these and the recommender system. This is often not the case in e-commerce applications like e. g. Amazon.com, where products with a high contribution to profit are placed by product managers next to real recommendations from other customers. Recognition of good cooperation within explicit recommender systems can be measured by reputation systems (for credence goods e. g. see [3]). A user point account tracks useful behavior (credit) and undesirable behavior (deduction of points). To keep users motivated an automatic discounting (decrease of points) over time is necessary. The quality of a review e. g. can be measured by the ratings of other users for this review.

5 Conclusions and Further Research

Scientific libraries hold a good strategic position to become digital information centers. Such information centers need to support library user interaction as well as information access beyond catalog searches. Recommender systems are a way to combine both. Different recommender systems support different user needs (e. g. finding standard literature or finding a specialized document for a specific topic). To amplify the described services the derived information is going to be stronger connected in the future. On one hand, e. g. the rating data can be used to further filter the behavior-based recommendations, on the other hand a different graph-based visualization approach that portrays the heterogeneous data from the different systems within one view is developed. Another way is a market-based approach to decide which information from which system should be offered to the user. The principle design of such a marketplace is described in [24].

All presented recommender systems are becoming regular OPAC features at the University Library of Karlsruhe. The introduction of the implicit recommender services is conducted in several steps. The first step comprised the technical development and launch of the services in the form described by this paper. To measure the intrinsic motivation of the users and to find the main obstacles for the users within the system, no technical incentive system like user point accounts was included, neither were any users directly asked to write reviews or give ratings. Although a lot of positive feedback for the systems itself was received, the free-riding problem can be hold responsible for the overall low information users have been put into the system. To overcome this situation, in the next steps the following is planned. First, students will be asked to write reviews on literature they are using for seminars to increase the number of quality reviews. Second, a reputation systems (list of best reviewers, best reviews, etc.) will be included and will be accompanied at an even later stage by a compensation system to raise extrinsic motivation.

Throughout all steps the evaluation of the quality of the ratings and reviews are of concern as well. Currently, the quality of reviews is measured by the ratings of reviews. No objective metric exists to measure the quality of scientific documents in an absolute way, the metric always depends on the function a document has to fulfill for a specific user. Once a reasonable number of submissions of ratings of documents exists, these ratings could be compared with data from other systems like Amazon.com, data from citation indices might correlate with ratings from scientists, and an evaluation by experts (lecturers, librarians, etc.) could lead to further insights as well. The most reasonable way to measure the effectiveness of the systems lies in observing the usage of the systems and asking the users, if the recommender systems (and thereby other users) helped them to find the right literature for the task they had in mind.

Acknowledgments. The author gratefully acknowledge the funding of the project "Recommender Systems for Meta Library Catalogs" by the Deutsche Forschungsgemeinschaft.

References

1. Adomavicius, G., Tuzhilin, A.: Toward the next generation of recommender systems: a survey of the state-of-the-art and possible extensions. IEEE Transactions on Knowledge and Data Engineering 17(6), 734–749 (2005)
2. Avery, C., Resnick, P., Zeckhauser, R.: The market for evaluations. American Economic Review 89(3), 564–584 (1999)
3. Emons, W.: Credence goods and fraudulent experts. RAND Journal of Economic 28(1), 107–120 (1997)
4. Fudenberg, D., Tirole, J.: Game Theory. MIT Press, Cambridge (1995)
5. Geyer-Schulz, A., Hahsler, M., Jahn, M.: Educational and scientific recommender systems. International Journal of Engineering Education 17(2), 153–163 (2001)
6. Geyer-Schulz, A., Hahsler, M., Neumann, A., Thede, A.: Behavior-based recommender systems as value-added services for scientific libraries. In: Bozdogan, H. (ed.) Statistical Data Mining & Knowledge Discovery. Chapman & Hall / CRC (2003)
7. Geyer-Schulz, A., Neumann, A., Heitmann, A., Stroborn, K.: Strategic positioning options for scientific libraries in markets of scientific and technical information – the economic impact of digitization. Journal of Digital Information 4(2) (2003)
8. Geyer-Schulz, A., Neumann, A., Thede, A.: An architecture for behavior-based library recommender systems. Information Technology and Libraries 22(4) (2003)
9. Herlocker, J.L., Konstan, J.A., Terveen, L.G., Riedl, J.T.: Evaluating collaborative filtering recommender systems. ACM Transactions on Informations Systems 22(1), 5–53 (2004)
10. Klatt, R., Gavriilidis, K., Kleinsimlinghaus, K., Feldmann, M.: Nutzung und Potenziale der innovativen Mediennutzung im Lernalltag der Hochschulen, BMBF-Studie (2001), `http://www.stefi.de/`
11. Kotler, P.: Marketing management: analysis, planning, and control, 4th edn. Prentice-Hall, Englewood Cliffs (1980)
12. Kunz, A.H., Pfaff, D.: Agency theory, performance evaluation, and the hypothetical construct of intrinsic motivation. Accounting, Organizations and Society 27(3), 275–295 (2002)
13. Milgrom, P., Roberts, J.: Economics, Organization and Management, 1st edn. Prentice-Hall, Englewood Cliffs (1992)
14. Narayana, C.L., Markin, R.J.: Consumer behavior and product performance: An alternative conceptualization. Journal of Marketing 39(4), 1–6 (1975)
15. Prendergast, C.: The provision of incentives in firms. Journal of Economic Literature 37(1), 7–64 (1999)
16. Resnick, P., Varian, H.R.: Recommender systems. Communications of the ACM 40(3), 56–58 (1997)
17. Rothschild, M., Stiglitz, J.: Equilibrium in competitive insurance markets: An essay on the economics of imperfect information. Quarterly Journal of Economics 80, 629–649 (1976)
18. Schafer, J.B., Konstan, J.A., Riedl, J.: Recommender system in e-commerce. In: Proceedings of the ACM Conference on Electronic Commerce, pp. 115–152. ACM, New York (1999)
19. Schafer, J.B., Konstan, J.A., Riedl, J.: E-commerce recommendation applications. Data Mining and Knowledge Discovery 5, 115–152 (2001)
20. Shapiro, C., Varian, H.R.: Information rules. Harvard Business School, Boston (1999)

21. Simon, H.A.: Designing organisations for an information-rich world. In: Greenberger, M. (ed.) Computers, Communications, and the Public Interest, The Johns Hopkins Press, pp. 40–41 (1971)
22. Spence, M.A.: Market Signaling: Information Transfer in Hiring and Related Screening Processes. Harvard University Press, Cambridge, Massachusetts (1974)
23. Spiggle, S., Sewall, M.A.: A Choice Sets Model of Retail Selection. Journal of Marketing 51, 97–111 (1987)
24. Wei, Y.Z., Moreau, L., Jennings, N.R.: A market-based approach to recommender systems. ACM Transactions on Informations Systems 23(3), 227–266 (2005)

On the Move Towards the European Digital Library: BRICKS, TEL, MICHAEL and DELOS Converging Experiences

Panelists

Massimo Bertoncini, Engineering Ingegneria Informatica, R&D Lab,
Massimo.bertoncini@eng.it

On behalf of BRICKS project

Thomas Risse, L3S
risse@l3s.de
Carlo Meghini, CNR-ISTI
carlo.meghini@isti.cnr.it

On behalf of TEL/EDL project

Jill Cousins, TEL Office
Jill.Cousins@KB.nl
Britta Woldering, CENL
woldering@dbf.ddb.de

On behalf of MICHAEL/MINERVAeC project

Rossella Caffo, Italian Ministery for Culture
rcaffo@beniculturali.it
David Dawson, MLA
david.dawson@mla.gov.uk

On behalf of DELOS Network of Excellence

Yoannis Yoannidis, University of Athens
yannis@di.uoa.gr
Donatella Castelli, CNR-ISTI
donatella.Castelli@isti.cnr.it

L. Kovács, N. Fuhr, and C. Meghini (Eds.): ECDL 2007, LNCS 4675, pp. 440–441, 2007.

Description

In the last few years, a deep paradigm shift has taken place in the Digital Library domain. From several independent online systems and closed library "silos" that store digital heritage content, digital library systems are evolving towards a networked service-based architecture built as a set of fully interoperable local digital library systems.

A ***digital library*** in this context refers to a network of services targeted to cultural heritage and/or scholarly institutions (libraries, archives, museums, etc.), allowing users to access and utilize globally distributed collections of multimedia digital content (text, images, and audio-video collections).

There are currently significant ongoing initiatives in the field such as BRICKS, TEL/EDL, MICHAEL, and DELOS) which have developed so far fundamental technologies on the road to the European Digital Library. Hence, this panel will begin with a comparative analysis of the state-of-the-art technologies, as made available by the different initiatives.

The main objective of the proposed panel will be to discuss to what extent the efforts so far have led towards a fully operational service for a European Digital Library, and what further challenges need to be dealt with, within the deadlines of the i2010 initiative.

Digital Libraries in Central and Eastern Europe: Infrastructure Challenges for the New Europe

Christine L. Borgman[1], Tatjana Aparac-Jelušić [2], Sonja Pigac Ljubi[3], Zinaida Manžuch[4], György Sebestyén[5], and András Gábor[6]

[1] Department of Information Studies,
University of California, Los Angeles
borgman@gseis.ucla.edu
[2] Department of Library and Information Science,
University J. J. Strossmayer, Osijek, Croatia
taparac@ffos.hr
[3] Croatian National and University Library, Zagreb, Croatia
spigacljubi@nsk.hr
[4] Institute of Library and Information Sciences,
Vilnius University, Lithuania
zinaida.manzuch@mb.vu.lt
[5] Department of Library and Information Science,
Eötvös Loránd University, Budapest, Hungary
lion@ludens.elte.hu
[6] Department of Information Systems, Corvinus University of Budapest, Hungary
gabor@informatika.uni-corvinus.hu

Keywords: Digital libraries, Central and Eastern Europe, systems design, cultural heritage, management, political reform, economics, education policy, libraries, museums, archives, information systems, technology transfer.

Description

The countries of Central and Eastern Europe (CEE) that were part of the Soviet Bloc or were non-aligned (Yugoslavia) entered the 1990s with telecommunications penetration of about fifteen telephones per hundred persons and a weak technical infrastructure based on pre-Cold War mechanical switching technology. They lacked digital transmission systems, fiber optics, microwave links, and automated systems control and maintenance. Until 1990, business, government, and education made little use of computers, although some mainframe-based data processing centers handled scientific and military applications. Communication technologies such as typewriters, photocopiers, and facsimile machines were registered and controlled to varying degrees in each country. The CEE countries could not legally make connections between their computer networks and those of countries outside the Soviet Bloc owing to the COCOM regulations and other embargoes imposed on the region by the West, although clandestine network connections were widely known to exist. In the fifteen-plus years since the collapse of the Soviet Bloc, these countries have made rapid advances in infrastructure and economics, and several already have become

L. Kovács, N. Fuhr, and C. Meghini (Eds.): ECDL 2007, LNCS 4675, pp. 442–444, 2007.

members of the European Union. Yet many challenges remain, especially with regard to infrastructure maturity, linguistics, and intellectual property.

This panel will address the special concerns for digital library research and development in the host region of the conference. Panelists will address three questions with respect to digital library efforts in their respective countries:

- What are the infrastructure concerns in developing digital libraries in the region?
- How do the linguistic concerns of the region (relatively small language groups, translation requirements, etc.) influence digital library design?
- What intellectual property issues most influence digital library developments?

Panelists:

C.L. Borgman, Introduction and Overview of Issues

Prof. Dr. Borgman, who was a Fulbright Professor in Hungary and a member of the Regional Library Program Board for the Soros Foundation Open Society Institute in the mid-1990s, will frame the panel discussion with political, technical, and historical background on digital library development in Central and Eastern Europe.

T. Aparac-Jelušić, Infrastructure and Content Management Issues in Digital Libraries: A Croatian Perspective

Prof. Dr. Aparac-Jelušić, who chairs the LIS programs at Osijek and at Zadar, Croatia, and also directs the annual conference in Dubrovnik, *Libraries in the Digital Age*, will set digital library research and development in Croatia in the context of education and research in the region. She will discuss policies to strengthen national information and communication technology infrastructure to increase Croatian participation in European information sector projects. She will explore how the Open Access movement in the research and academic community is addressing some of the concerns of small language groups. Intellectual property approaches are illustrated by new national programs to digitize Croatian heritage material and to build digital repositories of educational content. Distance education also is strongly influencing the development of digital libraries in the region.

S.J. Ljubi, Advantages of Being a Small Country: Croatian Experiences in Web Archiving

Ms. Ljubi, a Librarian at the National and University Library of Croatia, is a member of the research project team to harvest and archive Web-based Croatian publications. Over a period of 3 years, 1700 titles have been archived, most in multiple versions as they change over time, for a total of about 14000 instances. Each title may be a single discrete document or a whole government website containing thousands of pages. Among the issues to be addressed are cooperation with publishers, government agencies, and other institutions; intellectual property policies and technical mechanisms for providing access to archived content; architectural design of digital library services; and international efforts in cooperation and interoperability to preserve national cultural and scientific heritage.

Z. Manžuch, Building Cultural Heritage Libraries Online: Lithuanian Perspective in a Broad Context

Ms. Manžuch, a lecturer and doctoral student, will illustrate Lithuania's growing involvement in European digital library efforts with an ambitious project to create the *Integrated Virtual Library Information System* (IVLIS). It is a partnership among multiple memory institutions to provide access to the cultural heritage of Lithuania for in-country and foreign users. Establishing effective collaboration between the dispersed communities involved in digitization, including libraries, museums, archives, research institutes, and universities, is a core concern. Having made extensive investments in technological infrastructure, Lithuania is now addressing questions about the future of its libraries and about how digital libraries can be used to represent cultural identity, cultural diversity, and the dialog of nations and communities in a globalized world.

G. Sebestyén, Heading for a New Tower of Babel: Electronic Libraries in an Increasingly Globalized World

Prof. Dr. Sebestyén, who heads the Library and Information Science Department at ELTE in Budapest, will set regional developments in digital libraries in a global context. Hungarian is not part of the Indo-European language group, making it distinctively different from the languages of its continental neighbors. Hungary thus faces extra challenges in a multilingual and multicultural information society in which bridging the gaps of cultural relativism is a key issue. He will explore how users interpret digital library content in terms of their own cultures and ways in which DL interface design can address challenges of globalization.

A. Gábor: Digital Libraries in the Context of Modernisation of Higher Education Institutions

Prof. Dr. Gábor, who teaches management and computer science at Corvinus University of Budapest (previously known as the University of Economic Sciences, and during the Soviet period as Karl Marx University), will address the role of digital libraries in modernising higher education. Digital library services can contribute to the transformation of universities in the region by improving access to information for research and for teaching. Library infrastructure, with adequate investment, can support the management of research and development and can be integrated into project administration. Added value will come from active management of intellectual property rights, and from reporting, preserving, and disseminating project results. He will report on Hungarian national activities in business process analysis in higher education to improve library functions and services.

Electronic Work: Building Dynamic Services over Logical Structure Using *Aqueducts* for XML Processing*

Miguel A. Martínez-Prieto, Pablo de la Fuente, Jesús Vegas, and Joaquín Adiego

GRINBD, Depto. de Informática E.T.S. de Ingeniería Informática, Universidad de Valladolid
47011 Valladolid, Spain
{migumar2,pfuente,jvegas,jadiego}@infor.uva.es

Abstract. This paper presents, from e-book features, the concept of *electronic work* as a medium for publishing classic literature in different editions demanded by the Spanish educational system. The electronic work is an entity which, focused in its logical structure, provides a set of interaction services designed by means of *Aqueducts*, a processing model driven by XML data.

1 Introduction

The definition of what an *e-book* is, or has to be, is quite loose due to its complex nature. Even so, is accepted that an e-book is the result of integrating the classical book structure with features which can be provided within an electronic environment [5].

Although, there are many examples of e-books successfully exploited in real environments, we are interested in those focused in its *logical structure* for integrating concerns. An example of them, is the *Visual Hyper-TextBook* [5] that aims at a solid and flexible solution to allow the generation of hypertexutal versions with an appearance as close as possible to the printed paper book; it also provides advanced browsing and searching functionalities which facilitate the interaction with the e-book. From this experience, we believe that a specific model for describing the logical structure allows getting better e-books and suggest to use a *descriptive markup* that defines a high level of abstraction and reflects the function played by each fragment of text. This markup is build with a declarative language (XML[1]) that guarantees to preserve e-book contents.

Taking in account the main role played by the logical structure, we assume that its XML representation is the core of the e-book and it is used for building interaction services by means of a XML processing model. From this context, we introduce the *electronic work* as an approach of specific e-book focused in its logical structure, which is used for building interaction services with *Aqueducts* model.

2 Electronic Work: Concept and Logical Structure

This article shows preliminary results of the *BiDiLiC project* that designs a digital library to disseminate the Spanish literary heritage throughout the educational system, where the use of e-books has been substantial and continues to increase rapidly [6].

* This work was partially supported by the projects TIN2006-15071-C03-02 and TIN2005-25826-E from MEC (Spain).

[1] http://www.w3.org/TR/REC-xml/

L. Kovács, N. Fuhr, and C. Meghini (Eds.): ECDL 2007, LNCS 4675, pp. 445–448, 2007.

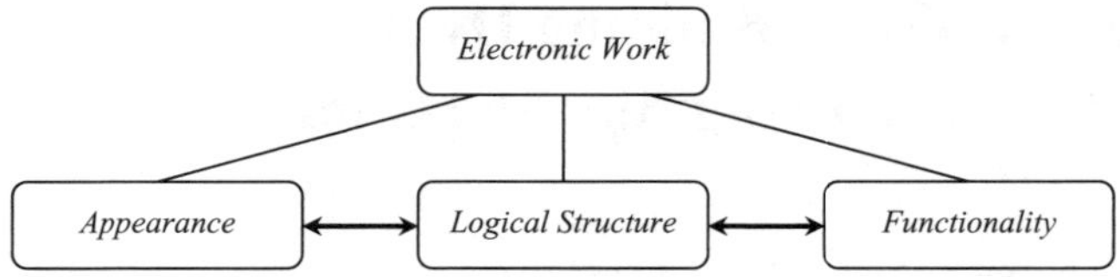

Fig. 1. An e-work as an integrator of concerns

2.1 Definition of Electronic Work

The *electronic work* (e-work) *is a literary entity in which a set of related editions are integrated next to the original text, with different services allowing a global interaction with the text and, independently, with each edition, fitting its appearance to the established issues of style*. An *open taxonomy* represents the specific semantics associated with editions that can be published in an *e-work*; this facilitates the concept's evolution which can add new classes of edition by means of the logical structure resources. Currently, the *e-work* allows publishing five classes of edition: *facsimile, palaeographic, modernized, updated* and *translated*.

The concept of *e-work* is designed from the e-book's features, so it is a dynamic and reactive element which can be made available in different formats in short periods of time. A low-level description (see *Figure 1*), presents an *e-work* as an integration of structure and services which define two main concerns: functionality and appearance. The *functionality* defines the logic of the service by means of a data guided processing which gets a generic result (represented in the same markup used for the logical structure) that is used by the *appearance* for building the visual result of the service according to the restrictions of the user's querying device.

2.2 A TEI-Lite Schema for Logical Structure Markup

An *e-work* is a single entity which publishes several classes of editions; therefore, the *descriptive markup* selected to represent its logical structure should facilitate the individual definition of every edition inside of the global structure of the *e-work*. This markup should be capable to describe all literary styles: prose, verse or drama.

We have choosen, for this purpose, an established norm as *TEI-Lite* [3], which suggests a markup for preserving the structure of underlying text obviating presentation issues; this feature allows us to mark contents independently of formats and styles used for showing them. The tagset of TEI-Lite is defined with XML, so the logical structure of the *e-work* has a high level of preservation and integrability in current environments, in which XML is considered as the *de facto* standard for the interchange of information.

Our approach of markup selects a specific subset of TEI-Lite for satisfying the *e-work's* needs, so it has two basic levels. On the one hand, a *global* level used to define information shared by all editions: metadata and critical and historic information of the *e-work* are marked with it. On the other hand, we suggest an *edition* level for describing the specific structure of each edition defined in the taxonomy of the *e-work*. This level contains two classes of elements, for *structural divisions* and for specific *contents* respectively. These entire elements share, amongst others, next attributes: *type* for defining the role that the element plays in the edition, *lang* for pointing out the language in which are expressed the contents that stores (required for translated editions) and *rend* for customizing (in palaeographic editions) the element's presentation style.

3 Aqueducts: A Pipelined Architecture for e-Work's Services

The *e-work* builds its interactive services by means of a XML data driven processing model: *Aqueducts*. It proposes a model for XML processing that abstracts semantics of *XProc*[2] conceptual model for representing it according to *pipe-filter* [4,7] features. This decision entails to define a *hierarchy of components*, based on *encapsulation*, which allows describing a *configuration* of pipes and filters as a higher-level entity.

3.1 Filter

The concept of filter abstracts (from the original's description of *filter* [7]) the syntactic and semantic features which inherit all components in this hierarchy. So, a *filter is a processor element which performs its specific computation over its XML input content for getting a XML output content which represents the result of its execution*.

A filter has two main components: the *interface of communication* which represents filter's role in the context of execution, and the *logic of process* which internally defines its computation features. This logic can be defined by means of an internal *finite state machine* (FSM) or by a complex FSM built over a configuration of pipes and filters.

3.2 Hierarchy of Components

This hierarchy differences *simple* and *complex* components according to the definition of its FSM. Moreover, each class of component has a specific semantic characterization.

A *structural step* is defined as *an atomic filter with an indivisible logic of process* (defined by an internal FSM) *in its context of execution*. We consider three classes: *generator* (as data source), *transformer* (as a generic filter) and *serializer* (as data sink).

A *construct* is defined as *a complex filter with a specific semantic to control and manage the contents flow inside an aqueduct*. We consider as constructs *sequences* of filters, *conditions* and *iterations* defined by means of boolean expressions, and, finally, mechanisms of *error handling* for managing errors happened during filter's execution.

An *aqueduct* is the high-level filter in the hierarchy. It is the unique component directly executed by the *e-work*. We define it as *a complex filter with an internal sequence of pipes and filters which is built upon a semantic associated with a software configuration in Aqueducts*. This semantic restricts the structure of an aqueduct:

1. The first filter executed in an aqueduct must be a *generator step* which provides content (TEI) from the logical structure of the *e-work*.
2. The core on an aqueduct is composed for *transformer steps* which defines the specific logic of process associated with the aqueduct.
3. The last filter executed in an aqueduct must be a *serializer step* which receives content generated and delivers it according to the request features.

[2] http://www.w3.org/TR/xproc/

3.3 E-Work in Action: Building Interactive Services with Aqueducts

In our current prototype of digital library, each *e-work* is stored in a XML file, so each service generates its content by means of a XPath[3] query performed on this XML file.

This content is successively transformed by means of XSLT[4] templates which represent the *functionality* concern of the service; all of these templates are designed according to the logical structure of the *e-work*. Next, the service achieves its final presentation format using a set of XSL[5] style sheets which represents the *appearance* concern of the service respect to the used TEI tagset. Finally, the content is serialized to the expected presentation format, guarantying that users can visualize the requested content independently of its querying device. It is an important challenge because services can be homogeneously rendered and, this is a weakness of e-books given the diversity of incompatible standards and the dependency of most e-books on specific devices [2].

4 Conclusions and Future Work

A concept of *e-work* describes an integration of concerns focused in its logical structure defined by means of a descriptive markup; these features show a robust and extensible solution with a competitive performance in real environments. So, this solution guarantees the preservation and exploitation of documents and allows us to publish other types of document through current *e-work* resources as indicated in the justification of the logical structure. Moreover, this structure facilitates the integration of concerns, allowing us to manage functionality and appearance in an independent way.

We are currently designing more services within an *e-work* which complement its current behaviour with specific features required in educational environments. For this purpose, we are using educational objects (associated with each *e-work*) which define different classes of activities that help students to assimilate important concepts.

References

1. Bia, A., Sánchez-Quero, M.: Diseño de un procedimiento de marcado para la automatización del procesamiento de textos digitales usando XML y TEI. In: Proceedings of II Jornadas Bibliotecas Digitales (JBIDI), Almagro, Spain, pp. 153–165 (November 2001)
2. Bry, F., Kraus, M.: Perspectives for electronic books in the world wide web age. The Electronic Library 20(4), 275–287 (2002)
3. Burnard, L., Sperberg-McQueen, C.M.: TEI Lite: An Introduction to Text Encoding for Interchange (1995), `http://www.tei-c.org/Lite/teiu5_en.pdf`
4. Buschmann, F., Meunier, R., Rohnert, H., Sommerlad, P., Stal, M.: Pattern-oriented software architecture: a system of patterns. John Wiley & Sons, New York (1996)
5. Crestani, F., Landoni, M., Melucci, M.: Appearance and functionality of electronic books. International Journal on Digital Libraries 6(2), 192–209 (2006)
6. Falk, H.: Electronic campuses. The Electronic Library 21(1), 63–66 (2003)
7. Shaw, M., Garlan, D.: Software Architecture: Perspectives on an Emerging Discipline. Prentice Hall, New Jersey (1996)

[3] http://www.w3.org/TR/xpath/

[4] http://www.w3.org/TR/xslt/

[5] http://www.w3.org/TR/xsl/

A Model of Uncertainty for Near-Duplicates in Document Reference Networks

Claudia Hess[1] and Michel de Rougemont[2]

[1] Laboratory for Semantic Information Technology, Bamberg University
[2] LRI, Universit Paris-Sud 11
claudia.hess@wiai.uni-bamberg.de, mdr@lri.fr

Abstract. We introduce a model of uncertainty where documents are not uniquely identified in a reference network, and some links may be incorrect. It generalizes the probabilistic approach on databases to graphs, and defines subgraphs with a probability distribution. The answer to a relational query is a distribution of documents, and we study how to approximate the ranking of the most likely documents and quantify the quality of the approximation. The answer to a function query is a distribution of values and we consider the size of the interval of Minimum and Maximum values as a measure for the precision of the answer[1].

1 Introduction

Digital libraries often contain duplicates, i.e., two or more representations of the same or nearly the same document. Duplicates are, for example, the pre-print and print, or erroneous copies of a document as in the metadata provided by CiteSeer[2]: only around 500,000 of the over 700,000 documents have a distinct title (almost identical titles are hereby not yet filtered). The fraction of duplicated pages on the web was estimated at 30 to 45% in [1,2]. Duplicates may be mirrors, but also be malicious copies by spammers, or crawling errors. When two heterogeneous document repositories are integrated, the merged collection may contain duplicates, too. Cleaning mechanisms try to avoid duplicates and hence define some identity between objects (e.g. [3]). Objects are merged if their similarity is above a certain threshold. However, a merge is not appropriate when documents differ too much with respect to their metadata, references or content.

We consider a Document Reference Network as a graph where nodes are documents and edges link one document with its references. PageRank [4] is the best known measure which analyzes document reference networks in order to rank the results of user queries. Measures on a document network may provide misleading results if the network contains duplicates. While a duplicate's citation list might be incomplete because not all references were correctly extracted, incoming references might point only to one of the duplicates. This could wrongly increase or decrease the rank of a document. We therefore propose a model of uncertainty for

[1] The work was supported by the German Academic Exchange Service.
[2] The CiteSeer metadata is publicly available at http://citeseer.ist.psu.edu/oai.html

L. Kovács, N. Fuhr, and C. Meghini (Eds.): ECDL 2007, LNCS 4675, pp. 449–453, 2007.

near duplicates. It follows the approach taken by probabilistic databases where alternative representations of the same real-world entity are available. As several nodes may represent the same document and link to different documents, one may first cluster similar documents and introduce probabilistic edges between the clusters. This simple model captures some of the difficulties to approximate queries in a digital library, and provides some measures of quality for the answers of relational and functional queries. The answer to a unary query is a distribution on documents, and we study how to approximate the sequence of most likely documents and propose a measure for the quality of the approximation. The answer to a functional query is a probabilistic distribution of values from a Min value to a Max value. The smaller is the interval [Min, Max], the better is the precision of the answer. To this end, the paper is structured as follows: section 2 presents the uncertainty model for graphs. Section 3 defines queries in this model and the main section 4 presents an efficient approximation of these queries.

2 Uncertainty Model for Document Networks

We extend the uncertainty model by Andritsos et al. [5] for relational databases to an uncertainty model for graphs. Table 1 shows an example database and figure 1 the corresponding graph with clusters. A cluster-based uncertainty graph is a structure $GC_n = (D_n, E, U_1, ...U_p, C_1, ...C_m)$ where D_n is the set of n nodes, $E \subseteq D_n \times D_n$ is the set of edges, $U_i \subseteq D_n$ is the set of labels, for $i = 1, ..., p$, and C_i are partial functions from D_n into $[0, 1]$ such that the domains of C_i partition D_n, and $\sum_x C_i(x) = 1$.

Table 1. Document Relation

	id	docID	references	prob
t1	d1	doc1	doc3, doc5	0.7
t2	d1	doc2	doc5	0.3
t3	d2	doc3	doc5, doc6	0.2
t4	d2	doc4	doc5	0.8
t5	d3	doc5		1
t6	d4	doc6		1

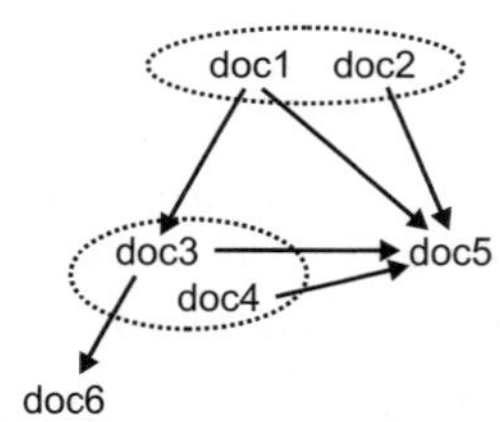

Fig. 1. Graph with Clusters

According to [5], probabilistic instances $\widehat{G}_i$ take one tuple t out of each cluster C_j from G with probability $C_j(t) = prob(t)$. Then $Prob(\widehat{G}_i) = \prod_{t \in \widehat{G}_i} prob(t)$ gives the probability distribution over all $\widehat{G}_i$. The answer to a query Q is defined as a probabilistic measure on tuples: $p_t = \sum_{\widehat{G}_i | t \in Q(\widehat{G}_i)} Prob(\widehat{G}_i)$. Our extension of the relational model indicates how to set edges from and to uncertain nodes in the probabilistic instances: there is an edge between C_i and C_j if the selected nodes $c \in C_i$ and $c' \in C_j$ were connected in GC_n.

We transform the graph with clusters on the nodes GC_n into a graph $G = (V, E_C, \mu_e)$ where V is the set of clusters. The probability μ_e of an edge $e \in E_C$

between two clusters C_i and C_j is the probability over the choices over $c \in C_i$ and $c' \in C_j$ that $(c, c') \in E$.

3 Queries to Uncertain Graphs

Definition 1. *A relational query of arity m on a graph G is a function* $Q : G \times V^k \rightarrow R$ *where* $R \subseteq V^m$.

In the cluster-based model, each instance $\widehat{G_i}$ provides a random variable $\widehat{R_i}$ and gives rise to a distribution $\mathcal{R} = \{(t, p_t)\}$ of tuples t with probabilities p_t, where $t \in R$ and $p_t = \sum_i \text{prob}(\widehat{G}_i)$ for i such that $\widehat{G}_i \models \widehat{R}(t)$.

Definition 2. *A function query f of arity k on a graph G is:* $f : G \times V^k \rightarrow \mathbf{R}$.

Each instance $\widehat{G}_i$ provides a function $\widehat{f_{\widehat{G}_i}}$ for f, giving a distribution of values (t, p_t) where $t \in \mathbf{R}$ and probability $p_t = \sum_i \text{prob}(\widehat{G}_i)$ for i such that $\widehat{G}_i \models \widehat{f_{\widehat{G}_i}} = t$. The expected function is defined as $E(f) = \sum_{i=1}^{m} \text{prob}(\widehat{G}_i) \cdot \widehat{f_{\widehat{G}_i}}$. We approximate the interval $I = [\alpha, \beta]$, where $\alpha = Min_{\widehat{G}_i} \widehat{f_{\widehat{G}_i}}$ and $\beta = Max_{\widehat{G}_i} \widehat{f_{\widehat{G}_i}}$.

4 Approximation

4.1 Approximation of Relational Queries

A unary relation query Q defines a distribution $\mathcal{R}$ on documents, and a sequence $s = d_{i_1}, d_{i_2}, ..., d_{i_n}$ ordered by decreasing probability. We want to approximate the k first answers, i.e. produce a sequence $s_k = d_{i'_1}, d_{i'_2}, ..., d_{i'_k}$ close to s. A classical distance between two sequences is the *Kendall Tau distance* which measures the number of misclassified pairs (see e.g. [6]). We relativize the weight of a misclassified pair with the difference of their probabilities. For each d in s_k, d' in s is *misclassified (mis.)* for d if d' is not a prefix of d in s_k and $d' > d$ in s.

Definition 3. *The peudo-distance between* s_k *and the sequence s associated with a distribution* $\mathcal{R}$ *is:*

$$d(s_k, s) = \frac{\sum_{d \in s_k} \sum_{d' \in s \ mis.} |Prob(d') - Prob(d)|}{N_k}$$

with $N_k = n - 1 + n - 2 + ...n - k$ *the maximal number of misclassified pairs.*

Definition 4. *A randomized algorithm* $\mathcal{A}(G_n, Q, k)$ *which outputs a sequence* s_k*,* ϵ*-approximates the answer* $\mathcal{R}$ *if* s_k *is* ϵ*-close to the sequence s, with high probability.*

Naive Sampling algorithm. Take N samples $\widehat{G}_i$, evaluate Q and obtain $\widehat{R_i}$. Let c the function which associates with a document d, the number of occurrences of d in $\widehat{R_1}...\widehat{R_N}$. Rank the documents according to c and select the k first answers.

Theorem 1. *The Naive Sampling algorithm ϵ-approximates any unary Least-Fixed point query Q in polynomial time.*

We now quantify the quality of the answer. Consider $s_k = (d_{i_1}, ...d_{i_k})$, where by definition $c(d_{i_j}) \geq c(d_{i_{j+1}})$ for $1 \leq j < k$ and each $c(d_{i_j}) \leq N$. The *quality* of s_k is $\sum c(d_{i_j})/N^2$ which is 1 if all k documents in s_k are present in the answers of all samples, and $1/N$ if each document is only present in one sample.

4.2 Approximation of Functional Queries

We show as an example the approximation of the length of the shortest path between two nodes, which is a basic function on graphs. Measures such as PageRank can be approximated in the same style. The approximation uses the graph G and conditional probabilities on the edges.

Definition 5. *An algorithm $\mathcal{A}$ which outputs $(\alpha, \ \beta)$ ϵ-approximates f if: (a) $f(\widehat{G}_i, u, v) \in [\alpha - \epsilon, \ \beta + \epsilon]$ for all $\widehat{G}_i$, (b) $\alpha - \epsilon \leq \min_{\widehat{G}_i} \ f(\widehat{G}_i, u, v) \leq \alpha + \epsilon$ and (c) $\beta - \epsilon \leq \max_{\widehat{G}_i} \ f(\widehat{G}_i, u, v) \leq \beta + \epsilon$.*

Shortest Path Approximation. We approximate the shortest path $SP(d_s, d_t)$ from a node d_s to a target d_t in GC_n. We aim to give an interval $I_{d_s \to d_t}$ such that $\widehat{\mathrm{SP}}(d_s, d_t) \in I_{d_s \to d_t} = [\alpha, \ \beta]$. SP is approximated by forwarding intervals in G from d_s to d_t in a naive way.

Interval Propagation Algorithm(GC_n, d_s, d_t). Compute the intervals $I_{d_s \to d_i}$ for d_i connected at distance 1,2,...i from d_s until d_t is reached or all nodes of the connected components C of d_s are reached. If $d_t \notin C$ then $I_{d_s \to d_t} = [\infty, \infty]$. By induction on the depth i we can prove that $\mathcal{A}$ satisfies the properties (a),(b),(c).

Theorem 2. *For each node d_i at depth i from d_s, $\mathcal{A}$ approximates SP with $\epsilon = 0$, after exploring at most n nodes.*

5 Conclusion

Most approaches to query answering over document networks assume networks without duplicates or incorrect links. However, these duplicates distort the results. We developed a model of cluster-based uncertainty for graphs. The answer to unary relational queries is a distribution of documents, and the answer to functional queries is a probabilistic distribution of values ranging from a Min to a Max value. We efficiently approximated these distributions and provided a quality measure for the answers.

References

1. Broder, A.Z., Glassman, S.C., Manasse, M.S., Zweig, G.: Syntactic clustering of the web. Computer Networks 29(8-13), 1157–1166 (1997)
2. Shivakumar, N., Garcia-Molina, H.: Finding near-replicas of documents on the web. In: Atzeni, P., Mendelzon, A.O., Mecca, G. (eds.) The World Wide Web and Databases. LNCS, vol. 1590, Springer, Heidelberg (1999)
3. Broder, A.Z.: Identifying and filtering near-duplicate documents. In: Giancarlo, R., Sankoff, D. (eds.) CPM 2000. LNCS, vol. 1848, pp. 1–10. Springer, Heidelberg (2000)
4. Page, L., Brin, S., Motwani, R., Winograd, T.: The pagerank citation ranking: Bringing order to the web. Technical report, Stanford Digital Library Technologies Project (1998)
5. Andritsos, P., Fuxman, A., Miller, R.J.: Clean answers over dirty databases: A probabilistic approach. In: Proceedings of the International Conference on Data Engineering (ICDE) (2006)
6. Fagin, R., Kumar, R., Mahdian, M., Sivakumar, D., Vee, E.: Comparing and aggregating rankings with ties. In: ACM Principles on Databases Systems, pp. 47–58. ACM Press, New York (2004)

Assessing Quality Dynamics in Unsupervised Metadata Extraction for Digital Libraries

Alexander Ivanyukovich[1], Maurizio Marchese[1], and Patrick Reuther[2]

[1] University of Trento, Department of Information and Communication Technology, Trento, Italy
a.ivanyukovich@dit.unitn.it, maurizio.marchese@unitn.it
http://dit.unitn.it/

[2] University of Trier, Department for Databases and Information Systems, Trier, Germany
reuther@uni-trier.de
http://dbis.uni-trier.de

Abstract. Current research in large-scale information management systems is focused on unsupervised methods and techniques for information processing. Such approaches support scalability in regard to present-day exponential growth in information processing needs. In this paper we focus on the problem of automated quality evaluation of a completely unsupervised metadata extraction process in the Digital Libraries domain. In particular, we investigate resulting metadata quality applying specific extraction methodology for scientific documents. We propose and discuss precise quality metrics and measure the dynamics of such quality metrics as a function of the extracted information from the repository and size of the repository.

1 Introduction

Digital Libraries offering access to scientific literature are a good starting point for researchers trying to identify relevant publications in specific areas. The creation, maintenance and evolution of digital libraries requires often a trade-off between quality and quantity of their content. The more data is collected the more problematic the task of assuring a high qualitative level. In practice a compromise between amount of data and quality needs to be found: CiteSeer.IST for example focuses on quantity by constant and substantial collection enlargement with a limited human intervention whereas DBLP, for example, is maintained with massive human effort in order to retain a high quality at the expense of publication coverage.

With the current exponential increase of information, the aspect of quantity becomes more and more important. Unsupervised metadata extraction from digital corpora is in fact an active research area. Many different services have emerged in the past years. CiteSeer.IST for example has tackled the problem of unsupervised metadata extraction using a combination of a pattern-based approach (regular expressions) and support from manually prepared external

L. Kovács, N. Fuhr, and C. Meghini (Eds.): ECDL 2007, LNCS 4675, pp. 454–457, 2007.

databases (DBLP and others). This provided high-quality metadata within known references. Subsequent metadata quality improvements in CiteSeer.IST were accomplished involving human-based information corrections. Application of statistical models - like Hidden Markov Model and Dual and Variable-length output Hidden Markov Model [1] - to unsupervised metadata extraction are reported to have nearly 90% accuracy. Further metadata extraction methods involves usage of Support Vector Machines techniques [2]. Although these methods demonstrate high accuracy, recall and precision, they require training set size of the same magnitude as a processing corpora.

In [3], we have proposed a notion of "information extraction pipeline", which described steps necessary to pass from digital object acquisition to its automatic annotation. The key feature of the pipeline is that each subsequent level in the pipeline is based on the information acquired on the previous level. In this paper we focus on the evaluation of the quality of the metadata extraction step in a completely autonomous Digital Library system - the ScienceTreks prototype[1].

2 Unsupervised Metadata Extraction Based on Maximal Re-use of Existing Information

Currently, the majority of modern scientific digital libraries are based around the concept of Citation Indexing and its derivatives [4]. This fact emphasizes that having only texts is not enough: text should be annotated and connected with other resources by means of citations. The ScienceTreks prototype that we use for our experiments, is not an exclusion from this rule. We have dedicated 2nd level of our information processing pipeline to citations extraction, processing and analysis. The most important steps of our approach can be summarized as **(1)** pattern-based citations extraction from references section of articles, **(2)** citations normalization and harmonization and **(3)** recognition of article's identity (title, authors, publication source and other similar metadata that uniquely characterize an article). The central assumption that guided us through the metadata extraction process was to benefit from maximal re-use of existing information present in each processing step. Further we will describe each of these steps in some details.

We have first manually analyzed a number of articles' texts and have identified common metadata elements based on their syntax and punctuation structure:

1. References section: can be described using a limited number of reference formatting styles that cover majority of the papers (IEEE, ACM, Springer, etc).
2. Table of contents section: can be distinguished on the level of punctuation and formatting, with additional sequence verification through-out the text.
3. Index section: can be easily distinguished on the syntactic level.

Processing of the References section using state-of-the-art implementation of specialized FSM-based lexical grammar parser [5] gave us the starting point for

[1] `http://www.sciencetreks.com`

further metadata exploration. Subsequent statistical correction of the extracted metadata (as described in details in [6]) allowed us re-using already extracted information for its own correction and further precision improvement.

The third and final step of our metadata extraction process covers recognition of the article identity - its title, authors, and other properties. In this article we concentrate on one of the methodologies we have developed for this step, that based on the maximal re-use of existing information. It suggests performing articles' identity recognition using only existing collection of the references obtained from the repository. This means we will identify only articles that have been cited by other articles in the collection. This approach normally makes sense only for big collections of articles, however, we can rely here on another usage pattern: it is quite common that authors of an article do use self-citation and/or citation within a group or community (research group, conference community, etc). In other words, we also rely on the expectation of some degree of overlap in the references set both of a single document or a group of documents (i.e. same parent URL - publications collected from home pages of an author, home pages of authors that belong to the same organization, etc.) The detailed identification procedure and all related algorithms can be found in [7].

3 Evaluation Methodology and Preliminary Evaluation Results

At present, ScienceTreks project contains about 500k documents. The order of magnitude of the base collection makes it clear that manual quality evaluation is not feasible [8]. Comparison of the methods used by other systems (CiteSeer.IST, GoogleScholar, etc) is complex due the fact that there is no common and a priory correct metadata publicly available - the "ground truth" set. In the domain of scientific publications DBLP is likely a good candidate for such "ground truth" metadata set - we have used an intersection of 45K between DBLP and ScienceTreks dataset for our experiments.

In our tests, we compare metadata extracted with our methods (see Section 2) with the "ground truth" metadata using Levenshtein distance metric. This comparison gives us a distribution of identified metadata over edit distances, together with average edit distance and related variance and deviation. Furthee evaluation was done varying a size of the "ground truth" set to assess the quality in respect to the growth of the dataset during evolution of the system - metadata quality dynamics. For more details on the preparation, representativeness evaluation of "ground truth" set as well as precise methodology of metadata comparison for titles and authors we refer to [7].

Results of the evaluation of extracted titles discovered a high percentage of exact match - ca. 37%. Thereafter, a relative shallow distribution is present in the range of Levenshtein edit distances 20-100, with a relative maximum around 45-50, and accounts for the remaining partially-recognized/unrecognized titles. Sequentially enlarging the documents sets we have observed that the overall shape of the distribution is unchanged, while the title recognition percentage linearly rises from 37% to 46% as the same time as we enlarged the document sets from 45k to 165k.

Results of the authors' identification quality within initial 45k set appeared to be better than titles' quality - ca. 53% of absolutely correct authors identification. Following from our simple boolean comparison for single author, the distribution of author's recognition is bi-modal with two sharp peaks at correct author recognition (value=1, 53%) and complete miss (value=0, 44%). The remaining - small - 3% consists of partially identified authors in the total number of authors of the article. Metadata quality dynamics in this case shows a limited variation: while enlarging the document set from 45k to 165K, the normalized author recognition value rises only a few percentages from the initial 53% up to 56%.

4 Conclusion

In this paper we have evaluated a novel method for unsupervised metadata extraction relying on maximal re-use of existing information within document repository. The method does not rely on any external information sources and is solely based on the existing information in the document and in the document's context (set of documents). Preliminary results show that our approach is capable of achieving a significant recognition quality level (ca 37% for title and 53% for authors) even within a limited document set (45k), without usage of human supervision or any external knowledge sources or training sets. Moreover, the recognition quality level for titles in our tests increase linearly with the size of the processed documents set.

References

1. Takasu, A.: Bibliographic attribute extraction from erroneous references based on a statistical model. In: Proceedings of JCDL, IEEE, Los Alamitos (2003)
2. Han, H., Giles, C.L., Manavoglu, E., Zha, H., Zhang, Z., Fox, E.A.: Automatic document metadata extraction using support vector machines. In: Proceedings of JCDL, pp. 37–48. IEEE, Los Alamitos (2003)
3. Ivanyukovich, A., Marchese, M., Giunchiglia, F.: Sciencetreks: an autonomous digital library system. In: ICSD (2007)
4. Garfield, E.: Citation Indexing: Its Theory and Application in Science, Technology, and Humanities. Wiley, Chichester (1979)
5. Kiyavitskaya, N., Zeni, N., Cordy, J.R., Mich, L., Mylopoulos, J.: Semi-automatic semantic annotations for next generation information systems. In: Proceedings of AISE. LNCS, Springer, Heidelberg (2006)
6. Ivanyukovich, A., Marchese, M.: Unsupervised metadata extraction in scientific digital libraries using a-priori domain-specific knowledge. In: SWAP (2006)
7. Ivanyukovich, A., Marchese, M., Reuther, P.: Assessing quality dynamics in unsupervised metadata extraction for digital libraries. Technical Report DIT-07-035, University of Trento (2007)
8. Reuther, P., Walter, B.: Survey on test collections and techniques for personal name matching. IJMSO 1(2), 89–99 (2006)

Bibliographical Meta Search Engine for the Retrieval of Scientific Articles

Artur Gajek[1], Stefan Klink[2], Patrick Reuther[1], Bernd Walter[1], and Alexander Weber[1]

[1] Department for Databases and Information Systems, University of Trier, Germany
{agajek,preuther,walter,aweber}@dbis.uni-trier.de
http://dbis.uni-trier.de

[2] Institute of Applied Informatics and Formal Description Methods, Universität Karlsruhe (TH), Germany
Stefan.Klink@aifb.uni-karlsruhe.de
http://www.aifb.uni-karlsruhe.de/

Abstract. The University of Trier maintains the DBLP (**D**igital **B**ibliography & **L**ibrary **P**roject) Computer Science Bibliography which offers bibliographic information about more than 870.000 scientific publications. This paper describes the *DBLP WebCrawler*, a meta search engine that is able to search for full text publications in PDF format for each DBLP entry on the web. Various search engines such as Google and Yahoo are used as data sources. The retrieved documents are additionally analysed and ranked according to their relevance. The proposed system differs from systems like CiteSeer in so far, that the DBLP Webcrawler builds upon metadata and tries to find relevant full-texts whereas CiteSeer mainly starts with full-texts and extracts metadata.

1 Motivation

Finding relevant bibliographical literature is a vital task for researchers around the world. While searching for bibliographical literature the Internet plays an increasing role. Many digital libraries and search engines specialise on the domain of scientific publications, e. g. io-port (http://io-port.net), the Collection of Computer Science Bibliographies (CCSB) (http://www.ira.uka.de/bibliography), CiteSeer or GoogleScholar. One of these libraries is the **D**igital **B**ibliography & **L**ibrary **P**roject (DBLP).

From a researcher point of view however it would be an added value if not only bibliographical metadata were supplied but also free and direct access to the content itself would be possible through the web service. DBLP faces this challenge by supplying links to electronic editions where the information is available. These links mostly point to publisher webpages where the users have the opportunity to buy the desired full text. The same behaviour can be seen in the portal io-port. In the result list a link to the full-text is given. If the user is a member of the publishers digital library, e. g. SpringerLink, ACM-DL or IEEE

L. Kovács, N. Fuhr, and C. Meghini (Eds.): ECDL 2007, LNCS 4675, pp. 458–461, 2007.

digital library, then the full-text is accessible. But most of the publications however are not only available through publisher websites but also on homepages of research institutes or the researchers themselves. The question arises if it is possible to automatically identify relevant full-texts for bibliographical records which would lead to an added value for researchers.

2 DBLP WebCrawler

DBLP WebCrawler is different to other approaches in so far that a bibliographic collection already exists. In fact where CiteSeer and GoogleScholar for example try to extract metadata from publications, DBLP WebCrawler already possesses high quality metadata and tries to identify the corresponding PDF files. Hence it can be seen as an added service to the already existing DBLP database.

For the DBLP WebCrawler the decision was made to design it as a meta search engine which makes use of already existing general search engines because on the one hand traditional libraries, although supplying more and more literature online, are not easily accessible and only offer a limited coverage. On the other hand specialised portals are not the preferred choice because access is often restricted to registered users and besides too many sources would have to be incorporated due to the different scope of the portals. Furthermore, general search engines are favoured because they often index indirectly publications from various specialised portals and additionally are characterised by huge indices.

Making use of the provided APIs the restricted amount of returned results per query are limited to 10 (Google), 50 (MSN) and 100 (Yahoo), respectively. This is sufficient for queries with a high precision, where the desired result is within the top ten.

For choosing individual search engines an empirical study was applied beforehand: Metadata for 300 publications including very old publications probably not available online as well as modern publications was randomly extracted from DBLP and used as a basis for queries. For 300 chosen records 97 correct full texts in PDF files could be identified. Figure 1(a) shows the results for different search engines. Because MSN and Exalead provided only few useful links they were not included into DBLP WebCrawler.

The DBLP WebCrawler sends queries to the search engines in order to obtain results. The queries are generated automatically from metadata available in DBLP. Empirical studies made by us have shown that using the title of the publication as well as the author names is sufficient for good results in most cases. However the more information is provided the lower is the recall but the higher is the precision. Therefore, queries should not necessarily consist of all available information or otherwise promising results might not be considered for further analysis. For DBLP WebCrawler queries were grouped according to the length of the publication title:

small title. Publications where the title has less than two words are excluded for full text search and consequently do not need a query generation. These short titles are not considered because the results are very poor.

Search Engine	Hits	excl. Hits
Google	69	5
Yahoo	58	3
MSN	14	0
Exalead	5	1
MetaCrawler	63	2
GoogleScholar	23	2
CiteSeer(Yahoo)	48	11
CiteSeer(MetaCrawler)	49	10

(a)

Rating	Results	Rel.	¬ Rel.	Ratio
87% - 100%	118	116	2	98%
66% - 86%	34	19	15	56%
0% - 65%	48	1	47	2%

(b)

Fig. 1. (a) Retrieved articles by search engines (b) Relevance Ratios of rating levels

average title. For publications whose title have an average length (three to four words) the first author of the publication was included into the query and an exact phrase search was applied for the title.

long title. For publications with long titles (more than four words) either the same approach as for average sized titles is applied if there are less than four stopwords in the title. Otherwise only the first maximal six non stopwords are used for querying because often search engines do not index stopwords.

Some search engines, e. g. Google, provide the possibility to search within the title (intitle/allintitle) of webpages or to specify the filetype of the results, e. g. `filetype:pdf`. If possible such specific options were made use of in the queries.

2.1 Analysis of Results Obtained with Queries

The DBLP WebCrawler provides for each search result a rating. The closer the rating is to 100% the higher is the probability that the search result is relevant. The search results are then ranked by the highest rating. To provide a good rating the text of the PDF documents is extracted with PDFBox, an open source Java library for PDF files (www.pdfbox.org). Ideally the PDF document should contain the same data as the corresponding DBLP entry. As small errors within the title are common the DBLP WebCrawler uses the Levenshtein Distance [1] [2] to verify that the article contains the correct title. Ideally the Levenshtein Distance should be smaller than five.

Instead of looking for the full name of the author, the program tries to find only the author's last name. This is done because the spelling of the first name may vary a lot in different scientific publications. One publication may quote its author as "Peter Müller", another may quote the same author as "P. Müller" [3][4]. Regular expressions are used for the search. Names with accents are often spelled differently. For example "Müller" can also be spelled as "Muller" or "Mueller". For the sketched example the regular expression should allow any character instead of the accent leading to the regular expression "M.{1,2}ller" instead of solely "Müller".

For evaluation of the rating system a further empirical analysis was performed. 200 search results obtained by the DBLP WebCrawler have been rated using the

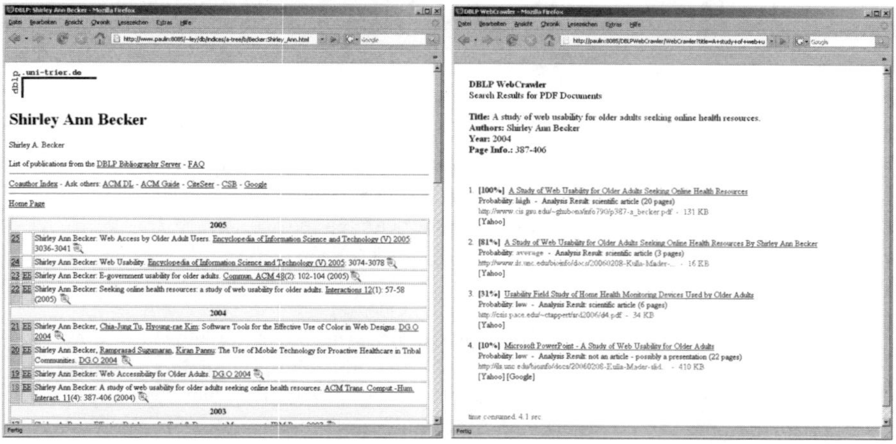

Fig. 2. (a) DBLP WebCrawler integrated into DBLP (b) Ranked Result List

above formula. Afterwards each search result has been compared manually with the DBLP entry to check if it was relevant. Actually, 98% of the search results with a high rating turned out to be relevant while only 2% with a low rating were relevant as well (see Fig. 1 (b) for details).

The DBLP WebCrawler in connected to the well-known DBLP service. For each of the more than 870.000 recorded publications users can search for the appropriate full-text PDF-file by just clicking an additional link button at the end of the publication entity (see Fig. 2 (a)). The DBLP WebCrawler generates an individual web-page including the results of the initiated search with the generated search query described above (see Fig. 2 (b)).

References

1. Levenshtein, V.I.: Binary codes capable of correcting spurious insertions and deletions of ones (original in Russian). Russian Problemy Peredachi Informatsii 1, 12–25 (1965)
2. Navarro, G., Raffinot, M.: Flexible Pattern Matching in Strings. Practical on-line search algorithms for text and biological sequences. Cambridge Univ. Press, Cambridge (2002)
3. Reuther, P.: Personal name matching: New test collections and a social network based approach. Universität Trier, Mathematik/Informatik, Forschungsbericht, 06-01 (2006)
4. Reuther, P., Walter, B., Ley, M., Weber, A., Klink, S.: Managing the quality of person names in DBLP. In: Gonzalo, J., Thanos, C., Verdejo, M.F., Carrasco, R.C. (eds.) ECDL 2006. LNCS, vol. 4172, pp. 508–511. Springer, Heidelberg (2006)

In-Browser Digital Library Services

Hussein Suleman

Department of Computer Science, University of Cape Town
Private Bag, Rondebosch, 7701, South Africa
hussein@cs.uct.ac.za

Abstract. Service models for digital libraries have looked into how services may be decomposed into modules and components for greater flexiblity. These models are, however, mostly aimed at server-side applications. With the emergence of Ajax and similar techniques for processing XML documents within a Web browser, it has now become feasible for a browser to perform far more of the computational tasks traditionally encompassed in server-side DL services. Among other advantages, moving computation to the client can result in improved performance and scalability. As a new twist on service oriented computing, it is argued in this paper that digital library services can be provided partially or wholly through applications that execute client-side. Two case studies are provided to illustrate that such in-browser services are feasible and in fact more powerful and flexible than the traditional server-side service model.

1 Introduction and Motivation

A recent development in Web technology is the widespread acceptance of richer user interfaces based on in-browser processing of XML within embedded Javascript on webpages. This technology, dubbed Ajax, has within the last 2 years been adopted widely by digital library systems (DLSes) to enhance user interactivity by providing users with an experience that closely mirrors that of desktop applications.

Ajax, often defined as Asynchronous Javascript and XML [2], is based on various technologies built into modern browsers, including Javascript, the XML/XHTML DOM parser and mechanisms to load XML documents asynchronously. Ajax applications typically use Javascript to load remote XML documents asynchronously, then update the user's view of a webpage without contacting the server for a page reload.

In digital libraries, there have been some attempts to use Ajax to support more dynamic user interaction. Licsár et al. [3] used Ajax in their construction of a gesture-recognising information retrieval system for music. Their system communicated with a server and a video capture subsystem from within the Web-based user interface. Feng [1] showed that it was feasible not just to create DLS interfaces using Ajax but also to design the workflows and interfaces themselves in a browser, using Ajax techniques.

L. Kovács, N. Fuhr, and C. Meghini (Eds.): ECDL 2007, LNCS 4675, pp. 462–465, 2007.

It can be argued, however, that Ajax techniques need not only be used for the uppermost veneer of DLSes (the user interfaces) and that it can be used also for service provision on the client's machine. This may have many advantages beyond the enhancement of user interaction. Firstly, the speed of interaction can be increased and the use of bandwidth decreased. More importantly, computation can be shifted to the client's machine, thereby freeing up the server and implicitly building greater scalability into the whole system. Figure 1 illustrates this shift in computation. In the traditional approach, most of the computation is concentrated on the server while in an in-browser service model, much of this computation happens on the client machine. In the latter case, the user interface is generated partially by server data and partially by the in-browser applications.

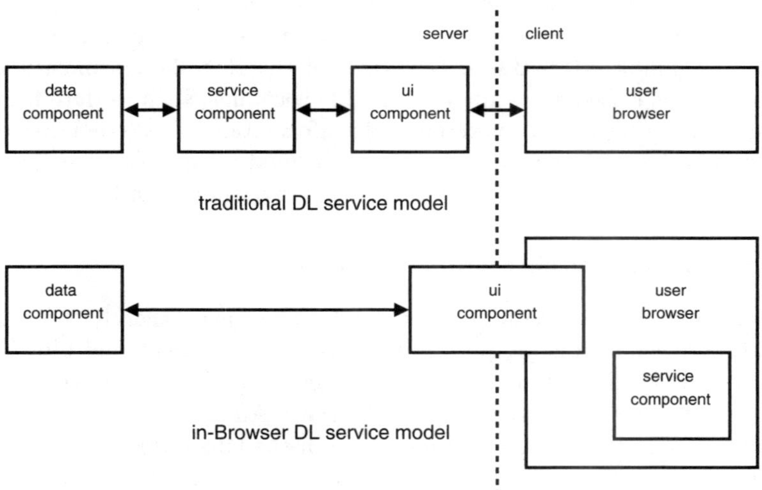

Fig. 1. Traditional and in-browser data/service provider models

Two case studies are discussed in this paper, illustrating how the notion of in-browser services can be effected using Ajax, as an alternative to server-side services.

2 Case Studies

2.1 RSS Validator

Really Simple Syndication (RSS) is a specification aimed at content syndication, where a data provider advertises a URL at which service providers may obtain a list of current or new content in a simple XML representation [6].

One of the biggest problems with RSS is a proliferation of specifications and some ambiguity about their interpretation, necessitating the use of external validators. Existing RSS validators are mostly server-side applications (e.g., http://feedvalidator.org/). An Ajax application was created to demonstrate similar functionality but as an in-browser service.

The RSS validator uses Ajax techniques to send a request for an RSS feed to a Web server. The XML response is then parsed and tested using a set of XML-DOM manipulations, with a report generated dynamically to the browser during the testing.

Security restrictions placed on Ajax allow only connections to the source (server or local disk) of the Web page. As a result, no Ajax-like methods will allow a user to load an XML document off a third-party server. This is not a problem in most digital library applications and third party validation was achieved in this case by using a simple HTTP proxy. If such a validation tool is packaged with DLS components, no proxy should be needed.

The validation tool was verified with 8 independently-coded local implementations from a simulated database of thesis metadata and 2 remote implementations (moodle, RSS Board Example) of the RSS 2.0 specification. Most implementations raised a few understandable warnings, such as date fields with incorrect formatting and inconsistent title information in different parts of the response. The level of error detection was deemed comparable to the existing online validation tools, but with all computation occurring in-browser.

2.2 In-Browser Search Engine

The Lucy Lloyd Archive Resource and Exhibition Centre recently commissioned the creation of a portable digital library system for the Bleek and Lloyd Collection [4]. This is a collection of notebooks and drawings that document the history and culture of some Bushman groups in Southern Africa. The data was collected primarily by Wilhelm Bleek and Lucy Lloyd in the late 1800s and serves as one of the few written records of this culture, which is widely recognised as among the oldest on our planet. This act of digital preservation has become far more urgent in light of the rapid assimilation of these ethnic groups into contemporary society [5].

The digital collection of notebook and drawing images is meant to be accesible online, offline or distributed on DVD-ROM, and should be usable irrespective of operating system or hardware architecture. This wide range of requirements is important to support the greatest possible audience of researchers wishing to use this data, even in remote parts of Africa. In this instance, Ajax was used to create a query service that is completely in-browser.

All data was first indexed by a standalone application and the inverted files and mapping of document identifiers to names (document index) were stored in static XML documents. Each inverted file includes part of the document index relevant to its documents. Thus, a single word query executes very efficiently as the document index is be optimal for it. Multi-word queries with overlap in document lists incur some penalty - it is known that most users prefer shorter queries so the problem ought to be minimal. This slight modification of a typical IR system increases the space required for the indices but decreases the time it takes to read in the document index for client-side applications.

3 Conclusions and Future Work

This paper has discussed an alternative approach to digital library services: that of executing service components on the client. By moving computation off the server, a number of benefits can be realised, including greater scalability and the possibility of self-contained in-browser digital library services. This also has implications for long-term preservation of services independently of the continued existence of service providers.

This refactoring of services has been demonstrated with 2 case studies using Ajax technology that is available in current browsers to convert typical server-side services into in-browser services. The case studies demonstrate that the idea of in-browser services is feasible in some cases and shows promise for a new twist on the paradigm of service-oriented digital libraries.

Ajax and similar client-side technology (such as XUL, Flash and Java) may offer particular benefits to DLSes and arguably should be integrated into current and future systems and design tools.

Acknowledgements

This project was made possible by funding from University of Cape Town, NRF (Grant number: GUN2073203) and the Lucy Lloyd Archive Resource and Exhibition Centre.

References

1. Feng, F.-Y.K.: Customisable Abstract Representation Layer for Digital Libraries, MSc Dissertation, Department of Computer Science, University of Cape Town (2006)
2. Garrett, J.J.: Ajax: A New Approach to Web Applications, Adaptive Path (February 18, 2005) (2005), Available `http://www.adaptivepath.com/publications/essays/archives/000385.php`
3. Attila, L., Szirányi, T., Kovács, L., Pataki, B.: Tillarom: an AJAX Based Folk Song Search and Retrieval System with Gesture Interface Based on Kodály Hand Signs. In: Proceedings of the 1st ACM International Workshop on Human-centered Multimedia (HCM '06), October 2006, ACM Press, New York (2006), Available `http://doi.acm.org/10.1145/1178745.1178760`
4. Lucy Lloyd Archive and Resource and Exhibition Centre: Lloyd Bleek Collection, University of Cape Town (2007), Available `http://www.lloydbleekcollection.uct.ac.za/index.jsp`
5. University of Cape Town: Jewel in UCT's crown to be digitised for world's scholars, Monday Paper (March 31, 2003) (2003), Available `http://www.uct.ac.za/print/newsroom/mondaypaper/?paper=114`
6. Winer, D.: RSS 2.0 Specification, Berkman Centre for Internet and Society (2002), Available `http://blogs.law.harvard.edu/tech/rss`

Evaluating Digital Libraries with 5SQual

Bárbara L. Moreira[1], Marcos A. Gonçalves[1], Alberto H.F. Laender[1], and Edward A. Fox[2]

[1] Department of Computer Science, Federal University of Minas Gerais, 31270-901 - Belo Horizonte - MG - Brazil
{barbara,mgoncalv,laender}@dcc.ufmg.br
[2] Department of Computer Science, Virginia Tech, Blacksburg - VA, 24061 - EUA
fox@vt.edu

Abstract. This work describes 5SQual, a quantitative quality assessment tool for digital libraries based on the 5S framework. 5SQual aims to help administrators of digital libraries during the implementation and maintenance phases of a digital library, providing ways to verify the quality of digital objects, metadata and services. The tool has been designed in a flexible way, which allows it to be applied to many systems, as long as the necessary data is available. To facilitate the input of these data, the tool provides a wizard-like interface that guides the user through its configuration process.

Keywords: Digital Libraries, Quality Evaluation, 5S, 5SQual.

1 Introduction

Digital libraries (DLs) are complex systems that offer information through content and services designed for specific communities of users. Since DL evaluations can be expensive and diverse (when evaluating quality, people interested in DLs focus on different aspects [1]), usually quality evaluations are conducted just when the system presents failures and the administrator should interfere immediately, contradicting the fact that evaluation should be a continuous process throughout the life cycle of a computer-based system [2]. For DLs to be more reliable and easier to maintain, it is necessary to find ways to perform, in practice, cost effective and automated quality evaluations of these systems.

In this work, we describe 5SQual, a tool we have developed to automatically assess various quantitative aspects of a DL according to the 5S quality model [3], a formal quality model for DL evaluation, built on top of the 5S framework. 5S, which stands for *Streams, Structures, Spaces, Scenarios* and *Societies*, is a theoretical framework to formally describe DLs [4,5]. The quality model provides a theoretical basis for developing and quantifying quality numeric indicators for 22 quality dimensions.

L. Kovács, N. Fuhr, and C. Meghini (Eds.): ECDL 2007, LNCS 4675, pp. 466–470, 2007.

2 5SQual Overview

The 5SQual development has been initially based on a subset of dimensions defined in the 5S quality model. These dimensions cover the evaluation of digital objects, metadata and services. The subset includes:

- Regarding digital objects - *accessibility* (given an actor x, the accessibility of a digital object is given by the percentage of the streams of the object that x is allowed to access), *significance* (indicates the importance of digital objects according to a certain factor, such as number of accesses, citations, downloads, etc.), *similarity* (estimates how related two digital objects are, e.g., we can use the co-citation measure as an indicator for this dimension), and *timeliness* (indicates how up-to-date the objects in the DL are. The numeric indicator for this dimension is the elapsed time between, for instance, the creation time and the current time).
- Regarding metadata - *completeness* (reflects how many metadata attributes, according to a standard schema, have values specified) and *conformance* (percentage of the attributes in the metadata that follows the rules defined by a standard schema).
- Regarding services - *efficiency* (reflects the response time of the services) and *reliability* (is proportional to the frequency of successful operations, among the total number of executions of a service).

Fig. 1 shows the 5SQual architecture. The necessary information for the evaluation resides in the DL and should be retrieved through the DL application layer.

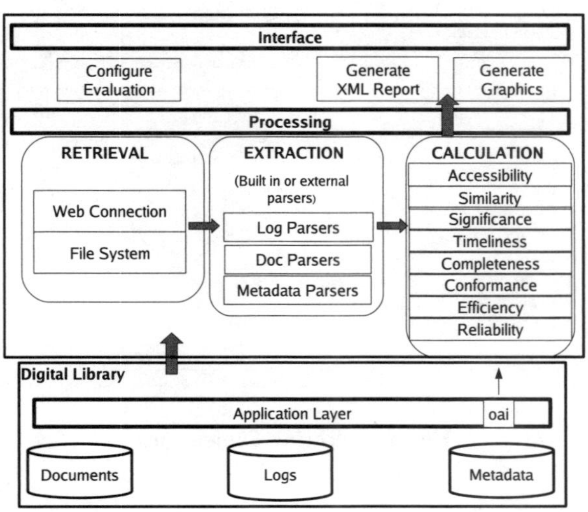

Fig. 1. 5SQual Architecture

The ***Processing Layer*** consists of three modules: the **Retrieval module**, which obtains data on the Web or from the local file system by collecting log files, metadata or documents; the **Extraction module**, which uses parsers to extract the necessary data from the collected files and converts them to a standard format required for each dimension (the set of built-in parsers includes content parsers, e.g., PDF and PS files, specific metadata format parsers, e.g., Dublin Core and RFC1807, specific log format parsers, e.g., the XML log format [6], and user-specified parsers for other file formats); and the **Calculation module**, which implements the set of numeric indicators for each quality dimension. The ***Interface Layer*** includes the **Configure Evaluation** module, which stores the parameters defined for the evaluation, and the modules **Generate XML Report** and **Generate Graphics**, which generate the outputs of the evaluations (XML reports and charts).

Before using 5SQual, a user, typically the administrator of a DL, has to configure the parameters for the evaluation. For this, we developed a setup wizard that guides the user through the necessary configuration steps. Fig. 2 shows one of the wizard's screens, used to select which dimensions to evaluate. Other parameters to be informed indicate where 5SQual should find information for the evaluation and how to extract them to calculate the indicators of the selected dimensions.

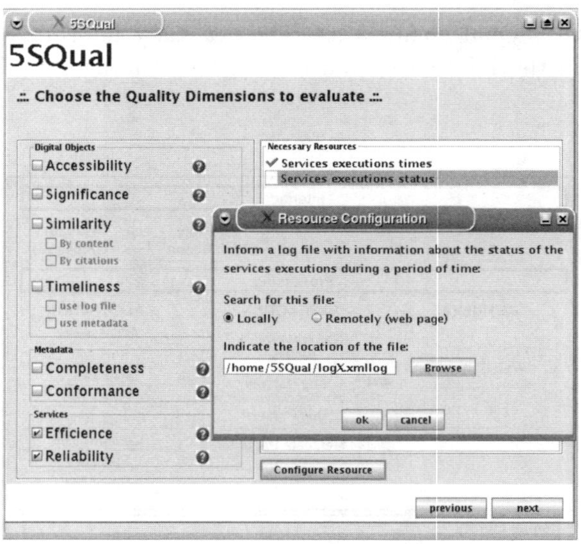

Fig. 2. Selecting Dimensions

To exemplify a 5SQual output, we show a chart generated as a result of the evaluation of *Timeliness* (see Fig. 3). Due to the lack of space, we just comment briefly about it. The **y** axis shows the number of objects that were created on a specific date, and the **x** axis determines the date when the objects

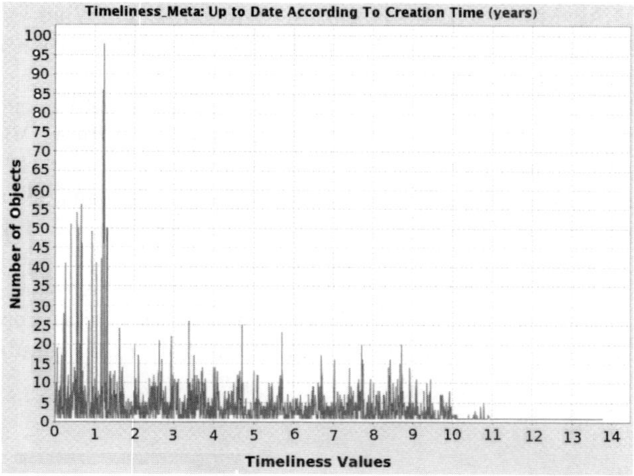

Fig. 3. Timeliness Chart

were inserted in the collection. Through this kind of chart, one can observe the creation pattern(s) that the digital objects present over time and also notice when different events happen (e.g., many objects were created at once).

3 Conclusions

5SQual has been developed to help administrators when building and maintaining a DL, thus providing data to guide its design, development and improvement continuously. To evaluate how useful the tool is, we conducted an interview with potential users (real DL administrators) to assess their expectations regarding its functionality. This interview has shown that the tool can be really useful while maintaining a DL, but that other aspects should also be covered in next versions, such as facilities for evaluating higher level components (e.g., collections and catalogs) and the availability of additional parsers.

Acknowledgments. This work was partially supported by the 5S-QV project (MCT/CNPq/CT-INFO grant number 551013/2005-2) and by the project grant NSF DUE-0121679.

References

1. Fuhr, N., Hansen, P., Mabe, M., Micsik, A., Solvberg, I.: Digital libraries: A generic classification and evaluation scheme. In: Constantopoulos, P., Sølvberg, I.T. (eds.) ECDL 2001. LNCS, vol. 2163, pp. 187–199. Springer, Heidelberg (2001)
2. Borgman, C.L.: NSF report on DELOS Workshop on DL evaluation. Technical report, Hungarian Academy of Sciences Computer and Automation Research Institute, Budapest, Hungary (2003)

3. Gonçalves, M.A., Moreira, B.L., Fox, E.A., Watson, L.T.: What is a good digital library? - defining a quality model for digital libraries. Information Processing and Management (to appear, 2007)
4. Gonçalves, M.A.: Streams, Structures, Spaces, Scenarios, and Societies: A Formal Framework for Digital Libraries and Its Applications. PhD thesis, Virginia Tech CS Department, Blacksburg, VA (2004)
5. Gonçalves, M.A., Fox, E.A., Watson, L.T., Kipp, N.: Streams, structures, spaces, scenarios, societies (5S): A formal model for digital libraries. ACM Transactions on Information Systems 22(2), 270–312 (2004)
6. Gonçalves, M.A., Panchanathan, G., Ravindranathan, U., Krowne, A., Fox, E.A., Jagodzinski, F., Cassel, L.: The XML log standard for digital libraries: analysis, evolution, and deployment. In: JCDL, pp. 312–314. IEEE Computer Society, Los Alamitos (2003)

Reducing Costs for Digitising Early Music with Dynamic Adaptation

Laurent Pugin, John Ashley Burgoyne, and Ichiro Fujinaga

Centre for Interdisciplinary Research in Music and Media Technology
Schulich School of Music of McGill University
Montréal, Québec, Canada
{laurent,ashley,ich}@music.mcgill.ca

Abstract. Optical music recognition (OMR) enables librarians to digitise early music sources on a large scale. The cost of expert human labour to correct automatic recognition errors dominates the cost of such projects. To reduce the number of recognition errors in the OMR process, we present an innovative approach to adapt the system dynamically, taking advantage of the human editing work that is part of any digitisation project. The corrected data are used to perform MAP adaptation, a machine-learning technique used previously in speech recognition and optical character recognition (OCR). Our experiments show that this technique can reduce editing costs by more than half.

1 Background

Indexing music sources for intelligent retrieval is currently a laborious process that requires highly skilled human editors [1]. Optical music recognition (OMR), the musical analogue to optical character recognition (OCR), can speed this process and greatly reduce the labour cost. In the case of early documents, the originals for which may not be available to a particular library, it is also important to have a digitisation system that can work with microfilm.

Aruspix is a cross-platform software program for OMR on early music prints based on hidden Markov models (HMMs) [2]. Like the Gamera project [3], it distinguishes itself from most commercial tools for OMR in that it is adaptive. Adaptive systems require training, however, and in order to train them, it is necessary to annotate a large set of images, dozens of images in our case, with complete transcriptions, known as ground truth. Furthermore, early documents suffer from a high and unpredictable level of variability across sources. The font shape varies considerably from one printer to another, and the noise introduced by document degradation or changes in the scanning parameters (e.g., brightness or contrast) may affect the accuracy of the recogniser as well. In these conditions, no single set of models can be expected to perform well for all books, and furthermore, a custom set of models optimised for one book would not necessarily perform well for another.

In a digitisation workflow, the consequence of these problems is that, in order to obtain sufficiently reliable models, one would need several dozen pages to

L. Kovács, N. Fuhr, and C. Meghini (Eds.): ECDL 2007, LNCS 4675, pp. 471–474, 2007.

be transcribed by hand every time a new book was to be processed. Similar issues are encountered in other domains, such as in speech recognition, where the problem is to deal with speaker variability. One common approach to solve the problem is to use dynamic adaptation techniques, such as MAP adaptation [4]. Outside of speech recognition, MAP adaptation has been brought successfully to a number of other fields, including handwriting recognition [5].

In this paper, we present a novel approach in OMR using the MAP adaptation technique. In a preliminary phase, a book-independent (BI) system is trained using pages taken from a number of different books. The BI system gives acceptable results in general but is not specifically optimised for a particular source. During the editing process, the BI system is optimised with MAP adaptation for the book that is currently being digitised. The main idea of the approach is to exploit editing work that has to be done during the digitisation process anyway in order to improve the recognition system. As soon as the editor has corrected the recognition errors on a newly digitised page, that page is used as ground-truth to adapt the BI models. Thus, when starting to digitise a new book, a book-dependent (BD) system can be obtained after only a couple of pages. The adaptation procedure is performed in a cumulative way so that at each adaptation step, it reads all of the pages of the book that have been digitised and corrected up to that point.

2 Experiments and Results

For our experiments, we used a set of microfilms of sixteenth-century music prints held at the Marvin Duchow Music Library at McGill University. They were scanned in 8-bit greyscale TIFF format at a resolution of 400 dots per inch using a Minolta MS6000 microfilm scanner. We used the Torch machine learning library[1] for both training of the BI system and MAP adaptation experiments. The BI system was trained using 457 pages taken from various music books produced by different printers. This set of pages was transcribed and represents a total of 2,710 staves and 95,845 characters of 220 different musical symbols (note values from *longa* to *semi-fusa*, rests, clefs, accidentals, *custodes*, dots, bar lines, coloured notes, ligatures, etc.).

To build BD models with MAP adaptation, we used five other printed music books: RISM[2] 1528-2, 1532-10, V-1421, R-2512 and V-1433 (see figure 1). For each of them, we transcribed 30 pages (150 in total), using 20 pages to build a training set and keeping the 10 remaining pages for a test set. For the training set, we took the first 20 pages of the book because the data become available in this order. For the same reason, we chose not to perform traditional cross-validation across the data set. The baseline for the evaluation was computed by using the BI models to recognise the pages of the 5 test sets.

OMR results are typically presented as symbol recognition rates. From a digitisation prospective, however, it is more beneficial to have an evaluation of the

[1] `http://www.torch.ch`

[2] `http://rism.stub.uni-frankfurt.de`

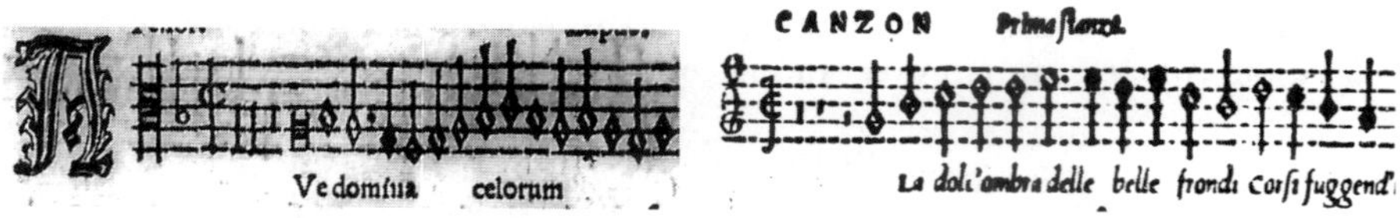

(a) RISM 1532-10 (Moderne, 1532) (b) RISM R-2512 (Gardano, 1575)

Fig. 1. Two prints used to experiment with MAP adaptation. Note the differences in font, line width, background, and overall scanning quality.

human costs. A human editor will always be required to correct the output to library standard, and the cost of this editor will outstrip the cost of the OMR processing time, software, and hardware in the long run. Based on our empirical experience with a human editor for this project, we estimated editing costs considering the following points: (1) deleting a wrongly inserted symbol is a straightforward operation, (2) changing the value of a misrecognised symbol takes twice the time of a deletion on average, and (3) adding a missing symbol is the most time-consuming operation, about four times the work of a deletion. In mathematical form, then, we propose the following average editing cost C per symbol:

$$C = 100 \left(\frac{1/4\, D + 1/2\, S + I}{N} \right) \tag{1}$$

where D is the number of symbols to delete (i.e., wrongly added symbols), S the number of symbols to replace (i.e., misrecognised symbols), I is the number of symbols to insert (i.e., missing symbols), and N is the total number of symbols on the page. Transcribing a page by hand, i.e., without any automatic recognition, would be equivalent to an insertion for every symbol ($C = 100$).

Using MAP adaptation in the digitisation workflow reduced the editing cost on all five sets we used for our experiments (see table 1). In the best case (1532-10, figure 1a), the cost was reduced by a factor of 2.24 with nearly a 15 percent gain in recognition rate. Even for the book where the recognition rate was 95 percent at the beginning (R-2512, figure 1b), our highest baseline recognition rate, MAP adaptation improved the recognition system further, approaching a recognition rate of 97 percent and decreasing the editing cost by 26 percent. On average, the editing costs were decreased by 39 percent. When comparing the results after MAP adaptation to the baseline, in most cases the improvement is already significant after only 5 to 10 pages; only with R-2512, the best-recognised book before adaptation, did it take more than 10 pages to obtain an improvement.

3 Summary and Future Work

When digitising early music sources on microfilm, checking and correcting the OMR output is a highly time consuming step of the workflow. To reduce the editing costs, and to deal with the high variability in the data, we experimented with MAP adaptation within the digitisation workflow. Our results show that

Table 1. Recognition rates and editing costs (see equation 1) before and after MAP adaptation. Adaptation improves editing cost in all cases.

Book	Recognition rate		Editing cost	
	Baseline	MAP	Baseline	MAP
RISM 1529-1	84.16	91.90	9.21	4.99
RISM 1532-10	74.95	89.39	13.52	6.05
RISM V-1421	92.35	94.50	5.26	4.08
RISM R-2512	95.10	96.97	3.46	2.56
RISM V-1433	91.31	95.72	5.56	3.08

this approach can improve the recognition system and reduce the editing costs even when using only a couple of pages, which means that the editors can very quickly glean time-saving side effects from their required work when starting to digitise a new book. At this stage, the dynamic adaptation procedure has been fully implemented and integrated into Aruspix.

Although our experiments focused on the digitisation of early music, the efficiency of dynamic adaptation in handling data variability suggest that the approach could be used fruitfully for digitising early documents in general, including books and maps. Dynamically adaptive methods such as ours promise to be a great boon to digital libraries and should significantly reduce the labour costs that affect all major digisitation projects.

Acknowledgements

We would like to thank the Canada Foundation for Innovation and the Social Sciences and Humanities Research Council of Canada for their financial support. We also would like to thank G. Eustace and M. Reckenberg for their help.

References

1. Bruder, I., Finger, A., Heuer, A., Ignatova, T.: Towards a digital document archive for historical handwritten music scores. In: Sembok, T.M.T., Zaman, H.B., Chen, H., Urs, S.R., Myaeng, S.-H. (eds.) ICADL 2003. LNCS, vol. 2911, pp. 411–414. Springer, Heidelberg (2003)
2. Pugin, L.: Optical music recognition of early typographic prints using hidden Markov models. In: Proc. Int. Conf. Mus. Inf. Ret., Victoria, Canada, pp. 53–56 (2006)
3. MacMillan, K., Droettboom, M., Fujinaga, I.: Gamera: Optical music recognition in a new shell. In: Proc. Int. Comp. Mus. Conf., pp. 482–485 (2002)
4. Gauvain, J.L., Lee, C.H.: Maximum a posteriori estimation for multivariate Gaussian mixture observations of Markov chains. IEEE Trans. SAP 2(2), 291–298 (1994)
5. Vinciarelli, A., Bengio, S.: Writer adaptation techniques in HMM based off-line cursive script recognition. Pat. Rec. Let. 23, 905–916 (2002)

Supporting Information Management in Digital Libraries with Map-Based Interfaces

Rudolf Mayer, Angela Roiger, and Andreas Rauber

Institute of Software Technology and Interactive Systems
Vienna University of Technology, Vienna, Austria
mayer@ifs.tuwien.ac.at, angela@roiger.at, rauber@ifs.tuwien.ac.at

Abstract. The *Self-Organising Map* (SOM) has been proposed as an interface for exploring Digital Libraries, in addition to conventional search and browsing. With advanced visualisations uncovering the contents and its structure, and advanced interaction modes as zooming, panning and area selection, the SOM becomes a feasible alternative to classical interfaces. However, there are still shortcomings in helping the user to understand the map – there are insufficient methods developed for describing the map to support the user in the analysis of the map contents. In this paper, we present recent work in assisting the user in exploring the map by automatically describing maps using advanced labelling and summarisation of map regions.

Keywords: Self-Organising Map, Interface, Summarisation, Clustering.

1 Introduction

The Self-Organising Map (SOM) [1] is an unsupervised neural network model that provides a topology preserving mapping from a high-dimensional input space to a low, often two-dimensional, output space. The output space consists of a grid of units, each associated with a weight vector of the same dimensionality as the input space. During the training process, the weight vectors are adapted to describe the input space as close as possible, arranging topically related inputs close to each other.

The SOM has been used in several applications to automatically organise documents in a Digital Library by their content. Examples are text, as in the WEBSOM project [2], the SOMLib Digital Library system [3], or in a map of news [4], music in the SOMeJB system [5], or pictures in the PicSOM project [6]. Advanced visualisations and interaction possibilities allow the user to fully exploit the potential of the SOM. An extension of the SOMLib system e.g. realises the symbiosis of traditional information retrieval using a search or list browsing interface with the explorative approach of the Self-Organising Map by providing a plug-in to the popular open-source Digital Library System *Greenstone 3* [7]. The user can exploit all the functionalities provided by Greenstone, and can benefit from the wealth of additional information the SOM mapping provides about the cluster structure of the documents matching the query results, and the whole collection itself.

L. Kovács, N. Fuhr, and C. Meghini (Eds.): ECDL 2007, LNCS 4675, pp. 475–480, 2007.

However, we still lack techniques to adequately help the user analysing the contents of the map. For large maps, containing several tens of thousands of documents on various topics, it becomes increasingly difficult to analyse the map. In this paper, we give an overview of existing uses of the Self-Organising Map in Digital Libraries and techniques to explore and interact with the map. Furthermore, we present recent work in automatically describing regions in the map, using clustering methods to identify topical areas and selecting representative labels and summarising the content for those regions.

2 Describing the Self-Organising Map Regions

In this section we present our work on identifying and describing regions in the SOM. As the SOM does not generate a partitioning of the map into separate clusters, we apply a clustering algorithm on the weight vectors of the units to identify the regions (Section 2.1). We then extract semantic labels for those regions (Section 2.2), that assist the user in getting a first glance overview of the contents of the map. To further support the analysis, we provide summarisation of documents using Automatic Text Summarisation methods (Section 2.3).

2.1 Clustering

Clustering is an unsupervised process of finding natural groupings amongst unlabelled objects. We cluster the units of a SOM using an agglomerative, hierarchical clustering algorithm on the weight vectors. In the beginning of this algorithm, every unit lies in its own cluster. In each subsequent step, the two nearest clusters are merged, until finally only one cluster remains. Specifically, we use *Ward's linkage* as one of the most performant within the linkage clustering families, where the distance of each pair of clusters is defined by the increase in the 'error sum of squares' if the two clusters are to be combined. The result of the algorithm is a hierarchy of clusters which the user can browse through. Increasing the number of displayed clusters means splitting existing clusters into two new ones, while reducing the number of clusters is achieved by merging two clusters into one. This is advantageous over a non-hierarchical clustering algorithm, where changing the number of clusters might completely change the layout of clusters. Moreover, hierarchical clustering allows us to display multiple layers with a different number of clusters at the same time.

2.2 Labelling Regions

To assist the user in interpreting the regions of the SOM, we automatically generate labels for the clusters we identified previously. The cluster labels are based on the unit labels generated by the LabelSOM method [8], which assigns labels to the units of the SOM describing the features of the data points mapped onto the respective unit. This is done by utilising the *quantisation error* of the vector elements, i.e. the sum of the distances for a feature between the unit's weight vector and all the input vectors mapped onto this unit. A low quantisation error characterises a feature that is similar in all input vectors to the weight vector. Thus the assumption is made that this feature describes the unit well. If the input vector contains a lot of attributes which are non existent and therefore have the value of 0, those attributes often also have a quantisation error of almost 0 for a unit. However, such features are in most cases not appropriate for labelling the unit, since they would describe what the unit does not contain. Therefore, we require vector elements to additionally have a mean value above a defined threshold. To choose a label for a region, we consider all the unit labels present in that cluster. We chose to determine the cluster labels based upon the unit labels as they are already a selection of features describing the contents of each unit. This method is faster in computation than checking all possible features. The user can specify whether he prefers labels based upon a low average quantisation error, a high mean value, or a combination of both. Utilising the properties of the hierarchical clustering we can also display two or more different levels of labels, some being more global, some being more local.

In the visualisation of the SOM, the labels are placed in the centroid of the cluster, which may result in some overlapping labels. To achieve a clear arrangement, labels can be manually moved on the map, or adjusted in their size and rotation. For some labels, it might be useful to edit their text, for example if the label text is only a word stem as in the experiment described below.

2.3 Region Summarisation

Even though labelling the map regions assists the user in quickly getting a coarse overview of the topics, labels can still be ambiguous or not conveying enough information. Therefore, we also employ Automatic Text Summarisation [9] methods. We provide the user with summaries of single documents (based on extraction methods), however, the main focus is to assist the user in quickly analysing the contents of the Digital Library by providing summaries of the previously identified regions using multi-document summarisation. The application allows the user to select whole regions, or manually any other rectangular shape or units along a path. From the documents on those units, the user can choose from several different summarisation algorithms using different weighting schemes to determine the importance of sentences for the summaries. Further, the user can specify the desired length of the summary, measured in percent of the original sentences. Thus, a somewhat more concise description of the topical areas is provided to the user.

3 Experiments

The following experiments were performed using the 20 newsgroups data set (`http://people.csail.mit.edu/jrennie/20Newsgroups`). It consists of 1000 newsgroup postings for each of its 20 different newsgroups, such as *alt.atheism* and *comp.sys.mac.hardware*. We used a bag-of-words indexing and Porter's stemming. Features for the input vectors were selected according to their document frequency, and the weights are computed using a standard $tf \times idf$ weighting scheme. This resulted in a 3151 dimensional feature vector for each document, from which the maps were trained. The specific map we will use in the remainder of this paper to illustrate our results is 75x55 units in size.

3.1 Labelling Regions

In our application it is possible to explore the clustered SOM interactively: to view the different levels of clustering and to zoom into the map to view the single postings. The user can browse the clustering levels either viewing only the cluster borders, or highlighting each cluster in a different colour. The former is shown in Figure 1, illustrating the steps from one to eight clusters. There is a special cluster in the lower right-hand corner with the a label also used on other clusters – 'god' in the fourth step, and 'gun' in the steps five to seven. This cluster is, however, not a separate one - when viewing the clustering with colours, it becomes apparent that this area is part of the disjoint clusters 'god' and 'gun', respectively, in the upper part of the map.

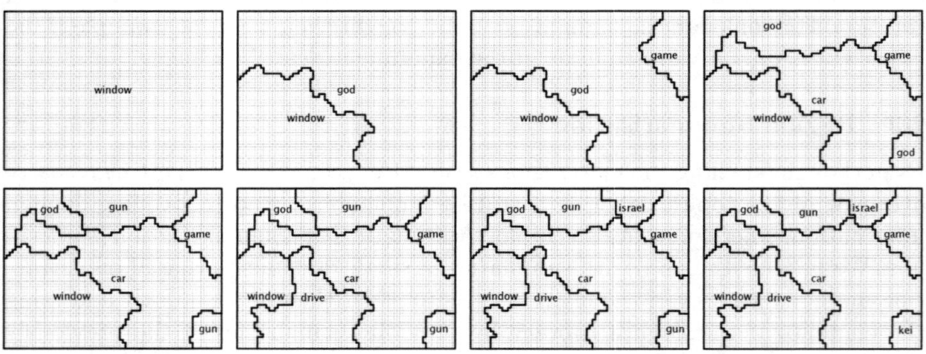

Fig. 1. 1 – 8 Clusters With Labels

Figure 2(a) shows an already labelled map, holding nine clusters with larger labels, and in addition 67 clusters with smaller labels. Again, there is one disjoint cluster, labelled 'david'. As a result of the stemming, the labels are sometimes not complete words that could be expanded to their original form.

In the top right-hand corner is a large cluster labelled 'game' containing most postings from the two sports related newsgroups. The large cluster next to it labelled 'israel' contains mainly postings from talk.politics.mideast. In the upper left-hand corner there is a cluster labelled 'god' containing all the newsgroups dealing with religion, i.e. alt.atheism, soc.religion.christian and talk.religion. misc. It is interesting to note, that, in contrast to the newsgroup hierarchy where these groups lie in three different top level hierarchies, they are combined into one cluster here.

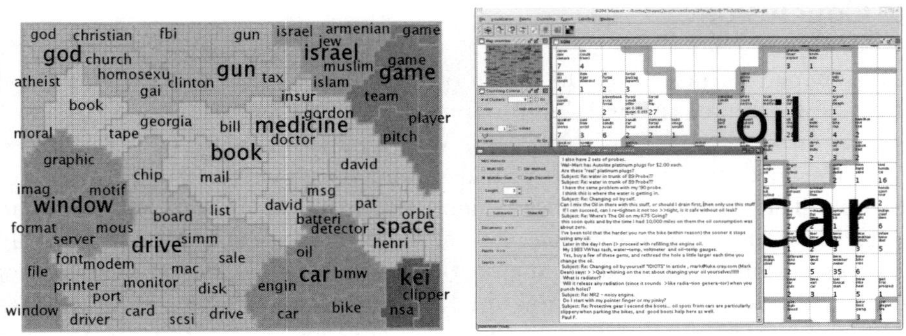

(a) (b)

Fig. 2. (a) 9 coloured and 67 smaller clusters (b) Summary of the cluster 'oil'

The large cluster in the middle labelled 'book' contains many of the smaller clusters of which only a few have meaningful labels. The clusters labelled 'insur' and 'doctor' suggest that they contain postings from the sci.med newsgroup and the cluster label 'orbit' relates to the newsgroup sci.space. The labels containing names such as 'gordon', 'david' or 'bill' do not help in identifying the underlying topics in those areas of the map. However, names cannot be easily automatically removed, as some common names as Mark or Bill are also a verb or noun respectively. Furthermore names can sometimes be useful labels, for example if they refer to a famous person. The small cluster labelled 'drive' lies in the cluster with the hardware topics but also directly next to the cluster labelled 'car'. It imples that in this area lies an transition of the word *drive* being used in the meaning of *hard disk drive* or in the meaning of *to drive a car.*

To enhance the comprehensibility of the map, the user can manually edit labels, e.g. add word endings, or improve the labels of areas that have diverse topics. For example the cluster automatically labelled 'car' could be extended to 'car & bike' to point out both newsgroups contained in this cluster. The cluster 'gun' containing the newsgroups talk.politics.guns and parts of talk.politics.misc and talk.politics.mideast could be adapted to 'politics'.

3.2 Region Summarisation

Figure 2(b) shows the summarisation of one of the regions in map, namely the cluster labelled 'oil'. The lower-left part of the interface shows the summarisation module, which allows the user to select a summarisation method, and the desired length of the summary. In our example, we use a multi-document summarisation extracting sentences considering their importance for the whole collection of documents selected, and chose 3% of the selected documents as desired summarisation length.

4 Conclusion

In this paper we presented the usage of the SOM as an interface to Digital Libraries. On top of this well-known approach, we presented methods to assist the user in interacting with the map. We employ clustering of the SOM to reveal hierarchical structures to provide a rough overview of the structure of the data. The clustering identifies regions, which we describe on the one hand by single descriptive words extracted from the document contents, and secondly by applying automatic text summarisation techniques to generate extracts of the contents. All methods are integrated into a single application that provides additional features such as visualisations and advanced interaction via zooming and panning, and selection of arbitrary regions of the map. With these tools available, the user can be greatly assisted in analysing the map and getting a quick overview of the contents of the Digital Library itself.

References

1. Kohonen, T.: Self-Organizing Maps. Springer Series in Information Sciences, vol. 30. Springer, Heidelberg (1995)
2. Kohonen, T., Kaski, S., Lagus, K., Salojrvi, J., Paatero, V., Saarela, A.: Organization of a massive document collection. IEEE Transactions on Neural Networks, Special Issue on Neural Networks for Data Mining and Knowledge Discovery 11, 574–585 (2000)
3. Rauber, A., Merkl, D.: The SOMLib digital library system. In: Abiteboul, S., Vercoustre, A.-M. (eds.) ECDL 1999. LNCS, vol. 1696, pp. 323–342. Springer, Heidelberg (1999)
4. Ong, T.H., Chen, H., Sung, W., Zhu, B.: Newsmap: a knowledge map for online news. Decision Support Systems 39, 583–597 (2005)
5. Rauber, A., Frühwirth, M.: Automatically analyzing and organizing music archives. In: Constantopoulos, P., Sølvberg, I.T. (eds.) ECDL 2001. LNCS, vol. 2163, Springer, Heidelberg (2001)
6. Laaksonen, J., Koskela, M., Laakso, S., Oja, E.: PicSOM-content-based image retrieval with self-organizing maps. Pattern Recogn. Lett. 21, 1199–1207 (2000)
7. Mayer, R., Rauber, A.: Adding SOMLib capabilities to the Greenstone Digital LibrarySystem. In: Sugimoto, S., Hunter, J., Rauber, A., Morishima, A. (eds.) ICADL 2006. LNCS, vol. 4312, pp. 486–489. Springer, Heidelberg (2006)
8. Rauber, A., Merkl, D.: Automatic labeling of Self-Organizing Maps for Information Retrieval. Journal of Systems Research and Inf. Systems (JSRIS) 10, 23–45 (2001)
9. Mani, I.: Advances in Automatic Text Summarization. MIT Press, Cambridge, MA (1999)

Policy Decision Tree for Academic Digital Collections

Alexandros Koulouris[1,2] and Sarantos Kapidakis[2]

[1] Central Library, National Technical University of Athens, 9 Heroon Polytechniou str., 15773 Polytechnioupoli Zografou, Athens, Greece
[2] Laboratory on Digital Libraries and Electronic Publishing, Department of Archive and Library Sciences, Ionian University, Plateia Eleftherias, Palaia Anaktora, 49100 Corfu, Greece
akoul@central.ntua.gr, sarantos@ionio.gr

Abstract. We present the results of a questionnaire survey for the access and reproduction policies of 67 digital collections in 34 libraries (national, academic, public, special etc) from 13 countries. We examine and analyze the above policies in relation to specific factors, such as, the acquisition method, copyright ownership, library type (national, academic, etc.), content creation (digitized, born-digital) and content type (audio, video, etc.); how these factors affect the policies of the examined digital collections. Responses were received from a range of library sectors but by far the best responses came from academic libraries, in which we focus. We extract policy (access, reproduction) rules and alternatives according to these factors that lead to a policy decision tree on digital information management for academic libraries. The resulting decision tree is based on a policy model; the model and tree are divided into two parts: for digitized and born-digital content.

1 Introduction

We propose a *policy decision tree* that contains flexible alternative access and reproduction policy solutions for *digital information management in academic libraries*. The *decision tree* is based on a conceptual policy model for digital information management, which is an evolvement and extension of our previous theoretical access and reproduction *policy model for university digital collections* [2]. The resulted *decision tree* may constitute a *map* or *guide* or policy *pathfinder*, for decision-makers and library managers in forming the policies (i.e. access, reproduction) and managing academic libraries' digital content.

2 Findings

We present the most important findings that were derived from the questionnaire survey and its data statistical analysis on collection level:

- The factors that mainly affect the access and reproduction policies are the acquisition method, the copyright ownership and the content creation type.
- Factors that affect less the previous policies are the content and library type.

L. Kovács, N. Fuhr, and C. Meghini (Eds.): ECDL 2007, LNCS 4675, pp. 481–484, 2007.

- The content creation type is independent from the library type.
- The library type diversifies the access policy structures (i.e. *off-campus*, *offsite*).
- Digital contents' acquisition method, especially in born-digital, diversifies access.
- Users' access diversification applies when other owners have the copyright.
- The libraries provide full off-campus onsite access for their own digital content, in which they have or administer the copyright.
- For the licensed content, and mostly for the born-digital, the libraries negotiate with the providers and they ensure *remote* access for their off-campus onsite users.
- When other owners have the digital contents' copyright, they restrict the full off-campus onsite access and they provide it in a limited sense.
- The libraries provide full offsite access for the digitized: *library* content, *free third-party*, *public domain* and *licensed* content; for the born-digital, they forbid it.
- In licensed content case, the provision of *limited* offsite access is widely used.
- The fact of copyright, especially when belongs to other owners, determines the kind of the (remote) offsite access (i.e. *full*, *limited*, or *not* provided).
- The user access rights' *clustering*[1] depends on digital contents' acquisition method.
- For the *library*, *free third-party* and *public domain* digitized content, users' access clustering is not applied.
- In the case of licensed digitized content, either *no*, or *common* clustering is applied.
- For the purchased digital content, *common* clustering is applied.
- Common clustering applies in born-digital content case, independent of the acquisition method used. Especially for the purchased content, except the *common*, *additional* clustering is also applied.
- When the copyright belongs to other owners, usually common clustering is applied or rarely additional clustering may applied.
- The users' clustering is related with the, a) access diversification between onsite and offsite users, b) offsite, c) off-campus onsite and d) on-campus onsite access.
- *Limited on-campus onsite access means additional clustering.*
- The private reproduction is usually free, independent of library type, acquisition method and copyright ownership.
- Libraries prefer providing their content with free private reproduction, either with a *credit* (mention) to the source, or by applying fair use provisions, but usually without enforcing written permission and/or fee, or any other additional restriction.
- The commercial reproduction is usually not authorized; it is mainly permitted from other library types (i.e. profitable private libraries).
- In most of the cases where the commercial reproduction is permitted, written permission and/or fee are required.
- The copyright owner gives, except few cases, the written permission and takes the fee for the commercial reproduction.
- The written permission is not always accompanied by fee payment.

---

[1] In this research, we categorize (*cluster*) the users according to their access rights. The *clustering* may have the values: *no*, meaning that onsite and offsite users have the same access rights; *common*, meaning that there is diversified access between onsite and offsite users and/or between onsite users (on and off-campus); and *additional*, meaning that there is diversified access between on-campus onsite users, even if inside library premises.

3 Proposed Policy Decision Tree for Digital Information Management in Academic Libraries: Rules and Alternatives

The rules and their alternatives that derived form the above findings result in a flexible (access and reproduction) *policy decision tree*, which is the *core* and *proposal* of this research. The *decision tree* is a *policy route map*, which offers alterative, flexible and effective access and reproduction policy solutions, according to the factors that apply on its case. It may have implications in building tools for making decision regarding policies and for managing the digital information.

The *decision tree* refers to the digital information life cycle focusing on its *creation* (digitized, born-digital), *acquisition* and *availability* (i.e. access, reproduction) – without excluding its *maintenance* (preservation). It simplifies and unifies already used practices, and converts them to efficient policy rules. Additionally, it offers new, flexible, extensible and innovative policy alternatives (*routes*, *paths*).

The *decision tree* is divided into two *parts*, for the *digitized* and for the *born-digital* content separately, which are not included due to format constrains. However, the *decision tree parts* are incorporated in *TR200701* technical report, available at http://dlib.ionio.gr/en/lab/treports.htm.

3.1 Policy Decision Tree for Academic Libraries' Digitized Content

We analyze some representative examples of alternative proposed *policy routes*. Academic libraries may follow four available alternative options for their digitized content acquisition: *library*, *third-party*, *public domain* and *licensed* content. When *library content* is involved, the library digitizes the content available on its collections, in which it has or administers the copyright. The access is full and free for all users. Private and commercial reproduction should be permitted to all users with a credit to the *source* (i.e. content *creator*, provider) and with written permission from and fees paid to the library respectively.

When the library digitizes *third-party* content, the *library* administers the copyright, or *other owners* hold it, or *library and other owners* mutually administer (share) it, or finally, it may varies from item-to-item. When the library administers the copyright two access alternatives are proposed: full for all users, or full for *onsite* (on and off-campus) only and *no* (forbidden) for offsite. The *private* reproduction should be permitted with a *credit* (mention) to the source or by applying *fair use* doctrine. The commercial reproduction has two alternatives; its provision with written permission from and fees paid to the library, or its examination on *case-by-case* basis.

When other owners hold the third party digitized contents' copyright, the access should be provided to onsite users only; and not to offsite. In this case, only onsite users have the content reproducing privilege, with a credit to the source for private, and with written permission, given by the owner, for commercial reproduction.

Variant and alterative access and reproduction policy routes are proposed when the third-party digitized contents' copyright is *shared* among library and other owners or varies from item-to-item. For instance, in case of copyright sharing, the access is *full* for onsite and it is *limited* or *not provided* for offsite users. Finally, the *licensed* or *public domain* digitized content has other alternative policy proposals.

3.2 Policy Decision Tree for Academic Libraries' Born-Digital Content

Examples of alternative proposed policy routes are analyzed. Academic libraries may follow four proposing alternatives for their born-digital content acquisition: *license*, *purchase*, *voluntary deposit* and *library* content. When occurs to purchased born-digital content, *other owners* hold the copyright or *library* and *other owners* mutually administer it, or finally, it *varies on item* basis.

When *other owners* hold the copyright, the proposing access policy *path* is full on-campus, limited off-campus and *no* offsite. The private reproduction should be permitted with a credit to the source or under fair use provisions, and the commercial should not be authorized. Two additional alternative reproduction policy paths may be considered, when library and other owners mutually administer the copyright; the *case-by-case* examination (private and commercial) and the provision of commercial reproduction with written permission from and fees paid to the owners.

When the copyright *varies* from item-to-item (encountered in *purchased* born-digital content), three proposing alternative access policy paths may be selected: a) *full on-campus, some off-campus and no offsite*, b) *full on and off-campus, some offsite* (i.e. fig. 1), and c) *full onsite and offsite*. Proposing paths for reproduction are its provision by mentioning (*credit*) the source or by applying fair use doctrine (*for private*), and its forbiddance (*for commercial*).

Academic libraries may alternatively select the *voluntary deposit* method for their born-digital content acquisition; having in mind that other owners control the copyright and normally impose policy (i.e. on *access*) restrictions. The proposing restrictive access (i.e. *full on-campus, limited off-campus, no offsite*) and reproduction (i.e. *permitted for onsite users only*) paths follow the logic of satisfying the content creators, and in accordance, ensuring the born-digital contents' voluntary deposit, viability and preservation.

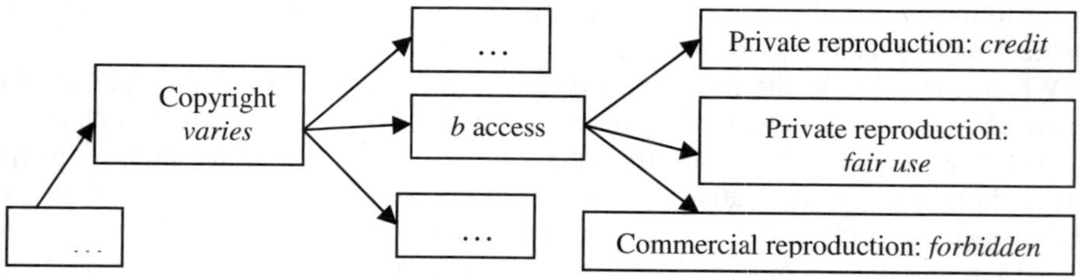

Fig. 1. Policy path examples of the decision tree for academic libraries' born-digital content

References

1. Ayre, C., Muir, A.: Right to Preserve? Copyright and licensing for digital preservation project Final Report, Department of Information Science, Loughborough University [Accessed 8-3-07] (2004), http://www.lboro.ac.uk/departments/ls/disresearch/CLDP/DOCUMENTS/Final report.doc
2. Koulouris, A., Kapidakis, S.: Policy Model for University Digital Collections. In: Rauber, A., Christodoulakis, S., Tjoa, A.M. (eds.) ECDL 2005. LNCS, vol. 3652, pp. 356–367. Springer, Heidelberg (2005)

Personalized Faceted Browsing for Digital Libraries*

Michal Tvarožek and Mária Bieliková

Institute of Informatics and Software Engineering,
Faculty of Informatics and Information Technologies,
Slovak University of Technology
Ilkovičova 3, 842 16 Bratislava, Slovakia
{Name.Surname}@fiit.stuba.sk

Abstract. Current digital libraries and online bibliographies share several properties with the Web and thus also share some of its problems. Faceted classifications and Semantic Web technologies are explored as possible approaches to improving digital libraries and alleviating their respective shortcomings. We describe the possibilities of using faceted navigation and its personalization in digital libraries. We propose a method of faceted browser adaptation based on an automatically acquired user model with support for dynamic facet generation.

1 Introduction

Present day digital libraries (DL) and bibliographies enable users to browse, search in and view their contents via web browsers, and can thus be considered a specific subspace of the Web. Consequently, they share several of its properties:

- *Size* – contemporary DL present large information spaces.
- *Changeability* – DL are much less changeable than the Web. While new titles are continuously added, the content of existing ones and their metadata (e.g., author, title, editor) remain the same. However, a diverse range of different DL exists ranging from simple publications to archaeological artifacts.
- *Complexity* – varying degrees of complexity are common ranging from relatively simply structured to very complex information spaces.
- *User diversity* – varies based on the target audience and DL type, with also the individual users' interests changing over time.

Unlike the current Web, DL display relatively good availability of metadata, which however does not prevent DL users from navigation problems and high recursion rate of navigation, which are common in the general Web [1]. Many existing DL allow users to browse entries by subjects or titles and also support

* This work was partially supported by the Slovak Research and Development Agency under the contract No. APVT-20-007104 and the Scientific Grant Agency of Slovak Republic, grant No. VG1/3102/06.

L. Kovács, N. Fuhr, and C. Meghini (Eds.): ECDL 2007, LNCS 4675, pp. 485–488, 2007.

search with limited personalization capabilities (e.g., ACM DL or IEEE DL). Others use simple faceted browsers that allow users to search for and navigate in available entries using multiple views (e.g., SpringerLink).

Since existing DL offer only limited support for advanced browsing and navigation in individual entries with minimal personalization features in terms of adaptation and user collaboration, new approaches were proposed to address information overload and insufficient search and navigation support. The Semantic Web incorporates shared semantics thus improving interoperability between systems [2], while faceted browsers take advantage of faceted classification and provide combined support for search and navigation as outlined in [3].

2 Adaptive Faceted Browsing for Digital Libraries

To address the disadvantages of faceted browsers insufficient personalization, difficult understanding of the size and content of the information domain, and access to popular topics, adaptation techniques were proposed in [4]. In this paper we explore and extend the possibilities of faceted navigation use in digital libraries and describe enhancements to faceted browsers by taking advantage of ontologies and adaptation based on an automatically acquired user model.

We first determine the relevance of facets and restrictions based on the in-session user behavior (i.e., user clicks), on the user model (i.e., user characteristics described by their *relevance* to the user and the *confidence* in their estimation) and based on global statistics (i.e., all user models). Next, we optionally generate new dynamic facets at run-time and lastly adapt the faceted browser interface in these steps:

1. *Facet ordering* – all facets are ordered in descending order based on their relevance with the last used facet always being at the top (i.e., most relevant).
2. *Active facet selection* – the number of active facets is reduced to 2 or 3 most relevant facets since many facets are potentially available. Inactive facts are used for queries but their contents are not restored, disabled facets are not used at all. Both inactive and disabled facets are still available on demand.
3. *Facet and restriction annotation* – active facets are annotated with tooltips describing the facet, numbers of instances satisfying each restriction and the relative number of instances satisfying each restriction via font size/type.
4. *Facet restriction recommendation* – the most relevant restrictions in a facet are marked as recommended (e.g., with background color or "traffic lights").

Adaptive views. Users can choose from several visualization options by selecting one of the available views – simple overview, extended overview or detailed view, which display increasingly more detailed information about individual search results. The attributes of the displayed instances are adaptively chosen based on their estimated relevance derived from the user model.

Information overload prevention. Based on facet and restriction relevance we reduce the total number of accessible items in order to allow users to find relevant facets and restrictions more efficiently without having to scroll several screens down. The selection of appropriate facet types and displayed restrictions is performed automatically based on their relevance in the user model and based on the current in-session user behavior so that it matches both long-term user interests and short-term user goals.

Query refinement. By using additional facets created by dynamic facet generation, users can refine their queries beyond what would by possible with statically defined facets. Furthermore, these are combined with additional functions often used in advanced search such as OR, NOT or braces. For example, if some users were interested in publications related to a given topic they would select that topic as the subject of the publication in a static facet resulting in publications which deal directly with the given topic. By using a dynamic facet generated from the domain ontology (i.e., one that was not anticipated by the system's administrator), users can instead select publications presented on conferences or in journals that deal with the given topic thus receiving a much broader set of publications which are still related to the given topic.

Orientation support. Since faceted classifications and large information spaces tend to be complex and hard to understand, we annotate facets and restrictions with additional information to aid users in orientation. Facet and restriction annotation includes the number of instances that satisfy a restriction and a textual description of their meaning. Individual restrictions can be further annotated with background color indicating e.g. their relation to users' field of work. Individual search results are annotated using background color, based on their relation to a given set of publications (e.g., already read or the author's own publications) by means of an external concept comparison tool [5].

Guidance support. The proposed method improves user guidance in several ways. First, we order the set of available facets based on their estimated user relevance thus recommending the most relevant facets. Next, we evaluate the relevance of individual restrictions and recommend the most relevant ones based on the user model, e.g. by means of background color. Moreover, we can recommend the most relevant search results by ordering them using external ordering tools [5,6] to evaluate the relevance of the final search results against the current user model and query.

Social navigation and recommendation. Since the domain of DL is somewhat closely related to social networks of e.g. authors, we take advantage of other users' preferences in the evaluation of concept relevance. *Global relevance* describes the overall "popularity" of concepts while *cross relevance* also considers the similarity between users. Thus we can recommend a publication if it is relevant for many researchers in a particular field and the user is also interested in this field, or a generic publication that seems to be relevant for many users.

Visual navigation and presentation. In order to improve the understandability of the domain and the available data a visual presentation method may be more suitable than pure text. Visual navigation in clusters [7] provides users with the necessary "global" overview of the respective information subspace selected in a faceted browser. Likewise, a seamless transition between an adaptive textual view with support for faceted navigation and a visual view, representing the selected information subspace (e.g., based on clusters), with successive visual navigation can provide users with a more intuitive browsing experience.

3 Conclusions

We presented a novel method of faceted browser adaptation with dynamic facet generation. We evaluated selected part of the proposed method in the domain of scientific publications (project MAPEKUS, `mapekus.fiit.stuba.sk`) by experimenting with developed adaptive faceted browser – *Factic*. Factic is evaluated as part of the personalized presentation layer proposed in [8] where it is integrated with tools aimed at automatic user action logging and characteristics acquisition. Preliminary evaluation showed that the adaptation of facets alleviates some disadvantages of faceted classification, such as difficult access to popular items, and significantly improves overall efficiency by reducing information overload.

Future work will include the design and evaluation of additional method enhancements, especially dynamic facet generation, social navigation in the faceted browser and recommendation based on user relationships.

References

1. Lavene, M., Wheeldon, R.: Navigating the World-Wide-Web. In: Lavene, M., Poulovassilis, A. (eds.) Web Dynamics, Springer, Heidelberg (2003)
2. Shadbolt, N., Berners-Lee, T., Hall, W.: The semantic web revisited. IEEE Intelligent Systems 21(3), 96–101 (2006)
3. Shen, R., et al.: Exploring digital libraries: integrating browsing, searching, and visualization. In: JCDL '06: Proc. of the 6th ACM/IEEE-CS Joint Conf. on Digital libraries, pp. 1–10. ACM Press, New York (2006)
4. Tvarožek, M., Bieliková, M.: Adaptive Faceted Browser for Navigation in Open Information Spaces. In: Proc. of WWW 2007, ACM Press, New York (2007)
5. Návrat, P., Bartoš, P., Bieliková, M., Hluchý, L., Vojtáš, P. (eds.): Tools for Acquisition, Organization and Presenting of Information and Knowledge, Research Project Workshop, Bystrá Dolina, Low Tatras, Slovakia (2006)
6. Horváth, T., Vojtáš, P.: Ordinal classification with monotonicity constraints. In: Perner, P. (ed.) ICDM 2006. LNCS (LNAI), vol. 4065, pp. 217–225. Springer, Heidelberg (2006)
7. Frivolt, G., Bieliková, M.: Topology generation for web communities modeling. In: Vojtáš, P., Bieliková, M., Charron-Bost, B., Sýkora, O. (eds.) SOFSEM 2005. LNCS, vol. 3381, pp. 167–177. Springer, Heidelberg (2005)
8. Tvarožek, M., Barla, M., Bieliková, M.: Personalized Presentation in Web-Based Information Systems. In: van Leeuwen, J., Italiano, G.F., van der Hoek, W., Meinel, C., Sack, H., Plášil, F. (eds.) SOFSEM 2007. LNCS, vol. 4362, pp. 796–807. Springer, Heidelberg (2007)

The Use of Metadata in Visual Interfaces to Digital Libraries

Ali Shiri

School of Library & Information Studies, University of Alberta
ashiri@ualberta.ca

Abstract. This poster reports on a study carried out to investigate and analyze a specific category of digital library visual interfaces that support information seeking, exploration and retrieval based on metadata representations, namely *metadata-enhanced visual interfaces*. This study has examined 21 metadata-enhanced digital library visual interfaces from the following perspectives: a) information access and retrieval features supported; b) metadata elements used; c) visualization techniques and metaphors utilized. The results show that visual interfaces to digital libraries enhanced with metadata are becoming more widespread. The study also demonstrates that the combined use of visualization techniques and metaphors is becoming increasingly prevalent as a design strategy to support users' information exploration.

Keywords: Visual interfaces, metadata, information visualization, digital libraries.

1 Introduction

Visual interfaces to digital libraries have recently found widespread attention. This development is mainly due to the fact that visualization techniques allow for rich representation of information bearing objects in digital libraries. This poster reports on a study of metadata-enabled visual interfaces to digital libraries based on the richness and variety of metadata elements, visualization techniques and metaphors.

2 Methodology

Borner and Chen [1] note that visual interfaces to digital libraries can support a range of information search and retrieval activities including the identification of the composition of a retrieval result, the interrelation of retrieved documents to one another, refine a search and to gain an overview of the coverage of a digital library to facilitate browsing. Shneiderman [2] identifies various visualization techniques based on data types and tasks. Based on the above research, this study has examined 21 digital library visual interfaces from the following perspectives: a) information

L. Kovács, N. Fuhr, and C. Meghini (Eds.): ECDL 2007, LNCS 4675, pp. 489–494, 2007.

access and retrieval features supported; b) metadata elements used; and c) visualization techniques and metaphors utilized. (Tables 1 and 2 feature the above elements).

Table 1. Metadata-enhanced Visual interfaces to Digital Libraries (1990s)

Visual interface	VT	Type of metaphor	Metadata Elements used	Focus on QF& MV	Focus on SRV	Focus on CRV	RV
Fowler et al. (1991) [3]	Net-work	Fisheye views & overview diagrams	Thesaurus terms, bibliographic elements	Yes	Yes	No	No
Envision (Fox et al., 1993, Nowell et al., 1996) [4, 5]	2D	Scatterplot graphs	Authors, date, title, document type, date, language	Yes	Yes	No	Yes
Lyberworld (Hemmje et al., 1994) [6]	3D, Cone trees	Spatial Navigation	Titles, associated keywords	Yes	Yes	Yes	Yes
Becks et al. (1998) [7]	2D	Spatial Representation (Map)	Abstracts	Yes	Yes	Yes	Yes
NaviQue (Furnas & Rauch, 1998) [8]	2D	Spatial metaphor	Type of photo, location, title, date	Yes	Yes	Yes	No
BALTICSEAWEB (Laitinen & Neuvonen, 1998) [9]	2D	Spatial representation (Map)	Geographic regions, cities, borders	Yes	No	Yes	No
VQuery (Jones, 1998) [10]	2D	Venn diagrams	Collection and item titles	Yes	No	No	No
LibViewer (Rauber & Bina, 1999) [11]	2D	Shelf position, document type, colour, size	Dublin Core (title, author, format, etc.	No	Yes	No	No
NIRVE (Sebrechts et al., 1999) [12]	2D & 3D	Map	Titles, clusters, keywords & concepts	No	Yes	No	No

Table acronyms:

VT: Visualization Technique
QF&MV: Query Formulation and Modification Visualization
SRV: Search Results Visualization
CRV: Collection Representation Visualization
RV: Relevance Visualization

Table 2. Metadata-enhanced Visual interfaces to Digital Libraries (2000s)

Visual interface	VT	Type of metaphor	Metadata Elements used	Focus on QF &MV	Focus on SRV	Focus on CRV	RV
Borner et al. (2002) [1]	3D	Treemaps	Item & collection titles, doc. types	No	Yes	Yes	No
VIBE (Christel, 2002) [13]	3D, Temporal, multi-dimensional	Maps, timelines , scatter plots	Transcripts & thumbnail images, geographic entities	Yes	Yes	Yes	Yes
Grokker (2002) [14]	Multi-dimensional	Venn diagrams, nested circles and squares	Title, author, source, date,	Yes	Yes	Yes	Yes
VisMeB (Klein et al., 2003) [15]	2D, 3D, multi-dimensional	Scatterplots, pie charts, bar charts, SuperTables	Server type, language, Date, relevance, title, abstract	Yes	Yes	Yes	Yes
FedStats Browser (Kules & Shneiderman, 2003) [16]	2D, Tree	Folders, trees, maps	Statistical metadata titles, collections, regions	Yes	Yes	Yes	No
Sumner et al. (2003) and Butcher et al. (2006) [17, 18]	2D	Semantic-spatial maps (Strand/concept maps)	Educational metadata such as grade levels etc.	No	Yes	No	No
Chang et al. (2004) [19]	2D	Ambient slideshows, thumbnails	Title, place, duration, media, Size, collection	Yes	Yes	Yes	Yes
NSDL Virtual spine (Dushay, 2004) [20]	2D	Scatterplots, folders	Creator, publisher, format, language, metadata provider, title, audience	Yes	Yes	Yes	No
Fluid interface (Good et al. 2005) [21]	2D	Treemaps	File type, file name, date, thumbnails	No	Yes	Yes	No
MedioVis (Grun et al., 2005) [22]	2D	Scatterplot, Tables, Spatial representationns	Title, author, year, media type, full text description	Yes	Yes	No	No
CombinFormation (Kerne, et al. 2006) [23]	2D	Text, image and temporal compositions	Title, URL, caption	No	Yes	Yes	No
SRS browser (Mane & Borner, 2006) [24]	2D	Association networks	Gene and protein metadata	Yes	Yes	Yes	Yes

The information access and retrieval features examined in this study were based mainly on the usage scenarios identified by Borner and Chen [1]. Concerning metadata elements, both manually and automatically generated metadata elements incorporated into visual interfaces were evaluated. To establish the visualization technique(s) used within a particular interface, the author relied on the information provided in the paper or prototype description as well as on the examination of the interface. In categorizing visualization techniques, the taxonomy suggested by Shneiderman [2] was utilized.

3 Results and Conclusion

The interfaces analyzed in this study represent digital collections in a wide array of subject areas ranging from computer science, medicine, biological sciences, earth sciences, to arts and media, geospatial and digital image collections. The study of the 21 visual interfaces developed in the 1990s and 2000s reveals some interesting patterns. One of the developments concerning visualization techniques lies in the increasing use of 3D and multi-dimensional visualization. Another observable development is the combined use of visualization techniques. Most visual interfaces developed in the 1990s employ real-world spatial metaphor and map-like representations of items and collections. A comparison between the interfaces developed in the 1990s and 2000s shows a noticeable shift towards the use of multiple visualization metaphors. In particular, metaphors such as Venn diagrams, pie charts and temporal representations are becoming increasingly popular. The study shows that the interfaces developed in the 2000s have increasingly made use of both manually and automatically generated metadata to overcome the challenge of knowledge representation. Of the 21 interfaces examined, 15 interfaces have incorporated query construction or modification features. Nineteen interfaces offer the search result visualization feature. The study also showed that 14 interfaces had visual collection representation facilities. Among the reviewed interfaces only eight of them have incorporated relevance visualization facilities.

This study demonstrated that metadata-enhanced visual interfaces are an emerging category of visual interfaces. Developers of information retrieval interfaces can take advantage of a combination of manually and automatically generated metadata within digital libraries to create content-rich visual interfaces to represent multimedia and multimodal digital libraries. Metadata has the potential to inform and enhance visualization techniques and metaphors and to suggest new frontiers in developing enriched visual information seeking and exploration facilities.

References

1. Börner, K., Chen, C.: Visual Interfaces to Digital Libraries. LNCS, vol. 2539. Springer, Heidelberg (2002)
2. Shneiderman, B.: The Eyes Have It: A Task by Data Type Taxonomy for Information Visualizations. In: Proceedings of the IEEE Symposium on Visual Languages, Boulder, CO, USA, pp. 336–343 (September 3-6, 1996)

3. Fowler, R.H., Fowler, W.A.L., Wilson, B.A.: Integrating query, thesaurus, and documents through a common visual representation. In: Proceedings of the 14th Annual International ACM/SIGIR Conference on Research and Development in Information Retrieval, pp. 142–151. ACM Press, New York (1991)
4. Fox, E.A., Hix, D., Nowell, L., Brueni, D.J., Wake, W., Heath, L.: Users, User Interface, and Objects: Envision, a Digital Library. Journal of the American Society for Information Science 44(8), 480–491 (1993)
5. Nowell, L.T., France, R.K., Hix, D., Heath, L.S., Fox, E.A.: Visualizing search results: some alternatives to query-document similarity. In: Proceedings of the Annual ACM Conference on Research and Development in Information Retrieval. Zurich, Switzerland, pp. 67–75 (August 1996)
6. Hemmje, M., Kunkel, C., Willett, A.: LyberWorld - A Visualization User Interface Supporting Fulltext Retrieval. In: Croft, W.B., van Rijsbergen, C.J. (eds.) Proceedings of the 17th Annual International Conference on Research and Development in Information Retrieval (SIGIR 94), pp. 249–257. Springer, Heidelberg (1994)
7. Becks, A., Sklorz, S., Tresp, C.: Semantic Structuring and Visual Querying of Document Abstracts in Digital Libraries. In: Proceedings of the 2nd European Conference on Research and Advanced Technology for Digital Libraries, Crete, pp. 443–458 (1998)
8. Furnas, G.W., Rauch, s.J.: Considerations for Information Environments and the NaviQue Workspace. In: Proceedings of the ACM Digital Libraries 98, Pittsburgh, PA, pp. 79–88. ACM Press, New York (1998)
9. Laitinen, S., Neuvonen, A.: BALTICSEAWEB - Geographic User Interface to Bibliographic Information. In: Nikolaou, C., Stephanidis, C. (eds.) ECDL 1998. LNCS, vol. 1513, pp. 651–652. Springer, Heidelberg (1998)
10. Jones, S.: Graphical Query Specification and Dynamic Result Previews for a Digital Library. In: ACM Symposium on User Interface Software and Technology, pp. 143–151 (1998)
11. Rauber, A., Bina, H.: A Metaphor Graphics Based Representation of Digital Libraries on the World Wide Web: Using the libViewer to Make Metadata Visible. In: Bench-Capon, T.J.M., Soda, G., Tjoa, A.M. (eds.) DEXA 1999. LNCS, vol. 1677, pp. 286–290. Springer, Heidelberg (1999)
12. Sebrechts, M.M., Cugini, J., Laskowski, S.J., Vasilakis, J., Miller, M.S.: Visualization of Search Results: A Comparative Evaluation of Text, 2D, and 3D Interfaces. In: Proceedings of the SIGIR'99: Proceedings of 22nd Annual International ACM/SIGIR Conference on Research and Development in Information Retrieval, Berkeley, CA, August 15-19, 1999, pp. 3–10. ACM, New York (1999)
13. Christel, M.G.: Accessing News Video Libraries through Dynamic Information Extraction, Summarization, and Visualization. In: Börner, K., Chen, C. (eds.) Visual Interfaces to Digital Libraries. LNCS, vol. 2539, pp. 98–115. Springer, Heidelberg (2002)
14. Grokker: http://www.grokker.com/
15. Klein, P., Müller, F., Reiterer, H., Limbach, T.: Metadata visualization with VisMeB. In: Proceedings of the 7th international conference on information visualization (IV 03), pp. 600–605. IEEE Press, New York (2003)
16. Kules, B., Shneiderman, B.: Designing a metadata-driven visual information browser for federal statistics. In: Proceedings of the 2003 annual national conference on Digital government research, May 18-21, 2003, Boston, MA, pp. 1–6 (2003)
17. Sumner, T., Bhushan, S., Ahmad, F., Gu, Q.: Designing a Language for Creating Conceptual Browsing Interfaces for Digital Libraries. In: Proceedings of the 3rd ACM/IEEE-CS Joint Conference on Digital Libraries, Houston, TX, USA, May 27-31, pp. 258–260 (2003)

18. Butcher, K.R., Bhushan, S., Sumner, T.: Multimedia displays for conceptual discovery: information seeking with strand maps. ACM Multimedia Systems Journal 11(3), 236–248 (2006)
19. Chang, M., Leggett, J.L., Furuta, R., Kerne, A., Williams, J.P., Burns, S.A., Bias, R.G.: Collection understanding. In: Proceedings of the ACM/IEEE-CS Joint Conference on Digital Libraries, Tucson, AZ, USA, June 7-11, pp. 334–342 (2004)
20. Dushay, N.: Visualizing Bibliographic Metadata - A Virtual (Book) Spine Viewer. D-Lib Magazine. 10(10) (October 2004), http://www.dlib.org/dlib/october04/dushay/10dushay.html
21. Good, L., Popat, A.C., Janssen, W.C., Bier, E.A.: A Fluid interface for personal digital libraries. In: Rauber, A., Christodoulakis, S., Tjoa, A.M. (eds.) ECDL 2005. LNCS, vol. 3652, pp. 162–173. Springer, Heidelberg (2005)
22. Grün, C., Gerken, J., Jetter, H.C., König, W., Reiterer, H.: MedioVis - A User-Centred Library Metadata Browser. In: Rauber, A., Christodoulakis, S., Tjoa, A.M. (eds.) ECDL 2005. LNCS, vol. 3652, pp. 174–185. Springer, Heidelberg (2005)
23. Kerne, A., Koh, E., Dworaczyk, B., Mistrot, J.M., Choi, H., Smith, S.M., Graeber, R., Caruso, D., Webb, A., Hill, R., Albea, J.: combinFormation: a mixed-initiative system for representing collections as compositions of image and text surrogates. In: Proceedings of ACM/IEEE-CS Joint Conference on Digital Libraries, Chapel Hill, NC, USA, June 11-15, pp. 11–20 (2006)
24. Mane, K., Borner, K.: SRS Browser: A Visual Interface to the Sequence Retrieval System. Visualization and Data Analysis. In: Proceedings of SPIE-IST Electronic Imaging, SPIE, January 15-19, 2006, San Jose, California, USA (2006)

Location and Format Independent Distributed Annotations for Collaborative Research

Fabio Corubolo, Paul B. Watry, and John Harrison

University of Liverpool, Liverpool, L69 3DA, United Kingdom
{corubolo, p.b.watry, john.harrison}@liverpool.ac.uk

Abstract. This paper describes the development of a distributed annotation system which enables collaborative document consultation and creates new access to otherwise hard to index digital documents. It takes the annotations one step further: not only the same types of annotations are available across file formats, but robust references to the documents introduce format and location independence, and enable the attachment even when the document has been modified. These features are achieved using standards of the digital library systems, and don't require modification of the original documents or impose further restrictions, thus being infrastructure independent. Integration into the Kepler workflow system allows annotating workflow results, and the automatic creation and indexing of annotations in document oriented workflows, which can be used as a flexible way to archive and index collections in the Cheshire3 search engine.

1 Introduction

In an era when digital documents are to a great extent replacing paper, there is a strong need for improved annotation tools which cover a range of annotation types, including good authoring tools, on a variety of common document formats.

The primary aim of this work is to use digital library resources as the basis for collaborative research; therefore, the investigation has looked into how existing digital library developments can be used to support distributed, *spontaneous collaborations*. In particular, technologies which will enable research community users to annotate documents and other peoples' data and share these annotations with others in a simple, spontaneous way. The result will support research collaborations within scholarly communities which are intellectually cohesive but geographically distributed.

Our work builds and extends Multivalent annotations [1], which will allow users to annotate shared documents, in numerous ways, and to share these annotations without any special prior arrangement or significant systems overhead and creates new access to otherwise hard to index digital documents, such as images.

The system, developed in the context of the JISC funded VRE programme, takes the annotations one step further: not only the same types of annotations are available across file formats, but robust references to the documents introduce *format and location independence*, and enable the attachment also when the document has been modified, thanks to a novel use of lexical signatures [2]. These features don't require modification of the original documents or impose further restrictions, and thus can be

L. Kovács, N. Fuhr, and C. Meghini (Eds.): ECDL 2007, LNCS 4675, pp. 495–498, 2007.

adopted without any additional infrastructures. The system can be inserted in many contexts, including situations where the original files do not support annotations or must remain intact, as in a digital preservation environment. Also, the casual users need not feel intimidated when adding annotations as there is no risk of altering the original document.

Integration of the key components into the Kepler workflow system [3] introduces the idea of annotating workflow results, and allows the automatic creation and indexing of annotations in document oriented workflows, that can be used as a flexible way to archive and index collections in the Cheshire3 search engine [4].

Due to the modular structure of the system, it will be possible to integrate alternative software components (e.g. a different workflow, database or document browser).

2 Methodology

The methodology followed aims to maintain a clear separation between the components and to adopt the *relevant standards*:

- Web services for the Cheshire3 workflow connector and the lexical signature service. These services are application specific, enabling reuse at a service level.
- The SRW standard search protocol for searching and retrieving the annotations.
- The XML Schema formally describes the annotations. The structure has been built to be extensible and application-agnostic.
- The XML Digital Signatures to assure provenance and authenticity. The signature is applied optionally by the client (the Fab4/Multivalent browser) to the entire annotation.

The *annotation schema* consists in an envelope for the annotation body, which is considered to be application dependant (in XML, text or binary format), containing:

- The generic annotation metadata, using Dublin Core and some specific metadata (annotation format, generating application, nature of the annotation).
- The digital signature applied to the annotation as a whole, so that both the body and the metadata are digitally signed.
- The annotated resource element, the main feature identifying the referenced document. This consists of multiple identifiers, permitting different levels of attachment. These include the document URI, binary digest, lexical signature [2], and textual contents digest.

The different identifiers, together, allow the attachment of the annotations according to different rules, which can be defined by the user (for example: attach to the same exact document, same location, same content, or similar document, in case of partial changes to the content).

The format independence is achieved using the textual content digest which normally does not change across file formats. Afterwards, an SRW query to the database system allows retrieving all the annotations for a specific textual content. Other advanced methods, involving the document structure, will be implemented in the future.

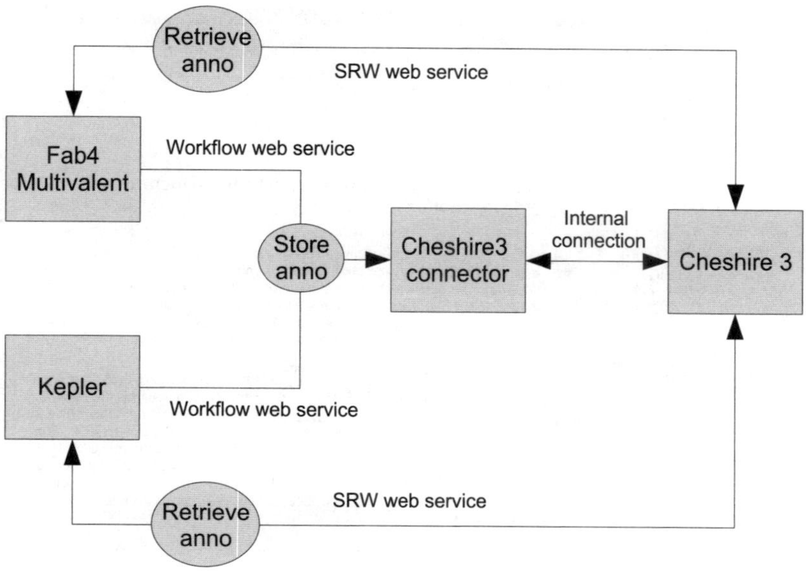

Fig. 1. The system connection diagram shows the interaction between the three main components. The infrastructure independency is highlighted by the use of web services.

Use cases considered during the development include: peer review, scholars needing to disseminate knowledge bases and virtual collaboration environments for students and researchers. An exemplar, based on the AHDS-derived "Designing Shakespeare" collection, has been developed; the Tavistock Institute has conducted a user study involving a community of students, researchers, and systems administrators.

3 Results

This system is now included in the default distribution of the Fab4 browser, publicly available [5].

The annotations are robustly attached, and thus:

- Location independent: the same file will always share the same notes, independently of where it resides (web server, local file system, email attachment etc.)
- Format independent: a PDF and text version of the same document share the same annotations.
- Robust to document changes: the same annotations can be attached to a document even if its contents are modified.

The annotations are always distributed to all the copies of the document, without the need to redistribute or modify the original file, a great advantage for spontaneous collaboration. This differs from other annotation systems which apply the notes to the original file and require the redistribution of the file on every annotation. Furthermore, the annotations are robustly attached to the contents of the document, using Robust Locations [6].

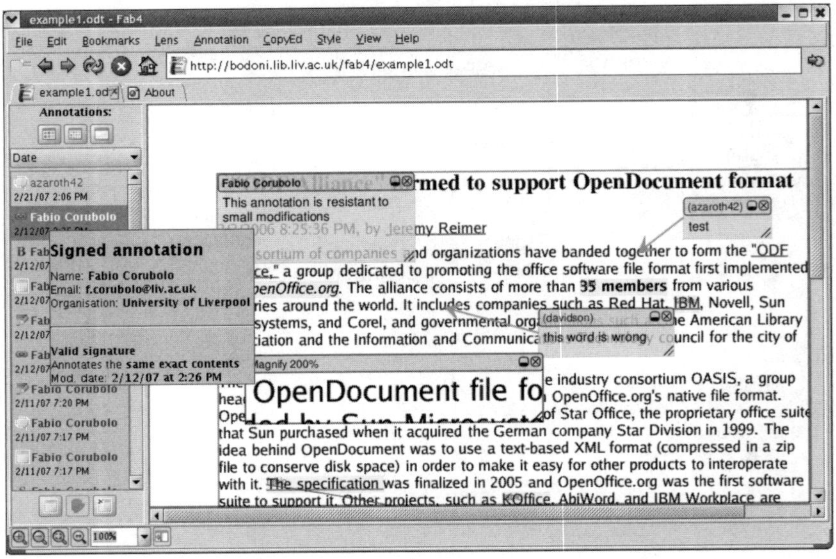

Fig. 2. A view of an annotated Open Document File in Fab4/Multivalent. In the annotations list on the left the trusted ones are highlighted.

The *digital signature* and a trust system guarantee the secure attribution and originality of the annotations so that the provenance can be trusted and proved. This could be further extended to enable the application of trusted actions to documents in a peer review system (e.g. "approved for publishing") or in other similar use cases.

A search interface, built on the Cheshire3 system, allows retrieval of the annotations, and, through them, of the referenced documents. This in fact creates new paths to the retrieval of digital objects.

Acknowledgements. This work was supported by the JISC VRE programme.

References

1. Phelps, T., Wilensky, R.: Multivalent Annotations. In: Procs. First European Conference on Research and Advanced Technology for Digital Libraries (1997)
2. Phelps, T., Wilensky, R.: Robust Hyperlinks: Cheap, Everywhere. In: Proceedings of Digital Documents and Electronic Publishing. LNCS, Springer, Heidelberg (2000)
3. The Kepler Project: http://kepler-project.org/
4. The Cheshire3 Information Framework: http://www.cheshire3.org/
5. The Liverpool VRE project web pages: http://bodoni.lib.liv.ac.uk/VRE/
6. Phelps, T., Wilensky, R.: Robust Intra-document Locations: http://www9.org/w9cdrom/312/312.html

NSDL MatDL: Adding Context to Bridge Materials e-Research and e-Education

Laura Bartolo[1], Cathy Lowe[1], Dean Krafft[2], and Robert Tandy[3]

[1] College of Arts and Sciences, Kent State University, 032 SRB,
Kent OH, 44242-0001 USA
{lbartolo, clowe}@kent.edu
[2] Department of Computer Science, Cornell University, 308 Upson Hall,
Ithaca, NY 14853-7501 USA
dean@cs.cornell.edu
[3] Department of Physics, Yale University,
New Haven, CT 06511 USA
robert.tandy@yale.edu

Abstract. The National Science Digital Library (NSDL) Materials Digital Library Pathway (MatDL) has implemented an information infrastructure to disseminate government funded research results and to provide content as well as services to support the integration of research and education in materials. This poster describes how we are integrating a digital repository into open-source collaborative tools, such as wikis, to support users in materials research and education as well as interactions between the two areas. A search results plug-in for MediaWiki has been developed to display relevant search results from the MatDL repository in the Soft Matter Wiki established and developed by MatDL and its partners. Collaborative work with the NSDL Core Integration team at Cornell University is also in progress to enable information transfer in the opposite direction, from a wiki to a repository.

Keywords: Materials Science, wiki, plug-in.

1 Introduction

The National Science Digital Library (NSDL) provides a dynamic, organized point of access to science, technology, engineering, and mathematics (STEM) education and research resources as well as access to services and tools that enhance the use of this content in a variety of contexts [1]. The NSDL Materials Digital Library Pathway (MatDL) is a consortium of organizations establishing an information infrastructure and assuming stewardship of significant content and services to support the integration of education and research in materials science (MS) [2].

MatDL provides the MS community with an open-source information infrastructure offering a variety services. This poster focuses on two of MatDL's services: the Repository (http://matdl.org) which uses the Fez content management system (http://www.library.uq.edu.au/escholarship/), a web front-end built on the Fedora (http://fedora.info) digital repository middleware; and the Soft Matter Wiki

L. Kovács, N. Fuhr, and C. Meghini (Eds.): ECDL 2007, LNCS 4675, pp. 499–500, 2007.

(http://matdl.org/matdlwiki), based on open-source MediaWiki (http://mediawiki.org) software. The Wiki enables communication and dissemination within the sub-domain of soft matter and facilitates expert community-driven development [3] of the publicly accessible site, ensuring that users have access to trustworthy, authoritative scientific information. Both services are stand-alone, but each contains resources relevant to the other service, making the development of a system of communication between installations a priority for MatDL. Currently, information regarding relevant research and teaching resources in the MatDL Repository is fed, via plug-in, into Soft Matter Wiki pages, providing additional, up-to-date context across topics bridging e-research and e-education.

2 Results and Discussion

A Fez search results plug-in has been developed for MediaWiki by extending its markup to include a <fez> tag, which is invoked with parameters indicating what to search for in the MatDL Repository and how to display results. Search results may be included on any MediaWiki page. Any desired search term can be used inside the <fez> tag and its arguments can be modified to customize aspects of the display, such as the maximum number of search results and whether or not to associate thumbnail images with each search result. Soft Matter Wiki users may choose to link directly to the resource in the MatDL Repository from individual search result titles or to link to the full search results list in the Repository.

MatDL is beginning to integrate its services both by bringing relevant results from the MatDL Repository into the Soft Matter Wiki, and by making resources originating in the wiki available in the repository. The NSDL Core Integration (CI) team at Cornell University is currently designing OurNSDL, also built on MediaWiki. OurNSDL will provide the ability to add newly created wiki pages along with simple metadata to a Fedora-based repository. MatDL is a co-designer and early adopter of the OurNSDL toolset, which will enable information flow from the Soft Matter Wiki into the MatDL and NSDL repositories.

Acknowledgments. This material is based upon work supported by the National Science Foundation under Grant Nos. DUE-0532831, DUE-0227648 and DUE-0424671. Any opinions, findings, and conclusions or recommendations expressed in this material are those of the authors and do not necessarily reflect the views of NSF.

References

1. Zia, L.: The NSF National Science, Technology, Engineering, and Mathematics Education Digital Library (NSDL) Program. D-Lib Magazine 8, 11 (2002)
2. Bartolo, L., Lowe, C., Sadoway, D., Powell, A., Glotzer, S.: NSDL MatDL: Exploring Digital Library Roles. D-Lib Magazine 11, 3 (2005)
3. Butler, D.: Experts Plan to Reclaim the Web for Pop Science. Nature 439(2), 516–517 (2006)

A Framework for the Generation of Transformation Templates

Manuel Llavador and José H. Canós

Dep. of Computer Science (DSIC)
Technical University of Valencia
Camino Vera s/n, 46022, Valencia, Spain
+34 963 87 70 00 Ext. 73588
{mllavador, jhcanos}@dsic.upv.es

Abstract. This demo shows a set of tools for managing and performing document transformations. These tools share a common infrastructure consisting on a set of Web Services and programming libraries to define semantic mappings and generate the corresponding transformation template automatically. The framework is currently being used on the Bibshare project to support the conversion between metadata formats, as well as in other domains related to Digital Libraries and Software Engineering.

Keywords: XML, Interoperability, Metadata Schemas, Document Transformation.

1 Introduction

Besides its use in other domains, XML[1] has been particularly successful in the field of Digital Libraries (DLs), specifically to cope with many interoperability problems coming from the heterogeneity of metadata formats. To convert metadata records from one format to another, we just need to have a well-defined transformation function expressed as an XSL transformation template. However, the definition of the transformation function and his implementation as a transformation template is not always easy. As a consequence, there is a clear need for tools that support the conversion definition and implementation processes.

In this demo, we introduce two tools that allow the (semi)automatic generation of XSL templates:

- Given two XML schemas S1 and S2, **XSWebMapper** generates the XSL template that transforms S1-valid documents into S2-valid documents. A typical example is the generation of the transformation template to transform records in a metadata format to records in another format.
- Given an XML schema S, and a language whose syntax is defined by a grammar G, where some non-terminal symbols come from elements of S,

[1] http://www.w3.org/XML

L. Kovács, N. Fuhr, and C. Meghini (Eds.): ECDL 2007, LNCS 4675, pp. 501–504, 2007.

DSLWebMapper obtains the XSL template that transforms S-valid documents into G-valid documents. For instance, it can be used to obtain the SQL database creation script from the XML schema corresponding to a given metadata format.

Although these tools were initially developed for the Bibshare project [1], they are general purpose tools as it corresponds to a generic language such as XML. Since both tools are implemented as Web applications, their software and hardware requirements are not restrictive. Section 2 describes the problem and the solution. Sections 3 present examples of XSWebMapper and DSLWebMapper use cases.

2 The Problem and a Solution

Sometimes, the definition of a transformation function is not easy; for instance, when source or target schemas are not well known by the user, or when the mappings between elements of the source and target schemas are not trivial. In other cases, its implementation as a transformation template is not easy because users do not know the template definition language.

We think that these two difficulties can be overcome by following a semantic approach for the definition of the transformation function, supported by graphical metaphors and following an automatic approach for the generation of the transformation templates. The main contribution of this work is the definition and implementation of a transformation framework based on:

- The graphical definition of transformation functions by the set of relationships between semantic concepts in source and target schemas. By semantic concepts we mean the set of different meanings of the data in the documents. Examples of semantic concepts in a bibliographic metadata format are *title*, *name* or *publisher;*.The meaning of several instances of data can be described by the same concept (for example the title of an article and the title of a book). Thus, every semantic concept is associated with the set of data binding or set of path expressions to the data that it describes.
- The automatic generation of the transformation templates from its transformation function definitions. This is done by automatic compilation techniques.

The main advantage of this approach is that users focus on the definition of the transformation in a more abstract way, therefore reducing implementation errors, enabling reusability, and making the definition of the transformation independent of the implementation. Furthermore, the automatic generation of the implementation enables an incremental description of the transformation function verifying that the solution is correct.

The transformation framework is composed of three web services and two programming libraries [2]:

- *XSDInferer* obtains the metadata schema of the source and target documents.
- *XPathInferer* identifies the semantic concepts and the data bindings of the source and target XML schemas.

- *XSLGenerator* takes as input the schemas and the semantic relationships and returns the corresponding XSL template that implements the transformation.
- *XMapBuilder.dll* and *Grammar.dll* implement the user interface of the XSWebMapper and DSLWebMapper, respectively, for the definition of the semantic relationships and the corresponding persistence classes.

The architecture of the framework and the process of definition of a transformation is presented in Fig. 1.

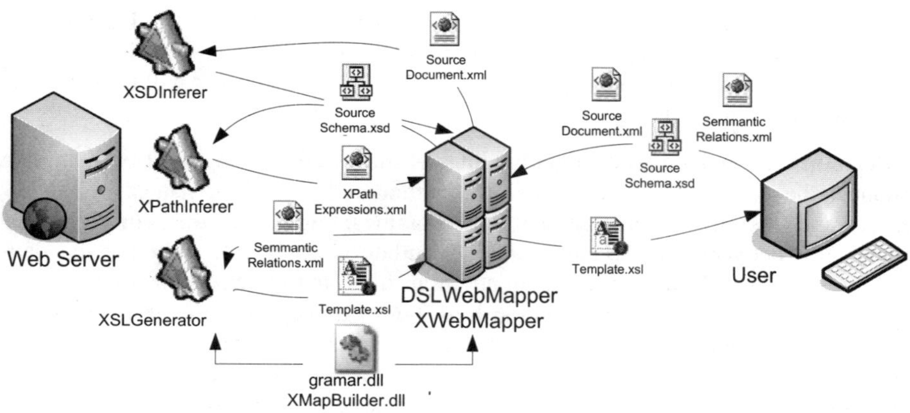

Fig. 1. Architecture of the framework and data flow during the generation of an XSL template that implements a transformation between two documents

3 XSWebMapper and DSLXSMapper Use Cases: Transformation Template from MODS to Simple Dublin Core and SQL Script

As an example of use of XSMapper, let us suppose we need to convert bibliographic records in MODS[2] to Simple Dublin Core[3] (DC). As we said above, the transformation template is generated automatically from the definition of the relationships between source and target schema semantic concepts. Hence, the first step in the process is the inference of the semantic concepts and the data bindings for both schemas. This task is done by the XPathInferer from the MODS and Simple Dublin Core XSD Schemas[4,5]. In cases where a XML schema is not available, XSDInferer generates it automatically from a sample document.

Next, the user defines the semantic relationships by using XSMapper that shows to the user the set of source and target concepts and data bindings and allows he or she to establish three kinds of relationships between them:

---

[2] http://www.loc.gov/standards/mods/

[3] http://dublincore.org/schemas/xmls/

[4] http://www.loc.gov/standards/mods/v3/mods-3-3-draft-for-final-review-april-13.xsd

[5] http://dublincore.org/schemas/xmls/simpledc20020312.xsd

- Same Concept: one (or more) source concept is semantically the same as one (or more) target concept. For example, the MODS.topic and DC.subject concepts belong to this category.
- Conversion: one or more source concepts must be converted to be the same as one or more target concepts. The allowed conversions are defined by the conversion functions provided by the transformation template definition language (in this case, the XSLT data conversion functions). For example, the DC.title concept is obtained as the concatenation of MODS.title and MODS.subtitle concepts.
- Constant: one or more target concepts will have a constant value. DC does not include any constant concept, but suppose we include a new DC field to describe the source metadata format, in this case this concept will have MODS as a constant value.

Relations can include all the data bindings of the concepts or a subset of them. For instance, the concept *name* describes the author and the editor names in MODS format and therefore includes two data bindings. However, the same concept relationship between MODS.name and DC.author is applicable only for the data binding of the MODS author name. In addition, filter and selection constructions are provided to define more precise relationships. For example, the name of the author in MODS is the name concept whose roleTerm value is "Creator", therefore the semantic relation described above for the DC.author should be labeled with a where condition that filters those MODS names whose roleTerm values are not "Creator".

Finally, XSLGenerator takes the semantic relationships and generates automatically the corresponding XSL template. This template can be used to convert source schema-valid documents into their corresponding target schema-valid documents.

The main difference between XSWebMapper and DSLWebMapper is that the first generates transformation templates whose target document is an XML, as the example presented above, and the second generates transformation templates whose target document is plain text (e.g. an SQL script). DSLWebMapper follows the same steps described above but replaces the graphical interface with a grammar edition tool that allow users to describe the syntax of the target (in this example the SQL script language for the creation of databases) with five possible elements: Text (constant strings that will be copied to the result document), Concepts (relations between source and target concepts), Rules (descriptions of the non-terminals of the grammar), and Enumerations (sets of ordered data from source document).

References

1. Canós, J.H., Llavador, M., Solís, C., Ruíz, E.: A Service-Oriented Framework for Bibliography Management. D-Lib Magazine 10(11) (November 2004)
2. Llavador, M., Canós, J.H.: XWebMapper: A Web-based Tool for Transforming XML Documents. In: Gonzalo, J., Thanos, C., Verdejo, M.F., Carrasco, R.C. (eds.) ECDL 2006. LNCS, vol. 4172, Springer, Heidelberg (2006)

MultiMatch – Multilingual/Multimedia Access to Cultural Heritage*

Giuseppe Amato[1], Juan Cigarrán[2], Julio Gonzalo[2], Carol Peters[1], and Pasquale Savino[1]

[1] ISTI-CNR, Area di Ricerca – 56124 Pisa – Italy
{giuseppe.amato, carol.peters, pasquale.savino}@isti.cnr.it
[2] UNED, Madrid, Spain
{juanci, julio}@lsi.uned.es

Abstract. Cultural heritage content is everywhere on the web, in contexts such as digital libraries, audiovisual archives, and portals of museums or galleries, in multiple languages and multiple media. MultiMatch, a 30 month specific targeted research project under the Sixth Framework Programme, plans to develop a multilingual search engine designed specifically for the access, organisation and personalised presentation of cultural heritage digital objects.

1 Research Agenda

Europe's vast collections of unique and exciting cultural heritage (CH) content are an important asset of our society. Much of this information is available in digital form and via the Internet. However, CH objects on the web are generally not found in isolation but as richly connected entities, equipped with very heterogeneous metadata, and with information from a broad spectrum of sources, some with authoritative views and some with highly personal opinions.

What means do users have to access these complex CH objects? How can they explore and interact with them in ways that do justice to the richness of the objects without being overwhelmed? Currently, users interested in accessing CH content - be it for educational, tourist, or economic reasons - are left to discover, interpret, and aggregate material of interest themselves.

The cultural heritage search and navigation facilities that we envisage would present users with a composite picture of complex CH objects. For instance, in reply to a request for information on Van Gogh, the MultiMatch engine could present certified information from multiple museums around Europe, in multiple languages, complementing this with pointers to Van Gogh's contemporaries, links to exhibitions and reviews, etc. The need to provide users in the CH domain

* Work partially supported by the European Community under the Information Society Technologies (IST) programme of the 6th FP for RTD - project MultiMatch contract IST 033104. The authors are solely responsible for the content of this paper. It does not represent the opinion of the EC and the EC is not responsible for any use that might be made of data appearing therein.

L. Kovács, N. Fuhr, and C. Meghini (Eds.): ECDL 2007, LNCS 4675, pp. 505–508, 2007.

with this kind of result poses a number of scientific challenges for information retrieval research in areas as diverse as web crawling, multilingual and multimedia access [2], semantic processing [3], and presentation design. The MultiMatch research agenda should make significant developments in each of these areas in order to arrive at a proof-of-concept implementation of a user-centered search and navigation engine for cultural heritage content.

2 Expected Results and System Functionality

Focused Search Engine. MultiMatch aims to take a significant leap forward from today's vertical search engines by offering "complex object retrieval" through a combination of focused crawling and semantic enrichment that exploits the vast amounts of metadata available in the cultural heritage domain, presenting both certified and non-certified information together (while clearly distinguishing one from the other).

Multilingual/multimedia indexing. Instead of returning isolated documents, MultiMatch will provide complex search results that put documents of various media types (text, audio, image, video, or mixed-content) and in multiple languages into context. This generates special challenges for indexing.

Information extraction and classification. MultiMatch will allow users to interpret the wealth of CH information by presenting objects not as isolated individual items, but with links to related context. A range of classifications, as well as various links to reviews, reports, and general background knowledge, will be provided.

Multilingual/multimedia information retrieval. Recent years have seen a significant increase in the investigation of information retrieval techniques for multimedia and multilingual document collections. Unfortunately, so far, there has been little transfer of research advances to real world applications. MultiMatch aims at bridging this gap. A major challenge will be to merge results from queries on language-dependent (text, speech) and language-independent material (video, image) [1].

User-centred interaction. Content-based access (e.g. video and image retrieval by visual content) still faces significant barriers when attempting to create truly effective and comprehensive retrieval with respect to user needs. The MultiMatch user interface will integrate automatic techniques for low level feature extraction and automatic concept classification. A key research problem for MultiMatch will be enabling the user to adequately formulate their query using the language of their choice and specifying both low-level and high-level multimedia features [5].

The main functionality of MultiMatch has been defined according to the user requirements collected during the first stage of the project [4]. The MultiMatch prototype is expected to offer powerful and flexible access to Cultural Heritage information available on-line, both on the generic Web as well as in specialized digital libraries or portals. The main user needs are related to (i) the quality of retrieved items – they must be relevant to the user request, and provided by *certified* sources – (ii) easy formulation of the user request, and (iii) easy visualization and aggregation of retrieved items.

The MultiMatch Search Engine will enable the user to retrieve cultural objects through different modalities:

- The simplest one is a traditional *free text* search. This search mode is similar to that provided by general purpose search engines, such as Google, with the difference that MultiMatch is expected to provide more precise results – since information is acquired from selected sources containing Cultural Heritage data – and with support for multilingual searches. This means that the user can formulate queries in a given language and retrieve results in one or all languages covered by the prototype (according to his/her preferences).
- Metadata based searches. The user will select one of the available indexes built for a specific metadata field – initially only *creators* and *creations* – and can specify the value of the metadata field (e.g. the *creator's name*) plus possible additional terms.
- A browsing capability will allow users to navigate the MultiMatch collection using a web directory-like structure based on the MultiMatch ontology.

Finally, MultiMatch will support multimedia searches, based on similarity matching and on automatic information extraction techniques.

From the results of the expert users survey we can conclude that, on average, CH professionals tend to classify searches for information about creators (authors, artists, sculptors, composers, etc.) and creations (works of art and masterpieces) as their most common search tasks. Therefore, in MultiMatch we have initially decided to focus on two types of specialized searches for creators and creations, although specialized searches focused on other relevant categories will also be considered.

MultiMatch searches can be made at three main levels of interaction: (i) Default search mode, (ii) Specialized search mode, and (iii) Composite search mode.

The simplest search mode is the *default* MultiMatch search level. This is provided for generic users, with a limited knowledge of MultiMatch system capabilities, or with very general search needs. In this case, no assumption is made on the user query, and MultiMatch retrieves information from all indexed material. In this way, given a general query, MultiMatch will retrieve all the cultural objects, web pages and multimedia content that best suit the query. Merging, ranking and classification of these results will be also performed by the system. This level of interaction involves the retrieval of not only cultural objects (i.e. creators and creations) but also web pages, images and videos related to the query.

Users with a more precise knowledge of MultiMatch system functionality, and with specific search needs, may use one of the *specialized* interaction levels available. These allow the user to query MultiMatch specific search services (for instance, video search, image search, etc.) and retrieve all the relevant information available via the selected search service. In this way, MultiMatch will include standalone image, video and metadata-based searches, each with its own search fields, display and refinement options. It will also include a set of browsing capabilities to explore MultiMatch content. This interaction level will allow the user to use specific query services, such as metadata-based search, image and video search or browsing.

The general idea of metadata based search is that, for a given type of cultural entity (for instance, creators), the whole collection of web pages can be used to mine information about each particular entity that is not present in the individual documents. For instance, the set of all documents talking about Van Gogh can be used to create a profile of the terms most closely associated (i.e. co-occurring more frequently) with Van Gogh. This profile can be subsequently used to compare Van Gogh with other creators. The implication is that for each type of entity considered, MultiMatch must have an index containing such descriptions.

The *composite search mode* supports queries where multiple elements can be combined. For example, it will be possible to search using the metadata fields associated with each document, but combining this restriction with free text and/or image similarity searches.

3 Conclusion

The MultiMatch project, funded by the European Commission under FP6 (Sixth Framework Programme), began in May 2006 and will finish in November 2008. A preliminary version of the MultiMatch search engine will be available in October 2007, while the final version is expected for October 2008. The consortium comprises eleven partners, representing the relevant research, industrial and application communities. The academic partners are: ISTI-CNR, Pisa, Italy (Coordinators); University of Amsterdam, The Netherlands; LSI-UNED, Madrid, Spain; University of Geneva, Switzerland; University of Sheffield, UK; Dublin City University, Ireland. Industrial members of the consortium are OCLC PICA, UK, and WIND, Italy. The cultural heritage domain is represented by Alinari, Italy, Sound & Vision, The Netherlands, and the Biblioteca Virtual Miguel de Cervantes, Spain.

More details on the project can be found at http://www.multimatch.org/.

References

1. Amato, G., Gennaro, C., Rabitti, F., Savino, P.: Milos: A multimedia content management system for digital library applications. In: Heery, R., Lyon, L. (eds.) ECDL 2004. LNCS, vol. 3232, pp. 14–25. Springer, Heidelberg (2004)
2. Chakrabarti, S., van den Berg, M., Dom, B.: Focused crawling: A new approach to topic-specific web resource discovery. Computer Networks 31, 1623–1640 (1999)
3. Ciravegna, F., Chapman, S., Dingli, A., Wilks, Y.: Learning to harvest information for the semantic web. In: 1st European Semantic Web Symposium, Heraklion, Greece (2004)
4. Minelli, S.H., et al.: User requirements analysis. Technical Report D1.2, MultiMatch Project, Internal project deliverable (restricted distribution) (2006)
5. Petrelli, D., Levin, S., Beaulieu, M., Sanderson, M.: Which user interaction for cross-language information retrieval? design issues and reflections. J. Am. Soc. Inf. Sci. Technol. 57(5), 709–722 (2006)

The Future of Large-Scale Evaluation Campaigns for Information Retrieval in Europe

Maristella Agosti[1], Giorgio Maria Di Nunzio[1], Nicola Ferro[1], Donna Harman[2], and Carol Peters[3]

[1] Department of Information Engineering, University of Padua, Italy
{agosti, dinunzio, ferro}@dei.unipd.it
[2] National Institute of Standards and Technology, USA
donna.harman@nist.gov
[3] ISTI-CNR, Area di Ricerca – 56124 Pisa – Italy
carol.peters@isti.cnr.it

Abstract. A Workshop on "The Future of Large-scale Evaluation Campaigns" was organised jointly by the University of Padua and the DELOS Network of Excellence and held in Padua, Italy, March 2007. The aim was to perform a critical assessment of the scientific results of such initiatives and to formulate recommendations for the future. This poster summarises the outcome of the discussion with respect to the major European activity in this area: the Cross Language Evaluation Forum.

1 Motivations for the Workshop

Since its beginnings, the DELOS Network of Excellence[1] has recognised the importance of R&D in the area of multilingual information access (MLIA) and has supported the activities of the Cross Language Evaluation Forum (CLEF).

CLEF began life as a track for cross-language system evaluation within the Text REtrieval Conference (TREC) series[2] but was launched as a separate European activity in 2000 with the goal of promoting the development of MLIA functionality, producing test collections for system benchmarking, and last but not least creating a multidisciplinary research community around this domain.

A major aim of a workshop held in Padua in March 2007 was to assess the achievements of CLEF over the years, and to discuss directions for an eventual continuation under FP7. Commonalities and differences between CLEF and TREC were also examined. This poster aims at stimulating further discussion and getting feedback on the future of CLEF.

---

[1] DELOS is currently running under the European Commission's Sixth Framework programme (FP6), see http://www.delos.info/

[2] TREC is the major initiative for information retrieval system evaluation in North America, see http://trec.nist.gov/

L. Kovács, N. Fuhr, and C. Meghini (Eds.): ECDL 2007, LNCS 4675, pp. 509–512, 2007.

2 Achievements of CLEF

When CLEF first started, the few existing cross-language information systems generally handled only two languages, one of which was normally English, and ran only for textual document retrieval. The long-term goal of CLEF has thus been to promote the development of truly multilingual, multimodal systems via a systematic study of the requirements of digital libraries and other globally distributed information repositories, and the design of tasks that meet these needs. Over the years, we have gradually introduced new tracks and more complex tasks to assess free-text and domain-specific cross-language retrieval, multiple language question answering, cross-language retrieval for speech and for image collections, multilingual retrieval of web documents, and cross-language geographic retrieval. For complete details of the CLEF 2000 - 2007 agendas, see the website at `http://www.clef-campaign.org/`.

From discussions at the Padua workshop, it was established that the main achievements of CLEF over the years can be summarised in the following points:

- implementation of a powerful and flexible technical infrastructure including data curation functionality;
- promotion of research in previously unexplored areas, such as cross-language question answering, image and geographic information retrieval;
- improvement in performance for cross-language text retrieval systems (from 50% of monolingual retrieval in 2000 to at least 85% in 2006);
- quantitative and qualitative evidence with respect to user interaction and best practice in cross-language system development;
- creation of important, reusable test collections for system benchmarking, covering 12 languages and three media (text, speech and image);
- building of a strong, multidisciplinary research community (94 groups from 5 continents submitted results in 2006).

Furthermore, CLEF evaluations have provided qualitative and quantitative evidence along the years as to which methods give the best results in certain key areas, such as multilingual indexing, query translation, resolution of translation ambiguity, results merging. For a more detailed assessment of CLEF, see [1].

It was agreed that CLEF has been crucial in stimulating research in multilingual IR not only in Europe, impacting both the information retrieval and the digital library research areas.

3 Recommendations for the Future

However, despite these achievements, it was recognised by the participants at the workshop that future editions of CLEF should not only continue to support annual system evaluation campaigns with tracks and tasks designed to stimulate R&D in the MLIA domain but should also (i) develop the facilities to further exploit the results of these campaigns by promoting in-depth studies and analyses of the outcomes, (ii) focus on areas of research previously ignored by CLEF mainly due to lack of resources, (iii) encourage the dissemination and technology transfer of the results obtained to the European digital library and related communities through the specification of best practices in MLIA system development.

With respect to the first point, it is recognised that the experimental data produced during an evaluation campaign are valuable scientific data, and as a consequence, should be archived, enriched, and curated in order to ensure their future accessibility and re-use. Nevertheless, current methodologies do not imply any particular coordination or synchronization between the basic scientific data and the analyses on them, which are treated as almost separate items. Researchers would greatly benefit from an integrated vision of data plus analyses provided by means of a scientific digital library system, where access to a scientific data item could also offer the possibility of retrieving all the analyses and interpretations on it [2].

As CLEF is run almost entirely as a voluntary exercise it is not always easy to find the necessary resources to follow a given line of action. However, if possible, we believe that efforts in the near future should be concentrated in the following key research areas:

- user modelling, e.g. what are the requirements of different classes of users when querying multilingual information sources;
- language-specific experimentation, e.g. looking at differences across languages in order to derive best practices for each language, best practices for component development and best practices for MLIA systems as a whole;
- results presentation, e.g. how can results be presented in the most useful and comprehensible way to the user.

We also need to identify new metrics specifically designed and tuned for use in a multilingual context and we need to study new methods for creating test collections quickly and efficiently [3]. So far, most CLEF evaluation methodologies have tended to adapt and reuse evaluation methodologies already experimented at TREC. We must move beyond topic-based relevance, absolute relevance of documents in isolation and mean average precision to include multi-valued criteria, such as diversity, novelty, authority, recency, and to address tasks which still do not have well-developed evaluation methodologies. In particular, we need to work on establishing realistic and scientifically well-grounded evaluation methodologies for interactive MLIA experiments and user studies [4].

In fact, a criticism made of CLEF at the workshop is that so far we have focussed too much on measuring overall system performance according to ranked lists of results while neglecting many other important aspects. As mentioned above, one area that needs to be addressed in far greater depth is that of user-centred evaluation; we need to know whether the system performance actually satisfies the user expectations? For this reason, we believe that, in the future the interactive track should be extended and more attention given to aspects involving user satisfaction issues. One question is whether average precision is really the best metric from the user viewpoint. In CLEF 2007, new metrics have been introduced into the ad-hoc track in order to favour systems that achieve a high precision of correct responses in the first ten results returned - rather than a good average precision. This is a user-oriented measure and we believe makes more sense in the Internet dominated world.

Another issue regards system response times. CLEF 2006 took a first step in this direction with the organization of a real-time exercise as part of the question-answering track. In the end, the question was whether the best multilingual question answering system was the fastest system or the most accurate one and, given the choice, would the user prefer a faster system over a slightly less accurate but slower one.

An important point made at the workshop was that there is still very little take-up of MLIA functionality by the market. In fact, although CLEF has done much to promote the development of multilingual IR systems, so far the focus has been on building and testing research prototypes rather than developing fully operational systems. One of the challenges that CLEF must face in the near future is how to best transfer the research results to the market place. In our opinion, if the gap between academic excellence and commercial adoption of MLIA technology is to be bridged, we need to extend the current CLEF formula in order to give application communities the possibility to benefit from the CLEF evaluation infrastructure without the need to participate in academic exercises that may be irrelevant to their current needs. We feel that CLEF should introduce an application support structure aimed at encouraging take-up of the technologies tested and optimized within the context of the evaluation exercises. This structure would provide tools, resources, best practice guidelines and consulting services to applications or industries that need to include multilingual functionality within a service or product.

In summary, CLEF should function as a center of competence for European multilingual information retrieval system research, development, implementation, and related activities.

Acknowledgements

The work reported in this paper has been partially supported by the DELOS Network of Excellence on Digital Libraries, in the Information Society Technologies (IST) Program of the European Commission (Contract G038-507618).

References

1. Agosti, M., Di Nunzio, G.M., Ferro, N., Peters, C.: CLEF: Ongoing Activities and Plans for the Future. In: Proc. 6th NTCIR Workshop Meeting on Evaluation of Information Access Technologies: Information Retrieval, Question Answering and Cross-Lingual Information Access, NII, Tokyo, Japan, pp. 493–504 (2007)
2. Agosti, M., Di Nunzio, G.M., Ferro, N.: A Proposal to Extend and Enrich the Scientific Data Curation of Evaluation Campaigns. In: Proc. 1st International Workshop on Evaluating Information Access (EVIA 2007), NII, Tokyo, Japan, pp. 62–73 (2007)
3. Sanderson, M., Joho, H.: Forming Test Collections with No System Pooling. In: Proc. 27th Annual International ACM SIGIR Conference on Research and Development in Information Retrieval (SIGIR 2004), pp. 33–40. ACM Press, New York (2004)
4. Ingwersen, P., Järvelin, K.: The Turn: Integration of Information Seeking and Retrieval in Context. Springer, Heidelberg (2005)

Digital 101: Public Exhibition System of the National Digital Archives Program, Taiwan

Ku-Lun Huang and Hsiang-An Wang

Institute of Information Science, Academia Sinica, Taipei, 115, Taiwan
{kulun, sawang}@iis.sinica.edu.tw

Abstract. Since the establishment of the National Digital Archives Program (NDAP), Taiwan in 2002, the five divisions and their accompanying projects have generated a huge amount of digital materials. The diverse content is available for multiple purposes, such as research, value-added applications and educational projects. The goal is allow the public to explore the achievements of NDAP in user-friendly ways. Digital 101, which is also called the Public Exhibit System (PES), serves to connect various groups interested in Taiwan's rich cultural heritage.

PES incorporates artistic, creative & interactive user interfaces and popular methods that allow the public to utilize the content of the NDAP. Through collaboration with local artists, PES provides special exhibits and thematic image galleries about Taiwan's rich culture. It is expected to become a gateway worldwide.

Keywords: Digital 101, Digital Archive, Public Exhibit System.

1 Article

The National Digital Archives Program (NDAP) [2], which was established in 2002, has digitized many cultural treasures and constructed hundreds of archive databases. To make these digital resources easily accessible to people in Taiwan and abroad, Digital 101 [1], which is also called the Public Exhibition System, was launched in 2005.

The main purpose of PES is to introduce the public to the NDAP. The objective of PES is two fold: "public exhibition" and "achievement gathering." To achieve these objectives, the following six functions have been implemented:

1. Thematic Image Gallery: The high-quality digital images collected from various organizations have been classified into the following four categories for exhibition: Chinese Treasuries, Cultural Taiwan, Ecology, and Oceania. A 'search' function is available to simplify usage. Each image can also be used as wallpaper and as a puzzle game by users.
2. Collection Catalog: This catalog, in conjunction with the Union Catalog [4], helps users browse collections according to the Content, Timeline and Geography, and link to the website and database of each content provider [3].
3. Special Exhibits: Special items of interest are selected for display by topic.

L. Kovács, N. Fuhr, and C. Meghini (Eds.): ECDL 2007, LNCS 4675, pp. 513–514, 2007.

4. System Directory: The NDAP contains various systems which are listed in the directory.
5. Teacher Center: This function allows elementary and junior high school teachers to incorporate the digital contents and related resources of the NDAP into their teaching programs.
6. Licensing & Value-added technologies: This function allows content holders to access newly developed, value-added technologies to increase their content demand. It also introduces companies to the available digital contents and opportunities for commercialization.

PES contains various types of resources, such as historical collections, archives, and information about the ecology of Taiwan and the world. It continues to accumulate immensely valuable cultural assets. In the future, more organizations/collections will be recruited to join PES. Furthermore PES will focus on selecting and presenting special exhibits via creative, interactive user interfaces to attract more users.

Acknowledgements. This research was supported in part by the National Science Council of Taiwan under NSC Grants: NSC95-2422-H-001-024, NSC96-2422-H-001-001.

References

1. Digital 101, Taiwan, http://digital101.ndap.org.tw
2. National Digital Archives Program (NDAP), Taiwan, http://www.ndap.org.tw/index_en.php
3. Tsai, Y.T., Chang, I.C.: Facilitating Resource Utilization in Union Catalog Systems. In: Proceedings of the 8th International Conference of Asian Digital Libraries, Bangkok, Thailand, pp. 486–488 (2005)
4. Union Catalog, http://catalog.ndap.org.tw

aScience: A Thematic Network on Speech and Tactile Accessibility to Scientific Digital Resources

Cristian Bernareggi and Gian Carlo Dalto

Università degli Studi di Milano – Biblioteca di Informatica
Via Comelico 39, 20122 Milano - Italy
cristian.bernareggi@unimi.it

Abstract. At present, digital scientific resources can be hardly read by visually impaired people. The systems to retrieve and download documents in digital libraries can be easily used also through speech and tactile assistive technologies. The main problems concern the digital formats employed to store documents. Therefore, visually impaired readers often find the right document, but they cannot read it. That often affects the learning process especially at university. In order to contribute to the preparation of guidelines to provide accessible digital scientific resources and to widespread best practices and best experiences achieved by university libraries and support services, the thematic network aScience was established. It is a two years project supported by the European Union eContentPlus Programme. The web portal www.ascience.eu delivers information about the thematic network activities and it will distribute sample documents of digital scientific literature accessible through speech and tactile assistive technologies.

1 The Problem

Digital scientific resources are usually delivered in electronic formats which can be hardly accessed by visually impaired readers. The main problems concern how mathematical expressions can be explored and understood and how graphical representations can be described in alternative formats (e.g. by embossing them on paper through tactile embossers). Most of the formats widely used to store scientific resources (e.g. PostScript files) do not enable software agents to easily extract the document structure to the extent of elements which constitute a mathematical expression (e.g. numerator, denominator, parenthesis structure, etc.). This high level of granularity is indispensable to generate high quality and meaningful speech descriptions of mathematical expressions. Furthermore, since there exists many national mathematical Braille codes, the Braille representation has to be generated according to the national rules which require extracting and rearranging specific structural elements. As for graphical representations, the possibility for software agents to process metadata linked to specific parts of the images, can make possible the production of alternative descriptions mainly based on the combination of tactile embossing and audio messages.

L. Kovács, N. Fuhr, and C. Meghini (Eds.): ECDL 2007, LNCS 4675, pp. 515–517, 2007.

2 Methodology

The methodology proposed to address the problem of accessibility to scientific resources by visually impaired university students is based on the establishment of the aScience thematic network on science accessibility by visually impaired students. The founding consortium is made up of institutions with long experience in accessibility issues: the co-ordinating Universita' degli Studi di Milano, Biblioteca di Informatica (Italy), the University of Linz, Institute Integriert Studieren (Austria), the Katholieke University Leuven (Belgium), the Comenius University, faculty of Mathematics, physics and informatics (Slovakia), the Union of the Blind in Verona (Italy) and the Pierre et Marie Curie Université (France). At first the network aims to share and make cross-country reusable working practices proven to be effective and efficient in the national institutions. At the same time emerging technologies are experimented, assessed and documented in order to come to the preparation of guidelines strongly related to the technological evolution. Furthermore, collaboration actions will be undertaken to involve interested institutions.

3 Sketching the Accessibility Solutions

As mentioned above, high level granularity in the document format is necessary to produce high quality speech and Braille output. Actually, software agents which process the document to produce the suitable output have to access to the parts making up the document in order to extract the mutual relations necessary for Braille and speech rendering. Therefore, only if the document is highly structured all of the parts needed by software agents can be retrieved, mutually related and rendered. The development line which has been analysed up to now is based on the delivery of scientific learning resources through the web. Web pages produced in compliance with the Web Content Accessibility Guidelines developed by the World Wide Web Consortium can be accessed by speech and Braille assistive devices. Nevertheless these guidelines do not focus on how to design web pages embedding mathematical content. Up to recently, mathematical expressions have been embedded in web pages as images. Images cannot be rendered by mainstream assistive technologies (e.g. screen reader and Braille display), consequently visually impaired people cannot read the content conveyed through graphical representations. Furthermore, even if a verbal description of the expression is provided together with the image (e.g. as alternate text or as a long description), it is often not enough to improve understanding because of the inherent structural complexity of many mathematical expressions. Speech and Braille screen readers should be enabled to provide several exploration techniques according to the complexity of the expression and to the exploration style of the visually impaired reader. Indeed, there exist many differences among visually impaired people. Those readers who can rely on residual sight usually read through magnification programs. Instead, totally blind readers usually employ Braille for reading. Both visually impaired and totally blind readers often rely exclusively on speech output or on magnification tools or Braille in conjunction with speech output. At present there exist many national mathematical Braille codes all over the world and the rules to vocally render a mathematical expression are different from country to country according to the national language. Therefore, what is needed is a markup language able to describe mathematical expressions, which can be embedded in web pages and rendered client side according to the user needs (e.g. Braille code, speech output, assistive device, etc.). These features can be achieved by using MathML markup language. Mathematical expressions can be embedded through MathML markup language so that software agents are enabled to access the expression structure thus producing high quality speech and Braille output [1] and implementing exploration strategies suitable for the reader's cognitive style. [2] Some emerging assistive tools (speech readers, Braille converters, etc.) to exploit MathML are available. Anyway, many extensions are necessary especially as for combination of national Braille codes and speech rendering of mathematical expressions in national languages. The aScience network will assess some of these emerging tools and document their use for reading scientific resources in educational contexts.

References

1. Soifer, N.: MathPlayer: web-based math accessibility. In: ASSETS05, pp. 204–205. ACM Press, New York (2005)
2. Schweikhardt, W., Bernareggi, C., Jessel, N., Encelle, B., Gut, M.: LAMBDA: a European System to access mathematics with Braille and audio synthesis. In: Miesenberger, K., Klaus, J., Zagler, W., Karshmer, A.I. (eds.) ICCHP 2006. LNCS, vol. 4061, pp. 1223–1230. Springer, Heidelberg (2006)

PROBADO – A Generic Repository Integration Framework

Harald Krottmaier[1], Frank Kurth[2], Thorsten Steenweg[3], Hans-Jürgen Appelrath[3], and Dieter Fellner[1]

[1] Graz, University of Technology
Inffeldgasse 16c, 8010 Graz, Austria
{h.krottmaier,d.fellner}@cgv.tugraz.at
[2] University of Bonn
Römerstraße 164, 53117 Bonn, Germany
frank@iai.uni-bonn.de
[3] OFFIS – Institute for Information Technology
Escherweg 2, 26121 Oldenburg, Germany
{thorsten.steenweg,appelrath}@offis.de

Abstract. The number of newly generated multimedia documents (e.g. music, e-learning material, or 3D-graphics) increases year by year. Today, the workflow in digital libraries focuses on textual documents only. Hence, considering content-based retrieval tasks, multimedia documents are not analyzed and indexed sufficiently. To facilitate content-based retrieval and browsing, it is necessary to introduce recent techniques for multimedia document processing into the workflow of nowadays digital libraries. In this short paper, we introduce the PROBADO-framework which will (a) integrate different types of content-repositories – each one specialized for a specific multimedia domain – into one seamless system, and (b) will add features available in text-based digital libraries (such as automatic annotation, full-text retrieval, or recommender services) to non-textual documents. Existing libraries will benefit from the framework since it extends existing technology for handling textual documents with features for dealing with the non-textual domain.

1 Introduction

Textual documents are very well integrated in the workflow of existing libraries. They are automatically indexed, metadata is almost automatically attached to these documents, and user interfaces are available for retrieving and working with them. However, multimedia documents stored in existing libraries suffer from the following problems: content is not indexed, it is still very difficult to retrieve these documents using well-known techniques (such as query-by-example), and no common tools are available to work with them.

It is the goal of the PROBADO project to make it as easy as possible for librarians and end-users to access and work with multimedia documents in real world digital libraries. To this end, PROBADO provides a tool set for content-based indexing, retrieval, and use of non-textual (or *general*) documents.

L. Kovács, N. Fuhr, and C. Meghini (Eds.): ECDL 2007, LNCS 4675, pp. 518–521, 2007.

2 Requirements and Assumptions

Nowadays, multimedia documents are stored in different types of *repositories* and are generally accessible via different types of interfaces and protocols. Repositories also attach some metadata (in e.g. Dublin Core format) to the content. As librarians want to provide stable and long-term access to content, almost all such repositories are hosted and maintained at the libraries themselves. Several different repositories for specific subject areas (e.g. large music-collections) already exist. However, there is no seamless integration of these repositories, no single point of user access, and no common "content-based query language".

To prove the design and functionality of a generic repository integration framework, PROBADO in its first project phase considers three particular but frequently used document classes: (1) music-documents, (2) e-learning material, and (3) 3D-documents. However, as one main focus of PROBADO is on developing *generic* tools, infrastructure, and interfaces for integrating repositories of arbitrary document types, repositories for other document types (e.g. video or images) may be easily integrated at a later time. Concerning retrieval functionality, users of the PROBADO framework are enabled to retrieve documents using standard text-based interfaces as well as specialized interfaces for content-based queries which depend on the particular document type.

It is obvious that types of metadata differ for every type of content. To facilitate cross-domain retrieval, we have identified a set of *core metadata* which can be assigned to most existing document types and which are frequently available in existing document collections. This core set of metadata is used to provide retrieval functionality that is independent of particular document types and follows the example of the Dublin Core metadata elements. Additionally, domain dependent metadata retrieval is possible using an extended search interface depending on the particular repository.

3 PROBADO-Architecture

The proposed architecture of the PROBADO framework is divided into 3 layers, see Figure 1. Communication between the layers is implemented using web services. Therefore it will be possible to expand the functionality as long as the PROBADO protocol is implemented.

The **frontend** (layer 1) is divided into two types. Both are capable of presenting result lists of user queries. The first type is a lightweight web interface for handling textual access methods like searching in the core metadata. Secondly, there are domain specific query clients, where each domain provides specialized interfaces for posing content-based queries. Examples are a query-by-humming interface for music retrieval or a complex sketch-based interface for searching in 3D-document collections.

The **core** (layer 2) is accessible through a well defined SOAP-API. In addition to the core metadata, this layer also contains administrative data about the connected repositories, data on user sessions (such as query results and relevance

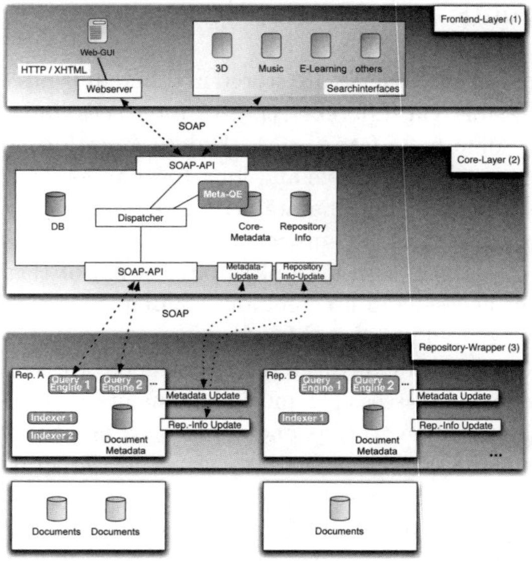

Fig. 1. Architecture of the PROBADO-framework

feedback), and user profiles. The key part of this core layer is the *dispatcher* which either schedules queries directly to the core layers' metadata query engine (for efficiency, the core metadata are mirrored in the core layer of PROBADO), or sends them to the appropriate query engines located at the repositories. Result lists returned by the repositories are aggregated by the dispatcher, previews (e.g. thumbnails) are integrated, and hyperlinks to special functionalities provided by the PROBADO framework (such as an annotation service for non-textual documents) are created.

The **repository wrapper** (layer 3) connects existing *repositories* to the core layer using well-defined SOAP-web services. This layer simplifies access to the different repositories connected to the core layer. Each repository stores document collections of specific subject areas (such as 3D-documents or music) and associated metadata. Access to each repository is provided by a set of *query engines*. Each connected query engine is registered with the core layer and provides a particular search functionality (like query-by-humming for music collections). By this means, the independently running repositories can provide their features to the framework using a wrapper without losing control over their documents.

4 Communication

To establish an open architecture, PROBADO implements communication between the layers using well-defined SOAP-web services as described in Section 3. The first step for a document repository to connect to the core layer is by delivering specific information. A repository may have several query engines for separate types of query operations. For each of its query engines, a repository has to declare a particular *query type* and the accepted *query format*. Whereas the query format specifies what kind of data the engine accepts as an input (e.g. text strings, SQL statements, or MIDI files) the query type describes what kind of retrieval it provides (e.g. full-text retrieval, SQL-based database search, query-by-example for symbolic music). In a second step, each repository has to provide the set of core metadata derived form the internal metadata set, to the core layer.

A user can access the PROBADO framework using either the lightweight web interface or one of the domain specific clients provided by layer 1. Each of these clients directs its queries (containing the query data itself, a session ID, a desired range of query results, and optionally particular repository IDs) to the core layer.

In the core layer, each incoming request is processed by the dispatcher. Queries on the core metadata are passed to the core's local query engine. All other queries are distributed to either the user-specified repositories or to all connected query engines accepting the particular query format as an input (alternatively, all repositories providing a particular query type can be used). Upon receiving a query, each query engine calculates a ranked list of query results.

While collecting the results of the queried repositories, the dispatcher merges these to a single result list. This list constitutes the basis for the response to a user query. It contains specific details for each matching document, particularly a document ID, rank, title, description, accessibility information, context information, document type, and associated links. Furthermore, global information for each query like the total number of results, the range of results, the session ID, the query data itself, and IDs of involved repositories are stored.

When getting a response the fontend is responsible for presenting the result list in an appropriate format. Again there are the standard web interface for a basic display of the results (default) as well as the specialized client applications for creating complex representations (e.g. playback of audiovisual content). Regarding the result list a user has different options. Beside the details page available for each match, PROBADO provides a document preview.

Acknowledgment

The PROBADO project started in February 2006 and is being conducted by the University of Bonn, Graz University of Technology, and the OFFIS Institute for Information Technology in Oldenburg, as well as by the German National Library of Science and Technology in Hannover and the Bavarian State Library in Munich. Currently, only parts of the architecture are implemented. A prototype will be available for public use in mid 2008. The system will be available at `http://www.probado.de`. PROBADO is founded by the German Research Foundation (554975 (1) Oldenburg, BIB48 OLof 01-02) and has a tentative duration of five years.

VCenter: A Digital Video Broadcast System of NDAP Taiwan

Hsiang-An Wang[1,2], Chih-Yi Chiu[1], and Yu-Zheng Wang[1]

[1] Institute of Information Science, Academia Sinica, Taipei, 115, Taiwan
[2] Department of Computer Science and Information Engineering, National Taiwan University of Science and Technology, Taipei, 106, Taiwan
{sawang, cychiu, wyc}@iis.sinica.edu.tw

Abstract. VCenter, a platform for broadcasting digital video content, was developed by the National Digital Archives Program (NDAP), Taiwan. The platform provides a number of functions, such as digital video archiving, format transformation, streaming broadcasts, editing, geotagging, and blogging. The concept of Web2.0 is conducted in VCenter to increase user participation and improve interaction between the system and the user.

For videos, VCenter adopts Flash technology because it has a multi-layer architecture and it can handle multimedia content. We can add watermarks or captions as layers to videos without changing the original video's content so that when users browse videos, the multi-layer overlaps the original video layer in real-time.

VCenter serves the Union Catalog system of NDAP as a video broadcasting platform. In addition to archiving the valuable videos of NDAP, it allows the general public to archive, broadcast, and share digital videos.

Keywords: blogging, digital archive, digital video, Flash, watermark, Web2.0.

1 Article

To date, the National Digital Archives Program (NDAP) of Taiwan [3], which was launched in 2002, has archived more than three million digital objects. All the metadata of digital collections is stored in the Union Catalog (UC) system [7]. Users can search or browse all of the NDAP's digital collections through the UC system.

Processing digital video data in UC is a complicated task. Because of the different digital video formats used by content providers, UC needs to transform digital videos into a uniform format for general viewing. In addition, to protect the copyright of digital video content, digital watermarks must be added and transmitted by streaming to reduce the risk of illegal use. As these processes consume an enormous amount of manual efforts and computing resources, we have developed the VCenter [8] system to process digital videos, and thereby enhance the capability of UC.

The most obvious difference between the VCenter platform and general multimedia content management systems is that VCenter is based on the concept of Web2.0 [2,4].

L. Kovács, N. Fuhr, and C. Meghini (Eds.): ECDL 2007, LNCS 4675, pp. 522–524, 2007.

The main objective is to increase user participation and improve interaction between the system and the user. Furthermore, as blogging is an important Web 2.0 application, we have incorporated a blogging function and interface in the design of VCenter.

In addition to offering basic functions, such as file uploading, digital video format transformation, digital video streaming, and file management, VCenter also lets content owners decide whether to make their digital videos available to the general public for viewing. After watching a video, users can comment on or rate it. Based on users' responses, VCenter then lists popular videos and recommends content on the homepage. The VCenter platform not only provides functions for users to query videos by entering keywords, it also incorporates the concept of Folksonomy [6]. Users can define a video's category tag themselves so that it is easy to search for or browse a video.

VCenter also provides online editing and geographic functions for videos. The online editing functions allow users to add digital watermarks, captions, and cue points to their videos in real-time on the Web without installing video editing software in the client computer. Meanwhile, to provide geographic capability, VCenter incorporates geographic information systems (GIS), such as Google Maps [5], which allow users to set the longitude and latitude of digital videos. As a result, users can search for digital videos by spatial search or by browsing digital videos on a map.

We adopted the Flash video (FLV) [1] format for VCenter; hence all videos uploaded by content providers are transformed into FLV format. The advantage of using FLV is that it has a multi-layer architecture, which allows us to add a new layer to video frames in real-time. The function also allows us to add watermarks and captions to videos easily and rapidly in different layers, without changing the original video's content. When users browse videos, the multi-layer overlaps the original video layer in real-time.

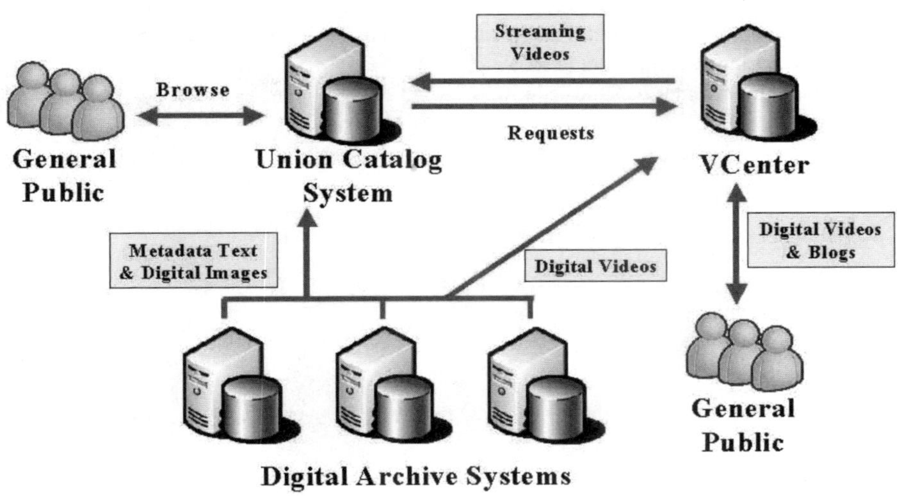

Fig. 1. The integration of VCenter with the UC system

VCenter serves UC as a platform for digital video broadcasts. When a user browses video content in UC, VCenter transmits video data to the user. In addition to archiving the valuable videos of NDAP, VCenter also allows the general public to archive and share videos. The integration of VCenter with the UC system is shown in Figure 1. By using the platform, content owners can edit and broadcast digital videos easily, which encourages the sharing of video content. In this way, more "folk" videos will be collected, and thereby increase NDAP's scope and impact on society.

Acknowledgements. This research was supported in part by the National Science Council of Taiwan under NSC Grants: NSC 95-2422-H-001-024, NSC 96-2422-H-001-001.

References

1. Emigb, J.: New Flash player rises in the Web-video market. Computer 39, 14–16 (2006)
2. Millard, D., Ross, M.: Web 2.0: hypertext by any other name? In: Proc. of the Seventeenth Conference on Hypertext and Hypermedia, pp. 27–30 (2006)
3. National Digital Archives Program, Taiwan, http://www.ndap.org.tw/index_en.php
4. O'Reilly, T.: What is Web 2.0 - design patterns and business models for the next generation of software, http://www.oreillynet.com/pub/a/oreilly/tim/news/2005/09/30/what-is-web-20. html
5. Pondar, H., Gschwender, A., Workman, R., Chan, J.: Geospatial visualization of student population using Google Maps™. Journal of Computing Sciences in Colleges 21, 175–181 (2006)
6. Russell, T.: Cloudalicious: folksonomy over time. In: Proc. of the 6th ACM/IEEE-CS Joint Conference on Digital Libraries, JCDL '06, North Carolina, USA, p. 364 (2006)
7. Tsai, Y.T., Chang, I.C.: Facilitating resource utilization in Union Catalog Systems. In: Fox, E.A., Neuhold, E.J., Premsmit, P., Wuwongse, V. (eds.) ICADL 2005. LNCS, vol. 3815, pp. 486–488. Springer, Heidelberg (2005)
8. VCenter, http://vcenter.iis.sinica.edu.tw/

Retrieving Tsunami Digital Library by Use of Mobile Phones

Sayaka Imai[1], Yoshinari Kanamori[1], and Nobuo Shuto[2]

[1] Department of Computer Science, Gunma University,
1-5-1 Tenjin-cho, Gunma 376-8515, Japan
{sayaka, kanamori}@cs.gunma-u.ac.jp

[2] Advanced Research Institute for the Sciences and Humanities, Nihon University,
Ichigaya Tokyu-building 6F, Kudan-Kita 4-2-1, Chiyoda-ku, Tokyo 102-0073, Japan
shuto-nobuo@arish.nihon-u.ac.jp

Abstract. We are developing a Tsunami Digital Library (TDL) which can store and manage documents about tsunami, tsunami run up simulations, newspaper articles, fieldwork data, etc. In this paper, we propose a public education against the tsunami disaster mitigation as one of TDL applications. For the education, we use mobile phones to retrieve TDL because we have to walk coast regions. Then, we have prepared summaries of documents and newspaper articles in TDL, and also developed query systems for mobile phone retrievals.

Keywords: Tsunami Digital Library, Mobile Phone, XML Database.

1 Introduction

We are developing a Tsunami Digital Library (TDL) which can store and manage documents about tsunami, news paper articles, tsunami run-up simulations, field work data, videos, etc., in Japan [1][2].

We have proposed a public education on the tsunami disaster which utilizes TDL for citizens in coast areas struck by the tsunami. We can visualize facts of tsunami disasters by clicking coast areas on the map in TDL. This shows a kind of virtual walking tours in TDL, and also is an effective public education. We can plan some walking tours in TDL based on spatio-temporal domain, the region or the era in Japan. For example, if you have any interest in the 1896 Meiji Sanriku Great Tsunami, you can travel Sanriku prefectures on the map, and see a lot of records on the tsunami by clicking villages, towns or cities along coasts in those prefectures. On the other hand, if one wants to know the tsunami disasters of a place where one is, he/she needs a PC which shows him/her the tsunami disasters. But its utilization is not useful at the open air. Therefore, we have developed a TDL environment using mobile phones. Furthermore, TDL will also contribute to a public education for tourists who go very occasionally sightseeing in the areas struck by the tsunami. This means TDL supports an actual walking tour.

L. Kovács, N. Fuhr, and C. Meghini (Eds.): ECDL 2007, LNCS 4675, pp. 525–528, 2007.

2 Retrievals by Use of Mobile Phones

We have developed the necessary TDL environments to support such walking tours as follows:

When tourists visit a coast area struck by a tsunami, a lot of facts of the tsunami disasters are automatically retrieved from TDL and displayed on mobile phones to attract their attention. Therefore, it is necessary to retrieve the region name of the place where tourists are in. We have obtained the place information from the area code when we use the i-mode [3] of NTT Docomo mobile phones. NTT Docomo provides Open i-area service. Open i-area is a function for i-mode that allows detection and collection of information about the location of tourists. When tourists access a web site which supports Open i-area, they can get the area code where they are. Japan is divided with 505 i-areas according to the base stations of mobile phones. The area code, which tourists receive, is based on the base stations of mobile phone which they access.

By using the area code, tourists can retrieve information about tsunami damage concerned with the place where they are. But there are restrictions of the number of display characters and the computing powers in mobile phones.

Only hundreds characters can be displayed in a mobile phone display. Because some documents about tsunami disasters include thousands of characters, it is hard to display the characters in a mobile phone display at a time. Then, we have to submit some remarkable contents, concerning the number of dead, destroyed houses and ships, and a summary of the document to mobile phones. We prepare summaries of tsunami documents and newspapers by using an algorithm based on sentence structures and weighted words [4].

3 Outline of Retrieval System

There are restrictions of the number of display characters and the computing powers in mobile equipments. We have to give some important contents to fit mobile equipments. Also, the network power of mobile phones is not so powerful. Therefore, we developed the retrieval system for mobile phones. In order to access to TDL and to retrieve contents of TDL, we prepared summaries of description of the tsunami disasters. Fig.1 shows the flow of database creation. At first we digitize the documents about tsunami disaster, and next, we create XML documents. XML documents are stored into whole text XML DB. Based on XML texts, summary XML texts are created by the summary creator. Summary XML texts are also stored into the summary XML DB.

Table 1. Iwate Prefecture damage list

City	Dead	Serious Injure	Destroyed House
Rikuzentakada	8	0	69
Oofunato	47	27	203
Kamaishi	0	0	17
Miyako	0	0	22
Ootsuchi	0	1	36
Total	53	28	347

On the other hand, the documents about the tsunami disaster include many lists about the dead, injured persons, damaged houses, and so on. We extracted the lists in documents about tsunami disasters. These data are very useful for people who are learning about tsunami disasters, to understand damages and power of the tsunami at each coast area. Table 1 shows a sample of a damage list.

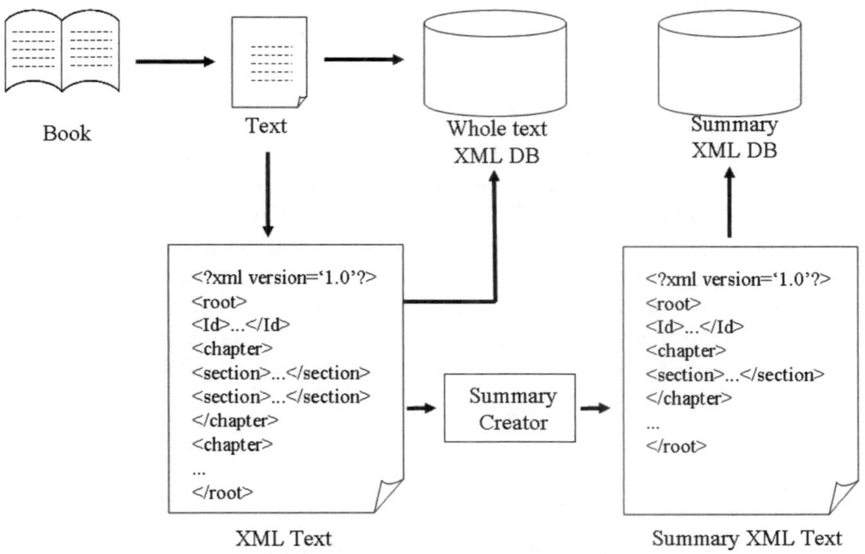

Fig. 1. Flow of whole text and summary XML database creations

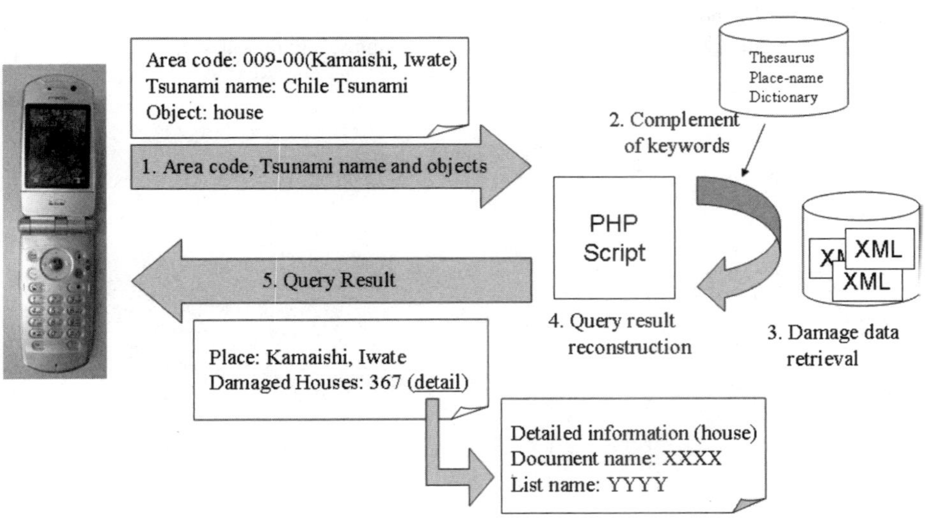

Fig. 2. Retrieval of damage list for the place "Kamaishi" in Iwate prefecture

PC users can get data as Table 1, but mobile phone users need not whole data. They need a part of damage data list concerned with their current place. So we developed retrieval system by using the place as a key. Fig.2 shows the retrieval of damage list for the place “Kamaishi” in Iwate prefecture. When a user accesses a web page of TDL by a mobile phone, the mobile phone sends an area code, where users are, a tsunami name and a damaged object. The system retrieves damage lists concerning a given place from XML DB.

4 Conclusion

By using mobile phones, people who visit a coast can get information about past tsunami disasters at the place. Now, we are only offering the character data because of the limits of the computing power in mobile phones. However, we think that videos or run-up simulations are more effective to the public education. In near future, our system will support such moving pictures. Furthermore, in order to support public education using mobile phones, the retrieval system needs to give the tsunami damage data depend on the age, the favorites and any other characteristics of the users. The retrieval system needs to get the information of user’s walking track by using GPS, and provide exact data.

References

1. Tsunami Digital Library: http://tsunami.dbms.cs.gunma-u.ac.jp
2. Imai, S., Kanamori, Y., Shuto, N.: Tsunami Digital Library. In: Gonzalo, J., Thanos, C., Verdejo, M.F., Carrasco, R.C. (eds.) ECDL 2006. LNCS, vol. 4172, pp. 555–558. Springer, Heidelberg (2006)
3. Docomo NTT i-mode: http://www.nttdocomo.co.jp/english/service/imode/index.html
4. Tsunami Digital Library for Mobile: http://tsunami.dbms.cs.gunma-u.ac.jp/iTDL/

Using Watermarks and Offline DRM to Protect Digital Images in DIAS

Hsin-Yu Chen, Hsiang-An Wang, and Chin-Lung Lin

Institute of Information Science, Academia Sinica, Taipei, 115, Taiwan
{kwakwai8, sawang, eddy}@iis.sinica.edu.tw

Abstract. The Digital Image Archiving System (DIAS) is an image management system, the major functions of which are preserving valuable digital images and serving as an image provider for external metadata archiving systems.

To enhance the security of images, DIAS enables online adding of watermarks to an image to protect the content owner's copyright. We use the Flash format to add watermarks because it has a multi-layer architecture and it can handle multimedia content. The function allows us to set the watermark as a layer that overlaps the original image. DIAS also provides an offline DRM (Digital Rights Management) mechanism to protect downloaded images. We package an image and its authorized information in an execution file for downloading. Then, when a user executes the file, the program validates the authorized information before showing the image. Using the watermark and offline DRM improves the security of DIAS images.

Keywords: digital image, DRM, Flash, watermark.

1 Article

The Digital Image Archiving System (DIAS) [2] is an image management system developed by the National Digital Archives Program (NDAP) [5], Taiwan. Its major functions are to preserve valuable digital images and serve as an image provider for external metadata archiving systems. Apart from providing basic digital image management and processing functions, DIAS also allows users to browse huge images on the Web and add watermarks to images online. In the past five years, DIAS has serviced nine NDAP metadata archiving systems and preserved approximately 670,000 images with a storage capacity of 2.3TB; the number of images continues to increase.

To prevent illegal use of images, DIAS provides a function that adds watermarks for content owner to indicate copyright [3]. The method adds a watermark to a certain part of an image; however, the drawback is that the watermark might disappear when the image is being zoomed into or moved in the viewer. We use Flash techniques to solve the problem [6]. As Flash has a multi-layer architecture and it can handle multimedia content, we implement an image viewer based on Flash technology, which can also be used to load images and overlay watermarks. By setting a watermark as a layer so that it overlaps the image, we can change the position and size of the watermark dynamically.

L. Kovács, N. Fuhr, and C. Meghini (Eds.): ECDL 2007, LNCS 4675, pp. 529–531, 2007.

Another feature is that, no matter how the image is zoomed into or moved in the viewer, the position and size of the watermark layer will not change and it will continue to overlap the image. In this way, the loaded image's data can be kept in the memory, instead of on a hard disk, which reduces the risk of the image being copied. Besides adding watermarks, we can easily add other layers, such as dialogue boxes or captions, to an image.

In the past, DIAS only used watermarks to protect stored images; it could not protect downloaded images. To resolve the problem, we use an offline digital rights management (DRM) mechanism to improve security [4]. The mechanism determines the authorized information about an image before downloading [1]. As shown in Figure 1, the information is divided into two parts: (1) identity information, which includes the hardware specification of the client PC, smart card information and user's ID/password to identify the user in the future; and (2) consent items, which include operations the image can be used for, and the days and times the image can be viewed. The image and its authorized information are then packaged in an execution file for downloading.

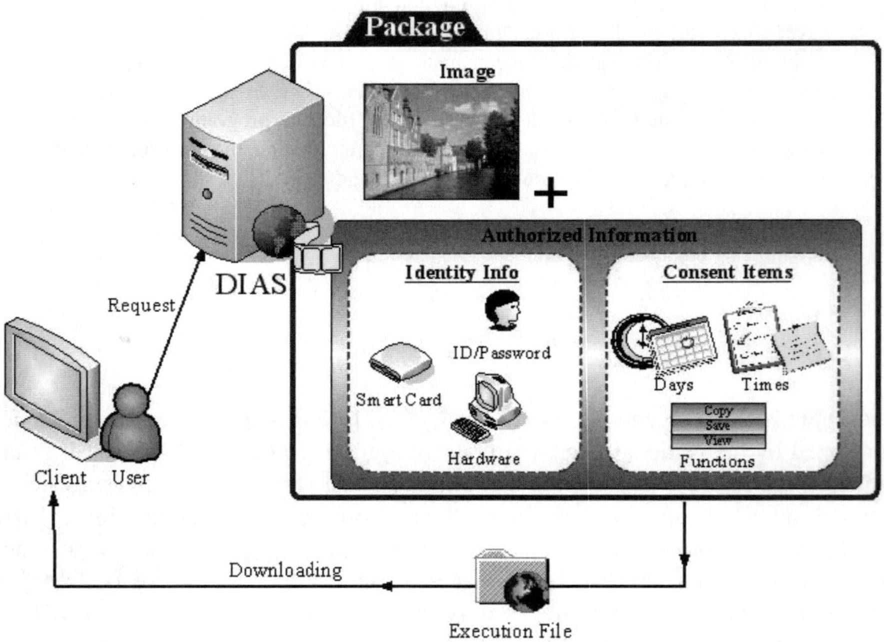

Fig. 1. The offline DRM mechanism of DIAS

When a user executes the file, the program loads the authorized information of the image in the file first. If the downloaded file passes the authorized information check, it will open the client's default application program to show the image; otherwise, it will not open the image. Every time a file is opened, the program records certain information in the client's PC, such as the time and date the image was viewed, which can be used to verify the authorized information the next time it is viewed.

We use the Flash format to improve the way watermarks are displayed so that images can be displayed more quickly. In addition, by using offline DRM to protect downloaded image files, we hope to enhance the security of DIAS so that it can provide complete protection for images.

Acknowledgements. This research was supported in part by the National Science Council of Taiwan under NSC Grants: NSC 95-2422-H-001-024, NSC 96-2422-H-001-001.

References

1. Chen, H.Y., Wang, H.A., Huang, K.L.: DIAS: the Digital Image Archiving System of NDAP Taiwan. In: Gonzalo, J., Thanos, C., Verdejo, M.F., Carrasco, R.C. (eds.) ECDL 2006. LNCS, vol. 4172, pp. 485–487. Springer, Heidelberg (2006)
2. Digital Image Archiving System (DIAS), http://ndmmc2.iis.sinica.edu.tw
3. Hsiao, J.H., Wang, J.H., Chen, M.S., Chen, C.S., Chien, L.F.: Constructing a Wrapper-Based DRM system for digital content protection in digital libraries. In: Fox, E.A., Neuhold, E.J., Premsmit, P., Wuwongse, V. (eds.) ICADL 2005. LNCS, vol. 3815, pp. 375–379. Springer, Heidelberg (2005)
4. Lin, C.L.: Wrapper-based digital rights management mechanism (In Chinese). Shih Hsin University, Taipei, Taiwan (2006)
5. National Digital Archives Program, Taiwan, http://www.ndap.org.tw/index_en.php
6. Schmitz, P.: Leveraging community annotations for image adaptation to small presentation formats. In: Proceedings of the 14th Annual ACM International Conference on Multimedia, Santa Barbara, CA, USA, pp. 671–674 (2006)

CIDOC CRM in Action – Experiences and Challenges

Philipp Nussbaumer[1] and Bernhard Haslhofer[2]

[1] Research Studios, Studio Digital Memory Engineering, Vienna, Austria
philipp.nussbaumer@researchstudio.at
[2] University of Vienna, Department of Distributed and Multimedia Systems
bernhard.haslhofer@univie.ac.at

Abstract. Integration of metadata from heterogeneous sources is a major issue when connecting cultural institutions to digital library networks. Uniform access to metadata is impeded by the structural and semantic heterogeneities of the metadata and metadata schemes used in the source systems. In this paper we discuss the methodologies we applied to *ingest* proprietary metadata into the BRICKS digital library network and to *process* CIDOC CRM metadata in terms of search and retrieval, and how we strove to *hide the semantic complexity from the end-user* while exploiting the semantic richness of the underlying metadata.

1 Introduction

When integrating multiple autonomous content repositories, the availability of metadata is not sufficient – *metadata interoperability* is required. Within the context of the BRICKS [1] project we have integrated metadata and content from a number of archaeological institutions. It was our intent to provide uniform access to their cultural assets via an end-user friendly application. Transparent handling of the structural and semantic heterogeneities was a key requirement.

In the literature one can find many definitions [2,3] and approaches [4] to achieve interoperability. We have chosen to use the CIDOC Conceptual Reference Model (CIDOC CRM) [5] to provide interoperability among the metadata of the archaeological institutions. The central idea of CIDOC CRM is to map each proprietary schema to a global ontology, tailored to the cultural heritage domain.

2 Methods and Techniques

The ingestion of metadata from the systems of the participating institutions involves two main steps: in the first step a domain expert identifies the metadata attributes to be mapped from the source schemes to the CIDOC CRM and defines unambiguous *mapping chains*. These are defined in a spread-sheet which then is semi-automatically transformed into an XSL style-sheet. In a second step, the importing process uses the style-sheet to transform the required metadata into RDF [6] and ingests them into the BRICKS network.

L. Kovács, N. Fuhr, and C. Meghini (Eds.): ECDL 2007, LNCS 4675, pp. 532–533, 2007.

Within the system the CIDOC CRM is represented as an OWL ontology [7], the metadata are persisted in a built-in RDF triple store and the field values are full-text indexed. Simple full-text search requests deliver the matching CIDOC CRM metadata descriptions – or rather a hierarchy of descriptions that reflect the CIDOC CRM chains that were initially defined during the mapping process. For targeted advanced search requests on specific metadata fields one must know the corresponding CIDOC CRM chain. As this involves expert knowledge, traditional advanced search mechanisms prove to be unsuitable in this application context.

On the user-application level we have introduced a set of pre-configured chains that cover the most relevant fields, in order to overcome the limitations of the previously mentioned advanced search issue. To provide a simple yet powerful means of searching – beyond full-text search – we offer a faceted-style, *guided search* interface which dynamically narrows the search result set with each user interaction.

3 Lessons Learned and Future Work

So far we have built a prototypical application which handles all the issues mentioned in the previous section and successfully integrated sample metadata from several archaeological institutions. We have noticed that the required integration effort decreases with every integrated institution. This is because existing mappings may be reused as templates for other scenarios.

As the CIDOC CRM abstracts from any implementation, some issues arise, such as the typing and embedding of data values, mapping of several chains to a single metadata attribute or handling possible ambiguities when the same chains are mapped to semantically distinct metadata attributes. This strong interdependency between the mapping process and the implementation requires several feedback cycles between the mapping experts and the application developers.

References

1. EU-FP6: BRICKS – Building Resources for Integrated Cultural Knowledge Services (IST 507457) (2007), `http://www.brickscommunity.org`
2. National Information Standards Organization (NISO): Understanding metadata (2004), `http://www.niso.org/standards/resources/UnderstandingMetadata.pdf`
3. ALCTS/CCS/Committee on Cataloging: Description and Access: Task force on metadata: Final report (June 2000), `http://www.libraries.psu.edu/tas/jca/ccda/tf-meta6.html`
4. Chan, L.M., Zeng, M.L.: Metadata Interoperability and Standardization – A Study of Methodology Part I + II. D-Lib Magazine 12(6) (June 2006)
5. CIDOC Documentation Standards Group: CIDOC Conceptual Reference Model (CRM) – ISO 21127:2006 (December 2006)
6. W3C Semantic Web Activity – RDF Core Working Group: Resource Description Framework (RDF) (2004), `http://www.w3.org/RDF/`
7. W3C Semantic Web Activity – Web Ontology Working Group: Web Ontology Language (OWL) (2004), `http://www.w3.org/2004/OWL/`

The Legal Environment of Digital Curation – A Question of Balance for the Digital Librarian

Mags McGinley

Digital Curation Centre, University of Edinburgh, Crichton Street,
Edinburgh EH8 9LE, Scotland UK
mags.mcginley@ed.ac.uk

Abstract. Digital curation is about maintaining and adding value to a trusted body of digital information for current and future use. This requires active management and on-going appraisal over the entire life-cycle of scholarly and scientific materials.

Whether there is a desire to make materials as open as possible or a requirement to keep them closed and private (for example in the case of sensitive personal data), legal elements can have a huge impact on the overall ability to effectively curate and preserve digital information over time.

The DCC advocates the development of a framework for any curation activity that includes consideration of legal matters throughout. - from copyright and licensing models, to freedom of information and data protection.

Keywords: Digital curation, copyright, licensing, freedom of information, data protection.

1 Description

Digital curation is a very wide ranging discipline, as is law. The legal areas you will need to consider will depend very much on the stage of the curation life cycle at which you operate (are you a data creator, data curator, data re-user?) and the type of data that is involved. There will also be a certain amount of balancing to be done between the often discussed desire to make resources as widely available as possible at low or even no cost (**open** environment) and the sometimes conflicting requirements to keep certain data or materials private or proprietary (**closed** environment).

2 Towards Openness

2.1 Copyright

Copyright is governed by the Copyright, Designs and Patents Act 1988 ("the CDPA"). It is the branch of intellectual property law that protects the expression of ideas. Copyright comes under a lot of criticism; especially from those involved in digital curation where the rights of the copyright holder can be seen as restricting vital curation

L. Kovács, N. Fuhr, and C. Meghini (Eds.): ECDL 2007, LNCS 4675, pp. 534–538, 2007.

activities.[1] However, there are certain exceptions to copyright and digital librarians should make full use of these. As well as the provisions aimed specifically at libraries and archives[2] the 'fair dealing' provisions are at your disposal.[3] They permit acts that would otherwise be copyright infringement in the case of research for non-commercial purposes, private study, criticism or review. It is important to note that at present the permission in section 29, applying to research and private study, does not apply to copyright in films, sound recordings, broadcasts or typographical arrangements. However, this was addressed in the recent Gowers Review of Intellectual Property ("the Gowers Review") where it was recommended that private copying for research be allowed to cover all forms of content.[4] The Gowers Review also recommended that the CDPA be amended so that libraries may format-shift archival copies to ensure records do not become obsolete.[5]

A further positive is that the framework provided by the CDPA can be used as a tool to enable greater levels of access through licensing, to which we now turn.

2.2 Open Licensing

Licences such as Creative Commons licences, the BBC Creative Archive licence and, for software, the GNU General Public licence have been developed to enable wider access to copyrighted works. Each has slightly different objectives and approaches which cannot all be described in detail here. To take Creative Commons as our example, its licences give a copyright owner the ability to dictate how others may exercise their copyright rights. Creative Commons describes this as moving from an "all rights reserved" position to "some rights reserved". It is achieved by applying a choice of elements: attribution; non-commercial; no-derivatives; and share-alike. The resulting licence attaches to the work and authorises everyone who comes in contact with the work to use it consistent with the terms.

2.3 Freedom of Information ("FOI")

In broad terms the FOI Acts[6] set out a right of access by the general public to all information held by public authorities. Information may be accessed by two means: via the public authority's publication scheme and via a statutory right to request information. FOI is not only enables but requires openness in regards to digital records.

---

[1] Muir, A., Digital preservation: awareness, responsibility and rights issues. Journal of Information Science, 30(1), 73-92.

[2] Sections 37-44 CDPA.

[3] Sections 29 and 30 CDPA.

[4] Recommendation 9, The Report of the Gowers Review of Intellectual Property. http://www.hm-treasury.gov.uk/independent_reviews/gowers_review_intellectual_property/gowersreview_index.cfm You can read the report of the Review at: http://www.hm-treasury.gov.uk/media/53F/C8/pbr06_gowers_report_755.pdf

[5] Recommendation 8, The Report of the Gowers Review of Intellectual Property. http://www.hm-treasury.gov.uk/media/53F/C8/pbr06_gowers_report_755.pdf

[6] There are two FOI Acts in the UK as Scotland has its own. Freedom of Information Act 2000 and Freedom of Information (Scotland) Act 2002.

The FOI Acts apply to electronic and paper records equally. Any recorded information can be requested which means that all applicable data has to be stored and retrieved effectively. Systems for organisation and retrieval are well established in the paper environment, but most records are now in digital format. A public authority's ability to comply with the legislation will be facilitated by effective electronic records management and thorough appraisal procedures.

In addition to this a record has not only to be retrievable but readable or useable over the long term. For this reason it needs to be preserved and curated. In some cases the FOI Acts have forced public authorities to tackle the question of longevity of data and allocate funds to support curation and preservation initiatives where they may not have otherwise done so.

2.4 Re-use of Public Sector Information

The relatively new law relating to re-use of public sector information was introduced in 2003 by a European Directive.[7] The Directive was implemented in the UK by the Re-use of Public Sector Information Regulations 2005 ("the Regulations").[8]

The aim of the Regulations is to encourage re-use of public sector information by removing obstacles that stand in the way of such action. The intention is that this will stimulate the development of innovative information products and services across Europe thereby boosting the information industry, as has been the experience in the United States. Re-use of information is described as the reproduction of documents in a way that was not originally intended when they were created. The scope of the legislation is very broad and its objectives are similar to those of digital curation.

It is important to note that at present the Regulations do not apply to archives, libraries, museums and cultural establishments or educational and research establishments.[9] However, this has been criticised and there is a strong chance that when the Regulations are reviewed in 2008 the bodies that they apply to will be extended. Also, as great re-users of intellectual property, libraries are well-advised to maintain a sound knowledge of the Regulations so as to be able to use them from the requestor's perspective.

3 Keeping It Closed

3.1 Data Protection

Data Protection in the UK is covered by the Data Protection Act 1998 ("the DPA")[10] and governs the handling of a living individual's personal data. It seeks to strike a balance between the interests of an individual in maintaining privacy over their personal details and the sometimes competing interest of those with legitimate reasons for using personal information. It gives individuals certain rights regarding information held about them, whilst placing obligations on those who process that data.

---

[7] Directive 2003/98/EC on the Re-use of Public Sector Information. http://europa.eu.int/eur-lex/pri/en/oj/dat/2003/l_345/l_34520031231en00900096.pdf

[8] S.I. 2005 No. 1515 http://www.opsi.gov.uk/si/si2005/20051515.htm

[9] Regulations 5(3)(b) and (c).

[10] http://www.opsi.gov.uk/ACTS/acts1998/19980029.htm

Data protection is relevant to digital curation from two different perspectives. Firstly, the DPA impacts the way those who have control over personal data can use it. If someone is curating or reusing data that is covered by the DPA (perhaps a researcher using medical or social science data) they will need to be aware of the legislation and take steps to comply with the Act. Although there are exemptions from certain of the data protection principles for, amongst other things, research use[11] an awareness of the constraints imposed by the legislation and how it impacts the way the data can be used is crucial. This becomes even more significant if the personal data is of the type defined by the DPA as 'sensitive personal data'.[12] In such cases more stringent rules apply.

From the other perspective, implementing robust curation practices in relation to digital data will be of great assistance not only in not falling foul of the legislation but in facilitating faster and more efficient compliance with the principles or any subject access request, thus requiring fewer resources in the long term.

3.2 Copyright Permissions

One of the more significant aspects of copyright for curation purposes is the fact that a user may not carry out an act restricted by copyright without the permission of the copyright owner. Preservation and curation of digital materials is dependent on a range of strategies that require the making of copies and modifications. It can therefore be appreciated that copyright's scope for hindering the curation of digital data is significant. Permission can be resource consuming to obtain. Licences such as those discussed above can go some way to alleviating this problem. However, in some cases it remains difficult. One such example of this is with orphan works which are works where it is not possible to request permission from the rights holder because they are not known or cannot be traced. Copyright permissions can also be difficult where it is not clear who owns the copyright, not because the owner cannot be traced, but because an employment relationship is involved or there are multiple authors.

Another important element to consider in relation to copyright permissions is that a single digital object may embody more than one copyright work, each with a different owner. For example a television programme may have literary, dramatic and musical copyrights for the script, screenplay and score respectively. There will then be further protection for the recording of the programme. In such cases permission will be even more burdensome to obtain.

3.3 Database Right

Much digital curation activity, especially in the scientific arena, involves databases. Unsurprisingly, the principal intellectual property right to look at when considering databases is the database right. This sui generis right was enacted relatively recently (in comparison to copyright's 400 year existence) as a result of Directive 96/9/EC on the legal protection of databases ("the Database Directive")[13] and then implemented in the UK by the Copyright and Rights in Databases Regulations 1997.[14] A key concern in

---

[11] Section 33 DPA.
[12] Section 2 DPA.
[13] http://europa.eu.int/ISPO/infosoc/legreg/docs/969ec.html
[14] http://www.opsi.gov.uk/si/si1997/19973032.htm

relation to the Database Directive has been a perception that the right it creates seems close to the grant of an intellectual property right in data and information per se, allowing only limited extractions for the purposes of non-commercial research. The result is that scientists may suffer restrictions on access to, and ability to re-use the raw data necessary for scientific progress.[15] Many of the considerations that apply to copyright also apply to the database right.

3.4 Digital Rights Management ("DRM")

DRM is an umbrella term referring to any of several technologies used to enforce pre-defined policies controlling access to and use of protected works. There is huge concern that DRM technology to protect content could lead to 'digital lock out' and the diminishment of the material freely available for use existing in the public domain. DRM can prevent a person from using a legitimate exception to copyright or the database right because it doesn't recognise that a user fits into one of the relevant categories. It is a significant issue for curation and preservation initiatives which may often rely on exceptions and who also hope to be the beneficiaries of future expansion of the exceptions as recommended in the Gowers Review.

[15] International Council for Science, Scientific Data and Information – A Report of the CSPR Assessment Panel, December 2004. Available at http://www.icsu.org/Gestion/img/ICSU_DOC_DOWNLOAD/551_DD_FILE_PAA_Data_and_Information.pdf

Demonstration: Bringing Lives to Light: Browsing and Searching Biographical Information with a Metadata Infrastructure

Ray R. Larson

School of Information
University of California, Berkeley
Berkeley, California, USA, 94720-4600
ray@sims.berkeley.edu

Abstract. In this demonstration we will show how a metadata infrastructure comprised of gazetteers, biographical dictionaries, and a "Time Period Directory" can be dynamically exploited to help searchers navigate through multiple web-based resources, and displayed in context with related information about "Who?, What?, Where?, and When?" and providing dynamic searches of those external resources. The demostration will show both a web-based interface and a Google Earth-based geo-temporal browser.

1 Description

Metadata is ordinarily used to describe documents, but it can also constitute a form of infrastructure for access to networked resources and for traversal of those resources. One problematic area for access to digital library resources has been the search for time periods and events, whether of historic import or of significance in individual lives. If there is a capability to search for time, it is usually a date search - a standardized and precise form but unfortunately rarely used in common chronological expressions. For example, a user interested in the "Vietnam war", "Clinton Administration" or the "Elizabethan Period" must either know the corresponding dates, or rely on simple keyword matching for those period names. In addition to this limitation, facilities for effectively browsing time periods are extremely limited.

In this demo we will show how chronological and geographic context can be displayed in order to facilitate browsing and interaction with conceptually related materials. This demo uses our prototype Time Period Directory[1], a metadata infrastructure for named time periods linking them with their geographic location as well as a canonical time period range, in conjunction with other local databases and web-accessible data. Both a conventional web interface and a Google Earth-based geo-temporal browser will be shown. As an example Figures 1 and 2 show examples of events on Budapest and biographically related information on the reign of Robert I of Scotland (also known as Robert the Bruce).

L. Kovács, N. Fuhr, and C. Meghini (Eds.): ECDL 2007, LNCS 4675, pp. 539–542, 2007.

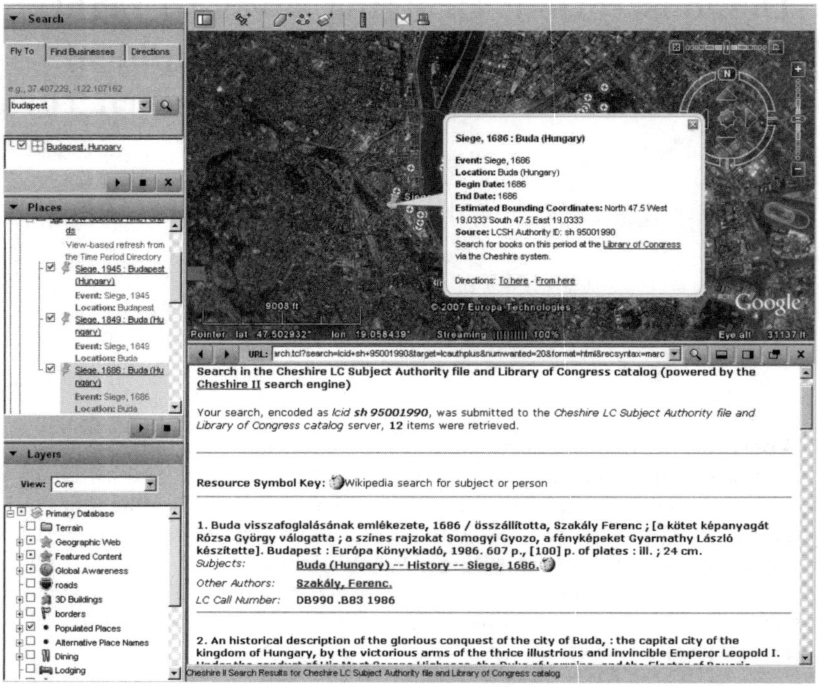

Fig. 1. Time Period Directory Entries in Google Earth

Chronological, geographical and biographical data lend themselves naturally to being connected: an event is associated with a place, a time and potentially with particular people; places are associated with different events and people; and individual people are also associated (in a variety of ways) with different places and events. One can foresee a plethora of relationships and possible search questions that a truly interconnected system should be able to answer. We have demonstrated with our Time Period Directory implementation that many different views and perspectives on the same data are possible and desirable.

Cultural heritage, history, and social sciences are fundamentally about human activity.

Everyone is interested in what other people do and have done.

Life-stories are hard to beat as a basis for narrative and for engaging interest, especially among young people. Biographies are regularly among the best-sellers. Not only History, but also Geography and most other subjects can come alive in the travelogues, journeys of discovery, and the life-stories of those involved. Science can be explained through the work of scientists. Engineering is routinely explained through the heroic struggles of inventors. Even natural history is often taught through the unfolding drama of the activities of an individual animal during its life-cycle or through the seasons of the year.

But mere narrative is not enough. Understanding the context differentiates education from memorizing. Building and supporting a community of learners

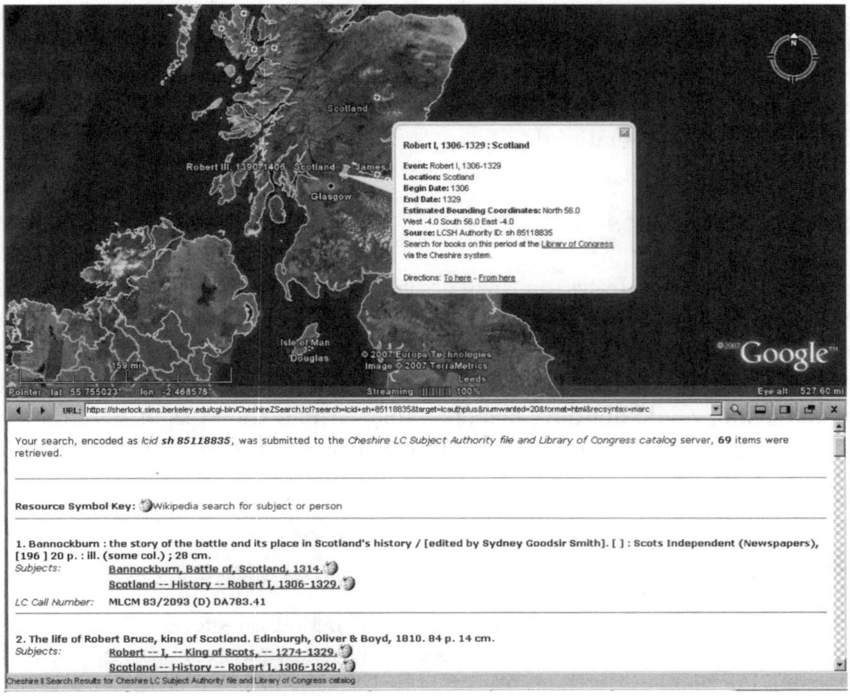

Fig. 2. Information on the Reign of Robert I of Scotland (Robert the Bruce)

needs more than facts. It is understanding the circumstances of people's actions that illuminates their lives, but there is a significant gap in the infrastructure developed by libraries, museums, and publishers in this area. We have standards for handling people's names, but not for their lives or events in those lives. There is, quite simply, no established standard or "best practices" for encoding what people do, nor for helping them to search out the resources that can provide the context to understand their actions and experiences.

Our objective in this project is to design, demonstrate, and evaluate techniques that would bring lives to light by revealing them in their contexts.

We are now at work further developing the biographical aspect to our framework. The Library of Congress Name Authority records are an obvious place to look - not only do they provide already structured data on persons and other corporate entities, they also inherently connect to a topical search applications (the library catalog), potentially easing our task of connecting the different informational aspects. Additionally, we are linking other sources of biographical data to our infrastructure. Various other resources (Wikipedia, EAD Archival Descriptions, etc.) are being mined to derive some prototype data to support the dynamic interaction of Time Period Directories, digital gazetteers, biographical data and ontological structures like thesauri and classification schemes, in combination with a variety of network-accessible digital library resources ranging from library catalogs to archival collections and digitized version of historical primary resources. Our vision is that in response to users' expressions of interest, their interaction with this system will construct a rich dynamic portal of interconnected resources with maps, biographies, timelines and chronologies, and primary research materials.

Acknowledgments

The work presented draws on two projects partially supported by Institute of Museum and Library Services National Leadership Grants: Support for the Learner: What, Where, When, and Who (http://ecai.org/imls2004/) and Bringing Lives to Light: Biography in Context (http://ecai.org/imls2006/). The system, and demo, would not have been possible without the work of Vivian Petras, Jeanette Zerneke, and Kim Carl, and the efforts of Co-PIs Michael Buckland and Fredric C. Gey.

Reference

1. Petras, V., Larson, R.R., Buckland, M.: Time period directories: A metadata infrastructure for placing events in temporal and geographic context. In: JCDL '06: Opening Information Horizons: 6th ACM/IEEE-CS Joint Conference on Digital Libraries 2006, pp. 151–160 (2006)

Repository Junction and Beyond at the EDINA (UK) National Data Centre

Robin Rice, Peter Burnhill, Christine Rees, and Anne Robertson

EDINA, University of Edinburgh

Abstract. EDINA has been funded to undertake a variety of repository-related development activities to enhance and support access to scholarly and learning objects in the UK. **JORUM** is a national learning object repository for sharing and repurposing educational materials. The purpose of **the Depot** is to ensure that all UK academics can enjoy the benefits of Open Access for their peer-reviewed post-prints by providing a repository for the interim period before every university has such repository provision. **GRADE** has been investigating and reporting on the technical and cultural issues around the reuse of geospatial data in the context of media-centric, informal and institutional repositories. With the **DataShare** project, by supporting academics who wish to share datasets on which written research outputs are based, a network of institution-based data repositories will develop a niche model for deposit of 'orphaned datasets' currently filled neither by centralised subject-domain data archives nor institutional repositories.

Keywords: repositories, open access, research outputs, learning objects, e-prints, data sharing.

1 Description

EDINA is a national data centre funded by JISC (UK Joint Information Systems Committee) to provide network-level services for UK Further and Higher Institutions. Under the Digital Repositories and Preservation Programme, JISC aspires to increase capacity of institutions to provide stewardship of their knowledge assets for long-term preservation and sharing, such as under terms of open access. Through the JISC RepositoryNet, key projects provide support and services to institutions in the development of their institutional repositories and to academics where local repository provision is not available. Four projects and services are described where EDINA, with its partners, have added to the national fabric of repository provision in support of the development of and access to 'community-generated content' within UK Further and Higher Education.

The **Jorum** repository service (http://jorum.ac.uk) supports the submission, sharing, reuse and repurposing of learning and teaching (L&T) materials in UK Further and Higher Education Institutions (F/HEIs). The Jorum is the first collaborative venture of this kind on a national scale in UK F/HE, and is in the long run likely to form part of a distributed e-learning architecture that supports many

L. Kovács, N. Fuhr, and C. Meghini (Eds.): ECDL 2007, LNCS 4675, pp. 543–545, 2007.

distributed repositories and user interfaces. The two JISC national data centres (EDINA in Edinburgh and MIMAS in Manchester) have worked together in this important policy area. The Jorum consists of two services: the Jorum Contributor Service, which takes in contributions of learning and teaching resources created within UK F/HEIs (started November 2005), and the Jorum User Service, which provides access to these contributions (started January 2006). Each service is open to all staff in F/HEIs, but not to students. In May 2007 there were over 2,000 resources and 2,800 registered users in over 360 institutions, of which 70 contribute content and 320 were registered for the user service.

The Depot facility (http://depot.edina.ac.uk) is based on E-Prints software and is OAI-compliant. Like other UK repositories, its contents will be harvested and searched through the Intute Repository Search project. It offers a redirect service, nicknamed UK Repository Junction, to ensure that content that comes within the remit of an extant repository is correctly placed there instead of in the Depot. Additionally, as IRs are created, the Depot will offer a transfer service for content deposited by authors based at those universities, to help populate the new IRs. The Depot will therefore act as a 'keepsafe' until a repository of choice becomes available for deposited scholarly content. In this way, the Depot will avoid competing with extant and emerging IRs while bridging gaps in the overall repository landscape and encouraging more open access deposits. The Depot is one of the supporting services of JISC RepositoryNet and works closely with SHERPA and the JISC Repositories Support Project.

The **GRADE** project (http://edina.ac.uk/projects/grade), part of the Digital Repositories Programme of JISC, found that a significant degree of informal geospatial data sharing occurs because of the lack of any formal mechanism, and that there is demand for a mechanism to legitimately share and reuse geospatial research data. Main barriers to more formal geospatial data sharing within the community are: perceived complexity of licensing and digital rights issues surrounding data (re)use in the UK; lack of quality metadata; concerns over the protection of depositors intellectual property; and lack of community-based mechanism(s) for sharing. Institutional repositories do not manage any geospatial content (and would not be capable of effectively doing so currently). The geospatial community would support data reuse but not necessarily (at present) within an institutional repository. More fine grained sharing mechanisms are preferred i.e. data sharing amongst peer group networks defined by the depositor. Main factors that would encourage geospatial data sharing and reuse are identified as the establishment of a specific geospatial repository infrastructure as part of academic Spatial Data Infrastructure plus less restrictive licensing. Over 150 datasets have been submitted into the demonstrator repository.

The **DataShare** project (http://www.disc-uk.org/datashare) is based on a distributed model in which each participating partner is responsible for the work on their own repositories, yet experience, support and knowledge are shared in order to increase levels of success. This builds on the existing informal collaboration of DISC-UK members (Data Information Specialists Committee) for improving their data libraries and models of data support at four institutions: Edinburgh, London School of Economics, Oxford, and Southampton. It will also bring academic data libraries in closer contact with e-prints repository managers and develop new forms of cooperation between these distinct groups of information professionals within academic environments. The advantage for the broader community is to provide exemplars for a range of approaches and policies in which to embed the deposit and stewardship of datasets in institutional repositories. Indeed, among the partners there will be exemplars for the three main repository solutions: EPrints, DSpace and Fedora. Project management is based at EDINA.

A Scalable Data Management Tool to Support Epidemiological Modeling of Large Urban Regions

Christopher L. Barrett[1,2], Keith Bisset[1], Stephen Eubank[1], Edward A. Fox[2], Yi Ma[1,2], Madhav Marathe[1,2], and Xiaoyu Zhang[1,2]

[1] Network Dynamics and Simulation Science Laboratory (NDSSL), Virgina Tech., Blacksburg, VA, USA 24061

[2] Department of Computer Science, Virgina Tech., Blacksburg, VA, USA 24061

{cbarrett,kbisset,seubank,mmarathe}@vbi.vt.edu,
{fox,may05,zhangx06}@vt.edu

Abstract. We describe the design and prototype implementation of a data management tool supporting simulation based models for studying the spread of infectious diseases in large urban regions. The need for such tools arises due to diverse and competing disease models, social networks, and experimental designs that are being investigated. A realistic case study produces large amounts of data. Organizing such datasets is necessary for effectively supporting analysts and policy-makers interested in various cases. We report our ongoing efforts to develop EpiDM—an integrated information management tool for interrelated digital resources, where the central piece is EpiDL(a digital library for efficient access to these datasets). The work is unique in terms of the specific application domain, which we are not aware of any such efforts and tools that can be generalized for simulation-based modeling of other socio-technical systems. EpiDL follows the 5S framework developed in the DL community.

Keywords: Computational Epidemiology, Public Health, Socio-technical and Information Systems, Simulation and Modeling, Digital Library.

1 Introduction

The spread of infectious disease depends both on properties of the pathogen and the host. Disaggregate or individual-based models [1,3,5,6] that have been developed recently represent each interaction between individuals, and can thus be used to study critical pathways. Simdemics [1,2,3,4] is a high fidelity agent based modeling environment for simulating the spread of infectious diseases in large urban regions and was developed by our group over last several years. It has been used extensively in a number of user-defined case studies. For example, recently, Simdemics was used as a part of a Dept. of Health and Human Services (DHHS) sponsored case study [7,8]. Simdemics details the demographic and geographic distributions of disease and provides decision makers with information about (1) the consequences of a biological attack or natural outbreak, (2) the resulting demand for health services, and (3) the

L. Kovács, N. Fuhr, and C. Meghini (Eds.): ECDL 2007, LNCS 4675, pp. 546–548, 2007.

feasibility and effectiveness of response options. See [1,3] for further details. Simdemics is in turn a part of Simfrastructure (a service oriented grid enabled modeling environment for integrating various simulation models).

Need for a Data Management Tool: High-resolution agent based models such as Simdemics require diverse and large amounts of input data, consist of a number of models, and produce diverse and large amounts of output data. To put this in perspective, Simdemics uses more than 35 different commercial and open source databases as inputs to its modeling framework. A large number of disease transmission and social network models are constructed based on the level of resolution and detail. The DHHS case study involved a factorial design consisting of more than 200 cells each containing more than 10 replicates. Efficiently storing and accessing such large volumes of multi-modal data that these simulations produce cannot be done in an ad-hoc fashion. An integrated data management tool can provide a natural way to store and retrieve these data sets and models. See http://ndssl.vbi.vt.edu/opendata/index.html for dataset examples produced by Simdemics.

Data Management Tool: We report ongoing work that is aimed at developing an architecture and a prototype implementation of a tool to support the above tasks. EpiDL is a digital library supporting epidemiological modeling. EpiDM is an integrated data management tool that contains beyond EpiDL. Architecturally, EpiDM resides within the data grid layer of Simfrastructure. EpiDL follows the 5S (Streams, Structures, Spaces, Scenarios, and Societies) framework that defines the meta-model for a minimal DL [8].

It stores streams of textual bits from files or databases and audio/video sequences. Challenges arise from enforcing proper structures over heterogeneously structured digital objects with close conceptual relationships. In our prototype implementation, we used RDF based metadata, which defines semantic contents of objects and relationships among them. The metadata constructs a knowledgebase for Simfrastructure, on which a browsing service could be based. Simfrastructure objects contain both textual information and real number parameters. We extended vector space model, where a simulation is viewed as segmented vectors with different weights. We used R-Tree [9] based index structures to efficiently access indexed simulations.

References

1. Atkins, K., Barrett, C.L., Beckman, R.E., Bissett, K., Chen, J., Eubank, S., Anil Kumar, V.S., Lewis, B., Macauley, M., Marathe, A., Marathe, M., Mortveit, H.S., Stretz, P.: NIH Chicago Case Study, NDSSL Internal Report No. 06-059
2. Barrett, C.L., Eubank, S., Smith, J.: If Smallpox Strikes Portland... Scientific American (2005)
3. Bisset, K., Atkins, K., Barrett, C.L., Beckman, R., Eubank, S., Anil Kumar, V.S., Marathe, A., Marathe, M.V., Mortveit, H.S., Stretz, P.: A High-Level Architecture for Simfrastructure NDSSL Internal Report No. 05-018 (2005)

4. Bisset, K., Atkins, K., Barrett, C.L., Beckman, R., Eubank, S., Marathe, A., Marathe, M., Mortveit, H.S., Stretz, P., Anil Kumar, V.S.: Synthetic Data Products for Societal Infrastructures and Proto Populations: Data Set 1.0, NDSSL Technical Report No. 06-006 (2006)
5. Eubank, S., Guclu, H., Anil Kumar, V.S., Marathe, M.V., Srinivasan, A., Toroczkai, Z., Wang, N.: Modelling disease outbreaks in realistic urban social networks. Nature 429, 180–184 (2004)
6. Ferguson, N.L., Cummings, D.A.T., Fraser, C., Ca jka, J.C., Cooley, P.C., Burke, D.S.: Strategies for mitigating an influenza pandemic, Nature (April 2006)
7. Germann, T.C., Kadau, K., Longini, Jr., I.M., Macken, C.A.: Mitigation strategies for pandemic influenza in the United States. Proc. of National Academy of Sciences (PNAS) 103(15), 5935–5940 (2006)
8. Gonçalves, M.A., Fox, E.A., Watson, L.T., Kipp, N.A.: Streams, Structures, Spaces, Scenarios, Societies (5S): A Formal Model for Digital Libraries. ACM Transactions on Information Systems 22(2), 270–312 (2004)
9. Guttman, A.: R-Trees: A Dynamic Index Structure for Spatial Searching. In: Proc. 1984 ACM SIGMOD International Conference on Management of Data, pp. 47–57 (1984)
10. Letter Report, National Academies Press (2007), http://www.nap.edu/catalog/11800.html
11. Synthetic Simulation Data Sets: http://ndssl.vbi.vt.edu/opendata/index.html

Living Memory Annotation Tool – Image Annotations for Digital Libraries

Wolfgang Jochum[1], Max Kaiser[2], Karin Schellner[3], and Franz Wirl[3]

[1] University of Vienna, Department of Distributed and Multimedia Systems
wolfgang.jochum@univie.ac.at
[2] Austrian National Library
max.kaiser@onb.ac.at
[3] Research Studios, Studio Digital Memory Engineering, Vienna, Austria
karin.schellner@researchstudio.at, franz.wirl@researchstudio.at

Abstract. Digital Libraries are currently discovering the full potential of web technologies in conjunction with building rich user communities and retaining customers. A visit to a digital library should nowadays offer more than passive consumption of content. Both the library and the user can benefit from moving forward from the "content provider" vs. "consumer" paradigm to the "prosumer" paradigm, thus allowing the user to produce and actively contribute content, interact with content and be part of communities of interest. We are presenting a smart annotation tool developed as part of the 'Living Memory' applications in the context of the EU-project BRICKS that supports the prosumer approach by inviting users to contribute new information by annotating content or commenting other annotations, thereby creating new knowledge in a collaborative way.

1 Introduction

Current applications in the domain of digital libraries focus on technologies and content, but in many cases do not exploit the full potential of web technologies to attract users and build user communities. Today's applications should be more user-centered and actively engage users by allowing them to participate and contribute. Libraries and related memory institutions will profit from applications that not only allow them to present content to their user groups, but also provide them with technologies which foster user communities around content. These communities of interest will see added-value in revisiting the digital library.

We are presenting a method of gaining user participation by introducing the "Living Memory Annotation Tool", which was developed as a core component of the Living Memory applications in the course of the EU-funded project BRICKS [1].

L. Kovács, N. Fuhr, and C. Meghini (Eds.): ECDL 2007, LNCS 4675, pp. 549–550, 2007.

2 Description

Although libraries and other memory institutions have discovered the added-value of user involvement and user contributions, they still require appropriate tools to monitor and control user input. In order to address this problem the Living Memory Annotation Tool provides an annotation management component that enables the organisation's staff to control content of annotations and access to annotations.

The annotation tool is a web-based application that allows the user to easily create and modify annotations on images as well as on parts of images. The selection of image parts supports different figures and styles. All annotations can be shared with and commented by other users, thereby building threads of annotations. Thus the creation of user communities around clusters of annotations is enforced and better insight into existing information can be gained.

Living Memory makes use of AJAX[1] technique, which allows the user to create annotations in an intuitive and user-friendly manner. Through AJAX, changes are presented to the user without any disturbing page reloads and communication with the back-end is streamlined. The user interface can be adapted to different languages by creating a translated version of the English language resource file.

The Living Memory Annotation Schema has been defined to meet requirements of digital library's visitors as well as curators of memory institutions. The application communicates with the BRICKS network via web services to retrieve, store and modify annotation data. Annotations are stored in the BRICKS Metadata Manager complying to the Living Memory Annotation Schema. The BRICKS Metadata Manager is based on RDF[2] and JENA[3] and supports keyword and schema based search; hence, image content can be discovered by searching through its text annotations.

3 Future Work

We intend to refine and extend our annotation tool in different directions. The major effort will go toward the integration of arbitrary taxonomies and ontologies. Creating structured annotations will support domain experts in classifying content resulting in enhanced retrieval results. In parallel, a zoom-tool will be added to the existing Annotation interface which will ease the annotation process and allow users to create detailed annotation areas on high-resolution images.

References

1. BRICKS: Building Resources for Integrated Cultural Knowledge Services EU-FP6 IST 507457 (2007), http://www.brickscommunity.org
2. W3C Semantic Web Activity – RDF Core Working Group: Resource Description Framework (RDF) (2004), http://www.w3.org/RDF/
3. Jena: A semantic web framework for java, http://jena.sourceforge.net/

[1] Asynchronous JavaScript and XML.

A User-Centred Approach to Metadata Design

Emma Tonkin

UKOLN,
University of Bath, BA27AY, UK
e.tonkin@ukoln.ac.uk
http://www.ukoln.ac.uk/

Abstract. The process of development of metadata elements and structures can be approached and supported in a number of different ways. We sketch a user-centred approach to this process, based around an iterative development methodology, and briefly outline some major questions, challenges and benefits related to this approach.

Keywords: Metadata, user-centred design, evaluation.

1 Introduction

Development of application profiles (APs) – a description of an application of a metadata set – and metadata vocabularies is well-documented from many perspectives, with research focusing on aspects such as interoperability concerns, modularity and reuse. We describe work arising from the JISC-funded IEMSR metadata schema registry project. IEMSR attempts to support the process of AP and metadata vocabulary development in Dublin Core (DC) and IEEE Learning Object Metadata (LOM) via desktop and Web-based client software that draw on the central registry as a resource[3]. As the IEMSR progresses from prototype towards evaluation, collection of user feedback and use in real-world contexts, we seek to align the software more closely with present-day best practice in metadata schema development. However, metadata development processes are often relatively informal, drawing on professional experience rather than a formally encoded process model. To inform this development, it was necessary to investigate current development methodologies and to develop a compatible approach, briefly sketched here.

1.1 Iterative Development

Our model is based on the star development life cycle[1], an iterative cycle that emphasises input from stakeholders and frequent evaluation stages, reflecting an underlying assertion that to speak of the usability of metadata is appropriate in a large subset of cases. The accuracy of this assertion depends on the specific context of use; for example, a metadata fragment destined for use only by software acts as an internal data structure, making developers the sole stakeholder group. By contrast, an AP may be in widespread use, often in several widely

L. Kovács, N. Fuhr, and C. Meghini (Eds.): ECDL 2007, LNCS 4675, pp. 551–554, 2007.

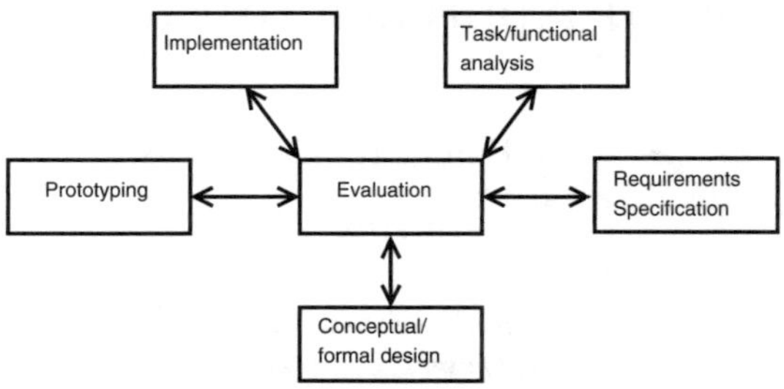

Fig. 1. The star development lifecycle

geographically distributed communities. This distributed usage pattern has a limiting impact on knowledge transfer and the available channels for feedback or repair, leading to circumstances in which usage patterns diverge. Iterative design methods are sometimes used at present for AP developments; most processes follow an essentially sequential model, although most permit ongoing application of minor changes and apply a corresponding versioning process (eg. [7]).

2 Activities

Application of the star methodology imposes prerequisites on the process of AP design. Stakeholders must be identified and approached, requirements (aims and objectives) identified, managed and encoded at each iteration. The evaluation stages of the methodology introduce additional challenges; evaluation of candidate APs or elements requires the identification of an appropriate technique for evaluating metadata structures. Evaluation methods have been proposed and applied for various aspects of digital library systems, eg.[2], [6]. Exploration of 'paper prototyping' approaches can permit exploration of metadata usage in context before development takes place, allowing issues to be identified at an early stage.

2.1 Supporting the Design Process

The schema registry may support this process in a number of ways – for example, by: promoting an appropriate methodology, providing the means to develop tools to support analysis of metadata use, and recording and allowing appropriate visualisation of changes made. It may also act as a focal point bringing together widely geographically distributed development communities.

2.2 Evaluation

Evaluation represents a key stage in this process. Marshall and Shipman[5] argue that users may be unwilling or unable to explicitly express information, and thus circumvent structures that require such formalisation. They describe many of the difficulties that this may cause, such as cognitive overhead and the need to develop, apply and consult a wealth of tacit knowledge during the process of developing a formalisation. The enforcement of a rigid, potentially misdesigned structure is characterised as a disincentive to make use of a system. They then outline an approach designed to minimise such problems, suggesting the following five principles:

- Designers need to work with users to reach a shared understanding of the use situation and the representations that best serve it.
- Designers must identify what other services or user benefits the computer can provide based on trade-offs introduced by additional formalization.
- Designers should also expect, allow, and support reconceptualization and incremental formalization in longer tasks.
- Taking a similar, computationally-based approach, designers may provide facilities that use automatically recognized (but undeclared) structures to support common user activities.
- Finally, training and facilitation can be used to help users effectively work with embedded formalisms.

We may add the following points:

- Designers must identify appropriate metrics for system evaluation.
- Metrics are required for detection and handling of systematic or random error in input. Consequences of error should be considered throughout the design phase.
- System repair and feedback methods should be considered; Marshall & Shipman invoke the need to handle semantic change.
- Approaches to error-handling and correction should be considered.

2.3 Means and Modes of Evaluation

There are various metrics that may indicate that a knowledge representation is failing the user. Dushay et al[4] demonstrate several in their analysis of DC metadata in use.

- Missing data
- Confusing or inconsistent data
- Incomplete data

Their approach to discovering flaws was based around a visual graphical analysis tool called Spotfire, and is designed for application by a human analyst rather than an as part of an automated system.

However, inconsistencies and missing data fields may generally be identified. For example, inconsistently applied encoding or syntax can be recognised using a variety of approaches, such as the use of sequence classifiers. Building and applying a limited set of partial grammars to describe the contents of a given field is possible; this is part of a general field of research covering the development and application of grammar checking techniques for natural or formal languages.

3 Future Work

Detailed user testing and evaluation is currently planned for the components making up the IEMSR. This will also enable detailed case studies to be undertaken regarding the development model described here, feeding into the development of a mature policy and guidance framework. We will also evaluate current developments in the area of computer-supported collaborative work, such as Web 2.0, for relevance to registry design. Particularly of relevance to the IEMSR project are developments in the areas of interoperability and architectural requirements.

References

1. Hix, D., Hartson, H.R.: Developing User Interfaces. Wiley, Chichester (1993)
2. Fuhr, N., Hansen, P., Mabe, M., Micsic, A., Sølvberg, I.: Digital Libraries: A generic classification and evaluation scheme. In: Constantopoulos, P., Sølvberg, I.T. (eds.) ECDL 2001. LNCS, vol. 2163, Springer, Heidelberg (2001)
3. Heery, R., Johnston, P., Beckett, D., Steer, D.: JISC Metadata Schema Registry. In: JCDL 2005 (2005)
4. Dushay, N., Hillman, D.I.: Analyzing Metadata for Effective Use and Re-Use. In: Proceedings of the Dublin Core Conference, September 28 - October 2, 2003, Seattle, WA (2003)
5. Shipman, F.M., Marshall, C.: Formality considered harmful: Experiences, emerging themes, and directions on the use of formal representations in interactive systems. In: Proc. Computer Supported Cooperative Work (CSCW) 1999, pp. 333–352 (1999)
6. Kralisch, A., Yeo, A.W., Nurfauza, J.: Linguistic and Cultural Differences in Information Categorization and Their Impact on Website Use. In: Proceedings of the Thirty-ninth Hawaii International Conference On System Sciences. January 4-7. Hawaii, USA (2006)
7. Kulvatunyou, B., Morris, K.C., Buhwan, J., Goyal, P.: Development Life Cycle and Tools for XML Content Models. In: XML Conference 2004 (2004)

A Historic Documentation Repository for Specialized and Public Access*

Cristina Ribeiro[1,2], Gabriel David[1,2], and Catalin Calistru[1,2]

[1] Faculdade de Engenharia, Universidade do Porto
[2] INESC—Porto
Rua Dr. Roberto Frias s/n, 4200-465 Porto, Portugal
{mcr,gtd,catalin}@fe.up.pt

Abstract. The web is currently the information searching and browsing environment of choice for scholars and lay users alike. The goal of most cultural heritage applications is to interest a large audience, and therefore web interfaces are being developed even when part of their functionality is not offered to the general public. We present a web-based interface for managing, browsing and searching a repository of historic documents. The documents pertain to a region which has been an important regional power in medieval times and their originals are under the custody of the Portuguese national archives. The challenges of the project came from its requisites in three aspects: rigorous archival description, the incorporation of document analysis and a flexible search interface. The system is an instance of a multimedia database framework providing both browse and retrieval functionalities to end users and configuration and content management services to the collection administrators.

Multimedia collections are more and more the rule. In digitally-born materials current environments favor the integration of video and audio materials with text, but cultural heritage collections can take advantage of media diversity to account for the sensory aspects of ancient objects. An extra challenge for cultural heritage materials comes from the need to analyze of their non-textual features and obtain useful descriptors in manageable formats.

To manage collections of multimedia documents it is necessary to identify abstractions which are useful for different kinds of objects and meaningful for the user interfacing the repository. The MetaMedia model [1] has been designed to satisfy these requirements and is organized around four main principles. The first one is that multimedia objects are organized in a *part-of hierarchy*. Each level has a set of attributes characterizing the corresponding set of items. The second principle is that of *uniform description*, whereby the same set of attributes is used for an individual object, for composite objects and for sets of related objects. The third principle is concerned with the internal structure of the individual

* Supported by FCT under project POSC/EIA/61109/2004 (DOMIR).

L. Kovács, N. Fuhr, and C. Meghini (Eds.): ECDL 2007, LNCS 4675, pp. 555–558, 2007.

documents and assumes they will be stored in one or more *segments* capturing components such as text or images. The fourth principle deals with document analysis and allows the association of *descriptors*, resulting from the analysis of some feature, as XML files to the segments.

The adopted principles have been embodied in a model capturing collection structure, standard-compliant description and content [1]. There is a strong integration between the base descriptors following description standards and the content descriptors resulting from content analysis; both are available from the interfaces offered to the collection managers and the end users. The platform has been designed as a web portal supported on a database system.

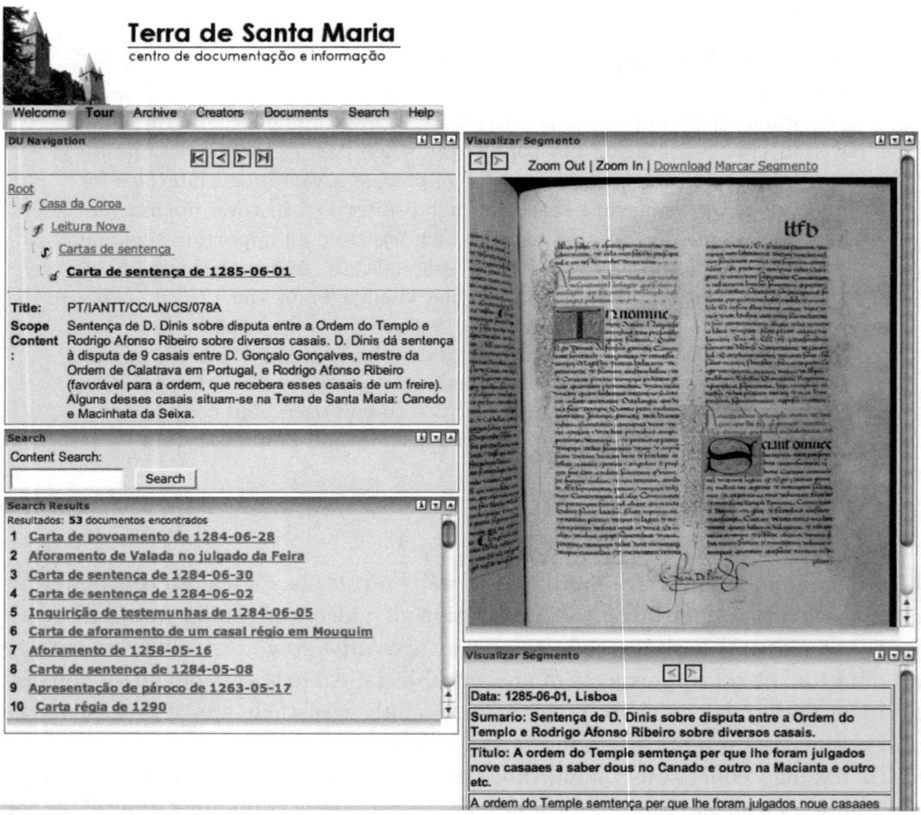

1 The Historic Documentation Repository

The Terra de Santa Maria historic documentation center [2] has been developed taking advantage of existing work by a team of medieval history specialists who have selected the documents and produced their transcriptions. The repository has been built on the multimedia database platform and used as a case study for the concepts of the model.

Information for a document in the repository includes three parts: the digitized image, the document transcription and the archival description according to the ISAD/ISAAR standards. The snapshot above of the collection "tour" shows a synthetic view of a single document; on the left we have its position in the hierarchy and part of the description and on the right the image and the transcription text.

When viewing a collection it is possible to have the complete descriptions for documents and sub-collections at any level, but also to move to the detailed view of the image and transcription for a single document.

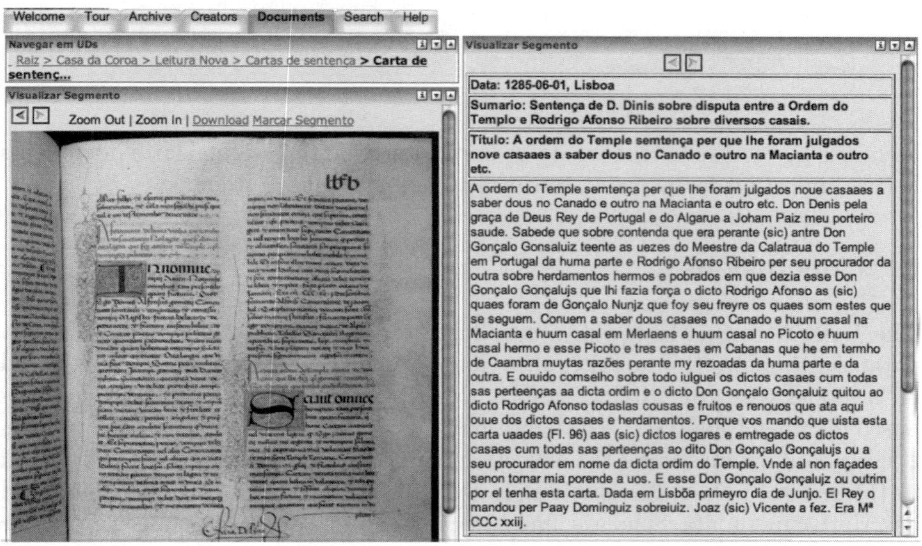

The interface offers several views on the document, intended for different kinds of users, their knowledge of the area and their permissions and is available in English and in Portuguese; the archival descriptions have only been generated in Portuguese.

On the *Archive* tab, it is possible to browse the hierarchy the archivists have designed and to edit the descriptions. The *Creators* tab has detailed information on the creators for the current unit.

The *Document* tab is intended for users who want to explore the contents of the documents. A medievalist studying one of the parchments uses this mode for observing the digitized image and its transcription side by side and possibly uploading his own analysis of the text.

Specialists need to search on specific items, while casual users require a simple keyword-based retrieval mode. Both are offered, and it is also possible to use the concepts marked up on the document transcriptions for search purposes. The figure below shows an excerpt of the available fields. Textual segments corresponding to the digital content are internally marked using XML. The markup

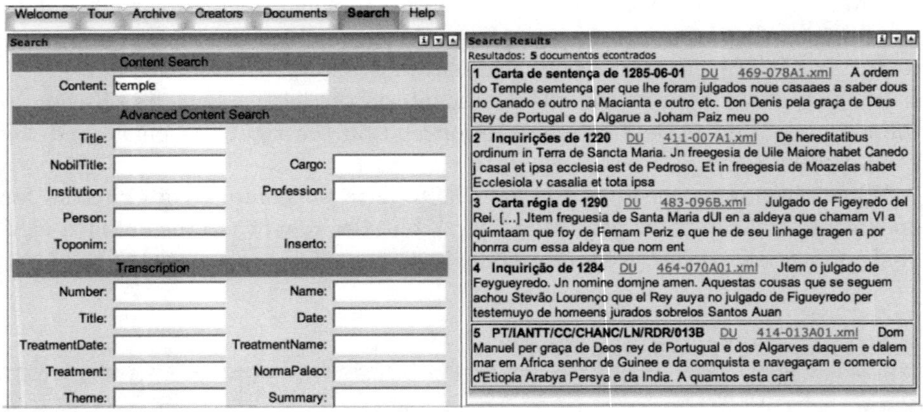

identifies key concepts that would be hard to spot on the original latin documents and is important for allowing retrieval to non-specialized users.

2 Conclusions

The Terra de Santa Maria repository illustrates the instantiation of a multimedia database framework in a cultural heritage application. The framework is based on a model where hierarchic uniform description is complemented by content-based document analysis. A web interface customizable for different user profiles is used both for managing the collection and for offering visits to specialists and to the general public. An archivist is able to create new subcollections and add descriptive metadata. Scholars may associate new or alternative transcriptions or translations to documents, or even upload some XML fragments resulting from an image processing tool. A collection administrator can manage user accounts, choose the items to highlight, add new documents and index the collection. Search modes range from search on the standard descriptors to keyword search on the full content and content search on the marked content.

References

1. Ribeiro, C., David, G., Calistru, C.: Multimedia in cultural heritage collections: A model and applications. Submitted for publication (2007)
2. Comissão de Vigilância do Castelo de Santa Maria da Feira: Centro de Documentação da Terra de Santa Maria. (2007), `http://www.castelodafeira.pt/`
3. Ribeiro, C., David, G., Calistru, C.: A multimedia database workbench for content and context retrieval. In: MMSP IEEE Workshop, IEEE Computer Society Press, Los Alamitos (2004)

Finding It on Google, Finding It on del.icio.us.

Jacek Gwizdka and Michael Cole

Department of Library and Information Science,
School of Communication, Information and Library Studies, Rutgers University
4 Huntington St, New Brunswick, NJ 08901, USA
ecdl2007@gwizdka.com, mcole@scils.rutgers.edu

Abstract. We consider search engines and collaborative tagging systems from the perspective of resource discovery and re-finding on the Web. We performed repeated searches over nine-months on Google and del.icio.us for web pages related to three topics selected to have different dynamic characteristics. The results show differences in the resources they provide to the searcher. The resources tagged on del.icio.us differ strongly from the top results returned by Google. The results also suggest the changes in the most recently tagged web pages may be associated with the level of activity in user communities and, indirectly, with external events.

Keywords: Folksonomy, Collaborative tagging, Resource discovery, Search.

1 Introduction and Motivation

Collaborative tagging of electronic resources has been described from the perspective of social navigation [4], distributed cognition [10], semiotic dynamics [1], and knowledge sharing and resource discovery [7]. In this project, we take the latter perspective and ask if delicious provides an additional dimension to information search resources on the Web. We pose our question in the context of communities as identified by users engaging in topical tagging activity. The users select Web resources and, by tagging them, provide an additional layer of information. We are interested in finding out if the selected Web resources are different from search engine results. We are also interested in examining changes in the kind and the level of tagging activity over long time periods.

2 Methodology

The Google and Delicious APIs were used make daily requests between 25.06.2006 and 1.01.2007, and then again in March 2007. The successful requests sent to Delicious and Google within a 6-hour window on the same day were paired. The Google results captured the top 19 documents. The Delicious results returned the tags related to the request and the most recent 27-30 URLs and the tags produced by users for those URLs. Five kinds of searches were conducted 1) `world cup`, 2) the phrase

L. Kovács, N. Fuhr, and C. Meghini (Eds.): ECDL 2007, LNCS 4675, pp. 559–562, 2007.

"world cup" on Google and `worldcup` on Delicious, 3) "web design" on Google and `webdesign` on Delicious, 4) `social tagging folksonomy`, and 5) `socialtagging folksonomy` (`"social tagging" folksonomy` on Google).

3 Results and Discussion

Overlap was calculated by counting exact matches of normalized URLs and for domains where any 'www.' prefix was stripped. Duplicates in a given day's data were removed for overlap and rank calculation. Table 1 compares the Delicious results with the top two pages (n=19) of Google results for submission of the same query over all days.

Table 1. Overlap of Delicious and Google search results

Query	worldcup	world cup	webdesign	social tagging folksonomy	socialtagging folksonomy
Total URLs	1402	3107	1129	1106	794
Total domains	1204	1762	1081	1081	723
URLs overlap %	1.5%	0.1%	0.6%	2.0%	0.0%
Domain overlap %	9.3%	8.3%	2.1%	8.2%	1.1%

Overlap between first page results from major search engines is low [2, 6]. Spink, et al. [9] found that 85% of the results were unique and the overlap between any pair of search engines was about 11%. They concluded that search engines appear to have different capabilities. We considered Delicious and Google as alternative search resources. Compared to Spink et al., we observed dramatically lower overlap even though overlap was calculated using only the top two pages of Google results. It seems unlikely Delicious users were tagging top ranked results retrieved from Google. This suggests users are tagging pages arrived at by other means, perhaps using very different queries to search engine, or by other Web search mechanisms altogether, for example recommendations or references in email or blogs. The mechanisms of user discovery of these pages may expose content that has not acquired (or was not designed to acquire) features that result in higher page ranks in the Google algorithm. It is also possible that taggers use search results but choose to tag only those items that are not in the top ranks, perhaps because they believe the top ranked results will remain easily found by the search engine. Future work includes considering Delicious overlap against multiple search engines.

Delicious users from the US tend to be better educated and wealthier than average [8]. Professionals or those with expertise in an area may be tagging information and resources relevant to their needs and specific interests. These documents are likely to have low ranks for search engine queries using general terms a non-expert might use in seeking relevant information on the Web.

We used 'world cup' to observe tagging activity on Delicious for a transient event, the 2006 FIFA World Cup. A rise in overlap was observed around the time of the conclusion of the event (July 9), when it might be expected that more of the new content produced by the event had been indexed by Google, and possibly that these new URLs had acquired sufficient link authority to be highly ranked. Figure 1 shows the development of activity in new Web resources being tagged with "world" and "cup" while the 2006 FIFA event was taking place and shortly afterwards. It is interesting to see that many new resources were tagged daily until shortly after the conclusion of the event, when tagging activity declined and the bookmarks stabilized. Tagging activity for other communities (`webdesign' and `social tagging folksonomy` not shown here) exhibit different dynamics, and we conclude that the level of activity may be used to characterize interaction within communities and how they are influenced by external events.

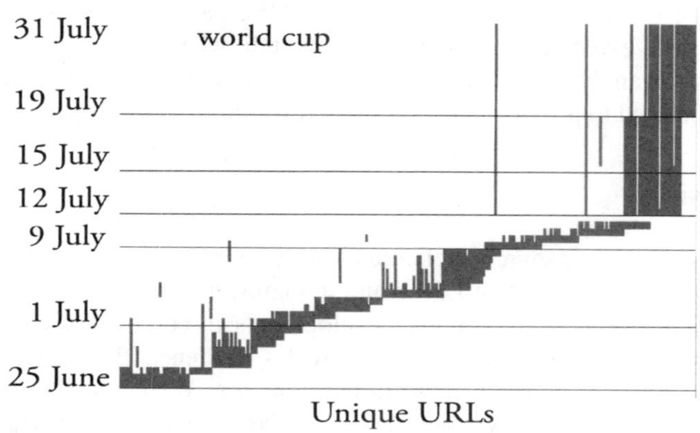

Fig. 1. *Unique URLs* (horizontal) being tagged on del.icio.us with "world" and "cup" over the period of five weeks (from June 25 to July 31,06). FIFA'2006 World Cup ended on July 9.

Fig. 2. Tags clouds with 64 most frequent words that co-occurred with "world" and "cup" in two month-long periods. July 2006 (FIFA World Cup in Germany) and March 2007 (Cricket world cup in Jamaica). "World" does not appear because it was on the stop-word list.

Figure 2 presents two tags clouds with 64 most frequent words that co-occurred with "world" and "cup". The clouds are shown for two month-long periods, during which two big world cup events took place. The co-occurring tags are quite different in each case. We can certainly learn a bit about a world cup event, or events that were taking place during each period. For example, it is clear that the first is related to soccer and FIFA (Federation of International Football Associations), while the second to cricket and ICC (International Cricket Council). Since the latter was during winter, we also note "skiing" among the tags. We can see what world cup taggers found of particular interest. The French football player Zinedine Zidane's infamous headbutt and the murder of cricket coach Bob Woolmer. We can identify countries that were involved in each event, but we cannot easily tell where each event was located. Clearly, this short analysis uses additional knowledge. Future work includes examining if tags could be used to provide machine support for information seeking tasks.

4 Conclusion

Considered as a search resource, Delicious results have very little overlap with the top pages of Google results, both in URLs and domains. The Delicious results appear to capture transient events and evolving developments in certain domains that are not reflected in Google's top results. This provides evidence that Delicious offers a resource that may provide a new dimension for Web searching beyond the collaborative tagging activity. Furthermore, Delicious may provide source of information about the level and the kind of activity in different communities.

References

1. Cattuto, C.: Semiotic dynamics in online social communities. The European Physical Journal C - Particles and Fields 46, 33–37 (2006)
2. Chignell, M.H., Gwizdka, J., Bodner, R.C.: Discriminating meta-search: A framework for evaluation. Information Processing and Management 35, 337–362 (1999)
3. Coenen, T., Kenis, D., Damme, C.V., Matthys, E.: Knowledge Sharing over Social Networking Systems: Architecture, Usage Patterns and Their Application (2006)
4. Dieberger, A., Dourish, P., H.K., Resnick, P., Wexelblat, A.: Social navigation: techniques for building more usable systems, vol. 7(6), pp. 36–45. ACM Press, New York (2000)
5. Golder, S.A., Huberman, B.A.: Usage patterns of collaborative tagging systems. Journal of Information Science 32(2), 198–208 (2006)
6. Gordon, M., Pathak, P.: Finding information on the world wide web: The retrieval effectiveness of search engines. Information Processing and Management 35, 141–180 (1999)
7. Macgregor, G., McCulloch, E.: Collaborative tagging as a knowledge organisation and resource discovery tool. Library Review 55(5), 291–300 (2006)
8. Rainie, L.: 28% of Online Americans Have Used the Internet to Tag Content. Pew Internet and American Life Project (2007)
9. Spink, A., Jansen, B., Blakley, C., Koshman, S.: A study of results overlap and uniqueness among major Web search engines. IP&M 42, 1379–1391 (2006)
10. Steels, L.: Collaborative tagging as distributed cognition. Pragmatics & Cognition 14(2), 287–292 (2006)

DIGMAP – Discovering Our Past World with Digitised Maps

José Borbinha, Gilberto Pedrosa, Diogo Reis, João Luzio, Bruno Martins, João Gil, and Nuno Freire

IST- Instituto Superior Técnico. Av. Rovisco Pais, 1049-001 Lisboa, IST - Portugal
jlb@ist.utl.pt, gilberto.pedrosa@ist.utl.pt, diogo.menareis@ist.utl.pt, bruno.martins@tagus.ist.utl.pt, joao.luzio@ist.utl.pt, j_gil@netcabo.pt, nuno.freire@ist.utl.pt

Abstract. DIGMAP is a project that will develop solutions for georeferenced digital libraries, especially focused on historical materials and in the promoting of our cultural and scientific heritage. The final results of the project will consist in a set of services available in the Internet, and in reusable open-source software solutions. The main service will be a specialized digital library, reusing metadata from European national libraries, to provide discovery and access to contents. Relevant metadata from third party sources will be also reused, as also descriptions and references to any other relevant external resource. The initiative will make a proof of concept reusing and enriching the contents from several European national libraries.

1 Description

DIGMAP is an international project co-funded by the European Community programme eContentplus[1]. This project will develop solutions for georeferenced digital libraries, especially focused on historical materials and in the promoting of our cultural and scientific heritage. The final results of the project will consist in a set of services available in the Internet, and in reusable open-source software solutions.

The main purpose of the project is to develop a specialized service, reusing metadata from European national libraries, to provide discovery and access to contents provided by those libraries. Relevant metadata from third party sources will be also reused, as also descriptions and references to any other relevant external resource. Ultimately, DIGMAP will pursue the purpose to become the main international information source and reference service for old maps and related bibliography.

2 DIGMAP Use Cases

DIGMAP proposes to develop a solution for indexing, searching and browsing in collections of digitised historical maps, according to the main use cases presented in

[1] http://www.digmap.eu

L. Kovács, N. Fuhr, and C. Meghini (Eds.): ECDL 2007, LNCS 4675, pp. 563–566, 2007.

the Fig. 1. It will be able to index maps by their geographic boundaries and will make it easy to classify, index, search and browse them with the support of multilingual geographic thesauri. DIGMAP will take also advantage of any available descriptive metadata to improve the services. Anther important service provided by DIGMAP will be a reference service, through which it will be possible to submit questions to be answered by experts registered in the system with specific knowledge in the area. This will be supported by in a controlled environment so that further access to previous questions and answers is facilitated and irrelevant questions can be discarded.

DIGMAP proposes also advanced features for the automatic indexing of historical maps, in order to make it possible to add to the collections and process new maps at very low human cost. Maps can be very rich in decorative and stylistic details, making them very different from, for example, photos, so new image processing techniques will be developed for this purpose.

The final service will offer also a sophisticated browsing environment for humans, with special features such as geographic browsing and timelines (for those maps where it is possible and easy to assess the date).

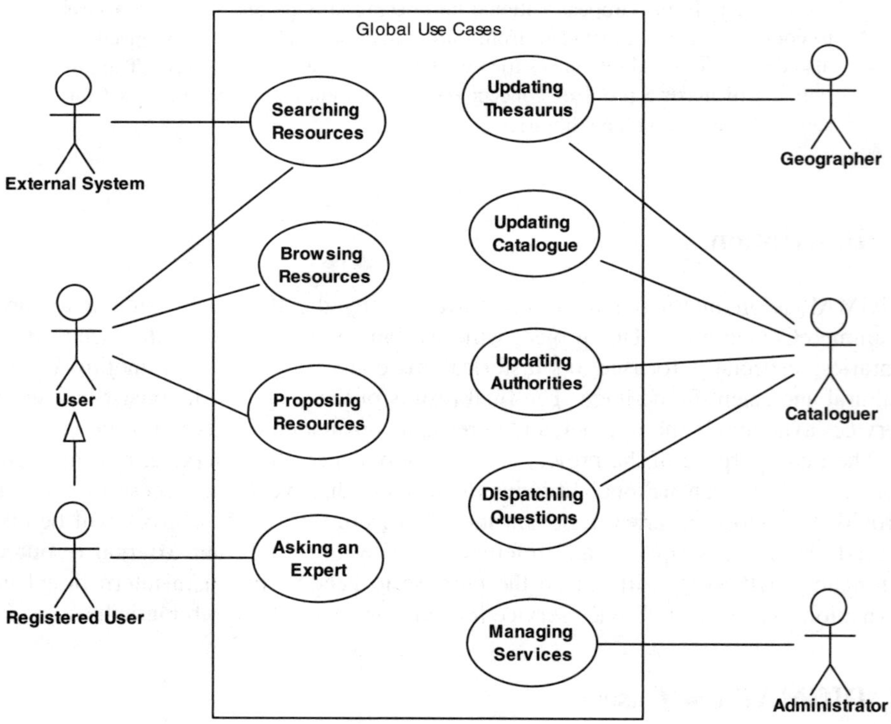

Fig. 1. DIGMAP schematic architecture

3 DIGMAP Architecture

All the software solutions produced in DIGMAP will be based on standard and open data models and will be released as open-source, so the results will be useful for local digital libraries of maps, as standalone systems, or as interoperable components for wider and distributed systems (as for example portal management systems). The generic architecture will follow the design represented in the Fig. 2.

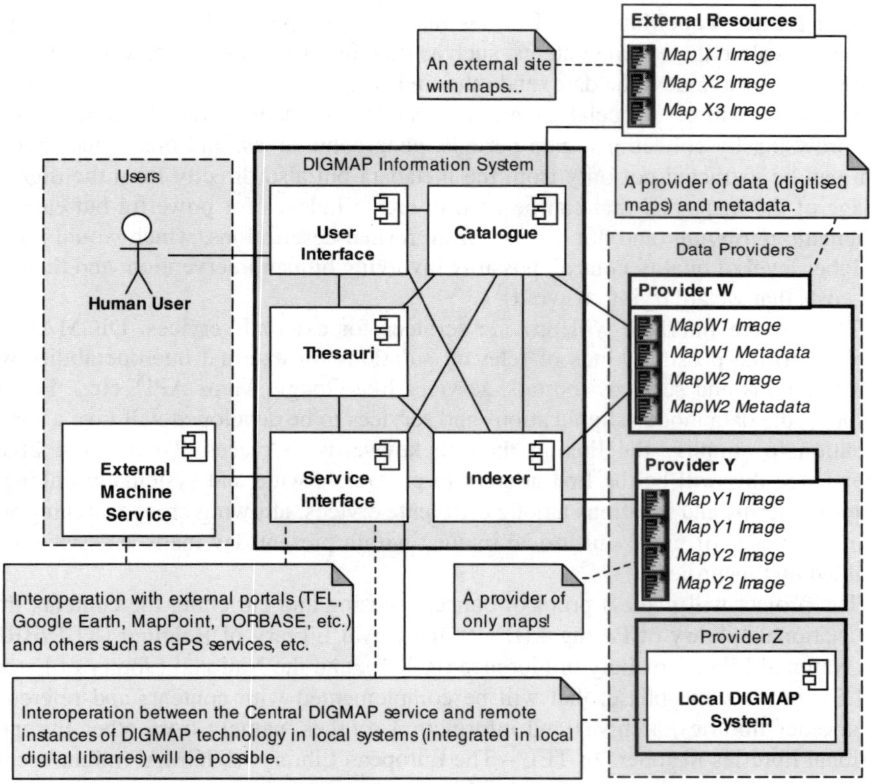

Fig. 2. DIGMAP schematic architecture

The Thesauri is the component of the System that registers auxiliary information for the purpose of indexing of Resources, searching be Resources and browsing for Resources. It will consist in a module able to manage information schemas compatible with the Authority Files created and used by libraries (mainly in UNIMARC[2] and MARC 21[3]), as also compatible with gazetteers as defined by the OGC[4]. In this sense, this module will be developed as a semantic information system, to manage and

[2] UNIMARC Forum – http://www.unimarc.net/

[3] MARC Standards – http://www.loc.gov/marc/

[4] Open Geospatial Consortium – http://www.opengeospatial.org

provide access to information relating to names of persons and organizations, concepts, geographic coordinates, names of places or areas, and historical events related with geographic points, places or areas (with dates or time intervals).

4 DIGMAP Service

The DIGMAP service will offer a browsing environment for human users. The interface will explore paradigms inspired by services and tools such as Google Maps[5], Virtual Earth[6], TimeMap[7], etc. Besides that, special specific functions will be provided to explore the actual contents, such as timelines (for those maps where it is possible and easy to assess the date) and other indexing features.

DIGMAP will give special attention to the development of visual clues, functions for browsing by collections, date periods, geographic areas, and other characteristic that can be extracted not only from the metadata but also directly from the digitised image of the maps and that can be used to create indexes for powerful but easy and pragmatic retrieving (and not forcibly from formal descriptions, which would require a higher level of quality control, possibly involving human intervention, and therefore the costs that we are trying to avoid).

The Service Interface will provide services for external services. DIGMAP will explore all the possible kinds of relevant solutions for external interoperability with other systems and services (portals, services like Google Maps API[8], etc.). For this purpose, the data models, applications and services to be developed will give a special attention to simplify the linking through keywords to places. To the best of our knowledge this will be the first attempt to promote a wide and systematic linking of historical terms and locations among different services, allowing cross searching with terms or places of mostly historical interest within present day maps, a service to be enabled by this project

The project will make a proof of concept reusing and enriching the contents from the National Library of Portugal (BNP), the Royal Library of Belgium (KBR/BRB), the National Library of Italy in Florence (BNCF), and the National Library of Estonia (NLE). In a second phase, that will be complemented with contents and references from other libraries, archives and information sources, namely from other European national libraries members of TEL – The European Library[9] (DIGMAP might became an effective service integrated with TEL - in this sense the project is fully aligned with the vision "European Digital Library" as expressed in the "i2010 digital libraries" initiative of the European Commission).

[5] Google Maps - http://maps.google.com
[6] MSN Virtual Earth - http://virtualearth.msn.com
[7] TimeMap Open Source Consortium - http://www.timemap.net
[8] Google Maps API - http://www.google.com/apis/maps
[9] The European Library – http://www.theeuropeanlibrary.org/

Specification and Generation of Digital Libraries into DSpace Using the 5S Framework

Douglas Gorton, Weiguo Fan, and Edward A. Fox

Department of Computer Science
Virginia Polytechnic Institute and State University
Blacksburg, VA 24061 USA
{dogorton, wfan, fox}@vt.edu

Abstract. While digital library (DL) systems continue to become more powerful and usable, a certain amount of inherent complexity remains in the installation, configuration, and customization of out-of-the-box solutions like DSpace and Greenstone. In this work, we build upon past work in the 5S Framework for Digital Libraries and 5SL DL specification language to devise an XML-based model for the specification of DLs for DSpace. We pair this way of specifying DLs with a generator tool which takes a DL specification that adheres to the model and generates a working DSpace instance that matches the specification.

Keywords: digital libraries, specification, generation, DSpace, 5S, 5SL.

In today's ever-changing world of technology and information, a growing number of organizations and universities seek to store digital documents in an online, accessible manner. These digital library repositories are powerful systems that allow institutions to store their digital documents while permitting the use, interaction, and collaboration among users in their organizations. Despite the continual work on DL systems that can produce out-of-the-box online repositories, the installation, configuration, and customization processes of these systems are still far from straight-forward.

Motivated by the arduous process of designing digital library instances, installing software packages like DSpace and Greenstone, configuring, customizing, and populating such systems, we have developed an XML-based model for specifying the nature of DSpace digital libraries. The ability to map out a digital library to be created in a straightforward, XML-based way allows for the integration of such a specification with other DL tools. To make use of DL specifications for DSpace, we create a DL generator that uses these models of digital library systems to create, configure, customize, and populate DLs as specified.

This is not the first work on DL specifications and generation. We draw heavily on previous work in understanding the nature of digital libraries from the 5S Framework for Digital Libraries [1]. That framework divides the concerns of digital libraries into a complex, formal representation of the elements that are basic to any minimal digital library system including Streams, Structures, Scenarios, Spaces, and Societies. 5S

L. Kovács, N. Fuhr, and C. Meghini (Eds.): ECDL 2007, LNCS 4675, pp. 567–569, 2007.

provides a universal way to understand the structure and characteristics that all DLs exhibit. 5SL is a language for the declarative specification of DL systems based on 5S using XML [2]. Also derived from this body of work is 5SGen, a generator that takes 5SL specifications and creates a set of tailored DL components that adhere to the specification [3]. In this work, we take a step beyond the theoretical, minimal DL towards practical DL systems like DSpace.

We reflect on this previous work and provide a fresh application of the 5S framework to practical DL systems. Our XML model for the specification of DSpace DLs provides the most commonly used functionalities and structures that the software furnishes. We divide our specification along the lines of the 5S's, into the aspects of the digital libraries based on DL structure, user related details, interface issues, and file type representations.

Our digital library generator is extensible and provides support for any digital library software for which generator classes are defined. The generation process takes a DL specification, checks it for validity against a corresponding XML schema, and goes through the various configuration, customization, and generation tasks specified including structure, users, import of content, and others.

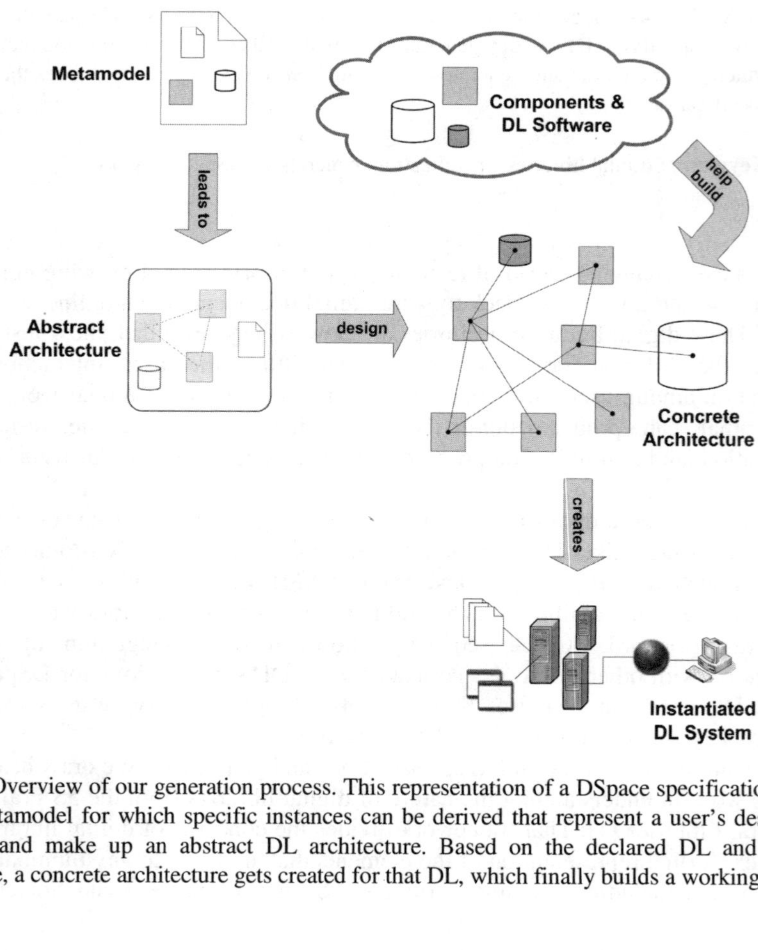

Fig. 1. Overview of our generation process. This representation of a DSpace specification serves as a metamodel for which specific instances can be derived that represent a user's desired DL system and make up an abstract DL architecture. Based on the declared DL and DSpace software, a concrete architecture gets created for that DL, which finally builds a working DL.

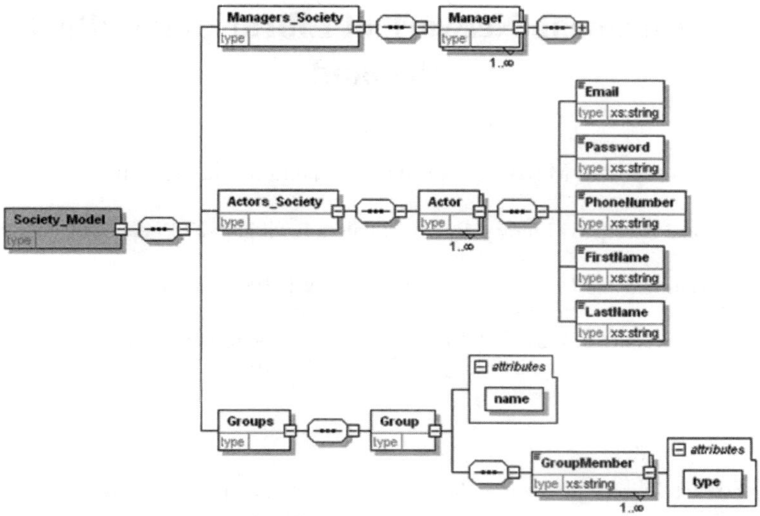

Fig. 2. An example of the structure of the Society sub-model of our DSpace specification method. Society related issues are defined here and include Managers, Actors, and Groups (which map to DSpace administrative users, regular users, and Groups respectively.)

We present this DSpace DL specification language and generator as an aid to DL designers and others interested in easing the specification of DSpace digital libraries. We believe that our method will not only enable users to create DLs easier, but also gain a greater understanding about their desired DL structure, software, and digital libraries in general.

Acknowledgments. We would like to thank and acknowledge the assistance and contributions of members of the Digital Library Research Laboratory in the design and implementation of this work as well as the support of NSF through grants IIS-0535057, IIS-0325579, DUE-0532825, DUE-0435059.

References

1. Gonçalves, M.A., Fox, E.A., Watson, L.T., Kipp, N.A.: Streams, structures, spaces, scenarios, societies (5S): A formal model for digital libraries. ACM Trans. Inf. Syst. 22, 270–312 (2004)
2. Gonçalves, M.A., Fox, E.A.: 5SL-a language for declarative specification and generation of digital libraries. In: JCDL'02: Joint Conference on Digital Libraries, July 14-18, 2002, pp. 263–272. ACM, Portland, OR (2002)
3. Gonçalves, M.A., Zhu, Q., Kelapure, R., Fox, E.A.: Rapid Modeling, Prototyping, and Generation of Digital Libraries - A Theory-Based Approach. Technical Report TR-03-16, Computer Science, Virginia Tech, Blacksburg, VA (2002)

EOD - European Network of Libraries for eBooks on Demand

Zoltán Mező[1], Sonja Svoljšak[2], and Silvia Gstrein[3]

[1] National Széchényi Library, Budavári Palota F wing, 1827 Budapest, Hungary
mezo@oszk.hu
[2] National and University Library, Turjaska 1, 1001 Ljubljana, Slovenia
sonja.svoljsak@nuk.uni-lj.si
[3] University of Innsbruck Library, Innrain 52, 6020 Innsbruck, Austria
silvia.gstrein@uibk.ac.at

Abstract. European libraries host millions of books published from 1500 to 1900. Due to age and value, they are often only accessible to users actually present at these libraries. EOD (eBooks on Demand) is a European wide service which gives an answer to this problem by providing eBooks on request from a wide range of European Libraries. The service is currently carried out within the framework of the EU project "Digitisation on Demand". EOD is an open network and every European library is welcome to join.

Keywords: eBooks, eBooks on Demand, Digitisation on Demand, Network.

1 The EOD Service Network

1.1 Introduction

Have you ever urgently needed a certain book in its original edition for an essay or out of mere interest? What was your reaction when this particular book was only available from a library many miles away to be borrowed exclusively on-site?

Even if some major digitisation projects have been underway in recent years, many of them only cover world languages like English and do not provide adequate solutions in terms of different languages, alphabets and cultures, even though this is of special importance for Europe with its variety of different countries and languages. European libraries host millions of books published from 1500 to 1900. Due to their age and value, however, access to those "treasures" is often limited to experts or people actually working in places of textual preservation.

In contrast, the Digitisation on Demand project, co-funded by the European Union, has been developing a more democratic, user-centred, approach for readers as it envisages a network of libraries offering every copyright-free book as eBook on a user's request. It hosts an electronic service by which the vast variety of public

L. Kovács, N. Fuhr, and C. Meghini (Eds.): ECDL 2007, LNCS 4675, pp. 570–572, 2007.

domain books from a consortium presently consisting of 13 European Libraries in 8 different countries can be accessed.[1]

In general, every user is able to order copyright-free books via common library catalogues for a certain fee. The respective library then makes a digital copy of the requested book and e-mails the download-link to the user. Books digitised in this way will then be incorporated into the online repositories of the participating libraries and will thus be accessible to everybody on the internet.

1.2 The Philosophy and Scope of Materials Offered Through the Service

The general aim of EOD eBooks service is to extend the general accessibility of rare library holdings. Most of the EOD libraries offer copyright free books printed between 1500 and 1900. Some libraries nevertheless also offer the digitisation of books beyond that timeframe, namely for special user groups in particular circumstances, e.g. for researchers or for people who are visually impaired or blind.

1.3 Ordering and Delivering eBooks Through EOD – From the Customer's and the Library's Point of View

All catalogue records of books available for digitisation via EOD contain a special order button. Whenever a customer sees this button, he can order an eBook directly from the online catalogue of a library.

Fig. 1. Example EOD button

After filling out the order form the customer receives a notification and is directed to a special tracking page where he is able to discern the status of his order and communicate with the library administrator.

The final product; the EOD eBook is a digitised book delivered as a PDF file. In the advanced version, the file contains the image of the scanned original as well as the automatically recognized full text. Marks, annotations and other notes in the margins of the original volume are also preserved in the digital version.

Central to the EOD network is a web-based software (Order Data Manager). It is hosted by the central service provider and offers all necessary components for order

[1] The EOD service is currently carried out within the framework of the eTEN program. The respective EU project "Digitisation on Demand" was launched in October 2006 with 13 libraries from 8 European countries and runs until spring 2008. Project partners are the Bavarian State Library, Humboldt-University Berlin, National Library of Portugal, National Library of Estonia, National and University Library of Slovenia, National Széchényi Library of Hungary, The Royal Library of Denmark, University Library of Bratislava, University Library of Graz, University Library of Greifswald, University Library of Regensburg, Vienna University Library co-ordinated by the University Library of Innsbruck. For additional information see http://www.books2ebooks.eu

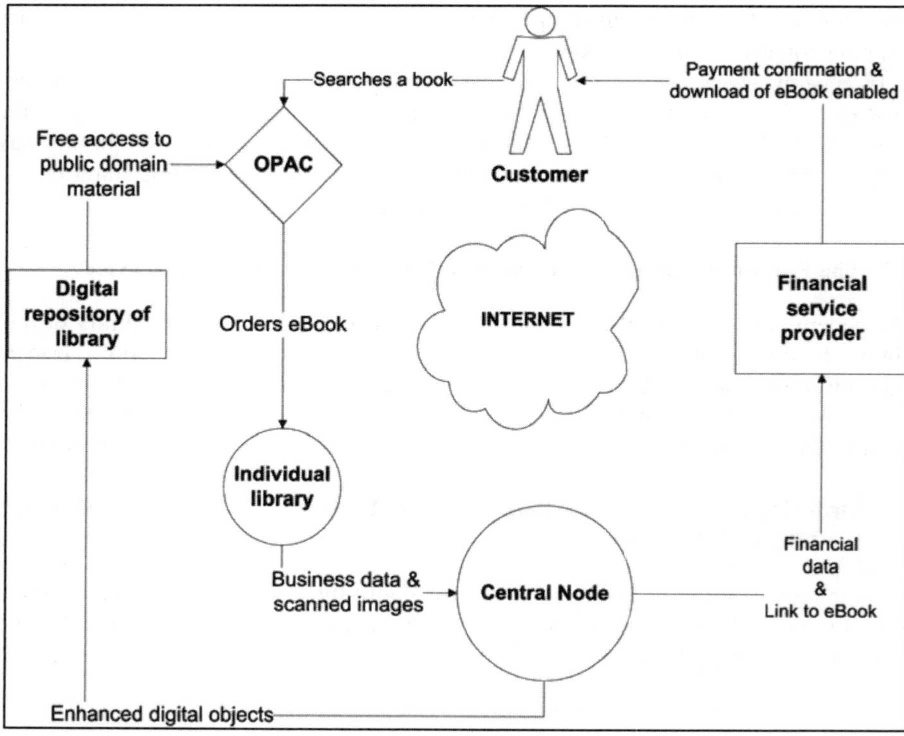

Fig. 2. EOD service – the architecture

management, customer relations, eBook creation (including OCR), eBook delivery and accounting.

1.4 Results and Outlook

The experiences and results of the service implementation at the University Library of Innsbruck, which is actually a middle-sized library, are reported representatively:

As far as this library is concerned an average of one eBook request per working day is currently being received either via direct order or via a cost estimation request. About two thirds of the overall cost estimations later become actual eBooks orders. Every second customer orders an eBook with automatically recognised text. About 80% of all customers prefer the downloadable eBook to postal delivery. About the same number of people choose credit card as a payment option.

As to the origins of eBook requests, the case of Innsbruck University Library shows a threefold division: one third of them are requests from Austria, another third from Germany and last but not least one third of requests come from other European countries and the rest of the world.

Semantics and Pragmatics of Preference Queries in Digital Libraries

El hadji Mamadou Nguer

LRI, Université Paris Sud
nguer@lri.fr

Abstract. As information becomes available in increasing amounts, and to growing numbers of users, the shift towards a more user-centered, or personalized access to information becomes crucial. In this paper we consider the semantics and pragmatics of preference queries over tables containing information objects described through a set of attributes. In particular, we address two basic issues:

- how to define a preference query and its answer (semantics)
- how to evaluate a preference query (pragmatics)

The main contributions of this paper are (a) the proposal of an expressive language for declaring qualitative preferences, (b) a novel approach to evaluating a preference query (c) the design of a user friendly interface with preference queries. Although our main motivation originates in digital libraries, our proposal is quite general and can be used in several application contexts.

1 Introduction

As information becomes available in increasing amounts, and to growing numbers of users, the shift towards a more user-centered, or personalized access to information becomes crucial. Personalized access can involve customization of the user interface or adaptation of the content to meet user preferences. This paper addresses the latter issue, and more precisely adaptation of the answer returned by a query to user preferences. We call *preference based query*, or simply *preference query* a usual query together with a set of preferences expressed by user, online, during query formulation. Such queries are useful in several application contexts where users browsing extremely large data collections don't have a clear view of the information objects . Rather, they are attempting to discover objects that are potentially useful to them in some decision making task, or in other words to identify objects that best suit their preferences. The main objective of this paper is to introduce a formal framework for specifying and evaluating queries in digital library. However, although our motivation comes from digital libraries [10], the results presented in this paper apply to other application contexts as well (e.g. e-shops, e-catalogues etc.). We consider a digital library catalogue essentially as a relational table describing various electronic

L. Kovács, N. Fuhr, and C. Meghini (Eds.): ECDL 2007, LNCS 4675, pp. 573–578, 2007.

documents through a set of attributes. Figure 1 shows an example of a digital library catalogue that we shall use as our running example. In the catalogue, each document is described by a reference (e.g. the document's URI), its year of publication, the (first) author's name, the subject category treated by the document, the language in which the document is written and the electronic format of document (such as Word, Pdf, and so on). In other words, we view the catalogue just like a table of a relational database, whose schema is **C(Ref, Year, Author, Subject, Language, Format)**, and in which each column is associated with a set of values (i.e. a domain). For simplicity, in Figure 1, we denote the references to documents by integers.

A query expressed by a user is of the form A=a, where 'A' is an attribute and 'a' is a value in the domain of A. For example, consider the following query:

$$\mathsf{Q_1} = [(\mathsf{Category} = \mathsf{Poetry}) \vee (\mathsf{Category} = \mathsf{Fiction})] \wedge (\mathsf{Language} = \mathsf{English})$$

To answer this query we must compute the set of documents having Poetry or Fiction as their Category attribute, then the set of documents having English as their Language attribute, and finally take the intersection of these two sets:

$$\mathsf{ans}(\mathsf{Q_1}) = (\{1,3,5\} \cup \{2,4,6\}) \cap \{2,3,5,6,8\} = \{2,3,5,6\}$$

Given that the size of the answer set might be too large to be exploited by a casual user, it would be interesting to present the returned documents in a decreasing order with respect to user preferences. The user can then inspect the most interesting documents first, and stop inspection when the documents become less and less interesting. However, in order to produce such an ordering of the answer set, the system must have access to user preferences, and this can be done in one of two ways:

1. The user declares *offline* a set of preferences to the system, or the system elicits user preferences by monitoring and analyzing previous queries; in either case, the set of user preferences is *stored* by the system - and referred to as the *user profile* (one talks then of profile-based queries).
2. The user declares *online* a set of preferences, together with the query; the set of preferences is not stored by the system but simply used to order the answer set during the processing of the query (one talks then of preference based queries).

It should be stressed that, no matter how user preferences are made available to the system, they influence strongly the presentation of the answer set. For example, consider the following statement of preferences over the attribute Category:

$\mathsf{P_1} : (\mathsf{Category} : \mathsf{Poetry} \rightarrow \mathsf{Fiction})$ [meaning that poetry is preferred to fiction]

We would like the previous query Q_1, together with the statement P_1, to return a result showing the documents about poetry before documents about fiction. In other words, we would like the answer to be presented as follows:

$$\mathsf{ans}(\mathsf{Q_1}, \mathsf{P_1}) = \{3,5\} \rightarrow \{2,6\}$$

It is important to note that the answer set of Q_1, processed alone, and the answer set of Q_1 processed together with the statement P_1 contain the *same* set of documents. The difference lies in the fact that, in presence of P_1, the answer set of Q_1 is partitioned into two subsets *ordered* so that the first subset contains documents about poetry and the second about fiction.

Oid	Author	Year	Category	Language	Format
1	A1	2001	Poetry	French	Word
2	A1	1998	Fiction	English	Pdf
3	A2	2000	Poetry	English	Pdf
4	A3	2001	Fiction	German	Pdf
5	A1	2002	Poetry	English	Word
6	A2	2000	Fiction	English	Word
7	A4	1998	Drama	German	Pdf
8	A2	2002	Comedy	English	Pdf
9	A3	2007	Comedy	French	Pdf

Fig. 1. A Digital Library Catalogue

In the previous example a preference was expressed in the form of a pair of attribute values (namely, Poetry and Fiction) with the understanding that the first value in the pair is preferred to the second. Expressing preferences in the form of pairs of attribute values is referred to in the literature as the *qualitative approach* [1,2,3,4,5,6,7,8,9].

The main contributions of this paper are (a) the proposal of an expressive language for declaring qualitative preferences, (b) a novel approach to evaluating a preference query by rewriting it into a sequence of standard queries whose evaluations constitute the answer to the preference query and (c) the design of a user friendly interface that allows users to express preference queries in two simple steps. The work presented here is part of my doctoral work and it is conducted in the context of the DELOS Network of Excellence in Digital Libraries, within WP-2, Task 2.10 (Information Access and Personalization).

2 The Definition of a Preference Query

As we have seen in the introduction, each attribute is associated with a set of values, called its domain. In order to simplify the presentation, we define the domain of two or more attributes to be the Cartesian product of the attribute domains. For example, the domain of Category, Format is defined as follows:

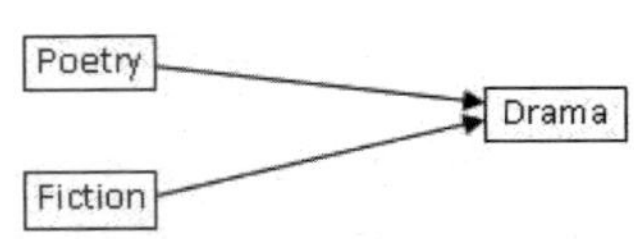

Fig. 2. P(Category) graph

Dom({Category, Format})= dom(Category)× dom(Format)

We define a preference over an attribute A to be any acyclic binary relation P(A) over the domain of A. For example, the following is a preference over the attribute Category:

P(Category)= {(Poetry, Drama), (Fiction, Drama)}

A pair (x, y) in a preference relation is interpreted as "x is preferred to y". So in our previous example Category is preferred to Drama and Fiction is preferred to Drama. Typically, a preference relation is of small size and is represented as a graph, called the preference graph (see Figure 4). As we mentioned in the introduction, a preference query is a standard query Q together with a preference relation P. Here, we make the following simplifying assumption: the query Q is always the disjunction of all values appearing in P (i.e. Q is implicit in P). Under this assumption a preference query is defined by simply giving a preference relation P. The problem then is how to evaluate P. In our approach, in order to evaluate P we rewrite it as a sequence of standard queries whose answers constitute the answer to P. We illustrate our approach in Figure 3, using our previous example:

First, consider the query Q which is implicit in P: Q=Poetry$\vee$ Fiction$\vee$ Drama.

As Poetry is preferred to Drama and Fiction is preferred to Drama, the documents returned by Poetry (considered as a query) should precede those that are returned by Drama (considered as a query), and similarly, the documents returned by Fiction should precede those that are returned by Drama. On the other hand, as Poetry and Fiction are not comparable, the documents that are returned by Poetry or Fiction should all precede the documents returned by Drama. Therefore, the following sequence of queries produces the answer to P:

The values appearing in P(Category) that is the nodes of the preference graph determine the tuple space

$$\underbrace{(Cat = Poetry) \vee (Cat = Fiction) \vee (Cat = Drama)}$$

Tuple space: { 1, 2, 3, 4, 5, 6, 7}

The arrows of the graph determine how the Tuple space is partitioned and ordered:

$$\underbrace{\underbrace{(Cat = Poetry) \vee (Cat = Fiction)}_{Q_1} \Rightarrow \underbrace{(Cat = Drama)}_{Q_2}}$$

Fig. 3. Evaluating a preference query

Q_1= Poetry$\rightarrow$ Fiction $\rightarrow$ Q_2= Drama

In other words, is rewritten as a sequence of two queries, Q1 then Q2, whose answers constitute the evaluation of P: { 1, 2, 3, 4, 5, 6} $\rightarrow$ {7}.

We have designed an algorithm that allows deriving the sequence of queries systematically. Our algorithm is based on topological sorting, and its application is illustrated in Figure 3. The complexity of the algorithm is linear to the size of the preference graph, where this size is defined to be the sum of the number of nodes and the number of edges. The algorithm described in Figure 3 applies also to preference relations defined over sets of attributes. Such "composite" preference relations are derived from "atomic" preference relations declared over two or more single attributes. For example, given a preference relation P(A) over attribute A, and P(B) over attribute B one can derive a composite preference relation P(AB) over A, B. The composite preference relation relates tuples over A, B. A complete account of the derivation process is given in the full paper.

3 The User Interface

An interface has been developed to allow users to define preference queries and exploit their answers in two simple steps. Here, we explain these steps briefly referring to the screen shot of Figure 3:

Step 1: Definition of preference relation P

1. The user is presented with the set of all attributes (i.e. the headings of the catalogue).
2. The user choose an attribute A and clicks the "+" button and the system shows a query field and preferences area where binary table with attributes L and R (for "Left" and "Right", respectively); the user then enters the desired pairs that constitute the preference relation P(A)[1]

   At the end of this step the system defines the preference relation and rewrites it as a sequence $Q_1 \rightarrow Q_2 \rightarrow \cdots \rightarrow Q_n$ of standard queries.

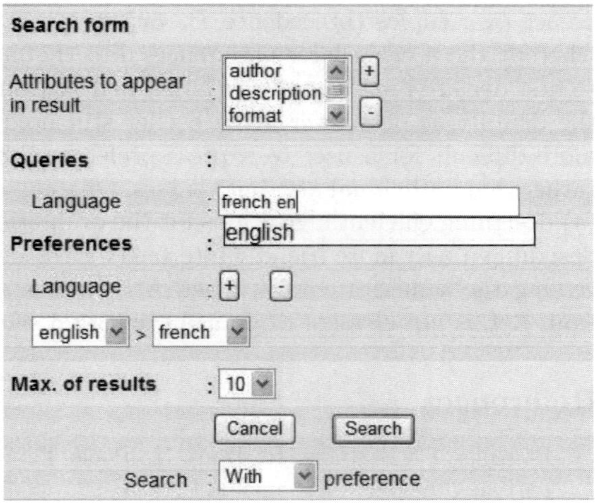

Fig. 4. P(Category) graph

Step 2: Exploitation of the answer

1. The user "clicks" on a button labeled "Search" and the system returns the answer to Q_1.
2. If the user is satisfied with the documents contained in the set ans(Q_1) then the session stops; otherwise the user clicks on "next" to receive the answer of the next query in the sequence.

It is important to note that this dialogue between the user and the system allows progressive evaluation of the queries in the sequence thus saving time: evaluation of the preference relation is controlled by the user, and it stops as soon as the user feels satisfied by the answers received so far.

[1] In case of composite preference this step is repeated as many times as there are attributes in the set defining the composite preference.

4 Future Work

We have presented a formal framework for the definition and processing of both, qualitative and quantitative preference queries, in a uniform manner.

For qualitative queries, in particular, we have introduced a language for expressing preferences, namely the language of precedence relations, which is strictly more expressive than the languages that have been proposed in the literature. Concerning the declaration of preferences (precedence or scoring) over multiple attributes, we have adopted the approach of letting the user make declarations over individual attributes, then choose a way of combining the declarations (Pareto or Lexicographic) and finally have the system derive the combined preference over tuples (precedence $P_\times$ or scoring $S_\times$). One can imagine a scenario whereby the user declares preferences directly on a set of tuples, without having to first declare preferences over individual attributes. Clearly, in such a scenario, the definitions of answer given earlier still hold. However, we think that it is more difficult for a user to express preferences by comparing or scoring tuples rather than individual attribute values. Ongoing research aims at two objectives: (a) designing efficient algorithms for the evaluation of preference queries and (b) designing a user more friendly interface for the declaration of preference (c) processing the same framework when A(i), where A an attribute and i an object from Ref, is not element of dom(A) but a set of dom(A).

References

1. Boutilier, C., Brafman, R., Hoos, H., Poole, D.: Reasoning with conditional ceteris paribus preference statements. In: UAI-99, pp. 71–80 (1999)
2. Chomicki, J.: Iterative Modification and Incremental Evaluation of Preference Queries. In: Dix, J., Hegner, S.J. (eds.) FoIKS 2006. LNCS, vol. 3861, pp. 63–82. Springer, Heidelberg (2006)
3. Chomicki, J.: Preference formulas in relational queries. ACM Transactions on Database Systems (TODS) 28(4), 427–466 (2003)
4. Chomicki, J.: Querying with Intrinsic Preferences. In: Jensen, C.S., Jeffery, K.G., Pokorný, J., Šaltenis, S., Bertino, E., Böhm, K., Jarke, M. (eds.) EDBT 2002. LNCS, vol. 2287, pp. 34–51. Springer, Heidelberg (2002)
5. Chomicki, J.: Semantic optimization of preference queries. In: Kuijpers, B., Revesz, P.Z. (eds.) CDB 2004. LNCS, vol. 3074, Springer, Heidelberg (2004)
6. Domshlak, C., Brafman, R.: reasoning and consistency testing. In: KR-02, pp. 121–132 (2002)
7. Hafenrichter, B., Kießling, W.: Optimization of Relational Preference Queries. In: ADC 2005, pp. 175–184 (2005)
8. Kießling, W.: Preference Queries with SV-Semantics. In: Haritsa, J., Vijayaraman, T. (eds.) COMAD. Computer Society of India, pp. 15–26 (2005)
9. Kießling, W., Köstler, G.: Preference SQL Design, Implementation, Experiences. In: Proceedings of 28th International Conference on Very Large Data Bases, Hong Kong, China, pp. 990–1001 (2002)
10. Spyratos, N.: A Functional Model for Data Analysis. In: Larsen, H.L., Pasi, G., Ortiz-Arroyo, D., Andreasen, T., Christiansen, H. (eds.) FQAS 2006. LNCS (LNAI), vol. 4027, pp. 8–10. Springer, Heidelberg (2006)

Applications for Digital Libraries in Language Learning and the Professional Development of Teachers

Alannah Fitzgerald

PhD Candidate in Educational Technology, Department of Education, Concordia University, Montreal, Quebec, Canada
alannah.fitzgerald@education.concordia.ca

Abstract. This poster presents plans for designing and developing learning support systems for end-users involved in the construction of a Language Learning Digital Library (LLDL). This is in conjunction with the LLDL project for developing stimulating interactive educational tasks that can be built on top of digital libraries made in Greenstone's open source software specifically to support language teaching and learning. The relevance of the proposed work includes the development of training modules and in-depth workshops for language teachers and students involved in the participatory design of stimulating educational activities that can be uploaded to create digital library collections. Digital libraries can support language teaching and learning through the use of authentic media, comprehensive searching capabilities, and automatically generated precision-targeted exercise material. They also provide social computing environments for teacher-to-student and peer-to-peer communications, along with opportunities to collaborate on group projects. What is more, teachers can build their own digital resource collections and these can be shared among online teaching communities which include annotations and reflections on how to best integrate the digital library technology into their teaching practice.

General Terms: Case Studies, Collection Development, Computer-Supported Collaborative Learning, Computer-Supported Cooperative Work, Educational Issues, Educational Applications, Information Retrieval, Interoperability, Knowledge Organization, Multilingual Issues, Multimedia.

Keywords: Digital Libraries, Computer-Aided Language Learning, Educational Issues, Corpus Linguistics, Participatory Design, Collection Building, Learning Support, Technology Integration, Case Libraries, Teacher Development.

1 Introduction and Motivation for Research

- Design and development of instructional programs for building end-user digital library collections for language teaching and learning
- Greenstone DL Software from the New Zealand Digital Library (NZDL)

L. Kovács, N. Fuhr, and C. Meghini (Eds.): ECDL 2007, LNCS 4675, pp. 579–582, 2007.

- Target participants: teachers and students of English as a second or other language (ESOL) in connection with a recently initiated research project for the development of a language learning digital library (LLDL)
- Recent developments in corpus linguistics for the use of authentic data in language teaching and learning
- A community computing model for the participatory design of digital learning objects
- Management and integration of digital libraries into language education
- A case library within the LLDL that can capture the experiences and reflections of the participants involved in the design, development and utilization stages of the LLDL for knowledge building and knowledge sharing, as a means to answering the following research questions:

What does it mean to empower teachers and learners?
Can we enable teachers/learners to be creative/innovative in the design of digital libraries?
How can we realise this vision of personalised participatory design for educational DLs?
How can digital library applications in language learning and teacher development help?

1.1 Educational Applications for Digital Libraries

This study has the long-term aim of informing the design of future digital language learning libraries, and the learning environments and scaffolds that can be designed around them to best inform and involve end-users. Here, we are viewing the proposed digital library as a repository of learning objects and case scenarios for the foreign language teaching and learning community and not as an institution or a service in the more traditional sense of a library [1]. Research into applications for digital libraries in education is less prominent than the abundance of literature from the library and information sciences on training librarians on the state of the art in building and managing digital libraries [2]. Too often teachers and trainers are offered very limited resources and incentives for participating in innovation and training in e-learning. What is more, some leaders in education are still slow to realize that it is technology that is leading educational innovation and not pedagogy [3]. Cross-sector collaboration is therefore needed to support those practitioners in the field of education to better engage with and exploit digital library applications in e-learning operating under the wider umbrella of technology integration in education.

1.2 Educational Affordances of the Greenstone DL Software

The proposed LLDL in the highly-adaptive Greenstone digital library software offers teachers and learners greater control over their language teaching and learning [4] as they are able to tailor the development of learning content to their curricula needs with "end-user collection building" facilities and more [5, 6].

Instructional sequencing and the amount of learner control reflect conceptions of teaching and learning which broadly speaking can be divided into two major approaches: the instructionist and constructionist approaches. In an instructionist approach the learner is a recipient of instruction whereby the learning program has been designed to deliver content and cover the course outline in a sequential fashion. Conversely, in a constructivist approach the learner engages in actively constructing new knowledge based on his or her prior knowledge wherein the learning program hands over a high degree of control to the learner. Further barriers to successful digital library applications in e-learning and language learning include traditional curricula that assess individual learners on rote memorization and the ability to reproduce knowledge in written exams. This does not account for constructivist approaches to learning that involve, among other things, computer supported collaborative learning. Striking a balance has become increasingly desirable.

2 Digital Collection Building for the Integrated-Skills Approach

Communicative language teaching and learning has been described as a "tapestry", consisting of the four primary language skills: listening, reading, speaking and writing. The tapestry also includes related skills, such as "knowledge of vocabulary, spelling, pronunciation, syntax, meaning and usage" [9]. According to Oxford, weaving all these skills together "leads to optimal ESL/EFL communication." This has become known as the integrated-skills approach.

The integrated-skills approach to teaching and learning is authentic because it reflects how we really use language. When we speak or write, we are almost always responding to something we have listened to, or read – or both. Therefore, in order to better help students learn to communicate in a second or foreign language, teaching materials as well as guidelines for curriculum design also need to have a strong focus on communicative competence – that is, they need to focus on language meaning as well as form [10]. As Oxford [13] points out, "Even if it were possible to fully develop one or two skills in the absence of all others, such an approach would not ensure adequate preparation for later success in academic communication, career-related language use, or everyday interaction in the language." Greenstone's open source digital library software affords the ability to plug in additional languages to achieve a multilingual interface and this is an area that will be further explored with the continued development of the LLDL.

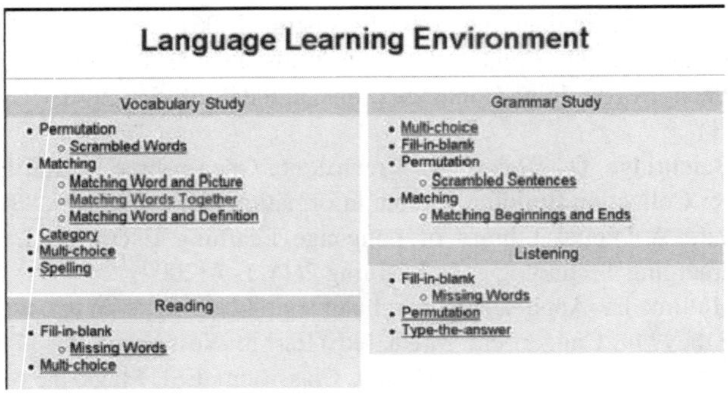

Fig. 1. Content development of language learning activity types enabled by Greenstone

2.1 Authentic Communication: Corpus Linguistics

Authentic communication skills can only be learned when the language, contexts, or tasks used to teach them are the same as, or closely simulate, those used in real situations. Corpus linguistics is a methodology that involves documenting real, authentic language, both oral and written, as it is used in the types of settings one is interested in. Major findings of Corpus Linguistics conclude that the traditional grammar-vocabulary dichotomy is invalid and that

- words need grammar for meaning and grammar has lexical restrictions;
- most 'used language' is composed of pre-fabricated word combinations; and
- intuitions about language are often unreliable.

For example, the word *reflect* has several meanings. Some of these are: to indicate that something is good or bad; when an action reflects a certain quality; e.g. what mirrors do; to think about something in a certain way, e.g. to reflect on a situation.

```
 evidence; arranging a mirror to reflect headlights, so forcing a driver
 painted. Isabella (whose bust is reflected in the mirror above left) was
 they turned the light inland and reflected it off a moveable steel mirror
a blackish silver cast. as though reflected in an old mirror. The sharp
```

Fig. 2. Concordance line for 'reflect' to be used in data-driven learning

References

1. Borgman, C.: What are Digital Libraries? Competing Visions. Information Processing and Management 35(3), 227–243 (1999)
2. Pomerantz, J., et al.: The Core: Digital Library Education in Library and Information Science Programs in D-Lib Magazine (2006)
3. Laurillard, D.: Rethinking University Teaching, 2nd edn., p. 288. Routledge, London (2002)
4. Wu, S., Witten, I.: Towards a Digital Library for Language Learning. In: Interactive Computer Aided Learning Conference 2006, Lifelong and Blended Learning. International Association of Online Engineering: Villach, Austria (2006)
5. Witten, I., Bainbridge, D., Boddie, S.: Power to the People: End-user Building of Digital Library Collections. In: Joint Conference on Digital Libraries 2001. Roanoke, Virginia, U.S.A. (2001)
6. Witten, I., Bainbridge, D., Boddie, S.: Greenstone: Open-source Digital Library Software with End-user Collection Building. Online Information Review 25(5), 288–298 (2001)
7. Wu, S., et al.: A Digital Library of Language Learning Exercises. iJET International Journal of Emerging Technologies in Learning 2(1), 1–7 (2007)
8. Brett, P.: Multimedia Applications for Language Learning – What are they and how effective are they? In: Dangerfield, M.e.a. (ed.) East to West pages, pp. 171–180 (1997)
9. Oxford, R.: Integrated Skills in the ESL/EFL Classroom. ESL Magazine 6(1) (2001)
10. Savignon, S.: Communicative Curriculum Design for the 21st Century. Forum 40(1), 2–7 (2002)

Author Index

Printing: Mercedes-Druck, Berlin
Binding: Stein+Lehmann, Berlin

Lecture Notes in Computer Science

Sublibrary 3: Information Systems and Application, incl. Internet/Web and HCI

For information about Vols. 1–4270
please contact your bookseller or Springer

Vol. 4740: L. Ma, M. Rauterberg, R. Nakatsu (Eds.), Entertainment Computing – ICEC 2007. XXX, 480 pages. 2007.

Vol. 4723: M.R. Berthold, J. Shawe-Taylor, N. Lavrač (Eds.), Advances in Intelligent Data Analysis VII. XIV, 380 pages. 2007.

Vol. 4715: J.M. Haake, S.F. Ochoa, A. Cechich (Eds.), Groupware: Design, Implementation, and Use. XIII, 355 pages. 2007.

Vol. 4675: L. Kovács, N. Fuhr, C. Meghini (Eds.), Research and Advanced Technology for Digital Libraries. XVII, 585 pages. 2007.

Vol. 4663: C. Baranauskas, P. Palanque, J. Abascal, S.D.J. Barbosa (Eds.), Human-Computer Interaction – INTERACT 2007, Part II. XXXIII, 735 pages. 2007.

Vol. 4662: C. Baranauskas, P. Palanque, J. Abascal, S.D.J. Barbosa (Eds.), Human-Computer Interaction – INTERACT 2007, Part I. XXXIII, 637 pages. 2007.

Vol. 4658: T. Enokido, L. Barolli, M. Takizawa (Eds.), Network-Based Information Systems. XIII, 544 pages. 2007.

Vol. 4656: M.A. Wimmer, J. Scholl, Å. Grönlund (Eds.), Electronic Government. XIV, 450 pages. 2007.

Vol. 4655: G. Psaila, R. Wagner (Eds.), E-Commerce and Web Technologies. VII, 229 pages. 2007.

Vol. 4654: I.Y. Song, J. Eder, T.M. Nguyen (Eds.), Data Warehousing and Knowledge Discovery. XVI, 482 pages. 2007.

Vol. 4653: R. Wagner, N. Revell, G. Pernul (Eds.), Database and Expert Systems Applications. XXII, 907 pages. 2007.

Vol. 4636: G. Antoniou, U. Aßmann, C. Baroglio, S. Decker, N. Henze, P.-L. Patranjan, R. Tolksdorf (Eds.), Reasoning Web. IX, 345 pages. 2007.

Vol. 4611: J. Indulska, J. Ma, L.T. Yang, T. Ungerer, J. Cao (Eds.), Ubiquitous Intelligence and Computing. XXIII, 1257 pages. 2007.

Vol. 4607: L. Baresi, P. Fraternali, G.-J. Houben (Eds.), Web Engineering. XVI, 576 pages. 2007.

Vol. 4606: A. Pras, M. van Sinderen (Eds.), Dependable and Adaptable Networks and Services. XIV, 149 pages. 2007.

Vol. 4605: D. Papadias, D. Zhang, G. Kollios (Eds.), Advances in Spatial and Temporal Databases. X, 479 pages. 2007.

Vol. 4602: S. Barker, G.-J. Ahn (Eds.), Data and Applications Security XXI. X, 291 pages. 2007.

Vol. 4592: Z. Kedad, N. Lammari, E. Métais, F. Meziane, Y. Rezgui (Eds.), Natural Language Processing and Information Systems. XIV, 442 pages. 2007.

Vol. 4587: R. Cooper, J. Kennedy (Eds.), Data Management. XIII, 259 pages. 2007.

Vol. 4577: N. Sebe, Y. Liu, Y.-t. Zhuang, T.S. Huang (Eds.), Multimedia Content Analysis and Mining. XIII, 513 pages. 2007.

Vol. 4568: T. Ishida, S. R. Fussell, P. T. J. M. Vossen (Eds.), Intercultural Collaboration. XIII, 395 pages. 2007.

Vol. 4566: M.J. Dainoff (Ed.), Ergonomics and Health Aspects of Work with Computers. XVIII, 390 pages. 2007.

Vol. 4564: D. Schuler (Ed.), Online Communities and Social Computing. XVII, 520 pages. 2007.

Vol. 4563: R. Shumaker (Ed.), Virtual Reality. XXII, 762 pages. 2007.

Vol. 4561: V.G. Duffy (Ed.), Digital Human Modeling. XXIII, 1068 pages. 2007.

Vol. 4560: N. Aykin (Ed.), Usability and Internationalization, Part II. XVIII, 576 pages. 2007.

Vol. 4559: N. Aykin (Ed.), Usability and Internationalization, Part I. XVIII, 661 pages. 2007.

Vol. 4558: M.J. Smith, G. Salvendy (Eds.), Human Interface and the Management of Information, Part II. XXIII, 1162 pages. 2007.

Vol. 4557: M.J. Smith, G. Salvendy (Eds.), Human Interface and the Management of Information, Part I. XXII, 1030 pages. 2007.

Vol. 4541: T. Okadome, T. Yamazaki, M. Makhtari (Eds.), Pervasive Computing for Quality of Life Enhancement. IX, 248 pages. 2007.

Vol. 4537: K.C.-C. Chang, W. Wang, L. Chen, C.A. Ellis, C.-H. Hsu, A.C. Tsoi, H. Wang (Eds.), Advances in Web and Network Technologies, and Information Management. XXIII, 707 pages. 2007.

Vol. 4531: J. Indulska, K. Raymond (Eds.), Distributed Applications and Interoperable Systems. XI, 337 pages. 2007.

Vol. 4526: M. Malek, M. Reitenspieß, A. van Moorsel (Eds.), Service Availability. X, 155 pages. 2007.

Vol. 4524: M. Marchiori, J.Z. Pan, C.d.S. Marie (Eds.), Web Reasoning and Rule Systems. XI, 382 pages. 2007.

Vol. 4519: E. Franconi, M. Kifer, W. May (Eds.), The Semantic Web: Research and Applications. XVIII, 830 pages. 2007.

Vol. 4518: N. Fuhr, M. Lalmas, A. Trotman (Eds.), Comparative Evaluation of XML Information Retrieval Systems. XII, 554 pages. 2007.

Vol. 4508: M.-Y. Kao, X.-Y. Li (Eds.), Algorithmic Aspects in Information and Management. VIII, 428 pages. 2007.

Vol. 4506: D. Zeng, I. Gotham, K. Komatsu, C. Lynch, M. Thurmond, D. Madigan, B. Lober, J. Kvach, H. Chen (Eds.), Intelligence and Security Informatics: Biosurveillance. XI, 234 pages. 2007.

Vol. 4505: G. Dong, X. Lin, W. Wang, Y. Yang, J.X. Yu (Eds.), Advances in Data and Web Management. XXII, 896 pages. 2007.

Vol. 4504: J. Huang, R. Kowalczyk, Z. Maamar, D. Martin, I. Müller, S. Stoutenburg, K.P. Sycara (Eds.), Service-Oriented Computing: Agents, Semantics, and Engineering. X, 175 pages. 2007.

Vol. 4500: N.A. Streitz, A. Kameas, I. Mavrommati (Eds.), The Disappearing Computer. XVIII, 304 pages. 2007.

Vol. 4495: J. Krogstie, A. Opdahl, G. Sindre (Eds.), Advanced Information Systems Engineering. XVI, 606 pages. 2007.

Vol. 4480: A. LaMarca, M. Langheinrich, K.N. Truong (Eds.), Pervasive Computing. XIII, 369 pages. 2007.

Vol. 4471: P. Cesar, K. Chorianopoulos, J.F. Jensen (Eds.), Interactive TV: A Shared Experience. XIII, 236 pages. 2007.

Vol. 4469: K.-c. Hui, Z. Pan, R.C.-k. Chung, C.C.L. Wang, X. Jin, S. Göbel, E.C.-L. Li (Eds.), Technologies for E-Learning and Digital Entertainment. XVIII, 974 pages. 2007.

Vol. 4443: R. Kotagiri, P.R. Krishna, M. Mohania, E. Nantajeewarawat (Eds.), Advances in Databases: Concepts, Systems and Applications. XXI, 1126 pages. 2007.

Vol. 4439: W. Abramowicz (Ed.), Business Information Systems. XV, 654 pages. 2007.

Vol. 4430: C.C. Yang, D. Zeng, M. Chau, K. Chang, Q. Yang, X. Cheng, J. Wang, F.-Y. Wang, H. Chen (Eds.), Intelligence and Security Informatics. XII, 330 pages. 2007.

Vol. 4425: G. Amati, C. Carpineto, G. Romano (Eds.), Advances in Information Retrieval. XIX, 759 pages. 2007.

Vol. 4412: F. Stajano, H.J. Kim, J.-S. Chae, S.-D. Kim (Eds.), Ubiquitous Convergence Technology. XI, 302 pages. 2007.

Vol. 4402: W. Shen, J. Luo, Z. Lin, J.-P.A. Barthès, Q. Hao (Eds.), Computer Supported Cooperative Work in Design III. XV, 763 pages. 2007.

Vol. 4398: S. Marchand-Maillet, E. Bruno, A. Nürnberger, M. Detyniecki (Eds.), Adaptive Multimedia Retrieval: User, Context, and Feedback. XI, 269 pages. 2007.

Vol. 4397: C. Stephanidis, M. Pieper (Eds.), Universal Access in Ambient Intelligence Environments. XV, 467 pages. 2007.

Vol. 4380: S. Spaccapietra, P. Atzeni, F. Fages, M.-S. Hacid, M. Kifer, J. Mylopoulos, B. Pernici, P. Shvaiko, J. Trujillo, I. Zaihrayeu (Eds.), Journal on Data Semantics VIII. XV, 219 pages. 2007.

Vol. 4365: C. Bussler, M. Castellanos, U. Dayal, S. Navathe (Eds.), Business Intelligence for the Real-Time Enterprises. IX, 157 pages. 2007.

Vol. 4353: T. Schwentick, D. Suciu (Eds.), Database Theory – ICDT 2007. XI, 419 pages. 2006.

Vol. 4352: T.-J. Cham, J. Cai, C. Dorai, D. Rajan, T.-S. Chua, L.-T. Chia (Eds.), Advances in Multimedia Modeling, Part II. XVIII, 743 pages. 2006.

Vol. 4351: T.-J. Cham, J. Cai, C. Dorai, D. Rajan, T.-S. Chua, L.-T. Chia (Eds.), Advances in Multimedia Modeling, Part I. XIX, 797 pages. 2006.

Vol. 4328: D. Penkler, M. Reitenspiess, F. Tam (Eds.), Service Availability. X, 289 pages. 2006.

Vol. 4321: P. Brusilovsky, A. Kobsa, W. Nejdl (Eds.), The Adaptive Web. XII, 763 pages. 2007.

Vol. 4317: S.K. Madria, K.T. Claypool, R. Kannan, P. Uppuluri, M.M. Gore (Eds.), Distributed Computing and Internet Technology. XIX, 466 pages. 2006.

Vol. 4312: S. Sugimoto, J. Hunter, A. Rauber, A. Morishima (Eds.), Digital Libraries: Achievements, Challenges and Opportunities. XVIII, 571 pages. 2006.

Vol. 4306: Y. Avrithis, Y. Kompatsiaris, S. Staab, N.E. O'Connor (Eds.), Semantic Multimedia. XII, 241 pages. 2006.

Vol. 4302: J. Domingo-Ferrer, L. Franconi (Eds.), Privacy in Statistical Databases. XI, 383 pages. 2006.

Vol. 4299: S. Renals, S. Bengio, J.G. Fiscus (Eds.), Machine Learning for Multimodal Interaction. XII, 470 pages. 2006.

Vol. 4295: J.D. Carswell, T. Tezuka (Eds.), Web and Wireless Geographical Information Systems. XI, 269 pages. 2006.

Vol. 4286: P.G. Spirakis, M. Mavronicolas, S.C. Kontogiannis (Eds.), Internet and Network Economics. XI, 401 pages. 2006.

Vol. 4282: Z. Pan, A. Cheok, M. Haller, R.W.H. Lau, H. Saito, R. Liang (Eds.), Advances in Artificial Reality and Tele-Existence. XXIII, 1347 pages. 2006.

Vol. 4278: R. Meersman, Z. Tari, P. Herrero (Eds.), On the Move to Meaningful Internet Systems 2006: OTM 2006 Workshops, Part II. XLV, 1004 pages. 2006.

Vol. 4277: R. Meersman, Z. Tari, P. Herrero (Eds.), On the Move to Meaningful Internet Systems 2006: OTM 2006 Workshops, Part I. XLV, 1009 pages. 2006.

Vol. 4276: R. Meersman, Z. Tari (Eds.), On the Move to Meaningful Internet Systems 2006: CoopIS, DOA, GADA, and ODBASE, Part II. XXXII, 752 pages. 2006.

Vol. 4275: R. Meersman, Z. Tari (Eds.), On the Move to Meaningful Internet Systems 2006: CoopIS, DOA, GADA, and ODBASE, Part I. XXXI, 1115 pages. 2006.

Vol. 4273: I. Cruz, S. Decker, D. Allemang, C. Preist, D. Schwabe, P. Mika, M. Uschold, L. Aroyo (Eds.), The Semantic Web - ISWC 2006. XXIV, 1001 pages. 2006.